D1733255

Windows Vista Administration
The Definitive Guide

Other Microsoft Windows resources from O'Reilly

Related titles

MCSA on Windows Server 2003 Core Exams in a Nutshell

MCSE Core Required Exams in a Nutshell

Microsoft Windows Vista Exam 70-620 Guide

What's New in Windows Vista?

Windows Vista: The Definitive Guide

Windows Vista for Starters: The Missing Manual

Windows Vista in a Nutshell

Windows Vista Pocket Reference

Windows Vista: The Missing Manual

Windows Books Resource Center

windows.oreilly.com is a complete catalog of O'Reilly's Windows and Office books, including sample chapters and code examples.

oreillynet.com is the essential portal for developers interested in open and emerging technologies, including new platforms, programming languages, and operating systems.

Conferences

O'Reilly brings diverse innovators together to nurture the ideas that spark revolutionary industries. We specialize in documenting the latest tools and systems, translating the innovator's knowledge into useful skills for those in the trenches. Visit *conferences.oreilly.com* for our upcoming events.

Safari Bookshelf (*safari.oreilly.com*) is the premier online reference library for programmers and IT professionals. Conduct searches across more than 1,000 books. Subscribers can zero in on answers to time-critical questions in a matter of seconds. Read the books on your Bookshelf from cover to cover or simply flip to the page you need. Try it today with a free trial.

Windows Vista
Administration
The Definitive Guide

Brian Culp

Beijing · Cambridge · Farnham · Köln · Paris · Sebastopol · Taipei · Tokyo

Windows Vista Administration: The Definitive Guide
by Brian Culp

Copyright © 2007 Brian Culp. All rights reserved.
Printed in the United States of America.

Published by O'Reilly Media, Inc., 1005 Gravenstein Highway North, Sebastopol, CA 95472.

O'Reilly books may be purchased for educational, business, or sales promotional use. Online editions are also available for most titles (*safari.oreilly.com*). For more information, contact our corporate/institutional sales department: (800) 998-9938 or *corporate@oreilly.com*.

Editor: Colleen Gorman
Production Editor: Rachel Monaghan
Copyeditor: Audrey Doyle
Proofreader: Rachel Monaghan

Indexer: Julie Hawks
Cover Designer: Karen Montgomery
Interior Designer: David Futato
Illustrators: Robert Romano and Jessamyn Read

Printing History:

June 2007:   First Edition.

 This book uses RepKover™, a durable and flexible lay-flat binding.

ISBN-10: 0-596-52959-7
ISBN-13: 978-0-596-52959-8
[C]

Table of Contents

Preface

Well, if you've gotten this far then that's about half the battle. Either the animal on the cover or maybe the spine caught your attention (kudos to the O'Reilly design team); or someone said something nice about the book; or you visited my web page and decided you had a few extra bucks to invest in your Vista education; or you read a good review online or ignored a bad one. Dude who wrote that one is crazy, anyway.

So now that you're here, I want to ask a favor: look at the bookshelves around you. Lots of other books on Vista, aren't there? So what makes this one any different from any of the other bicep builders you see either lining the shelves, or that have come up on a web page you're viewing right now? (I'm taking a flyer that this will be posted in the "Look Inside" section on Amazon or its equivalent.)

Not to get too egotistical about it, but the answer is *me*.

I want to take a bit of the brief space afforded by this preface to let you know that there's an actual person behind this book who will be a resource for you as you administrate Windows Vista computers and the networks that contain them. In fact, you can think of this book as the start of a conversation between me and you. The conversation continues on my web site, brianculp.com. That site is an essential companion for this title, if for no other reason than that you are able to reach me there and get answers to your Vista-related questions. I probably won't be able to solve every problem that's thrown my way, but I'll do my best.

There are some other great reasons for selecting this book. For one, it's very comprehensive. And here's another: it came out after Windows Vista hit the market. Why is that good? Because a lot of the books around you were drafted and even completed while Vista was still in beta, and beta doesn't mean the finished product.

Don't get me wrong; I drafted the book (most of it, anyway) using a beta copy of Vista as well. But in my subsequent review, I stumbled over dozens of things in chapter drafts that I had documented during the beta code that were just flat-out wrong once Vista released to the market.

Also, take a quick look at the Table of Contents and get a feel for the subjects this book covers. It's targeted toward a fairly high-level audience, but it can also serve quite nicely as a power user guide to some of Vista's more advanced features. In other words, you won't find a whole lot of discussion about Media Player 11, for example. There are many perfectly capable companion books for Windows Vista, no doubt, and you may want to read 50 pages on the Media Player. But if your goal is to learn about every possible button available in Media Player 11, I can save you time and frustration: this isn't the title you want. Windows Media Player plays MP3s. End of discussion.

Additionally, know beforehand that this book is not the blueprint for a stand-up comedy act. If I were you, I'd be a little wary of *computer* books that announce just how funny they are. In my experience, everyone has a great sense of humor. Just ask them. Also in my experience, people who tell you how funny they are tend to be anything but. Furthermore, not a single person has ever come up to me, or written me an email, expressing his or her opinion about how the computer book business was sorely lacking in hilarity. Yes, you might chuckle a time or two while reading this book, but I hold no illusions about why you've headed back to this section of the store in the first place. The Dave Barry books (whose own hilarity can be debated; I tend to like them) are elsewhere.

Another thing: this book is well written. I should know; I wrote almost every single word. That's not to say that every line of prose is letter-perfect. Despite my self-congratulations about the book not coming out until after Vista was released, its 800 pages still have to be produced too quickly for it to end up in the Literature section. But I do try to adhere to Wm. Strunk, Jr.'s mandate as frequently as possible—in essence, I don't use two words when one will do. Additionally, bear in mind that I worked for Microsoft, and I know bad writing when I see it. (I never realized that "best of class" or "360-degree view of the customer" had so many usages.) As far as computer documentation goes, believe me, you could do a lot worse.

Oh, and understand this before picking up this book: I am no Windows Vista expert. Yes, that sounds odd coming from someone who just spent several months writing a book on Vista administration, so let me add the following: I've used and administered and written about Windows operating systems for a long time now, so I have a baseline of understanding that's a bit greater than the average bear. But I haven't been exposed to Windows Vista a whole lot longer than any of you, or anyone else on the planet, for that matter. I may have a gotten a year's head start on Vista, but how on earth can I claim any *real* expertise? Although I've worked for Microsoft for the last two years, I certainly can't claim a direct lineage to Ballmer, Gates, Ozzie, et al.*

---

* Not that they'd do a much better job of explaining it anyway. I once attended a Ballmer speech while Vista was in beta where Ballmer exclaimed: "I can't really tell you everything it does, but just use it and you'll see." In print, that makes it look like he was kinda stumped by a simple question. But the thing about Ballmer, at least from my tiny little slice of time watching him speak, is that he's really smart and really dynamic, and I was genuinely excited to open up my laptop again and see what *else* Vista could do after he uttered that statement.

So instead I sit down, install the beta, then the release candidate, then the release-to-manufacturer (RTM) versions, and start clicking around. In the course of my clicking, I push Vista, poke it, ask questions of my colleagues, and read whatever I can get my hands on. In many ways, this book can be best described as a work of investigative journalism; i.e., although I can't claim a vast expertise with Windows Vista, what I do have is a good starting point.

And so then, now do you.

The Structure of This Book

There's really no right or wrong way to organize a book that covers this much ground. So because I have no magic formula, I just organized things based on how I would read a book on Vista administration.

Were I to read such a book, understand that I would never, ever, read the entire thing cover to cover; my bookshelf is chock-full of books pretty much exactly like this one, and I doubt I've ever read a single one cover to cover. I would first want to know what was new in the operating system, just to see what I was getting myself into, and Chapter 1 details many of the new features. I would then want to take the new features out for a test drive and see whether they were ones that would/could really enhance my time spent at the computer, and Chapter 2 addresses this question. Chapters 3 through 14 then look more specifically at certain administrative tasks, and how they are accomplished with Windows Vista.

So, then—here's what you'll find in this book:

Chapter 1, *What's New in Windows Vista?*
Consider this your official introduction to Windows Vista. As mentioned, this chapter examines the many new features of Windows Vista. In it, you'll see a discussion of the new Windows Search capability, look at parental controls, and be introduced to the many new security features, including User Account Control.

Chapter 2, *A Look at the Different Versions*
This chapter continues the discussion in Chapter 1 by looking at the five different versions of Windows Vista that most customers (or, more accurately, most readers of this book) will be able to choose from. In it, we dissect the Windows Vista Home Basic, Windows Vista Home Premium, Vista Business, Vista Enterprise, and Vista Ultimate editions. We will look at the various technologies included in each, and finally wrap things up with a discussion of the Tablet PC functionality. In Windows Vista, this is now a built-in feature rather than a separate operating system.

Chapter 3, *Networking with Windows Vista*
This is the mother of all chapters, as it deals with the rather broad topic of Windows Vista network administration. In fact, the entirety of the book could be called *Vista Network Administration*, for where else will administrators be

performing administrative tasks other than in a network environment? But this chapter focuses on the network part of Vista network administration. In it, we look at TCP/IP configuration, and even at TCP/IP version 6, support of which is now built into the Vista operating system. We will also look at common network tasks such as joining a Windows Server-based domain, and at securing a wireless connection.

Chapter 4, *Personalizing Vista*

Here we look at personalizing Windows Vista so that it behaves in a way that helps the end user get the most out of the operating system. This means simply that desktop icons will be where they are most useful for users, that the System Tray won't be clogged with too many program icons, and that Vista sends its display to the correct monitor—or monitors in a multiple-display setup.

Chapter 5, *Making Vista Easier to Use*

The focus of this chapter is to make Windows Vista easier to use. Like network administration, this topic could encompass much of the remainder of the book as well, but here we limit the discussion to tools such as Speech and Handwriting recognition, and changing Vista to work with multiple languages. The discussion of handwriting recognition, naturally, expands on topics first introduced in Chapter 2. Also, we discuss the new Accessibility options and the Sync Center, where we configure a host of synchronization relationships.

Chapter 6, *Vista Startup and Shutdown*

This chapter isolates startup and shutdown behavior, two areas of performance that administrators often spend a significant amount of time trying to manage. Here we look at ways to improve startup performance, ways to manage battery consumption with new Power Options Control Panel application. As with many chapters, new features are given more attention than those that have merely been updated. We discuss the new Sleep power mode in detail.

Chapter 7, *Working with Hardware*

After improving startup performance, we next turn our attention to enhancing hardware performance during operating system use. We look at the many device installation and management options here, then spend a good deal of time talking about management of a single device—the hard drive. We look at installation options, the difference between basic and dynamic storage, and at volume configuration choices, including drive shrinkage, a new feature available with Windows Vista. Finally, the chapter looks at the new printing options, including how to manage a Vista print environment with the new Print Management Microsoft Management (MMC) Console snap-in.

Chapter 8, *Working with Software*

Operating systems are intermediaries between the user and hardware, and also between the user and software. It logically follows, then, to now turn our attention from the hardware to the software. In this chapter, we'll look at software install/uninstall procedures, at how to configure default programs, and at application compatibility.

Chapter 9, *Deploying Windows Vista*

So far, this book on Vista administration assumed that the operating system was already deployed and ready to go. But simply deploying the software can present quite the administrative challenge. Chapter 9 looks at different deployment scenarios, and also discusses how to transfer data from an old computing environment into the new, Vista-based environment.

Chapter 10, *Internet Explorer 7*

There are many new applications/features built into Windows Vista, of course, as readers of the title have seen many times to this point. But it's a fair bet that there's one new application that will be the most-often *used* new feature, regardless of whether the discussion is about end users or administrators. It's Internet Explorer, of course, and version 7 ships embedded into Windows Vista. We'll examine the many new features of this Internet browser here, with an eye toward features that will make the Internet experience safer and more convenient than ever before.

Chapter 11, *Optimize Performance*

Operating systems often work like a dream the day you first take your computer out of the box or perform that clean installation on an existing machine. The goal of Chapter 11 is to introduce administrators and users to utilities and techniques that can help ensure the Vista environment works just as well down the road. In it, we examine the performance optimization tools such as Task Manager and the Reliability and Performance Monitor, and also look at some specific steps that can improve performance of computer subsystems such as processor, memory, disk, and applications.

Chapter 12, *Securing the Vista Environment*

Security is on the minds of many a Windows system administrator, no doubt, and was certainly foremost in the minds of many a Microsoft Vista developer. Vista introduces several new weapons to the administrative arsenal that will help run a more secure computing environment. Many of the technologies discussed here have been introduced at various times throughout the book, but they get the full attention they deserve here.

Chapter 13, *Vista and Group Policy*

Windows administrators will be adding millions of Vista computers to both new and existing Windows Server-based domains over the next few years, and doing so will open the door to have those computers governed by one or more Group Policy Objects. But as you'll learn in this chapter, deployment of Group Policies isn't limited solely to Server environments. Vista administrators can still manage standalone computers with this powerful administrative lever. If there's one chapter that encompasses the heart and soul of Vista (and Windows) administration, this is it.

Chapter 14, *Troubleshooting Essentials*

This chapter tries to get its arms around the nebulous topic of Vista trouble-shooting, the tools for which—for the most part—have been introduced in the preceding 13 chapters. Vista also includes several built-in, automated trouble-shooting routines (like Memory Diagnostics and Disk Diagnostics) that will work to keep real, roll-up-the-sleeves-and-submit memory-dump-files-for-parsing troubleshooting to a bare minimum. We will also examine here two utilities that are a vital part of remote computing—Remote Assistance and Remote Desktop—and look at scenarios where these can be used in a mixed Windows XP/Windows Vista environment.

Chapter 15, *Vista Tips and Tricks*

This chapter includes tips, tricks, and other cool stuff about Windows Vista that doesn't neatly fit into any certain chapter, but will help you use the new operating system more effectively. More tips such as these will be posted to brianculp. com on a regular basis. And, just because I've got a word processor, you'll also learn what I would change about Windows Vista were I in charge of Microsoft for a day. More importantly that just a forum to share my opinion, however, my hope here is that you're able to learn from my experience and plan for a few of the possible Vista gotchas that I've found.

How to Use This Book

The first two chapters are good—complementary pieces, really—and when taken as a whole will give you a rather comprehensive overview of what to expect from Windows Vista. They're very good, in fact. Also, Chapter 15 is very good—it has a lot of really cool tips and tricks, registry hacks, that sort of thing—and also contains some of my opinion about what's wrong or missing in Windows Vista so that you can be on the lookout for these shortcomings and plan accordingly (and remember, it's just one person's opinion here).

And, there's one tip in Chapter 15 that will more than pay for the entire price of the book. I won't tell you what or where it is, but I promise that this tip alone is one you'll repeat to friends, family, and coworkers.

So if I were you, I'd read the first two chapters, flip to Chapter 15, and then refer back to some of the other chapters as you see fit. Don't get me wrong: the rest of the book is very good as well, but it doesn't exactly make for light reading on the airplane or beach. It contains solid information that will help you use Vista and administer Vista networks, but I don't expect my agent will be fielding any calls about the movie rights to Chapters 3–14.

And don't think of this title as the be-all and end-all of Windows Vista administration, either. Instead, think of it as a starting point for a conversation. Me and you: talking about Windows administration, tips and tricks, etc. in an effort to deepen our understanding and, ultimately, make our computer networks run better than ever before. And in this, the book's second section, I offer the following to facilitate that conversation: my email address, *hmsbrian@brianculp.com*.

And here's the deal: I want you to write me with any questions you have about your computer problems. That's right; I said any, as long as Windows Vista is involved. My vision for this book is that the thing you're holding right now will be just the printed component of a much larger work. Why? Because no matter how many pages this or any book is, at some point the publishers have to take those words away from the author and lock them in place, glue the pages together, and ship the finished product to the bookstore so that they can begin to see a return on their investment. The problem, of course, is that operating systems are words, too, and as you know, those words change at a much faster pace than the words that document what they do. A book on Windows XP, for example, has little relevance if you've just purchased a computer running Windows XP with Service Pack 2. I don't have a crystal ball, but I expect that Vista will undergo similar overhauls over the course of its lifespan.

The good news is that this book has a companion web site, where documentation can change at almost the same pace as the operating system itself. Wait, I take that back. This title will have not a companion web site; instead, the web site will be an integral part of the work. It will ensure that you always have the most up-to-date information about Windows Vista administration. Oh, and the address, which you've probably deduced already from the email address, is *www.brianculp.com*.

Send me your questions and comments and I'll get back to you. If I end up fixing your computer network along with it, so be it. I've just saved you the cost of the book many times over.

So that's the deal. Purchase the book if you'd like and then write me—share your feedback, suggest a timesaving tip, or post a question. I'll get you a timely response. Together, we'll complete the remaining chapters of this book as the Windows operating system continues to evolve.

Conventions Used in This Book

The following typographical conventions are used in this book:

Plain text
> Indicates menu titles, menu options, menu buttons, and keyboard accelerators (such as Alt and Ctrl).

Italic
> Indicates new terms, URLs, email addresses, filenames, file extensions, pathnames, directories, and Unix utilities.

`Constant width`

> Indicates commands, options, switches, variables, attributes, keys, functions, types, classes, namespaces, methods, modules, properties, parameters, values, objects, events, event handlers, XML tags, HTML tags, macros, the contents of files, or the output from commands.

`Constant width bold`

> Shows commands or other text that should be typed literally by the user.

`Constant width italic`

> Shows text that should be replaced with user-supplied values.

 This icon signifies a tip, suggestion, or general note.

 This icon indicates a warning or caution.

Using Code Examples

This book is here to help you get your job done. In general, you may use the code in this book in your programs and documentation. You do not need to contact us for permission unless you're reproducing a significant portion of the code. For example, writing a program that uses several chunks of code from this book does not require permission. Selling or distributing a CD-ROM of examples from O'Reilly books does require permission. Answering a question by citing this book and quoting example code does not require permission. Incorporating a significant amount of example code from this book into your product's documentation does require permission.

We appreciate, but do not require, attribution. An attribution usually includes the title, author, publisher, and ISBN. For example: "*Windows Vista Administration: The Definitive Guide*, by Brian Culp. Copyright 2007 Brian Culp, 978-0-596-52959-8."

If you feel your use of code examples falls outside fair use or the permission given above, feel free to contact us at *permissions@oreilly.com*.

How to Contact Us

Please address comments and questions concerning this book to the publisher:

> O'Reilly Media, Inc.
> 1005 Gravenstein Highway North
> Sebastopol, CA 95472

800-998-9938 (in the United States or Canada)
707-829-0515 (international or local)
707-829-0104 (fax)

We have a web page for this book, where we list errata, examples, and any additional information. You can access this page at:

http://www.oreilly.com/catalog/9780596529598

To comment or ask technical questions about this book, send email to:

bookquestions@oreilly.com
hmsbrian@brianculp.com

For more information about our books, conferences, Resource Centers, and the O'Reilly Network, see our web site at:

http://www.oreilly.com

Safari® Enabled

 When you see a Safari® Enabled icon on the cover of your favorite technology book, that means the book is available online through the O'Reilly Network Safari Bookshelf.

Safari offers a solution that's better than e-books. It's a virtual library that lets you easily search thousands of top tech books, cut and paste code samples, download chapters, and find quick answers when you need the most accurate, current information. Try it for free at *http://safari.oreilly.com*.

Acknowledgments

Writing any book that makes its way onto a bookstore shelf is a team effort, and a big, thick, book on Windows Vista administration is all the more so because of its sheer size and the breadth of topics covered.

Yes, I've written much of what follows, but certainly not all. Along the way, I've received contributions for all or parts of several chapters from the following people. Each deserves a separate line or recognition in deference to the significance of his or her work:

Jennifer Hageman—Chapters 10 and 11

Peter Gregory—Chapter 12

Also: Mitch Roberson contributed a portion of Chapter 3 on Vista networking.

Further deserving recognition: Rex O'Neill, Scott Young, and Anad Iyer looked over a chapter or two each. These contributors provided valuable "second opinions," at times helping fill in topic discussions with a desperately needed paragraph or two.

I would also like to thank the people at O'Reilly who helped pull this entire project together. These people include acquisition editors Jeff Pepper, who was at the project helm at the time of its inception, and Colleen Gorman, who was there to see the project through to completion. They have both done a tremendous job shepherding this book. Thanks also to the production team—Audrey Doyle, copyeditor; Julie Hawks, indexer; and Rachel Monaghan, production editor.

Other folks who have made valuable contributions to this project include Chris Crayton and Pawan Bhardwaj.

Any errors and/or omissions and/or sentences that are just poorly written have nothing to do with the people just mentioned, but exist simply because there is a finite amount of manpower any one company can commit to clean up after one author.

CHAPTER 1

What's New in Windows Vista?

So here it is. Nearly six years since its release of Windows XP, Microsoft has released its latest operating system, and it's coming soon to a computer near you. And because you've picked up this book, chances are that said computer is the one you're using right now.

"But so what," you say. "What's so great about Windows Vista? Why should I upgrade my own computer to Windows Vista? Better yet, why should every single person in my corporate network upgrade? What's going to make this a cost-effective upgrade, and how am I going to justify the expense?"

What follows in this chapter are answers to some of these questions, by way of a brief discussion of some of Vista's new features. But note that the answers are certainly subjective in nature. Are Parental Controls vital to systems I administer? Is this Presentation feature going to save me money? Is Windows Flip 3D going to save time and confusion? Of course, the answers differ according to the needs of the individual and/or the enterprise.

Also realize that this chapter is by no means an exhaustive compendium of everything new in Windows Vista, but rather a guided tour of the significant changes as interpreted by one person. Microsoft has filled up hundreds of pages' worth of white papers covering these new enhancements; my job is to save you time and trouble by highlighting the most significant changes, and moreover, the most significant *features* of these changes.

We'll start with what's most obvious: the user interface, including features such as the new desktop and Sidebar. Later in the chapter, we'll examine a few new features with greater "administrative muscle," such as deployment and customization options. In fact, some of the features first introduced here will even merit further discussion during later chapters.

The Vista User Interface

I know what you're thinking: "Meet the new Windows desktop, same as the old desktop." And generally speaking, you're correct. If you have used a previous version of Windows (or any other operating system, for that matter), not a whole lot has changed—at least at first glance. Yes, the desktop background looks better, and yes, the Start button is now a Start "orb." But it's still located in the same place, and you can use it for basically the same purpose: to launch an application.

Because not much has changed with the Windows desktop, we won't spend a lot of time talking about it here. You know where the Start button is; you know how to launch a program with a desktop icon. Instead, I'll cover a few new bells and whistles, highlight some of the "eye candy," and focus on how to configure some of these options.

Windows Aero

Vista's most significant overhaul of the user interface can be summed up in a single word: *Aero.*[*] That is Microsoft's brand name for the new look and feel, although its functionality goes beyond just an improved desktop appearance. So, what exactly is Aero? It encompasses many characteristics, including:

Glass
> The program windows are now translucent, allowing users to see through programs to get an idea of what's on the window behind, as seen in Figure 1-1. If you maximize the program, the glass goes away and you get the Vista default application color of gray/black.

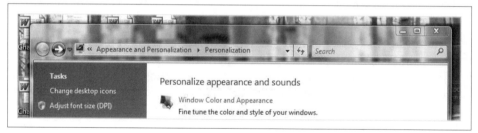

Figure 1-1. Aero's glass appearance lets you see through applications

---

[*] Luna was the brand name for the XP visual interface, by the way. One of the big differences between Luna and Aero is that Luna didn't really add any *functionality* to the Windows interface, especially when compared to Windows 2000—it just looked different. Aero, on the other hand, does add functionality—Windows Flip 3D, Live Thumbnails, and so on—that isn't available on a Vista machine that's not running Aero.

Glowing buttons

This isn't unique to Aero, but it is part and parcel of the new user experience. Buttons such as Minimize, Maximize, and Close now glow when your mouse hovers over them. You'll also see this behavior when using certain applications such as those in the Office 2007 suite. The glowing buttons make it just a little easier than before to be certain that your mouse click will carry out the action you intend. In other words, although it's a subtle difference, it's there to make the Windows experience more intuitive than ever. You see it even when you're not using Aero, which I'll explain in just a bit.

Windows Flip

Hold down the Alt-Tab keys to see Windows Flip in action. (I've seen it referred to as Windows Switcher as well. Whatever.) And if you're thinking, "That's not new, I could use Alt-Tab in lots of previous Windows versions," you're absolutely correct. The difference is that you can now see the program *contents* rather than just the program *icons*, which is why, I suppose, it gets its very own feature name now. Windows Flip lets users be more precise when switching between programs. If you're switching among five different PowerPoint presentations doing cut/copy/paste operations, say, this can really be a timesaver. Try it with a video running in Windows Media Player. Cool.

Windows Flip 3D

Taking Windows Flip one step further, Windows Flip 3D arranges all of the open programs in a Rolodex-style layered arrangement, again letting users actually look into each of their running applications. To use Windows Flip 3D, hold down the Windows key on the keyboard and then press the Tab key. Really cool. Impress-the-neighbors cool. (There's a Quick Launch shortcut for this as well, by the way, but the idea of both Windows Flip and Windows Flip 3D is that you can toggle between programs without having to reach for the mouse.)

Technically, all of this new eye candy is part of the Aero *appearance setting*, which you can change using a technique that should be pretty familiar to users of previous versions of Windows. This will also serve to answer a common question: can I set up my computer to look like an older version of Windows?

Changing from Aero to another theme

Here's how to change from Aero to another visual interface:

1. Open the Personalization Control Panel application. The easiest way to do this, in my opinion, is to just right-click an empty space on the desktop and choose Personalize.

2. Choose the Windows Color and Appearance link, opening the Color and Appearance dialog box.

3. From there, choose the "Open classic appearance properties for more color options" link. You will now see the Appearance Settings dialog box, as shown in Figure 1-2.

Figure 1-2. Change the appearance of Vista

This dialog box should look familiar to users with prior Windows experience, so I won't detail each possibility. With this dialog box, you can make Windows look more like Windows 2000, using the Windows Standard appearance, or even like Windows 98 with the Windows Classic setting.

Yeah, well, I don't see that dialog box. No, you may not. The Vista Aero appearance takes some significant processing horsepower to make it do its magic. Systems that are more than six months old, or laptops in general, might need an upgrade to unlock Aero's capabilities. As we'll discuss further in Chapter 2, though, computers can run Vista just fine even if they don't meet the hardware requirements to display the new Aero interface.

(Aero is actually part of what Microsoft calls the Windows Vista *Premium* experience, and if your system is Vista Premium Ready, it should be enabled as the default. If your system is merely Windows Vista Capable, you'll use the Windows Vista Basic appearance rather than the Windows Vista Aero appearance. The Basic appearance includes solid silver program windows and the redesigned buttons.)

You cannot enable the Vista Aero interface on a Vista Home Basic machine no matter how good your hardware is.

So, if you don't see the Windows Color and Appearance dialog box I just mentioned, you're experiencing a new engineering characteristic of Windows Vista. That is, if your system isn't speedy enough to support a certain feature, Vista won't even present you with the *opportunity* to turn it on. In fact, Microsoft even takes this concept one step further. According to Microsoft, a system running Vista will perform *faster* than the exact same system running Windows XP. Why? Because Vista does a better job of optimizing memory and disk usage, and does not allow graphics options to be turned on that the system cannot support capably.

Aero Wizards

Besides Aero, there's another way in which Windows Vista has changed user interaction. As millions of Windows users already know, most configuration, installation, and update tasks are performed with the aid of a wizard. The job of a Windows wizard is straightforward: it leads you through a series of questions designed to get the device, piece of software, or Windows component up and running the way you want. For example, if you want to back up files, you could open the Backup and Restore Center and choose the Back Up Files button. You will then see the opening page of a wizard, shown in Figure 1-3, which asks you a simple question: "Where do you want to save your backup?"

And although it may escape your notice at first, this Wizard dialog box represents a significant change over the way wizards used to work, the first such change to wizard behavior in roughly 10 years. I'll explain.

The standard for the Windows wizard interface design from the time of Windows 98 until now has been something known as Wizard 97. It is the standard still in effect for the wizards used in Windows XP and Server 2003. Vista Aero wizards give the wizards a major facelift, then, one that incoporates major updates to match the look and feel of the rest of Windows Vista. But I wouldn't bother mentioning this if it were just a matter of a prettier window. The Aero wizards also change how users interact with the wizard. How so? Look for these changes when completing a wizard:

- To enhance efficiency, Vista Aero wizards no longer use the Welcome and Completion pages that have been the standard of Wizard 97. (Geek side note: you can actually disable these Welcome and Completion pages in several current products, which use an "updated" Wizard 97 interface.)

- Aero wizard pages have a prominent main instruction that replaces page heading and subheading.

- Wizard pages are resizable. Wizard 97 dictated a fixed window size for content.

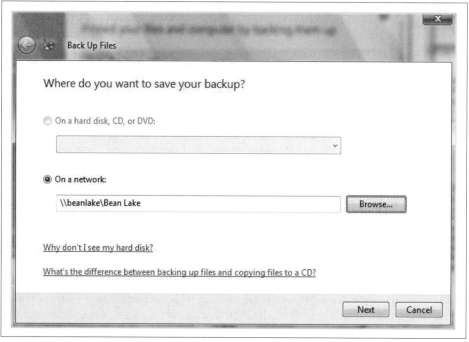

Figure 1-3. The opening page of a Vista wizard

- Aero wizards use a Back button that matches the appearance of other Vista windows, especially those used by Windows Explorer. The idea here is to focus on the Command choices, and not on clicking on a Next button repetitively in order to step through the wizard.

- A new control, known as a command link, allows for immediate and more expressive choices, carrying out most wizard functions with a single click per window.

- "Commit" buttons and pages, where the wizard explicitly states what will occur, are introduced. If there is no other information that needs to be communicated, these commit pages will be the last ones in the wizard. The result, Microsoft hopes, is more efficient decision-making and navigation flow.

- A "follow-up page" after some Commit pages can direct the user to take logical follow-up actions upon completion of the Aero wizard. After burning a CD using Windows Media Player 11, for example, the follow-up page might present the user with the option to either duplicate the disk or make a disk label.

And there's more: besides a change in the way users (and administrators) will interact with Vista's many configuration wizards, you will also notice a change in the way the new OS "talks" to you, both with the phrasing tone used and in the way the Security Center handles its notifications.

Vista's tone

According to the Vista User Experience Guidelines, Vista has also undergone a "personality change" of sorts by changing the language and overall tone of the user interface. The stated goal of the new tone is to make communication presented in Vista's many dialog boxes clearer, more precise, and even encouraging. Previous versions of Windows could have an inconsistent feel both in the way they instructed users to accomplish tasks, and in the way they made requests for information. Much of that has been remedied now with language that is more direct and user-focused.

What's more, Microsoft also encourages application developers to adopt a different tone in the applications built for Windows Vista. As a result, users should see much more consistency in how they are "spoken" to, whether they are using the operating system or an application running on it.

Windows System Tray notifications

You know them and love them (cough, cough): Windows System Tray notifications. Notifications allow an application or operating system component with an icon in the System Tray to create a pop-up window with some information about an event or problem. You've no doubt experienced System Tray notifications, which are commonly referred to as *balloons*, from applications like Microsoft Office (when a new email arrives, for example), or from the operating system (such as when a security setting is not as safe as it should be).

Th System Tray notifications were first introduced in Windows 2000 and have been the subject of much controversy and headache. I am routinely asked about how one can rid themselves of these balloons, and I share a few techniques in Chapter 15 and at other places throughout the book. The notifications can be particularly annoying to people who often run full-screen applications such as games, and can be a real mood-killer when one pops up during a PowerPoint presentation. As you'll soon see, however, Vista includes a "Presenter mode" for mobile computers that automatically addresses this very issue.

Windows Vista notifications aim to be less intrusive by gradually fading in and out, and by not appearing at all if a full-screen application or screensaver is being displayed—in these cases, notifications are queued until an appropriate time. Larger icons and multiple font sizes and colors are also introduced with Aero's notification windows.

 Even the OS font has changed. The Segoe UI font is the new default font for Aero with languages that use Latin, Greek, and Cyrillic character sets. The default font size is also increased from 8 points to 9 points to improve readability.

Lastly, one of the most important enhancements of Aero is its capability to deal with the high-resolution displays of the future by way of a resolution-independent UI. At present, monitors generally have a resolution of 96 dots/pixels per inch (dpi/ppi). Simply put, 48 × 48 icons are displayed on-screen in a half-inch square.

Future LCD screens, however, will support resolutions up to 240/320 dpi. Therefore, to be displayed at the same size without quality loss, icons must include much larger images. That's why Vista introduces a new standard for Windows icon size: 256 × 256 pixels.

Now that we've discussed some of Vista's new desktop features, let's spend a little time learning how to tailor the experience to your liking.

Adding an Icon to the Desktop

If you're performing a clean install, you'll notice that Vista likes the desktop as clean as possible. In fact, the Recycle Bin should be the only icon you see. To bring back old standbys such as My Computer, Internet Explorer, and the Network icons, follow these steps:

1. Open the Personalization Control Panel application. Again, you can just right-click an empty area of the desktop and choose Personalize.

2. In the left pane, choose the "Change desktop icons" link.

3. You'll see the Desktop Icon Settings dialog box shown in Figure 1-4. From here, simply check the checkbox for each icon that you want on. Clearing the checkbox will remove the desktop icon. Click OK to complete the operation.

And notice another change here: some of the desktop icon names have been changed. My Computer is now the more streamlined Computer. My Documents has been replaced by a checkbox called *User's Files*, but it still places a folder on the desktop that's the equivalent of the old My Documents folder. The *user* folder is physically located most typically at *C:\Users\username\Documents*. I like these changes.

Other desktop changes

Now that you've seen how to change the desktop icons, you're well on your way to modifying other areas of the desktop appearance. It all starts in the Personalization Control Panel application.

If you want to change the desktop background, for example, you follow the—what else?—Desktop Background link. To change Vista's screensaver, follow the Screen Saver link, opening the Screen Saver dialog box shown in Figure 1-5.

You can take it from here. The Personalization application also contains links to manage sound, mouse pointer, theme, and display settings. We will look at a few of

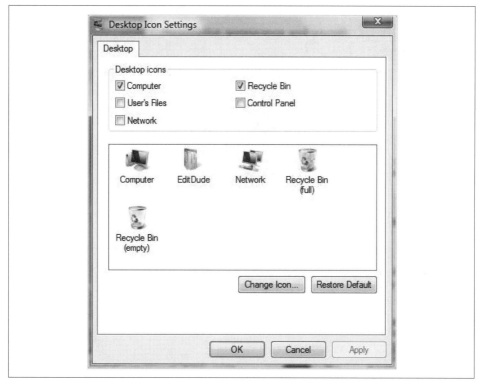

Figure 1-4. Add and remove common desktop icons

these later in the book, but only those that will have a direct impact on the life of an administrator. In other words, feel free to change the email notification sound, but don't look for click-step instructions amid these pages.

Because Vista is built especially to enhance the user experience for mobile systems, we will look at how appearance settings can affect laptop use.

Changing appearance settings on laptop computers. One interesting thing to note here is the Windows Mobility Center, which can also be accessed from the Personalization application. Just follow the link on the bottom section of the left pane. (There's a separate Control Panel icon for this as well.) Especially helpful on mobile computers, the Mobility Center represents not so much new technologies, but rather an easier way to get to these technologies.

As you will see in more detail later in this book, the Windows Mobility Center places key mobile computer display settings in one location, so you don't have to open each item separately. With the Windows Mobility Center, you can keep tabs on sync partnerships, battery life, and, most relevant to this section, external display and presentation settings. You can even change the laptop's own display settings by clicking on the "Displays connected" button, which looks like two flat-screen monitors side by side.

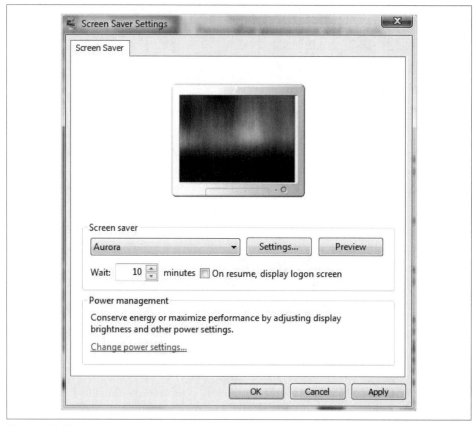

Figure 1-5. Change screensaver settings

But my job here is not to provide exhaustive desktop documentation, but rather to point you in the right direction. So, consider that task complete, and we'll leave the topic of the desktop for now. If you picked up this book for instructions on how to do things such as change desktop pictures or configure the screensaver, after all, you've chosen the wrong title.

Let's instead move to another new technology that's seen from the desktop: the Sidebar and its constituent gadgets.

The Sidebar and Gadgets

The Sidebar is new to Windows Vista. The Sidebar by itself really has no functionality; rather, it serves as a docking station for one or more gadgets.

Gadgets are little applications that can perform a wide variety of functions. They can display information gathered from your computer, such as memory/CPU usage and song playlists; information gathered from the Internet, such as stock, weather, and

RSS feed data; user-supplied information, such as the very handy Notes application; or none of these things, as is the case with puzzles and games.

By default, Vista ships with 13 gadgets: in alphabetical order, they include the Calculator, Clock, CPU Meter, Currency Conversion, Feed Viewer, Feed Watcher, Notes, Number Puzzle, Picture Puzzle, Recycle Bin, Slide Show, Stocks, and Timer. You can download additional gadgets at the Microsoft Live Gallery web site, which you can find easily by following a hyperlink in Vista's Gadget Gallery, detailed shortly.

Companies and individuals can also develop and submit their own gadgets. Does IT need a way to quickly update staff about network status? Gadgets might just be the perfect solution. Do you want to keep abreast of your fantasy baseball team during day games? Go ahead and write the gadget yourself. All that work time devoted to your fantasy team will likely earn you a promotion.

Of course, you don't have to use the Sidebar if you prefer not to. Fortunately, configuring Sidebar behavior won't present much of a challenge.

Gadgets are also leveraged when you are using something called the Windows SideShow. I explain the SideShow in the "Vista SideShow" section later in this chapter.

Changing Sidebar Behavior

This is pretty easy stuff. For the most part, just remember to right-click. If you right-click the Sidebar and choose Properties, for example, you'll see the Properties dialog box shown in Figure 1-6. This dialog box allows you to stop the Sidebar (and thus, the gadgets) from loading when Windows starts by clearing a single checkbox.

Note the options here that allow you to move the Sidebar display to the left or right of the monitor, and further to choose the monitor on which the Sidebar should appear.

What if you told the Sidebar to go away and now you have a change of heart? No big deal. There are two easy ways to get it back:

- Right-click the Taskbar notification icon for the Windows Sidebar (it looks like a tiny, tiny little desktop) and choose Open.
- Open the Control Panel, choose the Classic View, and then open the Windows Sidebar Properties application. Look under the Appearance and Personalization grouping if you're using the Standard View.

You cannot display a gadget without the Sidebar running. You can move a gadget from the Sidebar to the desktop and then hide the Sidebar, but the engine on which the gadget relies—the Sidebar—remains idling in the background.

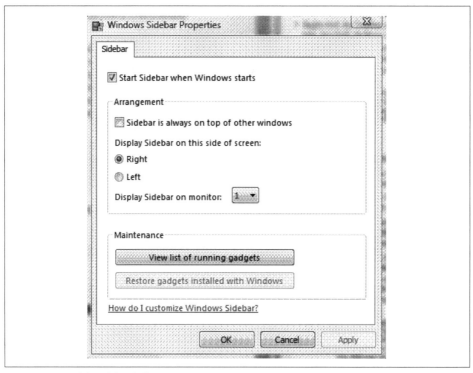

Figure 1-6. Modify Sidebar behavior

Adding a Gadget

Adding gadgets to the Sidebar is also fairly straightforward. Follow these steps:

1. Right-click the Sidebar and choose Add Gadget from the menu. The Gadgets Gallery appears, as seen in Figure 1-7.

2. Now all that's left is to choose which gadget to add. You can either double-click or just drag and drop to start using a desired gadget.

Note also that you can always "Get more gadgets online" by following that link in this dialog box. You'll be taken to the Microsoft web site where you can grab one or more of the hundreds of available Vista gadgets.

Finally, know that gadgets don't even have to live on the Sidebar at all. If you want to see a gadget on the desktop, just click and drag it off the Sidebar and place it wherever you want. When you bring a gadget to the desktop, it usually grows in size as well. (This is especially helpful with certain gadgets that display lots of information, such as the RSS feed watcher or the stock tracker, although this isn't nearly as helpful as it could be. See Chapter 15 for my full rundown on the Vista gadgets.)

Figure 1-7. Add one of the gadgets using this dialog box

 If you use gadgets regularly, commit this tip to memory. If the gadgets are hidden by program windows, press the Windows key and the G key simultaneously to immediately bring the gadgets to the top. This is great for when you've moved a gadget from the Sidebar to the desktop, but you can also use it to simply display the Sidebar if it's hiding behind other windows.

From there, the process of modifying individual gadget behavior will vary depending on the gadget. Generally speaking, though, just right-click the gadget itself and choose Options to begin the process.

Also, note that each gadget is installed locally on the user's computer, and is available for all users of the system. Gadget files are saved using the *.gadget* file extension, and can be emailed or distributed on the Web. A company can easily write a gadget to meet a specific purpose—displaying network status, for example—using HTML skills that should be old hat to most web developers.

Writing your own gadget

You write Vista gadgets using a combination of DHTML for visual layout, JScript and VBScript for functional code, and an XML file for defining the gadget's metadata (author name, description, etc.). This XML code is also referred to as the Gadget Manifest. As long as you've got a command of each of these three developer languages, you're on your way.

You then can distribute the gadget as a ZIP file with a *.gadget* extension. Displaying the gadget using DHTML allows the same gadget to be used on Microsoft's Live.com and Windows Live Spaces sites. Alternatively, on Windows Vista, the gadget can detect that Windows Presentation Foundation (WPF) is available and take advantage of its graphical capabilities to display in a different way from the Web.

Enhanced end-user functionality has been a major directive for Microsoft as it has created its newest operating system. Of equal, if not greater, importance has been creating a more secure computing environment. The next section of this chapter provides an overview of some of the more prominent features.

 Check out *http://microsoftgadgets.com/Sidebar/DevelopmentOverview. aspx#howGadgetsWork* for a great little overview on creating your own gadgets.

Security Features

So far, we've taken a quick tour of Aero—the new user interface—and Windows gadgets. These are two of the new features that will be most apparent to you when you glance at the Vista desktop for the first time. But what about other new features that aren't as readily apparent? Have they made as significant an impact? Absolutely, and we'll start here with a discussion of the new security features.

It is (or was, at the time of this writing) hard to find an article covering Vista that doesn't include some mention about Vista's many new security features. As most people who have even a trace of geek in their blood are well aware, Microsoft has been roundly criticized over the years for creating operating systems in which security was an afterthought. That's the prevailing wisdom, anyway: Microsoft cares more about usability and compatibility than security, and there are executives aplenty at Symantec and McAfee who have the vacation homes and trophy girlfriends to prove it.*

---

* That was a joke. Even better, it was funny, unlike the "humor" found in most computer books. I don't really know whether any Symantec or McAfee executives have trophy girlfriends, but I do know that most of this group is a) male, and b) well paid. You can do the probability calculations on your own. The point of the whole thing, really, is that a lot of people eat steak for dinner because of Microsoft's said security missteps. So be careful what you wish for.

But now, with Vista, Microsoft has made OS security its top priority. In fact, the Web is chock-full of articles that plagiarize Microsoft's own marketing statement about security on Windows Vista:

It's "engineered to be the most secure version of Windows yet."

So what does that mean, exactly? It means that Vista includes a number of features that complement one another to help users and administrators avoid security problems that have plagued previous Windows operating systems. This section looks at three of these that are now included with Vista:

- Windows Defender
- Windows Firewall
- Windows Vista Parental Controls

We will discuss each in its own subsection. There are others, such as User Account Control and BitLocker Drive Encryption, which merit a separate section's worth of discussion.

(The same prevailing wisdom that criticized Microsoft for not being secure enough, by the way, is now trying to have it both ways: the PW now is that security features, such as User Account Control, for example, make the operating system "too secure" for the average user, who will find himself nothing short of aggrieved at having to confirm steps that can reconfigure his system. For more thoughts/criticisms on the subject, please refer to Chapter 15.)

But I'm not here to repeat prevailing wisdom. Instead, I want to give you a decent overview of what some of these new security features are and how they will protect the user environment. Specific configuration steps will follow later in the book.

Windows Defender

Vista ships with a built-in antispyware tool called Windows Defender. Previously known as Windows Anti-Spyware (creative, eh?), Defender's mission is to prevent installation of malware, which is software that can either install itself or run without your knowledge or consent. It's sometimes difficult to determine whether malware has been installed—a well-written piece of malware calls little attention to itself—thus making detection and removal all the more critical. Why bother? Because malware has a job, and it's one you probably don't want it to do. After all, it's called spyware for a reason.

Malware applications can be written to gather information about online usage, including vital information such as login names, passwords, and credit card information. They can also change settings on your computer, such as Internet Explorer's home page, and/or just generally slow down performance. In a cruel joke to the uninformed, many of these malware programs are called *Internet optimizers*, or *spyware cleaners*, or something else that does not describe what they actually do.

And of course, there's the pop-up advertisement, brought to you courtesy of that old friend, adware. Although malware can define a broad range of code—worms, Trojans, viruses, and so forth—one of the things Defender works hardest against is the pop up. (Really nasty adware can display ads even when you're not connected to the Internet.)

Windows Defender helps to keep spyware off your computer—and remove it should it be there—using a three-pronged approach that includes the following:

Real-time protection
> How Defender helps prevent new installations of malware. Defender alerts you whenever potentially unwanted software attempts to install itself. The real-time protection also signals the user when programs attempt to change Windows settings. Both of these types of real-time alerts appear in the System Tray.

SpyNet community
> During Defender setup, you're given the opportunity to join the SpyNet community; it's checked by default. SpyNet is a good first line of defense against spyware, letting you see whether others have installed software that's not yet classified. If other members of SpyNet haven't allowed a particular piece of software, you can use that information when deciding whether to install. Your installation choices, then, close the feedback loop by helping other people choose what to do. It's recommended practice to join SpyNet during setup.

Scanning options
> Defender helps with malware that's already been installed. There are options within to scan manually and at regular intervals. You can also specify here what actions to take with any detected malware.

Configuring Windows Defender

We could spend an entire chapter discussing each and every feature of Windows Defender, but instead I'll concentrate on just two: automatic scan and Defender definitions. Once these two features are in place, Windows Defender works pretty much on autopilot: it carries out its job without much, if any, additional input from the user.

One of the most important components of the Windows Defender tool is its list of spyware. During a scan, Defender simply compares the list of installed software against the list of known malware and then detects (and most often deletes) software matching what's on the spyware definitions list.

Another important function of the antispyware tool is the automatic scan. After all, an updated list is of little use if it's not actually used in a scan. Fortunately, these two options are configured from the same location.

Here's how to make sure your malware definitions are always up-to-date, and that your system receives a regular scan:

1. Open Windows Defender. You can use several methods, including the Control Panel (its own app if you're using the Classic View). Alternatively, you can click the link in the Security Center.

2. Click the Tools link, and then the Options link.

3. Under "Automatic scanning," make sure the "Automatically scan my computer (recommended)" checkbox is selected, and set the scanning frequency using the drop-down boxes, as shown in Figure 1-8.

4. To make sure definitions are up-to-date, make sure the "Check for updated definitions before scanning" checkbox is selected.

5. Click Save. You may be prompted for administrative credentials if you're using User Account Control.

Figure 1-8. Set Windows Defender to protect your system automatically

Another technology that works in much the same fashion is Windows Firewall, which compares incoming and outgoing network traffic against a list of what is allowed and what is not.

Windows Firewall

Windows Firewall prevents the vast majority of Internet attacks from reaching your computer by closing off points of entry known as *ports*. And even if you're not worried about someone hacking into your system—let's say you're on a corporate network that's protected by its own firewall on the gateway router, for example—Windows Firewall can still help enhance network security by stopping your computer from sending out malicious software to other systems.

Before configuring Windows Firewall, a little history is merited. Windows Firewall is actually nothing new. It's been around, available for use on Windows 2000 and XP machines, for some time now. It just wasn't *enabled* by default—that is, until Windows XP's Service Pack 2.

 Port: an endpoint of a logical connection between two computers, designated by a number. The number helps the computer identify what application/protocol handles the incoming traffic. For example, traffic sent to Transmission Control Protocol (TCP) port 80 is handled, eventually, by the web browser because port 80 is the designation for HTTP.

Here's how to enable and disable Windows Firewall:

1. Open the Windows Vista Security Center. There are several ways to do this, including from the Control Panel. Alternatively, you can right-click the little "shield" System Tray icon (in the lower-righthand section of the taskbar) for the Security Center and choose Open Security Center.

2. On the left side of the Security Center, choose Windows Firewall.

3. On the left side of the Windows Firewall dialog box, follow the "Turn Windows Firewall on or off" link (you can also click the Change Settings button). You may be prompted for an administrator password if User Account Control is on.

4. The Windows Firewall dialog box appears, as shown in Figure 1-9. Choose the "On (recommended)" radio button and click OK.

You can then further configure firewall behavior with the two other tabs seen in the Windows Firewall dialog box:

- The Exceptions tab, as the name implies, allows you to configure exceptions to blocked traffic. This is important, as many applications need network connectivity in order to perform as written. To add an exception, simply click either the "Add program" or the "Add port" button and then complete the appropriate dialog boxes. To add a program, just select it from the list shown in Figure 1-10 and click OK. For a port, you'll name the port, select the protocol, and specify the port number.

  Under most circumstances, you'll only need to specify a program exception. You can find a list of well-known ports at *http://webopedia.internet.com/quick_ref/portnumbers.asp*.

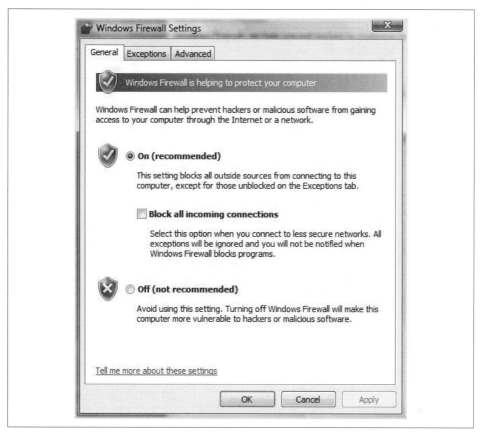

Figure 1-9. Use a firewall to prevent attacks from hackers and worms

- The Advanced tab isn't as advanced as the name implies, but rather just lets you adjust settings for an individual network adapter. If you're on a desktop system, you probably have only a single adapter. If you're using a laptop, however, chances are you have both a wireless and a wired adapter. By default, both are selected and firewall settings apply to both connections.

 You can also configure firewall settings at the domain level via a Group Policy Object (GPO) when the Vista computer is part of a Windows server domain. If this is the case, you'll see notification of such when configuring Windows Firewall. For instructions on how to configure Windows Firewall settings with Group Policy, please refer to Chapter 3.

Also note that average users don't normally have to configure the firewall using the method just described. During normal computer use, the firewall asks permission before allowing a program to access the Internet. If permission is granted, Windows

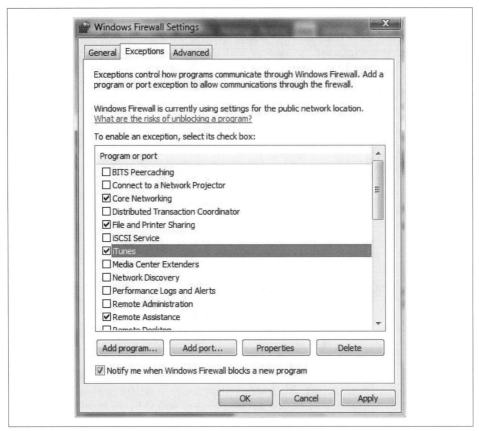

Figure 1-10. Adding a program to the list of exceptions in Windows Firewall

Firewall automatically configures the exception. To turn off this behavior, uncheck the "Notify me when Windows Firewall blocks a new program" checkbox in the Windows Firewall Settings dialog box.

An example of a firewall exception at work

So, you want to play *Halo* against friends online, or you want to listen to the radio on iTunes, or you want to allow Remote Administration of your computer, or, better yet, you want to do all three of these things. Windows Firewall prevents this activity until you configure it otherwise. As mentioned, it shouldn't be a problem under most circumstances; answer Allow the first time a program tries to access the Internet and you're on your way. If you've answered Block previously, though, you'll have to follow the steps listed earlier to configure an exception. Once you add *Halo* to the firewall's list of allowed programs, you'll be able to frag at will.

That is, unless someone has restricted access to *Halo* with Parental Controls.

Parental Controls

For a (relatively) long time now, computer administrators have been able to dictate how a computer could be used. Now Vista gives much of this administrative power to parents. (We'll use *parent* here to make things simpler.) Vista does this with a new feature called Parental Controls, which allows parents to set parameters for computer use. They make parents the administrators over their family's "domain."

The Vista Parental Controls can be set up to govern four key areas of computer use for any computer account. Although designed for parents to restrict kids' computer use, there's nothing that says these controls can't be used to keep a beloved spouse from gambling away the diaper money online, or at least to get a report of such behavior. They can be used to:

- Set time limits for computer use
- Limit Internet usage
- Prevent users from running certain programs
- Prevent users from playing certain games

And, probably most important, Parental Controls can keep a record of computer activity. We'll look at the configuration steps for each of these tasks in the following sections.

 Parental Controls are available only on the Home Basic, Home Premium, and Ultimate editions, and as such are mainly of interest to the home user looking to exert some administrative control over the home network. For the same kinds of control and reporting over program, game, and Internet usage with the Business or Enterprise edition, the solution is a GPO.

Limiting computer use

As mentioned, one of the ways to leverage Parental Controls is to set limits on hours of computer use. Options include setting limits for hours of the day, total hours of computer use, or both. Here's what to do:

1. Open the Control Panel (Start → Control Panel), and then open Parental Controls. If you're using the Classic View, there's an icon called Parental Controls. If you're using the Standard View, choose the link called "Set up Parental Controls for any user" under the User Accounts and Family Safety grouping. (You may be prompted for an administrator password.)
2. Choose the account for whom you'll be configuring time limits.

3. As seen in Figure 1-11, choose the On radio button under Parental Controls. Then click the "Time limits" link.

4. You'll now see a days/hours time grid. Click and drag to set blocked hours, which will appear in blue. To undo a blocked section, simply click and drag again.

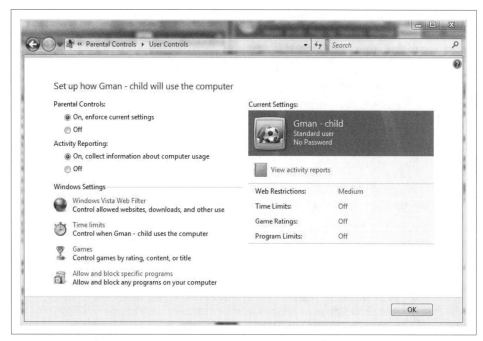

Figure 1-11. Configure time limits by first turning on Parental Controls

Limiting Internet usage

Parents also have the ability to constrain Internet usage. To do so, follow the steps outlined previously to access the Parental Controls application in the Control Panel. Then choose the Windows Vista Web Filter link. You'll get a dialog box with several options, as seen in Figure 1-12. Note that once you enable Parental Controls, certain behaviors are configured automatically. One such behavior is the Web Filter's action of "Block(ing) some websites or content."

The Block/Allow radio buttons in the top section work with the "Block web content automatically" radio buttons below. The Medium web restriction level is set by default, and Vista explains what the Medium level will block. The High level blocks all content except for web sites approved for children. Choosing the Custom level presents the parent with a set of checkboxes.

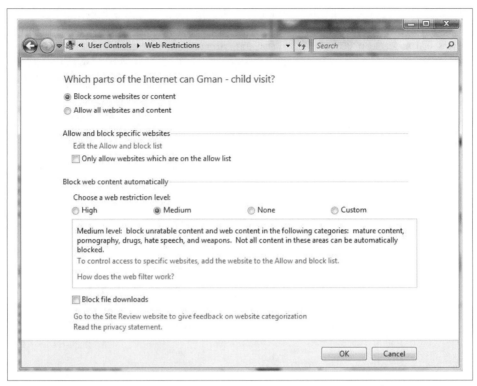

Figure 1-12. Configure web usage with the Vista Web Filter

You can further modify how these automatic filters behave by editing the "Allow and block list." Further, this list can be used with the None automatic filter and the "Only allow websites which are on the allow list" checkbox for ultimate micromanagement, taking any decision-making power away from Vista completely.

Editing the "Allow and block list," although tedious, is fairly self-explanatory. Just follow the "Edit the Allow and block list" link and use the ensuing dialog box to add sites to either the Allow or the Block section.

To speed up the process, you can use a list built on one Vista computer, on a second machine. Once you've built the "Allow and block list," export it with the Export button. On the second Vista machine, choose Import and then locate your *.weballowblocklist* file. (And yes, that's really the file extension.)

Preventing users from running programs

Prior to Windows Vista, it was a chore to restrict access to certain applications without third-party software. Now it's quite a bit easier thanks to Parental Controls. All you have to do is follow the "Allow and block specific programs" link from the User Controls dialog box, and you're on your way.

For example, if you don't want some nincompoop such as Banks Brockmore editing your hilarious feature film, you don't want him to be able to access the Avid editing software installed on your system. You can prevent him from doing so by selecting the "Banks Brockmore can use only the programs I allow" radio button. Then locate the program's executable (*.exe*) file and select its checkbox, as shown in Figure 1-13.

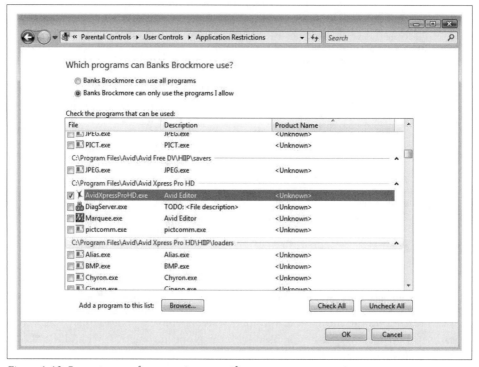

Figure 1-13. Prevent a user from running a specific program

Preventing users from running games

You can also limit what games are available to which users. Again, start in the Parental Controls section and choose the user account to be configured. Then, in the User Controls dialog box, click on the Games link, opening the Game Controls dialog box.

First, you've given a choice about whether the account can play games. Then you have two choices:

- Block (or allow) games by rating
- Block (or allow) games by name

There are links in each section. The "rating" link opens the dialog box shown in Figure 1-14.

By default, a user who is allowed to play games is able to play all games. The Rating dialog box lets you change this default behavior, letting the user play only those games that are rated for teens and younger, for example.

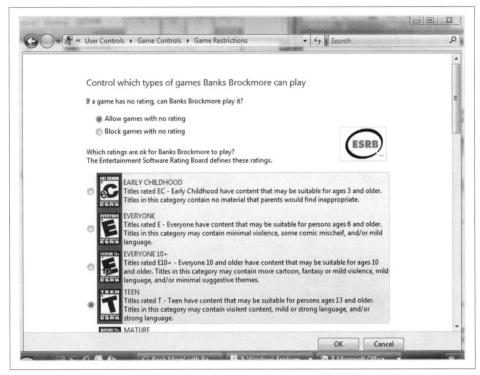

Figure 1-14. This user can run only those games with a maximum rating of Teen

The other link allows you to restrict certain game titles for the chosen account. If *Halo 2* is a bit too intense for your five-year-old, you can prevent its use by choosing its title from the list of games and then clicking the Always Block radio button.

 Explicitly blocking a game is usually not necessary because of the default setting in this list: User Rating Setting. This setting examines the game rating against the highest allowable level for the user. For example, if *Halo 2* has a rating of Mature (it does) and the maximum allowable game rating for that user is Teen, the user would not be able to play.

Activity reports

You can also enable and then view activity reports to see how much each person uses the computer. Here's what to do:

1. As before, open the Parental Controls application. You may be prompted for administrative credentials.

2. Choose the desired account (read: husband's) and then, under Parental Controls, click On.

3. In the Activity Reporting section, choose the On radio button to collect information about computer usage.

   To view a report on usage, just follow the "View activity reports" link from the same section. Vista then displays a report similar to what you see in Figure 1-15.

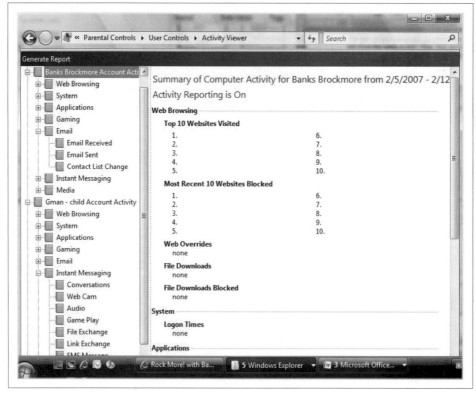

Figure 1-15. Vista activity reports let parents keep tabs on computer usage

As you can see, this report lets you then drill down to get a view of specific activity, such as web usage or game playing. Parents can use the activity reports to monitor incoming and outgoing email and Instant Messenger conversations, or even changes to a contact list; powerful technology for the parent/administrator, indeed.

And speaking of powerful technologies, another new feature included with Vista is User Account Control. Although its name might conjure up a very similar connotation as Parental Controls—that is, controlling the activity of an account—there is one significant difference. Parental Controls help *humans* decide what *activity* occurs on the system. User Account Control, on the other hand, is more about the *operating system* deciding what *applications and/or instructions* are executed by the processor. The next section details this further.

User Account Control

Here's the challenge for Windows administrators: your users have the ability to do *too much* with their computers. But that's a rather nebulous description, isn't it? What's too much? Too much, at least to an operating system, can encompass many things, including rendering a system all but inoperable (inadvertently, of course) by either deleting some crucial file or executing some program or script that tells the computer to do something you don't want it to do.

Why does this happen? It happens because in the past, most accounts ended up with administrative rights. In Windows XP, all accounts have rights as local administrators. The XP Setup Wizard is kind enough to place all users in the local Administrators group.

This means that all XP users, by default, have the ability to:

- Read, write, and execute permissions over every single file, including Windows system files
- Exercise all Windows rights (including, for example, the right to take ownership of a file and then change permissions at will)

Other accounts in Windows XP included standard user accounts, which had much more limited privileges over the computer—too limited for a lot of companies, in fact. For example, a standard user account in Windows XP could not install applications, creating many a headache for the end user trying to get that "mission-critical" ActiveX control installed in her browser.

But that's no longer the case. Now, Vista introduces User Account Control, making it easier for companies to limit the rights of the average user, while still protecting the computer from accidental installations of malware (read: mission-critical ActiveX control).

In Vista, there are now two basic kinds of user accounts:

Administrator accounts
> These accounts can perform any and all administrative tasks on the machine, including application installation and system setting changes.

Standard user accounts
> These are the equivalent of the standard user accounts in previous versions of Windows. Standard accounts *can* install applications, but not those that install into the *%systemroot%* folder. Also, they cannot change system settings or perform other administrative tasks.

 %systemroot% is a variable designating the installation directory for Windows Vista. On most computers, this will be *Windows*.

Now here's where Vista has made a big improvement over the past: a standard user can still perform administrative tasks if she provides proper account credentials. Figure 1-16 shows an example.

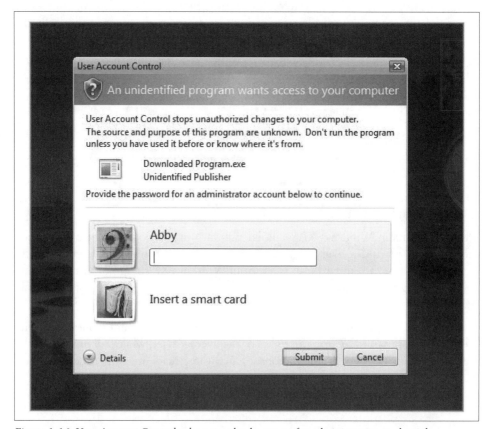

Figure 1-16. User Account Control asks a standard account for administrative credentials

And when User Account Control is enabled, even a member of the local Administrators group will be prompted to approve a process, whereas a standard user would be asked for administrative credentials. In other words, even the admin is treated as a standard user until trying to perform some administrative task, at which time Windows Vista asks permission, as shown in Figure 1-17.

Figure 1-17. With User Account Control, even the local admin is treated as a regular Joe

(If you investigate further by clicking the Details button, you'll notice the reason why Windows needs permission to complete this task: you're trying to launch an executable living in that darn *%systemroot%* folder.)

So even if it's the administrator who is trying to install that "mission-critical" ActiveX control, User Account Control ensures that, at the very least, said administrator is aware that she's installing a piece of software. Vista allows no access to the *%systemroot%* folder, for example, without permission to proceed.

Table 1-1 compares rights of standard accounts to rights of members of the local Administrators group.

Table 1-1. Comparing standard and administrator privileges

Standard user account rights	Administrator account rights
Establish a network connection.	Install and uninstall apps.
Modify display settings.	Install device drivers.
Play a CD or DVD.	Install Windows updates.
Burn a CD or DVD.	Configure Parental Controls.
Configure battery options.	Change a user account type.
Change your own password.	Add and delete user accounts.
Restore your own backup.	Configure remote desktop access.
Set up sync between devices.	Schedule automated tasks.
Connect a Bluetooth device.	Modify the User Account Control settings.

And because User Account Control is one of the most significant changes to the operating system, both from a usability standpoint and from an architectural standpoint, it's vital that any prospective Vista admin has a full grasp of its behavior. Here are a few things you should know about Vista's handling of User Account Control.

Disabling User Account Control

Now that you've learned all about User Account Control, how do you turn the thing off? How do you stop those constant reminders that you're about to install something, or make a configuration change? You're smart, after all, and you don't need some OS reminding you that you've sat down to install a new app. Here's what to do:

1. Open the Control Panel. There are lots of ways to do this; use the Start button and then choose Control Panel if you're lost.
2. Double-click User Accounts, and then choose the "Turn User Account Control on or off" link. Because User Account Control is on (right?), you'll have to grant approval for your action before getting to the next screen.
3. Uncheck the "Use User Account Control (UAC) to help protect your computer" checkbox. Already feel a little guilty, huh?
4. Click OK. You'll then need to restart your computer.

There are several other ways to do this, by the way. We'll hit on most of them throughout the course of the book. For now, all that's necessary is an understanding of User Account Control's implications.

With the User Account Control behavior off, you've made your brand-new operating system behave more like the old one, where users logged in as local administrators, carrying the full access token with them at all times.

(Note also that you're immediately warned about the utter stupidity of your action: the Security Center squawks a warning your way in the System Tray. Open the Security Center, and Vista even gives you a chance to atone for your transgression with a single click. Because you're disabling User Account Control, of course, you can ignore this warning.)

Before you take the step, however, I must pass along this word of warning, directly from Microsoft:

> While some non-UAC compliant applications may recommend turning UAC off, it is not necessary to do so since Windows Vista includes folder and registry virtualization for pre-Windows Vista or non-UAC compliant applications by default. Turning UAC off opens your computer to system-wide malware installs.

In other words, Vista will make "virtual" allowances for applications that want to run in the context of an administrative account. So there.

There is another new feature that takes protection one step further by protecting all data on the hard drive. It's called BitLocker, and the next section discusses how you can enable it.

BitLocker Drive Encryption

BitLocker is another new security feature that, well, locks up all the data, or bits, on the hard drive. This feature is especially handy if your computer's hard drive is ever lost or stolen, and the purpose of this section is to give you a brief overview of this feature and some of the key components needed. A more detailed discussion, including step-by-step instructions, appears in Chapter 12.

BitLocker Drive Encryption works by encrypting the entire Windows operating system volume. The keys needed to unlock the encrypted volume are stored on a Trusted Platform Module (TPM) chip, which is built into the motherboard.

Why is this significant? The encryption keys needed to unlock data on your entire Windows volume are removed from the hard drive and stored on the TPM chip. This prevents someone from stealing your hard drive, taking it to another machine, sticking it into an enclosure, and accessing all the data. The encryption keys needed to unlock this data are still back on the TPM chip, which sits on the motherboard of the laptop, which is back at your office, sans hard drive.

During Vista's boot process, the TPM releases the encryption key needed to decrypt data on the operating system volume, but only after operating system integrity has been established. (None of which is visible to the end user under most circumstances. The release of the encryption key happens without user input unless otherwise directed by Group Policy.) This ensures that no offline tampering has taken place.

For a properly configured system, BitLocker is either enabled or disabled using the Control Panel application shown in Figure 1-18. If you're using the Classic interface, there's a separate BitLocker Drive Encryption icon. If you're using the Standard interface, look under the Security grouping.

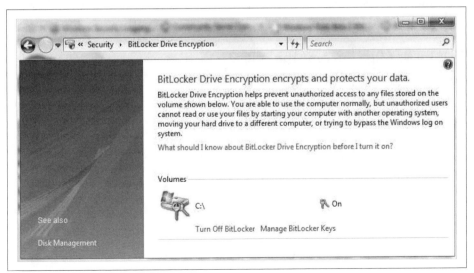

Figure 1-18. The Control Panel application displays whether BitLocker is on or off

And note that not every system can enable this feature. Before you implement Bit-Locker, make sure your system has the following components that meet BitLocker's minimum hardware requirements:

- A TPM microchip, version 1.2, turned on.
- A Trusted Computing Group (TCG)-compliant Basic Input/Output System (BIOS).
- Two NTFS drive partitions, one for the system volume and one for the operating system volume. The system volume partition must be at least 1.5 GB and set as the active partition.
- A BIOS setting to boot first from the hard drive, not the USB or CD drive.
- For any test that includes the USB flash drive, your BIOS must be configured to read and write to a USB flash drive during startup.

 I take back what I said about TPM: you can use BitLocker without a TPM chip. To do so takes some extra configuration, however. You must first either change the default behavior using Group Policy, or configure BitLocker using a script.

When BitLocker is used without a TPM chip, encryption keys are stored on a USB flash drive. You'll need this drive to unlock any data stored on the encrypted volume. We'll discuss the Group Policy edits necessary to implement BitLocker without TPM in Chapter 12.

For BitLocker to work, you'll first need to configure your computer with two volumes (sometimes referred to as *partitions*, although they're not technically the same thing). The first volume is the boot volume, and it contains essential Vista boot files on an unencrypted space. The second volume is the operating system volume, which holds the Vista operating systems as well as all user data. This is the one that Bit-Locker encrypts.

So Why Not Just Encrypt the Drive?

These questions come up all the time when I'm speaking to people about Vista's new features: "so what's the difference? Can't you encrypt the entire drive using the Encrypting File System (EFS) in Windows XP? How is that any different?"

In fairness, it can be very confusing. The objective, after all, is the same: to use encryption to protect files on your drive. One big difference, however, lies in the *scope* of the two technologies. With EFS, you encrypt files and folders (on an NTFS partition) on an individual basis. Further, the encryption is done per user. One user could log on and access all data on the drive except for encrypted data created by another user.

BitLocker, on the other hand, is more comprehensive. It encrypts everything, from the operating system to all user data. Table 1-2 shows some other significant differences between the two.

Table 1-2. Comparison of BitLocker and the Encrypting File System technologies

Vista's BitLocker	Windows XP's Encrypting File System
Encrypts everything on the operating system volume.	Encrypts only individual folders and files on any drive.
Requires two separate NTFS volumes.	Can be deployed on a single NTFS volume.
Does not associate the encryption with an individual user.	Associates encrypted files with a particular user account. Each user has the chance to encrypt files he owns.
Uses a TPM chip (or USB key) to store the encryption key.	Stores encryption keys within the operating system files. It does not require special hardware or software, but rather an NTFS volume on a Windows XP Professional machine.
Must configure BitLocker while logged on with administrator privileges.	No administrator account is necessary. Any user can encrypt files he owns.

Again, the main purpose of BitLocker is to prevent data access due to theft. You cannot slap a purloined BitLocker drive into another machine and boot up. And there's nothing that says the two technologies can't be used in harmony in an effort to protect your most sensitive information.

When implementing BitLocker Drive Encryption, each volume must be set up *before* proceeding with Windows Vista installation. Again, full implementation steps will be covered in Chapter 12.

Besides BitLocker, there's another new feature that protects files on your computer's hard drive. It's called Windows Service Hardening.

Windows Service Hardening

Windows services perform functions in the background. Usually, these services help automate a lot of tasks that make our computer life easier, and are an essential part of the operating system experience. If you've used Unix before, you might know these services as *daemons*. The Scheduling Service, for example, allows us to schedule maintenance operations such as an automatic backup or defragmentation of a drive.

But as with most things that make our lives easier, there's a potential downside. Sometimes malware is written to "piggyback" on these services, thus facilitating behaviors such as automatic software installation, duplication, changing of registry information, replacement of system files, and so forth. Windows Service Hardening works to prevent this behavior by reducing what Microsoft refers to as Vista's "attack surface."

Windows Service Hardening works by assigning a Security Identifier (SID) to each Windows service, which in turn allows Vista to better control access to the service. In other words, no access to the service is allowed other than what's specified by the SID. Also, services can now be further protected by utilizing access control lists (ACLs), which are private to the service, and which prevent both users and other services from accessing the resource. Windows Service Hardening also removes any unnecessary service privileges.

Further, Windows Vista services also now run in a less privileged account, such as LocalService or NetworkService, rather than the LocalSystem account, which has much greater reign over the computer. Previous Windows operating systems such as XP and Windows 2000 used the LocalSystem account to launch most applications.

Windows Service Hardening also grants a service write access only to those resources that have to be modified by the service. Any other modification, then, such as a registry modification requested by malware, will not be permitted.

An additional component of Windows Service Hardening is that services have a preconfigured firewall policy. This policy ensures that Windows services have only the minimum privileges needed to function properly.

The good news about Windows Service Hardening is that it's just a part of the operating system. There's little you should ever have to do to configure it.

New Ways to Search

One of the major overhauls in the Vista user interface is the (vastly) improved ability to search for (and locate) information on your hard drive. Good thing. With hard drives commonly ranging from 250 GB to 1 TB for personal storage, chances are pretty fair that you're now managing as much sheer data as many large companies—and even entire governments—did a mere quarter-century ago.

In this section, we'll look at some of the new search capabilities built into the Vista operating system. For me, these new search capabilities are like broadband Internet access—once you see them in action for the first time, everything that preceded them seems antiquated. I think you'll agree.

The Start Menu

For starters, there's the Start menu. This is certainly nothing new to Windows users—it's still there waiting to help you in the desktop's lower-lefthand corner by default, but it has been updated with some new features.

Using Instant Search on the Start menu

In general, the Start menu is designed so that your searches for files and folders on your computer are less "mouse-driven" than they were before. If you hold your mouse pointer over the All Programs folder, for example, the Programs submenu opens in the same Navigation Pane rather than in a cascading menu/submenu scheme. In other words, you'll spend less time (and aggravation) chasing submenus all over your monitor's screen.

But the biggest change is how Vista directs you to the new Instant Search. Click the Start menu, and the cursor blinks in the Search entry box, ready to help retrieve a program, a file, or just about anything stored on your computer. In other words, Instant Search is Vista's mechanism to accomplish the goal of reducing mouse-driven navigation.

Just type and locate. To get started using the new Start menu's Instant Search, just start typing. The best way to get a feel for how this works is to see it in action. Let's say, for example, that you're looking for a Word document about a new medicine that was emailed to you a few months back. Some questions can arise, however, that make retrieving that file problematic. These questions include:

- Is the title of the file *Medicine*, *New Medicines*, or some derivation thereof? What if it's named *Prescriptions* or something like that?

- Where did you store it? Is it in your Documents folder, or has it been moved elsewhere on your hard drive?

- Is it possible that you remember it being called "medicines" or something like that, but really the word appears only in the body of the document?

- Alternatively, what if you're a doctor or pharmacist, and you have 300 Word documents with *medicine* somewhere in the title? How are you going to locate the one file that's relevant to your search?

- You remember it being emailed to you. Are you sure you saved the attachment in the first place? Are you even sure it came as an attachment? Maybe someone just emailed you information about a new medicine but never typed it up formally in a Word document.

- Are you sure it's even a Word document at all? Could it have been a PowerPoint presentation instead?

The Start menu's Search can address all of this uncertainty, and more. With the new Search feature, you can focus on *what* you're looking for, and not worry about *where* it's stored.

Using the medicine example we've just agonized over, you can just start typing the word into the Search entry box and see what comes up. You don't even have to use the entire word. Typing **med**, for example, brings up the results shown in Figure 1-19.

Figure 1-19. Search starts looking even without the entire search term

Search quickly uses the Indexing Service to build a list of everything with *med* somewhere in it. Notice what the Start menu comes up with, handily divided into sections:

- The programs Media Center and Media Player (I'm using Vista Ultimate; the Media Center is included).

- In the next section, a list of files with *med* either in the title or in the *body of the document itself*. Search gathers all files indexed, but you could have limited your search to just Word documents.

- In the next section, if applicable, a list of all communications containing *med*. These will include items such as emails, appointments, and even RSS feeds. If your information was in the email itself and not a Word document after all, the Communications section would help you pinpoint that file here.

- If you don't see your item in the Start menu right away, it may be because there are more search results than can be displayed there. For a full listing, simply click the "See all results" link from the search results listing. The full tally will then be shown in an Explorer window.

- And, of course, the more letters you type in your search, the greater the chance that you'll be narrowing your search. If you keep typing the word *medicine*, for example, the Media Center will be eliminated from the search results by the time you get to the *c* in *medicine*.

 For a full discussion of the Indexing Service, including instructions on how to configure what gets indexed, please refer to Chapter 2.

Also, these same principles will carry forward to the discussion of Search integration into Windows Explorer, which is covered a little later in this section. For now, let's look at how to modify the Start menu to suit your needs.

Customizing the Start menu

Other than the new Search function, much of the new Start menu should look fairly familiar. The left side contains a list of frequently used programs, and the right pane contains a list of frequently accessed places such as the Control Panel and the user's Documents folder.

And, like before, it's fairly easy to customize what appears. Follow these steps to customize the Start menu's appearance:

1. Right-click the Start button and choose Properties from the context menu.

2. Choose the Start Menu tab (it should be selected by default) and then click the Customize button.

3. You'll see the Customize Start Menu dialog box, as shown in Figure 1-20.

Notice that most of the options here—Documents, Computer, Games, Pictures, and so on—are turned on by default, and that they are displayed as "links." If you're thinking *hyperlinks*, however, this is not exactly the case. If you've clicked on the Start button already, you've noticed by now that a Start menu link is really more of a button.

If you'd like to reset the Start menu back to the default settings, just click the Use Default Settings button in the middle of the Customize Start Menu dialog box.

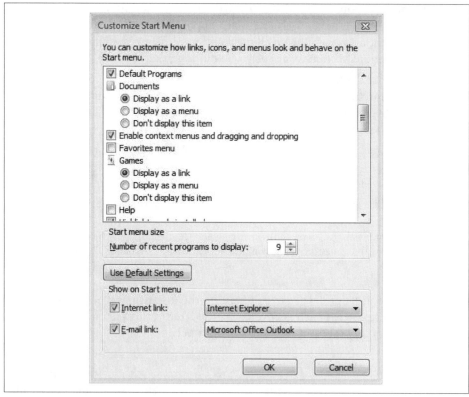

Figure 1-20. Choose your new Start menu options with this dialog box

Search with Windows Explorer

Another way to locate information on a Vista computer is through Windows Explorer, a feature that has been around on Windows computers for a while and yet another that has been almost completely redesigned.

Windows Explorer includes search capabilities in almost every nook and cranny. To see what I mean, take a look around the Windows Explorer view shown in Figure 1-21.

So then: meet the new Explorer. Same as the old Explorer, right? Actually, there's been a major overhaul, and almost all enhancements are designed to help you search faster and more intuitively. There are six features you can utilize to help you find what you're looking for:

- Navigation Pane
- Forward and Back buttons
- Address bar

- Headings
- Search box
- File list

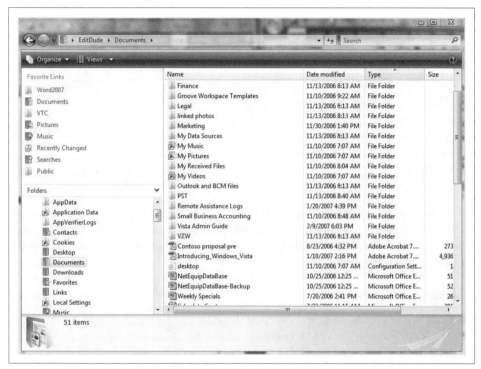

Figure 1-21. The Windows Explorer window provides several search possibilities

And although it may seem a bit elementary to use Windows Explorer, it is completely redesigned, so we'll spend a brief moment here looking at some of the individual search features.

Search Box

If you're looking for something in a specific location, the Search box is probably the fastest way to find that information. Thanks to the Windows Indexing Service, the Search box quickly locates files based on filename, text within the file, metadata tags (explained in a bit), and other data associated with that file.

In fact, if you look in Explorer's Address bar after performing a search, the "location" will be identified as "Search Results in *location*." This is actually displaying the contents of a Search Folder, also known as a virtual folder. You can save these Search Folders for easy file organization on an ad hoc basis. You can learn more about creating and saving Search Folders in Chapter 2.

Virtual folders have a green-blue color. Normal directory folders are shown using the old manila standby.

Let's say, for example, that you have a document in your Documents folder that's about auditing. But the file's actual title is something such as *Important Accounting Info.docx*. Can you still locate what you're looking for?

Yes, you can; just follow these two easy steps:

1. Choose the Documents folder using either the Navigation Pane or the list of Favorites (still technically in the Navigation Pane).

2. Type **audit** in the Search box. If *audit*—or any derivation thereof—appears anywhere in the body of the document, Search is able to retrieve the file. Alternatively, someone (you, possibly) may have entered a metadata tag that associates the word *audit* with the file.

This capability frees you from having to create an elaborate naming convention for all of your computer's folders and files. You don't have to have any naming system at all, in fact. You can just use a tag to identify the subject of some file, and let the indexing feature take care of the rest.

Changing a metadata tag

Take any file on your computer, and you'll see that lots of information is associated with it. Vista keeps track of the creation data: the author, the file size, and the last time the file was changed. Even the title itself is information referring to the file, but it is not necessarily part of the file, per se. It's metadata.

Metadata is information about a document—data that refers to the file itself. And Windows Explorer makes it easy to add your own custom metadata tags that the Indexing Service will track along with everything else. Here's what to do:

1. Make sure the Details pane is showing. To double-check, click on Organize in the upper-lefthand side of the Explorer window and choose Layout from the menu.

2. If it's not selected, choose Details Pane from the submenu.

3. You should now see a heading called Tags in the Details pane, and next to it you should see the text "Add a title," as shown in Figure 1-22.

Figure 1-22. You can add your own metadata tags right from within Windows Explorer

You can probably take it from here. Just click on the "Add a title" text, and it turns into an editable text box. Enter whatever you think will best help you locate the file later on.

 You need to have the proper administrative privileges to do this. Any user working in her own Documents folder should be able to add metadata tags to her files without administrative privileges, however.

Advanced searches

Typing a word into the Search bar and then pressing Enter is usually a pretty good way to quickly find what you're looking for. Every once in a while, though, the search returns too many items. To continue with the preceding example, if you're working at an accounting firm and you type **audit** in the Search box, you might get hundreds of documents returned.

There are a few search tricks to help you, however, so that the net you cast isn't quite so wide. The Search box lets you modify your searches to specify an exact file property for which to search. To use this feature, just type the property (metadata) you're searching for, followed by a colon, and then the search item itself. So, if you're looking for documents with *audit* in the title only, you would type **Name:audit**. If you just wanted the files with the metadata tag of audit, you can use **Tag:audit**.

And so on, and so on. How many file properties can you search for in this way? How about all of them! Like what? Right-click on an Explorer File List heading and choose More from the menu. Here; I'll save you the trouble in Figure 1-23. (Keep in mind, though, that just a few from the dizzying list of searchable file properties can be shown in a single screenshot.)

How about a movie folder that's organized according to favorite directors? In Windows Vista, it's entirely possible.

Boolean filters

I know. You want to use Booleans, right? You can. Booleans let you combine multiple search words or options using a simple logic tree. Booleans include the following:

AND
    Looks for files that contain both words used in the search

NOT
    Locates files that contain the first search word, but not the second

OR
    Looks for files that contain either word used in the search

Quotation marks
    Finds the exact phrase within the " "

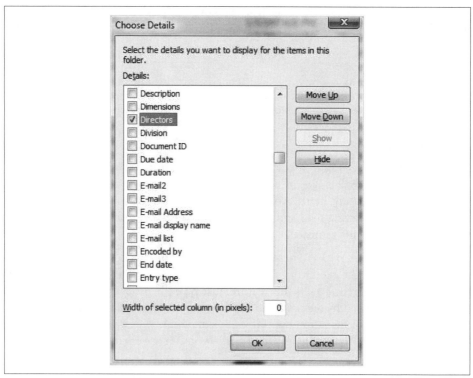

Figure 1-23. The Details dialog box provides a glimpse of all the searchable file properties

There's a reason I wrote the Boolean operators in all capitals in the preceding list. When conducting a Boolean search, you need to use all caps to let Vista know the word is a search argument, not a search word.

Natural language searches

Another cool new Explorer feature is that you don't have to speak to the computer using language the computer likes. You can use natural language instead. Once enabled, natural language searches let you use everyday speech to ask the computer to locate information for you almost the way you would ask a real person.

But as I mentioned, it must first be enabled. To use the natural language search, follow these steps:

1. From the Explorer window, click Organize → Folder and Search options.
2. Click the Search tab.
3. Select the checkbox labeled "Use natural language search," as shown in Figure 1-24.

Table 1-3 illustrates a few Boolean phrases turned into natural language requests.

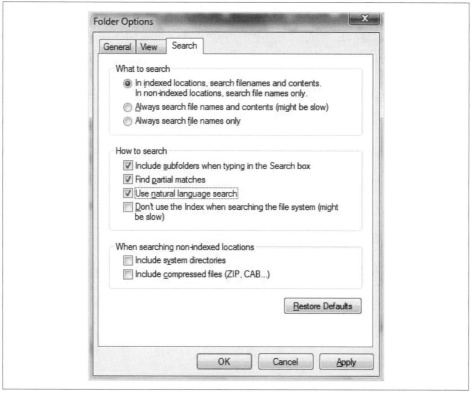

Figure 1-24. Enable natural language and put Booleans out to pasture

Table 1-3. Boolean phrases and their natural language counterparts

Boolean searches	Natural language searches
Kind:pictures author:Brian	Pictures by Brian
Kind:email subject:board meeting	Email about the board meeting
Kind:music artist:Pepe Deluxe	Music by Pepe Deluxe

File List Headings

Here's a feature you could use—more or less—in Windows XP, but only if you had the Details folder view enabled. Now it's available using all the Explorer views.

The File List headings are the items called Name, Date Modified, Type, Size, and so forth that appear across the top of the Explorer file listings. Again, these appear even if you're using Extra Large icons as an Explorer view (Views → Extra Large icons).

To sort using one of the headings, simply click it. Clicking Date Modified once, for example, stacks your file list in chronological order with the most recent items at the top. Clicking Date Modified again reverses the order, but files are still sorted by date.

And not only does Vista allow you to sort items with a click, but it also facilitates more sophisticated listings that allow you to filter and stack your views. The filter and stacking options vary by heading. You can use the filter and stacking options by using the drop-down menu that appears when you hover your mouse over one of the File List headings.

To use a listing filter, for example, you can click the drop-down arrow next to the Name File List heading. Selecting the Q–Z name filter narrows down the document listing to just those whose titles, quite obviously, start with the letters Q through Z.

Using a stack is similar, although no filtering is applied to the view. Stacking a folder according to name, for example, places all documents in the folder into discrete piles (or stacks); you'll get a better understanding of it from Figure 1-25.

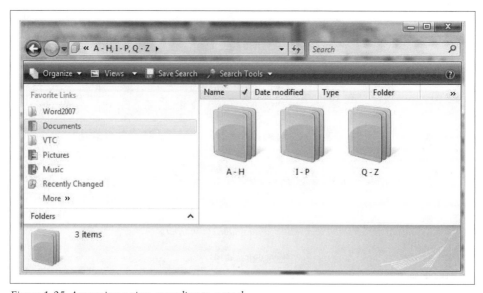

Figure 1-25. Arranging a view according to a stack

The New Task Scheduler

The Task Scheduler makes computing life easier by letting you automate certain routine jobs. This *ability* is not new to Windows Vista, although the Vista Task Scheduler *application* most certainly is.

As you will note, the Task Scheduler's "pane" appearance is much like that of Outlook 2003/2007, with a console tree in the left pane, the Task List in the middle pane, and an Actions pane on the right. The Task List is further divided into top and bottom panes, with the Task Preview (Properties) pane showing below a selected task in the top. So even though I describe how to access a task's Properties dialog box in the instructions that follow, there's really no need.

Further, you can show/hide the Task Scheduler pane with the toolbar buttons and the View menu options.

Scheduling a Task

Here's how to use the Task Scheduler to make life easier. Stepping through this procedure also serves as a good way to get familiar with the new interface and tone of the new Vista wizards:

1. Open the Task Scheduler. It's one of your system tools located under the Accessories grouping. You may be prompted for an administrator password if you're not already logged on as administrator.

2. In the Task Scheduler's program window, look at the Action pane on the right-hand side. These are the same actions you'd find under the Action menu. Choose Create a Basic Task.

3. Give the task a name and, optionally, a description. Note that every task must have a name and that the name must be unique to the task. Click Next.

4. You're now presented with several options:

   - For a calendar-based task, choose either Daily, Weekly, Monthly, or "One time." Click Next to specify the exact dates for the task.

   - For tasks based on particular events, such as "When the computer starts" or "When I log on," choose one of these two options.

   - For scheduling based on other nonrecurring events, choose the "When a specific event occurs" option. You'll then specify the event information after clicking Next.

5. As shown in Figure 1-26, the task can then perform one of three distinct actions. It can:

   Start a program automatically
   Choose "Start a program," and then Next, where you'll choose which program will run.

   Send an e-mail
   Select and click Next to specify both the message and the recipient. For example, you might use this kind of task to remind several users to submit reports for end-of-month activities.

   Display a message
   This message displays on the Vista desktop. Again, it's best used for reminders. Maybe you want to perform regular backups, but you want to perform them manually. You can configure this task to remind you and then perform the backup at a convenient time.

6. Click Finish.

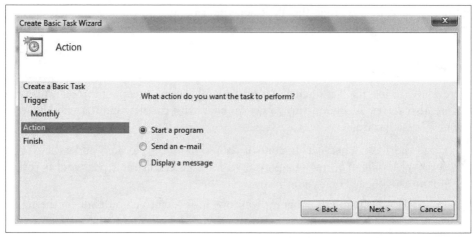

Figure 1-26. Basic tasks perform one of three actions

You should now be able to review and edit any user-created tasks by going to the Task Scheduler's left pane and choosing the Task Scheduler Library folder. To edit your task, right-click the task name and choose Properties. Other options, such as running the task manually or deleting the task, are also available by right-clicking, or by selecting the desired action in the Task Scheduler's right pane.

 You can export and import tasks that have been created on other computers so that you don't have to re-create tasks that might run on multiple systems, but the Vista tasks contain options and features that are more robust than in previous versions. For this reason, you cannot use a Vista-created task on a non-Vista computer. You can, however, use a task created on a Windows XP machine, for example, and import it into Vista's Task Scheduler.

Now let's look at one specific example where the Task Scheduler can be put to use.

Scheduling Disk Cleanup

One of the most common routine maintenance chores is to keep your hard drive free from clutter by removing files you no longer need. This task has two clear benefits: it frees up disk space for other applications, and it usually improves system performance. The Task Scheduler makes it easy to automate this task so that you never have to remember to do it.

Here are the necessary Task Scheduler steps:

1. Open the Task Scheduler. Try this: click Start, then type **task**. The Task Scheduler should be displayed in the Start menu by the time you've finished typing. Provide administrative credentials if prompted.

2. In the Action pane, click Create Basic Task.

3. Type **disk cleaning** in the Task Name dialog box, although you can use any name that suits your fancy. Add a description if you like, and click Next.

4. You'll now see the Task Trigger section of the Create Basic Task dialog box. Choose your desired calendar option and click.

5. Specify the exact schedule in the Trigger subsection and click Next.

6. In the Action section, choose the "Start a program" option and click Next.

7. Click the Browse button, and then type **cleanmgr.exe** in the "File name" box. Click Open to be returned to the "Start a program" subsection. Click Next.

8. Now you're done. Click Finish to exit the wizard. Select the checkbox to open the Properties dialog box for the task. (Doing so will let you immediately change some of the parameters you just set.)

As you may have noticed, you can also accomplish the same goals by choosing the Create a Task link rather than the Create a Basic Task option. By clicking Create a Task, you're given essentially the same options as in the Create a Basic Task Wizard. The difference is that the interface is a single dialog box with multiple tabs (Triggers, Actions, etc.) rather than the wizard's set of task questions.

No matter which interface you use, you should see configured tasks in the bottom of the Task Scheduler window, listed under the Active Tasks heading.

Vista SideShow

Another interesting new feature of Windows Vista that's worth a mention is something called the Windows SideShow. SideShow is a little tricky to explain; it clicks once you see a SideShow-enabled device.

For instance, you won't *see* the Vista SideShow on your laptop or desktop computer per se, but rather just configure it there using the dialog box shown in Figure 1-27. To launch the SideShow window, just type **side** in the Start menu's Search box. Windows SideShow should appear in the list of programs.

You can get a hint of what SideShow is used for by looking at this configuration window. From here, you'll tell one of the installed gadgets to send information to a SideShow-enabled device, which will be listed on the right. (Note that in Figure 1-27 I don't have a SideShow-enabled device.)

So, just what is a SideShow-enabled device, and why would I want one? Well, imagine reading your last few emails using a remote control. And I'm not talking about pointing the remote at a Vista computer with Media Center, mind you; I'm talking about checking email on a little screen *in the remote control itself*, while the Vista computer is turned off.

That's what Windows SideShow can do with a SideShow-enabled device. SideShow devices can let you perform simple little tasks such as checking your latest email, scrolling through a list of contacts, or looking through photos on your Vista

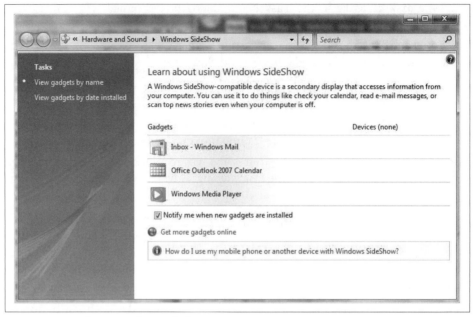

Figure 1-27. Configure Windows SideShow

machine, even while the machine where these files reside is powered off. SideShow-enabled devices include laptops, remotes, mobile phones, and even messenger bags with little external LCD screens built right in. Figure 1-28 provides a glimpse of a SideShow-enabled messenger bag in development from a company called Eleksen.

That's right. With a contraption such as this, you could look up a contact's mobile phone number without opening the laptop, or get the latest weather information courtesy of a Vista gadget that's sending information to SideShow.

Now, as of this writing, there aren't too many Windows SideShow-enabled devices. They should start arriving in stores around mid-2007. As a result, I can't really give a lot of setup instruction on configuring SideShow devices; steps will vary from device to device. Even the Microsoft help pages on the subject will tell you to refer to manufacturer documentation for installation steps.

Vista's New Printing Options

Vista even includes new options for producing printed output, thanks to a redesigned print architecture. The Vista print architecture is built on a technology called the Windows Presentation Foundation (WPF). WPF enhances printed content in several ways, including the following:

- Improved color management
- Removal of GDI-based print limitations

Figure 1-28. A SideShow-enabled device

- Better support of advanced print effects such as gradients and transparencies
- Enhanced support of color laser printers
- Easier printing of pictures
- Support for the XML Paper Specification (XPS)

Probably the most significant of these is the support for XPS. What's the big whoop? The XPS print path (XPS document writer) lets you create *.xps* files using any Windows program. You can then view these files on any computer that has an XPS viewer installed, *even if that computer doesn't have the program that originally installed the application.*

If the preceding description got you thinking Portable Document File, or PDF (I don't just use italics off the cuff here), you've pretty much got the idea, although XPS will not (at least for now) support every function available in a *.pdf*. Adobe wants to make money off its technology and all.

At any rate, here's how to print using the new XPS Document Writer:

1. First, open the file you want to print to the *.xps* format, and choose Print. (You usually can find this under the application's File menu, although some applications, such as Microsoft Word 2007, no longer have a File menu.)
2. Using the app's Print dialog box, select Microsoft XPS Document Writer, as shown in Figure 1-29.

3. Click OK.

4. Because you're printing to a file (logical) rather than to a print device (physical), you're now prompted for a filename and location where you want to save the *.xps* file. Your Documents folder is the default.

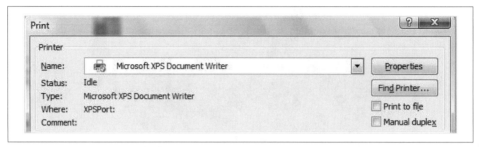

Figure 1-29. Print to XPS to facilitate easy document sharing

 For printers that support it, Vista makes the XPS print path available to physical devices as well. Microsoft claims that for What's On documents with intensive graphics, XPS printers are expected to produce better-quality prints than GDI printers.

The print subsystem in Windows Vista implements the new XPS print path as well as the legacy GDI print path for legacy support. For printers that support it, Vista will transparently make use of the XPS print path. Otherwise, it's the GDI print path for legacy support. For printers supporting XPS, this eliminates an intermediate conversion to a printer-specific language such as RAW, thus improving the fidelity of the printed output.

Using the XPS Viewer

So, if there's a way to create XPS files from any Windows application, surely there's a way to view these files built into Vista as well, right?

There is. It's called the XPS Viewer, although when you use it, you will be forgiven for thinking you're looking at Internet Explorer. That's because you are. When you open an XPS document, the viewer automatically launches inside an Internet Explorer window. You'll also see two additional toolbars, one above and one below. The XPS toolbars will allow you to perform these actions, among others, on the XML document:

- Save a copy
- Search for a word or phrase
- Go to a specific page
- Zoom

- Digitally sign the document
- Apply document permissions

Printing a Picture

Another enhanced printing feature is the way Vista handles pictures with a bundled application called the Windows Photo Gallery—not an essential administrative task, but worth pointing out.

The key, of course, is to first open the Photo Gallery application. It should appear in the All Programs menu after you click on the Vista Start button. Once there, use the checkboxes to select one or more pictures. With a picture selected, choose the Print option that appears in the Photo Gallery's toolbar. You'll see a dialog box such as the one in Figure 1-30.

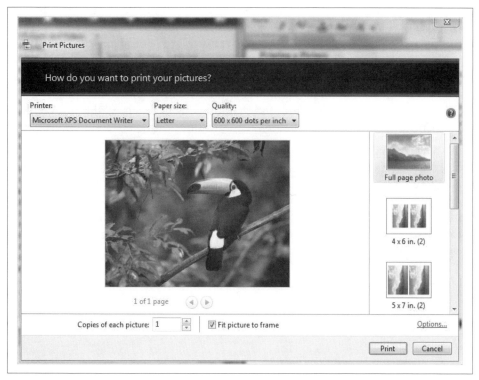

Figure 1-30. Vista greatly enhances photo printing options

You can take it from there. Of special note is the righthand pane. If you want to print four-up on 8.5 × 11-inch photo paper, just scroll down to the appropriate selection in the right pane.

One last thing

I want to leave this section on printing, and this chapter, with a little tip. This is not new to Vista, and it seems almost too elementary to include in this book, yet I find experienced computer users all the time who are unaware of this little printing time-saver, so I'm passing it on.

It's this: you don't have to open the file to print it. Just right-click the file wherever you find it in Vista—in its folder, in a Virtual (search result) folder, or even in an attachment in an email—and then choose Print. This will send the selected file to the default printer with just a click or two.

Summary

This chapter covered what's new and different in Windows Vista. We'd be here another 100 pages or so if I covered everything, so I just picked the things I thought were the most improved over previous versions, or would have the biggest impact on your Vista computing experience. The objective is to get you up and running as quickly as possible; we'll get more into the meat and potatoes of Vista administration in the chapters that follow. If this chapter helps you make the business case for your/your company's move to Vista, all the better. You've heard that Vista is going to be easier to use and more secure, and that it's going to be a breakthrough computing experience; now you can associate specific features with these descriptions.

One thing that Vista administrators must possess is a clear understanding of the different Vista versions. Right now, there are five distinct flavors of Windows Vista: Home Basic, Home Premium, Business, Enterprise, and Ultimate. In the next chapter, we'll look at each version in detail so that you'll be able to make more informed decisions about which version is right for your enterprise (it's probably not Home Basic). As you will see, not every version will support every feature, so it's vital to have this information before making your purchase.

CHAPTER 2

A Look at the Different Versions

In Chapter 1, we examined many of the new features that separate Windows Vista from its predecessors. There's a caveat, however: some of these new features that you're eager to put through the paces are available on only certain Vista versions.

Don't try to implement BitLocker, for example, on the Home Basic version. You won't find it there. And upgrading to Home Premium will bring you little satisfaction if BitLocker is the goal.

If you bring home your work-issued laptop and plan to use it to record television programs for later viewing because you heard Windows Vista includes the Media Center as a built-in application, you might be in for a surprise. Although you'd be correct in your assumption that Vista no longer treats the Media Center as a separate application, you didn't factor in the reality that this application isn't available on all Vista editions. There isn't necessarily anything *wrong* with the scenario just mentioned—you might want to record the local evening news, which is running a piece about your latest product release, for example—but you've brought the wrong tool for the job. In the example just mentioned, in which you want a computer to easily exist happily in both a home *and* a business environment, the Business edition won't fit the bill. Ultimate is the solution you're looking for.

This chapter, then, is a brief overview of the five different flavors of Windows Vista: Home Basic, Home Premium, Business, Enterprise, and Ultimate. In many ways, you can think of this chapter as a companion piece to Chapter 1's overview of new features; I just didn't want to create an opening chapter that ran into the 80- to 100-page ballpark. After all, there are a lot of features in the Windows Vista product suite, and keeping track of them can be a chore. Yet this is vital information to have when it comes to making purchasing and technology deployment decisions.

So, then, I've taken on the chore of briefing you on the Vista components so that they're all in one place. After reading the chapter, you'll be better able to recall which version supports what feature, information that can be a big help the next time you're about to get out your credit card at a retailer, or customize your system build from your favorite manufacturer's web site.

Five Vista Versions

As of the release-to-manufacturer (RTM) time—meaning that Microsoft has shipped the final code so that computer makers can start building systems with Vista preinstalled—five versions of Windows Vista are available in the U.S. market. The different editions are specifically tailored to meet the needs of varying operating system scenarios. Two are designed for the home user, two are meant to operate in a secure business environment, and one, Vista Ultimate, has the capability to happily exist in both. Here are the formal titles:

- Windows Vista **Home Basic**
- Windows Vista **Home Premium**
- Windows Vista **Business**
- Windows Vista **Enterprise**
- Windows Vista **Ultimate**

We'll discuss the characteristics of each under a separate heading, starting with the Home Basic edition.

 There are actually many more versions than this. My European readers, of whom there will be many, no doubt, may be using a version called Vista version N, which is essentially Vista with the Media Player stripped out of the default install in order to comply with an EU antitrust resolution. Also available in what Microsoft refers to as *emerging markets* is the Windows Vista Starter edition. Designed for users for whom Vista might be their first operating system, the Starter edition includes additional tools and tutorials to make it easier to use. The biggest difference in the Starter edition, however, is the price.

The Vista Starter edition is not available in "high-income" markets such as the United States, Canada, the European Union, Australia, and New Zealand. Features that apply only to the Starter edition will not be covered in this book.

Vista Home Basic Edition

The Windows Vista Home Basic edition is geared toward home users who want to take advantage of several of the new *security* and *search* capabilities included with Vista. In the following few sections is an overview of what to expect with a purchase of Home Basic.

Instant Search

I introduced the Instant Search capability in Chapter 1, in the section "New Ways to Search." This is because it's one of the most significant changes to the operating system, especially when compared to Windows XP. To briefly review, Instant Search is a huge boon in the age of the 300+ GB hard drive. (I'm referring mainly to desktops; by the time this book hits the shelves, no doubt, this median will apply equally to laptop machines as well.)

Not only does Instant Search make locating files on your computer much faster than before, but it also frees users from needing a complicated filing system. This will be a hard habit to break for a lot of users, but it's just not all that crucial a task anymore to organize your partitions into a series of directories and subdirectories. Just create a large "storage room" or two for your working files (Music, Pictures, and Documents, for example) and let Instant Search find them when it's time to work with them again.

An even harder habit to break, and yet another byproduct of Instant Search, is the practice of using the mouse to locate the program you want to open. Is the Task Scheduler under the Accessories program folder, or is it in Maintenance? Who cares? Just type **TASK** after clicking the Start button, and the Task Scheduler should appear before you've finished typing the word.

Instant Search is possible thanks to the Windows Indexing Service, a service that launches at startup time and runs in the background by default. What's even more convenient is the ability to modify the locations that the Indexing Service actually indexes. Here's what to do:

1. Open the Control Panel and then the Indexing Options application. If you're using the Classic View, you should see it as a standalone applet. With the Standard View, it's located under the System and Maintenance grouping.

2. The Indexing Options dialog box displays which locations are indexed. Click Modify to make changes.

3. Now, make your changes by checking and unchecking boxes in the Indexed Locations dialog box, shown in Figure 2-1.

Note here that you won't see all of your computer's locations by default. Outlook locations and offline folders are likely the only ones that appear. But you can easily manage all indexed locations by clicking the "Show all locations" button at the bottom of the dialog box. Showing all locations requires administrative rights, however; to proceed, you may be prompted for administrative credentials by User Account Control.

What might be even more powerful—and useful—is the Indexing Service's capability to catalog not only *where* to keep track of files, but *what* to keep track of, as you'll see in the next section.

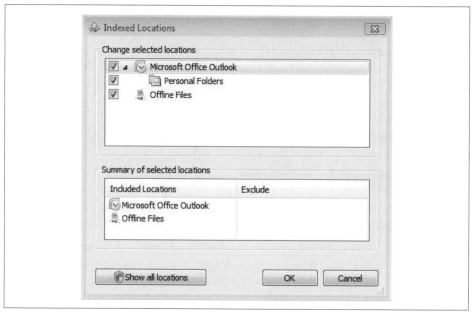

Figure 2-1. Fine-tune indexing behavior from here

Indexing file contents

When performing a search, you might also notice that sometimes the Indexing Service has the capability to look *inside* a file. Try this out to see what I'm talking about:

1. Open a Word document and type your name in the document.

2. Then save the file and name it whatever day of the week it is. Got it so far? You should now have a Word file on your system with a name such as *Saturday* whose contents are a single word such as *Brian*.

3. Now save and close the file, and then go to the Start menu. Click Start and type **Brian** (or whatever your name is; bully for you if it happens to be Brian, correct usage of the *i* and all).

What does the index find? Exactly. It'll find your file called *Saturday*. Why? Because the index—for certain files—catalogs not only the file *properties* (the title, author, date it was created, etc.), but also the file *contents*.

And, of course, you can change whether a file's contents are indexed at any time. Just open the Indexing Options dialog box again and choose the Advanced button. (User Account Control may prompt for administrative confirmation.)

Then, from the Advanced Options dialog box, choose the File Types tab and make your selections, as shown in Figure 2-2.

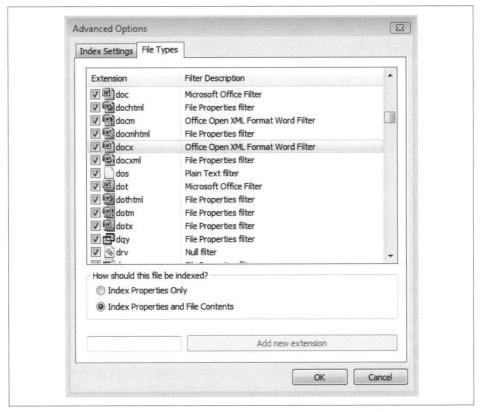

Figure 2-2. Decide whether to index file contents

If you wanted to search only for Word documents using the document titles, for example, choose the *.docx* extension (if using Word 2007), and then select the Index Properties Only radio button.

Once you've made a change to the index behavior, it's always a good idea to rebuild the index. If you don't take this step, you might not see the results you expect in your next search, as the search query will be carried out against an old index version.

To rebuild the index, just choose the Index Settings tab in the Advanced Options dialog box shown in Figure 2-3, and then click the Rebuild button.

You will be warned about speed during the reindexing process. Click OK to proceed.

And the choices continue. If you want to include a specific folder but not all of its subfolders, expand the folder and then clear any checkboxes for folders you don't want indexed. The choices will appear in the Exclude column when examining the "Summary of selected locations" list.

Also worth pointing out is the Indexing Options "reset" button. To undo *all* changes you've made to the indexing behavior, just access the Advanced Options dialog box as described previously. Then click the Restore Defaults button, as shown in Figure 2-3.

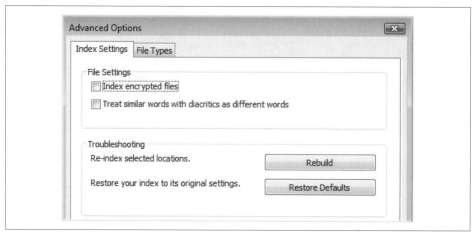

Figure 2-3. Rebuild the index after a significant change

Search Folders

Another feature new to all versions of Windows Vista, including Home Basic, is the ability to create and save Search Folders. Working in conjunction with Instant Search, Search Folders let you organize files without much, if any, preplanning on your part. The Search Folders keep you organized on an ad hoc basis by creating virtual storage locations that are easily accessed using Windows Explorer.

The best way to explain is with an example. Let's say that in the course of a busy work month, you've accumulated a bunch of *vital* files that have to do with fantasy baseball. Now, you want to quickly locate all those files that have to do with just one team, the Royals. And you want to refine your results to just those that mention a certain player, Brian.

Using the steps outlined in Chapter 1, you can create a search containing those two search criteria, and then choose the Save Search button in the Windows Explorer toolbar.

The virtual folder now appears as part of the user profile. Saved searches are stored under the directory called Searches, as shown in Figure 2-4.

What's more, you can go back to the Search Folder a week, a month, or even a year later and just give it a click. The search runs again, providing almost instant access to anything else you've added to your computer since the last search that meets the same criteria as the original search.

Figure 2-4. Using Search Folders is a simple and fast way to keep track of files without creating additional directories

And maybe best of all is that you can create and remove saved searches to help you keep organized on an ad hoc basis. Here's what I mean.

Have you ever performed a clean install with Windows XP and created folders for files? Of course you have, and you feel pretty darn organized when you do. But how does that same computer look six months later? If you're like me, you've now got folders everywhere, some called Contracts, some called Clients, some called Writing, Saved Sh#!, and so forth, and there are about 300 other files in the Documents folder that I'll get around to organizing "someday." Oh, and there are also three or four files that I can never find because they've ended up in some obscure Temp folder that has me thinking fondly of that scene from *Office Space* with the baseball bat and the fax machine.

But with Vista, I don't have to worry about creating and maintaining such an organized folder hierarchy. I can just create a few folders—Work, Personal, and Saved, for instance—and let virtual folders track down the information I'm looking for. I can keep organized and rearrange this organization system in a way that best suits my needs that day, and I can even use two organization systems simultaneously.

To delete a saved search that's no longer useful, just select it and click Delete. The virtual folder goes to the Recycle Bin, where it can later be retrieved if it's needed again. Deleting a virtual folder has no effect on the files themselves. It's like deleting a program shortcut; you are really just deleting a reference to the real thing.

Internet Explorer 7

Internet Explorer 7 isn't technically unique to Windows Vista—you can use it on a Windows XP machine, after all—but it is the Internet browser that is included with the Vista operating system. And because the browser is part of the operating system and all (just ask Netscape), it deserves a mention here. I won't discuss the basics of using a web browser, though. As always, my focus is on what's new and different in this latest iteration.

And, snarky parenthetical commentary about Internet browsers aside, I submit that Internet Explorer 7 *is* a great improvement over Internet Explorer 6 in several areas, including those listed in the following subsections:

Tabbed browsing. Although not necessarily new to Internet Explorer 7, this does significantly change the way you'll open and work with many different web sites. In the past, if you wanted to have multiple web sites open, you had to open each one in a separate window. Now, each site can be opened with only a single Internet Explorer 7 window instance. The difference is that each will open using a separate tab.

 Tabbed browsing is available in Internet Explorer 6 with the MSN Search Toolbar with Desktop Search. Of course, the look and feel are a little different from Internet Explorer 7, but the basic principles are the same.

Search. One of the best features of the new Internet Explorer is the one that is the easiest to explain: the new Search box, which lets you choose from multiple search providers without having to navigate to the provider's web site.

For example, the default search provider with Internet Explorer 7 is Live Search. To change it to Google, for example, click the arrow in the Search box and then choose "Find more providers" from the drop-down menu. You'll then see the web site shown in Figure 2-5.

As you can see, adding more providers is just a matter of clicking on the respective search icon.

It can also be extraordinarily helpful to create your own search favorite using the steps that appear on the righthand side of this page. If you're a doctor, lawyer, or just about any type of researcher, you can add search providers that will let you search a certain reference site, such as FindLaw, WebMD, or something like that (although WebMD is really geared toward patients, not doctors, but you get the idea).

RSS feeds. Internet Explorer 7 also lets you subscribe directly to Really Simple Syndication (RSS) feeds. An RSS feed allows users to stay on top of the latest changes to web site content. RSS feeds are all about personalization and customization of web

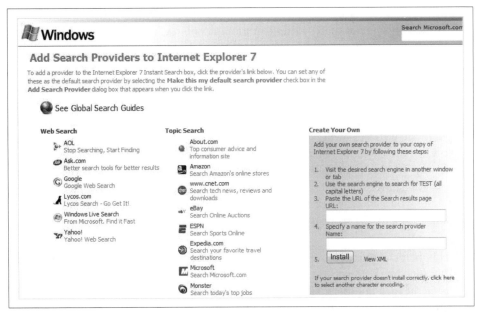

Figure 2-5. Internet Explorer 7 lets you quickly choose from multiple search providers

content that's important to you. What's more, this content is brought to you rather than you having to go out and browse for it. Internet Explorer 7 puts it all right at your fingertips.

Using an RSS feed, for example, you could be notified of price changes to an item you're shopping for, get instant scores from your favorite team, or receive news about a particular event. In the most common RSS implementation, a web site or other content provider publishes a feed link on its site that can be monitored by an *aggregator*, or news reader program. Internet Explorer 7 is one such aggregator.

To subscribe to a web page's feed, look for the little orange RSS feed button and give it a click (these buttons sometimes just say "RSS"). Once you've subscribed, Internet Explorer 7 queries the sites in the feed list to see whether they contain new content. If the site's feed list indicates that there is new content, Internet Explorer 7 notifies you.

One last thought on the latest Microsoft browser: yr. correspondent has used, and continues to use, competing browsers at times, and is therefore fully cognizant that some people decry the Microsoft browser as simply being a "me too" type of application. Firefox comes immediately to mind as one factor that seems to have driven many of the latest Internet Explorer 7 enhancements. This may be because Firefox is following a strategy that, until recently, only Microsoft has been able to pursue with regard to its browser: Mozilla doesn't seem to be concerned with making money with this application.

Security. Several new security enhancements are also built into Internet Explorer 7. We'll touch on some of these features in more detail in Chapter 10, but following are the security features worthy of note:

Security Status Bar

This provides a visual cue when web browsing presents a potential risk or is not recommended at all. The status bar displays a color-coded notification next to the Address bar and changes the color of the Address bar itself. Green signifies *good*; the web site owner has completed several identity and security checks. Yellow means *caution ahead*; information could be intercepted. Red can mean a variety of things, including that the site has been reported as a known fraudulent (phishing) site, or that the security certificate does not match the web site's name. You can easily display certificate and privacy detail information with a single click on the security status bar.

Phishing Filter

This helps protect you against either potential or known phishing sites—sites that *look* like real web sites but are designed to obtain personal information such as credit card numbers, addresses, and so on. The Phishing Filter also blocks the site if appropriate. Additionally, the Phishing Filter is updated several times per hour using the latest security information from Microsoft and other industry partners.

Fix My Settings

Internet Explorer 7 warns you with an information bar whenever current security settings could put you at risk. The information bar lets you instantly reset Internet security settings to the default Medium-High level. Just click the Fix My Settings option. Additionally, you will see certain critical items highlighted in red when they are unsafely configured in the Internet Options Control Panel applet.

Delete Browsing History

This is a streamlined, simplified dialog box where users can clear forms, cookies, passwords, and temporary Internet files. To access it, choose the Tools button and then click Delete Browsing History. You will see the dialog box shown in Figure 2-6.

And note that you can easily erase *all* Internet history with a single click of the "Delete all" button. A confirmation dialog box is then all that stands between you and the covering of your tracks.

Built-in diagnostics

Another great feature in Windows Vista Home Basic, and therefore in all editions of Windows Vista, is built-in diagnostics. Built-in diagnostics provides automatic correction for common errors such as hard drive failures, startup issues, and memory problems. In other words, Vista works harder than ever before to protect your vital data. As a result, you won't have to.

Figure 2-6. A centralized location for safeguarding web browsing privacy

What's more, the diagnostics functionality automatically conjures up the appropriate utility when a problem is detected. If Vista's built-in diagnostics detects a faulty RAM module, for example, it will automatically display a notification asking whether you'd like Vista to try to diagnose the problem. You don't have to curse your computer while guessing at what could be going on. (You can also run this diagnostics tool anytime you want by looking for an app called *mdsched.exe*. Better yet, just type **memory** at the Start menu prompt. The Memory Diagnostics tool should appear at the top of the list.)

The same applies for other subsystems that affect computer behavior: networking, processor, and the aforementioned hard drive.

Another nice new Vista utility is the Control Panel application called Problem Reports and Solutions. To open it, look for the System and Maintenance grouping if you're using the Standard View. (It's a standalone icon when you're using the Classic View.) You'll get a dialog box that looks like Figure 2-7.

The Problem Reports and Solutions center presents you with a variety of tasks in the lefthand side of this interface that help you identify problems and, more important, locate their solutions without clicking all over the Internet. Use is pretty straightforward: just follow an informational or solution link, and a page opens with instructions on how to address the problem. Often, you'll be taken to a web site where a patch or hotfix is available.

Again, these topics are discussed in full during Chapter 14's look at troubleshooting.

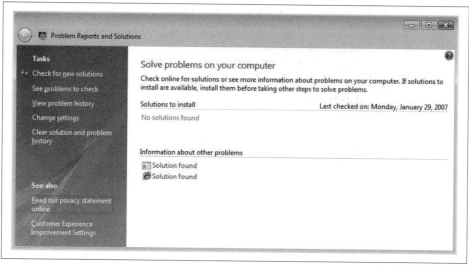

Figure 2-7. Fix issues automatically with the Problem Reports and Solutions application

Windows Firewall and Windows Defender

The Windows Vista Firewall and Windows Defender work in harmony to protect your computer from common Internet threats. These technologies were first introduced in Chapter 1 and will be revisited again in Chapter 12.

For the time being, just know that these two utilities are part of the enhanced security package that is built into every edition of Windows Vista, including Home Basic.

Vista Basic interface

Windows Vista Home Basic also comes standard with the Vista Basic interface. The Basic interface is less graphics-processor-intensive than its Aero counterpart, and therefore is also better suited for older machines that meet only the minimum recommendations for running Vista. (You'll see the difference between the Basic interface and Aero in starker detail in the discussion of Home Premium.)

Its graphics engine produces windows that, by default, are both silver and opaque. You won't see through these windows, just as you couldn't see through windows in previous editions of Windows. Application windows will generally look like what you see in Figure 2-8.

So far in this chapter, I've used screenshots using only this Vista Basic interface. Clever, huh? But the changes go beyond simply turning electric-blue windows into silver ones. Microsoft set out not only to improve the operating system's features, but also to improve operating system *performance*. According to Microsoft, a computer running Windows Vista *should* perform faster than the same machine running Windows XP.

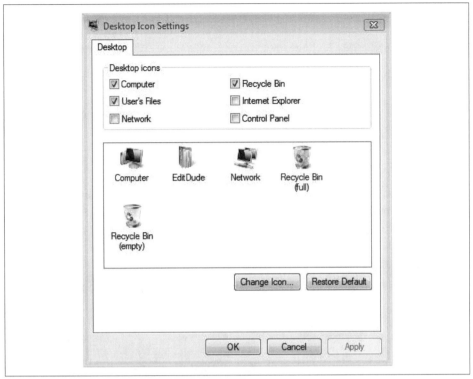

Figure 2-8. Opaque windows in Home Basic

So, then: if you use a computer mainly as a platform for productivity applications such as Microsoft Office, Internet Explorer, and so on, this is probably all the operating system you need, and it should provide you with snappier performance than ever before.

Windows Photo Gallery

Introduced in Chapter 1, the Photo Gallery makes it easy to manage your digital photography collection. Included are several organization choices so that you can set up a filing system that best suits your needs.

It would be beyond the scope of this book to delve into every aspect of the Photo Gallery in detail, but one feature I'd like to specifically point out is the Import Pictures and Videos Wizard. It lets you add keywords, or (metadata) tags, to your photos. These keywords can be an absolute godsend when you're trying to locate your pictures later on.

For example, say you're looking for pictures of the ocean in a directory that contains 2,000 pictures. Instead of sifting through your entire collection one photo at a time, add a tag to the picture by following these steps:

1. Right-click the photo and choose Add Tags from the context menu. (Alternatively, you could just select the photo from the library.)

2. The Info pane lists any existing tags, and lets you add more tags using the Add Tag link. You can also edit the picture's title using the bottom of this Info pane. Searching using a word in the title will work as well.

 If you don't see the Info pane, click on Info on the Windows Photo Gallery toolbar.

3. The Photo Gallery also lets you add keywords during the import process. To start the Import Pictures and Videos Wizard, choose File → Import from a Camera or Scanner. The Wizard runs, letting you add words about a specific picture's subject, scene, or event from the dialog box shown in Figure 2-9.

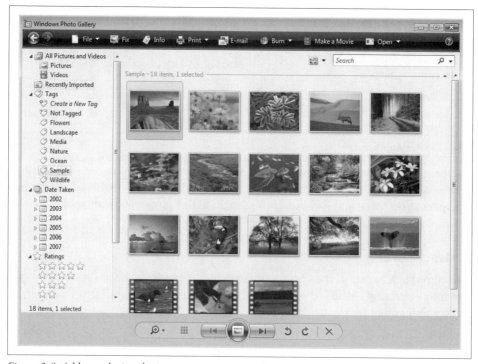

Figure 2-9. Add tags during the import process to speed up picture retrieval at a later time

Additionally, the Photo Gallery now lets you search for photos using "date taken" as a search criterion. Enter **Dec 2005**, for example, to quickly bring up images of a company party during which you performed that half-clothed dance that had everyone laughing, and which, examined with the aid of 2006's hindsight, you discover was equal parts outrageously hilarious and deeply regrettable.

The Date Taken category is automatically grouped by year and then by month on the lefthand side of the Photo Gallery.

One last cool thing about the Photo Gallery is the way you can quickly adjust the thumbnail size, another tool that can make finding pictures easier. Just click the magnifying glass icon at the bottom of the Photo Gallery window and then adjust using the slider control. Told you it was cool.

Hardware considerations

So what kind of machine should be running Vista Home Basic? Maybe *should* is the wrong word here. *Can* is more like it. First, let's examine the hardware requirements. Here are the minimum requirements to run this operating system version:

- An 800 MHz processor
- At least 512 MB of RAM
- A graphics card that supports DirectX 9
- At least 15 GB of free space on a 40 GB hard drive

And what about a really tricked-out Home Basic machine? The 32-bit version will support a single processor (although the dual-core procs count as only one processor), and they support 4 GB of physical RAM. The 64-bit version will support up to 8 GB of physical memory.

 Home Basic supports five simultaneous inbound network connections.

In summary, Windows Vista Home Basic is most similar to Windows XP Home edition. It is a solid operating system built for home users who want basic computer functionality while spending the least amount of money possible to get that functionality. It is a good choice, however, as a platform for almost any application the home user would want to run, and it includes a bundle comprising games, Internet Explorer 7, Media Player 11, and Windows Photo Gallery. It will run applications such as Adobe Photoshop and Microsoft Office with aplomb.

It does *not* include support for the Media Center, which provides advanced digital entertainment support. It also does not include Vista Backup, premium games such as Chess and Mahjong, and support for Tablet PCs. For these reasons, I find it difficult to make a strong case that someone should upgrade an XP Home machine to Vista Home Basic. The only exception to this is if you use a PC extensively for managing digital photos, in which case Photo Gallery is a slick little bundled app. But if you're going to *upgrade* a system, my recommendation is to upgrade to Home Premium.

Microsoft plans to support Home Basic until 2012.

Vista Home Premium Edition

Home Premium includes all of the features of Vista Home Basic. It adds several capabilities to this core set of features, though, that make it a better choice for computers handling a lot of digital entertainment such as pictures and movies. In fact, you can think of Home Premium as Home Basic with a few additional features turned on, because that's exactly what it is. Whether these additional features are worth the price, of course, is strictly up to you. (Allow me to help in your discernment here: they are.)

In addition to the Home Basic features listed previously, Windows Vista Home Premium also includes the following:

- Windows Aero
- Windows Movie and DVD Maker
- Windows Meeting Space
- Media Center
- Tablet PC support
- Mobility Center
- Xbox 360 Extender

 Vista Home Premium supports 10 simultaneous inbound network connections.

We'll examine each additional feature in the sections that follow.

Windows Aero

When most people think of the new features in Windows Vista, they're thinking of a user interface environment known as Windows Aero. When I get the question, "Hey, what's that thing where the applications do that swirly thing and you can see through them?" Aero is the answer. For sheer "wow" factor, this one's tough to beat.

It's tempting to call Aero "eye candy," but the characteristics of Aero go far beyond the enhanced visual appeal. Aero truly does make PC use smoother and more intuitive than it has been in the past (or, according to Microsoft, clearer and more confident).

Just because you purchase Vista Home Premium doesn't mean you can automatically use Aero. One vital component of the Windows Aero discussion is that your hardware must support it in order for you to use it. When compared to the Windows Vista Basic interface, Aero requires a heck of a lot more horsepower. Here are the hardware minimums for Aero, which in turn pretty much define the minimums for Windows Home Premium. I don't think many folks will want to run Home Premium without using the Aero interface:

- A 1 GHz processor
- At least 1 GB of physical RAM
- At least 128 MB of memory on the graphics card
- A graphics card driver that supports DirectX 9 and uses a Windows Display Driver Model (WDDM) driver
- At least 15 GB of free disk space on a 40 GB hard drive

As you can see, the graphics card is going to present the biggest performance hurdle for users upgrading older machines, with the 1 GB of physical memory requirement running a close second. (When I started this book, only one of my two *desktop* machines had 1 GB of RAM.) Most cards with 128 MB or more of memory from video card manufacturers ATI and NVIDIA support this WDDM standard, but check before you buy.

 OEMs will advertise their systems as Windows Vista Premium Ready if they support the Aero minimums.

Whatever adjectives are used to describe Aero, here's what to expect when using a computer running this new Vista interface.

Glass window appearance. The first thing to note about the new Windows interface is, well, the appearance of the windows themselves.

The default Aero color scheme is clear glass. Much like real glass (think the kind that's used in a lot of shower doors), this glass appearance allows you to see other items *behind* your window through a slightly blurred, translucent effect.

As with so many other aspects of the Windows interface, the glass appearance is completely customizable. If clear glass is not for you, you can easily "tint" your windows by selecting from these glass options:

- Graphite
- Blue
- Teal
- Red
- Orange
- Pink
- Frost

To access these appearance options, just right-click the desktop and choose Personalize, which replaces the Properties option that's been available on the Windows desktop for years. Then choose the Window Color and Appearance link at the top to open the configuration window. As shown in Figure 2-10, the sliding bar lets you adjust the level of glass opacity. There's even an advanced glass setting that allows you to disable transparent glass altogether.

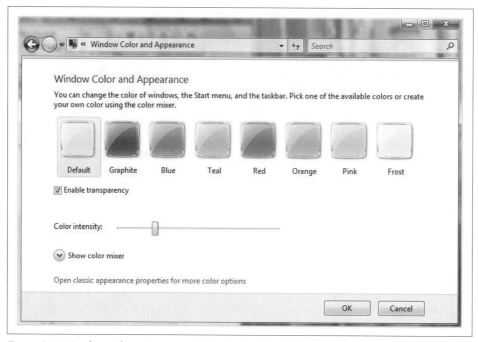

Figure 2-10. Configure the appearance of Aero's glass windows

You can even fine-tune glass color by using the color mixer at the bottom. This will let you make adjustments based on hue, saturation, and brightness. If you turn down the brightness, for example, you can *really* see through your windows.

Live taskbar thumbnails. Another navigation aid that's part of the Windows Aero interface is something called *live taskbar thumbnails*. Let's say you have multiple instances of windows open, and you want to use the time-honored Windows method of switching among programs: you want to click the Taskbar program button.

The problem, though, is that you're currently working with 10 windows, and the taskbar is too crowded to see the window titles. With previous Windows versions (and in the Vista Basic interface, for that matter), switching to the desired program window was a hit-or-miss proposition.

Now, however, the taskbar thumbnail in Aero gives us a fighting chance. By hovering the mouse pointer over a taskbar button, you'll see a thumbnail, which in turn displays the contents of that window, as shown in Figure 2-11.

Figure 2-11. The live thumbnail helps sift through a cluttered taskbar

The live thumbnail is displayed regardless of whether the window is minimized, and will show everything the program window contains—photos, documents, and even running videos. The live thumbnails are particularly helpful when maneuvering among multiple windows of the same application.

Windows Flip and Flip 3D. I covered these two features in Chapter 1, so we won't spend much time on them here. To review, these are navigational aids that complement the taskbar thumbnails:

- To use Windows Flip, hold down the Alt-Tab key combination, pressing Tab repeatedly to choose among open applications. As with the taskbar thumbnail, you see a live preview of each window rather than the standard program icon.

- For Windows Flip 3D, hold down the Windows key and the Alt key in a similar manner. You can also use the scroll wheel on your mouse to flip through the open windows. Release the key combo to make the desired application the active window.

Windows Movie Maker and DVD Maker

Another nice addition to the Home Premium bundle are the Movie Maker and DVD Maker applications. I'm treating them as a single Vista feature because they will work hand in hand on most occasions. In other words, you'll first edit a movie in Movie Maker and then burn it to a DVD using the DVD Maker. As with the Photo Gallery application, a full discussion of Movie Maker and DVD Maker capabilities is beyond the scope of this book. It's *fairly* easy to get started creating a home movie, but it will probably take a few trips to the help files to gather a full understanding of the tools available. As you can see in Figure 2-12, I was able to get a movie of Vegas snapshots thrown together with little trouble, adding music and transitions between pics.

Once you're done creating the movie, you have the opportunity to see how easily Movie Maker and DVD Maker work together. When you choose the DVD option in the list of "Publish to" tasks, Vista will immediately open the DVD Maker application

Figure 2-12. Create a movie using Windows Movie Maker

with your movie loaded up and ready to burn. Once the media have been added, all that's left is to choose the menu style and then click Burn. Naturally, you'll need a DVD burner attached to your system in order to create a new DVD.

 I want to again emphasize that I'm just pointing out the features of Home Premium, and not trying to provide instructions or recommendations on either of these two apps. Video editing is a highly specialized field, and professional editors don't edit with either of these two tools. These features exist to help the average home user make a home video that won't bore everyone to tears.

Windows Meeting Space

Despite the relative ease with which a Windows computer can share information in a network, true real-time collaboration can still be a challenge. For example, what would you do if you were preparing a PowerPoint presentation, and you wanted to do a dress rehearsal in which you could solicit a few last-minute comments from several coworkers? If you're like most small- and even medium-size companies, you might save the *.ppt* (or *.pptx*) file to a flash drive and hand it to one coworker at a time. Or you could send your coworkers the file using email or Instant Messenger. Paper handouts are not uncommon, either.

But what if you could just set up a shared virtual meeting space for those same co-workers, allowing them to easily see what's on your computer and offer comments and/or edits without anyone leaving his computer? You can do just this with Windows Meeting Space.

To get started with a Windows Meeting Space session, click the Start menu, and then Windows Meeting Space. Type **meet** in the Search bar if you don't immediately see it in the Start Menu. If this is the first time you're using Windows Meeting Space, you'll be asked whether you want to enable People Near Me and File Replication. Answer "Yes, continue setting up Windows Meeting Space," and you'll be prompted for your People Near Me screen name.

Now you can start a meeting session using the dialog box shown in Figure 2-13.

Figure 2-13. Get productive using Windows Meeting Space

The Windows Meeting Space session gives you several meeting options. For starters, you can simply share your desktop or a specific application with other meeting participants. Click the Share button on the meeting session's window to get started. Participants will then be able to see your desktop without leaving their computers.

You can also "project" an application or desktop to any Windows Vista-compliant Network Projector. You could also share a file with the meeting group by creating a handout. Creating a handout allows meeting participants to make edits on the fly, eventually leading to a "collaborated" version of the file. The original handout item will not be changed.

You also can use Windows Meeting Space with Vista Home Basic, but only kinda. Basic users can only view meetings.

Windows Media Center

Once treated as a separate operating system by Windows XP, Windows Media Center serves as a "digital dashboard" for easy access to home entertainment content. This dashboard makes it easy to perform such tasks as calling up a movie, creating a slideshow of photos, or recording and then watching a TV show, using a remote control from your couch. Windows Media Center is optimized to make enjoying your photos, home movies, and TV a better experience than ever before, supporting widescreen and HD formats. And Windows Media Center lets you organize digital entertainment in many ways. As seen in Figure 2-14, Windows Media Center includes options such as thumbnail pictures to help you quickly identify which CD, photo, movie, or TV show you're looking for.

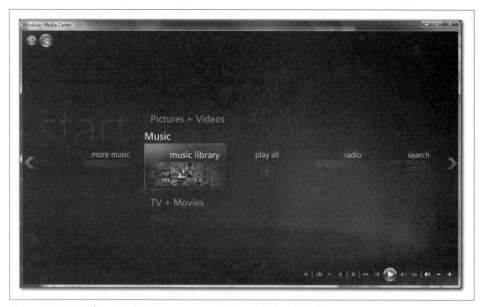

Figure 2-14. Windows Media Center can make Vista the hub of a home entertainment system

Another nice feature is the capability of Windows Media Center to handle multiple media sources at once. For example, you can easily search through your digital photo collection or change the selected *.mp3* playlist while continuing to view the movie, TV show, or other photos already on your screen. (Again, Windows Media Center is really just the dashboard; Windows Media Player is the engine that handles the files.)

What's more, you can extend the Windows Media Center experience to multiple rooms. Vista's version lets you enjoy all your digital entertainment, not only on your PC but also on up to five TVs, through the use of Media Center Extenders. That means you can be *working* on your PowerPoint presentation for the next day in your home office while the rest of the family is *watching* a movie hosted on the same computer on a 42-inch plasma display in the living room. Cool, yes?

In my mind, this represents the most compelling reason to use Home Premium over Home Basic whenever possible. You can even extend this Media Center Extender to the Xbox 360 as well—more on that in a separate subsection covering the Xbox Extender.

If it's all set up correctly, you can sit down at any TV in your house and see the same Media Center digital dashboard, and thus have easy access to your entire digital universe.

Windows Mobility Center

The Windows Mobility Center represents not so much a new technology, but rather a new location to obtain easy access to a host of technologies. And as fate would have it, all of these technologies have something to do with mobile computing.

For example, it's often necessary to change multiple settings over the course of a mobile computing day. You may want to conserve your battery by adjusting usage patterns or screen brightness while using your mobile computer on a plane. When conducting a presentation, often you need to make a display tweak or two once the external display has been attached. In the past, such changes were made using different applications in the Control Panel. They still are, technically, although it's easy to access all of them at once using the Mobility Center.

Here are the areas of mobile computing the Mobility Center lets you modify:

Presentation settings

I'm listing this one first because it is a new bell and/or whistle. The rest are in alphabetical order.

Click the Turn On button (insert your own tasteless joke here; yr. correspondent, despite hours upon hours in front of the computer, has resisted temptation) to send output to an external projector. You can then adjust presentation settings with the Projector button, opening the Presentation Settings dialog box shown in Figure 2-15. Note that, among other things, you can quickly change the desktop background should you decide your Vegas vacation pics aren't exactly congruent with the company's mission statement during that presentation to shareholders.

When presenting, you'll see a System Tray presentation icon. You can right-click that icon to stop the presentation instead of opening the Mobility Center again. Once the presentation stops, changes such as the desktop background return to the way they were before the presentation.

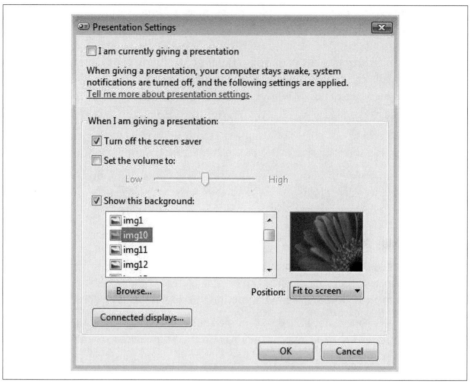

Figure 2-15. Change presentation settings easily with this dialog box

Battery status

Here you get a quick visual indication of how much charge remains on your battery. You can also easily change power plans from the drop-down menu.

Brightness

Use the slider to adjust display brightness. Note, though, that this is a temporary setting, and is not the same as adjusting brightness of a *power plan*. To adjust the brightness settings for your power plan, use the Power Options tile and follow the Change Plan Settings link from the Control Panel applet.

External display

This allows you to quickly connect an additional monitor to your laptop computer. Click the display icon to open the Display Settings dialog box to adjust resolution.

Screen rotation

You'll see this only if you're running a Tablet PC computer. It allows you to change the orientation of your screen.

Sync Center

This displays the status of any file sync in progress, and lets you configure new sync partnerships. Clicking on the Sync Settings button opens the Sync Center Control Panel applet.

Volume

Use the slider to adjust speaker volume (or mute the speakers altogether). You can also click the Speaker button to configure more advanced volume settings, such as that of the recording device.

Wireless network

This shows the status of the wireless connection. You can toggle the wireless adapter on or off from here as well.

You can access the Mobility Center in one of two ways. The first is by using the Control Panel. Just look for the Mobility Center icon when you're using the Classic View. (In the Standard View, look in the Mobile PC grouping.) Also, you can right-click the Battery Status icon in the System Tray and choose Windows Mobility Center from the context menu. Either way, you'll see a Mobility Center much like the one shown in Figure 2-16.

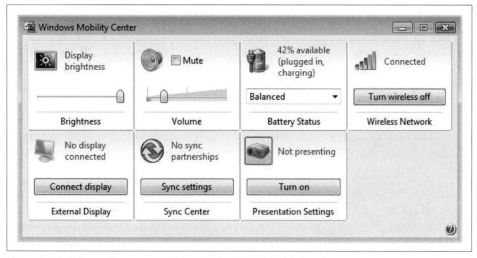

Figure 2-16. Oft-used laptop controls are gathered in the Mobility Center

  Not every laptop will show all of the Mobility Center options listed here. It will depend on your hardware and, more vitally, whether the drivers for that hardware cooperate with Windows Vista.

Xbox 360 Media Center Extender. You might not think that mention of the Xbox belongs in a title focused mostly on Vista, and then more so on Vista *administration*, but I'd argue otherwise. I can't say for sure what's going on inside the heads of Gates, Ballmer, et al., but I can speculate based on what I've seen and heard in my years at Microsoft. I'd posit that the future sphere of influence will move from simply Windows/Office to something more like Windows/Office/Windows Mobile/Xbox/Live/Zune, all connected, all seamlessly integrated to make information, productivity, and recreation independent of a particular device. That's what they're working on, anyway (more specifically, it's my interpretation of what it seems they're working on).

(They're gonna have to punt and redo Zune, however. Its deficiencies have been well chronicled, and I won't rehash them here other than to wonder why you can't just buy a song and play it. You first have to purchase Microsoft points, then do the mental gymnastics that help you convert 79 points into 99 cents, and then wonder what on earth you're gonna do with those leftover points. If they're not taking applications in the Zune division, they should be.)

Plus, a lot of home users are opting for the Xbox 360–Windows Media Center Edition experience already, and many of these home users are willing to pay handsomely for a home entertainment center that connects movies, games, and computing with the latest flat-screen TV and thumping, THX-grade sound system. Thus, it becomes part of administration for the home network.

So, then: a brief word about the Xbox 360 Extender. Essentially, it allows the Xbox to behave almost exactly like the Windows Vista machine when you are accessing digital entertainment through Windows Media Center. In other words, you could be sitting at your TV and calling up a movie or Media Center playlist as easily as you could from your Vista computer. The Media Center interface would look exactly the same. The only difference between the two is that whereas you use the mouse in Windows Vista, you use the Xbox controller (or remote) while accessing the same content through your Xbox.

The appeal for home networks, of course, is that you can have one room (say, the home office) hooked up to the Windows Vista machine, and you can be playing music or surfing the Internet on that machine. Meanwhile, the kids in the basement are using the Xbox to watch a movie. And where's the movie stored? On the hard drive of the Vista computer. In theory, it sounds really cool. In practice, it's even better.

Fortunately, the setup is very easy. All you have to do to get started is to visit the Media tab from the Xbox Dashboard and then select the Media Center selection. You'll be prompted to verify your network connection settings (it goes without saying that for this to work, the Windows Vista machine and the Xbox need to be connected to the same network; a wireless router is the method of choice for most home networks), and then eventually you'll be prompted to visit the following web site from the Vista machine:

http://www.xbox.com/pcsetup

You'll see the Internet page shown in Figure 2-17. From there, just select the proper operating system link, and you're on your way. Steps will vary depending on whether this is your first connection to the Xbox or you are replacing an existing relationship.

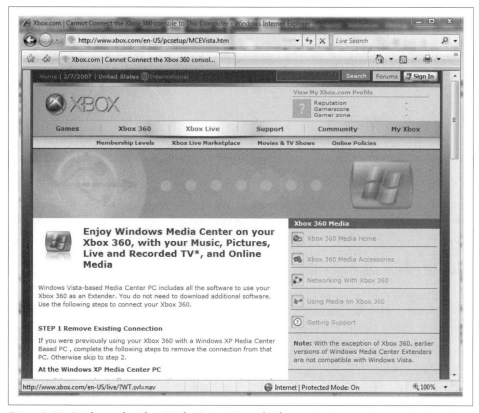

Figure 2-17. Configure the Xbox Media Center Extender for room-to-room entertainment

 You can also connect an Xbox to a Windows Vista machine without the Media Center software, such as Vista Home Basic. The setup procedure is fairly similar, but we won't cover the details here. Email me if you need additional setup instructions.

Vista Home Premium also includes Tablet PC support. Other Vista editions include such support, so I'll discuss this separately, later in the chapter.

Vista Business Edition

The Vista Business edition is built for, well, business use. More specifically, it is targeted to meet the needs of small- and medium-size businesses.

Similar to Home Premium and Home Basic, the Business edition includes all the features of Home Basic: Windows Defender, Windows Firewall, Instant Search, and so forth. In addition, here's what else you get with Windows Vista Business edition:

- Aero
- Mobility Center
- Tablet PC support
- Windows Meeting Space
- Advanced backup and diagnostics
- Remote Desktop Connection

Because we already covered Aero, the Mobility Center, and Tablet PC support, there's no need to cover that ground again. Instead, we'll focus on features that set the Business edition apart from the others.

Advanced backup and diagnostics

As mentioned, one of the design goals for Windows Vista was to make the operating system perform better than ever before. And for most users, better performance translates simply into more speed.

But it also means better reliability, especially where administration is concerned. Vista users should also see fewer hangs, crashes, and similar disruptions than users of Windows XP, if for no other reason than the fact that many of the common causes of such problems have been discovered and resolved, with the resolutions working their way into the Vista operating system code. There are also several new features that work toward this reliability goal.

One of these features is built-in diagnostics. This technology warns you of such disasters as impending hard drive failures and applications that are running out of virtual memory, advising you about corrective actions to take before data is lost.

Another is the new and streamlined backup interface presented in the Vista Backup and Restore Center. The backup options here let you easily configure either a backup of critical data or a complete backup of the entire Windows PC. To access the Backup and Restore Center, look to the Control Panel, then to the System and Maintenance grouping.

You can create an image of the entire Vista machine with the "Back up computer" button, as shown in Figure 2-18.

We'll look at the Backup and Restore Center options in further detail in Chapter 14.

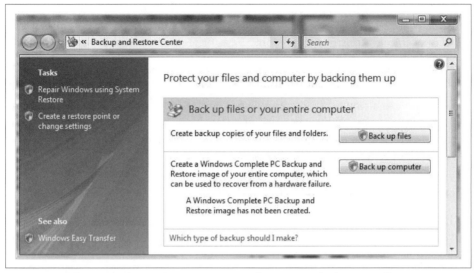

Figure 2-18. The new Backup and Restore Center makes it easy to back up your files

Remote Desktop Connection

Another feature available in the Business edition but not in either of the Home editions is Remote Desktop Connection, which is perfect for telecommuters. We'll flesh out the details of how to set up a Remote Desktop Connection in Chapter 3.

Remote Desktop Connection lets telecommuters (or business travelers, part-time workers, etc.) access their office desktops from another computer running Windows. In other words, you can sit at your home computer and use your office computer, many miles away, as though you were sitting right in your office. This feature can work in a wide variety of network scenarios, but it will most often be implemented over an Internet connection.

There are a couple of quick pointers here concerning Remote Desktop Connections. For everything to work:

- The remote computer must be turned on.
- The remote computer must have a network connection.
- The Vista Remote Desktop must be enabled.
- You must have permission to connect.

The remote session then opens inside a separate window, looking and behaving much like any other running application. It's easier than it sounds, and again, we discuss the specific click-steps in the next chapter.

Let me tell you about a couple of important things, though, before moving on.

First, the computer hosting the connection—the one being remotely connected to—must be running Windows Vista Business or higher. You cannot use a Remote Desktop Connection to control a Vista Home Basic or Home Premium system.

Also, you can create outgoing connections to Vista Business machines from computers running the aforementioned operating systems.

Finally, you can also use Vista to establish Remote Desktop Connections to computers running Windows XP Professional. You can't establish a Remote Desktop Connection to computers running Windows XP Home, though. We'll touch on Remote Desktop Connection in more detail in Chapter 14.

Vista Enterprise Edition

If the Business edition is meant for small- to medium-size businesses, that of course leaves the Enterprise edition as the most likely candidate for large enterprise organizations. Such organizations often have many offices, sometimes spread around the globe, and can utilize highly complex IT infrastructures. With more than 70,000 employees and offices in virtually every country in the world, Microsoft itself comes immediately to mind as a likely "early adopter" of the Enterprise edition.

You can't purchase the Vista Enterprise edition at your local retailer. Enterprise is available only to Microsoft Volume Licensing clients. If you know what Volume Licensing is, I'm guessing you work for a firm that has purchased the Enterprise edition. If you don't have a clue what I'm referring to, you can start to find out more at *http://microsoft. com/licensing*.

(Notice that I said *start to find out more*. In the interest of full candor here, I must say that I count myself as one of the aforementioned clueless folks, and I worked for the company for more than two years. A lot of the Microsoft licensing folks couldn't really explain it when I asked, either.)

As mentioned, it's one of the two versions of Vista built specifically for business use. But it can do a few things that the other can't.

Here are the features available in Vista Enterprise that are not available in Vista Business:

- BitLocker Drive Encryption
- Application compatibility
- Multilanguage support

As before, we'll deal with each in a separate heading.

BitLocker Drive Encryption

With Vista Enterprise edition, users have the ability to encrypt their entire hard drives using Windows BitLocker Drive Encryption. This new technology is especially meant to guard against data compromise in the event of a hard drive loss or theft (including theft of the entire machine).

BitLocker separates itself from previous file encryption tools by taking advantage of Trusted Platform Module (TPM)-compliant machines. These machines can store the encryption keys on the hardware of the computer itself instead of storing them on the hard drive. Other key storage possibilities are available, but BitLocker is designed to work best on TPM machines.

A more complete discussion of the BitLocker technology appeared in Chapter 1; I'll cover it again in Chapter 12.

Application compatibility

Another new enhancement of the Vista Enterprise edition is improved application compatibility. This application compatibility works with applications built for previous versions of Microsoft operating systems, of course, but it also includes tools for compatibility with Unix operating systems.

One of these tools is Virtual PC Express, which lets users run an operating system other than Windows Vista. The legacy application then runs in its native environment simply because it has no idea that it's really running on Vista. The feature is especially valuable to CIOs, who can decide to move to Windows Vista with confidence. Much of the worry about migrating legacy applications is taken out of the equation.

 There's a catch, of course, regarding Virtual PC Express and Vista Enterprise. The Virtual PC Express software is actually free of charge. What's not free are the software licenses for running other operating systems inside those Virtual PCs. Vista Enterprise, however, lets you run up to four additional versions of Enterprise inside a Virtual PC free of charge to facilitate help desk use, training, or application testing.

The other tool that is critical for Unix compatibility is something called Subsystem for Unix-based Applications (SUA). With the SUA, Unix administrators can now run both Windows Unix applications on a single Windows Vista Enterprise machine.

The SUA is not available on the Business edition. For additional discussion of how to configure application compatibility, please refer to Chapter 8.

Multilanguage support

Another important consideration for many large corporations, for which the Vista Enterprise edition was designed, is the ability to "speak" in multiple languages.

The built-in multilanguage support means the language a user sees—in the Start menu, the help system, the management tools, and so on—appears in the language native to the end user. Vista Enterprise includes all available interface languages in one offering. Access to all worldwide Windows interface languages means that global organizations can create just a single image that they can then deploy to individual PCs around the world. This same image can present an English interface to users at headquarters in Kansas City, and a German interface to a sales force logging in from Munich.

And speaking of an operating system that's ready to easily deploy worldwide, we come at last to the biggest and baddest of all Vista editions, Windows Vista Ultimate.

Vista Ultimate Edition

So what does Vista Ultimate contain? In a word, everything. The whole shebang. The kitchen sink. With the lone exception of the Virtual PC Express licensing feature mentioned with Vista Enterprise, every single possible feature of Windows Vista is included in the bits of this operating system install. For that reason, you won't see any Vista Ultimate "features" discussed in this section. We've already covered them all.

In other words, if it's been identified in this chapter, you can be assured that it's in Vista Ultimate. BitLocking? Check. Media Center? Check. Meeting Space? Check. Remote Desktop Connection? Tablet PC support? Aero? You get the idea.

And here's what's really interesting: even if you've purchased the Home Basic edition of Windows Vista, you have all the *software* of Vista Ultimate. That's right: the only real difference between Home Basic and Home Ultimate is the product key.

"So what?" you say. "Who cares what bits are on the DVD I've got here if I can't use them?" The big deal is that the upgrade from one version to another is a whole lot smoother than ever before. If you've upgraded from Windows XP Home to XP Professional, you know what I'm talking about. Technically, you didn't upgrade. You reinstalled. Same goes for taking a machine running XP Home to the XP Media Center edition. Separate operating systems. Separate operating system installs.

But no more. Upgrading from Home Basic to Premium, or to Ultimate, for that matter, is simply a matter of entering a new product key. You won't have to reinstall applications and drivers, restore data, and perform similar tasks that make changing XP operating system flavors such a pain.

At any rate, back to the Ultimate edition. So, who would want to install the Vista Ultimate edition anyway? Somewhat ironically, Ultimate is geared mostly toward the *small* business user or owner. I know, weird, huh? Here's why.

Vista Ultimate is ideal for users who want to have a powerful home PC that is also capable of serving as the hub for home entertainment—surfing the Web, recording TV shows, managing photos, editing movies, and creating DVDs. But these same users also want to be able to have this computer do some business heavy lifting as well: they want it to connect to a corporate network, run productivity applications, protect their data easily, and secure network communications.

What kind of user did I just describe? That's right, the small-business owner/ombudsman, who can't justify the expense of carrying two computers, one for business and one for home. The Ultimate edition gives users such as these the most power and the most options—and, more important, perhaps the most *cost-effective* solution for small-business users.

And let's not forget Tablet PC functionality, now included in several of Vista's editions rather than sold as a separate operating system (the Ultimate edition comes to mind). With Vista, Tablet PC computing is more powerful than ever before.

Windows Vista on a Tablet PC

Computers are great at handling typed text, no doubt: typing is neat, clean, and easily digitized, which means that text can then be easily saved, reproduced, and transmitted to others.

So in the 21st century, there's no longer any need for handwriting, right? Every time a human needs to write something, he can just look for his nearest laptop computer. Countless trees can be saved, and we'll never lose that important phone number we scored last night when doing a load of laundry.

Not so fast. Humans are tactile creatures, and there are still lots of instances in which nothing beats grabbing a pen and sheet of paper to scribble down a thought or two. Besides the mission-critical task just referenced, handwriting usually trumps keyboard and mouse in these situations:

- A doctor visits a patient and writes notes about care or a prescription.
- A mother takes notes while on the phone with her child's teacher.
- A husband jots directions to a florist he'll visit on the way home.
- A foreman updates project information while visiting a construction site.
- A student follows along with her professor's lecture.
- A secretary takes notes at a company meeting.

What's more, many of these tasks can be enhanced by the ability to leverage a computer's capability to save, recall, and transmit that handwriting. Would it be easier for the student to refer to class notes if they were stored on a computer rather than in a spiral notebook? How about the foreman with his notes on construction progress? Would it be easier to email notes to a supplier, or travel back to the office, transpose, and then do the same? What about those directions? Maybe you don't have time to run that errand today. How likely are you to find that Post-it note a week later?

The answer to many of these quandaries, and more, is a Tablet PC, of course, which seeks to bridge the gap between the digital and analog worlds of communication, making computer use as effortless as possible. It is also the focus of this chapter's second part.

And further, as you've already noticed, there's no longer a separate Tablet PC edition of Windows Vista as there was in Windows XP. Instead, all Tablet PC functionality is bundled into the Vista operating system itself, and is enabled automatically when Setup detects that the computer it's installing on is tablet-capable.

Why is this a big deal? Because in the Windows XP world, businesses that wanted to deploy both laptop and Tablet PC computers had to maintain (at least) two different images for deployment: one image for the laptops running Windows XP Professional, and one for the Tablet PC devices running Windows XP Tablet PC edition. Now, corporations need only maintain one image and can deploy no matter what the platform.

And before reading any further, know that Home Basic is *excluded* from the discussion of Tablet PC functionality. All other Vista versions support use of a Tablet PC, but not Home.

Furthermore, the tablet functionality in Windows Vista has changed in several ways over Windows XP, as I'll discuss in the next sections.

The Tablet PC Input Panel

For starters, consider the Tablet PC Input Panel (TIP). It has changed so that it's now out of the way until you need it. Move the TIP anywhere on the left or right side of the screen, and it will remain hidden there with just enough of the edge showing so that you can open it when needed. Figure 2-19 shows the TIP hidden.

Figure 2-19. The TIP remains hidden until you call for it

The TIP still shows on the screen automatically when the pen is in a text input area.

As you might expect, however, this is configurable behavior. To modify how the TIP appears, follow these steps:

1. Select Preferences from the Tablet Input Panel Options dialog box.

2. Choose (or tap; it's a tablet after all) Tools, and then choose Options on the TIP toolbar.

3. Now select the Opening tab of the Options dialog box. Here you'll see several options governing TIP behavior under the "Input Panel icons and tab" section, as shown in Figure 2-20.

Figure 2-20. Configure tablet input behavior with these options

If you leave the defaults alone, note that you can also drag the TIP to the location of your choosing with a simple click-and-drag operation.

 The ability to write on your computer improves as Vista becomes more adept at recognizing your particular style of handwriting. In Chapter 4, we'll explore the handwriting recognition feature of Tablet PC computing in more detail.

Back of Pen Erase and Scratch-Out Gestures

Some Tablet PC pens have an eraser on one end. Why would a manufacturer put an eraser on the end of a digital pen? For the same reason that Faber-Castell puts an eraser on the end of its Number 2 pencils. Again, assuming your Tablet PC has the right hardware, you should be able to delete words in the writing pad, character pad, and correction area with the pen's "eraser."

What's more, Vista introduces new *scratch-out gestures* to allow you to delete handwriting or recognized text in the Input Panel. The tablet scratch-out feature lets you use a more personal style of crossing out text when using the Input Panel. Some of the new scratch-out gestures include:

Strikethrough
> A horizontal line drawn across a word

Vertical
> A mark in the pattern of an *M* or *W*

Circular
> A circle around a word or letter

Angled
> A diagonal hash through deleted text

And if you're used to deletions using the Z-shaped gesture in vogue with the Windows XP Tablet PC edition, you are able to use that as well. In fact, you can instruct Vista to recognize only the Z-shape as the deletion command.

Changing Screen Orientation

You may have already noticed another handy Tablet PC feature during our discussion of the Windows Mobility Center: it's the Screen Orientation feature. There are actually four possible settings here that help users get the most out of their Tablet PC writing area:

Primary landscape
> This is the default orientation. When you use the primary landscape settings, the taskbar appears at the bottom of the screen, with the top of the desktop positioned at the top of the display.

Secondary landscape
> This reverses the primary landscape orientation, placing the taskbar at the top of the display instead.

Primary portrait
> This configures the Tablet PC display so that it's more like a traditional sheet of writing paper, moving the taskbar to the left edge of the display.

Secondary portrait
> This is the inverse of the primary portrait orientation.

Other general Tablet PC settings

As you get started using a pen rather than a keyboard, you'll probably want to configure handwriting settings. If you have used the XP Tablet PC version, you'll see that Vista offers quite a few more of these options than XP does. Your starting point will likely be the Control Panel's Mobile PC console. Once here, choose the Tablet PC Settings link (in XP, it was the Tablet and Pen Settings link), which will open the dialog box shown in Figure 2-21.

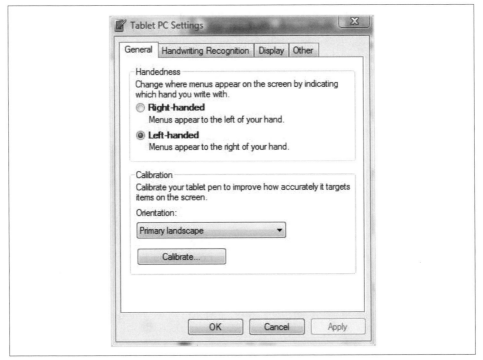

Figure 2-21. Configure Tablet PC settings, including handwriting recognition, here

Another way to quickly locate it is to use the integrated Search—just type **tab** at the Start menu. The Tablet PC settings should appear in the list of programs.

Once here, you'll note that the General tab is essentially the same as the old Settings tab found in Windows XP. Also, the Display tab is identical to its predecessor. However, there is a new Handwriting Recognition tab, which contains two sections:

Personalization
> You can provide Vista with samples of your handwriting. This increases the accuracy of the handwriting recognizer (the feature that converts handwritten text into typed text), but only when the Use the Personalized Recognizer checkbox is activated.

Automatic Learning

This feature collects information about your writing, including the words you write and the style in which you write them. Note that this applies not only to your handwriting—the ink you write in the Input Panel, the recognized text, and the corrected text—but also to your typing, including email messages and web addresses typed into Internet Explorer. To use this feature, activate the Use Automatic Learning option.

 I address this in more detail in Chapter 5, but the Automatic Learning feature stores information on your computer as part of the user profile. If you're concerned that this might expose sensitive data to people who might hack or steal your system, you should turn off this feature.

Pen Cursors

When using a Tablet PC, it can be a challenge knowing whether you've clicked, double-clicked, or right-clicked. Pen cursors provide crucial feedback to help lessen the confusion. For example, when you hover the pen above the screen, a small dot appears. This little dot provides crucial feedback to help you point to *exactly* the button you want to—otherwise, selecting something with your pen can involve more than a little guesswork. Also, once you make the tap (equivalent to the left-click), a small ripple appears. Right-clicking produces an even stronger ripple, bordered in white.

To configure these pen cursor options, access the Control Panel and then open the Pen and Input Devices applet. If you're using the Standard View, it's located in the Mobile Computing grouping.

Next, follow the "Change pen settings" link, and you'll see the dialog box shown in Figure 2-22.

By default, all pen cursor actions are selected, but of course, you can change any or all of these by unchecking the appropriate boxes.

Pen flicks

Also, notice that next to the Pointer Options tab in the Pen and Input Devices dialog box is the Flicks tab. Flicks are natural, handwriting-esque (I may have just made up a word) motions that help you use your pen more effectively by essentially transforming it into a magic wand.

Using pen flicks, you can scroll a window up or down or navigate forward and backward on the Web with a quick little wave of the pen. With the second option, "Navigational flicks and editing flicks," you can also perform tasks such as paste, delete, and undo.

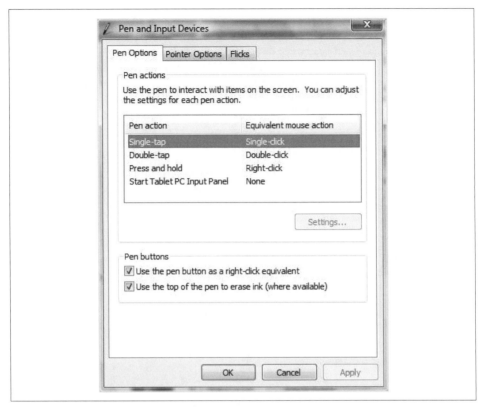

Figure 2-22. Change pen cursors from here

What's more, these pen flicks are completely customizable to better suit your Tablet PC usage needs. In fact, you can use a pen flick to perform any action you can carry out using a keyboard shortcut. Just tell Vista what the pen flick means, and then use the flick to make Tablet PC usage more efficient than ever.

Here's how to tailor pen-flick behavior to your liking:

1. As before, open the Control Panel and then select Pen and Input Devices. Choose the Flicks tab.

2. Choose "Navigational flicks and editing flicks," and then click on the Customize button.

3. As shown in Figure 2-23, the Customize dialog box lets you select from a dropdown menu of predefined flick actions. Alternatively, you can choose Add to associate any key combination with a particular flick.

4. On the same tab, adjust the sensitivity of your flicks to give the best performance without triggering a flick accidentally.

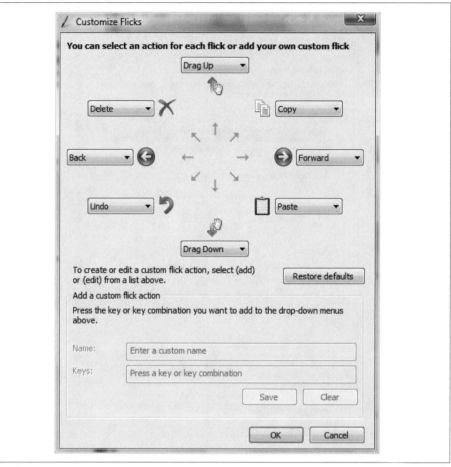

Figure 2-23. Specify what happens with a pen flick

During normal Tablet PC usage, you might perform an action that could be performed more quickly using pen flicks. If so, you should receive a notification from a learning wizard regarding help with pen flicks. Vista will send such a notice only once in a 24-hour period. If you don't use the help, this reminder will go away after the third notification.

Summary

This chapter has a single purpose. It exists to help answer one question: what's the difference between the versions of Windows Vista? As you can see, that answer has many components, and you've really gotten only a brief introduction to the topic.

We spend the time here to categorize the Vista versions for several reasons: it helps us understand the choices we have when making a purchase. If you're buying a laptop computer for home use, do you want Vista Home Basic or Home Premium? Hopefully now you'll be able to make a more informed decision. If you're purchasing for a company upgrade with 70 users, is it OK to get the Business edition, or might it be a better investment to look into Microsoft Volume Licensing to get the Enterprise version? And how does Ultimate fit into this picture? Might it be more cost-effective to just get the entire Vista code base?

Also, this chapter works in conjunction with the previous chapter to help set the foundation for the rest of the book. In the chapters that follow, you'll see further discussion of BitLocker Drive Encryption, the new Backup and Restore Center, and how to enable network sharing of documents. But on which editions of Vista will these features apply? With this chapter as a reference, you'll be able to quickly jog your memory.

In the next chapter, we'll leave the foundation-setting behind and start rolling up our sleeves, delving into some everyday Vista administrative tasks. We'll start with a look at Vista network administration, including how to join a domain and how to set up a wireless connection.

CHAPTER 3

Networking with Windows Vista

During the course of your Windows Vista administration, I'll guess that roughly half of your work will fall under the guise of what could more generally be described as *network* administration—getting Vista computers to talk to other Vista computers, to other Windows computers, and just to other computers in general.

You can achieve this using a wide array of methods, some of which may require a wide range of computing know-how. That's exactly the focus of this chapter. Obviously, it's a big topic, one to which entire books have been devoted. There's a reason this chapter is longer than the others in this book.

It could be argued—convincingly, in my opinion—that the network is the "killer app" that spurred the revolution that Bill Gates famously envisioned back in his days as a Harvard undergrad: a computer on every desktop. The network was the reason many people purchased their first PC, and the same remains true today. A large portion of the globe is still discovering the power of sitting at one computer and grabbing information stored on another.

There have been several significant changes to the networking behavior and tools employed by Windows Vista, and certainly we'll spend time on many of these new features, such as native support for IP version 6, the new Wireless connection window, and the Network and Sharing Center.

Fortunately, however, many of these changes are "under the hood" and probably won't require any significant changes in the way you *administer* Vista networks. For most connections, you'll enable a Windows Vista machine as a Dynamic Host Configuration Protocol (DHCP) client, and then you'll make sure it belongs to the proper logical grouping of computers. Just like before, you'll have two options: to join either a workgroup or a domain.

But, of course, real Vista network administration just gets started at the point where most Vista users stop thinking about it altogether. You sometimes won't want your system to use an automatic IP address, and you'll have to configure some connections manually.

More important than just making the network connection is actually *using* that connection. In other words, the bulk of the chapter deals with the answer to a single question: what do you want your computer to *do* on the network?

The (abbreviated) answer to that question takes only about 75 pages to answer.

Joining a Windows Server Domain

Vista setup, especially if you're upgrading a computer from Windows XP, assumes that you have an active network connection. And for the time being, so will I. Along with the ability to communicate with other computers comes an important setup decision: whether the computer will join a Windows workgroup or a Windows server-based domain.

But before making this decision, we must first understand the difference between a domain and a workgroup. Along the way, we also answer a central question: should I join a domain, or is a workgroup network configuration all I need? OK, fair enough. That was two questions.

Let's look at the differences now.

Windows Domains Defined

A *domain* is a logical collection of computer *things*. What kinds of things? Users, computers, groups, printers, shared resources, and the objects and services that manage them are things that are collected, stored, and managed within a Windows server domain.

And, of course, the key word in that last sentence was *managed*. A domain is a collection, but more important, it represents a security *boundary* that is used to help administrators of companies maintain all the computer systems within their environment. The domain is distinguished by three chief hallmarks:

- **One user, one account**, which leads to
- **Centralized administration**, which leads to
- A more **secure computing** enterprise

In practice, a domain allows administrators to set up user accounts in one central location: the domain controller. (Multiple domain controllers can be deployed throughout the domain, by the way, but they will all store a copy of the same database of domain accounts.)

Users can then use these accounts from any computer that is also part of the domain because logon requests are fielded not by the client computers, but centrally, by the domain controllers.

Finally, administrators can secure these accounts throughout the environment using policies that control the security, appearance, permissions, and overall use of the computing resources. All of these policies are (can be) created from a centralized location: again, the domain controller.

A Windows server domain environment also affords administrators greater flexibility. When a change is necessary—a person makes a *physical* change by moving to a new department or city and now requires access to a different set of documents, printers, computers, and so forth, for example—the domain admin can move the logical *user* domain object via a centralized management console. The person arrives at the new location and will be granted access to those necessary enterprise resources.

There are a couple of significant requirements to note before a Windows Vista computer can join a domain. One is the operating system version. Only these three Vista versions can participate in a Windows server domain:

- Business
- Enterprise
- Ultimate

The other requirement is Windows Server: either 2000, 2003, or whatever they end up calling Longhorn at the time of its release. To create a Windows domain environment, you must install a suite of services called Active Directory. You cannot set up Active Directory on any version of Windows Vista.

The conversation about domains is mostly focused on the Windows server operating system. And as you have just seen, such a discussion excludes a few of the Vista versions. Because of this, this book will mostly focus on Windows Vista in a workgroup implementation, which is also sometimes referred to as a *standalone* system.

There will still be plenty of discussion focusing on Windows Vista in a domain, however. The trick will be in trying to keep the discussion as inclusive as possible for all possible Vista versions.

Vista Workgroups Defined

A *workgroup* is also a logical grouping of computers, albeit one without any centralized database of user accounts, such as is found in a Windows server domain. Similar in objective to a domain, workgroups are set up by administrators to facilitate easy sharing of resources, such as documents and printers, with other computers and users in the workgroup.

The difference is the decentralization of user accounts. In a workgroup environment, every computer is an "island" and has to have separate user accounts set up for each user that might need access to the data on that system. In other words, all accounts are *local* accounts, which in turn can lead to confusion as the workgroup grows.

For example, imagine a Vista workgroup of just two machines: one called Kansas and another called State. I have an account called Brian on Kansas, which I use to log on and perform my everyday work.

But there's a shared folder on State that I need access to. Can I access it? Not using the Kansas\Brian account. I would have to access the shared resource using some account that exists on State, not on Kansas, and in most workgroup implementations, I would set up an account: State\Brian.

You see the problem, yes? One user, Brian, and *multiple user accounts* called Brian. Further, each account would have a separate set of rights and permissions. As the workgroup expands, I might end up with 10, 12, or 15 user accounts called Brian, and each one is a separate object to manage.

For this and other reasons, the 10-user threshold is usually where administrators consider a domain implementation.

Nevertheless, many of the tools available to domain administrators are also at the disposal of workgroup administrators. For example, they can still leverage Group Policies to govern computer and user behavior, but again, each policy and configuration will be distinct for the local machine.

In many real-world implementations, workgroup configurations are set up with just a single account (technically, multiple accounts, all given the same name and password) being used by everyone. This avoids the confusion of having 12 Brian user accounts, but it has a potentially devastating side effect: it greatly increases the likelihood of security breaches later on.

To briefly summarize, here are the pros and cons of a domain:

- Centralized, flexible administration.
- Better security.
- Limited choices of client operating systems (XP Professional and the Vista versions mentioned).
- Increased cost, at least in terms of software (Windows Server is more expensive than the desktop OSs) and, usually, hardware.

Meanwhile, here are the pros and cons of a workgroup:

- No additional cost.
- You can implement workgroups using multiple types of operating systems (all Vista versions, XP versions, and even 9x and Server OSs can join a workgroup).
- Easy, easy, easy, to set up and share resources.
- No centralized administration, which can cause confusion.
- Security can be configured only on a onesey-twosey basis.

So, which is best? It all depends on your particular computing needs. (I may have coined the *onesey-twosey* phrase. At least I've never seen it in print.)

If you're in a home/home office/small company environment, you will usually deploy a workgroup. When using Vista in a corporate environment of 15 users or more, however, chances are that Vista will be participating in a domain.

But to do so, Vista must first add its computer account to the domain. Once it does, it will then be able to take advantage of the benefits of the domain environment.

Joining a Domain

To join the domain, you will need to go to the System Control Panel application. There are many ways to open the System application. Here are three:

- From the Start menu, right-click Computer and select Properties.
- From the Start menu, select Control Panel and then select the System icon.
- From the Welcome Center, click More Details in the upper-right corner.

However you get there, you now see the System Control Panel application shown in Figure 3-1.

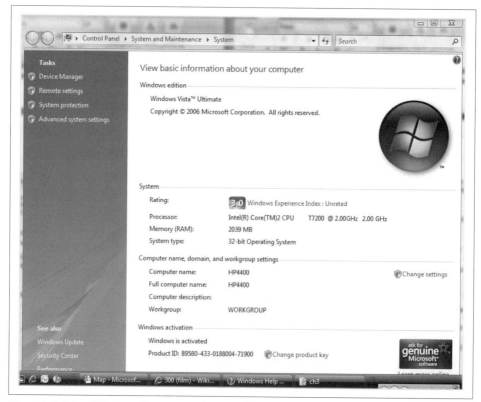

Figure 3-1. Join a Windows Server using this console

Now, in the System console, you should see the "Computer name, domain, and workgroup settings" area. Click on "Change settings," and you'll be prompted for administrative confirmation if User Account Control is turned on.

You will now see the System Properties dialog box. As seen in Figure 3-2, you have two choices here:

- Network ID
- Change

Figure 3-2. The System Properties dialog box

Network ID walks you through a wizard to help you join the computer to the domain.

The Change option can accomplish the same goal without using the wizard.

When you select Change, you see the "Computer name/domain changes" box. Here you can select the radio button for Domain, and then enter the domain name you want to join.

 You can't join just any domain you'd like. You must have permissions to create a computer account in the domain, and you will usually be prompted for administrative credentials for the target domain. Also, your Vista computer must be able to communicate with a domain controller in the target domain. If not, joining the domain will fail and you will see a corresponding message informing you of such.

Domain administrators can grant you the *right* to add only your computer to the domain, or you can be given rights to join multiple computers to the domain. How? By configuring and deploying a Group Policy Object (GPO) that would grant this right. Performing Windows server administrative tasks such as this are a little beyond the scope of this book, but you can get a pretty good feel for GPOs by turning to Chapter 13. Also, I'd be more than happy to send you instructions on how to do this in a domain environment. Just go to *http://www.brianculp.com* and drop me an email.

When the process completes, you should receive a dialog box that says "Welcome to (*the domain*)." You now need to reboot the computer for the changes to take effect.

 As mentioned, choosing the Network ID button will step you through the Join a Workgroup or Domain Wizard. It will accomplish the same thing, but it is meant for users who don't necessarily understand the distinctions between the two.

Joining a Workgroup

Unless you're upgrading an existing XP installation, Vista automatically joins itself to a workgroup called WORKGROUP at setup time. For some people, especially home users, this default setting will work just fine.

But thousands upon thousands of computer networks out there are already called WORKGROUP. You may want a more private grouping, and in fact, Microsoft recommends that you make this change. However, changing the workgroup name will not automatically *hide* the workgroup from being detected by other workgroups.

To change workgroup affiliation, follow these steps:

1. Open the System Control Panel application by typing **System** at the Start menu.
2. Once there, click "Change settings." You'll be prompted for administrative confirmation if User Account Control is enabled.
3. As before, you have two choices: Network ID and Change.
4. Choose Change, select the radio button for Workgroup, and enter the desired workgroup name, as seen in Figure 3-3.

   Note here that you won't be prompted for any kind of administrative permissions to join a workgroup.
5. The last step is just to click OK. You will then have to reboot for the changes to take effect.

 You don't technically have to join a workgroup, either. You can set up any old workgroup you like by changing the workgroup's name using the technique just described.

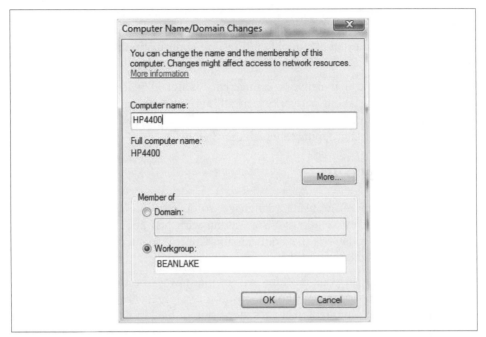

Figure 3-3. Changing workgroup membership

Changing the computer name

There's really only one naming rule that you have to follow when putting a Vista workgroup together: no two computers can share the same name (this is also true of assembling a domain, by the way).

Fortunately, changing your computer name is easy, and the steps have not really changed when compared to Windows XP. Here's what to do:

1. Open the System Control Panel application and then click "Change settings."

2. In the "Computer name" entry box, type a new computer name. Click OK and then reboot. Easy as a divorce.

> This can be confusing, but the computer's NetBIOS name and its Fully Qualified Domain Name (FQDN) are two different things because they denote two different name spaces.
>
> NetBIOS is an older Windows networking technology in which names are restricted to 16 characters or less. NetBIOS uses a "flat" namespace. FQDNs are standards-based names that appear in the host.subdomain.domain.top-leveldomain format. FQDNs use a "hierarchical" namespace. They are the computer names that have been used by the Internet forever, and now represent the standard naming convention used by Windows domains. NetBIOS is kept around for backward compatibility.

At the beginning of this section, I mentioned that we would assume a network connection was in place. We won't be able to join a domain, for example, if our computer can't send out a request to join, and receive confirmation that the request has been accepted.

So now, let's assume that network connectivity is not in place. Let's pretend we don't know anything about networking at all, and start to explore just how Windows Vista communicates with other computers in a network in the first place, regardless of the logical grouping to which they belong.

Configuring TCP/IP

Just as people communicate using a language, so do computers in a network. And the language spoken by Windows Vista—along with just about every other computer on the planet today—is the Transmission Control Protocol/Internet Protocol, better known by its acronym, TCP/IP.

The TCP/IP settings on your machine will in many ways be the foundation for a happy computing experience. Without them, you can forget about sending an email, surfing the Web, chatting, remote access, accessing a shared folder, receiving a software update, letting a gadget receive a weather update...OK, I've made my point, and you already know all this anyway.

Without a fairly good understanding of TCP/IP, administrators are very limited, and will likely spend many laborious hours of troubleshooting to get computers to talk to one another.

Fortunately, not much has changed in the upgrade to Windows Vista in terms of basic functionality. Yes, there are some new features, and yes, some of them are quite significant, such as the inclusion of IP version 6. But functionally speaking, if you know how to install a network card and set it to "Obtain an IP address automatically," most of the time you'll be in good shape. (Chapter 7 includes the instructions for installing hardware devices.)

In other words, although the click-steps and tools might take a bit of getting used to, the underlying goal of the administrator will remain the same.

Vista and TCP/IP

One of the most interesting new changes to the Vista operating system is its support of IP version 6. Why IP version 6? In short, because it was feared at one time that the world would run out of IP addresses as more devices and households and companies attached themselves to the Internet. In fact, that fear exists because indeed, we will run out of IP version 4 addresses. Someday. (I still think this is rather amazing: when you're connected to the Internet, you're connected to *every single* other computer on the Internet as well. I didn't say it was terribly relevant, just that it was amazing.)

That day hasn't arrived yet, however, because of the many complementary IP v4 technologies, such as Network Address Translation (NAT) and proxy servers (which in turn run NAT). These technologies not only have helped to keep company and other networks more secure, but have also provided the added benefit of reducing the number of public IP addresses needed for communication. An entire company of 100 computers might need only a single IP address to provide all external connection requirements. Multiply this by the millions, and you can see where this technology has helped to conserve the world's pool of IP addresses.

For example, let's take my home-based business. It's not without some sense of shame that I admit there are no less than six devices in my house that access the Internet. I have more computers than humans in my house. But for all these devices, my house needs only a single IP address: the address assigned to my cable modem. All other devices that use this Internet connectivity are assigned private IP addresses in the 192.168.*x*.*y* range.

In other words, as Mark Twain once observed about himself, reports of IP version 4's demise have been exaggerated. In fact, you might not need to ever enable its updated version, IP version 6. Furthermore, many home and small-business networks do not support IPv6 as of this writing.

 So, what happened to IP version 5? Interesting story: IP version 5 was assigned to an experimental protocol called ST (Internet STreaming Protocol). It was thought that IP version 5 would be a complement to IP version 4. IP version 6, on the other hand, can be used instead of IP version 4. IP 5 has never been introduced for public usage. OK, it was a mildly interesting story.

You select the IP versions for a network card by accessing its Properties dialog box, as shown in Figure 3-4.

Note here that IP version 6 is not bound to the network card because it's not needed. Even though this is a laptop and it connects in a multitude of network environments, all of the devices this computer connects to support IPv4.

And because you'll be managing and/or troubleshooting IPv4 networks at least for the time being, it's important for any network administrator worth his or her salt to at least have a good general understanding of this communication protocol. Following, then, is a brief primer.

Understanding IP Version 4

To get started, open the network card's Properties dialog box, as discussed previously, highlight the IP version 4 selection, and click the Properties button. You then see a dialog box like the one in Figure 3-5.

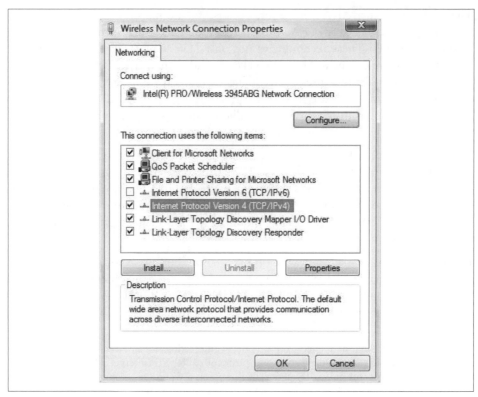

Figure 3-4. Selecting IP 4, IP 6, or both, on the network card

From here, you see two basic configuration parameters. You can configure the network card to either one of the following:

- "Obtain an IP address automatically," which is the default and uses the services of a DHCP server somewhere on the network
- "Use the following IP address," wherein an administrator configures a static IP address by typing specific IP parameters

Which parameters are needed? Administrators choosing a static address will generally type in four main configuration parameters, as suggested by the entry boxes that are available here. They are:

- An IP address
- A subnet mask
- A default gateway
- A primary (and sometimes a secondary) Domain Name System (DNS) server address

Here's what to keep in mind when configuring IP settings manually.

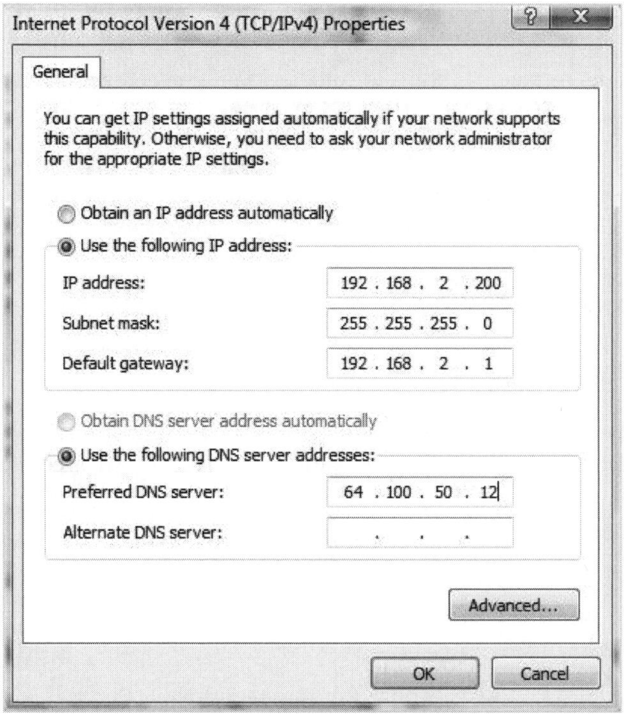

Figure 3-5. Configure IPv4 properties

When configuring TCP/IP, an IP address and a subnet mask are absolutely required. You usually will configure the other two parameters, which are essential for communicating on larger networks such as the Internet. Each one gets individual attention in the sections that follow.

The IP address

As you know, computers speak to one another using numbers, and the IP address is simply a number that identifies your computer on the network as a unique entity, much as a telephone number does for phones.

And, much like part of the phone number (the area code, for example) identifies which network the phone lives on, so too does the IP address: it identifies what *network* your computer lives on.

The IP address is a 32-bit binary address—a string of thirty-two 1s and 0s—that humans work with by breaking them up into four octets (each octet composed of eight bits) that are then converted into decimal equivalents and separated by periods. In other words, to a human an IP address looks something like this:

```
192.168.2.200
```

But to the computer, it's just a string of thirty-two 1s and 0s:

```
11000000101010000000001011001000
```

We're not going to worry about 1s and 0s. Let the computer take care of that. Instead, let's focus on the decimal equivalents.

Every IP address is composed of two parts: the *network ID* and the *host ID*. The network ID represents the network to which the computer belongs, and the host ID portion uniquely identifies the computer itself. The addressing rules are straightforward, and they go like this:

- Every network ID on a TCP/IP "Internetwork" (such as the Internet) must be unique.
- Every host ID on each network must also be unique.

Easy, right? Again, think of the phone system. Two phone numbers can be 555-7911, sure, but two phones with this number cannot exist in the 913 area code.

So, if that's the case, there must be a way to separate the IP address into a network portion and a host portion. But how does IP do this? How does the computer know which part of the IP address is the network identifier and which part is the host identifier? Read on.

The subnet mask

The subnet mask is used to *divide* the IP address into the network portion and the host portion. Just as the IP address is also a required TCP/IP setting, without the subnet mask, the computer has no idea what network it belongs to.

The subnet mask is also a 32-bit binary number broken into four octets for easy human consumption. A subnet mask might look like this to us:

```
255.255.255.0
```

To the computer, the same string would look like this:

```
11111111111111111111111100000000
```

But again, the binary notation is simply to provide a frame of reference. The significance of the decimal number 255 is that it is an octet of eight binary 1s. The decimal value of 0 is a string of eight binary 0s.

The job of the 1s in the subnet mask, then, is to *mask out* the network number—they identify which of the thirty-two 1s and 0s in the IP address are the network ID. As for everything else that lines up with the 0s in the subnet mask? You guessed it: that's the host ID.

So, using the IP address and subnet mask example here, we get a network ID of:

```
192.168.2.
```

and a host ID of:

```
200.
```

So, why do Vista administrators need to know this? This information is vital if you're configuring IP addresses manually, and if you want those computers to work. The correct IP addressing conventions are needed for the successful delivery of information to the proper network.

Even computers that are assigned dynamic IP addresses by DHCP servers sometimes use static addresses for their alternative configurations. You'll find more on alternative IP configurations later in the chapter.

So, then: once a TCP/IP packet is prepared for delivery, Vista decides where the packet needs to be delivered. If the network IDs for source computer and destination computer match, the packet is delivered to the local segment of computers.

If Vista sees that the destination address is on a different network, however, it delivers this packet to the default gateway for routing.

The default gateway

Here's another key ingredient in IP configuration. Although the default gateway parameter is not technically required, your network communication would be very limited without it.

A *default gateway* is the IP address of the *router*, which is the pathway to any and all remote networks. To get a packet of information from one network to another, the packet is sent to the default gateway, which helps forward the packet to its destination network.

Without default gateways, Internet communication is not possible, because your computer doesn't have a way to send a packet destined for any other network. Typically, this default gateway information is handed out as part of DHCP configuration, but if you're configuring a static address, it is necessary for Vista admins to have the IP address of the default gateway close at hand.

There's one additional address they should have on a Post-it note nearby as well, which we'll cover in the following subsection.

The DNS server

Type **Microsoft.com** into your browser, or **Oreilly.com**, or **Brianculp.com**. If you're connected to the Internet, you'll see a web page in short order. But why? Don't computers need numbers? The answer lies in the DNS. Simply put, the job of DNS is to provide translation between humans and computers. Humans like names, whereas computers like numbers.

DNS servers, then, are used to resolve computer names—sometimes called FQDNs—into IP addresses. So unless you can remember the unique IP address of every computer you want to communicate with, administrators must remember to configure this name-resolution technology.

When getting an IP address automatically from most Internet Service Providers (ISPs), the primary and secondary DNS servers are also assigned automatically. Type **ipconfig /all** at the command prompt to see which DNS servers are currently providing name resolution.

DNS serves as the default name-resolution technology used by Microsoft operating systems since Windows 2000, and will continue to be for the foreseeable future. In fact, logging onto a Windows Server Active Directory domain from a Vista machine is not even possible without a DNS server in place. As a Vista network admin, the sooner you learn DNS inside and out, the better.

 Vista computers can still use the *HOSTS* file for FQDN resolution, but don't look for it using the Vista search indexing engine. *HOSTS* is in an operating system directory that is not indexed by default. You can find the *HOSTS* file by navigating to *%systemroot%\system32\drivers\etc*.

CIDR notation

You shouldn't normally have to worry about this when configuring a Vista client machine, but I'm mentioning it for background purposes. There is another way to express the IP address without having to spell out the subnet mask in octets of 255s and 0s, as you do when specifying a static IP address.

This alternative method is known as Classless Inter-Domain Routing (CIDR) notation. Using CIDR notation, an IP address and subnet mask are specified using an abbreviated notation that appends the IP address with a forward slash and then notes the number of contiguous 1s used to mask the network number. If you noticed in the previous example, there were twenty-four 1s in the subnet mask, followed by eight 0s. Using CIDR notation, that same IP address/subnet mask combination would look like this:

    192.168.2.200/24

In other words, the /16 part of the CIDR notation informs any routing device that the IP address has a subnet mask in which the first 24 bits are set to 1. Twenty-four 1s leaves you with a decimal subnet mask of 255.255.255.0.

Why mention this? For three reasons:

* You might stumble on it in your role as network admin, because CIDR notation is used to simplify entries on routing tables. It is the notation used by a majority of backbone Internet routers.
* It can be used during the creation of DHCP *address pools*, which are simply a collection of possible IP addresses that can be handed out during automatic configuration.
* It can specify subnet masks whose decimal equivalents can be 255.254.0.0, or 255.255.224.0, or something other than a series of 255s followed by 0s.

CIDR's main function in life, by the way, is to cut down on the number of wasted IP addresses in the class B address space. If you understand the significance of that, fine. If not, that's fine, too; the object of this section is just that you can recognize a CIDR notation when you see it. There are lots of other places to read up on CIDR notation, and a full discussion is a bit beyond the scope of this book.

At any rate, you now have a fairly good foundation on which to configure the TCP/IP settings on your Windows Vista network. As mentioned, most users will *never* configure Vista's TCP/IP settings, because so much is automated. By default, Vista will *bind* IPv4 to any and all network adapters, and will configure them to automatically obtain address settings.

Normally, these IP address settings come from a DHCP server. But Vista will even obtain an IP address automatically when a DHCP server is not available.

Automatic Private IP Addresses

When a DHCP client is unable to locate a DHCP server, the Vista machine picks out a random IP address from an Automatic Private IP Address (APIPA) range.

The APIPA range consists of an IP address of 169.254.x.y, with a subnet mask of 255.255.0.0. Why is the APIPA range considered to be *private*? Because that set of network numbers is not in use on the Internet; it is also *random* because the client generates an arbitrary host number (the x.y part) for that 169.254 network.

Let's say, for example, that the client picks a host ID of 100.23. The client will then announce to the network with a broadcast packet that it wants to use the IP address of 169.254.100.23. If no other computer responds that the IP address is already in use, Vista registers that IP address and binds it to the network card.

So what? The significance of APIPA is that Vista machines that are DHCP clients will still assign themselves an IP address even when they cannot find a DHCP server. This is better than no IP address at all, as the 169.254 address will allow them to communicate with other computers on the same subnet that cannot find a DHCP server, either (and that also assign themselves an APIPA address).

In other words, APIPA allows for (limited) network communication when the DHCP server is either down or just plain not there. Note, however, that APIPA does *not* assign a default gateway, and therefore it cannot communicate with any computers that live on the other side of a router. A Vista computer with an APIPA-assigned address will therefore not be able to access the Internet or any other computers that live on other subnets.

APIPA is not a new feature to Windows Vista. A mixed workgroup of Vista and XP systems will be able to use APIPA and communicate with one another using the 169.254.x.y address range.

In summary, here are the signs to look for when networking with an APIPA address:

- An IP address of 169.254.*x.y*. Administrators can open a command prompt and type **ipconfig** to look up IP address information.
- The ability to communicate with other DHCP clients on the same subnet.
- The inability to communicate with any other computers, including those on the Internet.

Because computers with APIPA addresses cannot (typically) check their email, it might be better for administrators to configure Vista clients with an alternative IP address in the event that the DHCP server is down.

You don't need to do anything to configure APIPA; it's configured by default. Here's how to double-check:

1. Open the Network Connections Control Panel application under the Network and Internet grouping.
2. Right-click the desired network adapter and choose Properties. Now select Internet Protocol Version 4 and click the Properties button.
3. In the IPv4 properties dialog box, choose the Alternate Configuration tab, as shown in Figure 3-6.

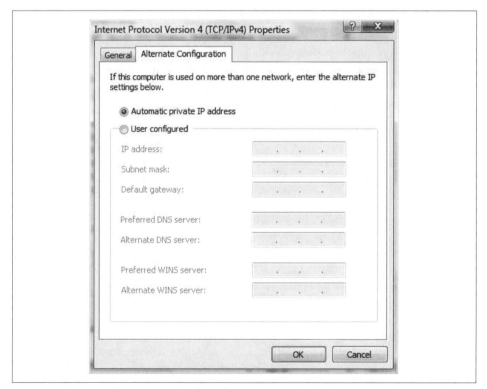

Figure 3-6. Using an alternative network configuration

This is the tab that Vista uses to govern networking behavior when the computer cannot obtain its IP address information automatically. To use APIPA, ensure that the "Automatic private IP address" radio button is selected.

We'll use this same dialog box in the next section's discussion of alternative IP addresses.

Using an alternative IP address

Because of the aforementioned limitations (no Internet access, for example), you might not want your computer to use an APIPA address if a DHCP server cannot be found.

For example, let's say you bring your laptop to work, where you know the IP address of the router and the pool from which the IP addresses are being handed out—you know the default gateway is at 192.168.2.1, and the pool is from the 192.168.2.2– 254 range. In that case, you're going to lose all network connectivity if the DHCP server is down and Vista pulls an APIPA address.

This might be a perfect opportunity to use an alternative configuration with a static address. In the event that your system is unable to get an IP address automatically, Vista will switch over to whatever you've configured on the Alternate Configuration tab, as shown in Figure 3-7.

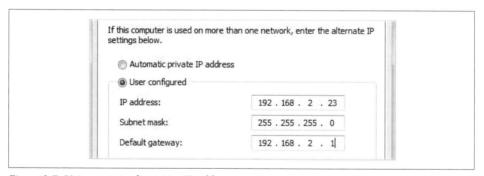

Figure 3-7. Using a static alternative IP address

And note here that you can still configure other parameters, such as the DNS and Wins name resolution servers.

The "IP address" box is where you can add multiple IPs to the same network interface. This can be helpful in many circumstances, but it is generally considered bad practice. However, many people do it for many reasons. Some applications require two IP addresses for communications.

The automatic metric

In most cases, the automatic metric is fine. However, in unique circumstances, there are times when two network cards are being used and traffic needs to flow out of a specific card for whatever reason. In this case, you can manually set the card's metric.

For instance, say you have two network cards, as follows:

NIC 1

> IP address of 192.168.66.16; subnet mask of 255.255.255.0; and a gateway of 192.168.66.1

NIC 2

> IP address of 192.168.66.17; subnet mask of 255.255.255.0; no gateway (you should have only one gateway in most configurations)

Let's also say that you have an application that needs to see traffic coming from this computer on 192.168.66.7. However, because the gateway is on 192.168.66.6, most of the traffic will go out from 192.168.66.16, so you metric 192.168.66.17 to a 10 and 192.168.66.16 to a 20. This will cause all internal traffic to go out from 192.168.66.17 and all traffic to the Internet to use 192.168.66.16, which has the gateway in place. This is not a best practice, but it works very well.

Understanding IP Version 6

One of the new features of Windows Vista is its default installation of IPv6. The configuration tasks—should you find yourself in an environment that uses IPv6—are almost exactly the same as for IPv4. In fact, IPv6 should prove to be even *less* of an administrative hassle than IPv4. How?

One big advantage that IPv6 has over IPv4 is the sheer number of possibly unique addresses. How many? 128 bits' worth of addresses. If that doesn't sound like a lot, consider that IPv4 uses only 32 bits' worth of possible addresses, and further consider that adding a single bit *doubles* the number of binary possibilities. In other words, 233 is twice as many as 232. How many more is 2,128 than 232? I don't even want to count that high.*

This means there are plenty of addresses to go around, and IPv6 clients are almost always configured to obtain an address automatically. So, for an administrator, just about the only IPv6 configuration task that needs to be done on a Vista machine is to make sure IPv6 is bound to the network card and that it is using automatic configuration.

---

* Fine, I'll count that high: 2,128 can describe 3.4×10^{38} possible unique addresses, which, by the way, is more than I'm being paid to write this book, even in pennies. I know. Hard to believe.

Here's how:

1. From the Network Connections Control Panel console, access the Properties dialog box for the desired network card.

2. Choose the Internet Protocol version 6 selection and click Properties. You'll be prompted for administrative confirmation if User Account Control is turned on.

3. As shown in Figure 3-8, from the IPv6 Properties dialog box, make sure the "Obtain an IP address automatically" radio button is enabled.

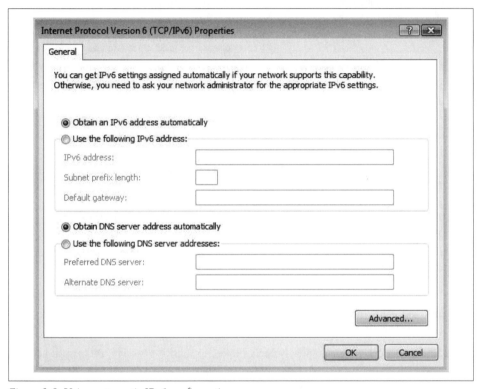

Figure 3-8. Using automatic IPv6 configuration

You *can* still specify a static IPv6 address should your network environment require one. It will look something like this:

```
2001:0:4136:e37c:3075:2a00:3f57:fdf3
```

And, of course, there are significant differences between IPv4 and IPv6 other than the larger address space. For the curious, Table 3-1 shows a quick rundown of these differences.

Table 3-1. Differences between IP version 4 and IP version 6

IPv4 features	IPv6 features
Source and destination addresses are 32 bits (4 bytes) in length.	Source and destination addresses are 128 bits (16 bytes) in length.
IPSec support is optional.	IPSec support is required.
Header includes a checksum.	Header does not include a checksum.
Header includes options.	All optional data is moved to IPv6 extension headers.
Internet Group Management Protocol (IGMP) is used to manage local subnet group membership.	IGMP is replaced with Multicast Listener Discovery (MLD) messages.
Broadcast addresses are used to send traffic to all nodes on a subnet.	There are no IPv6 broadcast addresses. Instead, a link-local scope all-nodes multicast address is used.
Must be configured either manually or through DHCP.	Does not require manual configuration or DHCP.
Uses a smaller packet size that is possibly fragmented.	Uses a larger packet size that is not without fragmentation.

What is the net of all this? Much like the Vista operating system includes many evolutionary improvements that make it easier to use and more secure, IP version 6 includes many feature enhancements and introductions that help make the Internet Protocol more secure, easier to configure, and more supportive of modern computer communication.

 IP version 6 is also available in other Microsoft operating systems such as Windows Server 2003 and XP with Service Pack 2. The difference with Vista is that it is installed and enabled by default. The next version of Windows Server, Longhorn, will also carry forward this design change.

You can find a lot more information about IP version 6 at oreilly.com. Look for a book there called *IPv6 Essentials*, by Silvia Hagen (O'Reilly).

In addition to new technologies, which make networking easier and more secure, Vista also introduces new tools to help achieve these objectives. One of the new tools is Vista's Network and Sharing Center.

The Network and Sharing Center replaces the functionality of the Network Properties dialog box from Windows XP, and represents a more intuitive way to connect to network resources. It is among the many tools discussed next.

Vista Networking Tools

Even though Vista includes support for a relatively new networking protocol, you'll probably still use an older protocol—IP version 4—to connect to and exchange data with most of the other network computers you encounter.

With the Vista networking tools, however, you will definitely be using some of the new bells and whistles. But once you see these tools in action, I think you'll agree that they represent a more intuitive and yet more powerful way of both setting up and managing network connections.

Here are some of the many new Vista networking tools and technologies:

- The Network and Sharing Center
- The Network Map
- Network Discovery
- Wireless Network Connection
- Creating a Network Location

Let's examine each of these now, starting with the hub of all Vista network activity, the new Network and Sharing Center.

The Network and Sharing Center

The new Network and Sharing Center is designed to assist the home user in setting up and sharing her documents and printers securely from one easy location. It's available on all Vista versions, but will likely be put to use most often in these flavors:

- Home Basic
- Home Premium
- Ultimate

There are several ways to quickly open the Network and Sharing Center, including these:

- Choose Network in the Start menu, and then click the Network and Sharing Center button located in the Windows Explorer toolbar.
- Double-click the Network and Sharing Center icon in the Control Panel.
- Right-click the Network item on either the Start menu or the desktop (if applicable) and choose Properties.
- Click the little network icon in the System Tray and then choose Network and Sharing Center from the context menu. (A right-click will work as well.)

No matter how you open it, you'll end up seeing the dialog box shown in Figure 3-9.

So what's here? As do many Control Panel consoles, the Network and Sharing Center features an extensive list of tasks on the lefthand side. Naturally, the ones in the Network and Sharing Center have to do with connecting to resources and sharing resources on the local machine. Using these links in the Network and Sharing Center, users or administrators will be able to perform the following actions:

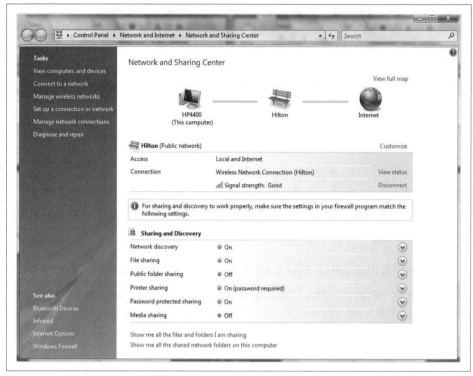

Figure 3-9. The new Vista Network and Sharing Center

- View computers and devices
- Connect to a network
- Set up a connection or network
- Get a visual representation of the network with a Network Map
- Change the network discovery options
- Change the network name, type, and icon
- Manage network connections
- Diagnose and repair network connectivity issues

Choose the "View computers and devices" link, for example, and you will be taken back to a Vista Explorer view where you'll see a list of devices found by the network discovery mechanism. As we will discuss in further detail in just a bit, this is a form of link-layer topology detection that runs by default within Vista. Figure 3-10 shows an example of what you might see when you click the "View computers and devices" link.

Figure 3-10. Using the Network Vista Explorer window

From this Vista Explorer page, you can then access other computers and resources the same way you access resources on your own system: by clicking and double-clicking on a graphical, hierarchical object and folder list.

> You do need the appropriate user permissions to access resources on these other computers, however. In many cases, you'll be prompted for user credentials when double-clicking a network resource.

In fact, there's actually a name for the location of this list of network resources. It's called, appropriately, the Network window.

The Network Window

This same Explorer screen also shows you devices that are within your network if they have firmware that is new enough to support Universal Plug and Play (UPNP), including any routers that support UPNP.

As shown in Figure 3-11, you can easily access and configure router properties using the Vista Explorer view. All you have to do is right-click and choose Properties from the context menu.

Figure 3-11. Access vital information about routers

This can really be a timesaver when it comes to troubleshooting. By accessing device properties, you will have access to a lot of vital configuration information concerning the device, including (oftentimes) a link to the device's configuration web page.

This is often a starting point for troubleshooting efforts with ISPs, and can save you from either a trip under the desk or rifling through the company's wiring cabinet.

Managing Network Discovery

This ability to see other computers—and to have those other computers see you—is a function of a new networking feature called Network Discovery. Whether Network Discovery is on or off by default depends on which type of network you're connected to. And how is that determined? Well, the first time you connect to a network, Vista asks you to choose a network location or type. This selection will prompt Vista to then automatically set the appropriate firewall settings based on the network type you just selected.

This is a new feature in Windows Vista. As you can see in the Network and Sharing Center, Vista lets you know what type of network you're connected to. It will be one of three types:

- Home (a Private network type)
- Work (also Private)
- Public Location

If you select either Home or Work, Network Discovery is turned on, and other computers will be able to see your system in the Network window, as you saw in Figure 3-11.

Microsoft recommends that you choose either of these network types when you know and trust the people and devices on the network. These network types, and the subsequent discovery that is enabled, are meant for home-office or small-business networks.

If you're connecting in a coffee shop, on the other hand, you almost *always* want to use the Public network type, as this disables the network discovery by default. The Public network type is designed to keep your computer from being visible to other computers around you. In other words, you generally don't want the curious in a coffee shop to just pull up an Explorer window, see your computer, and then access it with a double-click.

Also, turning off Network Discovery can help protect your computer from any malicious software looking for a port on which to land.

But just because these are the defaults doesn't mean they are set in stone. You can always turn Network Discovery on or off for a given network type as you please.

Here's what to do:

1. Open the Network and Sharing Center, and then look in the Sharing and Discovery section.
2. Expand the Network Discovery item and then use the radio buttons to toggle the feature on or off, as shown in Figure 3-12.
3. Once you've made the change, click the Apply button. The Security icon there signals what comes next: you're prompted for administrative confirmation if User Account Control is turned on.

And note that there's a way to change the network type from the Network and Sharing Center as well.

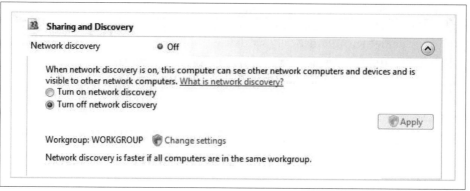

Figure 3-12. Changing default Network Discovery behavior

Customizing the network

When opening the Network and Sharing Center, you'll notice that Vista has automated several network parameters without your intervention. Here's what you should see under the mini Network Map:

- A name of the network, usually the same as the SSID of whatever network you're connected to
- The network type, which usually depends on the type chosen when establishing the connection
- A network icon, also a function of the network type chosen

But naturally, all of these are configurable options of the network *profile*. To change any of these settings, click the Customize link to the right of the network name.

You'll now see another of Vista's new networking utilities, the "Customize network settings" dialog box, shown in Figure 3-13.

From here, you can set the network type as either Public or Private, and even change the Network icon if it helps you differentiate among networks. And note that Vista does a pretty good job of letting you know the significance of the Public versus Private selection. Just remember that, counter to what the name might suggest, a Private network allows you to see computers and devices, while at the same time making your computer discoverable to others.

Click Next and then Close to commit the network changes.

In a domain setting, you cannot change these network settings. The domain administrator sets these options.

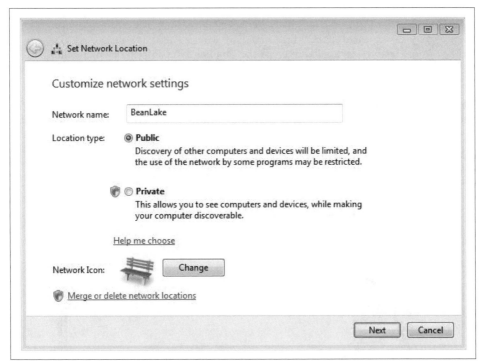

Figure 3-13. Customizing the network profile

Finally, don't confuse the network name with the workgroup name. The workgroup name describes a logical collection and is used to define a security and sharing entity. The network name describes the connection topology. It is possible to have two (or more) workgroups exist in the same network, and it is also possible to have a single workgroup span multiple networks.

The Network Map

The Network and Sharing Center also provides a link that allows administrators to view a full map of the network. If you click on this link, you'll see other computers and devices that have the Link-Layer Topology Discovery (LLTD) responder installed on them. Windows Vista machines have this responder installed by default.

In most cases, you can connect to and then perform administrative tasks on these devices. If you're using a mixed Vista–Windows XP environment, you need to download the LLTD responder for Windows XP at the TechNet web site, *http://technet2. microsoft.com*.

The LLTD specification describes how the LLTD protocol operates over wired (802.3 Ethernet) and wireless (802.11) media. LLTD enables device discovery via the data-link layer to help determine the physical makeup of a network.

As shown in Figure 3-14, the Network Map gives administrators a powerful troubleshooting tool that lets them literally see what devices are connected to what other device. Often, this information alone can help pinpoint the source of trouble.

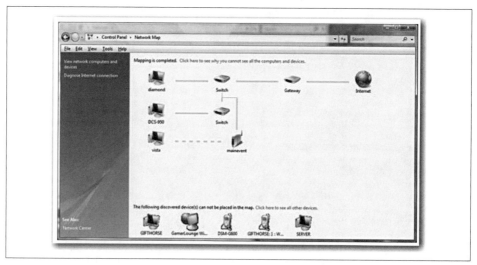

Figure 3-14. A sample Network Map

Be aware that LLTD is not a routable protocol. It was designed to assist with home and small-business networks. It will only see and discover devices on the same subnet.

Creating a Network Connection

The Network and Sharing Center also makes it easy to access and manage your computer's network connections, including any virtual private network (VPN) and personal area connections that are facilitated by Bluetooth. Most Vista-capable laptops today have at least two network connections built in.

To get started, click the "Manage network connections" link from the Network and Sharing Center. You will then see the Network Connections dialog box, which is really an Explorer window.

As seen in Figure 3-15, this dialog box displays a list of all of your network cards, VPN connections, and dialup connections.

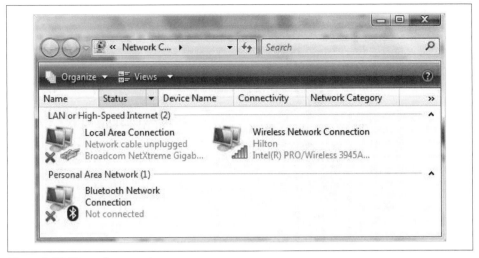

Figure 3-15. Network connections

Notice that all wired Ethernet connections are called Local Area Connection. If your system has more than one wired controller, I recommend renaming these to something a little more user-friendly. To rename a connection, simply right-click and choose Rename from the context menu.

Network Card Options

Although Vista does a pretty good job of configuring network connections automatically, administrators—especially in corporate settings—sometimes have to adjust settings manually.

Here's what to do:

1. Open the Properties dialog box for the selected network adapter. There are three ways to do this:

   - Double-click on the connection, which brings up the status of that network card. Then, in the lower-right corner, select Properties.

   - Right-click the connection icon and select Properties.

   - Double-click on the network icon in the System Tray. This brings up the status dialog box for the network card, from which you can open the Properties dialog box, shown in Figure 3-16.

2. To configure the settings of the network connection, click the Configure button. This opens the same dialog box you'd see if you were using the Device Manager to investigate the card's configuration.

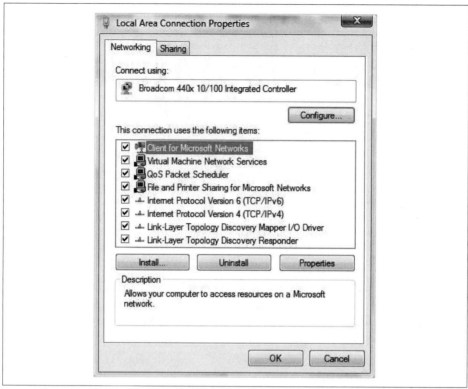

Figure 3-16. Properties of the Local Area Connection

The dialog box you see now will differ slightly depending on the card your system uses, but all should have the following configuration tabs:

- General
- Advanced
- Driver
- Details
- Power Management (least likely, although most modern cards should include Power Management options)

We'll discuss each configuration tab in the following section.

Network card properties

The General tab provides information about the device type, manufacturer, and location, as well as a notification about the status of the device. If you've lost product documentation, or you are dealing with a device you've never seen (an integrated wireless adapter, for example), this can prove to be helpful troubleshooting information.

The Advanced tab provides additional manufacturer-specific information. The properties you see here will vary from device to device.

During device troubleshooting, the Driver tab is probably the most frequently visited tab. Shown in Figure 3-17, it contains options for viewing, updating, uninstalling, and rolling back device drivers. For additional information about updating a device driver, please see Chapter 7. Use of the Driver tab doesn't really vary from device to device.

 Windows Update will also perform a regular check for updated drivers by default. Type **update** from the Start menu to begin to examine and configure Windows Update.

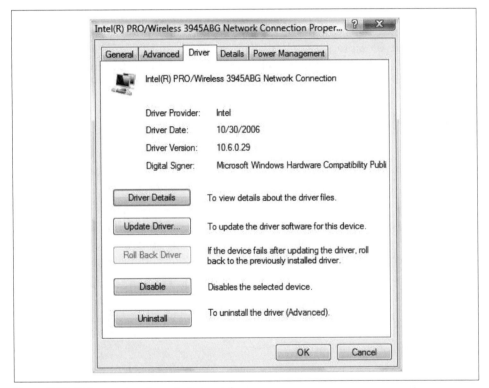

Figure 3-17. Using a network card's Driver tab

And remember when using the Driver tab that you can perform a rollback only if the device has not been uninstalled and there has been a previous driver.

One thing to remember about this tab is the uninstall. Often I see engineers, including myself, pull out a network card and replace it with another network card without uninstalling the drivers. This can cause many problems; for example, in some cases, the network address, if assigned statically, will stick and give an error message that says, "IP is already assigned to another NIC, do you wish to continue?" Usually you can go right past this, but if the other NIC is ever plugged back in, you could have a problem.

Occasionally, drivers from previous NICs cause compatibility issues with new NICs. It is recommended that you uninstall any device prior to removing it from your computer. This ensures that there will be no compatibility issues or conflicts with other drivers.

Vista stores lots of information about the network card; the Details tab is where you can retrieve that information. It provides a drop-down menu where you can select from a huge list of device properties, such as Manufacturer. The property value will then display in the Value portion of this tab.

The Power Management tab provides a few selections that will help the network card save battery life on laptop computers. This is usually most significant for wireless network cards, and may configure behavior such as allowing Vista to turn off the card to save power.

Wireless Networking

As you've seen already, Windows Vista includes a number of specific improvements geared to the mobile user, and few things are more convenient and beneficial to the mobile user than the ability to connect to a wireless network.

Vista has indeed introduced several changes to the process of connecting to a wireless network, all geared toward making the experience easier but without sacrificing security. After all, just because you connect to a Wi-Fi hotspot while swilling a latte doesn't mean you want all those other bohemians hacking your personal information.

What's more, many home network admins don't realize that in setting up a wireless network, they have just provided free Internet access for their neighbors as well. If you're inclined not to care about this and see it as your small way of sticking it to the man, fine, but also realize that an open wireless network can provide a means to access personal information as well.

At the very least, Vista administrators should be aware of the risks involved when setting up wireless networks. They should also be able to take a few countermeasures against hackers when necessary.

Connecting to a Wireless Network

Making a connection to a wireless network is easier than ever with Windows Vista. As in Windows XP, most users will start the connection process by right-clicking the Network icon in the System Tray. In Vista, the next step is to choose "Connect to a network" from the context menu.

In fact, if you're not already connected, the System Tray even notifies you when a wireless network is available.

Here's the entire process:

1. In the System Tray, right-click the Network icon and choose "Connect to a network" from the context menu. Alternatively, you can use the Start menu and click on the Connect To item. Either way, you'll see the dialog box shown in Figure 3-18.

Figure 3-18. Connecting to a wireless network

2. As you can see, the connection process from here is straightforward. All you have to do is select the desired network and click Connect.

3. If the network is *unsecured*, you'll see the yellow shield icon beside it. If the connection is security-enabled, you'll be prompted for the preshared key, as seen in Figure 3-19.

This preshared key is like a little password for the network.

After successful connection, the next dialog box lets you save the network for future automatic connection. If this is a wireless network you frequently use, such as a home or office wireless access point (WAP), or a favorite coffee shop, leaving this checked will allow Vista to connect without your intervention in the future.

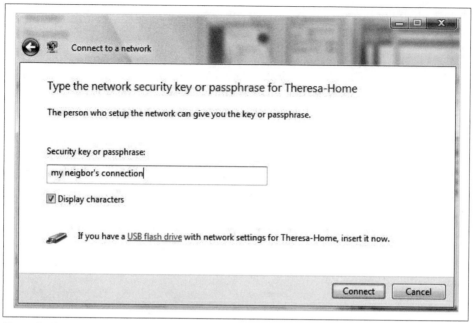

Figure 3-19. Connecting with a preshared key

Finally, click Close. You should now see one last dialog box the first time you establish communication with this network: the selection of whether the location is Home, Work, or Public. We discussed the significance of these options earlier in the chapter. You will be prompted for administrative confirmation if User Account Control is turned on.

One last thing: you will be able to connect to a WAP using the just-described method only if that WAP is broadcasting its SSID. How do you know whether a WAP is broadcasting? If you see it listed in the Connect To dialog box, it is.

But some WAP admins disable this behavior as a security measure, and you might do the same on a home WAP. In that case, a few other selections are necessary to connect to a WAP whose SSID is hidden.

Here's what to do:

1. Open the Connect To dialog box using any of the procedures previously introduced.

2. Choose the "Set up a connection or network" link at the bottom, and then choose "Manually connect to a wireless network" from the ensuing dialog box.

3. Now, in the dialog box shown in Figure 3-20, provide the following connection information:

Network name
> The SSID of the network

Security type
> The security protocol used

Encryption type
> How data is encrypted while in transmission

Security Key/Passphrase
> The password needed for a connection

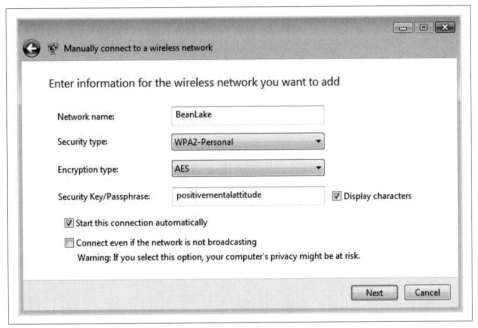

Figure 3-20. Connecting to a nonbroadcasting WAP

And note that just as when connecting to a broadcasting network, you can start the connection automatically the next time the Vista computer is in range. Heed the following word of caution, however, about the "Connect even if the network is not broadcasting" checkbox, as its implications can be confusing.

A network can be broadcasting its availability even if it is *not* broadcasting its SSID. When you enable the "Connect even if…" checkbox, you're telling Vista to send requests for the network to see whether it's in range. This request is not encrypted, though, and it can be read in all its plain-text glory by anyone capturing packets sent over the air.

On most WAPs, I'd say that isn't a terribly big deal, but on networks where the administrator has gone to the trouble of hiding the SSID, leaving data to pass unencrypted can significantly circumvent this security measure. So, best practice says to leave this unchecked when connecting to a non-SSID-broadcasting network.

When following the steps to connect to a hidden wireless network, you might also have noticed some other connection options.

Other network connections

Using the same dialog box shown previously in Figure 3-18, you also have the option of setting up several types of network connections for the first time. Following the "Set up a connection or network" link generates a list of several network connection choices, including:

- Connecting to the Internet
- Set up a wireless router or access point
- Manually connecting to a wireless network
- Setting up a wireless ad hoc (computer-to-computer) network
- Setting up a dial-up connection
- Connecting to a workplace
- Connecting to a Bluetooth personal area network (PAN)

The options from here will depend on the selection you've made. If you select "Set up a wireless router or access point," for example, you'll be taken through a wizard that will try to configure settings for a WAP.

This wizard will try to detect the WAP and automate its configuration for such tasks as sharing files and printers. If the wireless router supports a technology called Connect Now, the Vista wizard will detect the wireless router and then help you set up both it and the wireless network card on the client machine.

The wizard will ask whether you want to connect *other* computers and offer you the ability to save the configuration to a USB key. The advantage here is that once you've saved the configuration on the USB key, you can then take it to additional computers that will use the same network configuration and automate network setup.

 You can also take this same executable to a Windows XP SP2 machine to set up its wireless connection.

If Vista is unable to detect the wireless router automatically, you will likely have to configure it manually. Refer to manufacturer instructions for how to connect. Once the access point and the wireless connection are configured successfully, they should automatically connect when in range.

And note that when configuring either WEP or any of the WPA personal settings (both of which I'll discuss in more detail shortly), Vista can create the passphrase for you automatically. As seen in Figure 3-21, the passphrase is a randomly generated string of 20 characters that can then be copied to the WAP's security configuration.

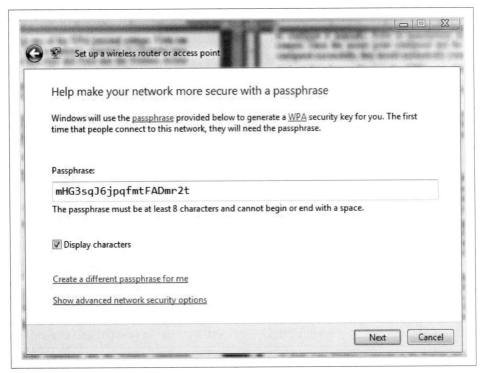

Figure 3-21. Securing a wireless connection automatically

Once all configuration parameters are in place, Vista stores these settings in an executable file, which is in turn saved to a USB flash drive. Administrators can then easily reuse this USB drive on another machine for quick wireless configuration.

This is but one example of the kinds of networks that can be quickly configured using Vista's new Connect To options. Another worth mentioning is an ad hoc network, which can be used to allow a few Vista computers (usually wireless-enabled) to quickly form a network for the purposes of conducting a meeting or exchanging files.

Setting up a VPN connection

VPNs are a convenient way to connect to a private company network over a public network such as the Internet. Once connected, the end user accesses all network resources using the same methods he uses when physically in the office.

What's more, the data sent over these connections is private, even though the network used to transmit that data is public. This is because information sent over a VPN is encrypted so that only sender and receiver computers (the end points of the VPN *tunnel*) are able to decipher what's being sent.

In practice, VPNs are deployed mostly to facilitate telecommuting. However, VPNs have fallen out of vogue over the past few years as alternative technologies have stepped in to accomplish much of what VPNs were used for, but with lower administrative overhead.

For example, many VPNs were deployed simply to allow email access. Now, that same functionality can be deployed natively with a Microsoft Exchange server. Exchange has two features built in:

Outlook Web Access (OWA)
> Allows users to use a web browser such as Internet Explorer 7 to view much of what they would normally view in Outlook.

RPC over HTTPS
> Stands for Remote Procedure Calls over Secure HTTP. It lets the full-featured Outlook client securely connect to the Exchange Server over the Internet. This is a really nice feature; there's no difference between using Outlook on the corporate network and using it on an Internet connection.

Also, Microsoft technologies such as SharePoint Server and Remote Desktop as well as third-party utilities such as GoToMyPC provide much of what VPNs were originally intended for. You can easily grab a file from a SharePoint site, for example, or perform desktop administration remotely through a Remote Desktop or GoToMyPC session.

All that notwithstanding, some administrators and companies still opt for a full-fledged VPN, which allows much more comprehensive corporate network access. Let's say, for example, that you need access to application installation files that are posted to your company's fileserver. In that case, a VPN is still probably the best way to go.

Configuring a VPN is very similar to setting up a wireless connection. The Connect To Wizard prompts you for all the information needed to establish the connection.

Here are the steps:

1. From the Start menu, click the Connect To option and then the "Set up a connection or network" link.

2. From the next dialog box in the wizard, choose "Connect to a workplace" and then click Next.

3. You now have two options, as seen in Figure 3-22. For a VPN connection, obviously the choice is "Use my Internet connection (VPN)."

4. Now just provide the appropriate credentials. You will then be prompted for a username and password, as well as a domain, if necessary.

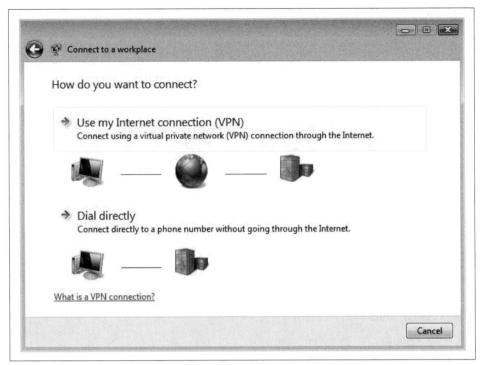

Figure 3-22. Establishing a VPN connection

Note that you can have Vista remember your password. This is not the most secure option, however.

Allowing a VPN connection

Flipping the connection topology around, you can also set up Vista to host an *incoming* VPN connection. Here's what to do:

1. Open the Network Connections Control Panel window.

2. Hold down the Alt key, and then choose File → New Incoming Connection. You'll be prompted for administrative confirmation if User Account Control is enabled.

3. Now, just select who can connect and how they can connect. The wizard will guide you through the process, enabling the appropriate protocols and opening the appropriate ports on the router.

Other users will now be able to establish a VPN connection to your machine using the steps mentioned in the previous section.

Setting up an ad hoc network

Let's say, for example, that you're conducting a meeting in which you want to get approval on some web site artwork you've been creating, or have a client review a commercial. What are your options? One is to burn the media on CD or DVD, and hand the client a copy. Another is to build an FTP site and have the client connect and download.

 You can only set up ad hoc networks using wireless connections, not wired connections.

But neither of these options is terribly personal, and can involve a lot of background administration. What if your system doesn't have a DVD burner? What if the file is too large for convenient posting to FTP?

Another option, then, is to meet the client at just about any convenient location and bring laptops in tow. Once connected to the same network (this can include APIPA), you can then use the Connection Option Wizard to quickly set up an ad hoc network.

To get started, follow these steps:

1. After clicking the "Set up a connection…" link, choose the "Set up a wireless ad hoc (computer-to-computer) network" option and click Next.

2. After the informational dialog box, you now see the dialog box shown in Figure 3-23. From here, give the temporary network a name, a security type, and a password if desired.

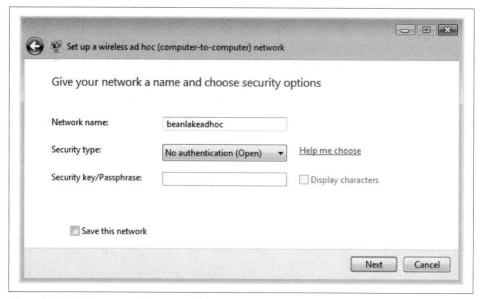

Figure 3-23. Setting up an ad hoc network

This is one of those instances in which it can help to understand the difference between a network and a workgroup. To set up an ad hoc network, both machines must be on the same network. They don't necessarily have to be in the same workgroup.

For the least amount of hassle/least amount of security, choose the "No authentication (Open)" option. Any other computer on the network will then be able to join.

What's more, your system will then be connected to that network as well. This may mean that you are now part of a network that doesn't have Internet access, by the way.

Disconnecting from a network

To disconnect from the ad hoc network, or from any other network, for that matter, open the "Connect to a network" dialog box once again, select the network you're connected to, and choose Disconnect. You'll see the dialog box shown in Figure 3-24.

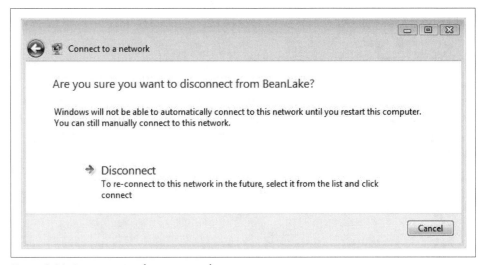

Figure 3-24. Disconnecting from a network

Alternatively, you can use the right-click method on the System Tray Network icon and choose the "Disconnect from" context menu selection.

Additionally, know that ad hoc networks are automatically deleted under these two circumstances:

- After all users disconnect from the network, or
- When the person who set up the network disconnects and goes out of range of other users of the administrator ad hoc network

There is one exception to these two rules: if the person who set up the administrator ad hoc network has selected the option to make it a permanent network, other users can still connect to and use it.

The key with all these "Connect to a network" options, of course, is to understand which kind of network you want to set up and then simply follow the instructions in the wizard.

Managing wireless networks

Keeping track of all these network connections can pose a challenge. Because of my travel schedule, in fact, I currently manage more than 20 wireless connections.

Or at least Vista does. Truth be told, I don't really have to manage any of them; it's all pretty much automated for me. How? With the Manage Wireless Networks console.

To access the Manage Wireless Networks console, follow these steps:

1. Open the Network and Sharing Center, and then choose the Manage Wireless Networks link.

2. You now see the Manage Wireless Networks console shown in Figure 3-25.

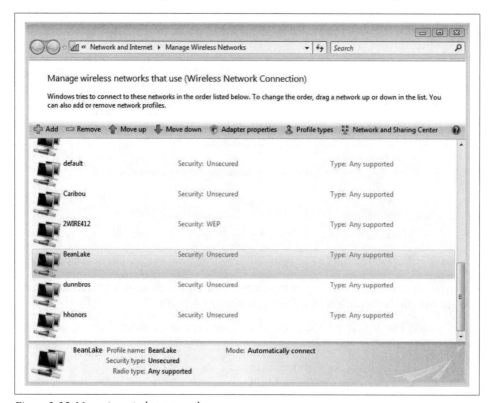

Figure 3-25. Managing wireless networks

There are really only two occasions when you might need to access this dialog box and change settings.

One is when your system is routinely in range of more than one WAP. You prefer to connect to network A over network B, but you don't want to delete network B altogether. In that case, it helps to know that Vista will connect to wireless networks in the order in which they appear on the list. To always connect to network A first, make sure it appears above network B. To do so, just highlight network A and use the "Move up" arrow in the toolbar.

Instance two is when security settings have changed for one of the WAPs. If the network's preshared key has changed, for example, you can update settings by right-clicking the network and choosing Properties from the context menu. In the network's Properties dialog box, there are two tabs: Connection and Security. As seen in Figure 3-26, choose the Security tab, select the security type, and then enter the new passphrase.

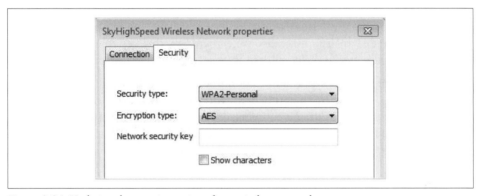

Figure 3-26. Updating the security settings for a wireless network

Now that I've introduced wireless security and some of the ways to connect to secure networks, let's turn things around a bit and look at security from the administrator's perspective. What options do administrators have to secure wireless connections, and how can they be configured?

We begin with a general overview of wireless security principles.

Wireless Security on Windows Vista

One of the ways to secure wireless communication is to encrypt the data passing through the airwaves. Vista offers three wireless protocols to secure the wireless connection:

- Wired Equivalent Privacy (WEP)
- Wi-Fi Protected Access (WPA)
- 802.1x authentication

Note that WPA security includes four subcategories: WPA-Personal, WPA2-Personal, WPA2-Enterprise, and WPA-Enterprise. You could argue that this leaves Vista with six different wireless security technologies, but we will treat WPA as a single protocol here.

No matter what protocol you use, one of the biggest administrative challenges is to know when to use a particular protocol. The next three sections discuss each wireless protocol individually.

WEP

Wired Equivalent Privacy has been widely used in many wireless deployments for years. As the name suggests, it provides a level of security that is equal to what's available on a wired network. Vista makes this technology available as well, which essentially requires a known password between the sending and receiving devices before communication is possible (just like when a wired user must log on to a computer using a password before using the wired network).

To perform its magic, WEP uses a preshared key that has to be set up on each access point and then on each Vista machine. WEP then uses this key to encrypt all information exchanged between the computer and the WAP.

WEP was designed for encryption and not authentication. Although WEP is a good encryption method, its strength and overall security can be weakened by not changing the shared secret. It is difficult to manage, and because it uses a shared secret to create additional keys, it is theoretically possible for a person to catch enough packets in a busy network and therefore determine the shared secret.

WPA

Wi-Fi Protected Access is the preferred method of securing a wireless connection. As mentioned, WPA supplies four types of possible wireless connections:

- WPA-Personal
- WPA2-Personal
- WPA-Enterprise
- WPA2-Enterprise

WPA and WPA2 are similar in design and setup, although WPA2 is the newest version and has some added security features and functionality. WPA2 may not be supported on some older wireless equipment, however, so network administrators may find themselves in a situation where the available hardware dictates the use of WPA instead of WPA2.

WPA or WPA2 Personal and Enterprise differ in their deployment methods and security. Personal is designed for the home or small office. It uses a preshared key to create the security encryption. It is still subject to dictionary-type attacks and password hacks. In order to strengthen the personal mode of WPA, you should use longer pre-shared keys. Fourteen random characters should be the minimum for the preshared key; 22 characters is the preferred length. Windows Vista will randomly generate a 20-character preshared key for you. We recommend you use the random passphrase generator.

WPA Enterprise allows administrators to specify both the encryption and the authentication types used by the connection. Two types of encryption are available for WPA Enterprise:

AES (Advanced Encryption Standard)
> This is a more advanced encryption method than Data Encryption Standard (DES). It was adopted by the U.S. government and is now the default standard within Windows Vista.

TKIP (Temporal Key Integrity Protocol)
> TKIP was designed to replace WEP without replacing any hardware. TKIP provides each packet with a different key, sometimes known as key mixing, so that each packet has its own unique encryption key.

Several selections will affect how users will prove that they are who they say they are:

Smart card or other certificate
> A smart card allows you to use smart cards and/or computer certificates to authenticate the connections between the WAP and the client. However, you need to have a RADIUS server installed as part of the implementation.

Protected EAP (PEAP)
> PEAP is designed to protect the beginning sessions of wireless client authentication. When they are using the Extensible Authentication Protocol (EAP) by default, the beginning packets of an EAP startup are sent in clear text so that they can establish the type of encryption and authentication to be used. PEAP initiates a TLS/SSL encryption prior to transmitting the beginning of the EAP stream.

Note further that in Microsoft's implementation of PEAP, you have PEAP with MS-CHAP v2 and PEAP-EAP TLS. In both cases, you will need a RADIUS server EAP-TLS computer or user certificates (smart cards) for authentication. For PEAP-MS-CHAP v2, you will need a server certificate on the RADIUS server and the clients need to have the CA trusted root certificate to establish the TLS connection for the protected portion. But then it uses the user's credentials to authenticate the connection through RADIUS.

Wireless single sign-on

In corporate environments, wireless networking can sometimes be a challenge because users first have to attach to the wired network and cache profile settings before establishing wireless access. Obviously, this can present a problem for a mobile or virtual workforce that might be issued only a laptop computer.

Microsoft has addressed this with a technology called single sign-on, which is actually an advanced feature of WPA2. If it's enabled, users can sign on to the corporate wireless network without having previously signed on using the wired connection.

Here's how it works. Users authenticate to the WAP using 802.1x prior to opening their domain profile. They do so using the same credentials they enter during normal sign-on. In other words, the changes to wireless domain sign-on versus wired domain sign-on should be apparent only to the administrator. Users can now perform a domain login using a device they have never used before, and wireless single sign-on will eventually allow them on the domain

 To implement wireless single sign-on, administrators must be using a Windows server domain environment with 802.1x enabled.

There are three methods to deploy a wireless single sign-on environment.

Method one. Network administrators preconfigure the wireless computer to the domain, configuring wireless single sign-on using a bootstrap wireless profile. With this method, an IT administrator joins the wireless computer to the domain before distributing it to the user. When the user starts the computer for the first time, the credentials specified for user logon are used for two purposes: to establish a connection to the wireless network, and to log on to the domain.

Here are the configuration steps:

1. An administrator joins the new wireless computer to the domain (for example, through an Ethernet connection that does not require IEEE 802.1x authentication) and then adds a bootstrap wireless profile to the computer with the following settings:
   - PEAP-MS-CHAP v2 authentication
   - Validate RADIUS server certificate disabled
   - Single Sign On enabled

2. In the bootstrap wireless profile settings, the administrator then specifies that single sign-on performs 802.1x authentication immediately before user logon.

3. The administrator distributes the new wireless computer to the user.

4. The user now starts the computer. Vista prompts the user to enter his domain user account name and password. Single sign-on will then use domain user account credentials to first establish a connection with the wireless network and then log on to the domain.

Method two. The user configures his wireless computer with a bootstrap wireless profile using an XML file and joins the domain. He uses an XML file and script that have been configured by an IT administrator.

Here are the implementation steps:

1. An administrator configures another Vista-based wireless computer with a bootstrap wireless profile that uses PEAP-MS-CHAP v2 authentication with the validation of the RADIUS server certificate disabled.

2. The administrator then extracts the bootstrap wireless profile to an XML file with the `netsh wlan export profile` command and creates a script file to execute that will automatically add the profile on the user's computer.

3. The wireless computer is then distributed with the script and XML file containing the bootstrap wireless profile. The script file contains the `netsh wlan add profile XML_File_Name Connection_Name` command. USB flash drives are commonly used to distribute this information.

4. The user starts the computer and performs a logon using a local computer account.

5. The user runs the script file to add the bootstrap wireless profile.

6. After the script is run, Windows Vista attempts to connect to the wireless network. Because the settings of the bootstrap wireless profile specify that the user must provide credentials, Windows Vista prompts the user for an account name and password.

7. The user types his domain user account name and password, and the Windows Vista client computer connects to the wireless network.

8. The user joins the Active Directory domain.

Method three. The user manually configures a wireless computer with a bootstrap profile and joins the domain. He manually configures the bootstrap wireless profile based on instructions provided by IT staff.

Here is the general procedure:

1. An administrator distributes instructions for configuring a bootstrap wireless profile that uses PEAP-MS-CHAP v2 authentication with validation to the RADIUS server certificate disabled.

2. The user starts the computer and logs in using a local computer account, and then follows the instructions to configure the bootstrap wireless profile.

3. With the bootstrap wireless profile now configured, Vista prompts for a domain username and password. If authentication is successful, the Vista client connects to the wireless network.

So, just how do you create a bootstrap profile, then?

Creating a bootstrap profile

Here's the procedure to create a bootstrap profile:

1. Open the "Connect to a network" dialog box using the previously discussed methods. From there, choose the "I don't see what I want to connect to" option and click Next.

2. From the "Select a connection" dialog box, choose "Set up a network."

3. You'll now see a dialog box for the new wireless connection where you can enter the following information:

   - The network name
   - The security type (WEP [802.1x], WPA-Enterprise, or WPA2-Enterprise)
   - The encryption type (WEP, TKIP, or AES)

4. Click Next, and then choose "Change connection settings." From the Security tab, select the Protected EAP (PEAP) method.

5. Click Settings under the "Choose a network authentication method" section.

6. Finally, from the Protected EAP (PEAP) Properties dialog box, clear the "Validate server certificate" checkbox. Click OK twice, and then click Close.

Now the administrator needs to export the settings of this bootstrap wireless profile to an XML file so that it can easily be reused.

Enter the following at the command prompt:

```
netsh wlan export profile XML_File_Name Profile_Name Connection_Name
```

Note here that *XML_File_Name*, *Profile_Name*, and *Connection_Name* are variables that define the XML file that will store the profile settings, the wireless profile name, and the name of the wireless adapter being configured.

Among all the discussion of encryption settings and preshared keys, one area of network security is often overlooked: simply locking down the computer so that few people, if any, have network access to it in the first place.

After all, if your laptop computer is meant to be used by you and only you, there's no sense in opening it up for the curious network user by enabling all of the file-sharing options. Fortunately, Vista places this security measure just a few clicks away.

This capability is just one of the features we look at as we now turn our attention to leveraging the network to be more productive.

Using the Network

As we've discussed already, many of the new features of Vista have focused on making the desktop and networking experience more secure than ever before. And with good reason: studies indicate that as many as 80 percent of PCs are unprotected, and thus are candidates to be used by hackers to send spam and advertisements.

But most of Vista's new security features are turned on by default, ensuring that even the most casual user experiences a more secure environment.

For example, Vista installs with the firewall enabled. It also includes a new Network and Sharing Center that makes configuration changes much easier. As seen in Figure 3-27, it is now quite easy to quickly see whether file and printer sharing is enabled. You can then disable or change settings with just a few clicks.

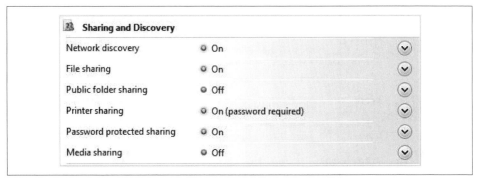

Figure 3-27. File and printer sharing options in the Network and Sharing Center

Locking Down the System

One big change in the way users connect to networks is the selection of the network *type* at connection time. As we examined previously, when connecting to a network for the first time, you're asked whether you're connecting to one of three types of networks, as listed here and shown in Figure 3-28:

- Home
- Work
- Public

The Windows Firewall blocks all incoming traffic until you specify a setting. The most secure default choice is to use the *public* setting. This selection hides your system and turns *off* automatic discovery protocols so that other computers nearby cannot access your system using a browse list.

In any network where you don't have complete knowledge of the settings, I recommend the public network setting.

Why does this dialog box provide such a big improvement over past connection behavior? Because in previous Windows versions, the firewall and network sharing settings would not adapt to the network. You could open ports on your computer to enable file and printer sharing when connected to work, for example, but those same ports would still be open when using the network at a hotel. Now, Vista lets you change network configuration with a single click.

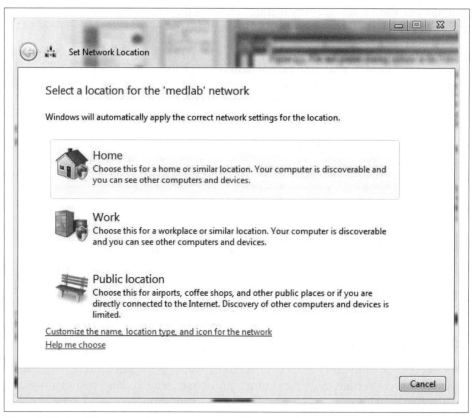

Figure 3-28. Specifying network type to configure default security settings

And you can still modify the default behavior very easily with just a few clicks in the Network and Sharing Center. Under the Sharing and Discovery section, expand the Public folder sharing button. You will see three options for governing public folder behavior:

Turn on public folder sharing so anyone with network access can open files
> This allows others connecting across the network to read and view any documents or pictures in the public folder.

Turn on sharing so anyone with network access can open, change, and create files
> This opens up more security risks because now you have allowed systems to write to your system. If, by chance, a computer that has a virus on it connects to this share, it can pass the virus, which will be transferred to your computers.

Turn off sharing (people logged on to this computer can still access this folder)
> This stops systems on the network from seeing the public folder; however, anyone logged on to this PC will still have access to the public folders.

Other sharing options appear beneath these three, and are fairly self-explanatory. Printer sharing is either on or off, for example, and can be secured with the password options that appear just below that option.

Note that when you use password protection, that option will affect all accounts accessing the printers and any public or file shares. Anytime a user connects to a shared resource, she will be prompted for an account and password for the local computer.

Keep in mind the reason we set up computer networks in the first place: to share resources, including the data housed in the many files and folders stored on our hard drives.

Sharing Files and Folders

In this chapter—and really, in the entire book so far—we have focused on what can be described as the *client* capabilities of Windows Vista. But the terms *client* and *server* describe what a computer is *doing* in the network, not the name of the operating system. It's very possible, for example, for a small business (or home) to have all of its file and print server capabilities met by a single Windows Vista machine.

In fact, several sharing capabilities are included with Windows Vista, more than in any previous version of the Windows desktop operating system. Again, it starts with a look at the Network and Sharing Center. As you can see in Figure 3-29, now five different file-sharing types can be enabled and then managed:

- File sharing
- Public folder sharing
- Printer sharing
- Password protected sharing
- Media sharing

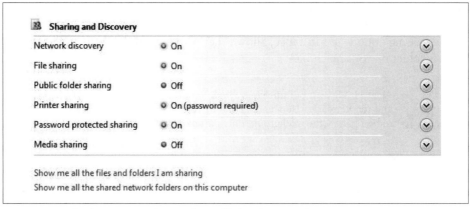

Figure 3-29. File-sharing types that can be enabled and managed

To configure any of the options here, just expand the option using the "chevron" button on the right, and then enable/disable it with the appropriate radio button.

For example, the "Public folder sharing" option lets users quickly share files by dragging them to a special folder called—what else?—Public. You can then configure the following three options for Public folder sharing:

Anyone with network access can open files
> This shares out the Public folder, but users can only read files within. This would let a user play a music file or play a movie, for example, as well as leverage a series of subfolders in the Public folder for easy organization. Figure 3-30 shows this subfolder hierarchy.

Anyone with network access can open, change, and create files
> This also shares the Pubic folder, although users have much more control over the files within. Use this option, for example, to facilitate easy collaboration within the confines of a workgroup, or when setting up an ad hoc network.

Turn off
> Self-explanatory.

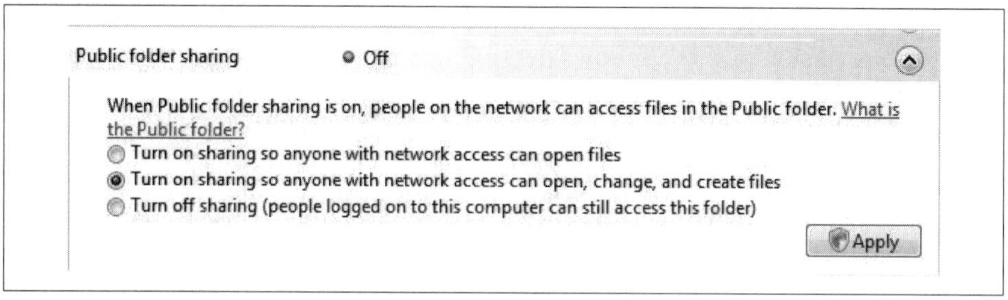

Public folder sharing   ○ Off

When Public folder sharing is on, people on the network can access files in the Public folder. <u>What is the Public folder?</u>
○ Turn on sharing so anyone with network access can open files
◉ Turn on sharing so anyone with network access can open, change, and create files
○ Turn off sharing (people logged on to this computer can still access this folder)

Apply

Figure 3-30. Options for Public folder sharing

Other sharing options in the Network and Sharing Center are fairly straightforward, as they are meant to be. The options here are designed to let users easily share resources without any of the background knowledge presented in this chapter. (The Printer sharing options, for instance, allow other people on the network to access the Printers folder on your machine.)

> Again, it's worth pointing out the difference between the workgroup and the network. Users connecting to your Printers folder don't have to be a part of the workgroup, only part of the network.

For this reason, we won't spend any more time on it here. What is important from an administrative perspective is to understand the implications of more traditional Server Message Block (SMB) sharing, discussed next.

Sharing for Administrators

As we've just seen, Vista facilitates very simple resource sharing by allowing users to share public folders and/or printers. But administrators want some more robust choices for network sharing rather than just the ability to turn it on or off for a single folder. Fortunately, Vista has carried forward almost all of the technologies of previous versions, allowing you to share out other folders on an individual basis using traditional folder sharing as well.

Here's what to do:

1. To share out using traditional Windows folder sharing, first ensure that File Sharing is enabled in the Network and Sharing Center. Expand the File Sharing selection and click the "Turn on file sharing" radio button.

2. Then use Windows Explorer to navigate to the folder you want to make available. Right-click it and choose Share from the context menu.

3. You'll now see the dialog box shown in Figure 3-31. From here, select the user or group you want to share the folder with using the drop-down selection. You also have the ability to create a new user from here (assuming appropriate user rights).

4. Now, click Share. You'll be prompted for administrative confirmation if User Account Control is turned on.

5. After sharing has been enabled, you're shown a confirmation dialog box that displays the full Universal Naming Convention (UNC) path to the share. From here, you can email a link to the share to facilitate an easy connection. You can also copy the link onto the Windows clipboard for use in other applications.

Figure 3-31. Creating a folder share

You can now share individual files using the same techniques mentioned here. Just navigate to the file, right-click, and then choose Share to get started.

Advanced sharing

Although the preceding section provided the steps to perform the *function* of "traditional" Windows folder sharing, you can still use the familiar *interface* as well. To get started, follow these steps:

1. Right-click the folder you'd like to share (or one that's already been shared using the new method) and choose Properties from the context menu.

2. Now, from the folder's Properties dialog box, click the Share tab. There are two buttons here:

    Share

    This launches the Sharing Wizard, taking you to the file-sharing dialog box that was discussed in the preceding section.

    Advanced Sharing

    This opens the Advanced Sharing dialog box, shown in Figure 3-32. From here, click the "Share this folder" checkbox. The additional options let you give the share a name and set the number of simultaneous connections.

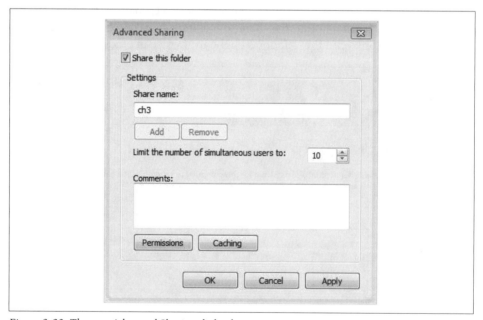

Figure 3-32. The new Advanced Sharing dialog box

You can also be very granular with the folder permissions from this Advanced Sharing dialog box by clicking on the Permissions button. This will open the more traditional Windows folder sharing dialog box that is seen in Figure 3-33. As the security shield indicates, you'll be prompted for administrative confirmation if User Account Control is turned on.

Figure 3-33. Configuring sharing using the traditional folder sharing dialog box

Again, this dialog box will look familiar to administrators who have used previous versions of Windows, and the Allow and Deny behaviors will be the same. You can add individual users and groups and then assign appropriate permissions as you see fit (more on this in the next section).

Also note that administrators can configure offline file options by clicking on the Caching button from the Advanced Sharing dialog box. There are three options here, as shown in Figure 3-34:

- Only the files and programs that users specify will be available offline.
- All files and programs that users open from the share will be automatically available offline.
- Files or programs from the share will not be available offline.

You can access the Advanced Sharing options with or without the Sharing Wizard turned on, but it can reduce confusion to turn it off. To do so, access the Folder and Search options from any Vista Explorer window (Organize → Folder and Search Options) and click the View tab. Once you're there, uncheck the Use Sharing Wizard option.

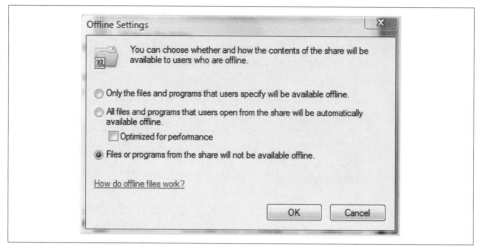

Figure 3-34. Caching settings

We will discuss offline file behavior later in the chapter. For now, however, we will continue with the ways administrators can secure shared folders and files.

Securing a Shared Folder

Sharing also provides a limited form of network security through the use of share permissions, which define what kind of access a user has when connecting to a share over the network.

It's also important to note here that two kinds of permissions are available on Vista computers: share permissions and NTFS permissions. It's even more important that you not confuse the two.

Share permissions define what happens only when a user is connecting to a resource *from over the network*. These permissions are meaningless if that same user were to sit down and log in locally. To control *local* access, you need to implement NTFS permissions. We'll tackle NTFS permissions in the next section, though.

For any given user or group with access to a shared folder, three types of share permissions define the level of access. Table 3-2 describes the three options.

Table 3-2. Share permissions

Permission	Characteristics
Read	Allows a users to view files in a folder; lets users execute programs in the shared folder.
Change	Allows users to change the data in a file; lets users delete a file within a share (so be judicious about who has change permission).
Full Control	Allows full access to the shared folder, including all permissions from Change; allows users to change permissions on the share.

Further, these three permissions are restricted by two conditions:

Allow
> Grants the specific permission to a shared resource. This is the default selection for a permission setting.

Deny
> Will explicitly *block* the permission from being applied to a resource. This condition adds another layer of complexity to shared resources and should be used sparingly.

For example, it is possible to deny a user read access to a resource while still allowing change access to be in effect. It's not good practice, and it's a nightmare when you're troubleshooting access permissions, but it is possible. The result would be a folder in which a user could delete a file that he could otherwise not read.

To configure share level permissions to a network resource (or NTFS permissions, for that matter), you will edit the resource's access control list (ACL). The ACL is a list of user accounts and groups that are allowed to access a resource, and it lists what level of access is allowed. Vista tracks an ACL for each and every object every time an account needs access to that object, and shared resources are no different. Examples of objects include folders, files, network shares, and printers.

When you first share out a folder, note that the ACL consists of only one entry: the Everyone group is granted read permission. If you want to edit the list of users and groups who can access the share and how they can access it, click the Add button and you can add a group or individual account. You can also remove groups by selecting them in the ACL and clicking Remove.

After the user or group appears in the ACL, you can modify its level of access by either checking or unchecking the appropriate checkboxes.

Bear in mind that it's possible for a user to be a part of two or more Vista security groups. When groups have different levels of access to a resource, the share permissions for that user are cumulative; they are added together. If a user was part of the Everyone group with read access, and was also a member of the Administrators group with full control, for example, the effective permission would be Full Control.

Note, though, that Deny is the trump card. If a user is part of a group with the Deny setting, Deny becomes effective.

As a last thought, remember that you can implement sharing on both FAT and NTFS partitions, and can even share out resources from an optical drive or just about any other storage device that's attached to your system.

If sharing is all about making a resource available, NTFS permissions—as we'll discuss next—are all about securing these resources.

NTFS File Permissions

Unlike shared folder permissions, NTFS permissions can be configured at the folder level *and* at the individual file level. What's more, they are effective no matter how a user accesses a resource. They are just as effective locally as when the resource is accessed over the network.

To access and configure NTFS permissions, right-click the file or folder and choose Properties. From there, choose the Security tab, where you'll see an ACL that looks very similar to what you saw when dealing with share permissions. Figure 3-35 shows this ACL.

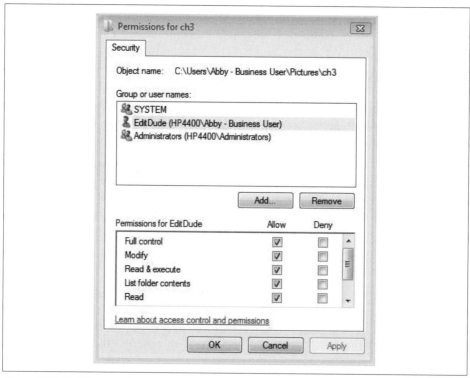

Figure 3-35. NTFS permissions

Upon further review, however, you'll notice that there are many more options than just the three share level permissions.

What's more, the permissions you see here are really just collections of several attributes that define behavior. Let's take a closer look, in Table 3-3.

Table 3-3. Standard folder permissions

With this NTFS folder permission...	A user can...
Read	See files and subfolders and view folder ownership, permissions, and attributes.
Write	Create new files and subfolders within the folder, change folder attributes, and view folder ownership and permissions.
List Folder Contents	See names of the files and subfolders within a folder.
Read and Execute	Move through folders to reach other files and folders, even if she doesn't have permission for those folders; perform actions permitted by the Read permission and the List Folder Contents permission.
Modify	Delete the folder, and perform actions permitted by the Write as well as the Read and Execute permissions.
Full Control	Change permissions, take ownership, and delete subfolders and files, plus perform actions permitted by all other NTFS permissions.

As with share permissions, each standard NTFS permission has an Allow setting and a Deny setting. Also, as with shares, the Deny setting trumps the Allow setting. If you want to quickly deny *all* access to a user or group for a particular resource, deny the Full Control permission. This turns off all other access to the resource.

Here we'll deal with just the collection of standard NTFS permissions, not the full list of individual NTFS attributes. Configuring individual NTFS attributes is rather complicated, especially with Vista's redesign, which has added even more complexity to this process, including some nonsensical, find-the-McGuffin-like dialog boxes.

For example, to edit the standard NTFS permissions, you would naturally gravitate toward the Edit button, right?

Not so fast. On most resources, this just lets you *view* the ACL. This list is not editable until you first remove the inherited NTFS permissions on the resource. So, you have to click Cancel to get out of that dialog box.

To remove the inherited permissions, then, you have to click the Advanced button from the resource's Security tab, which then gives you the dialog box shown in Figure 3-36. Now you can remove inherited permissions, right?

Wrong again. This also just lets administrators see a list of NTFS permission entries. To remove the entries that are there, you must then click Edit, which gives you pretty much the same dialog box as what you were just looking at.

Instead, you have to perform one more step: clear the "Include inheritable permissions from this object's parent" checkbox. You'll then get a dialog box that lets you do one of the following:

- Copy the entries that are already there
- Remove all ACL entries to start from scratch
- Cancel out of the operation

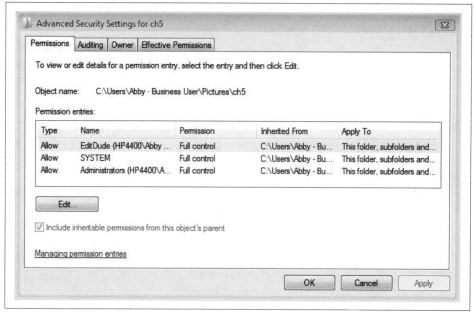

Figure 3-36. Advanced NTFS settings

Now you're finally done with the convoluted operation, and you're ready to at least *view* the ACL entries for the resource. To do so, make a selection on the Permissions area and then click Edit again. At last, you have the ability to view and edit the individual NTFS attributes in all their glory, as seen in Figure 3-37.

Exhausted? Try writing about it. The point of this rather lengthy segue is that you should perform 90 to 100 percent of your NTFS permission editing using the standard NTFS permissions as detailed in Table 3-3.

Oh, and so you don't get your hopes up, it's not all that simple to just edit standard NTFS permissions, either. You will have to go through many of the steps just detailed to remove the inherited NTFS permission before being able to make any edits.

 All of the foregoing instruction assumes, of course, that you have the proper permissions to access these Properties pages in the first place. A user with read access, for example, would not be able to see this information.

One of the big advantages of NTFS permissions is that they can also be used to secure individual files, not just the folders that contain them. The NTFS file permissions look almost exactly the same as the folder permissions, with a few exceptions. Table 3-4 sums up the activity that a given standard file permission will allow.

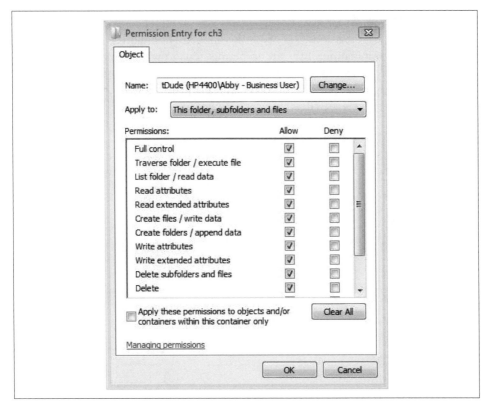

Figure 3-37. Individual NTFS entries

Table 3-4. Standard NTFS file-level permissions

With this NTFS file permission...	A user can...
Read	Read the file and view file attributes, ownership, and permissions.
Write	Overwrite the file, change file attributes, and view file ownership and permissions.
Read and Execute	Run applications and perform the actions permitted by the Read permission.
Modify	Modify and delete the file, plus perform all actions permitted by the Write as well as the Read and Execute permissions.
Full Control	Change permissions and take ownership, plus perform the actions permitted by all other NTFS permissions.

As you can see, the only significant difference between folder and file permissions is that List Folder Contents is not one of the standard file permissions.

NTFS permission behavior

Like shared folder permissions, NTFS permissions are cumulative: a user's effective permission is a combination of the group permissions to which an account has been assigned, plus any individual permissions specifically assigned to that user. A user that is part of a group that's been assigned read access and a group that's been assigned full control gets the effective permission of Full Control.

 If you investigate the Advanced Properties of the ACL, you might notice a handy little tab that helps keep all of this straight: it's the Effective Permissions tab, and it displays just that: the effective permission for the user or group selected in the ACL. Figure 3-38 shows what information can be obtained on the Effective Permissions tab.

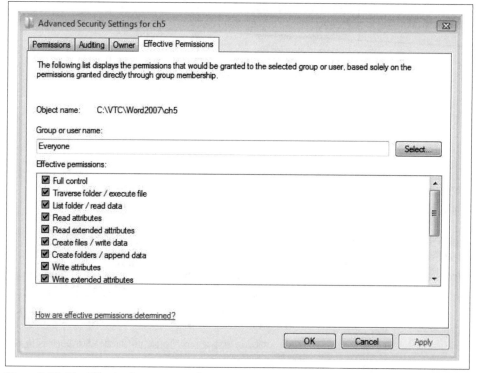

Figure 3-38. The Effective Permissions tab

Administrators also need to keep in mind that NTFS file permissions *override* folder permissions. A user might have just the Read permission to a folder, for example, yet have Full Control permission to one or more of the files within that folder.

Comparing share versus NTFS permissions. Vista administrators should also be able to discern the differences between NTFS and share permissions. We covered some of this earlier, but the two levels differ from each other in these significant ways:

- NTFS permissions are effective locally.
- Share permissions apply only over the network.
- NTFS permissions can be applied to both folders and individual files.
- Share permissions can be granted at the folder level only.
- NTFS permissions apply only on NTFS resources.
- Share permissions can secure resources independent of the filesystem.

What else? Oh yeah, there's another significant factor, one that I've seen become part of many a head-scratching session when troubleshooting resource access. Here it is:

- When share and NTFS permissions are combined, the most *restrictive* permission is the effective permission.

See? It's so important that it gets a separate bullet point. So, lock that one in the old noodle.

Incidentally, the permissions behave this way because each ACL is evaluated independently. Vista is, in effect, saying, "You have *this* set of permissions at this level, but you have only *that* set of permissions at another level. So, I suppose, you're really supposed to have only *that* level of permission, aren't you?"

Or something like that. This is the computer talking.

Permissions best practices

So, then, when you're setting up traditional sharing, my advice is this: share your network resources from an NTFS volume, and then use NTFS permissions to tighten down security. You can configure share permissions as wide open as you please; NTFS permissions will take care of any access to the resource, and you'll essentially have just a single ACL to worry about.

Another reason to deploy network resources such as this is that the security will also be effective even if the resources are accessed locally.

Accessing a Network Resource

Earlier in the chapter, we examined how computers send information to one another using TCP/IP. We then looked at how to leverage those network connections to make resources available.

Now we turn our attention to the result of getting these computers to talk to one another. What can we access, and how can we access it, once we enable computer communication?

There are actually several methods for accessing information and resources that are stored on network computers. They include the following, starting with the most-often used:

- Browsing using Internet Explorer
- Browsing using the Network node of Vista Explorer
- Mapping a network drive
- Using the NET USE utility from the command line
- Using the Address toolbar in the taskbar
- Using the Run entry box

It's all pretty straightforward, and the more that networks and operating systems evolve, the more that *all* networking will look like the first example cited: following hyperlinks in an Internet browser.

A few networking methods in Vista still require an understanding of UNC syntax. At other times, using UNC is just plain easier.

UNC syntax locates resources in a Windows computing environment with addresses that look like this:

```
\\servername\sharename
```

where *servername* is the NetBIOS name of the server, and *sharename* is the name of the resource that's being shared. This syntax is used exclusively by the NET USE utility and when mapping a network drive.

It can also be used in the Run entry box (or the Start menu's Search box itself), and can even be used in the address bar of Internet Explorer 7. In fact, we were exposed to this UNC syntax earlier in the chapter, when we configured a share using the Sharing Wizard. Recall that at the end of the wizard, we were prompted to send an email to other users notifying them of the UNC path to the new share.

You don't even have to type in the full path of the share. If you just want to see what resources are available on the Beanlake computer, for example, you could simply type **\\beanlake**.

In the Start menu's Search box, you will now see a window similar to what's shown in Figure 3-39.

Mapping a drive

Another connection option is to *map* a drive to a network resource. The advantage here is that Vista assigns a drive letter to the mapped resource so that it looks like just another drive resource on your system.

Here's how to map a drive. From a Vista Explorer window, right-click the Network item and choose Map Network Drive. You'll now see the Map Network Drive dialog box shown in Figure 3-40.

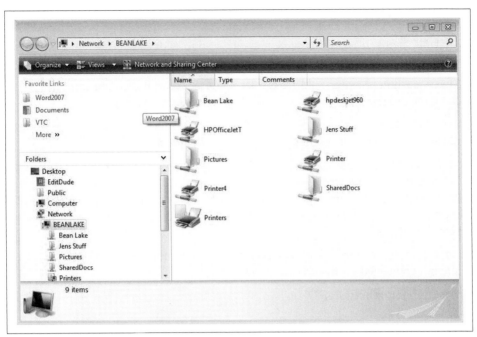

Figure 3-39. Results of browsing the network

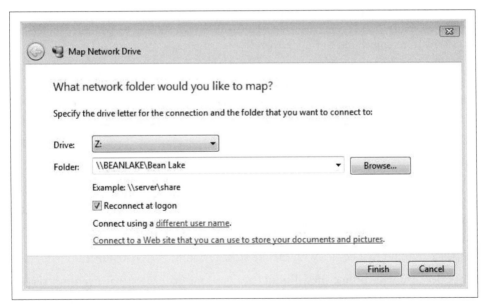

Figure 3-40. Mapping a network drive

From here, you simply select a drive letter and then specify the UNC path to the resource. If you don't know the UNC path, click Browse and search in a little browse window. Click Finish to commit the changes.

Another compelling reason to map network drives is one of permanence. If you keep the "Reconnect at logon" checkbox checked, you won't have to go browsing or typing in UNC paths to access the same network resources day after day.

What's more, some older (really old) programs rely on data that must be stored on the local machine. Mapping a drive can let you use a centralized data store while still tricking the program into thinking it's dealing with a local resource.

But at the end of the day, mapping a drive on a Windows Vista machine should really look no different from previous versions of Windows.

So, then, accessing resources on a Windows Vista network is pretty easy stuff. Just click around and you'll find you can connect to what's out there. You can store vital files in a centralized computer that runs a scheduled backup, and you can rest easy knowing that if your laptop is ever stolen, you'll have a copy of your most precious files back in the office.

What's even more impressive, however, is accessing these same files even when you're not connected to the network. How?

This is a job for offline files.

Offline Files

With offline files, you can work with files stored on a network server even if you're not connected to that server, allowing you to access the same set of data regardless of whether you're connected to the network.

For reasons that are self-evident, this is especially helpful when using a laptop, but it will not be available on every laptop. Use of offline files is available only for these editions:

- Business
- Enterprise
- Ultimate

I know. It stinks that Microsoft didn't include it on the Home Premium edition. Keep this factor in mind when tricking out your new laptop, by the way—you might want to save up and get the upgraded version of Vista. It's a Home Premium deal-breaker for me. I know that my life is barely possible without offline files, if only for the peace of mind that comes with the file storage configuration just mentioned.

Why? Because with offline files, I'm *always* working with files that live on a server back in my home office, regardless of whether I'm actually connected to that server. And most of the time, I'm not.

When I reconnect to the server, the new Vista Sync Center makes sure that these offline files are then synced to the server, so I'm always working with the most recent version of the files, and I don't have to keep track of which version is on what computer.

If you're using one of the three offline files-capable operating systems, it should be enabled by default. Here's how to check, just in case.

From the Control Panel, open the Network and Internet application. Then choose the Offline Files link. You'll see the Offline Files dialog box shown in Figure 3-41. If it's disabled, you'll see a button called Enable Offline Files.

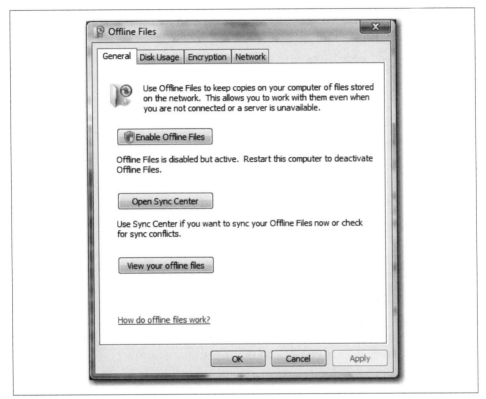

Figure 3-41. The Offline Files dialog box

Note that when you make a change, you're affecting all users of the system. You'll be prompted for administrative confirmation if User Account Control is turned on.

Once you've confirmed that the Offline Files feature is ready for use, the next step is to actually make a network resource available. It's breathtakingly simple. Here's how:

1. Use any of the connection techniques to locate the server that holds the share you want to make available. For example, you could type **\\server** at the Vista Start menu.

2. Right-click the share you want to make available, and choose Always Available Offline from the context menu.

Vista now displays a dialog box letting you know the status of the offline file operation. Once complete, the files are now synchronized and available for offline use. Vista indicates any offline files with a Sync icon next to the folder, as shown in Figure 3-42.

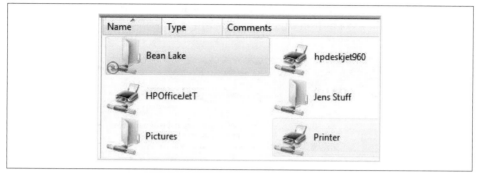

Figure 3-42. Folders that are available offline

 Administrators can be very specific about whether and how offline files are used by deploying a GPO that defines settings. I'll discuss Group Policies in more detail in Chapter 13, or you can drop me an email and I'll point you in the right direction.

There are now two ways to work with the offline files:

Access the files using network syntax, just as when working with them online
With this method, you do the same thing to access the offline files as you do the online files. If you type **\\beanlake** online, you type **\\beanlake** offline as well. You'll see a Vista Explorer window with just the offline folders displayed. I prefer this method, as I always use a consistent means of locating files.

Use the Vista Sync Center
This is a new technique for working with offline files, replacing the Offline Files folder that was present in Windows XP (XP systems can still use the first method), except that it's almost exactly the same as using the Offline Files folder under Windows XP. In essence, not much has changed.

As shown in Figure 3-43, you can open the Vista Sync Center (type **sync** from the Start menu) and access any offline files by double-clicking the Offline Files folder here.

The improvement over the Windows XP version of this tool is that the Vista Sync Center shows a graphical display of sync status. You can know immediately when looking in the Sync Center whether a sync has occurred, and when.

The other advantage is that the Sync Center makes it a bit easier to configure regular synchronizations among your sync partnerships. You had this same ability in Windows XP, by the way, but now Vista includes a few additional scheduling options. Here's how to put it to use:

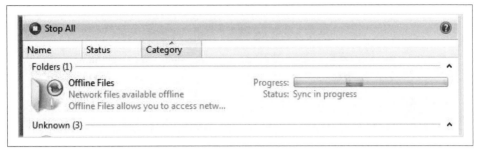

Figure 3-43. Offline files in the Vista Sync Center

1. Start the process by clicking the Schedule button once you've selected a sync partnership in the Sync Center.

2. The Sync Schedule dialog box appears, letting you choose to which items in the Offline Files folder the schedule will apply.

   You have two choices here:

   - A scheduled time
   - On an event or action

The wizard's choices will vary, depending on which path you select. If you want to sync every time you log on to your computer, for example, choose the "event or action" path and then the "I log on to my computer" checkbox, as shown in Figure 3-44.

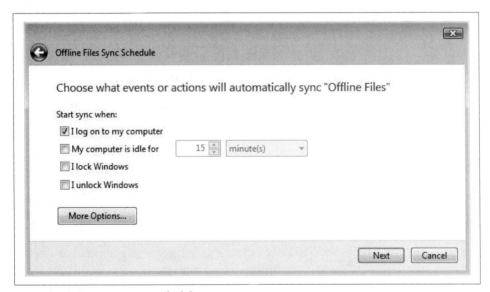

Figure 3-44. Setting up a sync schedule

When you're done, give the schedule a name and then click Finish. For most offline file uses, syncing on the logon event is a good way to update the server with the latest changes made while offline.

 You can also manually sync at any time by right-clicking the Sync Center System Tray icon and choosing Sync All from the context menu.

Synchronization Conflicts

If both the online and the offline copies of the files have been changed, you'll be notified by a Sync Conflicts Have Occurred message from the Sync Center.

In that case, click the message. You'll then have three options for how to handle the conflict (or a specific conflict, should there be more than one). You can:

- Keep the network version.
- Keep the offline version.
- Keep both versions.

Best practices dictate that you keep both versions. You can always look at each file at a later time and decide which one is safe to discard.

Removing offline files

Once you no longer need access to the server files offline, simply reverse the previous procedure. Connect to the server resource once again, and this time, clear the Always Available Offline checkbox.

 You can easily encrypt offline files, which is a good idea. This will prevent a laptop thief from accessing potentially sensitive server data if he takes the drive and looks at it on another computer. To encrypt offline files, use the Encrypt tab on the Offline Files Properties dialog box, as shown previously.

Sharing a Printer

Another kind of resource you can share from your Windows Vista computer is any and all of the installed printers. That's because the printer is really a disk resource, just like a file or a folder. The thing that produces paper with ink? That's a print device.

For now, just know that in order to use printer sharing, you must first enable it in the Network and Sharing Center. You can probably figure it out on your own by now, but just to jog your memory, here are the steps:

1. Open the Network and Sharing Center using any method you choose. I prefer typing **net** at the Vista Start menu.

2. Expand the Printer Sharing section under Sharing and Discovery.

3. Make sure the Turn on Printer Sharing radio button is selected.

Now you can open the Printers folder in the Control Panel and share one or more of your attached printers. What's the easiest way to do this? Just type **print** at the Start menu, and then follow these steps:

1. Right-click the desired printer and choose either Sharing or Properties from the context menu. (The Sharing choice will take you directly to the Sharing tab.)

2. Now, just select the "Share this printer" checkbox.

3. If the checkbox is grayed out, click the "Change sharing options" button.

4. You should now see the printer's Properties dialog box, where you can select the sharing option.

5. Type in a name for the shared printer, as shown in Figure 3-45. By default, Vista uses the entire brand name of the printer, which can be long. I recommend using a more user-friendly name, such as Basement, Photo Printer, and so on, as this is the name users will see when accessing the printer over the network.

Also selected by default is the option to have print jobs rendered on the client computers. If you uncheck this, the printed object is sent to the Vista machine sharing the printer. If people use the Vista print server, this is generally not a good idea. If you're setting up a dedicated Windows Vista print server, this can offload work from client computers.

You can also add additional drivers for print clients with this dialog box. For instance, you can add 64-bit drivers to enable 64-bit clients to print, or even older NT4 drivers if need be. This makes it much easier to share and use printers because the print clients will automatically download the appropriate driver from the Vista print server machine instead of making you install drivers manually.

Firewall considerations

As a final note on folder and printer sharing, know that the Windows Firewall must be properly configured to allow file and print sharing traffic, both incoming and outgoing.

This should be automatically configured when enabling sharing in the Network and Sharing Center, but it's worth checking firewall settings if you run into trouble.

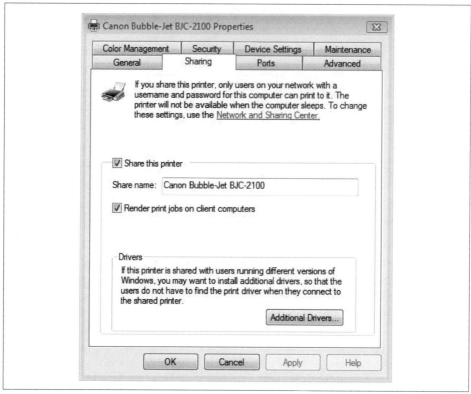

Figure 3-45. Sharing a printer on Windows Vista

Here's what to do:

1. Open the Windows Firewall. You can find it in the Security grouping in the Control Panel, or just type **fire** from the Vista Start menu.

2. Click the Change Settings button. You'll be prompted for administrative confirmation if User Account Control is turned on.

3. From the Firewall Setting dialog box, choose the Exceptions tab.

4. Now, ensure that the File and Printer Sharing option is selected, as shown in Figure 3-46.

Figure 3-46. Making sure the Windows Firewall enables file and printer sharing

Also, don't forget about other possible firewalls that may be installed on your machine. Many computer manufacturers install their own firewall products, and many antivirus programs install a "security suite," which typically includes a firewall as well. Vista can run just fine with more than one firewall; it can lead to configuration confusion, though.

Creating a User Account

All activity on a Windows Vista machine is done in the context of a user account, and it is a best practice to create an account for every user of the machine. The benefits of individual accounts for each user are almost too numerous to detail here, but if you want to be able to specify certain behaviors for certain users, you need to leverage separate user accounts.

For example, tracking activity with Parental Controls is done with user accounts. An administrator account sets it up, and individual computer use is then tracked for standard accounts you specify. But how do you create additional user accounts in Windows Vista?

Here's one method:

1. Open the Control Panel and then click User Accounts. By default, this will call up the settings page for the account currently in use.

   Several options are available from this window. You can:

   - Create a password.
   - Change the picture.
   - Change the account name.
   - Change the account type.
   - Manage other accounts.
   - Turn User Account Control on or off.

2. The task list on the left provides even more options. To get started creating another account, choose the "Manage another account" option, which will open the Manage Accounts dialog box.

3. Now, click the "Create a new account" link to create an account, revealing the dialog box shown in Figure 3-47. From here, you name the account and select whether you want the user to be a standard user or an administrator.

Note that Vista does *not* allow users without passwords to access resources that have been shared. So even in the least secure of environments, such as a home network where everyone trusts one another and no one is concerned about data security, you must set up the network to use accounts with passwords in order to facilitate sharing.

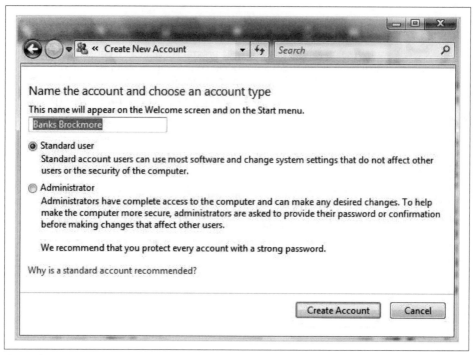

Figure 3-47. Creating a new user account

 If a user tries to access a network resource with the same username and password as an account on the machine where the shared resource lives, the user is not prompted for a password. Otherwise, the user sees a Connect To dialog box where she is prompted for user credentials.

Standard User Account

Even if you're a Vista administrator, Microsoft recommends that you create a standard account for all of your normal everyday tasks. You can then use an administrative account to make changes to the computer that may affect other users. When you install new software, for example, you can log on as an administrator or simply use User Account Control and provide administrative credentials.

This is a good security practice because it stops malicious content from being run without your permission. By stopping programs from executing without your permission, you can help to maintain security for you and the rest of the Internet.

Another good security practice—even on home computers (maybe *especially* on home computers)—is to create standard user accounts for children. Home admins can then restrict certain web site and/or game usage, for example, leveraging Parental Controls.

Remember that you have to combine this with configuring passwords for administrator accounts. If you don't set passwords for administrator accounts, any user can turn off these safeguards as easily as they can be enabled.

Administrator Account

An administrator account has privileges to install and make changes to everything on the local machine. These settings can, and often do, affect every user that works on that PC.

One of the main differences between Vista and previous Windows versions, of course, is how User Account Control affects the default behavior of administrator accounts. When using the computer normally, User Account Control runs all administrator accounts in a standard user state. Then, as you've seen already, it prompts you for confirmation when performing a task that makes a systemwide change. Instead of being prompted for the administrative username/password, though, you're prompted only for confirmation.

 First available with Windows XP, Fast User Switching is enabled by default on Windows Vista as long as it is not part of a domain. Fast User Switching allows users to remain logged on with all programs running while another person uses the computer. When the environment is then switched back to the original user, the user gets the desktop just as it was, as though it's resuming from sleep mode.

There's really nothing to configure with Fast User Switching. To use it, click on the Start menu and then the arrow next to the Sleep and Lock buttons. You'll see the "Switch user" command on the menu. Keep in mind that each user logged on will be consuming resources, however. Using Fast User Switching with more than two users can place a significant strain on performance.

Using Vista with Live OneCare

At the risk of turning this chapter into more marketing material from Redmond, I would be remiss not to mention a new set of Windows operating system technologies called Live OneCare. You can find out about it by visiting *http://onecare.live.com*.

It includes antivirus, firewall, tune-up, and backup capabilities; can be used on Vista and Windows XP systems; and is available for download or purchase in a retail store.

Once installed, OneCare turns *off* the Windows Firewall and turns *on* its own firewall. The OneCare Firewall provides a slightly greater level of control over the Windows Firewall version. OneCare also offers wizard-based backup—a welcome addition to users of the Home Basic and Home Premium editions, which don't include the Vista Backup utility (not that you'd use the Vista Backup utility anyway; see Chapter 15 for more).

From the Live OneCare console, shown in Figure 3-48, you get a quick glance of system status and a list of recommended actions to take. The Live OneCare console home page lets you easily start a virus and spyware scan, for example.

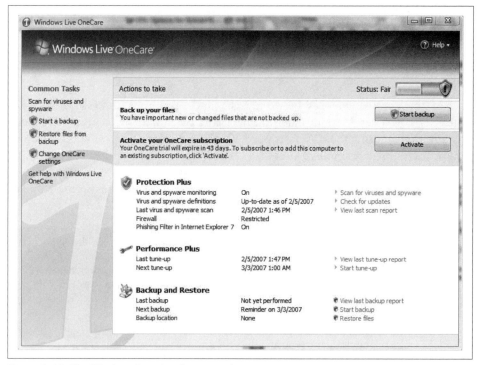

Figure 3-48. The Windows Live OneCare console

From the OneCare home page, use of the tool(s) is fairly intuitive. You can scan your system for viruses and spyware by following the "Scan for viruses and spyware" link, for example. You will then see options about what kind of scan to perform. Options include:

- Quick scan
- Complete scan
- Custom scan

These antivirus scanning options are not terribly different from those found with other antivirus programs from vendors such as McAfee, Norton, and Trend Micro. Probably the most important point to take from this section is that Vista still relies on third-party software for antivirus capabilities. Now, with Windows Live OneCare, that third party can be Microsoft itself.

Summary

Although the word is still used, almost no one uses a *standalone* computer anymore. It could be argued, in fact, that the network, above all else, has been the killer app driving the PC revolution. And certainly no IT administrator is going to administer for very long without installing, configuring, or troubleshooting a network connection.

This chapter should provide a good foundation, then, for understanding how to network with a Vista machine. Although many of the networking technologies have been automated now, and Vista should communicate properly if backend services such as DHCP and DNS have been properly configured, administrators will need to know how to manually configure settings should the need arise.

You now have a better understanding of how to manually configure a network connection, how to connect to a wireless network, and how to create a VPN connection to a corporate network. You have also learned about some of the technologies that can help secure this communication.

Also, you've seen discussion about many of the related features that depend on network connectivity. You now know how to leverage a network to share resources among computers, and you can use the offline files capability to keep shared resources close at hand, even when no network connection is present.

The next chapter looks at personalizing the Windows Vista environment. In it, we'll take a look at how to make the desktop environment behave just as you want it to. As always, we'll focus mostly on features that are new to Windows Vista.

CHAPTER 4

Personalizing Vista

A common request from users is to change the user interface. Wait. Strike that. A common *task* carried out by users is to change the user interface. Your job as administrator, then, is to walk over to the user's cubicle, figure out what in the name of William Gates he did to make his system look like that, and then figure out how you can put the Vista interface back in order.

This chapter looks at many features that will affect how users navigate the operating system. In it, we examine such things as working with multiple monitors, customizing menus, and using virtual folders.

A few of the topics discussed here may seem a bit elementary to some, but then again, brain surgery is elementary to brain surgeons. So consider some of what follows as Anatomy 101 of the Windows Vista desktop. You have to know this stuff fairly well to go on to bigger and better topics. Don't worry; more than a few nuggets here will raise the eyebrows of all but the most experienced Windows network admins. (For example, do you know what to do if you delete the Quick Launch toolbar's Show Desktop icon? You will find out in the pages herein.) If you like to dive into the registry as some sort of display of bravado, you will find plenty to like here.

And for all you English majors/part-time IT admins out there, the chapter's underlying theme will be relatively easy to spot: it's all about *control*—control of the desktop, control of the Start menu and taskbar, and control over the output to one or more monitors. After digesting this entire chapter, you have my permission to armchair-psychoanalyze how this chapter serves as a transparent glimpse into my id, ego, or otherwise by emailing any comments to this address: *hmsbrian@brianculp.com*.

We'll begin by looking at how to take command of the new and improved Vista Start menu.

Controlling the Start Menu

As we discussed briefly in Chapter 1, one of the major changes to the Vista Start menu is that it now incorporates the Windows Desktop Search. In fact, all you have to do to initiate a search is to click the Start menu button and start typing. (For even quicker searches, use the Windows key on the keyboard.) Vista then presents you with a list of the best possible choices based on the characters in your search.

For example, if you want to find the Character Map—where *was* that thing stored in Windows XP, anyway?—just press the Windows key and type **char**. Boom. There it is, listed first in your list of programs. Select it and launch.

And just to reiterate, the new expanded Search will also present results in a wide variety of file types besides program executables. The search results will also include Internet favorites and history, contacts, email messages, and even appointments you've set in Outlook. And as you have seen and marveled at previously, the Windows Desktop Search also includes the *body* of the file in the search. Using the search phrase just mentioned, Vista's Start menu search will also return any email messages or Word documents that mention your favorite *American Idol* contestants.

Now, let's talk about other Start menu options in more detail.

Changing Between the Classic and Simple Start Menus

You don't have to use the new Vista Simple Start menu. If complicating your computing environment (as Microsoft Start menu nomenclature would tell it) appeals to you, you can switch back to the Classic Start menu that was used by previous Windows operating systems such as Windows 2000.

Follow these steps:

1. First, right-click on the Start button or on an empty area of the taskbar (an area not hosting a program bar) and choose Properties from the context menu.

2. Use the Start Menu tab, shown in Figure 4-1, and select the "Classic Start menu" radio button.

3. Of course, to switch back from the Classic to the Simple Start menu, select the "Start menu" radio button. Click OK to commit the changes.

Note here that if you change to the Classic Start menu, you're not changing things back to the way they were in Windows XP. Save for the circular Start button, the Classic Start menu resembles the one that's been around since Windows 95.

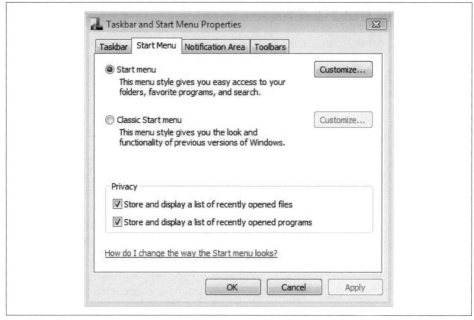

Figure 4-1. Change to the Classic Start menu from here

Customizing the Classic Start Menu

Because the Start menu interface has been around for so long, most people won't have any trouble figuring out how to change the look and feel. You can add and remove Classic Start menu commands just as before. Here's what to do:

1. As before, right-click on the Start button or on an empty area of the taskbar and choose Properties from the context menu.
2. Make sure the "Classic Start menu" radio button is selected and then choose the Customize button.
3. As shown in Figure 4-2, the Customize Classic Start Menu dialog box allows users to configure what's displayed.

For example, many admins like to have easy access to the administrative tools. As with previous Windows editions, you can access these tools by checking the "Display administrative tools" Advanced Start menu option.

In my opinion, changing to the Classic Start menu really highlights the power of the newly designed Start menu with the Windows Desktop Search incorporated. Now try to find the Character Map, or that email you got three months ago with directions to that meeting.

Figure 4-2. Customizing the Classic Start menu appearance

Table 4-1 provides a brief summary of how each selection in the Advanced Start menu options changes Classic Start menu behavior.

Table 4-1. Using the Advanced Start menu options

Setting	Purpose
Display Administrative Tools	As mentioned previously, it displays a submenu full of Vista's administrative tools.
Display Favorites	Shows the Favorites menu from the Start menu. This is helpful when users frequently navigate using the Favorites menu.
Display Log Off	Adds and removes the log off command. If this option is not selected, users must press the Ctrl-Alt-Delete key combination to log off.
Display Run	Shows users the run command from the Start menu, which is not present by default in Windows Vista.
Expand (Documents, Pictures, Network Connections, Printers, Control Panel)	These are individual choices, but they all perform the same function. They cause the selection to appear as a submenu rather than in its own window when clicked.
Show Small Icons in Start Menu	This reduces the Start menu program icon sizes.
Use Personalized Menus	This option causes only a partial display of menu contents, hiding less frequently used programs behind a down arrow at the bottom of the menu.

Customizing the Vista Simple Start Menu

If you've spent time exploring the Classic Start menu options, you're off to a good start getting a handle on the Simple Start menu ones. That's because all the options available with the Classic Start menu are present with the Simple Start menu. The difference is that Simple Start menu users also get some additional features not available with the Classic version.

As I've opined, I think you'll really get a lot of practical use out of these new features. Here's how to change some of the default settings:

1. Right-click the Start menu and choose Properties from the context menu.
2. Choose the "Start menu" radio button (refer to Figure 4-1) and then click the Customize button.
3. From the Customize Start Menu dialog box, shown in Figure 4-3, you can select from an array of choices to help users get the most from the Start menu.
4. Make the desired changes and click OK twice to commit the changes.

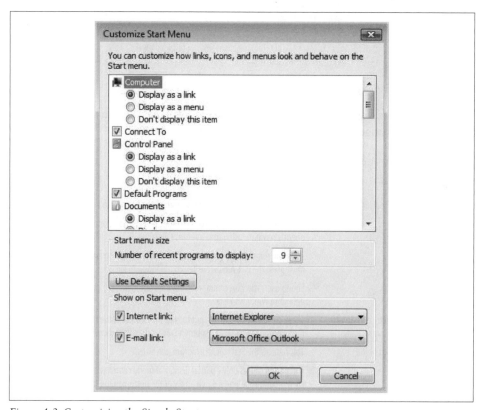

Figure 4-3. Customizing the Simple Start menu

Notice here that most of the options have three choices:

- Display as a link
- Display as a menu
- Don't display this item

Choosing to display as a link causes another window to open when the link is clicked. For example, note that this is the default option for the Control Panel display. That means when you click this link (it glows more like a button, really, but then again, I wasn't consulted when writing the code for the Start menu options dialog box, surprisingly), the Control Panel opens in its own window. If you select "Display as a menu," the Control Panel Start menu option will then cascade a list of possible applets that can be launched right from there.

Choosing not to display a certain item can be an administrative option for reducing the temptation to launch certain Start menu items such as the Control Panel or the Network Configuration window. Note, however, that this is not the same thing as restricting access to each of these tools. To restrict access, use a Group Policy Object (GPO). We will discuss GPOs in Chapter 13.

Here are some other Start menu customizations of note, along with their default settings:

Enable context menus and dragging and dropping (enabled)
This allows users to right-click a Start menu item to bring up a list of actions. You can use the context menus to, among other things, open a file or application, or pin the application shortcut to the Start menu so that it's more readily available. Obviously, it also allows dragging and dropping to rearrange Start menu items. One of these context menu items, by the way, gives you the ability to delete the selected Start menu item. Administrators might consider disabling this option to prevent accidental reconfiguration of the Start menu. (There's also an interesting note about dragging and dropping on the Start menu, which I'll address in a bit.)

Highlight newly installed programs (enabled)
This option draws attention to new programs by highlighting them in the Start menu.

Open submenus when I pause on them with the mouse pointer (enabled)
This simply means that users don't have to click to open a program group submenu. You might want to consider unchecking this if you're using the "submenu" display options rather than the "Display as a link" option for items such as the Control Panel and documents. When disabled, you will only see the cascading submenu after clicking.

Search (enabled)

This shows the Search option in the Start menu. Using it will bring up a dialog box such as the one seen in Figure 4-4. Because the Windows Desktop Search is built into the Start menu anyway, administrators can safely disable this link without any loss of functionality.

Use large icons (enabled)

This default setting uses large icons in the Vista Simple Start menu. As the name implies, unchecking this box reduces the size of Start menu icons, but will not affect the overall size of Vista's Start menu.

Start menu size (default of 9)

Located just below the main dialog box section, this absolutely *can* control overall Start menu size. It determines how many recently used programs are listed. You can set this value all the way up to 30, but the Start menu will then likely take up the entire left side of the screen.

Sort all programs by name (enabled)

By default, Vista lists contents of the All Programs Start menu folder alphabetically. Unchecking this makes it so that programs are listed in order of installation. This is a subtle yet welcome change from older Windows Start menus that had to be sorted by name manually to make programs easier to find.

Internet and mail links (Internet Explorer and Windows Mail by default)

These will be the top two shortcuts in the most recently used program list. Users have the option here to change the program displayed (if other mail and/or Internet browsers have been installed), or to disable the program links altogether.

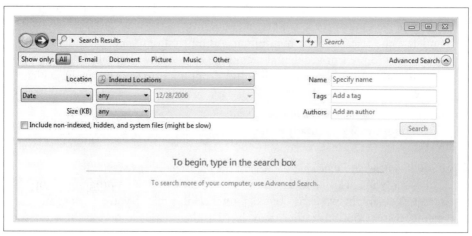

Figure 4-4. The Vista Search dialog box with advanced options expanded

 By default, only users with administrative privileges can drag and drop to rearrange the Start menu.

Other Customizations

Besides the Windows Desktop Search, probably the next easiest way to launch an application is to choose its program icon from the Start menu. Fortunately, the Vista Start menu carries forth an innovation first introduced in Windows XP where the most frequently used programs reside in a list on the Start menu's lefthand side. I discussed a couple of options for changing what's displayed here in the previous section.

The list is actually divided into two parts: programs that appear in the bottom division are the most recently opened applications, and just how many appear depends on the customization settings discussed earlier. The ones living in the upper section have been *pinned* to the Start menu and will always show there, no matter how often they are accessed.

For example, Windows Mail might appear in your Start menu even if you've never opened the program because that's what the Mail link specifies in the Start Menu Customization dialog box.

But as with Windows XP, you have complete control over what is pinned to the Start menu and what is not. You can place other program shortcuts in the pinned section by right-clicking the Start menu icon and choosing Pin to Start Menu from the context menu.

To remove a program from the pinned section, right-click its shortcut and this time choose Unpin from Start Menu. Remember, neither option will change anything else about the program besides how easy it is to find in the Start menu. And if you pin a frequently used program, Vista is smart enough not to show it to you twice in the program list.

Setting the Start menu back to the defaults

As you've seen, it's quite easy to tailor the Start menu. This ease of use can be the proverbial double-edged sword, however. A user who has configured all sorts of Start menu options to best suit her working style may be passing on a computer that is difficult for another person to use if she leaves the company or is simply issued a brand-new machine.

Fortunately, there's also an easy way to set the Start menu back to its defaults without having to go through either a reinstall or a lengthy reconfiguration process. Here's what to do:

1. Right-click the Start menu and choose Properties from the context menu.

2. Choose the Start Menu tab, and then click Customize.

3. In the Customize Start Menu dialog box, click Use Default Settings, as shown in Figure 4-5. Click OK to finish the procedure.

Figure 4-5. Quickly resetting the Start menu to its defaults

 Changing the Start menu back to its default settings does not affect any programs that have been pinned to the Start menu. Removal of pinned programs must be done manually.

The Start menu and the filesystem

So just where does this Start menu *live* anyway? Can I dig through the filesystem to see all of the program shortcuts? Or is it a registry setting?

The general answer to both of these questions is "yes."

It's just another folder in the filesystem. What a user sees in his Start menu is actually a byproduct of two file locations merging together at logon time. Here's what happens:

Some of the program shortcuts are available to all users of the computer. Which programs, you ask? The ones stored in this file location:

> %systemdrive%\ProgramData\Microsoft\Windows\Start Menu

Other program shortcut groups are available only to the user who is currently logged on. Which ones are these? You can find them here:

> %UserProfile%\AppData\Roaming\Microsoft\Windows\Start Menu

where %systemdrive% is the drive letter where the Windows Vista operating system exists, and %UserProfile% is the path to the user's unique set of environment folders.

 Both folders just mentioned are hidden folders. To display them, you have to change the Windows Explorer Folder options by choosing Organize → Folder and Search Options, and then selecting "Show hidden files and folders" on the View tab of the ensuing dialog box.

It's governed by the registry. This is also true, but we'll have to tackle that topic in a separate section in just a bit. For now, too much still needs to be said about the Start menu folders.

At startup, Vista merges the contents of these two Start menu folders and presents the user with a single Start menu, of course. For each folder stored in one of the Programs folders, as shown in Figure 4-6, Vista builds a Program Start Menu group and associated shortcuts.

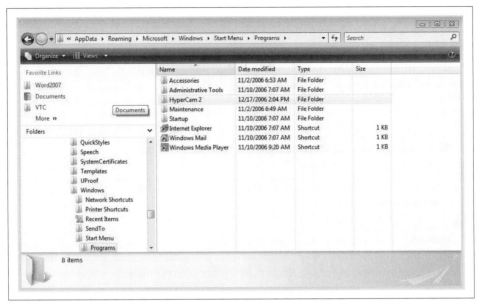

Figure 4-6. Editing a Start menu shortcut from the folder location itself

The point here is that if you're more comfortable configuring the Start menu by using the filesystem locations, by all means go ahead. Open the desired Start menu folder location (remember to enable viewing first) and add or remove application shortcuts as you see fit.

In fact, this can present an administrator with a very powerful option for configuring a system that multiple users will access. Let's say, for example, that you run an organization with a mobile sales force, and that every person on the sales force checks out computers as needed rather than using a company-issued laptop. You want to place a program icon onto the Start menu so that anyone on the sales team can easily find and launch an application you sell, and therefore, you want it always present on the Start menu's list of recently used programs.

To carry out the task, simply open the following folder and add a shortcut:

> *%systemdrive%\ProgramData\Microsoft\Windows\Start Menu*

The shortcut you add will now appear for all users of the system.

Adding and changing a menu

Not only can you change the program icons shown in Vista's Start menu items, but you also can change the very nature of the menus themselves. You can add, rename, or remove the menus altogether if you want to.

As introduced in the previous section, all you have to do is know where to look. If you're adding a menu for a particular user, for example, you need to access the user's Start Menu folder at:

%UserProfile%\AppData\Roaming\Microsoft\Windows\Start Menu

Once there, you can perform the following menu tasks:

Add new menus

To create a new menu, just add a folder to the Start menu hierarchy. This new folder will appear as a separate item in the Vista Start menu.

Change existing menus

You can modify the contents of existing menus by moving folders or shortcuts to new locations.

Rename folders and/or shortcuts

This one's self-explanatory. You can rename an item here just as you can any other file on your hard drive. Alternatively, you can right-click the item from the Start menu itself and choose Rename from the context menu.

 Two Start menu items shouldn't be renamed, moved, or deleted. They are the Startup folder and the Administrative Tools folder. In the case of the Startup folder, altering its properties can prevent Vista from using it. As for the Administrative Tools folder, any changes, such as whether or not the administrative tools display, should be performed using the Taskbar and Start Menu Properties dialog box, as discussed multiple times in this chapter.

Adding Administrative Tools to the Vista Start Menu

Earlier in this section, we discussed the Classic Start menu and its familiar way of adding the administrative tools to its list of possible programs. I know from experience that this is a favorite of many a Windows administrator, and it is even the reason that many still use the Classic Start menu interface.

But it's also easy to add the administrative tools to the Vista Simple Start menu as well. When you add them to the other ease-of-use benefits of the new Start menu, this helps make the new way of doing things all the more compelling.

Here's how to set it up:

1. Right-click the Start button and choose Properties from the context menu, launching the Taskbar and Start Menu Properties dialog box.

2. Select the Start Menu tab and then the Customize button.

3. Scroll down the list of customization options. As seen in Figure 4-7, you'll see two possible choices regarding the display of administrative tools:

- Display on the All Programs menu
- Display on the All Programs menu and the Start menu

4. Click OK twice to complete the action.

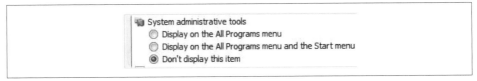

Figure 4-7. Displaying options for the administrative tools

Now the entire range of administrative tools is but a click or two away.

Changing the Start menu picture

Now for some more fun features. If you've been shipped a computer with Vista preinstalled or have recently upgraded to Vista, you have likely noticed a picture associated with the user account located in the Start menu's upper-righthand side, just above the username.

You can change this picture if you want. Here's how:

1. From the Control Panel, open the User Accounts applet. In the Standard View, look under the User Accounts and Family Safety grouping.

2. Once there, choose the "Change your picture" link. You'll now see a group of preinstalled pictures. As shown in Figure 4-8, simply click the picture you want to use, and then click Change Picture.

Boring. More fun: use a picture of your own by choosing the "Browse for more pictures" option, and then navigate to the picture you want to use. Select the picture and then click Open.

Controlling Start menu behavior with the registry

As mentioned, what appears on the Start menu is also a byproduct of certain registry settings, and you can control the Start menu by making direct edits to the registry. The registry is a database of information that tells the operating system—in this case, Vista—how to behave.

To edit the registry, first you need to open the Vista registry editing tool. It's the same one used in previous versions of Windows—Regedit—and opening it is pretty straightforward. From the Start menu, simply type **regedit**, and the utility should appear in the program list.

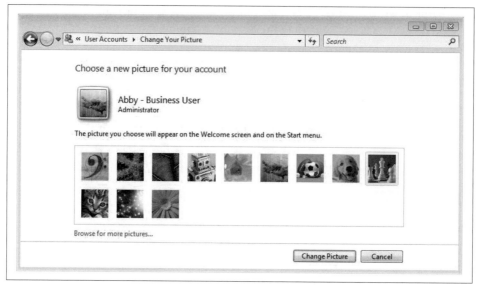

Figure 4-8. Changing the Start menu picture

Now that the Registry Editor is open, navigate to this key, shown in Figure 4-9:

*HKEY_CURRENT_USER\Software\Microsoft\Windows\CurrentVersion\Policies\
Explorer*

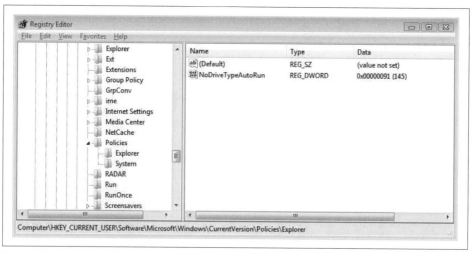

Figure 4-9. Start menu changes can also be performed by editing the registry

Once there, you can add something called *DWORD values* to the Explorer key to modify Start menu behavior. To add a DWORD value, follow these steps:

1. Use the Registry Editor's Edit menu, or just right-click in the Details (righthand) pane, and choose New → DWORD (32-bit) value.

2. The new DWORD value appears, with a name similar to "New Value #1." Rename this value using a name from Table 4-2.

3. Now, assign the DWORD a value. Fortunately, we have only two options for the values discussed here: 1 or 0. In other words, the feature will be on or off, with 1 signifying on and 0 indicating off. Either setting can be used to force an administrative change.

For example, if you want to make sure the username is removed from the Start menu, add the DWORD NoUserNameInStartMenu and set the value to 1. If you want to make sure the username is always displayed, on the other hand, add the same DWORD and set the value to 0.

Now, refer to Table 4-2 for other Start menu changes that you can force through the registry.

Table 4-2. Start menu changes you can force through the registry

DWORD	Description
NoSimpleStartMenu	Disables the new Simple Start menu and forces the Classic Start menu.
NoStartMenuPinnedList	Removes the pinned programs list from the Start menu.
NoStartMenuMFUprogramsList	Removes the frequently used programs list from the Start menu.
NoRecentItemsMenu	Removes the list of recently used items from the Start menu.
NoSMPictures	Removes the Pictures item from the Start menu.
NoStartMenuMusic	Removes the Music item from the Start menu. Also removes the corresponding checkboxes from the Taskbar and Start Menu Properties dialog box.
NoWindowsUpdate	Removes the Windows Update link from the Programs list. It also prevents access to *http://windowsupdate.microsoft.com*.
ClearRecentItemsOnExit	Deletes all shortcuts in the Recent Items menu as users log off.
DisablePersonalDirChange	Prevents users from changing the Documents folder directory path.
NoNetwork	Removes the Network item from the Start menu. Also removes corresponding items from the Taskbar and Start Menu Properties dialog box.
NoSMHelp	Removes the Help item from the Start menu. Users can still access help files, however.
NoChangeStartMenu	Prevents changes to the Start menu by dragging and dropping. Other methods of customizing are still enabled.
NoSetTaskbar	Disables access to the Taskbar and Start Menu Properties dialog box.
NoUserNameInStartMenu	Removes the username from the Start menu.

You can then go back and safely remove any DWORD values you've added by accessing the following registry key and then simply deleting the DWORD itself:

HKEY_CURRENT_USER\Software\Microsoft\Windows\CurrentVersion\Policies\Explorer

 Deleting registry keys is generally not a good idea. You're in effect performing brain surgery on Vista when you do, and the wrong deletion can leave Vista with the equivalent of a lobotomy, or worse. In fact, Vista warns you about these implications every time you delete a registry entry, and now you've been warned in this book as well.

As a final thought, also note that all of the preceding will change if you're using the 64-bit version of Windows Vista, but not by much. Instead of adding 32-bit DWORD values, you'll add 64-bit QWORD values. The names of the entries themselves should remain the same.

 You can also change the Start menu power button behavior, but I think that fits better in the discussion about startup and shutdown, including a full mention of hibernate, sleep, and so on. Chapter 6 covers these topics.

Controlling the Taskbar

So just what is that thing at the bottom of the screen there? You know, the thing that holds all of the program buttons, the Start menu button, and all those other little icons on the far-righthand side. Does it even have a name?

It does, and as most admins are already aware, it's called the taskbar. Configuring taskbar behavior can present a little more of a challenge than just remembering its name, however. It may seem like a trivial, almost inconsequential, part of the greater Vista picture. But before you dismiss it, consider what a huge impact the taskbar has on overall Vista usability. It provides quick access to a wealth of operating system and application information, and it is *the* key navigational tool for most users when switching among applications.

Given its vital role, then, it's important that administrators understand how to customize taskbar behavior to best suit not only their needs, but also the needs of users in the enterprise. This section tackles the many methods administrators can use to tweak taskbar behavior.

 Recall that one nice enhancement of the taskbar is the ability to see a live thumbnail of the application contents, as shown in Figure 4-10. This is predicated, however, on using the Vista Aero interface.

Figure 4-10. Live thumbnails in the taskbar

Changing Taskbar Size and Position

You already know about the taskbar's default location: at the bottom of the screen. By default, it's wide enough to contain one row of application buttons. But you can change both of these characteristics with a few simple clicks of the mouse.

To change the taskbar *size*, move the mouse pointer over the edge of the taskbar until you see a double-headed arrow. Now just click and drag to increase the taskbar real estate. This might be especially handy if you decide not to group taskbar items together, as discussed later on.

To change the taskbar *location*, left-click an empty taskbar area and drag. The taskbar can be housed on the left, right, or top of the desktop area, as well as in its default location at the bottom of the screen.

 Each technique requires that the taskbar not be locked, because you cannot change the taskbar while it is locked. To unlock the taskbar, just right-click an empty area and make sure there's no check next to the Lock the Taskbar menu option.

Grouping Similar Items on the Taskbar

Just as Vista works to keep the desktop as clean as possible, it also does the same with the taskbar. The technique for doing this is to group related program items into a single button that expands when you click it.

For example, if you have seven Word documents open at once, chances are (barring a *really* large taskbar and no other open programs) that Vista will group these Word instances into a single taskbar button. This reduces the overall number of taskbar buttons, in turn reducing taskbar clutter. Click on the Word button, and all the open documents appear in a list.

Of course, whether you use the taskbar grouping is entirely up to you. If you want each document represented by its own taskbar button, you can instruct Vista not to use the grouping behavior. Here's how to change the default Vista settings:

1. Open the Taskbar and Start Menu Properties dialog box as instructed previously. (Fine; those instructions were to right-click the Start button and choose Properties.)

2. Select the Taskbar tab.

3. Clear the "Group similar taskbar buttons" checkbox, as seen in Figure 4-11. Naturally, you can reverse this procedure by ensuring that it is checked.

Figure 4-11. Turning off grouping of taskbar buttons

(To turn off grouping, clear the "Group similar taskbar buttons" checkbox.)

 Changing the grouping behavior will not affect the Windows Flip or Windows Flip 3D method of switching among open files. In the case of seven Word documents open at once, as previously introduced, each one still appears as its own item in Windows Flip.

Also, the grouping comes into play only when there's no more room on the taskbar for additional buttons. If you've got only two instances of an application open and nothing else, they won't group.

Not only can the taskbar house buttons to let you switch among open applications, but it also can host entire *toolbars* that can add a significant amount of functionality. One example of such a toolbar is the Quick Launch toolbar, discussed next.

In Windows XP, you could add the Desktop Search toolbar. Because of the integration of Desktop Search in Windows Vista, this toolbar is not available on Vista machines.

Working with the Quick Launch Toolbar

It's been a favorite way for me to launch programs for some time, and it can certainly be used from the Vista desktop as well: the Quick Launch toolbar. It stores program shortcuts in a little icon, and it allows for single-click launching of the applications you use most frequently.

This taskbar toolbar should be enabled by default at Vista installation time, but you might be inheriting a computer in which it's been turned off. In that case, you'll probably need the appropriate click-steps.

Here's how to display the Quick Launch toolbar:

1. Right-click an empty area on the taskbar and point to Toolbars.
2. To add the Quick Launch toolbar, just make sure there's a check next to the Quick Launch menu option. To remove the Quick Launch toolbar, remove the checkmark.

By default, you should see three icons in the Quick Launch toolbar: Show Desktop, Switch between Windows, and Internet Explorer. But of course, the idea is to place frequently used programs at your fingertips without even having to open the Start menu, as seen in Figure 4-12.

Figure 4-12. Using the Quick Launch toolbar

Adding a program to the Quick Launch toolbar

Of course, users can manipulate the Quick Launch toolbar to contain the programs that are most helpful to them. Fortunately, it's very easy to add more programs to the taskbar.

Here's how:

1. Locate the program you want to add on the Start menu or on the desktop.
2. Right-click the program icon and drag it to the Quick Launch toolbar. A context menu appears, giving you the option of moving the item or copying it. (A left-click should work as well when dragging to the Quick Launch toolbar, although you won't get any choices in a context menu.)

You can do this with just about any program shortcut, from just about anywhere on your computer. One alternative method is to let programs install desktop shortcuts (many will if you don't customize the installation), and then just left-click and drag the shortcut to the Quick Launch toolbar.

Removing the Quick Launch item, then, is a breeze. Just right-click the Quick Launch shortcut and choose Delete from the context menu.

Restoring Show Desktop in the Quick Launch toolbar

If deleting a Quick Launch icon is easy, how about restoring one? If you're using a shortcut to an application, the procedure is the same as adding a new shortcut: just drag and drop the shortcut from some other location. Easy cheesy.

But what about the Show Desktop button? This is a very useful Quick Launch button, as it minimizes all open windows with a single click, saving users the labor of minimizing and/or resizing windows to access something on the desktop, such as a recently downloaded file. And once the desktop has been shown, the button can be used again to quickly toggle back to the working environment, again saving a bunch of window recalls and/or resizing.

But although this is cool and very functional, the Show Desktop Quick Launch button isn't really an application, is it? In reality, it's just a pointer to a *script*, and although it's not necessarily easy to re-create the Show Desktop button, you can do it by following a few simple steps. After all, other than looking for a way to enhance your biceps, that's why you picked up this book.

To restore the Show Desktop button, you will need to re-create a file called *Show Desktop.scf* and make sure it's stored in the right location. Here's what to do:

1. Open Microsoft WordPad (in the Accessories folder) and then enter these lines of text:

   ```
   [Shell]
   Command=2
   IconFile=explorer.exe,3
   [Taskbar]
   Command=ToggleDesktop
   ```

2. Now, save the file in the following location:

   %UserProfile%\AppData\Roaming\Microsoft\Windows\InternetExplorer\ Quick Launch

   and name the file *Show Desktop.scf*.

As discussed previously, *%UserProfile%* is a variable designating the user's profile filesystem location. Usually, the profile is stored under the *C:\Users\username* directory. If you're not sure where the profile is located, you can find out by opening a Command Prompt window and typing **set userprofile**. The command returns the path for the currently logged-on user.

Controlling the Toolbars

Another way you can customize the Vista taskbar is by adding (or removing) one or more toolbars. The idea of a toolbar is to place commonly accessed information within easy reach. By default, users have these toolbars available:

Address toolbar

This places an address box directly in the taskbar, similar to what is seen in Internet Explorer. In fact, it's used in the same way. Users can simply type a Uniform Resource Locator (URL) into the Address bar for any given resource. This resource can exist on the local machine, the Web, or the local network.

Once the path is specified, Vista automatically launches the appropriate application for viewing the file (i.e., if the URL specifies a web page, Vista calls Internet Explorer; if it's a path to a PowerPoint presentation stored on a network share, Vista launches PowerPoint instead). And just like the Address bar in Internet Explorer, the taskbar's version also tries to suggest possible locations after the first few letters, saving the user from having to type the entire path. With frequent use, the Address bar can save a lot of time when accessing frequently used files and web sites.

Links toolbar

If you find yourself using the Favorites folder often as a way to get quick access to the web sites you need, you might consider adding the Links toolbar. This provides access to the Links folder in the Favorites menu of Internet Explorer. You can then add links to other resources, no matter where they live, by dragging and dropping shortcuts onto the Links toolbar. For example, users could quickly access a fileserver's folder of working files simply by creating a shortcut on the Links toolbar, making the resource only a few clicks away.

Desktop toolbar

If desktop shortcuts are your thing, you might find it very useful to use the Desktop toolbar. This toolbar places all the desktop shortcuts you've created into one toolbar. This comes in especially handy when you're working with several windows that are hiding your normal desktop shortcuts. The Desktop toolbar provides easy access to all these shortcuts without having to minimize all open windows, thus interrupting your work.

Quick Launch toolbar

This wonderful little toolbar provides one-click access to commonly used applications. Also, this is the only taskbar toolbar shown by default. We'll discuss the Quick Launch toolbar in more detail in the sections that follow.

So, how do you use any/all of these toolbars? It's easy; just right-click on an empty area of the taskbar, point to the Toolbars menu item in the context menu, and then place a checkmark next to the toolbar you want to use. Uncheck the item to remove the toolbar.

Note also that all of the taskbar toolbars have a title to go along with them, with the exception of the Quick Launch toolbar. If you'd like to hide the toolbar titles, just right-click the toolbar and deselect the Show Title command, as seen in Figure 4-13.

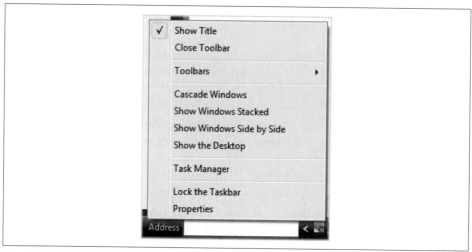

Figure 4-13. Deselecting the toolbar titles

In most computing environments, you'll see more than just the Address, Links, Desktop, and Quick Launch toolbars. Several other applications also create their own taskbar toolbar at installation time, and you can enable and disable these other toolbars using the techniques previously discussed. Media playback applications such as iTunes and Windows Media Player come immediately to mind. Applications such as Microsoft's Encarta also create a toolbar at installation time.

Adding a custom toolbar

You can create a custom toolbar to suit almost any shortcut purpose you can envision. These custom toolbars are based on existing folders, and the toolbar shortcuts are then determined by the folder contents.

Here's how to create a personalized toolbar for either yourself or other users to obtain easy access to resources:

1. As before, right-click an empty area of the taskbar and choose the Toolbars menu option. Click New Toolbar.

2. You'll now see the New Toolbar dialog box, shown in Figure 4-14. Use the Explorer interface to select a root folder for the toolbar.

Once you click OK, the selected folder becomes a new toolbar that you can toggle on and off just as you can any of the other taskbar toolbars. The toolbar contents are the same as the folder contents. And remember that the toolbar root folder doesn't necessarily have to exist on the local machine. Creating a custom toolbar can be yet another easy way to get quick access to network files.

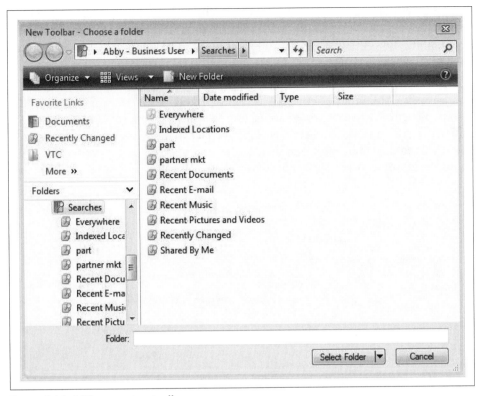

Figure 4-14. Adding a custom toolbar

Once you create a custom toolbar, though, it's good practice to lock the taskbar (right-click and choose Lock the Taskbar from the context menu). That's because the toolbar, unfortunately, doesn't become part of the user profile. When you close the custom toolbar, Vista loses track of it, and you must re-create it to use it once again.

Controlling the System Tray

Look to the lower-right side of the taskbar (unless you've moved the taskbar location). There, among other items, you'll see the system clock, the volume indicator, and maybe a battery indicator on a laptop machine. There's a name for this taskbar section as well. The flotilla of icons you see there is called the System Tray, also known as the Notification Area (presumably because Vista, like Windows XP, has a habit of displaying little balloon notifications from this area).

The System Tray is populated by icons that indicate applications, or at least certain application *components*, that were loaded at startup. Hovering the mouse pointer over one of these icons should produce a little ScreenTip that lets you know the purpose of the icon.

To manipulate application behavior, just right-click the desired application icon. For example, you can adjust sound properties by right-clicking the speaker icon and choosing the appropriate action (if you want to turn the volume up or down, try the Volume Mixer).

Several other programs, such as Windows Live Messenger, also load at startup time and place an icon in the System Tray. By right-clicking on the System Tray icon, you can usually either open the program itself or get quick access to a properties dialog box where you can tweak startup behavior. In the case of Windows Live Messenger, you can open the application, and then access an Options dialog box from the Tools menu where you can tell the application not to load every time Vista starts up (see Figure 4-15).

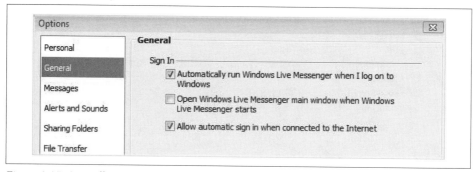

Figure 4-15. Controlling application startup behavior via the System Tray

Why is all this important? Because each background application that shows in the System Tray is also using at least some system resources. Governing which applications load in the background can be an important part of tuning startup and shutdown performance (open applications close during a normal shutdown), and the System Tray is a great indicator.

 Just because an application loads at startup time doesn't necessarily mean it also places a corresponding icon in the System Tray. To get a better handle on what programs load during system startup, use the Msconfig utility (msconfig.exe). I discuss the Msconfig utility in Chapter 6.

There are a couple of ways to manage what happens in the System Tray. One is to change the properties of the application so that it doesn't load and place an icon there in the first place. But we just discussed that. For icons that aren't necessarily applications that load, such as the system clock, you can also change the behavior of the System Tray, which we'll discuss next.

Changing System Tray Behavior

To change the general behavior of the System Tray, you can access the Notification Area tab in the Taskbar and Start Menu Properties dialog box. If you've been reading this chapter, you already know how to get there. If not, follow these steps:

1. Right-click the Start button or an empty area of the taskbar and choose Properties.

2. The Taskbar and Start Menu Properties dialog box appears. Make sure the Notification Area tab is chosen.

3. As seen in Figure 4-16, there are a couple of options here that determine general System Tray activity.

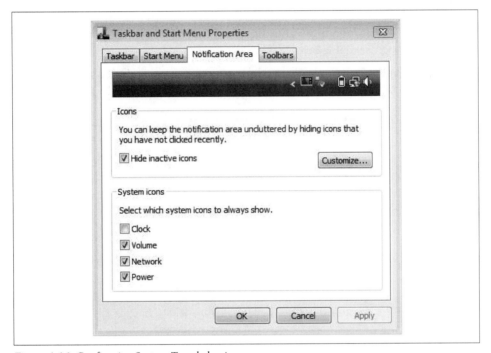

Figure 4-16. Configuring System Tray behavior

You can turn off icons for the volume, clock, power, and network by unchecking the appropriate checkboxes in the "System icons" section of the Notification Area screen.

The big one here is the default setting to "Hide inactive icons." Checking this box (or, more technically, leaving it checked) hides most of the System Tray icons behind a little arrow button. Clicking this arrow button expands the full list of System Tray icons. Unchecking this box can have a significant effect on the usable space available to the rest of the taskbar.

For additional manipulation of just the system clock, you can right-click an empty area of the System Tray (or the time reading) and choose Adjust Date and Time. The Date and Time dialog box opens. Use the Additional Clocks tab to configure more options.

In this same dialog box, you may have also noticed a Customize button, discussed in the following section.

Customizing System Tray Icon Behavior

You can be even more specific about System Tray conduct by configuring actions on just the icons of your choosing. If you're following along from the preceding section, just click the Customize button from the Notification Area tab of the Taskbar and Start Menu Properties dialog box.

Otherwise, right-click an empty area of the System Tray and choose the Customize Notification Icons menu item. Either way, you'll see the dialog box shown in Figure 4-17.

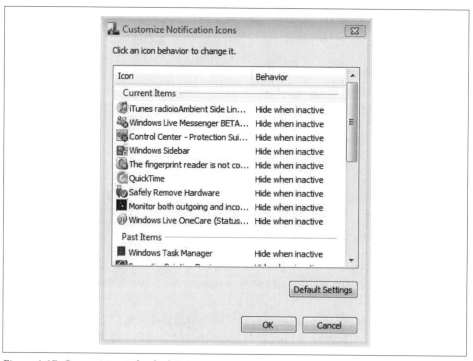

Figure 4-17. Customizing individual System Tray icon behavior

To configure icon behavior, just select one of the items in the list. The Behavior column then becomes a drop-down list where the options are as follows:

- Hide
- Show
- Hide when inactive

Current items are the ones loaded at the time you open this dialog box. Past items were at one time loaded in the System Tray, and may yet be loaded again. For example, if you don't want to see the Windows Task Manager icon in the System Tray the next time you use this utility, choose it from your Past Items list, and then choose the Hide option.

Again, it's worth pointing out that just because you don't *see* an icon in the System Tray doesn't mean the application hasn't *loaded*. Hiding an icon has no bearing on the item's startup behavior (other than whether the icon shows up in the System Tray).

There's even a registry edit that will hide all icons permanently if you'd like to handle all of the System Tray icons with a bigger stick.

Hiding All System Tray Icons

A relatively simple little registry edit can hide all System Tray icons, leaving the area displaying only the system time and date (and of course, you can disable these as well, as we've just seen).

Here's what to do:

1. Open the Registry Editor by typing **regedit** at the Vista Start menu.
2. Navigate to this key:

   HKEY_CURRENT_USER\Software\Microsoft\Windows\CurrentVersion\ Explorer

   and add a new DWORD value called NoTrayItemsDisplay.
3. Double-click the new DWORD value and assign it a value of 1 (true).
4. Exit the Registry Editor and reboot your computer. Now, the System Tray should look like what you see in Figure 4-18.

To reenable the display of System Tray icons, you can either delete the NoTrayItemsDisplay DWORD value or set its value to 0.

Turning Off the System Tray Notifications

The tab on the Taskbar and Start Menu Properties dialog box is called the Notification Area, and it's called this for a reason. As users discover almost from the moment they first use their Vista computer, another function of the System Tray is to host application and operating system notifications that appear in the form of pop-up balloons. (OK, *pop-up* has a bad connotation; let's say they fade in and out instead, shall we?)

Figure 4-18. No more Notification Area icons

It seems you can't do anything about these balloon tips. Or can you? Can you turn off Vista's capability to interrupt you with a notification?

As it just so happens, you can disable the balloons. To do so, you need either a registry hack or a piece of freely available software. I'll discuss each.

Using the registry

As you know by now, registry settings define how the Vista operating system behaves, and that includes whether balloon tips display. To disable the notifications from appearing in the Notification Area, just follow this recipe:

1. Open the Registry Editor by clicking the Start menu and typing **regedit**.
2. Now, navigate to this key:

   *HKEY_CURRENT_USER\Software\Microsoft\Windows\CurrentVersion\
   Explorer\Advanced*

3. Create a new DWORD key called EnableBalloonTips, and set the value to 0 (false), as shown in Figure 4-19.

Now, exit the Registry Editor and reboot. You should no longer receive Vista's notifications in the System Tray.

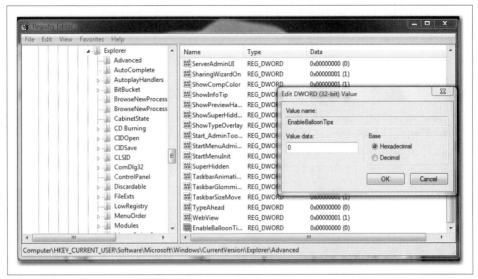

Figure 4-19. Turn off balloon tips with this registry edit

Using separate software

You can also change Notification Area behavior with applications such as TweakUI.

At least I think you can. I'm taking a bit of a flyer here; Vista authors had to start writing Vista books long before the operating system was made public, and long before related utilities such as TweakUI were updated to include support for Vista.

At any rate, TweakUI is part of a suite of utilities called PowerToys. (As of this writing, the full name is PowerToys for Windows XP.) PowerToys are available for free download from this web site:

> *http://www.microsoft.com/windowsxp/downloads/powertoys/xppowertoys.mspx*

Before you get carried away, note that TweakUI, as with the rest of the PowerToys, is *not* considered part of the operating system, and therefore is *not* supported by Microsoft. In fact, here's the caveat emptor from Microsoft's web site:

> We take great care to ensure that PowerToys work as they should, but they are not part of Windows and are not supported by Microsoft. For this reason, Microsoft Technical Support is unable to answer questions about PowerToys. PowerToys are for Windows XP only.

Despite the warning, you can use the PowerToys utilities for a wide variety of tasks; disabling the Notification Area's balloons is just one of them. And even though I've pointed you to a Windows XP resource, I'm told that they *should* be updated to include support for Windows Vista as well—as in by the time this title is nestled into your bookshelf, I'm betting.

Controlling Desktop Theme and Appearance

As mentioned briefly in Chapter 1, a user or administrator can control virtually *every single aspect* of the Windows Vista desktop. This includes the desktop backgrounds, colors, screensavers, sounds, and icons that can personalize the computing environment.

The most sweeping changes to the desktop environment can be applied through the use of *themes*, which serve, essentially, as combinations of backgrounds, colors, sounds, and so forth. A few are included with the Vista installation, and you can download more still. To change a theme, follow these steps:

1. Open the Personalization application from Vista's Control Panel. You can shortcut this by right-clicking on the desktop and choosing Personalize.

2. Follow the Theme link toward the bottom of this Personalization console, opening the Theme Settings dialog box as shown in Figure 4-20.

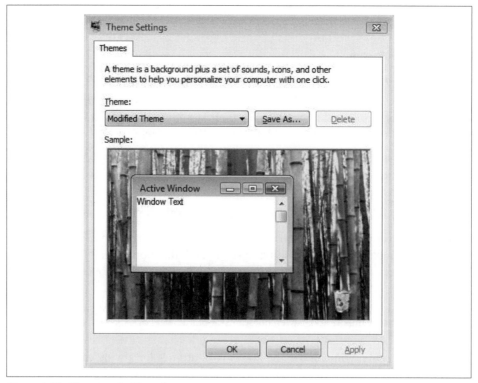

Figure 4-20. Changing the Vista theme

The cool thing here is the Save As feature. Any changes you've made to any part of the desktop environment can now be saved as part of a new, customized theme. In fact, notice that if you do something such as change the desktop background (to the green bamboo wallpaper shown in the figure—very attractive), you will then see the theme listed as Modified Theme. Just click Save As from here for the ability to change back to this background (and any associated sounds, icons, etc.) at any time without going through the extra click-steps.

Although I don't want to belabor the point, I do want to be clear about what components are part of a theme. Here are the primary settings that, once changed, can be saved as part of a new theme. Also included are instructions about how to change each element. It's fairly straightforward stuff; if you've changed a desktop background in Windows XP, 2000, or 98, you should be able to figure out what to do. But just in case:

Screensavers

From the Personalization Control Panel application, choose the Screen Saver link. Then, in the Screen Saver Settings dialog box, choose the desired screensaver from the drop-down menu. You then have a few other ways to govern behavior, such as the amount of time before the screensaver takes over.

Some screensavers, such as the 3D text screensaver, have additional settings you can configure.

Sounds

Follow the Sounds link from the Personalization Control Panel application to open the Sound dialog box, shown in Figure 4-21. Here, from the Sounds tab, you can select almost any Windows action and then preview or change the default sound associated with the action. You can then save a list of customized sounds as a Sound Scheme with the Save As button to allow for quick toggling among different sets of Windows sounds without having to manually reconfigure.

Mouse pointers

To change the look and behavior of the mouse pointer, follow the Mouse Pointers link in the Personalization Control Panel application. From here, you will see the Mouse dialog box with several tabs to fine-tune mouse settings, some of which will be hardware-dependent. For example, if you're using a laptop, you'll probably see two Buttons tabs: one for the touchpad built into the laptop, and one for the mouse you may connect when you're not on the go. Other mouse pointer options include mouse speed and visibility options.

Desktop background

For changes to the desktop background, follow the—you guessed it—Desktop Background link in the Personalization Control Panel application. Now you'll see a selection drop-down list that lets you specify a picture location (the default is the Windows Wallpapers location; *%systemroot%\Web\Wallpapers*) and then choose the desired picture. And of course, you can select any picture on your hard drive as the desktop background by browsing to it.

Color schemes

From the Personalization Control Panel application, choose Window Color and Appearance to change options that affect window colors. Note also that this dialog box will change depending on whether Areo is the selected color scheme. If so, you see options that can change the color and transparency of the glass. If not, you see an Appearance dialog box similar to what has been available in previous versions of Windows.

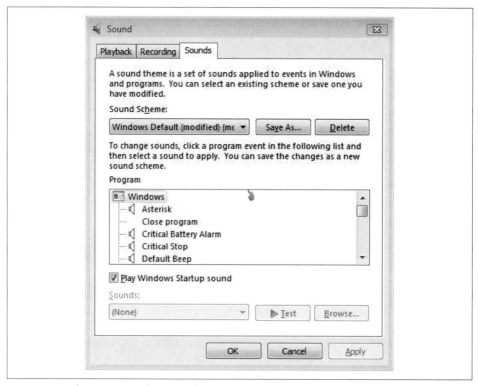

Figure 4-21. Changing a Windows sound

And remember, once you've spent a few hours making changes to elements that comprise a Vista theme, make sure to *save your changes* by accessing the Themes link and saving—a big timesaver when you want to apply the same settings some time in the future.

Something Cool About Vista Desktop Backgrounds

Here's something that makes the preceding a little more worthwhile, an interesting nugget that can help you take even more control over the desktop environment—particularly when it comes to setting desktop backgrounds.

The list of Windows wallpapers you see when clicking the desktop background link in the Personalization Control Panel application is divided into sections such as black and white, light auras, paintings, textures, and so on. Where do these divisions come from, and can we add our own little Windows wallpaper grouping?

They come from the metadata tags associated with the pictures. To see what I mean, open a Vista Explorer window, look in the *%WinDir%\Web\Wallpaper* folder, and then look at the pictures there.

Select the painting of the carp image, for example, and then note the image properties in the Details pane (if the Details pane isn't showing, click Organize → Layout in Vista Explorer and make sure the Details pane is turned on). There, you should see that the tag associated with the painting of the carp is called Paintings. Vista uses this tag information when grouping the Vista wallpapers in the Desktop Background dialog box.

So, how can you put this to use? If you add a picture to this directory, you can edit the metadata tag associated with this picture to either add your own custom Windows wallpaper groups, or just add pictures to existing groups.

Note, however, that you need to grant yourself special permission to perform this action. Because this folder lives in the Windows directory, not even administrators have permission to edit metadata tags by default.

And no law says you have to add a metadata tag. If you just want the convenience of having all possible Windows wallpapers in one place, simply copy or move the pictures to the *\Web* folder. If no tag is specified, there will merely be an "Unspecified" wallpaper grouping in the Desktop Background dialog box, as seen in Figure 4-22.

Now that you understand how to manipulate elements of the Vista desktop to your liking and then save these changes as part of a desktop theme, surely there must be a way to undo things. There is, as we explore in the next couple of brief sections.

Restoring the Default Theme

You can easily reset the theme to what it was during the "out-of-box" experience. To restore Vista to the default theme, just follow these three steps:

1. Access the Control Panel's Personalization application by right-clicking the desktop and choosing Personalize.
2. Click the Theme link to open the Theme Settings dialog box.
3. From the drop-down menu, choose the Windows Vista theme and click OK to complete the change.

If you don't want to keep a saved theme around any longer, there's a way to get rid of it.

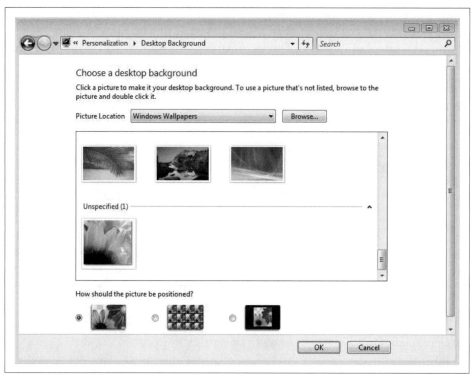

Figure 4-22. Creating your own wallpaper categories

Deleting a theme

We've spent quite a bit of time here discussing how to customize the Vista desktop appearance and then save those changes as a theme. But what if you want to delete a theme? It takes only a few steps:

1. Open the Personalization Control Panel application (right-click an open area of the desktop and choose Personalize), and then choose the Theme link.

2. From the Theme Settings dialog box, select the theme you've slated for deletion in the drop-down menu and click the Delete button. Vista removes the theme definition file and all related media that may be associated with the custom theme.

Theme files, by the way, are stored in the *%WinDir%\Resources\Themes* folder by default, but you shouldn't delete theme files manually. Use the steps just outlined instead.

Disabling Theme Changes

Sometimes themes can be the bane of an administrator's existence. Users end up losing icons and can't figure out how else to launch favorite applications, or they change the wallpaper to something that's, shall we say, less than business-appropriate, and so on. Inevitably, they end up calling *you* over to set things back to the way they were—a loss of productivity, to say the least.

Fortunately, there's a way to *enforce* that a particular theme be used. More specifically, there's a way to prevent changes to any part of the Vista desktop so that whatever settings have been configured for the user will remain unaltered.

The technology answer here is to use a GPO, and configure a policy setting that prevents any desktop changes. Here's the procedure to follow:

1. Open the Microsoft Management Console by typing **mmc** from the Start menu. You will be prompted to continue if you're using User Account Control.

2. A blank MMC console opens. This console has zero functionality right now, but it will be functional once we add a snap-in. To do so, click File → Add/Remove Snap in.

3. The Add or Remove Snap-ins dialog box appears, as seen in Figure 4-23. From the list, choose the Group Policy Object Editor and then click the Add button (in the middle) to snap it into the blank console.

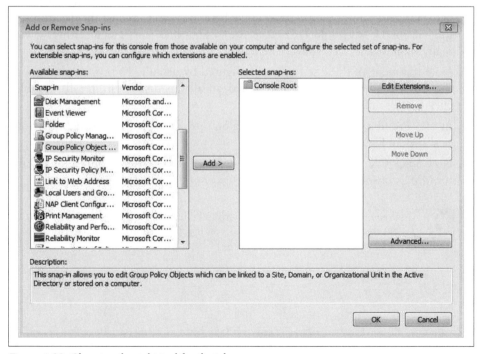

Figure 4-23. Choosing the right tool for the job

You're now asked to which object the GPO will be *linked*. In a Windows server domain environment, you can link GPOs to domains, sites, and organizational units (OUs). To manage a single computer, choose to link the GPO to just the Local Computer where the setting will apply. If your Vista computer is not part of a domain, you'll only get one choice: the Local computer.

Now the MMC console appears with a snap-in loaded called Local Computer Policy. There are two main groups of policy settings here:

Computer settings
> These settings configure computer behavior, such as startup and shutdown activity.

User settings
> These control user behavior, such as actions at logon and logoff time.

As you might imagine, there can be a lot of overlap when configuring settings for a particular desired behavior.

There are hundreds of possible Group Policy settings (and that's just for the Local computer; never mind ones available in a Windows server domain), so we'll focus here on just the desired result: preventing user changes to the desktop. To do so:

1. Expand the Group Policy by selecting User Settings → Administrative Templates → Desktop → Desktop.

2. Here you see just a few of the possible desktop settings that *could* affect user behavior. (And not to beat a dead horse here, but these are just the desktop settings in the Desktop folder. Look at the taskbar and Start menu settings if you really want to start feeling overwhelmed.)

3. Note that none of these settings is configured by default. To prevent changes to the Desktop theme (that is what kicked off all this discussion, recall), double-click the "Prohibit changes" setting.

4. In the "Prohibit changes Properties" dialog box, click the Enabled radio button, as shown in Figure 4-24.

5. Now, click OK. The setting should be enabled in the Group Policy Object Editor MMC console.

 If you're wondering whether the Group Policies can apply to one user but not another user, the answer is yes. If you're waiting for me to tell you how, you'll have to look ahead to Chapter 12.

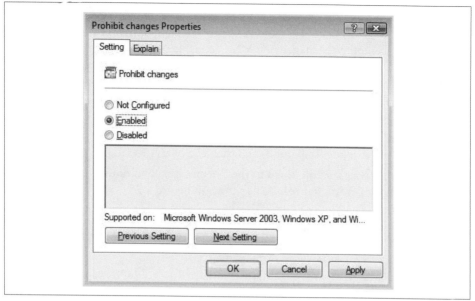

Figure 4-24. Prohibit changes to the desktop with a GPO

Disabling themes, Part two

There's another way to disable theme changes without quite as much heavy lifting as is the case when editing and applying a Local GPO. Because Vista's themes are controlled by the Themes service, all you have to do to disable theme changes is to stop the Themes service. Sneaky, but hours of fun.

There are actually two ways to do this. One is by stopping the Themes service from the Command Prompt. The proper command is net stop themes.

To restart the Themes service from the Command window, use the command net start themes.

The advantage of this is that it's a rather efficient method for turning off themes without changing anything about the underlying theme configurations.

 This command must be performed from an elevated Command Prompt. For instructions on how to automatically start a Command Prompt with elevated permissions, see the tips in Chapter 15.

The other way to stop the Themes service is to use the Computer Management MMC console. Here's what to do:

1. Open the Computer Management MMC console. As with so much else, there are several ways to do this. You could right-click the "Computer" item in the Start menu and choose Manage from the context menu, for instance. As always, you could also type something like comp at the Start menu instead.

2. There are three main nodes here: System Tools, Storage, and Services and Applications. Because we're trying to stop a service, we want to focus on the Services and Applications node. Expand it, and then click Services.

3. In the list of services, scroll down to the Themes item and double-click it to open the Themes Properties dialog box, as shown in Figure 4-25.

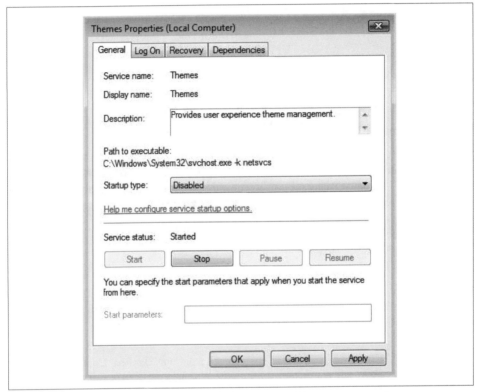

Figure 4-25. Stopping the Themes service with the Computer Management console

Now, you can use this dialog box to configure several actions for the Themes service. To stop it immediately, click the Stop button.

You can also prevent the Themes service from loading at startup time by selecting Disabled in the "Startup type" drop-down menu. This will prevent all future theme changes until an administrator either changes the Themes service startup behavior or starts the service manually.

Stopping the Themes service will have an immediate and dramatic impact on the Vista interface. It will cause you to lose use of even the Windows Vista Basic theme, and you will now be using a Vista machine that looks a whole lot more like Windows 2000. The Start button, for example, will now be square instead of round, and window buttons will change to a more retro look. And don't even think about using Aero; an investigation of the Window Color and Appearance options after stopping the Themes service will turn up options that are quite different from those that are possible with the Themes service running.

To regain use of Vista's many themes, including Aero, just select the Themes service once again and click Start. It's also probably best to let the Themes service load at startup.

Using Vista's Color Scheme

Vista's Aero color scheme changes the game somewhat when it comes to tweaking the appearance of windows and other elements such as the Start menu.

First, let's revisit how to enable the Aero interface in the event that it's turned off. And remember that Aero is enabled by default if your computer has the hardware guts to support it. To turn on the Vista Aero color scheme:

1. Open the Control Panel's Personalization application.
2. Follow the Window Color and Appearance link.
3. From the Appearance Settings dialog box, choose Windows Aero.
4. After a brief wait, you should now be dealing with transparent windows, live preview thumbnails, and all other elements that describe the Aero color scheme.

Now, then: the point of this section is not to detail turning on and off the Windows Aero color scheme, but rather to point out the differences in the Window Color and Appearance dialog box once Aero is on.

With Aero enabled, and after following the steps just listed, you will see a very different Window Color and Appearance dialog box. In fact, it will look much like the one shown in Figure 4-26.

As you can see, several color options here let users select a color of glass to use and then set a level of transparency with a single click. The Transparency slider can change how easy it is to see through the current window.

For even more options that will dictate window color, click the "Show color mixer" button, as I did before grabbing the screenshot shown in Figure 4-26. With these options showing, users can manipulate the hue, saturation, and brightness of the window color by using the corresponding slide controls.

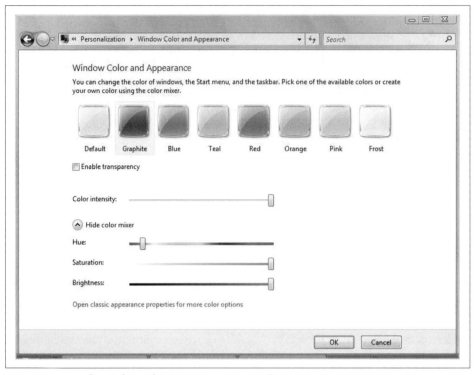

Figure 4-26. Window Color and Appearance options with Aero

Additionally, users still have the ability to manipulate any of the individual Vista graphical elements no matter what theme (if any) they are using. If you want to configure a different look and feel for message boxes, for example, or if you want to change how the application title bars display their text, you can. Just follow these steps when using Aero:

1. Open the Control Panel's Personalization application, and then follow the Window Color and Appearance link.

2. From the dialog box shown in Figure 4-26, click the "Open classic appearance properties for more color options" link.

3. In the Appearance Settings dialog box, click the Advanced button.

4. You now see the Advanced Appearance dialog box, as shown in Figure 4-27.

From this dialog box, it's now just a matter of selecting the item from the drop-down menu and then using the other configuration options to make the desired changes.

Note that not every element will use every configuration option. You won't configure a font, for example, for the Desktop item (and it's probably worth mentioning that changing the desktop color won't have any effect on appearance if you're using wallpaper for a desktop background). Select the ToolTip item, on the other hand, and you can then specify a font, size, and color for the displayed ToolTip text.

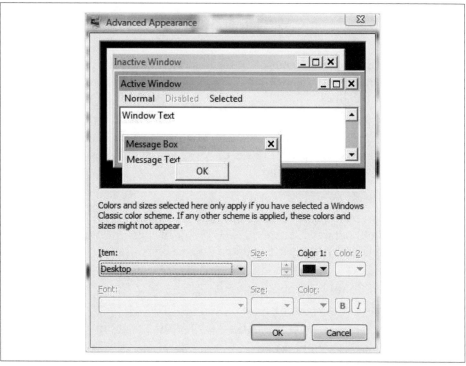

Figure 4-27. Configure appearance for specific window elements here

In previous chapters, we discussed how to use Windows Flip 3D. But there are a few items worth pointing out that let you customize how this program's switching functionality works.

Limiting the number of windows available in Windows Flip 3D

As mentioned previously in this title, Windows Flip 3D is a function of Vista's new Areo interface. As such, it won't be available on every computer out there. Your computer must meet certain hardware specifications that designate it as "Windows Vista Premium Ready." At the time of this writing, that didn't include a whole lot of existing computers, especially if we're talking about laptop systems.*

---

* At the time of this writing, Microsoft was being sued in the state of Washington for deceptive advertising. The claim: Microsoft marketed computers as being "Vista Capable," when in fact they were only capable of running Windows Vista Basic. But what do you see in the marketing campaign? Aero, of course, and as you now know, Vista Basic is not "capable" of running Aero or Media Center or many of the other features that make Vista worthwhile. Personally, I think the lawsuit has merit—how is the average computer consumer supposed to know or understand that there are 15 different versions of a single operating system? I'd guess that 95 percent of Microsoft employees don't realize there are that many, much less have the ability to articulate the differences among the multiple versions. To the average Joe watching an advertisement, a computer either runs Vista or it does not.

Moreover, the Aero interface won't be available on every Vista version, either. To review, Aero is available on Vista Home Premium and higher. It's not available on Home Basic.

Because of the hardware requirements for the Aero interface, some users might experience a considerable performance hit if their system hardware just barely meets Vista Premium capabilities.

If you have several open windows, Flip 3D has to render each window when switching among programs. As a result, some users might notice glitches in performance when several windows are open. If this is the case, you might consider limiting the number of windows displayed in Flip 3D.

Here's what to do:

1. From the Start menu, type **regedit**, and then launch the Registry Editor application from the Programs list. Alternatively, you can press the Windows key and the R key and then type **regedit** from the Run dialog box.

2. Choose Allow when asked permission to launch the Registry Editor (assuming User Account Control is enabled).

3. Now, navigate to this registry key:

   HKEY_CURRENT_USER\Software\Microsoft\Windows\DWM

   and create a new DWORD (32-bit) entry; give it the name Max3DWindows.

4. Then, as shown in Figure 4-28, double-click to open and set the DWORD value to the maximum number of windows you want displayed by Vista's Flip 3D. For low-end Vista Premium machines, try a maximum of 5. For more robust machines, 10 should work without a performance hiccup.

5. Click OK and exit the Registry Editor.

In Chapter 6, we'll discuss the Windows Experience Index (WEI). This will allow you to get a good score for your computer's performance at a glance. The tips discussed here might be a good idea if your system's WEI score is 3 (less than that, and it won't be able to run Aero anyway).

Controlling the Display

Sure, the Vista computer you're using makes a lot of calculations and handles a lot of tasks that make modern life and business possible. But you don't spend all day looking at the CPU and chipset, do you? Of course not. Humans stare at the monitor for feedback, and controlling what and how this output displays is a very important part of computer use. The last main section of this chapter deals with changing display properties.

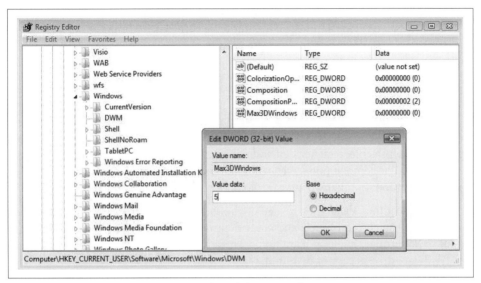

Figure 4-28. Configuring a maximum number of Flip 3D windows

Changing Screen Resolution

One of the most critical factors that affects Vista display is the screen resolution. The *screen resolution* is defined as the number of pixels (picture elements) that are shown on the monitor, represented in a reading of the *number* (of pixels horizontally) × (by) the *number* (of pixels vertically).

Most monitors today have screen resolution capabilities of at least 1,024×768, with fallback settings of 800×600 and 640×480. Higher-end monitors can use resolutions of 1,280×1,024; 1,600×1,200; and even 2,048×1,536. The higher the screen resolution, the more screen area the user sees. Users who work with a lot of open windows tend to gravitate toward higher resolutions.

There's a trade-off however. At higher resolutions, text becomes smaller and harder to see, especially for those with vision problems. For those with perfect vision, high resolutions create tiny, tiny, tiny text, which in turn can lead to eyestrain, eventually leading to vision problems (capital *I* irony, huh?). Fortunately, this book gives you the tools to adjust text size, which is just one of the reasons it's so good (even though a rather mundane discussion of screen resolution contains valuable information that will help you get the most out of your computer).

To adjust Vista text size, use the Personalization Control Panel application and then click the "Adjust font size (DPI)" link on the list of tasks to the left. Flip to Chapter 15 for the specific instructions.

At any rate, there is no ideal screen resolution; it's just whatever works best for the individual user and what kind of work she wants to perform. One thing's for sure, though: using a higher resolution requires more hardware horsepower than using lower resolutions, including both the display adapter and the monitor itself.

Also affecting computer display is the color depth, which represents the number of colors that can be simultaneously displayed. Color depth can range from 16 colors for standard VGA monitors to 4 billion simultaneous colors for most monitors in use today (4 billion = 232, or 32 bits' worth of distinct colors). And as you might guess, higher color depths place higher demands on computer hardware. A video card capable of 32-bit color depth at one screen resolution may be capable of only 16-bit depth at a higher resolution. In other words, the two performance benchmarks are interrelated.

At installation time, Vista tries to detect the video adapter and monitor, and then configures the screen resolution and color depth at optimal settings. Moreover, there are fallback settings, such as installing a "generic Plug and Play" monitor, used in case hardware drivers cannot be found.

After Vista installation or after a hardware/driver update, you can change both screen resolution and color depth from the same dialog box. Here's how:

1. Open the Personalize application in the Control Panel by right-clicking the desktop and choosing Personalize. Follow the Display Settings link.

2. In the Display Settings dialog box, choose the monitor you want to configure if multiple monitors are detected.

3. As shown in Figure 4-29, use the Resolution slider to specify screen resolution, and use the Colors drop-down menu to specify color depth.

4. Click OK to apply your changes and exit.

Figure 4-29. Changing screen resolution and color depth

Besides setting the optimal screen resolution for the particular user and work tasks, another important setting is the monitor's refresh rate. A high refresh rate can improve your comfort level when you're sitting in front of a computer all day.

Changing Display Refresh Rate

The light-emitting diodes (LEDs) that make up your computer's display don't hold their images forever; the refresh rate determines how long the screen is redrawn by your video card each and every second you're at your computer.

The lower the refresh rate, the more the image will flicker, and even though you might not notice it when staring at the screen, flicker can cause eyestrain over time. The converse is also true: the more the screen redraws itself, the less strain computer use places on your eyes.

You should, therefore, strive to set a refresh rate as high as your video card's settings will allow. To configure Windows Vista's display refresh rate, follow these steps:

1. Open the Control Panel's Personalization application and click the Display Settings link.

2. Select the monitor you want to configure (if multiple monitors have been detected) and choose the Advanced Settings button.

3. On the Adapter tab, choose the List All Modes option. A list of all resolution/refresh rate modes supported by the monitor should appear in the List All Modes dialog box.

4. Now choose the desired refresh rate on the Monitor tab's drop-down menu, as seen in Figure 4-30. You should notice from the List All Modes dialog box that not every refresh rate will be available for every screen resolution.

Figure 4-30. Changing screen refresh rate

Now that we've gotten some of the basics out of the way, let's move on to some more advanced display settings, such as having Windows Vista utilize multiple monitors at once.

Using Multiple Monitors

Thanks to the magic of Plug and Play and the generally standardized interfaces among video cards and monitors (either VGA or DVI connections), using a second monitor for Vista output is usually just a matter of hooking up the second monitor to your computer.

Vista then does its level best to detect the new monitor and apply the video settings best suited for it, guessing at an ideal screen size, screen resolution, and color depth for the new monitor.

Additionally, you should see a handy little dialog box the first time you connect. In this dialog box, shown in Figure 4-31, you're given the option about how you want this second monitor to handle the Vista desktop.

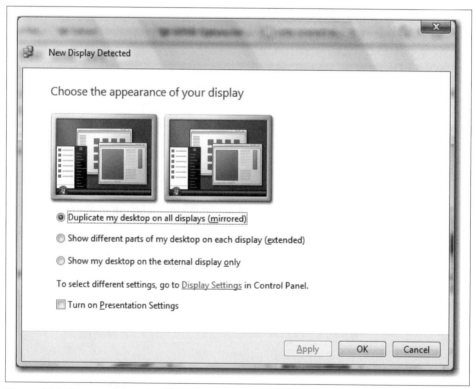

Figure 4-31. Choosing how to handle the second monitor

You have three choices about what to do in the New Display Detected dialog box:

Mirrored
> This option simply duplicates the existing desktop on each display you connect, and it is the default option. This will be the likely choice when you're using a laptop computer for a presentation by connecting an external projector or other fixed display such as a flat-screen monitor in a conference room.

Extended
> This option extends the Vista desktop across all displays, retaining just the single logical desktop, increasing overall desktop area. Once you select it, you can move program windows between the displays.

External display only
> This selection displays the Vista desktop only on the external display and not on the laptop's native LCD. Why this option? If using the Media Center capabilities from a laptop, for example, this will likely be the best choice when playing a DVD or recorded TV program. Additionally, using "External display only" will conserve battery power by turning off the mobile PC display.

Once you make your choice from the New Display Detected dialog box, you get the chance to preview your selection. Click Apply to preview on the newly connected monitor; choose OK to confirm.

Again, the default is to mirror the display. If you cancel out of this dialog box, Vista will use the default setting.

> You will see the New Display Detected dialog box only when you're using two displays. If you're trying to set up three or more displays, you must manually designate your primary display and apply display settings to all monitors manually using the Display Settings dialog box.

What's nice about the New Display Detected dialog box is that Vista remembers your settings here and uses them the next time you connect that monitor. When you disconnect the recently added monitor, Vista reverts to the original display settings.

> I've got no scientific evidence to back this up, but I'd guess that most use of multiple monitors happens on laptops, which usually come configured with an external video port somewhere in the back. Also, laptops can easily be attached to docking stations that send output to a bigger, better monitor. In other words, the practice is a little more prevalent on laptops because nothing has to be added.
>
> This isn't the case on most desktops, however, which about 98 percent of the time are configured with a single video card. Some video cards have the capability to connect multiple monitors, but usually a second video card is needed to send desktop output to a second monitor.
>
> You can find more information about video cards that support multiple monitors at *http://www.nvidia.com* and *http://www.ati.amd.com*.

Using Multiple Monitors Manually

Here's how to use multiple monitors to create a single logical Windows Vista desktop:

1. Open the Control Panel's Personalization application and then click the Display Settings link.

2. In the Display Settings dialog box, select the secondary monitor. Usually, it will be displayed as "2" in the dialog box.

3. Choose the "Extend the desktop onto this monitor" option, as shown in Figure 4-32.

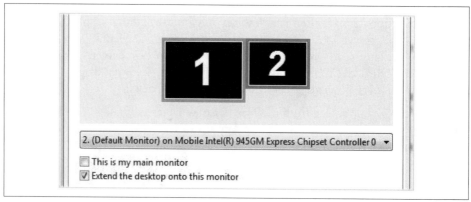

Figure 4-32. Using a single logical desktop on multiple monitors

Click either Apply or OK to commit your changes. You should now see the Start button on the lower-left side of your primary monitor, and a whole lot of desktop real estate out on your second monitor. If you're using the Vista Sidebar, these should appear on the right side of the second monitor by default.

Multiple-monitor considerations

Speaking of setting up a desktop computer with multiple video cards to support output to multiple monitors, it's important to note one important caveat regarding multiple-monitor use on Windows Vista.

If you want to take advantage of the Aero user interface across multiple displays (one desktop, multiple monitors), Vista requires that *all* video cards use the same driver. In most circumstances, you can't even mix and match different cards from the same manufacturer.

Again, I highly recommend visiting the major video card manufacturers' web sites before making a purchase, and furthermore, that you consider a single card with multiple video out ports for this purpose. If you're using two separate cards, try to make sure that both come from the same manufacturer.

You *can* still use video cards from different manufacturers, but you won't be able to use Aero. You'll be limited to the Vista Basic interface.

 Support for multiple monitors even extends to the use of Remote Desktop. A Remote Desktop Protocol (RDP) client that is using one logical desktop will still get the Terminal Services session over multiple monitors.

Configuring multiple monitors with UltraMon

It's fairly easy to configure a Vista system to use 2 monitors, but what about 3, 4, or even 10? To be sure, some users want and need this many monitors to maximize efficiency. Another challenge of dealing with a single desktop over multiple monitors is that it can be difficult to drag and drop all the information you want to work with among the array of monitors. In these instances, third-party software can usually help.

One popular example of such a utility is called UltraMon, from Realtime Soft. UltraMon performs helpful little tasks such as adding a taskbar to each monitor, and adds a button to the title bar of every window. Users can click on the button to move the active window to a different monitor, which then lets them quickly switch among different monitor configurations. Its strength really shows when you're using monitor configurations of *more* than two monitors. For more information on UltraMon, visit *http://www.realtimesoft.com*.

You can tailor UltraMon with keyboard shortcuts to speed things up even more. Pressing one keystroke combo can move an active window to the right display, for example, and another can move it to the left. Other options include the ability to precisely send a window to the monitor of your choosing, as shown in Figure 4-33.

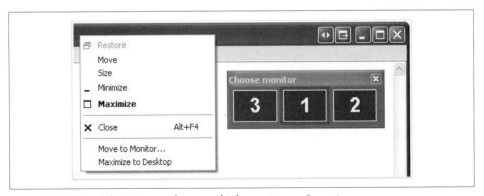

Figure 4-33. Using UltraMon to enhance multiple-monitor configuration

The screenshot shown in Figure 4-33 is from Windows XP, of course, but the application behavior should be the same on Windows Vista.

Originally developed for older Windows operating systems, version 2.7.1 currently supports Vista with a few limitations; look for full Vista support with version 3.

Summary

So now you know how to tweak just about every aspect of the Vista desktop environment exactly to your liking, and therefore to the liking of the users in your enterprise.

In this chapter, we looked at how to control three significant areas of the user interface: the Start menu and taskbar, the desktop itself, and the display. Along the way, we covered some fairly basic stuff, such as changing the monitor's refresh rate, but we also delved deeper into some serious Vista administration. Changing the System Tray with a registry edit isn't something you'll do every day in your life as a Vista administrator, after all.

I think you'll find both the elementary and the relatively advanced topics presented in this chapter very valuable, and that you'll even make some new friends in HR when you show them that one cool tip that will help make their desktop *just so*.

In the next chapter, we'll look at some configuration techniques that will make Vista even easier to use than what comes in most default installations (you'll learn about custom deployments later, in Chapter 8).

CHAPTER 5

Making Vista Easier to Use

Although this chapter's name might imply that using Vista is somewhat cumbersome, and that average users need some kind of treasure-trove full of tips and hacks just to get around their systems, nothing could be further from the truth. As we have seen in the preceding chapters, many of the new Vista enhancements already achieve the goal of making Vista easy to use. Searches are now performed much more quickly, the operating system environment is secured more automatically, the gadgets place information at our fingertips more readily, and so on.

This chapter looks at several features that can take this ease of use to the proverbial next level. Let's say, for example, that you need to use a computer while on your feet rather than sitting at a desk. You might be a doctor making rounds; you might be a project manager visiting a construction site. In that case, wouldn't it be easier to interact with your Vista computer the same way you do with a clipboard—in other words, with a pen rather than a keyboard? With just one of Vista's usability technologies—handwriting—you can.

And what if either you, or the users for whom you're configuring a Vista system, face physical challenges such as limited vision, or impaired use of arms or hands? Are options available that still allow for productive time using Vista? There are, and in this chapter, you'll learn how to set up some of these as well.

Another feature that helps make Vista easier to use is its capability to synchronize data among other devices such as mobile phones or network storage locations. Such synchronization makes it possible to have but one set of working data for any given user, rather than multiple versions of files stored across multiple devices. This chapter includes discussion of the Vista Synchronization Center, where you can view all of these sync relationships and sometimes manage them using a centralized interface.

But first, we begin this chapter with yet another usability technology: the capability for Windows Vista to "speak" in just about any language on the planet.

Changing Language and Regional Settings

Vista lets you easily change the language used to display menus, wizards, dialog boxes, and so on.

Editions:

- Enterprise
- Ultimate
- Home Basic, Home Premium, and Business with the Language Interface Pack (LIP) installed, as explained shortly

You need to make sure you have the appropriate language files available, however, before proceeding with the steps that follow. In Vista, there are two types of language files, each discussed separately in the next two sections.

The Windows Vista Multilingual User Interface (MUI) Pack

Because most multilanguage scenarios involve companies with a global span, the Vista MUI is available only with the Enterprise and Ultimate editions, and provides a translated version of the Vista user interface. MUIs require a license.

Advantages of the MUI pack with Vista Enterprise and Ultimate include the following:

- Built-in support for 36 languages.
- The ability to simply toggle among the languages installed.
- The ability to install a single deployment image on multiple computers whose users speak a different language. Also, this same image can be deployed on a variety of form factors, such as desktops, laptops, tablet devices, and so forth.
- Reduced deployment cost to companies by reducing the number of images needed to meet language requirements.

In other editions of Windows Vista that don't have the MUI available, you still have the ability to switch among different languages. Vista Business, Home Premium, and Home Basic can take advantage of the Language Interface Pack, or LIP.

The Windows Vista Language Interface Pack (LIP)

The Vista LIP is slightly less robust than its MUI cousin and provides a translated version of the most commonly used area of Vista's interface. The good news is that you can download a LIP from the Microsoft web site free of charge (just go to microsoft.com and search for "Language Interface Pack"). Further, most LIPs can be used on any Vista edition.

The drawback—although if you noticed, you'd probably need the MUI files anyway—is that the LIPs require at least one parent language. Don't worry about committing this to memory; you're instructed about all the necessary parent language requirements when you download a LIP (I'm making *absolutely* no calculated stab at humor here; sometimes computer book sentences just come out looking a bit, well, odd). Just think of the parent language as whatever your native tongue is.

As mentioned, user interface components that are not translated into the LIP language are instead displayed in the parent language. When you download a LIP, you are given the parent language requirements for that language. One of these is that you need to install the parent language pack before you can install the LIP.

So, when is it ideal to use a LIP? Anytime a company needs multilanguage capabilities but doesn't want to take on the expense associated with an OS upgrade. For example, small firms with a bilingual workforce may be able to get by just fine with the LIP instead of taking on a license agreement required to obtain the Enterprise edition of Vista, and thus the license for Multilingual User Interface files.

You can get these language files from additional locations, such as the Windows DVD, a network share, or your computer's hard drive.

Installing Additional Languages

Now that we've got the background out of the way, we can begin the task of using another language. Follow these steps to make another language available using the LIP:

1. Open the Regional and Language Options applet from the Control Panel. If you're using the Standard View, look under the Clock, Language, and Region grouping.
2. Choose the Keyboards and Languages tab.
3. In the Display Language section, click the "Install/uninstall languages" button. After a warning asking whether User Account Control is enabled, you'll get a dialog box such as the one shown in Figure 5-1, where you can choose to either install or remove a given language.

From there, it's a matter of locating the appropriate language installation files using the Browse button in the next dialog box. Follow the instructions in the wizard to complete the installation process.

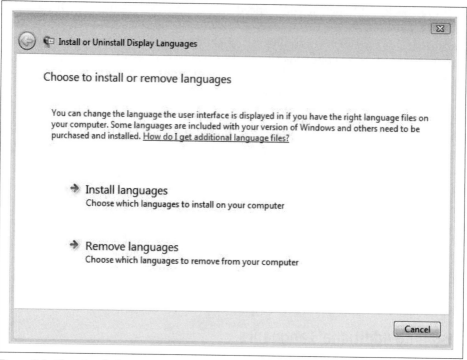

Figure 5-1. Changing the language Vista uses

Changing languages

Installing the language pack is just half the battle, however. To complete the process, you need to instruct Vista to use the newly installed language. Here's what to do:

1. Again, you'll use the Regional and Language Options dialog box. Make sure the Keyboards and Languages tab is selected.

2. As shown in Figure 5-2, choose a language from the list of display languages, and then click OK.

Now you should see the Vista menus and dialog box in whatever language you've just chosen.

If you're using Vista Enterprise or Ultimate, the operation is a little less strenuous thanks to the MUI. If you're using one of these two versions, you could do this:

1. Open the Regional and Language Options dialog box, and choose the Administrative tab.

2. Click the "Change System locale" button. You might then be prompted for administrative credentials.

3. In the Regional and Language Settings dialog box, shown in Figure 5-3, change the system locale from the drop-down list.

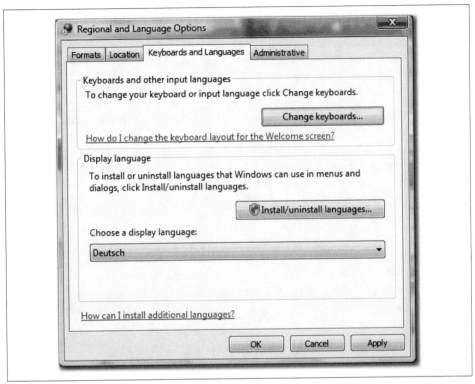

Figure 5-2. Telling Windows Vista to switch languages

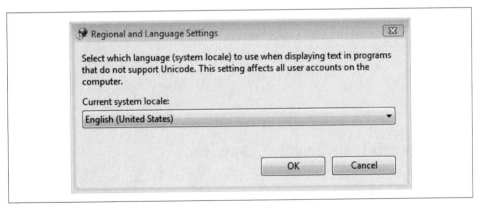

Figure 5-3. Changing system locale

Not only is Vista conversant in multiple languages, but it also understands input from sources other than the keyboard and mouse. One of these is good, old-fashioned handwritten text, which we'll examine in the next section.

Using Handwriting Recognition

As with many technologies, the first versions of Tablet PCs—along with their enabling feature, handwriting recognition—represented the shaky first steps of a toddler just learning to amble about.

Problems were twofold: they included hardware that was powered mostly by Pentium III processors, which led to battery life that did not exactly complement mobile computing, at least not for very long. Tablet PC software, likewise, had drawbacks that included a Tablet PC Input Panel (TIP) that was anchored at the bottom of the screen. Moving text from this early iteration of the TIP to the application and back could become quite tedious. Also, the handwriting recognition didn't kick in until after you were finished writing, so you had to go back and make corrections to your text afterward instead of making them on the fly.

Now each limitation has been addressed as the hardware/software platform continues to evolve. Hardware makers such as Intel have since released the Centrino chipset/Pentium M combination, which considerably improves battery life. Microsoft, for its part, has continually upgraded the Tablet PC operating system (and even reorganized its business structure to facilitate this at an organization level; the Tablet PC group was moved into the Mobile Computing group).

Now Tablet PC software includes improvements such as a floating TIP and real-time handwriting recognition.

And, of course, with Windows Vista, the Tablet PC functionality is no longer treated as a separate OS install.

Editions:

- Home Premium
- Business
- Enterprise
- Ultimate

Enhancements to the Tablet PC Experience

In addition to the general improvement of the Tablet PC hardware/software platform, some specific features have been developed for Windows Vista that should have handwriting aficionados cheering.

AutoComplete

Now, the TIP can behave just like programs such as Microsoft Word and Outlook when performing AutoComplete operations. For those unfamiliar with AutoComplete in the aforementioned applications, it works like this: as you start typing,

AutoComplete suggests possible matches based on the first few letters. You can then select from a list and press Enter to accept the suggestion, saving you time and effort at the keyboard. It's a real timesaver.

Vista extends this into the TIP as well. As you write a letter or series of letters, Auto-Complete lists possible matches based on text you've entered before. You can then simply tap to accept the suggestion. This can really cut down on having to hand-write long entries such as URLs, email addresses, and filenames.

Ink erasing

Just as typists need the Backspace and Delete keys, handwriting practitioners need the eraser. But how do you "erase" text on a tablet? There are several methods, actually, and Windows Vista makes it easier to make a correction to handwritten text.

In Windows XP's Tablet PC Edition, users scratched out a letter or word with a z-shaped gesture. With Windows Vista, however, users now have additional options, including a vertical scratch-out in the pattern of an M or W, a circular scratch-out, and an angled scratch-out. Further, Vista includes support for a hardware-based "eraser" featured on some manufacturers' Tablet PCs. That means with some tablets, you can just flip your pen over and erase as though using a writing tablet made by Big Chief, say, rather than by Hewlett-Packard. Cool.

TIP positioning

As introduced in Chapter 2, even the TIP's positioning has made for easier use of the tablet platform. When the Input Panel is closed, the tab appears on the left edge of your screen by default, neatly tucked away to the point where it's almost entirely hidden. To open the Input Panel, simply tap the Input Panel tab, and it slides out from the edge of your screen. When you close the Input Panel, the tab slides back to the edge of the screen.

You can then move the TIP tab by dragging it along the right or left edge of the screen. Whenever you tap, the Input Panel opens along the same latitude as the tab. This is a considerable improvement over the days of anchoring the Input Panel at the bottom of the screen.

Helping Vista Improve Handwriting Recognition

If you want to use a pen as an input device, it's imperative that you help Windows Vista recognize what you're writing in any way you can. Your chicken scratch may look considerably different from mine, after all; Vista has the unenviable task of deciphering when you write a 2 and when you write a z.

Two components help Vista recognize what you're scribbling in the TIP. Fortunately, neither requires a lot of work on your part. They are:

Automatic learning

Automatic learning allows Vista to gather information about the words you write and how often. Enabling this feature is a no-brainer; turn it on if you're using the Tablet PC functionality.

The Handwriting Recognition Personalization tool

This lets you manually provide handwriting samples that Vista uses to improve handwriting recognition. You should provide these samples as often as is convenient.

As mentioned, neither tool is difficult to set up or configure. Here's what to do:

1. Open the Tablet Input Panel. If you don't see it on your screen for some reason, choose Start → All Programs → Accessories → Tablet PC. It's listed there.

2. Choose Tools and then Personalize Handwriting Recognition. As shown in Figure 5-4, you then have two choices:

Target specific recognition errors

This option lets you provide handwriting samples for specific characters or words that are being recognized incorrectly. Think 2 and *z*.

Teach the recognizer your handwriting style

This option allows you to provide more comprehensive handwriting examples for Vista to learn from.

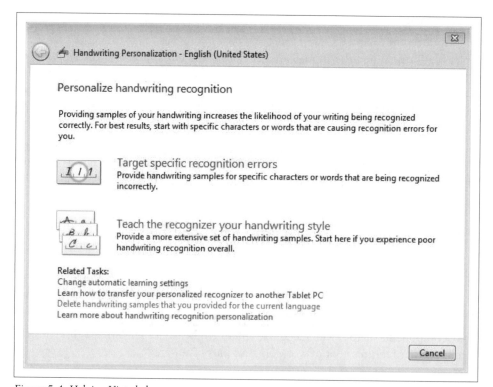

Figure 5-4. Helping Vista help you

Options differ depending on the paths selected. Essentially, they all involve you writing something—a word, a letter, a number—and then telling Vista exactly what you meant.

You then can turn on automatic learning with a single radio-button click. First open the Tablet PC Settings in the Control Panel. Look to the Mobile PC settings if you're using the Standard View.

Then, from the Tablet PC Settings dialog box, choose the Handwriting Recognition tab shown in Figure 5-5.

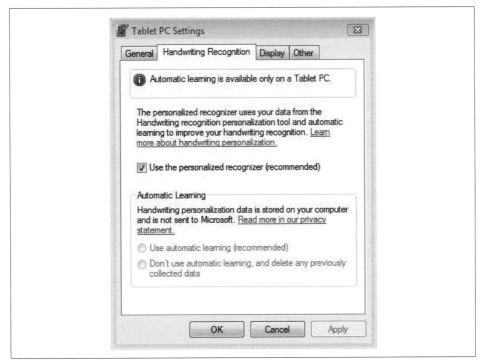

Figure 5-5. Turn on automatic learning when using a Tablet PC

Now, just choose the "Use automatic learning (recommended)" radio button. If it's grayed out, you're not using a Tablet PC. (If it's grayed out, there's probably no reason for you to be reading this section anyway. And note that the machine on which I'm composing this book is *not* a Tablet PC. We'll deal with it, though; the click-steps are no different.)

About the only instance when automatic learning would *not* be a good idea is when the same Tablet PC will be used for multiple users. For example, let's say you're running a veterinary clinic and multiple vets use the Tablet PC to enter diagnoses and prescription information about their patients. If only one person uses the Tablet PC, though, it will save a lot of handwriting correction in the long term: the more it's used, the better it gets at recognizing your particular writing style.

Transferring Your Handwriting Personalization to Another PC

So, you've gone to great pains to personalize your handwriting recognition, and now Vista recognizes pretty much every word you scratch into the TIP despite your tendency to write as though you're a physician dispensing a prescription (and maybe you *are*).

But now you want to switch computers. What happens to all that work? Will you have to train your new system all over again?

Good news: the handwriting personalization information is stored as data, and if you can get other data from one computer to another, you should be able to get the handwriting recognition data transferred as well. More good news: that data is part of the user's *profile*. So, if you recall from Chapter 1, the answer to "Will you have to train your new computer all over again?" is a resounding "no."

All you have to do is use the Windows Easy Transfer tool. Once you start the Easy Transfer process, just make sure you bring over all the information stored in the user profile.

To start Windows Easy Transfer, begin at the new system and then click Start → All Programs → Accessories → System Tools → Windows Easy Transfer. Alternatively, you can just do a Start menu search for *tr*, and Windows Easy Transfer should be the first program that appears.

Here's the information that will be migrated to the new system:

- Any handwriting samples that you've provided to the handwriting recognition personalization tool

- Any automatic learning information (data collected about the words you use and how you use them)

- Any options selected in the Handwriting Recognition tab of the Tablet PC Settings applet in the Control Panel

Full details about migrating from old to new computers, including click-steps for Windows Easy Transfer, are given in Chapter 7.

 If you're currently using a Windows XP Tablet PC edition, you can just upgrade to Windows Vista. All handwriting personalization information will be saved for use in the new Vista machine.

Personalizing Handwriting for Another Language

Vista also gives you the option of training it to recognize languages other than English. As of late 2006, handwriting personalization is also available for Japanese, Chinese (Traditional), Chinese (Simplified), and Korean.

There are a few caveats if you use these other languages, however:

- Teaching the recognizer your handwriting style is available for English only.
- Automatic vocabulary learning is available for English only.

Personalization steps for languages other than your native language are exactly the same as described earlier. All you need to do is make sure the correct input language is selected in the TIP. Follow these steps:

1. Open the Tablet Input Panel and use the Language bar to choose a different input language. The TIP should change similar to what you see in Figure 5-6.

2. Now, just choose Tools → Personalize Handwriting Recognition and follow one of the two paths provided in the wizard (at the time of this writing, you aren't able to personalize German). Same as before, just a different language.

Figure 5-6. Personalization of another language starts here

Using Vista to translate

Once you have additional language files installed, you can use your computer as a translator between languages, even when you're using applications such as Microsoft Word (or maybe especially when using Microsoft Word).

All you have to do is remember the right-click. For example, if I select the following block of text in Word:

> I've got Positive Mental Attitude! Ask me why.

and then right-click, I will see a Translation menu option. To use this Translation option, first select a language, and then choose the Translate selection. Word should display the Research pane, as shown in Figure 5-7.

The Research pane presents several options. The Translation section should be up to the task, however. Note that you can translate the entire document by choosing the appropriate options in the From and To drop-down menus here.

Underneath the "Translate a word or sentence" section, you're presented with the results of the selected translation. For example, using WorldLingo to translate the aforementioned block of text, I get:

> J'ai l'attitude mentale positive! Demandez-moi pourquoi.

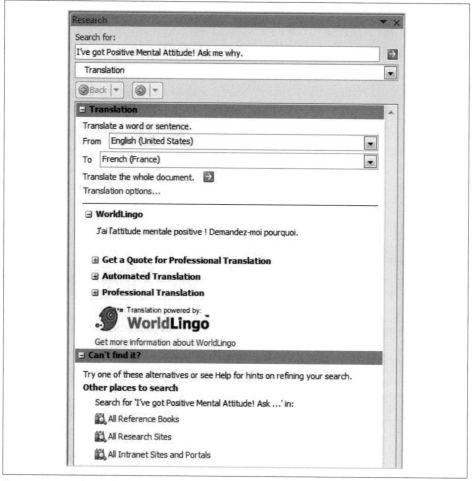

Figure 5-7. Word can also serve as a translator for multiple languages

because I selected French before performing the translation. Other translation options appear in that section of the Research pane as well.

Word uses online language dictionaries to perform translation; you need to be online for the translation to work.

Tablet PC Usage and the Windows Journal

As we have seen so far, the TIP allows Tablet PC users to convert handwriting into typed text in just about any Windows application. Instead of typing out your morning's emails, for example, you can just "TIP" them into Outlook if that saves you time.

Editions:

- All Windows Vista Editions support handwriting recognition.
- Tablet PC "pen" features are on Home Premium, Business, Enterprise, and Ultimate.

But there's another program *specifically* designed to handle handwriting, called the Windows Journal. With it, you can use *ink* (aka *handwriting*—you'll most likely use the Windows Journal with a pen device) over a larger canvas than in the TIP. If you're in the practice of taking notes with a spiral notebook, a legal pad, or a coffeehouse napkin, you might never go back to paper again. (In fairness to the much-maligned coffeehouse napkin, I think Jim Clark wrote the business plan for Netscape on the back of a napkin, and that turned out pretty well, at least during the IPO. Or am I thinking of J.K. Rowling and the Harry Potter books? At any rate, it had something to do with napkins, handwriting, and coffee.)

 So far, I've written this assuming that you're using a Tablet PC's pen device to input handwriting. Although that's certainly the norm for handwriting recognition, there's no law against using the mouse. Notice that when the mouse hovers above either the Windows Journal or the TIP, the cursor changes into a point. You can then click to deposit a drop of "ink." If you click and hold, you can draw letters, numbers, and so on, and insert those into documents as either converted text or as is. Again, I'm not recommending that you write using your mouse; it's just there if you need it.

To open the Windows Journal, just type **jo** from the Start menu—it should be the first thing you see. (Select Start → All Programs → Accessories → Tablet PC if for some reason it isn't.)

Also, before we jump into the full discussion, know that Journal handwriting won't work unless handwriting recognition is turned on. This is a default setting for the Windows Journal, but just in case, you can double-check by going to Tools → Options and opening the Options dialog box. As shown in Figure 5-8, choose the Other tab and verify that the "Enable handwriting recognition" checkbox is active.

Converting Handwriting to Typed Text

Once you've got the Windows Journal open, you'll see something that looks like a sheet of paper in a notebook or legal pad, fairly begging for some heavy-duty scribbling. So go ahead. That's exactly what the Windows Journal is for.

As mentioned, the Journal's job is to handle handwriting; you can then do just about whatever you want with it. You can leave the handwriting right where it is and save it for later reference, convert it into typed text for use in another program, or use it as is and place it into another application as a text box.

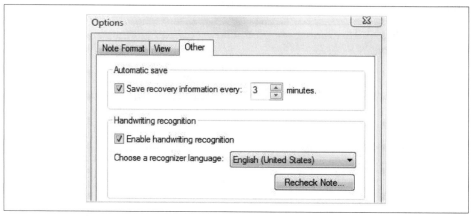

Figure 5-8. Ensuring that handwriting recognition is enabled

Here's what to do:

1. Using the Pen tool, write some text or just simply doodle. (I really don't care, and neither does the Journal. Let the proverbial muse be your guide.) The Pen tool is selected by default when you open the Windows Journal, and you will see pen options by clicking the drop-down arrow next to the Pen toolbar button.

2. Now that you've got some text to work with, use the Pen toolbar to choose the Selection tool (it looks like a little red lasso).

3. Using the Selection tool, "lasso" the handwriting that you want to convert.

4. Choose the Actions menu, and then the Convert Handwriting to Text option.

5. The Text Correction dialog box displays, shown in Figure 5-9. You have several choices here about what to do with your text:

   • The Options button, for example, lets you decide what to do about line breaks. If your original handwriting had line breaks that are important to the finished output, such as an outline of meeting minutes, or better, the poem you wrote while at said meeting, use the "Preserve line breaks" selection. If you've just scribbled down a paragraph as quickly as possible and you don't care about the line breaks, naturally you should clear this option.

   • The "Converted text" section allows you to manually change the recognized text. The Alternative section lets you point and tap from a list (which is *very* helpful if you'd have to flip the screen back around to make a manual correction).

   • The handwriting that was lassoed appears in the "Ink from note" section. If the handwriting is not being recognized as you expect, it could be because you didn't quite lasso what you thought you did.

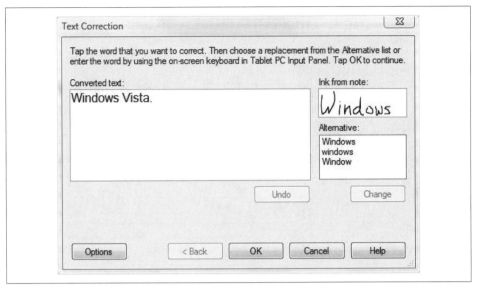

Figure 5-9. Choose what to do with your selected handwriting

6. Click OK when you're satisfied with the recognized text. Now you're presented with two options about what to do with the text:

- "Copy to the Clipboard" allows you to paste your text into another program, and the Windows Journal's original handwriting remains. A checkbox with this selection makes this the default behavior, and you will not be prompted again when converting text.

- "Insert in the same Journal note" inserts the converted text into the Windows Journal note using a text box, as seen in Figure 5-10. The handwriting is deleted.

7. Choose Finish to complete the operation.

 You can also make manual changes without flipping the screen around with the TIP. Just select the On-Screen Keyboard button, located on the TIP's upper-lefthand side.

If you've chosen the Clipboard option, you can now use that copied text anywhere else you can paste from the Clipboard.

Also, if you don't need to be specific about what text to convert—say, if you've been assigned meeting minutes duty and are converting everything—there's no need to lasso. Just use the Edit menu to select all of your handwriting before doing the conversion.

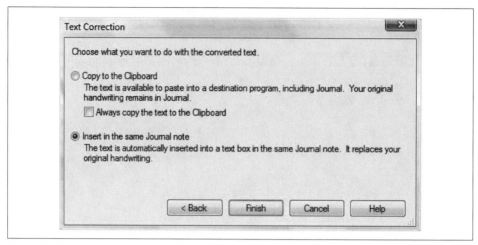

Figure 5-10. Handwriting converted into a Windows Journal text box

 You might have noticed that there's a highlighter in the Windows Journal, too, but you will only be able to convert ink to text when using the Pen tool. Converting to text won't work with the highlighter, even if you use it to make letters and such. (If this note actually applies to you, by the way, you can stop reading right now and go back to drawing in the margins with your crayon.)

Using the handwriting only

As mentioned previously, you can choose to use just the handwriting itself. This can help add a personal or visual flair to a written document, or draw special attention to a comment or annotation.

To paste your chicken scratch into another application:

1. Start by selecting the desired passage (or doodle) with the lasso, as before.

2. Now, just perform a right-click and choose Copy. A *picture* of the handwriting is now on the Clipboard, free for pasting wherever you'd like.

You can even paste it into a really, really cool book on

Beats the pants off napkins, huh?

I just blew your mind, didn't I?

Using a Recognizer Language

The Windows Journal uses its own *recognizer language* to help identify handwritten text. Furthermore, this language can be completely separate from the Vista interface language discussed previously in this chapter.

Obviously, using the recognizer for the same language you're taking notes in will make your handwriting recognition as accurate as possible. If you're writing in a language that's not available in the recognizer, the engine is more prone to errors when interpreting your writing. If this is the case, it's probably best to turn off the Journal's handwriting recognition.

Here's how to change or turn off the recognizer language:

1. From the Journal window, choose the Tools menu, and then Options.
2. Select the Other tab, and as shown in Figure 5-11, select or clear the "Enable handwriting recognition" checkbox under the Handwriting Recognition section. Choose OK to commit the changes.

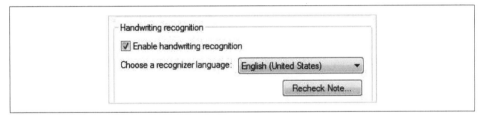

Figure 5-11. Enabling the handwriting recognizer

This action will prevent unexpected selections when you tap words to select them. But note that this will also prevent you from converting your handwriting to text.

Writing an Email; Really, Writing It

Unless you've just turned to this particular section, you probably already noticed from the preceding section that you can also convert Journal text into an email. Here are the steps:

1. Just as before, use the Pen tool to write the note you'd like to send as email. Then, choose the Selection tool and lasso your desired note.
2. Click the Actions menu, and then Convert Selection to E-mail.
3. In the Convert to E-mail dialog box, shown in Figure 5-12, choose the Options button to determine what to do about the note's line breaks. You can:
   - Preserve line breaks from notes.
   - Keep the note as a single paragraph of text.

- Include the selected ink. This is checked by default, and it saves the selected ink as an enhanced metafile (*.emf*) file and attaches this to the email message.
- Attach a graphics file to the email. The attached file consists of the original ink selection, which just about any graphics program can view. It should render in Outlook just fine, for example.

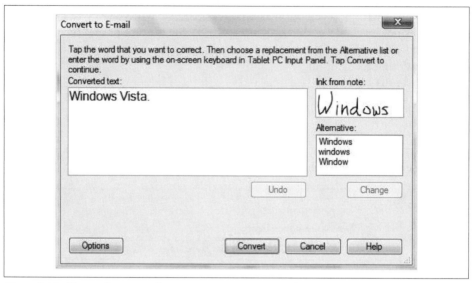

Figure 5-12. Choose the options for converting text to an email

Now make corrections as necessary. Again, we've covered this before, so I won't detail it here. The "Converted text" box lets you make corrections with a simple tap and edit; a green background means the word may need to be corrected. Alternatives let you select and tap Change.

To complete the procedure, choose Convert. The Windows Journal now communicates with the default email program, and you'll see a new email window open. The message body will contain the converted text. The original ink selection will also appear if you have included it with the Options button during the conversion procedure.

 Before trying this out, make sure you have an email program set up for the Journal to send the note to. The Windows Journal does not actually handle the email, but rather just converts the text to a picture that is then sent with a separate application. The Journal returns a "quit unexpectedly" error if it does not detect an email program.

The fact that Vista can so readily recognize handwriting is well and good, but it's of practical use only when you're using a Tablet PC. Wouldn't it also be great if you could just speak to the operating system and have it obey your commands? It can, of course, and I break down the details in the section that follows.

Working with Speech Recognition

Computers are dumb. They carry out instructions brilliantly, mind you, but we have to tell them what to do. In fact, they're so dumb that until very recently we haven't even been able to truly *tell* them what to do. Instead, we have had to type commands at a keyboard, one letter at a time, using language specific to the computer.

But as is the case with handwriting recognition, that is slowly changing (this is debatable; some would argue that they are changing rapidly indeed). Software is better able to work with spoken language, and the hardware needed to process distinct sonic waves into computing actions—opening a program or placing a word into an email, for example—is catching up.

With Windows Vista, you can use your voice to control your computer as never before. Generally speaking, you can use your voice to ease computer use in one of two ways. You can:

- Speak commands that the computer carries out.
- Dictate and edit text in applications.

This speech recognition capability can be a boon both for end users and for companies, and I have heard stories in which the Speech Recognition feature alone has saved companies countless thousands of dollars, and has saved some users their livelihoods.

Editions:

- All

Languages:

- English (U.S.)
- English (U.K.)
- German (Germany)
- French (France)
- Spanish (Spain)
- Japanese
- Chinese (Traditional)
- Chinese (Simplified)

You can probably think of several instances in which using your voice is a better option than the keyboard. For example, people who have to do a lot of typing throughout the day can quite literally avoid injury by speaking instead of typing (think of a customer service rep who deals mostly with emails, or a paralegal who has to prepare contracts and motions throughout the day). Speech recognition capability can subsequently save these workers from filing for workers' compensation, which in turn can save companies big time in lost productivity and insurance benefits.

On a more mundane level, think simply of the slow typist whose productivity can be enhanced significantly if he could only talk instead of relying on his fingers.

So yes, it's a good thing. But there are some setup considerations to note.

Before you get started using Windows Speech Recognition, of course, you'll need to set up a microphone. Sometimes this involves a driver installation, although such an occasion would be fairly rare. Once the microphone is set up, you can then train your computer to better understand you by creating a *voice profile*. Vista then uses the voice profile to recognize your voice and spoken commands.

Setting Up Speech Recognition

The Windows Vista Speech Recognition engine provides excellent voice recognition whose accuracy improves over time (i.e., the more you talk to your Vista machine, the better it will get at understanding what you're saying). But before you can use it, there are a few setup hoops to jump through.

Basically, configuring Vista Speech Recognition involves three steps. They can be summarized thusly:

1. Set up your microphone.
2. Learn how to talk to your computer.
3. Train your computer to understand you.

And as this is a complete *guide*, I'll now guide you through each step in the following subsections.

Setting up your microphone

Here's how to get started with speech recognition. You'll first configure your microphone using these steps:

1. In the Control Panel, open the Speech Recognition Options applet. If you're using the Standard View, look under the Ease of Access grouping and then follow the Start Speech Recognition link.

2. Click Next to set up your microphone. As seen in Figure 5-13, you will choose what type of microphone to set up. As explained shortly, you'll probably have better success with a headset microphone.

3. Now just follow the instructions throughout the remainder of the wizard. One of the significant steps to look for here is whether to run speech recognition at startup.

 As you might guess, speech recognition correlates directly to the fidelity of the microphone. Users of headset microphones will generally experience better performance. Because the microphone is closer to the mouth, headsets are less sensitive to external room noise. For additional information about microphones, visit the Microsoft web site and search for *microphone*.

Figure 5-13. Selecting the microphone

Once you've successfully set up the microphone, it's vital that you learn how to communicate verbally with your computer.

Teaching yourself how to talk to your computer

Now, on to the second part. After you've set up the microphone, you're given the option of running through the speech tutorial that will help get you started. The tutorial takes about 30 minutes, and it's highly recommended that you take the time to complete it.

But you don't necessarily have to take it during microphone setup. You can take it later if time doesn't allow right after the mic setup. Follow these steps to run the speech training tutorial:

1. From the Control Panel, open the Speech Recognition Options applet, and then follow the Take Speech Tutorial link. (Remember, you can just start typing what you're looking for using the Start menu's Search.)

2. A woman with perfectly shaped eyebrows leads the demonstration. Follow the instructions to complete the tutorial. Again, although somewhat time-consuming, this tutorial is an important step in the speech recognition process, as it helps improve accuracy right from (almost literally) the word go.

Common speech features

I generally don't like to place two large tables back-to-back, but this is a reference book, after all, so I've gathered two tables available from separate Microsoft sources and combined them into Table 5-1. Hopefully, having all this information in one place will help you better understand Vista's Speech Recognition so that you can learn it faster. You won't have to research the many speech recognition features because I've already gone to the trouble for you.

We'll start with a consolidated list of the most commonly used Vista Speech Recognition features.

Table 5-1. Vista Speech Recognition features

Feature	Description
Commanding	"Say what you see" commands allow you to naturally control applications and complete tasks, such as formatting and saving documents; opening and switching between applications; and opening, copying, and deleting files. You can even browse the Internet by saying the names of links.
Correction	Efficiently fix incorrectly recognized words by selecting from alternatives for the dictated phrase or word, or by spelling the word.
Dictation	Dictate emails and documents, and make corrections and save your work by voice.
Disambiguation	Easily resolve ambiguous situations with a user interface for clarification. When you say a command that can be interpreted in multiple ways, the system clarifies what you intended.
"How do I" help (U.S. English only)	You can say "How do I" followed by a task you want to perform with your computer. For example, "How do I change my desktop background?"
Innovative user interface	The new user interface provides a simple and efficient experience for dictating and editing text, correcting mistakes, and controlling your computer by voice.
Interactive tutorial	The interactive speech recognition tutorial teaches you how to use Windows Vista Speech Recognition and teaches the recognition system what your voice sounds like.
Personalization (adaptation)	Ongoing adaptation to both your speaking style and your accent continually improves speech recognition accuracy.
Support for multiple languages	Windows Vista Speech Recognition is available in eight languages/dialects.

And now that you've seen some of the speech capabilities, let's look at some of the specific commands that will let you literally tell Vista what to do.

Common speech commands

Table 5-2 lists many of the commands that Windows Vista uses to carry out the specified action.

Table 5-2. Vista's speech commands

Desired action	Speech commands
Choose a menu item using its name	File; Start; View
Choose an item	Click Recycle Bin; Click Computer; Click File
Double-click item	Double-click Recycle Bin; Double-click Computer; Double-click File
Switch to an open program	Switch to Paint; Switch to WordPad; Switch to program name; Switch application
Scroll direction	Scroll up; Scroll down; Scroll left; Scroll right
Insert a new paragraph or new line in a document	New paragraph; New line
Select a word in a document	Select word
Select a word and start to correct it	Correct word
Select and delete specific words	Delete word
Show a list of applicable commands	What can I say?
Update the list of speech commands that are currently available	Refresh speech commands
Make the computer listen to you	Start listening
Make the computer stop listening to you	Stop listening
Move the Speech Recognition microphone out of the way	Move speech recognition
Minimize the microphone bar	Minimize speech recognition

Now, all that's left is to train Vista to better understand your voice. As with handwriting recognition, the more you use it, the better it will become at understanding you.

Teaching Vista's Speech Recognition to Better Understand You

One of the most vital components to using the Vista Speech Recognition features is to help Vista adapt to your particular speech style and cadence. To get the most out of Windows Speech Recognition, use the Voice Training Wizard to train your computer to recognize your speech.

Again, you have the option of either training at microphone setup time, or coming back later to complete this step.

Here's what to do:

1. Open the Speech Recognition Options applet from the Control Panel (see the previous sections for how to locate it).

2. Choose the "Train your computer to better understand you" link.

3. The wizard leads you the rest of the way. Essentially, you read a series of passages to the system and Vista makes recognition adjustments as necessary (see Figure 5-14).

Figure 5-14. Using the speech training feature

There's yet another, more ad hoc method for training Vista's Speech Recognition, which is to correct text in the midst of dictation. Vista is bound to recognize a word incorrectly; telling the recognition engine what you meant can really help fine-tune things, leading to a higher success rate.

Here's what to do:

1. First, open Vista's Speech Recognition. Depending on the options you selected at setup time, it may be opened when you start up your computer. If it isn't, you can just type **spee** from the Start menu. It should appear at the top of the list.

2. Now, while dictating text in an application (Microsoft Word, Microsoft Outlook, Notepad, etc.), simply say "correct that" to correct the last thing you said. You now have two choices:

   • To correct a single word, say "correct" followed by the word you want to correct.

   • In the Alternates Panel dialog box, shown in Figure 5-15, say the number next to the item you want.

 You can even change a specific selection in the Alternates Panel dialog box by saying "spell" followed by the item's number.

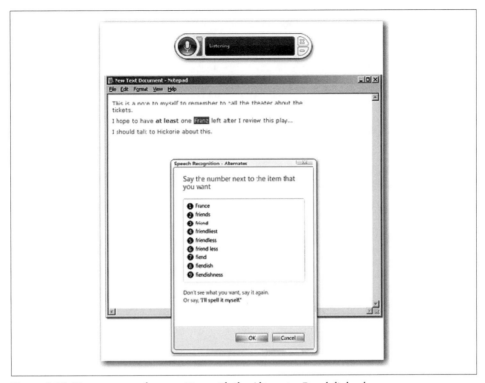

Figure 5-15. Fine-tune speech recognition with the Alternates Panel dialog box

Training Speech Recognition using the Speech Dictionary

The Vista Speech Recognition engine uses a dictionary to do its magic. When you speak a word, Vista checks the aural pattern against the dictionary, and if there's a match, the word is placed in the application.

You may also use words that don't appear in the Vista Speech Dictionary. People's names, brand names, and industry jargon are examples of frequently used words that won't be in the dictionary by default.

But as you might expect, you can add words to the Speech Dictionary so that Vista will recognize these as well. Here's what to do:

1. With Vista Speech Recognition open, say "open speech dictionary."

2. Now, you have the following options, as shown in Figure 5-16:

   - You can add a word to the dictionary by saying "add new word" or by clicking on the Add button. Follow the instructions in the wizard.

   - You can also *prevent* the Speech Recognition engine from recognizing a particular word. Click or say "prevent," and then follow the wizard's instructions.

   - Lastly, you can correct one of the dictionary's existing words. Click or say "change existing words," and then follow the instructions in the wizard.

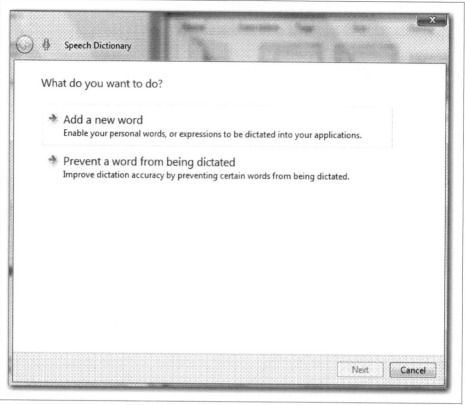

Figure 5-16. Changing the Vista Speech Dictionary

Now you can better use Speech Recognition to dictate that letter instead of typing it—and let's face it, you're not exactly Mavis Beacon. This should save you a lot of time and effort.

You can use the dictation in applications that mostly handle text. Examples include Microsoft Word, Outlook, and Notepad. Just about any program that's built into Vista is supported.

But you can't use it in *every* application just because said application handles text. This mostly encompasses third-party applications, but it includes a few from the Microsoft Office suite as well. Examples include:

- Microsoft Excel
- PowerPoint
- WordPerfect
- Eudora
- Lotus Notes

Running Speech Recognition at Startup Time

As seen when setting up the microphone, you have the option of automatically starting Speech Recognition as Vista starts. This, too, is configurable behavior. If, for example, you discover that it's easier to quickly dictate responses to the first few emails, but you have previously chosen not to have Speech Recognition start automatically, you can change course with just a few clicks of the mouse.

Here's what to do:

1. Open the Speech Recognition Options applet from the Control Panel.
2. Choose the "Advanced speech options" link in the lefthand pane, opening the Speech Properties dialog box.
3. As shown in Figure 5-17, just make sure the "Run Speech Recognition at startup" checkbox is selected.

Note that these settings are specific to the user profile. If another user logs on, she won't see the Windows Speech Recognition tool unless she's also configured it for automatic startup.

Accessibility Options

In addition to handwriting and speech recognition, Microsoft has long made an effort to include built-in options that make it easier for someone to see, hear, and use his machine. Options available in previous versions of Windows have empowered users with physical challenges such as visual problems, hearing loss, and limited use of hands and arms.

Vista is no different, and it builds on the work of previous Windows operating systems' accessibility features in exciting ways. Replacing the functionality of the Accessibility Wizard in Windows XP, all of Vista's main accessibility tools are now gathered in one place, called the Ease of Access Center. Here, you will find the improvements on options that make it easier to see and hear your computer. There are new utilities as well.

Editions:

- All

Ease of Access Center

Shown in Figure 5-18, Vista's new Ease of Access Center gathers accessibility tools into a centralized location that facilitates easy use and configuration of each. Upon first launching it, you will notice a quick access section, which places all of the common accessibility tools within easy reach.

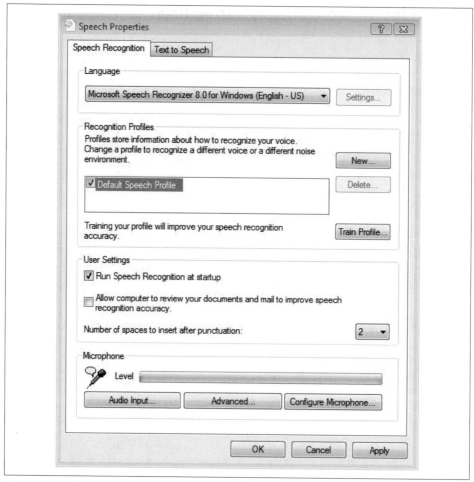

Figure 5-17. Change your mind about speech at startup

The Narrator tool even reads the Ease of Access text aloud, and you can then launch other tools by pressing the Space bar rather than clicking a mouse. Below the common tools are the rest of Vista's accessibility utilities, organized into seven categories.

To launch the Ease of Access Center, either look in the Control Panel or press the Windows key and the U key simultaneously. (And of course, typing **eas** also works in the Start menu.) The Ease of Access Center is also available at logon by selecting the little blue Control Panel icon in the logon screen.

A questionnaire is even provided that can help you select the right options for your particular needs. This can be an especially big help to administrators setting up a computer for someone else's use.

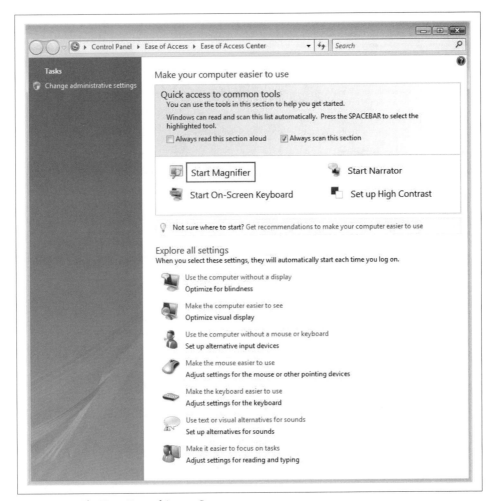

Figure 5-18. The Vista Ease of Access Center

Recommendations for accessibility settings

Just under the common tools is a link labeled "Get recommendations to make your computer easier to use." This is the official replacement for the Windows XP Accessibility Wizard, and it is meant to help users find the best options to address their physical limitations. Based on the answers given, the Ease of Access Center provides a custom list of recommended accessibility settings. Figure 5-19 shows an example.

Furthermore, you can come back to this questionnaire at any time, adjusting settings along the way or adapting the accessibility options for another user.

Again, administrators might find it more useful to walk a user through the questionnaire, at least for the first time. A blind user, for example, will not be able to see the

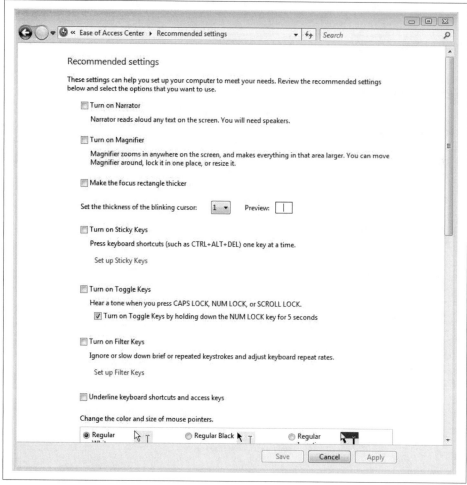

Figure 5-19. The Ease of Access Center can recommend settings for the user

"I am blind" response to the questionnaire's first section. During subsequent questionnaires, however, the Vista Narrator (discussed shortly) will likely be turned on for that user, so she should be able to make adjustments without further administrative help.

Settings checked after the recommendations questionnaire will fall under one of the seven accessibility categories. A few of these merit an additional paragraph or two.

Magnifier. As the name implies, the Magnifier lets users enlarge a section of screen real estate to allow for easier viewing of screen contents. The computing equivalent of large-print books, it's meant for users with poor eyesight.

Users can magnify part of their screen up to 16 times the original size using the option shown in Figure 5-20.

Figure 5-20. Using the Vista Magnifier

You can also set the Magnifier to track the mouse, keyboard, or text editing, and even invert the colors for better screen legibility. By default, whatever the Magnifier is enlarging is located at the top of the screen, but this is configurable as well.

Narrator. The Vista Narrator turns screen text into spoken language, and is ideal for users facing more significant visual impairments. You can listen to an example of the Narrator at work when you open the Ease of Access Center for the first time. As long as the "Always read this section aloud" checkbox is selected, Microsoft Anna (the Narrator) will speak the window contents.

You can toggle the Narrator on or off by choosing the Start Narrator button under the common tools. You can also launch it by following the "Use the computer without a display" link. To configure additional Narrator options, use the checkboxes in the dialog box that follows, shown in Figure 5-21.

The Vista Narrator is improved over Windows XP in a couple of subtle ways: it now can read menus without leaving the active window, and can do so in a more pleasant, natural-sounding voice. You can even speed up or slow down the rate at which Anna reads by clicking the Set up Text to Speech link as you configure the Narrator. Another dialog box opens, letting you tweak this option.

Once enabled, you'll hear "Initializing Narrator," and the Narrator mini-dialog box opens in the lower-righthand corner, as shown in Figure 5-22.

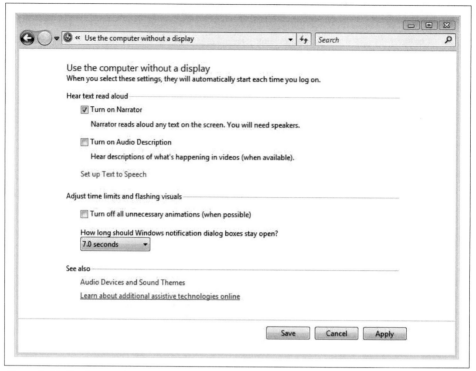

Figure 5-21. Configuring Narrator options

Figure 5-22. Adjusting Narrator preferences

Options here include whether to read aloud keystrokes, system messages, and scroll notifications. Adjust settings as necessary.

On-Screen Keyboard. The On-Screen Keyboard, shown in Figure 5-23, is a virtual keyboard rather than a physical keyboard, and it lets users make selections with a mouse or other pointing device instead of by pressing keys with their fingers.

Figure 5-23. The On-Screen Keyboard

The On-Screen Keyboard provides several additional configuration options, most of which you can access from the Settings menu.

For example, users can hover above a key to select it instead of making a mouse click; this can be especially helpful for users who have difficulty using their fingers. The On-Screen Keyboard can also be useful for kiosk computing situations in which a keyboard might not be attached. Users at the kiosk can use a touch screen or mouse instead.

Other options. For the hearing impaired, one good assistive choice is "alternatives for sounds," which you can find by clicking on the link of the same name in the Ease of Access Center. The sound alternatives can use visual cues to replace Vista system sounds, such as warning notifications. The sound alternatives can also provide captions for any spoken text, as shown in Figure 5-24.

Additionally, Microsoft has worked closely with partners from around the world to ensure that specialized products meet specific assistive needs. These products include voice recognition software, screen readers, screen magnifiers, and on-screen keyboards that have different/additional capabilities than those built into Windows Vista.

As of this writing, more than 300 assistive technology products are compatible with Windows Vista, with improved technologies in continuous development. Administrators looking for more information on assistive technology products can visit *http://www.microsoft.com/enable/at*.

Once here, administrators can search for a specific assistive technology, using either product types or specific products as search criteria. Keep in mind that it is crucial to select products that are compatible with existing software, and that will address specific needs. Obviously, choosing a solution that is incompatible with Vista is of little

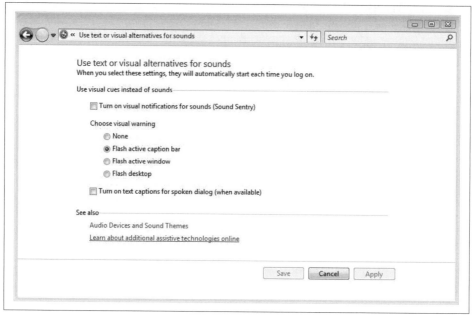

Figure 5-24. You can set alternatives for the Windows sounds

use. Fortunately, though, a link on the righthand side of the Assistive Technology web page takes you to a list of companies that are certified compatible with Windows Vista.

In other words, Microsoft will do what it can to help you find the solution that's right for your enterprise, big or small.

Syncing Devices

A modern computing environment—even for the single user—usually involves data being stored across multiple devices. But the end user wants a single set of working data, not multiple versions of working data on each device or storage location.

Home users, for example, want to hook up a smartphone and keep email, contacts, and maybe even a Word document or two on the phone. They also want to attach removable drives to both expand storage and back up data.

Enterprise users have similar data synchronization needs. They might want to connect their laptops to a personal digital assistant (PDA) to keep sales leads at their fingertips wherever they go. An administrator may have redirected her Documents folder to a network location, and thus is using Offline Files to keep server-based data on her laptop at all times.

But how is all this data synchronized? In the past, each data storage device had a separate synchronization routine. Users were faced with configuring separate sync relationships using separate utilities.

Now, however, Vista offers the Sync Center, shown in Figure 5-25, where you can manage all sync relationships from a central location.

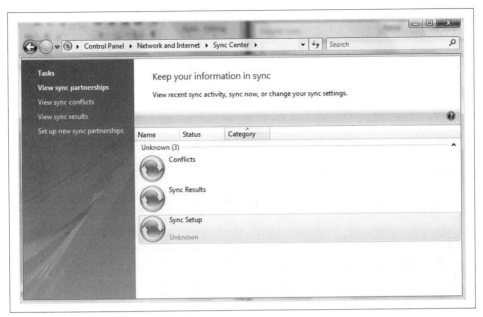

Figure 5-25. The Vista Sync Center

The Sync Center's job is to let users initiate a manual sync, stop a sync that's already in progress (such as when a device is first connected and syncs automatically), view the status of current sync activities, and receive notifications about sync conflicts.

Note that the Sync Center doesn't replace the actual synchronization utilities themselves. Most of the Sync Center's duties are informational.

Offline Files, for instance, still synchronize using the Offline Files mechanism—copies are pulled down from the network share and are stored locally under the Windows directory. If you want to specify which data sets of Outlook are synchronized to your Windows Mobile Device—Contacts, Calendar, and so on—the Sync Center will direct you to the Windows Mobile Device Center. Alternatively, in the case of a partner device, you're steered to a third-party utility (think Palm or BlackBerry devices).

In this way, the Sync Center behaves much as the Windows Security Center; the utility just serves as a dashboard that directs you to the underlying utilities themselves. The Windows Firewall, for example, is a separate application from whatever antivirus program you're using, but the Windows Security Center can provide the status of each and let you launch the Windows Firewall configuration utility.

But this is not always the case, as discussed in the following section.

Setting Up a Partnership with the Sync Center

Under most circumstances, you'll configure your sync relationships elsewhere, and then either view the status or perform manual syncs with the Sync Center.

You can initiate certain kinds of sync relationships using the Sync Center, however. One such relationship is Offline Files.

Here's what to do:

1. Open the Control Panel, and then the Sync Center. If you're using the Standard View, look under the Mobile PC grouping. (You can also use the Vista Mobility Center.)

2. In the list of tasks, click the "Set up new sync partnerships" link.

3. Now you can choose from the list of possible sync relationships. Choose the Offline Files relationship.

4. A Setup button appears above the list. Click it and a dialog box appears, providing instructions on how to establish the Offline Files partnership, as shown in Figure 5-26.

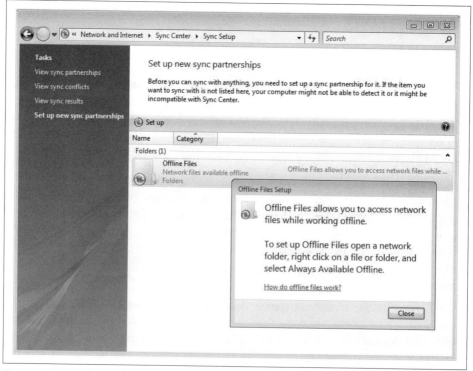

Figure 5-26. One method of setting up a sync partnership

Follow the instructions here to complete the sync relationship.

Using Bluetooth Devices

Bluetooth is a wireless specification for personal area networks (PANs) that provides a way to exchange information among a variety of devices: PCs, keyboards, mice, PDAs, printers, and video game consoles. Most famously, Bluetooth is used in mobile phones to send voice digitally between handset and headset.

Because it's a wireless specification, it's sometimes easy to confuse Bluetooth with IEEE 801.11 wireless networks, otherwise known as Wi-Fi. The way I like to think of it is that Wi-Fi is an *Ethernet* replacement technology (I know this is not *technically* correct; they are Ethernet packets, after all), whereas Bluetooth is a *cable* replacement technology.

Another way to think about it is in terms of power and devices. Wi-Fi connects only Ethernet network devices—NICs to wireless routers. But it does so using relatively high power, so Wi-Fi cards can maintain communication over rather large distances. 801.11g networks can work in ranges of 100 feet or more. 802.11n networks can project a signal nearly twice that far.

Bluetooth is also a wireless specification defined by the IEEE—802.15. In terms of devices, Bluetooth supports a much wider variety: printers, cameras, phones, and so on, as mentioned before. Another big difference is in power consumption, and therefore, range. Bluetooth is generally meant for devices that are relatively close together, with most devices having a range of 10 meters and consuming only 2.5 milliwatts of power, although recent Bluetooth classifications—which consume *a lot* more power—have extended this to 100 meters.

Windows Vista supports Bluetooth technology natively. Setting up a connection involves three basic steps, as follows:

1. Add a Bluetooth adapter to your computer.

   Many of today's computers come with Bluetooth adapters built in. This is especially true on laptop computers, where both Wi-Fi cards and Bluetooth adapters are being built into the chipset. Otherwise, the physical connection between a Bluetooth adapter and a computer is a USB port. The drivers for most Bluetooth adapters should install automatically.

2. Configure the device so that your system can locate it. This in turn involves two relatively elementary steps:

   a. Turn on the device.

   b. Make it discoverable. This usually involves just a single click of a checkbox, typically done during installation time. Check the manufacturer's documentation for exact instructions on how to make a device discoverable.

3. Finally, install the device using Windows Vista. For most devices, you can use the Bluetooth Devices applet in the Control Panel. You'll take these two steps:

   a. From the Control Panel's Classic View, choose the Hardware and Sound grouping, and then click Bluetooth Devices.

   b. As seen in Figure 5-27, click Add, and then follow the instructions in the setup wizard.

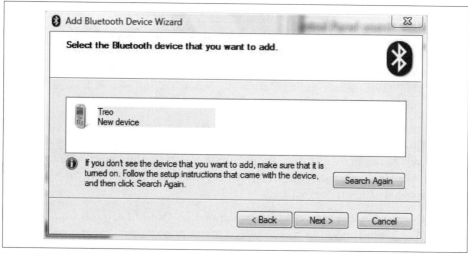

Figure 5-27. Establishing communication for a new Bluetooth device

A discoverable Bluetooth device sends out radio signals to advertise its location to other devices and computers.

 You won't see a Bluetooth Devices applet in the Control Panel unless you've first added a Bluetooth adapter to your computer.

Bluetooth and the Passkey

Some Bluetooth devices require a passkey in order to facilitate communication. Think of a passkey as a password or PIN that isolates communication only to passkey holders, and not to other Bluetooth devices that happen to be in range.

It can be very wise administration—both for individual users and for those who implement Bluetooth devices within an enterprise—to configure passkeys. Such passkeys enable "pairing" of Bluetooth devices, and the devices can even exchange encrypted data from there.

A passkey need not be entered every time initial communication is established. And because the Bluetooth address is permanent, the pair is preserved even if the device's name changes. The pair can be deleted, however, at any time and at either device.

 So what's with that Bluetooth logo? It's actually a merge of the Nordic runes for H and B, which stands for Harald Bluetooth, who as everyone knows was the king of both Norway and Denmark during the 900s, known for bringing together Danish tribes that had a history of fighting with each other. He was able to do this in large part thanks to his innovative invention, the Palm Treo 700. (I'll have to double-check the historical accuracy of that last part.)

Surfing the Net Using a Bluetooth Phone

If one tip by itself might be worth the price of this (very reasonably priced) book, it's this: most times, you can use a Bluetooth-enabled phone as a means of connecting to the Internet. If the phone can be used as a modem, chances are that it can also be used to provide Internet access for your Vista laptop (desktops as well, but this will more commonly be used for laptops).

Just follow these steps to get started:

1. Open the Network and Sharing Center from the Control Panel and choose the "Connect to a network" task in the Tasks list.

2. In the Connect to a Network Wizard, choose Connect to the Internet and then click Next.

3. You may already be told that you have an active Internet connection (especially true on a laptop where a wireless connection has been previously set up). Click the "Set up a new connection anyway" option.

4. On the next screen, shown in Figure 5-28, choose the Dial-up option, and then follow the steps in the wizard. The crucial step here is that you select the Bluetooth-enabled phone as the dial-up modem.

5. On the "Type the information from your Internet service provider (ISP)" page, in "Dial-up phone number," type the carrier code or phone number.

You may need to then contact your mobile carrier for the required username, password, and carrier code credentials.

Troubleshooting a Bluetooth connection

Bluetooth devices don't always set up the way you envisioned. Bluetooth issues can have several causes, although the good news is that troubleshooting usually requires only a few relatively simple procedures.

The subsections that follow outline a few things to look for.

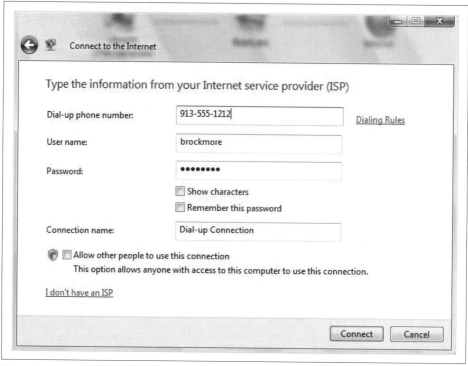

Figure 5-28. Choose the Bluetooth-enabled phone as the Internet connection

Remove and reinstall. This sounds like just unplugging and plugging in again, but in practice it involves removing the software rather than just the device itself. Here's what to do:

1. Turn off the Bluetooth device or make it undiscoverable using the manufacturer's instructions. Usually, there's just a button to push or a checkbox to unclick.

2. Open the Control Panel and look for the Bluetooth Devices applet.

3. Choose the Bluetooth device that's not working, and click Remove.

4. Now choose Add, and re-enable the Bluetooth device. Select the "My device is set up and ready to be found" checkbox, as shown in Figure 5-29, and then click Next.

5. Once Vista discovers the device, select it and click Next.

6. Complete the instructions in the wizard to finish setting up the device. If the device is discovered and installed, it should now work.

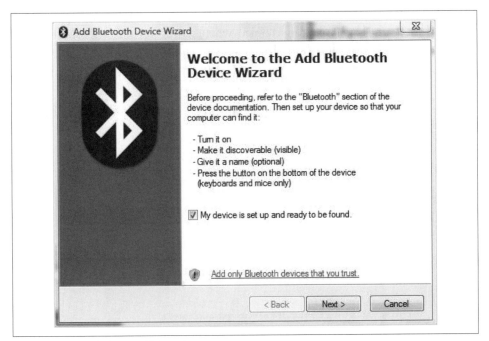

Figure 5-29. Ready for install (again)

As Bluetooth devices require power to send and receive communications, they also require a power source. When troubleshooting, don't overlook the fact that the device needs to be turned on and have batteries with a charge.

Ensure proper device communication. As mentioned in this section's introduction, a Bluetooth device has a finite range, usually around 10 meters. If the devices are farther apart than this, naturally communication can be affected.

Another thing to check is whether the Bluetooth device is already hosting connections. Most devices can support only a set number of simultaneous connections, and cannot communicate when they are too busy servicing other communication sessions. To alleviate this, you could try one of two things:

- Wait for the device to become less busy, and then try the communication again.
- Configure some of the devices so that they are not discoverable. A discoverable Bluetooth device can start "chatting" with others in the area without your knowledge.

If you've configured a paired connection, make sure you are using the correct passkey, and entering the passkey within the time limit (if applicable).

You should also ensure that Vista has been configured to *accept* incoming Bluetooth connections. It should have been enabled when setting up the Bluetooth-enabled adapter, but it may have since been disabled. Here's how to check:

1. Open the Control Panel, and locate the Bluetooth Devices applet. Look under the Printers and Other Hardware grouping if you get lost.

2. As seen in Figure 5-30, choose the Options tab, and select the "Allow Bluetooth devices to connect to this computer" checkbox.

3. Click OK to commit the changes.

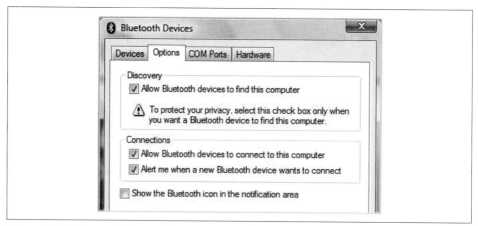

Figure 5-30. Make sure Vista is allowing incoming Bluetooth connections

Ensure proper Bluetooth device location. As a final troubleshooting note, know that Bluetooth technology uses radio frequencies to communicate. And so do a lot of other things in your house or office. Microwaves, remote controls, cordless phones, Wi-Fi networks, and even lighting can interfere with the Bluetooth signal. And to make matters worse, Bluetooth uses relatively little power to get its signal through the surrounding noise.

The solution doesn't require a lot of computer know-how, but rather what many call "the sense God gave a horse." If you suspect interference with Bluetooth communication, try moving the nonworking device to a better location.

Summary

This chapter was an exploration of tools and technologies that make Windows Vista easier to use. Such technologies include handwriting, voice recognition, and accessibility capabilities. Not only did we examine each of these technologies in detail, but we also looked at how we can configure these technologies to best meet our usability needs. As you've seen, Vista includes some powerful tools that administrators can use to allow for computer use for a variety of users: some with limited physical capabilities, and some who just want to dictate rather than type.

We also looked at the Vista Sync Center, and how we can use it to set up and manage sync relationships between devices that store our working data. One such device could be a Bluetooth-enabled smartphone, of course, so it made sense to include a section about how to set up and configure a Bluetooth connection. You even saw how you might be able to use that smartphone as a backup (or primary) Internet connection for your Vista system.

In the next chapter, we'll look at how to govern Vista's startup, shutdown, and power-management behaviors.

CHAPTER 6

Vista Startup and Shutdown

Starting up and shutting down. Sounds fairly elementary, right? How can an entire chapter be devoted to the topic? Well, to answer the first question, these actions can be elementary, and the typical user generally doesn't have to give them much thought. But typical users don't pick up 800-page books, and users such as yourself know that a lot occurs at startup and shutdown that can have a huge impact on the computing environment. This chapter is for you.

In it, we'll look at what happens during normal startup and shutdown, and then at some ways you can dictate exactly what occurs. Throughout, we'll keep an eye out for tools and methodologies we can use to improve Vista's startup and shutdown performance.

Controlling startup can also be a very valuable troubleshooting aid, so we'll look at some of the steps and tools that can help you isolate a problem.

And because the main focus of this chapter is on Vista performance (at least during startup and shutdown), I figure it's probably a good idea to begin with a discussion of how Vista's performance is *rated* starting right from the time Vista first starts up. The performance rating is given using a new—oh, what is it, exactly?—I guess we'll go with *technology*, called the Windows Experience Index.

It's a discussion that could fit just about anywhere in this book; it works here just as well as in any other chapter. As the chapter starts, we'll examine how the Windows Experience Index might impact purchasing and configuration decisions, and we'll look at how we might improve this rating.

Your Computer's Performance Rating

While we're on the topic of computer performance, we'd better start with a look at your computer's overall performance *score*. You read that correctly: Vista has introduced the Windows Experience Index (WEI), ostensibly to help you gauge your system's performance capabilities.

The WEI assigns a numeric score to each of five different computing subsystems:

- Processor
- Memory (RAM only; we'll discuss why I even bring this up later in the chapter)
- Graphics
- Gaming graphics (i.e., the 3D capabilities)
- Primary hard disk

Windows Vista then takes all of the scores and comes up with your system's *base score*, which is kind of a least common denominator for the performance of your computer. How so? Because Vista takes the lowest subsystem score and uses this to set your computer's overall WEI score. If your processor rates a 3.7, for example, and your gaming graphics subsystem ranks a 1, your computer's overall, or base, score will be a 1. In fact, you might see exactly this score if you open the Performance Information and Tools applet from the Control Panel, as shown in Figure 6-1.

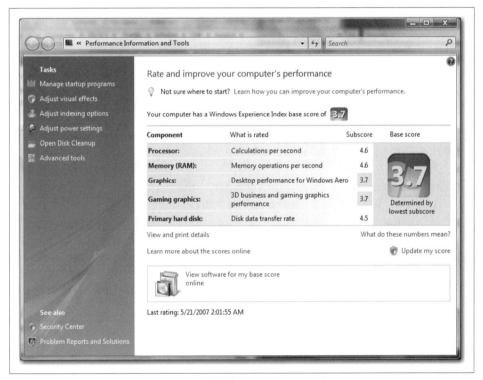

Figure 6-1. Vista assigns your computer a Windows Experience Index score

Look under the System and Maintenance grouping if you're using the Control Panel's Standard View. And remember that you can always type **perf** at the Start menu to bring it right up.

So a score for every component. I get it. Something like the star rating for movies: one star equals bad, four stars equals good. Or something like that, right? Maybe a scale between 1 and 10?

Ha. If only it were that simple. Here's how the rating system actually works: each component gets a ranking from 1 to—get this—5.9, and best of British luck figuring out why. The official reason for now is that no hardware is capable of rating a 6, but that might not be the case in the future. If Moore's Law is any predictor, you should see machines that rate a 6 sometime in the summer of 2007. (Such discussion tempts me to craft some kind of "turn it to 11" witticism/nod to Spinal Tap and Nigel Tufnel, but I'll instead leave that to your vastly superior creative abilities.*)

So, what exactly does the base score mean? Well, on the system I'm currently using, it means I can run Vista, but that's about it. No Aero, just the Windows Vista basic user interface, thank you very much, and I shouldn't even *think* about multiplayer online gaming for a while, either (don't worry, I never will).

Here are a few of the capabilities of your computer based on the WEI score:

1 or 2

This indicates a computer that can handle general computing tasks. It can handle running Microsoft Office and most other line-of-business applications, can participate in a domain, and can search the Internet with aplomb. A computer with a base score of 1 or 2 won't be powerful enough to run Windows Aero, however, nor will it have horsepower to tackle some of the more advanced multimedia experiences. If you're running a system with the Windows Vista Home Basic edition, this is all the performance you need.

3

This is a run-of-the-mill score for a computer running Windows Vista, and most significantly indicates that the computer will be capable of using the Windows Aero interface. Further, it should also be capable of handling some advanced features, although there's a chance that these features will run with a reduced level of functionality. For example, if you've purchased Vista Home Premium mainly because you want to record and play back television content, be aware that a machine with an overall rating of 3 might struggle with the playback of high-definition content.

---

* And I will write a check for $10 to the first person who can actually work that into a witticism; $20 if you can fit in a reference to "Hark, Beowulf: A Fusion Opera," which as everyone knows was Derek Smalls' reworking of the epic poem about the great hero who slew Grendel. For winner information, go to *http://www.brianculp.com*.

4 or 5

These are the tricked-out bad boys you want to show off to your neighbors. A Vista system with an assigned base score of either 4 or 5 should be capable of handling all Windows Vista features with full functionality. A score of 5, for example, means that the system will be capable of running the Vista Aero interface on multiple monitors without any performance snags. It will be capable of high-end graphics-intensive work such as digital video editing, multiplayer 3D gaming, and recording/playback of HDTV content.

Note that just because your system starts with a given WEI score doesn't mean it's stuck with that score forever. If your gaming graphics score is a 1, for example, you can improve it in one of two ways:

- Update the driver.
- Get a new video card.

Once you've improved the new subsystem, visit the Performance Information and Tools Control Panel applet once again. Then, under the base score rating, click the "Update my score" link, as shown in Figure 6-2. You'll be prompted by User Account Control for permission to continue, and then Vista will scan your system and update the WEI score if necessary.

Figure 6-2. Updating the WEI score

 You never have to update your computer's WEI. The WEI rating is generated during Vista installation, and is there for your information only. You can still gain the benefit of an upgraded component without updating the WEI.

Keep in mind, however, that the score is determined by the lowest subsystem score. Using the graphics card example from earlier, upgrading the system memory so that it reads a 5 won't improve the overall score. The only way to boost Vista's base score in this case would be to upgrade the graphics card.

How Does the Windows Experience Index Score Help?

You've learned so far about the new WEI, and how it can give you feedback about the performance of your Vista machine. But just how do you put this information to use?

A good question. Supposedly, this WEI information comes into play when evaluating and purchasing new PCs. It all comes down to an attempt to simplify the labeling system now in use for hardware components and software applications; it's supposed to help the average consumer make sense out of product description lists full of MHz, MB, and other acronyms. Now, consumers are presumably able to look at the side of the software box, and instead of cogitating on something like this:

Minimum requirements:

1.2 GHz Pentium 4 microprocessor

512 MB of RAM

DirectX 9.0 or higher

Etc.

they will be able to look for a single value, for a label that will look more like this:

Minimum requirements:

WEI: 4

I think it's a great idea.

How practical is this on the retail shelves? Who knows? I have yet to see any hardware manufacturer tout its laptop's overall score when selling (or even custom-building) a system, nor have I seen any software boxes utilizing the WEI. But it's still early.

WEI and Software

Another way the WEI helps is that it can aid in matching application software and options to best suit your computer's performance. When buying software, knowing your PC base score is very useful. Microsoft is currently working with software vendors to use the base score and subscores for recommended system requirements rather than the aforementioned big, hairy list of component requirements.

Consumers should end up with software packaging whose labels are a lot more consumer-palatable, such as the example shown in Figure 6-3.

Software vendors are now supposed to publish this recommended information, letting consumers know at a glance whether their systems will be capable of effectively running the application.

In fact, Vista includes just such an example of how this process works. To see what I mean, open the Games Explorer by typing **game** at the Vista Start menu. You'll see a dialog box that displays all the games installed on your system. A WEI score should also appear for each game.

Simply choose one of the games—*FreeCell*, for example—and you'll see a WEI rating for the game in the Games Explorer's right pane, as shown in Figure 6-4.

The recommended minimum rating for the game is a WEI of 2. My (current) system is rated a 1. So will the game run? Yes, because right below the game's *recommended* minimum is the *required* minimum.

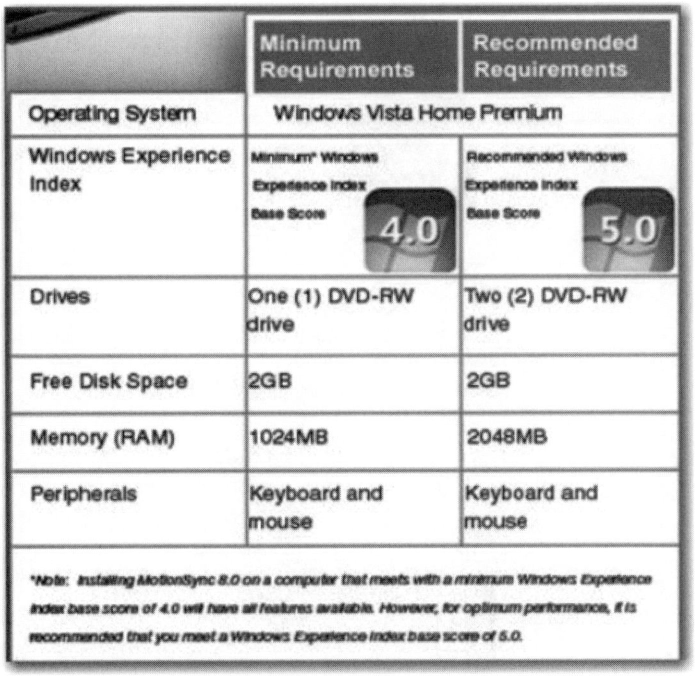

	Minimum Requirements	Recommended Requirements
Operating System	Windows Vista Home Premium	
Windows Experience Index	Minimum Windows Experience Index Base Score **4.0**	Recommended Windows Experience Index Base Score **5.0**
Drives	One (1) DVD-RW drive	Two (2) DVD-RW drive
Free Disk Space	2GB	2GB
Memory (RAM)	1024MB	2048MB
Peripherals	Keyboard and mouse	Keyboard and mouse

Note: Installing MotionSync 8.0 on a computer that meets with a minimum Windows Experience Index base score of 4.0 will have all features available. However, for optimum performance, it is recommended that you meet a Windows Experience Index base score of 5.0.

Figure 6-3. A possible WEI-equipped software label

So, if I've got a Vista machine that's not exactly setting new performance benchmarks, where should I begin the upgrade process? I want to play *FreeCell* the way it was *intended* to be played.

The answer, of course, is "it depends." Again, the WEI score comes in handy in helping you make the upgrade that will most improve performance. Beyond that, however, you need to have a general understanding of which computer subsystem has the biggest *impact* on what you want the computer to do. The following matrix should help:

Office productivity

If you use your computer almost exclusively for email, word processing, surfing the Net, spreadsheets, and so forth—what is generally called office productivity—you want high subscores in the CPU and memory categories. Subscores of 2 or higher are usually sufficient in the hard disk, desktop graphics, and gaming graphics categories.

Gaming and graphic-intensive programs such as video editing, 3D animation, and computer-aided design (CAD)

If you use your computer for applications that demand a lot of your computer's video rendering capabilities—think *Halo*, or *Half Life*, or Adobe Premiere—high scores in the RAM, desktop graphics, and gaming graphics categories are what you want. Subscores of 3 or higher are usually sufficient in the CPU and hard disk categories.

Figure 6-4. The Vista Games Explorer

Media Center

If you intend for Vista to serve as a home entertainment hub—recording television, playing HD movies, and such—maximize your system's subscores in the CPU, hard disk, and desktop graphics departments. The hard disk is especially a premium component here, as it stores all the content you watch, and not much of that content is going to be stored in system memory. Subscores of 3 or higher are usually sufficient in the memory and 3D graphics categories.

All of these performance subsystems also play a role in how fast your Vista computer starts up. System startup is something we take for granted, but as with so many other performance areas, it is something that savvy administrators can control and improve.

The next section starts the examination of this process.

System Power Up

Because this chapter deals mostly with improving startup and shutdown performance, it's a good idea to start with an overview of these processes. This section doesn't include many click-steps, but it will give you some good background information, and it will help to provide the answer to a fundamental question: exactly what happens under the lid of my computer when I press that Start button?

System power up is more commonly referred to as *boot up*, a phrase that refers to the computer supposedly picking itself up from its bootstraps without much help from any outside source. In reality, though, hundreds of programmers have contributed thousands of lines of code so that computers can be personified in such a manner. At its core, a computer's system startup (or restart, for that matter) involves a very simple core objective: it must load the operating system.

How this objective is carried out varies from machine to machine, and can depend on factors such as whether the system is booted from a disk drive, a network, or some other source. For illustration purposes, let's look at the most common startup scenario: a PC/AT computer booting from the files stored on its hard drive. Here's the usual sequence of events:

1. The computer's Basic Input/Output System (BIOS) software, which is stored within the chipset of the system's motherboard, reads something called the Master Boot Record (MBR).

2. The BIOS hands control of the boot-up process to the MBR code.

3. The MBR transfers control to the code that is responsible for loading the rest of the operating system. In previous versions of Windows, that code was a little program called Ntldr.

4. The Ntldr program doesn't work alone. Among other things, it calls a simple little text file called *boot.ini*, which helps to steer Ntldr to the operating system installation directory. It also displays a list of possible operating systems to the user on a dual-boot machine (technically, however, *boot.ini* doesn't display anything; Ntldr displays *boot.ini*'s *contents* in a boot-up screen).

5. Ntldr then begins initialization of the operating system files based on where *boot.ini* indicated that these were stored, and does so according to potential boot options configured in *boot.ini*.

So, like I said earlier, it's *really* simple.

 The generic term *PC/AT* refers to a computer motherboard and power supply standard that's been in use since IBM released its second-generation PC (IBM tried, unsuccessfully, to trademark the name). It now describes just about every desktop computer utilizing an x286 or faster processor, and it describes the ATX motherboard/power supply specification, released by Intel and in much more common use today.

Although PC/AT machines are much, much more common today, another firmware standard may become the norm over the next 10 years. It's called the Extensible Firmware Interface (EFI) standard, and its boot process is quite different from the process just described. For instance, the EFI boot process does not use the *boot.ini* file at all, but rather a set of boot configuration options that are stored in the chipset's Non-Volatile RAM (NVRAM). It's expected that the EFI will replace traditional BIOS in the coming decade.

What's New with Vista Startup

At any rate, the Windows Vista startup process is new and improved, different even on systems that use BIOS (i.e., most of them) today. It introduces a technology called boot configuration data (BCD), which essentially replaces the function of the *boot.ini* file.

Here's the big difference: the BCD abstracts the underlying firmware and provides a common programming interface to manipulate the boot environment for all Windows-supported computer platforms. Further, the BCD supports both PC/AT BIOS and EFI systems, making it well positioned to be used on a wide variety of platforms at present and into the foreseeable future.

But, the BCD interface is also *extensible*, giving it the capability to support other types of firmware in addition to the two discussed here.

Moreover, several new boot applications are included with Windows Vista. They include the following:

Bootmgr
> Most closely analogous to Ntldr, bootmgr controls the overall boot process. On a dual-boot machine, it is now bootmgr's job to display the list of possible operating systems to the user.

Winload.exe
> This performs the chore of actually loading the Vista operating system—loading the Vista kernel, the hardware abstraction layer (HAL), and the boot drivers into memory. If more than one instance of Vista is installed (or Vista and Server Longhorn, for that matter), each instance gets its own winload.exe program. The operating system loader creates the execution environment for the operating system and loads the OS files into memory.

Winresume.exe
> The Vista resume loader program does for restores what winload.exe does for system startups. Its job is to return Vista to a running state when a computer resumes from hibernation.

And what happened to the venerable Ntldr, you ask? It is still used on systems that load from BIOS and need to dual-boot into an earlier version of Windows. The older operating systems cannot take advantage of Vista's new boot-up technologies.

On a dual-boot machine running an older version of Windows, the BCD is used to describe Ntldr and the boot process for loading previous versions of Windows, but these operating systems are ultimately loaded by Ntldr and therefore must still use the *boot.ini* file to store boot options.

 If you're configuring a dual-boot machine with an earlier version of Windows, install the earlier version before installing Windows Vista. If you don't, the older operating system will not recognize Vista as one of the available boot options.

Startup and the BCD

As I've mentioned, the BCD provides a mechanism for changing the boot environment that is independent of platform, and is now used by Vista to perform two key tasks:

- Loading the operating system
- Running boot applications used for diagnosis and troubleshooting

For example, when you run the Memory Diagnostics tool (type **mem** from the Start menu; Memory Diagnostics should appear in the list of programs), as shown in Figure 6-5, you're calling on the BCD to hand off the startup procedure to the Windows Memory Diagnostics tool.

Figure 6-5. The Windows Memory Diagnostics tool runs during startup—before Vista loads, in fact

As you can see, running Windows Memory Diagnostics requires a reboot. Clicking either of the options here *extends* the normal function of the BCD; it causes the BCD to call for an application. Only after the application finishes its work does the BCD load the Vista operating system files.

 When running a diagnostics tool such as Memory Diagnostics, you're prompted for elevated credentials if you're not logged on as an admin. Manipulating the BCD requires elevated permissions.

Later versions of Windows, including Windows Server Codename Longhorn, will also use the BCD to perform these tasks.

Modifying the BCD

So, if the BCD is extensible, exactly how can administrators extend it? Essentially, there are two thoroughfares for modifying settings contained in the BCD:

- Use one of several tools provided by Windows Vista. The Memory Diagnostics tool is one such example. Precisely what gets modified in the BCD depends on the tool used.

- Write a change manually with the BCD Windows Management Instrumentation (WMI) provider. The WMI provider is a unified programming interface that you can use for both local and remote management of BCD stores. Developers can use this technique to change the BCD manually, and because the WMI is independent of the underlying firmware, one application can be used on a wide variety of systems.

Because this book assumes that you're not a developer, we won't spend any time on WMI programming. Instead, we'll focus on three main tools that the average administrator has at his disposal to change the BCD information.

BCD Editor #1: The System applet in the Control Panel. In the Control Panel lives the System applet, which you can find as its own applet using the Classic View; otherwise, look under the System and Maintenance grouping. You also can launch this configuration dialog box by right-clicking on the computer icon/button on either the desktop or the Start menu. However you get there, it looks like what you see in Figure 6-6.

You can locate the BCD control by choosing the "Advanced system settings" link, which launches a System Properties dialog box. You will be asked for permission to continue if User Account Control is on.

Now, select the Advanced tab and then click the Settings button under the Startup and Recovery section. You'll see a Startup and Recovery dialog box as shown in Figure 6-7.

There are two global BCD elements for which you can configure the value in this dialog box:

- The default operating system and configuration
- The boot manager's timeout setting

BCD Editor #2: The System Configuration utility (Msconfig). Per Microsoft, msconfig.exe is *primarily* used by its own product support service (PSS) department for handling troubleshooting calls. But we know better, don't we? We know (at least now we do) that it represents another way to manipulate BCD settings without having to write code.

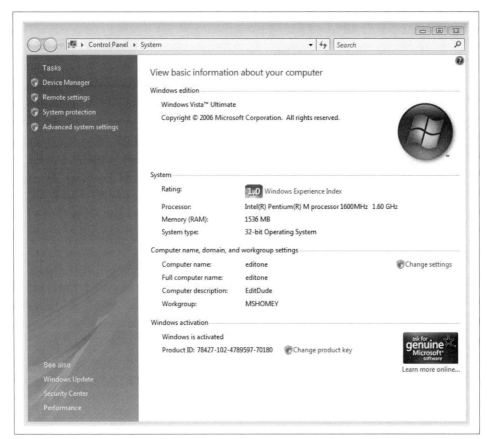

Figure 6-6. The System applet

To launch the System Configuration utility, open the Start menu and type **msconfig**. The executable should appear at the top of the Programs list. You will be asked for permission to continue if User Account Control is on.

There are several tabs in the System Configuration utility. To change the BCD, however, concentrate on the Boot tab, as shown in Figure 6-8.

You can use the Boot tab to change the boot loader display (if applicable) and the Safe Mode options. Advanced options let you configure how many processors are recognized by Vista at boot-up time, and configure where to send debugging information.

We will discuss the System Configuration utility in further detail later in this chapter.

BCD Editor #3: The BCDEdit utility. The third way to edit BCD information that's within reach of administrators is the BCDEdit command-line tool. This is an advanced tool, however, and is most often used by support professionals and developers. BCDEdit serves essentially the same purpose as Bootcfg.exe on earlier versions of Windows.

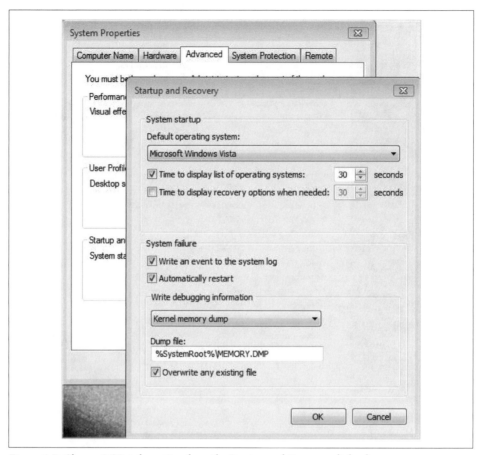

Figure 6-7. Change BCD information from the Startup and Recovery dialog box

Bootcfg is still available on Windows Vista, but you can use it only to edit boot information on previous versions of Windows on a dual-boot machine. It will have no functionality on a Vista-only computer. Only BCDEdit can directly edit the BCD for Vista and later versions.

There have been two main enhancements of BCDEdit over Bootcfg.exe:

- BCDEdit exposes a wider range of boot options than Bootcfg.exe.
- BCDEdit has improved scripting support.

The command-line utility is designed primarily to perform single changes to BCD information. For example, it can quickly add a new boot menu option, create a new BCD store, or modify an existing store. For more complex operations, administrators should consider using the BCD WMI interface to create customized startup tools.

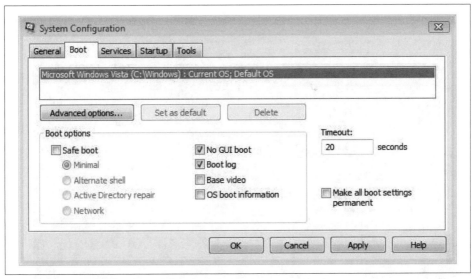

Figure 6-8. Alter the BCD with the Boot tab options

As with changing the BCD using the Msconfig and System Properties tools, you need administrative privileges to use BCDEdit.

The basic syntax for BCDEdit is as follows:

```
BCDEdit /Command [Argument1] [Argument2] ...
```

You can also get help on proper usage of BCDEdit by typing:

```
bcdedit /?
```

at the command prompt. You'll get an extensive set of usage notes, as shown in Figure 6-9.

The BCD's data is stored in a registry hive, but Microsoft strongly recommends that you do *not* edit that data store with the Registry Editor, regedit.exe. Interaction with the underlying firmware occurs in the supported BCD interfaces.

For more information about the BCDEdit utility, go to *http://www.microsoft.com* and search for "bcdedit faq." A page enumerating BCDEdit capabilities should appear at the top of the search results.

Now that we have a little background about the Vista startup procedure, we're about ready to get down to business. As administrators, we want to ensure a reliable startup procedure. More than that, though, we want users to have access to their desktops as quickly as possible. Governing startup performance, therefore, becomes a top priority.

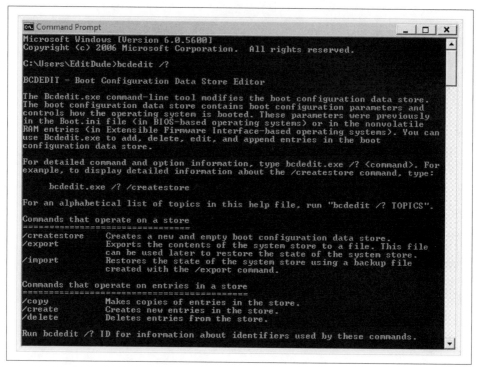

Figure 6-9. Using the BCDEdit utility

Startup Performance

The problem is familiar: you push the power button on your computer and you wait. You shut down the computer and you wait. Developers walking the hallowed halls of Microsoft's Redmond campus have computers, too, and they don't like waiting for startup and shutdown any more than you or I do.

The difference between you and the developers at Microsoft, of course, is that they get to try to do something about it, and the product of their labor should be apparent every time you press the on and off buttons.

Not only does Windows Vista makes system startup and shutdown a speedier process (at least by design; whether you actually experience this improvement can depend on multiple factors, some of them subjective), there are even some new technologies that will help speed things up quite dramatically when putting the computer to "sleep."

During normal usage, users should have to reboot their systems only once in a while. And even when users have to perform a "cold boot," Vista handles most of the system initialization chores—loading startup services, programs, and so forth—in the background, providing users with a working desktop faster than ever before.

Startup Performance and Memory

Quick introductory anecdote (I don't do many of these; indulge me): I used to teach an MCSE class (this would have been the NT4 track, back in the 1970s), and I had a student who absorbed lesson after lesson about domains, about TCP/IP, about configuring one-way trust relationships, and the like. He summarized each day's lessons about configuring/tweaking/controlling the admittedly Byzantine Windows NT4 administrative environment thusly: "So…just add more memory, then."

As you can no doubt imagine, it got funnier with each repetition—except the thing was that for the most part, he was correct. What's more, that's still pretty much the case. Adding system memory remains the most surefire way to improve performance. Why? Because to an operating system or a program running on that operating system, memory is nothing more than a bunch of addresses. Programs then use these addresses to store data. But the programs don't have any way of knowing the physical location of these addresses. The programs ask for space, and the operating system allocates this space.

Further, these addresses can exist in one of two storage locations: the RAM or the hard drive. When they're on the hard drive, it's known as *virtual memory*, because physical RAM has been virtualized in hard disk storage.

The problem with virtual memory, of course, is that hard drives are slow—obscenely so, even—when compared to physical RAM. The more physical RAM you have, the more information that is readily available for the processor to process. But upgrading memory can be difficult, costly, impossible, or some combination of all three. What's more, some machines have limited memory expansion capabilities. In many laptops, for example, there's only a single expansion slot.

But you know this already. The good news is that Windows Vista lets you address this in an exciting new way.

Windows ReadyBoost

One of the really cool things about Windows Vista is how easy it can be to add memory. That's because you don't even have to "crack the case" to add RAM. How's that? A technology called Windows ReadyBoost makes it possible to take a flash drive—yeah, like the one around your neck and/or on your keychain right now—and use it as Vista system RAM.

Told you it was cool.

ReadyBoost allows a flash memory device—aka a thumb drive—to serve as additional space for memory addresses. It's not quite as fast as system RAM, mind you, but it's a lot better than the hard drive. Windows ReadyBoost relies on the intelligent memory management of Windows SuperFetch and can significantly improve system responsiveness.

Oh, and it can also work with Secure Digital (SD) memory cards as well. Many of today's laptops come with SD ports built in.

 Almost any drive can be used with Windows Vista for storage, but not every flash drive works with ReadyBoost. Certain performance requirements must be met for Vista to be able to use the device as memory. Look for an "Enhanced for Windows ReadyBoost" tag when you're looking for a flash drive to ensure its use for this purpose.

Using ReadyBoost

Here's how ReadyBoost works. Insert the memory device of choice—again, a USB flash drive or an SD memory card will work—into the appropriate port. Vista will now run a check to see whether its performance is fast enough to work with Windows ReadyBoost.

If the device is a match, you are asked whether you want to use this device to speed up system performance, as shown in Figure 6-10.

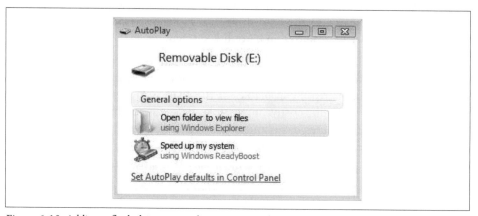

Figure 6-10. Adding a flash drive to speed up system performance

 I've heard anecdotes about folks who have tried this step and have received a dialog box stating that the memory stick was not capable of being used as memory. They then retested and were able to use the device as RAM. Could just be one of those quirks. If this has happened to you, report your experience at *http://www.brianculp.com*.

Following are some common questions about the use of ReadyBoost.

What if I've already got files on the flash drive? That's fine. You don't have to use the entire thing. If you've got a 4 GB jump drive that you use as a backup device and a laptop with 512 MB of RAM, you can easily allocate just a gigabyte or two from your jump drive for ReadyBoost memory and leave the remainder for file storage.

Note that in the preceding figure, you can configure device usage with the sliding scale in the middle of the Memory tab.

What happens if I yank out the flash drive in the middle of doing something? Will I lose information? Will my computer crash? In brief, nothing will happen. ReadyBoost technology is durable, meaning that you can remove the memory device at any time without loss of data or any other negative impact to system stability. The Vista memory manager detects when the flash drive is removed, and it turns things over to the hard drive. No user action is required.

The only caveat here is that you lose the performance-boosting capability of the flash drive. When memory is stored on the hard drive, system performance will suffer as a result.

I work on confidential files on my laptop. What happens if I lose the USB drive? Is the data secure? (and go back and change "if" to "when," if you could). Yes, people lose USB keys. Don't worry: the data stored by ReadyBoost on the flash device is encrypted. A stolen USB key will reveal no company secrets; at least none that were part of virtual memory. Any other files stored on the drive are fair game.

How long will the USB drive last when I start using it as memory, especially seeing how that data stays on the drive, just like all the other files I've got stored on that thing? The Vista memory manager uses an algorithm to optimize wear patterns so that the USB device can be used to enhance performance for many years, even when used heavily.

In fact, here's what Microsoft's operating system president, Jim Allchin, has to say on the entire matter, pretty much neatly summarizing my preceding Q & A section. From an entry on the Microsoft Windows Vista team blog:

> I should be clear that while flash drives do contain memory, Windows ReadyBoost isn't really using that memory to increase the main system RAM in your computer. Instead, ReadyBoost uses the flash drive to store information that is being used by the memory manager. If you are running a lot of applications on a system that has limited memory, Windows ReadyBoost will use the flash drive to create a copy of virtual memory that is not quite as fast as RAM, but a whole lot faster than going to the hard disk. What is very cool here is that there is nothing stored on this flash disk that isn't also on the hard disk, so if you remove the flash drive, the memory manager sees the change and automatically goes to the hard disk. While the performance gain from ReadyBoost is gone, you don't lose any data and there is no interruption. And because the Windows ReadyBoost cache on the flash drive is encrypted using AES-128, you don't need to worry about exposing sensitive data if the flash drive is stolen or lost. Also, the memory manager compresses the pages before writing them into the cache on the flash disk, which means you'll get more mileage from each MB.

See? Even Allchin thinks it's cool.

And even if you don't use the new ReadyBoost technology, Vista also includes a new way to improve the performance of that good old standby, the system RAM. It's called SuperFetch, and it's discussed in the following section.

Windows SuperFetch

Here's the issue: you boot up your computer first thing in the morning, and programs work fine. System response is snappy, and you're cruising through your day's work.

Then it's lunchtime, and when you get back to your desk, it's as though your computer spent the lunch hour gorging on turkey sandwiches just as you have. Programs are slow; you click and it takes several seconds for the menu to appear. So, what's the deal?

The problem lies in the way memory is managed—a problem that has, for the most part, been largely addressed by Windows Vista. Vista now includes a new memory management technology called SuperFetch, which helps the system to use physical RAM more efficiently. Essentially, it all comes down to math.

To wit: most existing memory management schemes utilize an algorithm known as Most Recently Used (MRU). The MRU memory management technique dictates that the content last accessed remains in RAM until it's replaced by something else. The problem with MRU is that when users leave their machines for an extended period of time—say, 15 minutes or more—background applications often use this as a chance to execute actions such as indexing, virus scans, or system management.

Under the MRU algorithm, the data that these background applications use remains in memory. The user now comes back to the computer after lunch and wants to check email, but the information used by the email program has been tucked away to the hard disk by the MRU algorithm.

Which explains the sluggish-return-from-lunch thing. It also helps you anticipate how SuperFetch helps to alleviate this problem. If you're thinking "new algorithm," you're ahead of the game.

Vista's SuperFetch will help to improve system responsiveness with a new memory management algorithm that assists in two ways:

- It prioritizes user applications over background tasks.
- It adapts to how each user works. It can even anticipate usage demands based on factors such as time of day and day of the week.

The SuperFetch technology still allows background tasks to run on system idle. The difference between SuperFetch and the MRU algorithm, though, is that once the background task is done with its work—Windows Defender runs its system scan for malware, for example—SuperFetch will put things back in order, as it were. Whereas MRU will leave the Windows Defender malware definitions, search results, and so forth in physical RAM, SuperFetch will retrieve the user's email data, placing it into RAM. The user returns to an email application whose responsiveness is a lot snappier than it would be under MRU.

SuperFetch repopulates memory with the data the user was accessing before the background task ran, so when the user returns to her desk, her applications continue to run as quickly as before.

And as mentioned, SuperFetch also tries to learn from your computer usage patterns so that it can better retrieve the data you need to work with before you're at your computer, asking an application to carry out a task. It will (should) get better over time.

All of this leads to an important performance question relating to whether you can make SuperFetch perform better *right now*.

 Remember back in Chapter 2 when I mentioned that Vista should perform better than XP even on the same hardware? Of course you don't; you've got a social life, however impaired it may be by your love of computers, and you aren't reading this book cover to cover. Well, this is one of the technologies that helps Microsoft back up this claim. So although folks can trot out one benchmark test or another proclaiming that XP outperforms Vista for a certain task, Vista—thanks to enhancements such as ReadyBoost and SuperFetch—should be the better performance choice for normal everyday use.

According to Microsoft.

So how do I configure SuperFetch behavior, then?

You don't. SuperFetch is, after all, an algorithm, and there's really no way—at least through Windows Vista—to trick it out.

There is another performance technology, however, that is configurable, and that can also help speed up computer performance, especially at startup time. It's called ReadyDrive, and it's discussed next.

Vista ReadyDrive

ReadyDrive is a performance-boosting technology that essentially lets Vista utilize systems equipped with a new kind of hard disk called a *hybrid hard disk*. What's a hybrid hard disk, you ask?

Here's how the technology works: the hybrid drive works in much the same way that hybrid cars work—it combines two technologies to offer better overall performance. In the case of hybrid cars, of course, the performance boost is in fuel efficiency. In the case of hybrid hard drives, the boost comes in the form of greater I/O speed.

A hybrid hard disk combines a standard hard disk with a relatively large amount of NVRAM—RAM like the kind used by motherboards to store BIOS information, which won't lose its information when it loses power. Think a gigabyte or more on the typical hybrid drive.

As you might suspect, this NVRAM provides a host of speed-related benefits because much of the drive's frequently used information ends up getting cached on the NVRAM. With ReadyDrive, you can expect to be able to boot up and resume from various sleep and hibernation states much faster than before. Computer performance in general should be snappier with a hybrid drive.

Hybrid drives also provide the less obvious benefit of improved battery life. Why? Because the most-often-used information is stored in NVRAM, the computer doesn't have to spend as much time—and thus, power—spinning the hard drive's platters when accessing data.

It can even improve hard drive reliability. One common way that drives can become damaged is when they are moved while spinning. Because data is stored on NVRAM, it reduces the likelihood that the disks will be spinning the next time you're working and have to be on the move quickly.

So because this hybrid hard drive stuff is a hardware component, any old system can put it to use, right? Well, no, at least not for now. Prior versions of Windows won't be able to utilize these hybrid hard drives unless drive manufacturers include drivers that enable such support.

That's where Vista's advantage really shines—there's a reason the feature has its own brand name, after all. With Vista's ReadyDrive, there's nothing to add or configure. If you have such a drive, Windows ReadyDrive will just plain-old *work*.

One problem, though: there really aren't any PCs at the time of this writing that are using the new hybrid drives. Reports are that Samsung will be the first manufacturer to release the hybrids commercially, and you should start seeing new laptops with Samsung hybrids by the first quarter of 2007.

No matter what hard drive you use—Parallel EIDE, Serial ATA, or one of the fancy new hybrids—you will be able to realize better performance if you keep the drive defragmented. This used to be a chore with previous versions of Windows, but it doesn't have to be once you upgrade to Windows Vista.

So far in this chapter, we've discussed a number of startup behaviors and improvements in Windows Vista that should help you get up and running faster than ever before.

What comes next, then? On most Vista systems, the next tollbooth that stands between you and your use of the operating system, of course, is system logon. We tackle that next.

Logging On to Windows Vista

At Vista installation time, you're asked to create at least one account—the administrator account—which is used to install the operating system. You can then supply username and password credentials for other users if necessary.

What's more, the options you supply here will have an impact on default logon behavior. You will see one of two options at logon time:

- If you did not provide a password for the single user of the computer and the system is not part of a Windows server domain, Vista logs on the user automatically. This is a fine choice if you're not concerned about data theft should the computer be lost or stolen.
- If you did provide a password, or if you created multiple standard users at installation time, you will see the Vista Welcome screen, as seen in Figure 6-11. Use of this screen is uncomplicated: the user clicks on his corresponding username (and picture), and is then prompted for a password.

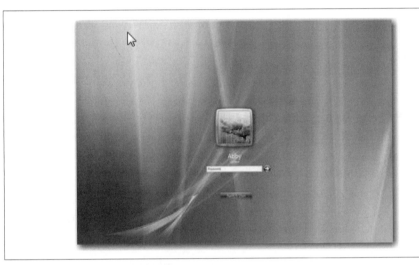

Figure 6-11. The Vista Welcome screen

Note here that the Vista Welcome screen is significantly different from that of Windows XP Professional or Home. As you might guess, administrators have several ways to manipulate this logon behavior. The next sections look at the hows and whys.

Logging On to a Domain

In Chapter 3, we looked at how to join a Windows Vista computer to an Active Directory domain. When you do, users then have to not only supply correct username and password credentials, but they also have to specify which domain they are logging on to. Domain users have two choices for carrying out this logon task:

- They can use their email address in the form of *username@domainname*. Obviously, you can't use just *any* of your email addresses here, but one that matches the domain you're trying to log on to. The part after the @ symbol tells Vista where to submit the *username* credentials. For example, to log on as *brian* on the *brianculp.com* domain, you could use *hmsbrian@brianculp.com*.

- They can use the NetBIOS domain name and then the username in this syntax: *NetBIOS domain\username*. Using the same example, the logon credentials would be *brianculp\hmsbrian*.

Keep in mind that administrators must have the proper name-resolution technologies in place for speedy and successful logons. The *username@domainname* form relies on the Domain Name System (DNS) for name resolution (the same as Active Directory, by the way), and the NetBIOS naming convention usually relies on WINS to forward logon requests across a routed environment. There's no right or wrong way to log on, but generally speaking, the bigger the network, the more likely it is that admins will instruct users to use the DNS conventions (*username@domainname*) for domain logon.

Of real significance here is that this Vista Welcome screen replaces the Classic Windows logon with which almost every corporate user has become familiar. What's the Classic Windows logon? I'll answer that with another question: have you ever pressed Ctrl-Alt-Delete? If you have, you've used the Classic Windows logon, which is no more with Windows Vista.

With the Classic Windows logon, users could simply select from a drop-down menu the domain they wanted to log on to. Alternatively, they could choose the *computername* selection and submit logon credentials locally. Now, users have to type in this domain or computer information.

 For this reason and a few others, I'm not real crazy about the changes in the Vista Welcome screen when it comes to logging onto a domain. For more, see my notes toward the end of Chapter 15.

To reiterate, then: it's no longer necessary under Windows Vista to press the Ctrl-Alt-Delete key combination to access the Welcome screen. There is still a way for administrators to *require* Ctrl-Alt-Delete before users see the Welcome screen, however.

Requiring Ctrl-Alt-Delete

Known in some circles (usually not the ones I travel in, mind you) as the "three-finger salute" or even (definitely not the ones I travel in, ever) the "Vulcan nerve pinch," Ctrl-Alt-Delete was a security measure built onto the Windows NT (then 2000 and XP) logon process whose purpose was to prevent certain types of hacking, notably presenting the user with a counterfeit logon screen that could be used to swipe user credentials.

Its use as a security measure is not terribly relevant anymore, but it can still be required as part of the Vista logon routine.

Here's what to do:

1. Open a Run dialog box (type **run** at the Start menu or press the Windows key and the R key simultaneously), and then enter the following:

   ```
   control userpasswords2
   ```

2. You'll now see the User Accounts dialog box. Choose the Advanced tab, and then click "Require users to press Ctrl+Alt+Delete" in the Secure logon section, as shown in Figure 6-12.

Figure 6-12. Requiring the Ctrl-Alt-Delete combination at logon time

3. Now click OK to commit the change. Notice here the text of the dialog box: the security provided by Ctrl-Alt-Delete is that it "guarantees (an) authentic Windows logon prompt."

While pointing out how to maximize security for the Vista logon process, I suppose it's also necessary to point out the complete and total converse of what I just discussed: to have the local Administrator account log on *automatically* each time Vista starts up.

Configuring Administrator auto-logon

Now, before even going into click-steps, know that configuring an Administrator auto-logon is the least, *least* secure method of using your Vista computer, and it leaves it wide open for anyone to pick it up and subsequently perform *any* administrative task, not to mention access *any* piece of information stored on the system. Ballmer would be fairly apoplectic if he saw you doing this.*

But as long as you understand the consequences, and you are certain that no one else will be accessing the computer, it can actually be quite a convenience. When combined with startup programs, it allows you to hit the power button, walk away for five minutes or so, and then come back to a desktop that's completely ready for the workday.

At any rate, there are actually two ways to configure this auto-logon behavior. One is to use the User Accounts dialog box. Use the steps just mentioned to open it, and then:

1. Clear the "Users must enter a username and password to use this computer" checkbox.

2. Click Apply. You should now see an "Automatically log on" dialog box where you will be prompted for the user credentials that will be automatically submitted, as shown in Figure 6-13.

3. Click OK, and OK again, in the User Accounts dialog box to commit your changes.

The other set of click-steps requires a trip to the registry. Here's what to do:

1. Launch the Registry Editor by typing **regedit** at the Start menu. You have to type the entire string, and you're prompted for administrative credentials once you do.

2. Navigate to this registry key:

    HKLM\Software\Microsoft\Windows NT\CurrentVersion\Winlogon

3. Now, perform the following three tasks:

    a. Double-click the AutoAdminLogon REG_SZ (String Value) setting and set the value to 1. Figure 6-14 shows this step.

    b. Create a registry String Value called DefaultUserName and set the value to the administrator username you want to log on automatically.

    c. Create a registry String Value called DefaultPassword and set the password value for the user.

 If you're logging onto a domain automatically, you can also create a DefaultDomainName value and set its value to the domain you will log on to automatically.

---

* I mean more apoplectic than normal.

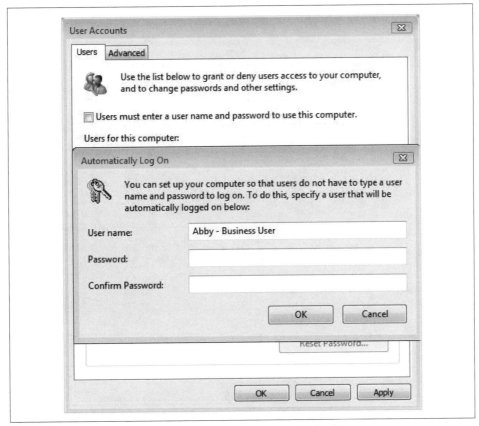

Figure 6-13. Configuring auto-logon using the User Accounts dialog box

You can override auto-logon for a given logon attempt by holding down the Shift key as Windows (not the computer) starts up.

Now that you've seen some of the ways to govern startup behavior, including how to access the desktop automatically, let's turn our attention to a way to ensure that Vista's performance is as speedy as possible once we're using that desktop to carry out our daily tasks.

Automatic Disk Defragmentation

You already know the importance of disk defragmentation: over time, a hard disk's files get spread out over large plots of disk real estate. Part of the file is in one place, another part is in another place. The disk's read/write heads, therefore, have to travel (relatively) long distances to both parts of that file. And in practice, of course, a file can be stored in tens or even hundreds of locations. A single Word document chock-full of graphics can end up getting stored in multiple hard disk sectors, as shown in Figure 6-15.

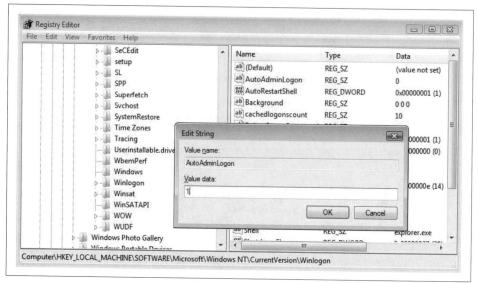

Figure 6-14. Configuring administrator auto-logon

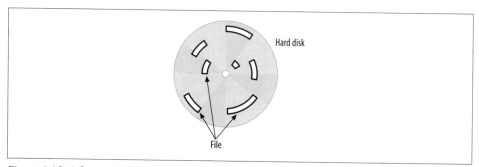

Figure 6-15. A fragmented file spread among many disparate sectors (bad)

Wouldn't disk performance improve, then, if all of these locations were consolidated so that the read/write heads could travel to just one location instead of having to fan out all across the drive to locate one file?

The answer is a resounding yes, and the Disk Defragmenter performs just this kind of hard disk housekeeping. Where possible, it will bring a file's sectors together so that the same Word document referenced earlier will be stored in a way that is more like that shown in Figure 6-16.

With the file (and thus, all files) rearranged in such a way, the hard drive can work much more efficiently. Microsoft has recognized this for some time, and has included a version of the Disk Defragmenter utility with every version of Windows since Windows 9x. As a part of regular maintenance, users could open the utility and perform the defrag, usually with only a few clicks.

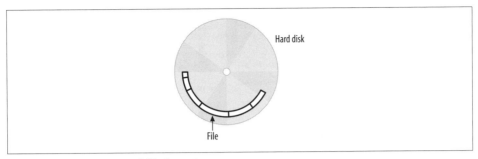

Figure 6-16. A defragmented file (better)

Ah, but therein lies the rub. It was up to the user to remember to run the Disk Defragmenter, or at the very least to configure a Scheduled Task so that it would be run with regularity.

But that's no longer the case. In Vista, the Disk Defragmenter runs at a weekly interval by default when your computer is turned on, so you don't have to remember to carry out this vital housekeeping task.

Here's all you have to do:

1. Open the Disk Defragmenter utility. There are a number of ways to do this; the easiest is to type **defrag** at the Start menu. The Disk Defragmenter appears at the top of the list. If User Account Control is on, you'll then be prompted to continue.

2. The Disk Defragmenter window appears, as shown in Figure 6-17. Note here that the tool is already configured so that it will run automatically.

3. To change the schedule, click the "Modify schedule" button and choose the appropriate options from the ensuing drop-down menus. You'll see selections for how often, what day, and at what time of day to schedule the defragmentation.

4. Click OK, and OK again, to commit your changes.

By default, the Disk Defragmenter runs every week. Unlike with previous versions of Windows, you don't really need to worry about it any further. You can change how often it runs, and at what time of day, but it is recommended that you let the Disk Defragmenter do its magic once a week—as configured—during typical computer usage.

After the Disk Defragmenter does its work and leaves your disk in relatively pristine condition, it's time to make sure your disk—and thus, the operating system—does the same when it's time to walk away from the computer. As with starting a computer, there is, of course, more than meets the eye.

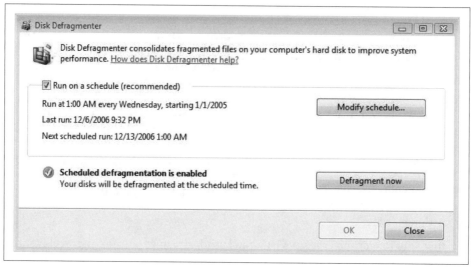

Figure 6-17. The Disk Defragmenter runs automatically

System Shutdown

For every beginning, there is an ending. Or something like that. Shutting down a Vista machine is every bit a part of computer use as is starting it up. System shutdown is necessary both for altruistic purposes, such as saving energy, and for reasons that are of more immediate concern to the end user and administrator. Proper shutdown helps make sure that working data is safe and secure. It also helps your system start quickly the next time you use it.

And because it's a task that is done so frequently, it's important to understand what occurs at shutdown, what options are available, and how these options affect system performance.

The button-pushing part of shutting down a system is very easy. Just click the Vista Start button; the shutdown buttons appear just to the right of the Windows desktop Search box. From left to right, then, the first button is called the Power button. It either shuts down your system or puts it to sleep (another sentence that just sounds funny without any labor on my part to wisecrack), and can even switch between the two functions depending on circumstances. I'll explain more in a bit. To the right of the Power button is the Lock button, which, as the name suggests, locks the system. The third is a simple arrow that brings up your full menu of shutdown options.

There are as many as seven shutdown options, some of which don't really shut down the computer at all. From top to bottom, they are:

- Switch User
- Logoff
- Lock

- Restart
- Sleep
- Hibernate
- Shut Down

In the sections that follow, we'll look at each option individually.

Switch User

Switching users lets two (or more) people share the same computer with a minimum of hassle. Each user can have a completely separate desktop, with different programs accessing two completely different sets of data. The advantage over logging off is that nothing has to be closed before doing the switch. User A can be working on a rather lengthy Word document, for example, and can let User B (*quickly*) check her email by switching users, as is happening right at this very moment. I'll be right back…

…upon switching back, User A will see his work exactly as it was prior to the switch.

To perform the switch, just choose the Switch User option, and then select the user who wants to use the computer.

 Even though switching users does not require saving data before making the switch, it's always a good idea to do so. Another user with the rights to shut down the system could do so and wipe out unsaved work in the other user's session. The user will be warned about this before proceeding, though.

The Switch User feature is a byproduct of something called Fast User Switching, which was also available in Windows XP and is likewise enabled by default in Windows Vista.

In fact, one significant difference between XP and Vista when it comes to participating in a domain is that Fast User Switching is always enabled with Vista, even when joined to a domain. Under Windows XP, Fast User Switching was disabled when joined to a domain, and there was an option to turn it off when part of a workgroup.

Under Windows Vista, you should always have the ability to switch users.

Logoff and Lock

Logging off a session forces any open programs to close. The computer remains turned on, and other users can log in and begin a session.

The main advantage of logging off is that you don't need to worry about another user shutting down the computer and losing your data. Logging off causes the data you're working on to be tucked away safely to the hard drive.

To log off, click the Start button, and then use the menu to choose Log Off.

Locking a computer prevents access to the desktop until the currently logged-on user (or the administrator) comes back and unlocks the computer with the appropriate credentials.

Especially in secure environments, it should be common practice to lock the machine before leaving it unattended. Administrators can even configure Group Policies that lock the computers automatically after a given idle time.

To lock the computer, just click the Start button and choose the Lock selection.

Restart

Restart performs what's known as a *warm* or *soft* reboot of the machine. Software controls the restart process, and power to the machine is never severed. Restart represents an orderly shutdown and restart of the Vista operating system.

Restarts are often necessary after software installations, especially those that involve a hotfix or patch of the operating system. Some utilities, such as the Memory Diagnostics tool, also require a system restart. To initialize a restart at any time, click the Start button and choose the Restart menu option.

Sleep

Here's where it gets more interesting, as the Sleep option represents a new feature of Windows Vista. Sleep, at least when speaking about a Vista machine, is a new power state that offers two great benefits. These benefits are essentially a combination of two power states that were available with Windows XP (and that are still available under Vista). By putting a computer to sleep, a user gets:

- The quick shutdown procedure of Standby—although the computer doesn't really do this; the working environment is stored in memory
- The data protection of Hibernate

When your computer sleeps, Vista automatically manages memory using Windows SuperFetch, a new memory technology discussed earlier in this chapter. In fact, the work of SuperFetch is highly noticeable when resuming from Sleep, as users can get their entire working environment back from Sleep in usually just a matter of seconds.

As you might guess, Sleep's benefits are especially noticeable on laptops, where frequent interruptions of the working environment (an hour here or there in the hotel room, airport, or coffee shop [make that two hours in the coffee shop] is the norm).

Power savings in Sleep mode

Placing a laptop in Sleep mode—or configuring the Power Options so that it goes to sleep after a brief idle period—can have a dramatic impact on battery life. And this power savings can be put to use on a desktop as well. While asleep, a desktop uses only a fraction of the power it uses when running under full power. If your company's users typically leave their computers on when leaving the office, implementing a policy that puts the computers to sleep can save a significant amount of power, which, as anyone who's ever written a check to the power company knows, isn't exactly free. Multiply this power savings by the number of computers in the network, and Sleep can mean a huge cost savings as well.

In fact, I'll turn once again to Jim Allchin, who wrote a white paper that summarizes power consumption and the Sleep mode in this way (my emphasis on the numbers here, which is why I've borrowed the quote):

> A typical Pentium 4 PC with a 17" LCD monitor draws about 102.6 watts of power (think about a 100-watt light bulb). That same PC and display in a sleep state draws only 5.6 watts, or 97 fewer watts. If you figure that a PC is used for active work for 10 hours a day, 5 days a week, 52 weeks per year, that is 2,600 operating hours. With 8,760 hours in a year (365×24), there are actually 6,160 potential idle hours per year. Since sleep mode uses 97 fewer watts than full power mode, the total savings is 597 kWh per year—and by the way, the impact is obviously even greater (760 kWh) if you use a CRT monitor since they draw more power than LCDs...
>
> ...The paper uses an estimate of $0.0931 per kWh from the U.S. Department of Energy, so for a home user with one PC, the savings amounts to $55.63/year (more if the PC is used less than 10 hours a day). While that is great savings for a home user, think about an enterprise with **10,000 desktops** where the potential **cost savings would be $556,300/year**...
>
> ...each PC that moves to Windows Vista generates 926 fewer pounds of carbon dioxide or about 8 percent of what the EPA estimates that a typical car generates in the course of a year—so for every 12 and a half PCs that are running with Windows Vista's new power management capabilities, it's like having one less car on the road.[*]

Seeing the numbers behind Sleep mode is much more powerful than simply describing what it is and how it works. Also, I emphasized the bottom-line cost savings to help you associate some kind of concrete dollar figure to the Sleep function.

You can, of course, scale this cost savings to fit your particular situation. A company with 1,000 PCs, for example, can expect savings of roughly $56,000. Meanwhile, the 100-person firm might realize a $5,600 net benefit. This is to say nothing of the possible air-conditioning costs that could also be factored in—computers and monitors produce heat. These kinds of cost savings in power consumption alone can go a long way toward justifying the Vista investment to a CFO. Will some expense be associated with an upgrade to Windows Vista? Yes. Might this upgrade pay for itself in terms of electric-bill savings? Here also, the answer might be yes.

Keep in mind that Sleep requires at least *some* draw on power, however. On a mobile system, Sleep typically uses one to two percent of battery power per hour. But even at this reduced rate, it will eventually drain the battery completely. To prevent loss of data, Vista automatically transitions into Hibernate mode before the battery dies.

---

[*] From *http://www.windowsvistablog.com*.

But I don't see Sleep on my computer

You may not. Sleep's availability depends on several factors. If you don't have the Sleep shutdown option available, it could be due to one of these limiting factors:

The video card doesn't support it
> In order for a computer to sleep, the video card must support this feature. But just because it doesn't right now, don't despair. Sleep is new, and all that could be standing between you and Sleep is a driver update.

Your system administrator isn't allowing Sleep
> Vista Business, Enterprise, and Ultimate computers can join a Windows domain. This means they can also be managed by Group Policy Objects (GPOs) and GPOs can enforce restrictions about usage, including the ability to sleep.

Sleep is disabled in the computer's BIOS
> Your BIOS may have the Sleep function disabled, preventing Vista from utilizing it as well. The good news, though, is that this is usually the easiest to fix. To enable Sleep, restart the computer and then enter the BIOS setup program. (Refer to the manufacturer's instructions on how to launch BIOS setup. Usually, you just press a key such as F10 or Delete.) Change the necessary BIOS setting and then save and exit.

A lot of desktop computers, especially older ones, do *not* support the Sleep option. You should also know that on a mobile computer that supports it, sleep is the default action for *both* the Power button and the Start menu, and when you simply close the lid of your computer.

The only exception to this is when Vista has recently downloaded and installed operating system updates. In this case, the Power button changes to a shutdown, except there's the little Security Center shield icon over it. This indicates that updates have been installed, and that the computer needs to be shut down and restarted for these changes to take effect. Clicking on the Power button in this instance does just that.

Changing Sleep options on mobile computers

You can also configure this behavior by changing Vista's Power Options:

1. Open the Power Options Control Panel application. One easy method is to right-click the power meter in the System Tray and choose Power Options.

2. From the "Select a power plan" page, follow the "Choose what closing the lid does" link.

3. In the "Define power buttons and turn on password protection" page, shown in Figure 6-18, look to the third option in the list of possible actions.

    The drop-down choices here let you specify what happens when you close your laptop. Note that you can configure different options for when the system is on batteries and for when it is plugged in.

4. Click "Save changes" to complete the procedure.

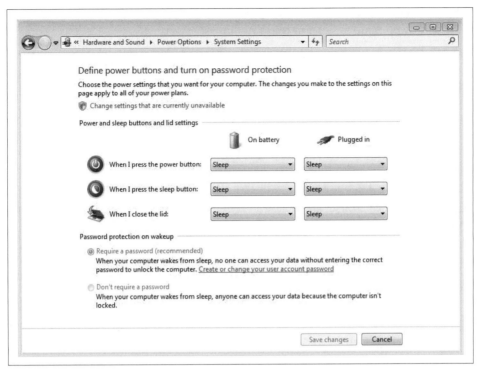

Figure 6-18. The default action for closing the lid is to sleep

 A full discussion of Power Options appears in the section "Vista Power Management," later in this chapter.

Hibernate

Hibernate is another power-saving state that allows a user to come back to the work environment just as he left it. The difference between Hibernate and other low-power options such as Standby and Sleep is that the computer is actually turned off so that there's no drain on power. You can use Hibernate on a Friday at 5:00 p.m., for example, and come back to the same work space the following Monday at 8:00 a.m.

Hibernate writes the entire contents of memory to a file called *hiberfile.sys*, and then it stores this file on the hard disk. Upon resume, Vista retrieves these contents and regenerates the desktop just as it was. So, if you hibernated while in the middle of a Word document, you'd get the same document when resuming, down to the cursor's insertion point.

It's a great feature, and it can save a lot of time when re-creating your work environment as compared to a full shutdown. The drawback of Hibernate is speed. Because

Hibernate writes a file and stores it to the hard disk, it can take a minute or so to retrieve it. Sleep is much faster at restoring the user's session.

To put a computer into Hibernate mode, choose it from the Shut Down menu options.

Shut Down

Shut Down describes not one process, but really a series of processes. When a computer shuts down, it closes all open programs, then closes Windows Vista itself, then turns off your monitor, and then finally kills the power to your computer. And note that shutting down a computer does *not* save all work, although many programs ask you to save before *they* are closed by Vista.

The advantages, of course, are in power savings and data protection. Short of theft, it's all but impossible to access data on a system that's not on.

To shut down, choose the bottom selection on the Shut Down menu. Also, you might see a power button that looks like this:

This is different from the Sleep button, which is the default. Why would you see a Power button rather than a Sleep button? There are three possible explanations:

- Your system does not have Sleep capability, or the option has been disabled in the system BIOS.
- Your system is being governed by a Group Policy setting that forces you to always shut down the computer.
- As described earlier, the computer needs a restart to finish installing software updates. In that case, the Power button looks like this:

If you're using a laptop computer, these should be the only times you see the Shut Down button on the Start menu.

Unless, that is, you've configured the Vista Power Options so that the default behavior of the button is changed. Just how do you change the Start menu's Power button behavior, you ask? The answer merits a quick segue into a discussion of Vista's new Power Management options. We could have segued into this section in a dozen different places; here works just as well as anywhere else.

Vista Power Management

As I mentioned at least a couple of times in this title, Microsoft has focused much of its re-engineering efforts to make Vista a significantly better choice for laptop computers. Putting the computer to sleep rather than in Standby or Hibernate mode is just the tip of the iceberg, though. There are several other improvements in how Vista handles power options, and users now have much, much more control over what options are configured and when.

Note that this power management capability extends to administrators as well, of course. Not only can admins specify Power Options on an individual computer basis, as we will discuss in this section, but also several new Group Policy settings can manage Power Options for entire groups of computers. For more on these new Group Policy options, turn to Chapter 13. For now, we'll concentrate on the options that you can configure per individual machine.

To get started, open the Power Options console from the Control Panel. You can find it under the Hardware and Sound grouping, but the easiest way to locate this console is to simply type **power** at the Vista Start menu. The Power Options should appear at the top of the Programs list. As seen in Figure 6-19, you will now see three possible power plans to choose from:

Balanced
> This tries to give battery life and computer performance equal weight.

Power saver
> This plan tries to use processing power at as low a rate as possible in order to extend battery life as long as possible.

High performance
> This plan maximizes computer performance without regard to battery life. The computer should perform almost as speedily as it does when plugged in.

Vista chooses the Balanced plan as the default.

 Another way to quickly access the Power Options console is to right-click the battery icon in the System Tray and choose Power Options.

But choosing one of these three preconfigured power plans is just the beginning. Each plan comprises numerous individual power behavior settings, each of which you can adjust to your liking by following the "Change plan settings" link.

Or you can create your own power plan from scratch, using one of the three preconfigured power plans as a starting point. To get started, follow these steps:

1. Open the Power Options console using the steps previously described. On the left side of the console, click the "Create a power plan" link.

2. In the "Create a power plan" dialog box, choose the template plan and give your new power plan a name. Click Next.

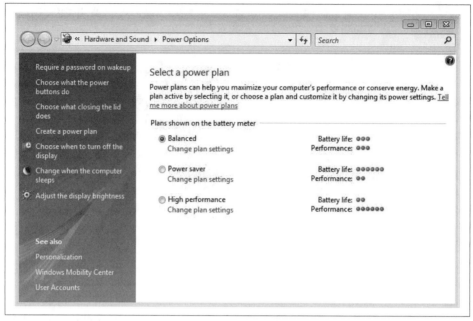

Figure 6-19. Choosing from one of the three Vista power plans

3. Now all that's left is to configure these options for when the computer is running on battery and when it is plugged in:

    Turn off the display
        Most power plans specify that the system should turn off the display when on batteries sooner than when it is plugged in.

    Put the computer to sleep
        This is the interval when the system automatically goes into Sleep mode.

    Adjust screen brightness
        Dimming display brightness on battery power will conserve battery life.

4. Now just click Create to save your new plan; you should see the Power Options console once again.

5. To really get into the inner workings of the plan, however, you'll want to click the "Change plan settings" link and then click "Change advanced power settings" on the ensuing dialog box.

6. As shown in Figure 6-20, you will not see the "Advanced settings" Power Options dialog box. You will see 12 additional power management options, and these are just the ones you can see at the outset. To see all possible power options, click the "Change settings that are currently unavailable" link. You'll be asked for administrative confirmation if User Account Control is turned on.

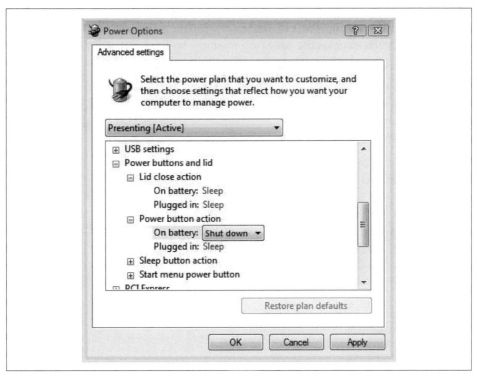

Figure 6-20. Changing advanced power options

7. Once you've gotten to this "Advanced settings" dialog box, using it is just a matter of expanding an option and then configuring with a drop-down menu. For example, if you want to change the Start menu Power button so that the laptop shuts down rather than sleeps, expand the "Power buttons and lid" selection and then the "Power button" action.

For most actions, such as the lid close and power button options shown in Figure 6-20, there are choices about behaviors both when the laptop is plugged in and when it is on battery power.

 I recommend that you do not modify any of the three plans so that they can be used as templates for other custom plans. This also provides a way to press the Reset button when you've made several changes to a customized power plan without having to back out of each individual change.

One last thing, which is just an interjection of my opinion: I *really* like the changes Vista has made with the Power Options. It's great to have that much control over individual power consumption options, and it can really help to extend battery life when deployed properly. The Power Options console is a bit overengineered, though. Several of the links on the lefthand side take you to the same dialog box, which is exactly the same as the one you get when choosing any of the "Change plan settings" links. Only the "Create a power plan" link *needs* to be there.

Now that we've examined the different options you have as you shut down and manage power consumption on the Vista computer, it's time to move into a discussion of what options are available as Vista starts up. As you will soon see, there are even more startup choices than there are at shutdown.

Advanced Startup Options

You have additional startup possibilities other than just pressing the Power button and waiting for the login screen. Advanced options give you more control over startup behavior, and are an invaluable troubleshooting aid.

To access the Advanced Startup options, turn on the system and press F8 before Windows starts. As shown in Figure 6-21, you have several options:

- Repair your computer
- Safe Mode
- Safe Mode with Networking
- Safe Mode with Command Prompt
- Enable Boot Logging
- Enable low-resolution video
- Last Known Good Configuration
- Directory Services Restore Mode
- Debugging Mode
- Disable automatic restart on system failure
- Disable Driver Signature Enforcement
- Start Windows Normally

Note that your system might not display every Advanced Startup option. Only computers that have been joined to a domain, for example, will have the Directory Services Restore Mode available.

We discuss the uses for each Advanced Start option in the subsections that follow.

Repair Your Computer

Hopefully, your time as a Vista administrator won't include having to use this startup option. *Probably*, it will. Choosing the "Repair your computer" option displays a list of system recovery tools that you can use to accomplish a variety of tasks, including diagnosis and repair of a startup or of an entire system restore.

```
                    Advanced Boot Options
Choose Advanced Options for: Microsoft Windows
(Use the arrow keys to highlight your choice.)

   Safe Mode
   Safe Mode with Networking
   Safe Mode with Command Prompt

   Enable Boot Logging
   Enable low-resolution video (640x480)
   Last Known Good Configuration
   Directory Services Restore Mode
   Debugging Mode
   Disable automatic restart on system failure
   Disable Driver Signature Enforcement

   Start Windows Normally

Description: Set or reset the display resolution. Start Windows in
            low-resolution display mode (640x480).


 ENTER=Choose                                        ESC=Cancel
```

Figure 6-21. Vista's advanced startup options, which you can access by pressing F8

Note that this is one of the options you may not see at your Advanced Startup Options screen, at least not right away. These are available only if the repair tools are first installed on your computer's hard disk. If you have access to the Vista installation disc, however, they reside there as well.

For immediate instructions on how to install these recovery tools to the hard drive, please refer to Chapter 8.

Safe Mode

You can always tell that your Vista computer is running in Safe Mode because the screen will look horrible and the words "Safe Mode" appear in all four corners of the desktop. So yeah, that's how you can tell you're in Safe Mode.

Safe Mode startup loads Vista with *just* enough services and drivers to run the operating system (i.e., only those drives and services that—in theory—ensure safe operation).

Safe Mode's purpose is to help with troubleshooting. If an administrator cannot duplicate a problem when booting into Safe Mode, he can eliminate the default settings and basic device drivers as possible causes. In such a case, the administrator can use Safe Mode to disable or reinstall the suspected program or driver.

If the problem *does* reoccur while in Safe Mode, however, it lies with Vista itself, and an operating system reinstall is often needed (or at least is the most expedient course of action, in my experience).

Of course, the process of elimination can help track down the offending program or service. Just start the programs you typically use, one at a time, followed by the

Windows services. Reproducing the problem is a great thing in terms of trouble-shooting; Safe Mode can get you started on that path.

What gets loaded in Safe Mode. As I've mentioned, Vista loads the bare minimum needed to get the computer up and operational when booting into Safe Mode. But just what, exactly, does that mean? Obviously, users and administrators who are troubleshooting still need to see the screen, so some kind of video driver is loaded. But it will be a very basic video driver, and probably not the one shipped with your computer.

Besides a VGA display adapter that loads so that Vista can generate output to a monitor, Vista also loads drivers for the following drives during a Safe Mode boot-up:

- Floppy disk drives (internal and USB)
- Internal CD-ROM drives (ATA, SCSI)
- External CD-ROM drives (USB)
- Internal DVD-ROM drives (ATA, SCSI)
- External DVD-ROM drives (USB)
- Internal hard disk drives (ATA, SATA, SCSI)
- External hard disk drives (USB)
- Keyboards (USB, PS/2, serial)
- Mice (USB, PS/2, serial)

And although the system doesn't load every service, some are essential for Vista to operate properly. Also, Vista loads services such as the Event Log service to facilitate information gathering. Safe Mode will also load these vital Windows services:

- Event logs
- Logical disk manager
- Plug and Play
- Remote procedure calls
- Cryptographic services
- Help and Support
- System restore
- WMI

Furthermore, Safe Mode startup comes in more than one flavor. Choices include opting for network support and the command prompt. The following sections look at the differences between each, and help to identify instances in which a particular choice would be appropriate.

Safe Mode with Networking. Everything about Safe Mode with Networking mimics Safe Mode, with the exception that the system can utilize its networking capabilities. In other words, Safe Mode with Networking is a superset of Vista Safe Mode.

Furthermore, there are certain services the Vista networking stack can't live without when using Safe Mode with Networking. Quite obviously, the network adapters need to load in order to make the networking capabilities possible. Here are the other networking services that come into play:

- Computer Browser
- Dynamic Host Configuration Protocol (DHCP)
- DNS
- Netlogon
- Network connections
- Servers
- Terminal Services
- TCP/IP-NetBIOS Helper
- Upload Manager
- Wireless Zero Config

Safe Mode with Networking can be crucial to enabling troubleshooting, as solutions such as updated drivers and/or Known Good Configuration files can exist on other computers on a network, or on servers connected to the Internet.

Safe Mode with Command Prompt. The Safe Mode with Command Prompt presents administrators with a command prompt rather than the Vista desktop. Notice that I said *Command Prompt*, not *Command Prompt window*.

When using Safe Mode with Command Prompt, you won't see a Start menu, Windows Explorer, or any other familiar components that people associate with Windows. All you get are a directory location and a cursor.

Diagnostic tools for Safe Mode. If the whole idea of a Safe Mode boot-up is to allow computer admins the ability to isolate and troubleshoot computer problems, it follows that at least a few tools will be available for this task.

In fact, many are available, including these:

Control Panel
> The hub of Vista configuration; you will use the tools herein to change a multitude of Windows settings.

System Restore
> You can use this to roll back a Vista configuration to a specific point in time.

Device Manager

This lets administrators examine and uninstall hardware, and allows for update of device drivers.

Event Viewer

A repository of what the system has reported about itself can provide valuable information concerning system activity.

System Information

As shown in Figure 6-22, this displays basic, at-a-glance information about the computer's hardware components and drivers, and serves as a dashboard for other troubleshooting tools such as the Device Manager and Advanced Settings.

Command Prompt

This allows admins to run testing utilities they might not otherwise be able to with the GUI; it can be a great place to start network troubleshooting with utilities such as PING, IPCONFIG, and NETUSE.

Registry Editor

This allows for direct editing of registry information, which serves as Vista's central nervous system. When using the Control Panel, users are technically making registry edits.

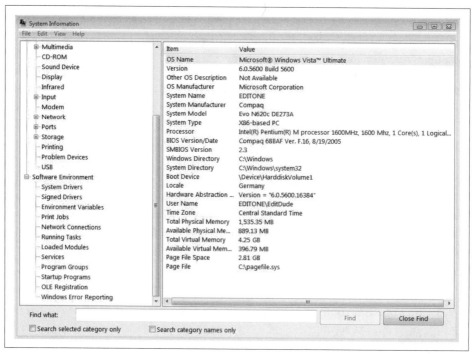

Figure 6-22. The System Information tool

Each tool gets further discussion, including instructions about use, in Chapter 12.

Enable Boot Logging. When starting with boot logging enabled, Vista creates a logfile called *ntbtlog.txt*. This file lists all the drivers installed during startup time, and that information is then used to help isolate which drivers are actually loaded. Administrators use this file for advanced troubleshooting.

Enable low-resolution video. This changes Safe Mode boot-up slightly in that it loads Vista using your video card's native driver, but it does so using a 640×480 resolution and a very low refresh rate.

This startup option is useful when a bad video driver is suspected as the cause of trouble.

Last Known Good Configuration. Each time your computer starts up, Vista stores configuration information about itself in a registry key called LastKnownGood. This serves as a repository of system settings that are known to work properly. Last Known Good is an advanced startup option that uses these configuration settings at startup time, supposedly guaranteeing a rollback point for Vista that always works.

Last Known Good comes in handy when you're having trouble that's keeping you from starting your computer, but you were able to start correctly the last time you used it.

 If you are having problems with startup, it's a good idea not to log on to the desktop. If you do, the Last Known Good registry key is rewritten, problems and all.

Note that the Last Known Good Configuration resets your *Windows* settings to an earlier point in time, but does not do the same for your *personal data*.

So what? Well, this is extremely good news because you may have created and saved several pages in a new book you're working on, for example, since your last good startup. When using the Last Known Good Configuration, the data remains unchanged so that even though you're using settings from three days ago, you will still be using the data from three minutes ago.

If you're experiencing erratic behavior while logged onto the desktop, another troubleshooting weapon that behaves similar to Last Known Good is System Restore. Like Last Known Good, System Restore resets Vista to an earlier point in time when things worked correctly. Unlike Last Known Good, however, the changes made by System Restore can be undone. Also, System Restore presents the opportunity to restore to many different points in time. Last Known Good restores only to the last good startup.

To use the Last Known Good Configuration, press F8 during computer boot-up before the Windows logo appears. From the Advanced Startup Options page, use the arrow keys to highlight the Last Known Good Configuration, and then press Enter.

More details about Last Known Good Configuration and System Restore appear in Chapter 12.

Directory Services Restore Mode. You won't see this on a Vista computer, but rather only on Windows servers running Active Directory. Such a server is also known as a *domain controller*, because it stores and synchronizes a copy of the Directory Services database. The Directory Services restore mode can help recover the Active Directory database on one of these machines.

It's included here because it is one of the *possible* Advanced Startup options that you might run across as a network administrator, although it won't be detailed in this title.

Debugging Mode. Debugging Mode starts Vista in an advanced troubleshooting mode intended for troubleshooting professionals and system administrators.

You can also enable Debugging Mode by editing the BCD, as discussed earlier in this chapter. To turn on kernel debugging, you can use the following syntax from the BCDEdit command-line utility:

```
bcdedit /debug on
```

Disable automatic restart on system failure. This option prevents Windows from automatically restarting in the event that Vista is failing and restarting. This can sometimes cause the computer to become stuck in a loop—the problem causes a restart, which causes the problem, which causes the restart, and so on.

You can usually break this loop without tossing the computer across the room by pressing the F8 key after system BIOS and then selecting the "Disable automatic restart" option.

Another way to disable the automatic restart on system failure behavior is by editing the Advanced Startup options. As seen previously in this chapter, start by opening the System Control Panel applet and follow the "Advanced system settings" link.

From there, choose the Advanced tab and then click the Settings button under the Startup and Recovery section.

Now look at the "System failure" section, as shown in Figure 6-23. Uncheck the "Automatically restart" checkbox to disable the default restart behavior.

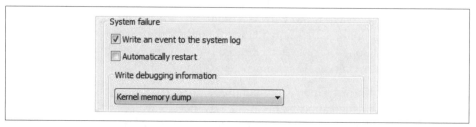

Figure 6-23. Disabling Vista's automatic restart

Note here that you can also control debugging behavior.

Disable Driver Signature Enforcement. This option is not recommended as a first line of troubleshooting, but it can help isolate a problem to a particular driver. If you have a security policy that does not allow for unsigned or improperly signed drivers, this will override that security policy. If the system starts without incident, administrators may have to consider relaxing the policy about unsigned drivers.

Start Windows Normally. As the name implies, this starts Windows Vista with the full complement of drivers and services.

Change the Default OS When Dual-Booting

I have made a couple of references in this chapter so far about using a dual-boot system. A dual-boot machine gives the user the opportunity of booting into two (or more) operating systems, each one installed on its own partition, in its own system directory.

When dual-booting, though, one OS will be the default; it will be the one chosen if the user isn't there to make a selection. So then, here's how to change the default operating system that launches when you do nothing at the boot selector screen:

1. Open the Control Panel's System applet. Again, type **sys** at the Start menu and there it is, among your list of programs. You may be prompted for administrator credentials or confirmation.

2. Choose the "Advanced system settings" link.

3. From the Advanced tab, under Startup and Recovery, click Settings.

4. As shown in Figure 6-24, look under the "System startup" section. Then, in the "Default operating system" list, click the operating system that will run when you turn on or restart your computer.

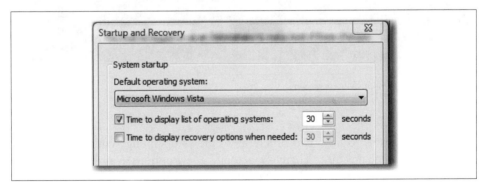

Figure 6-24. Choosing the default operating system

If you don't configure a time value in this dialog box, the computer will simply boot up into the selected operating system. (An administrator could use this as a way to "hide" an operating system selection for a given computer. Maybe the computer is used for general office computing, but you want to use a previous operating system for certain tasks. You could quickly change the default OS options here and then reboot, selecting the other operating system.)

If you'd like to be able to select which operating system will run, choose the "Time to display list of operating systems" checkbox, and then set the number of seconds that you want the list displayed.

The results will be evident when using the boot selector menu, as shown in Figure 6-25.

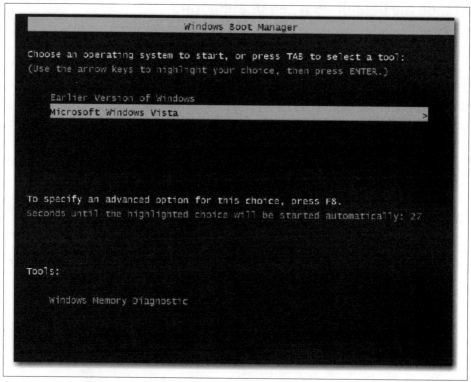

Figure 6-25. Vista's boot selector screen

Dual-boot considerations

It is entirely possible to have two different Windows operating systems living side-by-side on the same machine. There are actually a few options available today. One of these is the ability to run another operating system such as Windows XP inside a "virtual" machine. The other is to configure a dual-boot machine, where only one operating system can be used, or "booted up," at a time.

But setting up a dual-boot machine is not without its pitfalls. Specifically, there are two issues that can plague Windows Vista machines when also trying to boot with previous editions of Windows. They are:

- When you install an earlier version of Windows, such as Windows XP, after installing Vista first. In this case, you'll find that Vista no longer starts. Only the earlier version of the Windows system starts.
- When you install a second instance of Windows XP on a computer where you have already configured a Windows XP–Windows Vista dual-boot configuration. If this is the case, you may receive a "Disk read error has occurred" message.

Why would you run into either of these issues? It's all about the new way that Windows Vista uses Boot Configuration Data (BCD) to boot up rather than a *boot.ini* file, as was the case with Windows XP. In other words, the new boot-up procedure is incompatible with the old. When you install Windows XP onto a computer that's already running Vista, the XP setup procedure overwrites everything from the existing Master Boot Record (MBR), boot sector, and the boot files. What's the big deal? The big deal is that this old boot configuration method is unable to locate or load anything related to Windows Vista. It's as if the original Windows Vista installation is gone.

So there it is in a nutshell: to set up a dual-boot machine, you should install the older Windows (Windows XP) OS before installing Windows Vista.

Also, note that the edition of Windows Vista is irrelevant when you're setting up a dual-boot environment.

Improving System Startup

If you notice that your computer seems to shut down slowly (or not at all), start up slowly, or refuses to enter power-saving mode, it might be due to a program or device driver interfering with Windows power settings. You can use Performance Information and Tools Control Panel application to try to detect these programs or device drivers.

Follow these steps to begin investigating startup performance issues:

1. Start by opening the Performance Information and Tools Control Panel application.
2. Choose the "Advanced tools" link under the list of tasks on the left. You'll now see the Advanced Tools dialog box, as shown in Figure 6-26.
3. From here, you may see a performance issue or two listed under the top heading. (In my screen capture, none was listed.) Choose any of the ones listed to see a dialog box explaining more about the issue. You may also see a button here that can begin corrective action, such as the one shown in Figure 6-27.

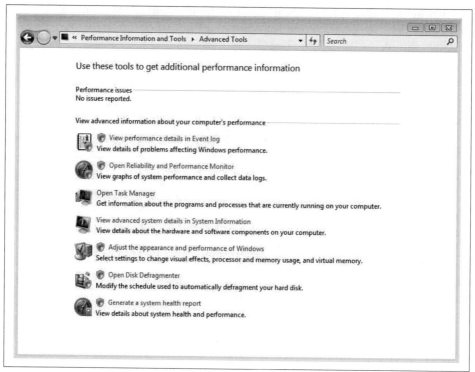

Figure 6-26. Use Advanced Tools to help improve system startup

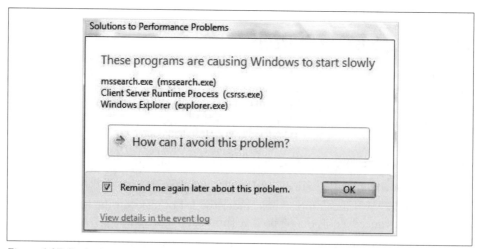

Figure 6-27. Beginning a corrective action

Of course, the options presented from here will depend on the particular problem Vista is detecting.

The Performance Information and Tools Control Panel application may also report a problem with a driver or program that's preventing your computer from quick startup. In that case, you can look to these possible solutions:

Manage which programs run at startup
Some programs start automatically as Vista finishes booting. If the System Tray is stretching all the way across the taskbar, this is likely the cause of a slow startup process. Although you might be tempted to use the System Configuration tool (msconfig.exe) to manipulate startup items, the safest choice is Windows Defender's Software Explorer. Stopping a program from running automatically can be an easy way to speed up startup performance.

Locate an updated or alternative driver
Hardware manufacturers are constantly updating drivers. A newer driver version might include a resolution to the problem.

To use Windows Defender to manage startup items, follow these steps:

1. Open Windows Defender by typing **def** at the Start menu. Alternatively, you can right-click the System Tray icon and choose Open.

2. From the Windows Defender home page, choose Tools, and then Software Explorer. The Software Explorer dialog box appears, as seen in Figure 6-28.

3. Now, select the Startup Programs category in the drop-down menu at the top, and then select the desired startup application in the list below.

4. To disable a startup program, simply click the Disable button. To remove it permanently, choose Remove. (Try Disable if you're trying to troubleshoot a slow startup. That lets you try a variety of startup options without reconfiguring startup applications.)

Just as programs or drivers can slow down computer performance at startup time, these components can prevent Vista from turning off quickly as well. You can try these options to address the slowdown:

Close the application prior to shutting down
Sometimes Vista has a hard time killing an application. This is usually accompanied by a dialog box the gives you the option of "ending now," but that's not always the case. Simply shutting down applications before shutting down can address the situation.

Locate an updated or alternative driver
Sound familiar? Newer drivers can help shutdown just as they can startup.

If these options fail to resolve the problem, the program or driver might be incompatible with Vista. Naturally, you should remove a program or device that you no longer use.

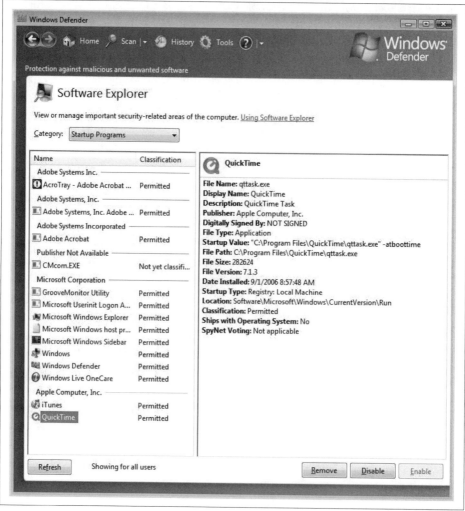

Figure 6-28. Disabling a startup item with Windows Defender

Startup Repair

New to Windows Vista is something called the Startup Repair Tool (SRT). This tool includes the capability to automatically fix many common problems encountered at startup time. It also helps system administrators perform diagnostics on more complicated issues, and can even help repair these situations as well.

There is a caveat, however: the SRT may not be installed (see the upcoming note). You can still get access to this tool even if this is the case (also discussed shortly). The SRT might be preinstalled on your system if it comes with preinstalled recovery options.

The automation works like this: when Vista detects a boot failure (also known as a Stop error), it will automatically restart into the SRT. The SRT then performs a series of diagnostic routines, including these:

- An analysis of startup logfiles
- A check of the hard drive for corrupted files
- A check of registry entries for unwanted processes
- An inspection of startup programs that could cause execution of programs such as spyware, viruses, and automatic dialers

And here's the magic: if the SRT is able to locate the source of the startup failure—it detects a corrupted Vista system file on the hard disk, for example—it then attempts to fix the problem automatically, saving Windows administrators lots of time, and thus, lots of money.

If the SRT is not able to isolate the problem, it will then try a reboot using the Last Known Good configuration. Also, the SRT can provide system administrators with valuable diagnostic information and support options to make troubleshooting easier.

 The SRT is not included on every computer because some hardware manufacturers either customize or replace this tool altogether. For more information, refer to your manufacturers' documentation.

As mentioned previously, the SRT should launch automatically upon detection of a Stop error. If it doesn't, however, you have the option of running it manually.

Using the SRT

If your system has the SRT installed, you can run it anytime you like. Here are the steps to use the SRT:

1. First, remove disks—floppy and optical—from the computer, and restart. Then take one of these two actions:
   - If the computer has a single operating system installed, press the F8 key as the computer restarts, and before the Windows logo appears.
   - If the computer is a dual-boot machine, use the arrow keys to select the operating system you want to repair at the boot selector menu. With the desired operating system selected, press the F8 key.

2. You now should see the Advanced Boot Options menu. From this screen, use the arrow keys to select "Repair the computer," and then press Enter.

3. Choose the appropriate keyboard layout and click Next. You are now prompted for a username and password.

4. In the Startup Recovery Options menu, click Startup Repair. Click Finish once the SRT has completed the repair process.

If the computer doesn't have the SRT preinstalled, you can still use it. All you need is the Windows Vista installation disc. Here are the steps to follow:

1. Insert the Vista installation disc and then restart using the disc as the boot-up media. You may have to edit the system BIOS to enable booting to the optical drive.

2. After restart, choose your language settings, and then click Next.

3. From the ensuing window, choose "Repair your computer."

4. Now, simply choose the operating system you want to repair, and then click Next.

5. From the System Recovery Options menu, choose Startup Repair.

Once again, the SRT begins its scan and diagnosis of the startup procedure. Click Finish to complete the repair process.

Also note that the SRT cannot address every computer failure, especially those due to hardware failures or virus attacks. Nor is it a backup tool; it won't be of any use in retrieving lost or damaged music, photos, or documents. (Backup options are discussed in Chapter 14.)

If the startup repair is unsuccessful, you'll see a summary of what happened as well as links where you can obtain further assistance.

Vista also includes a startup configuration tool administrators can use during an active Vista session. If you use this utility to maximize startup performance, the hope is that you will rarely, if ever, have to resort to the SRT.

System Startup with System Config

The Vista System Configuration utility—we'll truncate it to System Config—is a handy little utility that can control what happens at startup.

It's a very powerful tool, though, too powerful even to be located in the Control Panel. You won't find it there. Nor will you find it by simply digging around the Start menu. Although it can rightly be considered a system tool, don't go looking in the Vista Accessories → System Tools location. Because of its power, Microsoft hides System Config's executable in the Windows (technically the *%Systemroot%*) directory, and does not advertise this utility's presence.

But that's why you picked up this book, isn't it?

To use the System Config tool, open the Start menu and type **syst**. The System Config tool will appear in the list of programs at the top of the Start menu. You can also open the Run dialog box and type **msconfig**. Users who have used the System Config tool in previous versions of Windows will note that the executable filename has remained unchanged. If User Account Control is on, you will be prompted to click the Continue button.

The application window, shown in Figure 6-29, should also look familiar to users who have worked with this tool before.

Figure 6-29. System Config utility

The System Config tool can also prove its worth when it comes to troubleshooting. With the Selective Startup option, users have the ability to enable or disable startup services and/or programs on an individual basis.

Here's how to enable selective startup:

1. Choose the General tab, and then click the "Selective startup" radio button as shown in Figure 6-30.
2. Now, clear the "Load system services" and "Load startup items" checkboxes.
3. Select the "Load system services" checkbox, and click OK. You'll now be asked to restart your computer. (Obviously, the startup options will be a moot point until your system actually does some starting up.)

There are essentially two troubleshooting tasks that administrators can perform with selective startup.

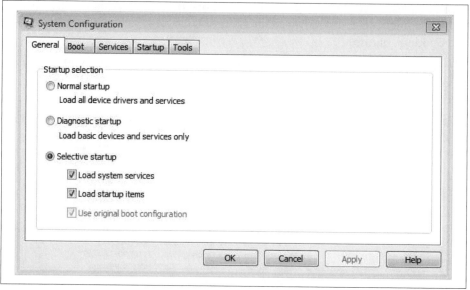

Figure 6-30. Troubleshooting by choosing "Selective startup"

Isolating the system service causing the problem

This generally involves starting only one startup service at a time. To perform the troubleshooting, follow these steps:

1. Use System Configuration's Services tab, shown in Figure 6-31, and choose the "Disable all" option.

2. Select the first service listed, and then restart the computer.

3. If the problem occurs, you've just targeted the guilty startup service. If the computer starts without incident, you need to repeat the process for each service listed.

4. Assuming the computer has started normally, choose the second service listed and make sure all others are unchecked. Restart the computer again.

As you can see, this can be a somewhat tedious process that involves several computer restarts (thank goodness the Vista startup process has been sped up). Eventually, though, you should be able to pinpoint the startup service causing the problem.

If you can't reproduce the problem, though, you may have to look to a startup program as the source of the trouble, which of course leads to the second thing the selective startup is good at.

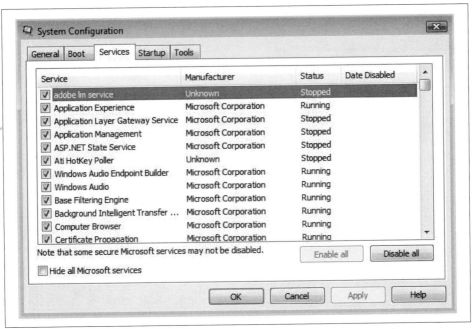

Figure 6-31. Disabling startup services with the System Configuration's Services tab

Isolating the startup item causing the problem

This looks at any applications that may be causing the issue. To perform startup item troubleshooting:

1. Open the System Config utility and with the General tab selected, choose the "Load startup items" checkbox.

2. Now, on the Startup tab, shown in Figure 6-32, click "Disable all."

3. One at a time, choose the startup items listed in this tab and restart the computer.

4. Like before, if the problems occur while just one of the startup items is checked, you've got your culprit. If the computer starts just fine, you need to choose a different startup item.

As you can guess, unchecking a checkbox disables the startup item, whereas leaving the box checked will tell Vista to continue to load the service or startup program.

 System Config is a great tool for helping to target startup problems, but it is not officially meant to manage the startup environment. If you don't want a program to run at startup time, you should change its properties using the "Uninstall or change a program" Control Panel application.

We'll look at the "Uninstall or change a program" application in more detail in Chapter 7.

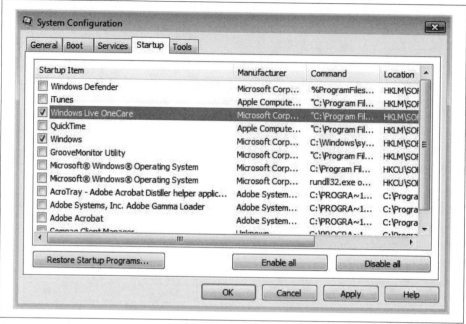

Figure 6-32. Choosing startup programs one at a time

Summary

In this chapter, we examined a few of the capabilities that can speed up Vista performance, especially at startup and shutdown. We started with an overview of Windows Vista performance and how the Windows Experience Index tries to encapsulate this into a sort of grading system. This WEI score will hopefully reduce confusion about the capabilities of both hardware and software when it's time to make a purchase.

But by far, the bulk of this chapter dealt with Vista startup and shutdown performance. After an overview of what happens at startup and shutdown, we examined many of the utilities that let administrators manipulate what happens during these two occurrences.

We looked at the Advanced Startup options, which can prove very valuable when admins run into startup difficulty, and we looked at the many options available for when it's time to put the computer away, both for a few minutes and for a few days.

Finally, we examined the System Configuration utility, and we learned about some of the ways in which it can modify the startup environment. We learned that it can be used to control not only Vista's startup programs, but also startup services as well.

In the next chapter, we will look extensively at how to work with Vista as a *platform*—how it can be managed and manipulated so that it best works with all the devices connected to it and all the applications running on it.

CHAPTER 7

Working with Hardware

As you are probably already aware, an operating system's main function is to serve as an intermediary—between hardware and applications, between hardware and users, and between applications and users.

In the next two chapters, we'll take a closer look at this role, and especially at instances in which a Vista administrator can and should step in. Although we start off with a general discussion of adding and updating any old hardware device, the majority of this chapter deals with just two main components: the hard disk drives and the printers. System administrators typically spend a good deal of time with these two components, especially in comparison with other hardware devices.

And there's a good reason why: many more administrative considerations go into optimizing deployment of these two hardware components than almost any other. Are you going to deploy basic or dynamic storage? Are you going to use a printer pool to serve the needs of your network? Are you going to take a disk out of one computer and access its data on another?

The answers to these questions represent just a bare minimum of the hardware choices faced by admins every day. Let's get started, then, with a look at how to install a new hardware component. You'll install many in your day, no doubt; you should know how Vista can help with the task.

Installing a Device

One of the great things about using the Windows platform is the ability to upgrade your hardware with a minimum of hassle. For the most part, stuff just attaches and works. After all, one of the most significant factors in Microsoft's rise to the top of the PC world has been the interoperability of Windows with such a wide array of software programs and hardware devices.

As of this writing, in fact, Microsoft boasts that Windows Vista is compatible with more than a million different hardware components.

So, as you might guess, if I detailed the click-steps for installing every imaginable piece of software, we'd be here for another 500 pages or so. This book is comprehensive, but not *that* comprehensive.

Fortunately, Vista makes it pretty easy to install most devices, and the click-steps don't vary a whole lot whether you're connecting a new monitor, a new hard drive, a new sound card, or a digital camera. Instead, I'll offer generic instructions on how to install a device—any device—and let you take it from there.

The first step in setting up a new device is to physically attach it. If you're upgrading a sound or video card, for example, first you need to shut down your Vista computer, open the case, and insert the card into the appropriate motherboard slot— PCI, PCI Express (PCIe), or AGP.

Then turn on the computer again. Depending on what you attached, Vista should now automatically detect the device and install appropriate drivers, as many hundreds of hardware drivers are included with the standard Vista installation.

What's more, if you've got Windows Update configured to allow for driver upgrades as part of the regular update routine, Vista will check for any newer drivers when you connect this device for the first time. Also, you may need to use Windows Update's "Check for updates" button to manually check for updated driver software.

The New Hardware Wizard

Another possibility is that Vista detects the newly installed device and launches the Found New Hardware Wizard, which walks you through these steps:

1. In the Found New Hardware Wizard Welcome dialog box, click the "Locate and install driver software (recommended)" option, as shown in Figure 7-1.

2. The wizard then searches both the Vista installation and the Internet (if connected) for appropriate drivers. If none is found, you're prompted to insert the driver disc that shipped with the device. You have two options:

   - If you have the disc, insert it and follow the wizard's prompts. The device should be set up properly when you're done (see Figure 7-2).

   - If you can't locate the installation disc, choose "I don't have the disk. Show me other options." Then follow the remaining prompts. Usually, the other option you have is not to use the device until you can track down the appropriate drivers (see Figure 7-3).

3. You can also browse your computer for drivers using the Browse button in the Found New Hardware Wizard. This might be helpful if you've already downloaded or transferred the right driver files, but you have stored them in a location that Vista doesn't normally search.

Figure 7-1. Vista can find driver software automatically

Figure 7-2. Installing a driver

4. If the driver install goes smoothly, you get a confirmation dialog box telling you that the process has worked. If not, you get a dialog box informing you of such. If the wizard cannot install the device, there might be a problem with the hardware itself. Nine times out of 10, however, the problem rests with the drivers.

Hardware manufacturers usually document setup instructions just fine. Sometimes they want you to install the drivers before attaching the device. If you can follow their instructions, really, you should never have a problem with a new piece of hardware on Windows Vista, assuming it's compatible in the first place.

The bottom line is this: either the device will install or it won't, and it usually isn't worth a whole lot of administrative calisthenics to get the device up and running. Hardware manufacturers have (presumably) tested their devices before they box them up and ship them out to stores, so if you can follow the manufacturer's instructions, everything should work out just fine.

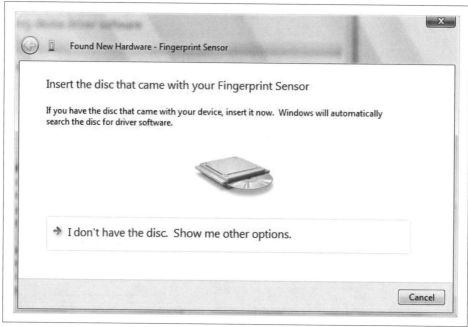

Figure 7-3. *Manually installing from disk*

If the thing doesn't work, my general advice is to take it back to where you got it. Wrestling with hardware is one of those time equals money equations that will never work in your favor. Something else is probably on the shelves that will do what you want it to do for a few bucks more.

The real administrative task, then, is to understand how to manage your hardware devices once they're installed, and that's what the rest of the chapter is all about.

We start with the Windows tool that's been used for hardware management for years: the Device Manager.

Using the Device Manager to Monitor Devices

Once you've set up the hardware on your Vista machine, the main tool used to further manage these devices is called the Device Manager. This utility provides a detailed list of all devices attached to the computer, and can even be used to perform hardware management on remote systems (instructions to follow). The Device Manager should look pretty familiar to previous Windows administrators, and both the look and the function of the Device Manager remain essentially unchanged.

Here's a brief overview, then, for those who are using Windows for the first time. This could also be relevant information for those who have used Windows for years, but are just now donning the hat of system administrator.

To access the Device Manager, you simply type **dev** from the Start menu. Although it's a Control Panel application, it should appear as a separate entity at the top of the Start menu's Programs list. You can also find it in the Administrative Tools grouping. You now may be asked for administrative confirmation.

The Device Manager console now displays, as shown in Figure 7-4. The tree hierarchy displays the computer, followed by a list of all attached, installed devices. You can navigate the Device Manager much like Windows Explorer: just click the plus sign (+) next to the device type to see a more detailed list of devices.

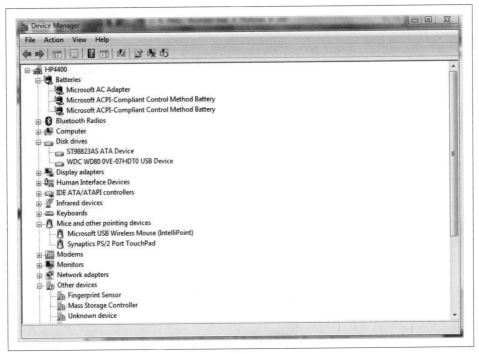

Figure 7-4. The Device Manager shows all connected hardware

There's yet another way to access the Device Manager, and that's through the Computer Management MMC console. To do so, right-click the Computer icon or button (if available) and choose Manage. Otherwise, type **comp** from the Start menu and the Computer Management item should appear.

The advantage of accessing the Device Manager through the Computer Management MMC console is that it lets you access remote systems, as mentioned previously. To connect to another system, right-click the Computer Management item in the console tree and choose Connect to Another Computer. You are then prompted to browse for another system; you also have the option of simply typing the Fully Qualified Domain Name (FQDN) for the computer, as seen in Figure 7-5.

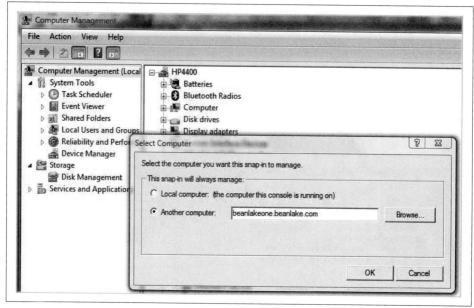

Figure 7-5. In the Computer Management MMC console, you can use the Device Manager on another system

A handy troubleshooting aid in the Device Manager is that you will see warning icons if there are problems with a detected device. For example, if you have an improperly installed driver, the icon looks like Figure 7-6.

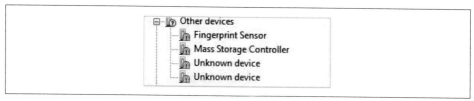

Figure 7-6. There is a problem with these devices; access the Properties dialog box to find out more

And if the device has been disabled, the notification icon looks like a little down arrow instead, as shown in Figure 7-7.

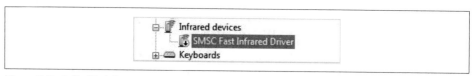

Figure 7-7. A disabled device

As I've mentioned, you can perform several management tasks from the Device Manager, and just about every single one starts with a right-click. Depending on the device, the right-click allows admins to:

- Uninstall the device.
- Disable the device.
- Enable the device.
- Scan for hardware changes (this is useful for when you attach a device and its drivers are not immediately installed).
- Update the driver.

And let's not forget the option to access a set of properties for the device, revealing a host of additional options. To access the Properties pages, just right-click the device and choose Properties from the context menu. You get a dialog box similar to the one shown in Figure 7-8, although options vary somewhat from device to device.

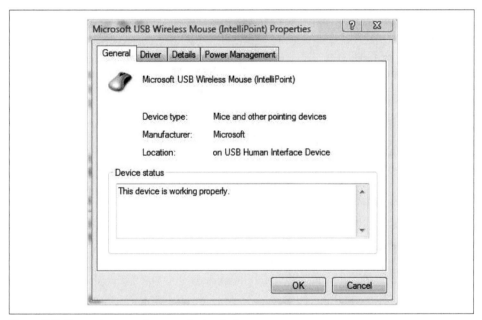

Figure 7-8. Properties pages for a particular device

Again, depending on the device, you can gather lots of information and/or take administrative actions from here.

The Device Manager makes itself even more useful by allowing administrators to change the views on connected hardware. By accessing the View menu choices, you can examine the following:

Devices by Type

This is the default view seen previously, grouping items by device type. Expand a type to view and manage specific devices.

Devices by Connection

This shows devices by connection type. For example, you could use this view to look at everything connected to the Serial ATA bus, as shown in Figure 7-9.

Resources by Type

This shows which devices are using which resources. Resources used by a device include Interrupt Request (IRQ) lines, memory addresses, input/output (I/O) ports, and direct memory access (DMA) channels. I'll discuss DMA a bit more later on.

Resources by Connection

This shows all allocated resources by the connection type instead of the device type.

Show Hidden Devices

This reveals any non-Plug and Play devices. It is also very useful at showing devices that have been physically removed, yet whose device drivers still remain. You can then use the Device Manager to remove unneeded device drivers (although in most cases, they won't do any harm if you don't remove them).

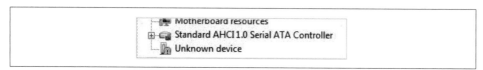

Figure 7-9. Displaying resources by connection

Use the Windows Update Driver Settings

Another significant driver setting function is telling Vista what to do when a new device is connected. You will do this with a dialog box called the Windows Update Driver Settings. You will have three options each time a new device is connected:

- Check for drivers automatically (recommended)
- Ask me each time I connect a new device before checking for drivers
- Never check for drivers when I connect a device

This driver update setting can be found using the System Properties dialog box. To open it, follow these steps:

1. Open the System Control Panel application, then follow the Advanced System Settings link from the left.

2. In the System Properties dialog box that follows, choose the Hardware tab.

3. Click the Windows Update Driver Settings button and make the selection from the dialog box that appears.

Using DMA

DMA is a critical component of modern systems. It allows storage devices such as hard drives and optical drives to have direct access to memory addresses without the CPU having to get involved and spending a lot of time and processing power simply copying data from one location (the drive) into another (memory). This frees up the CPU to execute other tasks while data is on the move.

Besides hard drive and optical drive controllers, lots of other hardware devices take advantage of DMA: graphics cards, network cards, and sound cards. We'll deal with just the hard drive instructions here, as they will have the biggest impact on performance.

Under most circumstances, administrators don't have to perform much configuration of DMA. By default, Vista will enable DMA for devices that support it. However, there are times when you might need to turn it on manually. This can include instances in which the device was improperly installed, or when a system error has occurred at installation time.

To manually turn on DMA, then, just follow these steps:

1. Open Vista's Device Manager. It's a Control Panel application with its own icon if you're using the Classic View. You can also find it pretty easily from the Start menu by typing **dev**.

2. If you're using User Account Control, you will be prompted for administrator confirmation.

3. Direct memory comes into play for Integrated Drive Electronics (IDE) devices, so click the plus sign next to "IDE ATA/ATAPI controllers" to expand it.

4. Look for items with the word *Channel* in their labels. Access the Properties dialog boxes for each of these by right-clicking and choosing Properties.

5. In the Advanced Settings dialog box, shown in Figure 7-10, look in the Device Properties section and either select or clear the Enable DMA checkbox.

6. Click OK and close the Device Manager to commit the changes.

Installing a USB Device

In most cases, installing a USB device will be one of the most trouble-free hardware installations you perform. That's because USB largely fulfills the promise of Plug and Play—as in you *plug* it into the computer, and then you can use it (*play*) right away. (There's another way to phrase what I just wrote, but the connotations are just too puerile.)

Anyway, here's what *will* happen when you attach a USB device: Vista *will* automatically install the proper driver software for that device and you'll be able to use it right away. Now, after subsequently removing the device, you can freely connect and disconnect it at any time without Vista having to perform a driver install every time.

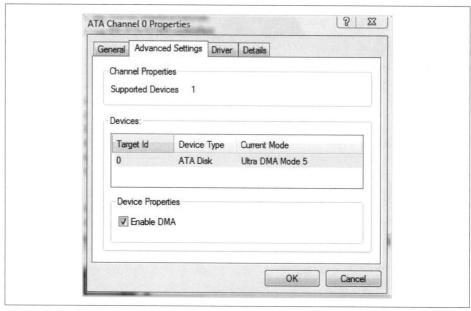

Figure 7-10. Manually setting the DMA attributes for the device

OK, let's go back and replace *will* in that preceding paragraph with *should*. It *should* work just as advertised, but books like this aren't written because computers and operating systems always behave as expected.

As your mother could warn you, it's always a good idea to read the instructions that came with the USB device you're trying to connect. Some can be finicky about how they're installed. For example, many require that you turn on the power *before* you connect the device, but others want you to power the devices *after* making the physical connection. Moreover, many devices come with driver software that won't be included with Vista's set of drivers; in this case, it's almost always recommended that you install the drivers *first* before connecting the device. With the drivers already part of the Vista filesystem, successful USB device installation is all but ensured.

Removing a USB device

As with installation, removal of a USB device usually requires the same mechanical know-how as turning off a toaster. Just unplug the thing. The only caveat, really, is to make sure you're not in the middle of a data transfer.

This is where the Safely Remove Hardware System Tray icon comes into play. If you see this icon in this area, you can use it to ensure that a device you want to remove has completed all operations in progress and is ready to be removed.

To use it, just give it a click. You're now presented with a list of devices. Choose the device you want to remove. Vista then gives you a notification dialog box telling you that it's safe to remove, as seen in Figure 7-11.

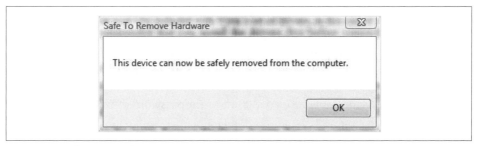

Figure 7-11. The coast is clear

Troubleshooting USB device installation. Besides what I've already covered, the handiest piece of advice I can pass along regarding USB device installation is that it's also a good idea to try different ports if you're certain that the drivers have been properly set up, but the device still won't work.

In my days under many a cubicle desk (stop it), I've seen lots of occasions where a device will work when plugged into one USB port but not another. For instance, the USB hard drive works when attached to the front ports, but not the rear ones. Usually this is because of an improper physical connection, and usually this is not worth troubleshooting. You'd have to shut down, crack open the case, and reconnect a bunch of tiny wires.

In these instances, just remember that the nature of the USB bus allows you to connect multiple devices over a single port. Pick up a USB hub for $2.99 and bingo—problem solved.

Updating Hardware Driver Software

Sometimes it's necessary to update device driver software even if everything is working smoothly. This is normally because an upgrade of another component or software installation may not be compatible unless you have the latest driver.

Although not really a hardcore administrative reason, the most common one I've seen is when a new game requires an update of the video card driver. If that's the case, you need to know how to perform this update.

There are actually two ways to update driver software for a device that's already in use. One is to use Windows Update to install the new driver automatically. The other is to manually update the driver using the Vista Device Manager. Both methods are described here. Once again, we'll deal with a generic situation, because that's all that's necessary; the steps for updating driver software don't differ significantly from device to device.

Both of these methods assume an active Internet connection.

Here's how to update a driver using Windows update:

1. Open the Control Panel's Windows Update application. If you're using the Standard View, look for the link under the Security grouping. Typing **update** at the Start menu works like a charm as well.

2. You may now be prompted for an administrator password or confirmation.

3. In the left pane of the Windows Update dialog box, click the "Check for updates" link. Vista then checks online for any available updates.

4. After the scan, look at the righthand side of your screen. In the main section of the Windows Update window, you should also see a notification regarding whether any updates are available. If you see one (or more), follow the "View available updates" link to the right. Figure 7-12 is an example of what this will look like.

5. Next, in the Windows Update dialog box shown in Figure 7-13, any updated drivers are listed. From here, just check the driver update you'd like to apply and then click Install.

6. Once again, you will be prompted for an administrator password or confirmation if you're using User Account Control. Vista doesn't allow access to vital system components without authorization.

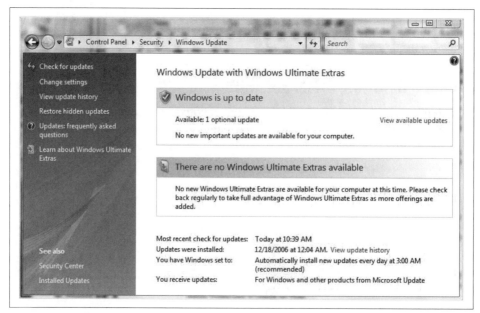

Figure 7-12. Updates are available

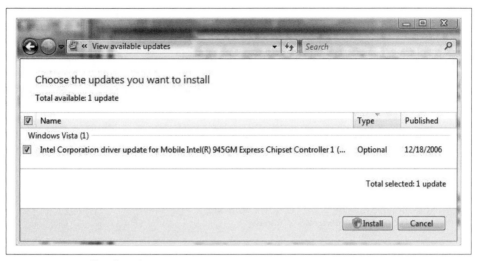

Figure 7-13. Install updates here

 By default, Windows Update is configured to check for updates automatically. You may not have to actually scan for updates, but rather just use this tool to view and install available ones. (In other words, you can pretty much ignore steps 1 through 3 in most cases.)

Now that we've covered the automated way of updating a device driver, let's examine the steps to do the same thing manually.

Updating drivers manually

Here's what to do:

1. Open the Device Manager Control Panel application. Once again, typing **dev** from the Start menu will find it quickly. You may be prompted for an administrator password or confirmation.

2. In the Device Manager window, find the device you want to update, and then access its Properties dialog box with a double-click.

3. In the device's Properties dialog box, choose the Driver tab, and then click Update Driver. (A shortcut: right-click the device you want to update. Either way, you'll end up at the next step.)

4. You now should see a dialog box asking you how to locate the updated driver software. There are two choices here: to either search automatically for updated software or browse for the driver file manually, as seen in Figure 7-14.

Each choice will result in different completion paths. The process is not too difficult, though; just follow the on-screen prompts and you shouldn't have any trouble.

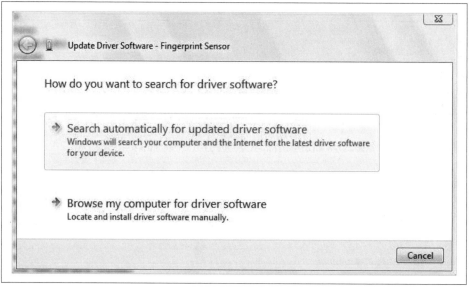

Figure 7-14. Updating driver software

Restoring a Driver to a Previous Version

At times, updating a driver causes the opposite effect of what was intended. Instead of making computer performance better, it mucks things up. For example, you may find that the new driver causes an application to crash, interferes with normal output to the monitor, or just generally causes slow performance.

In that case, you can easily *roll back* the driver, restoring it to its previous version. Here's what to do:

1. Open the Device Manager from the Control Panel. If User Account Control is enabled, you are prompted for administrative confirmation.

2. Expand the device category for the device giving you trouble, and then access the device's Properties dialog box by either right-clicking and selecting Properties, or by double-clicking.

3. Select the Driver tab, shown in Figure 7-15, and then click the Roll Back Driver button.

4. You are then shown a confirmation dialog box warning you about the procedure. Click OK to officially restore the old driver.

 You can also roll back a driver after booting to Safe Mode. In fact, it can even be necessary to boot to Safe Mode first before rolling back the driver—the driver problem being such that Vista is unable to boot normally. For further details about Safe Mode, see Chapter 8.

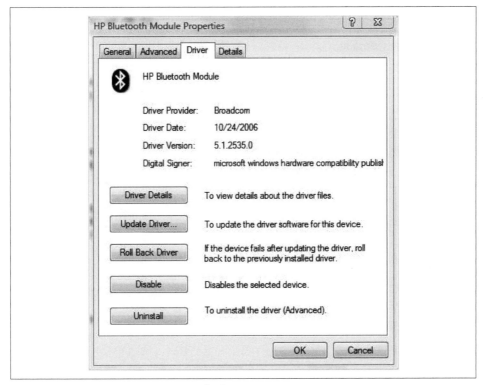

Figure 7-15. Restore a previous version of a driver

Finally, notice that for some devices, the Roll Back Driver button will be unavailable. If a driver hasn't been updated, the option to restore the original won't be available, either.

So far, we've covered some basic device installation and upgrade steps. With most devices you attach to your Vista computer, the objective is merely to get this thing working. When you're connecting some devices such as a hard drive, getting it to work is only half the battle. You need to make a host of other administrative decisions regarding how that hard drive space will be used, as you will see in the pages that follow.

Driver Signing Options

To hear Microsoft tell it, bad drivers are the bane of a stable computing environment, and one of the biggest contributors to operating system crashes.

As a countermeasure, then, Microsoft has developed the Microsoft Hardware Qualifying Lab. Part of this lab's job is to test hardware devices and drivers for compatibility and stability.

If a particular driver is approved, it bears the Designed for Windows logo and is *digitally signed*. Drivers carrying a digital signature appear with a little green checkmark and diploma thingamajig.

Figure 7-16 shows a driver that's been digitally signed.

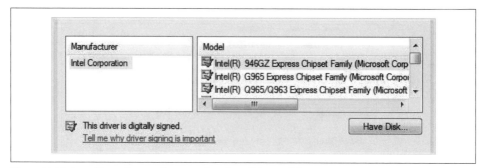

Figure 7-16. Installing a legacy device with a digitally signed driver

So, what happens if you install a driver that isn't digitally signed? You get a dialog box with two options:

- Don't install the driver.
- Install the driver.

I didn't say it was complicated. So, which will you choose? You will install the unsigned driver, of course, Microsoft's warnings about bad device drivers notwithstanding. After all, you purchased the new device for a reason: you want to see whether the thing will run. What's more, many drivers, at least in the early days of Vista's rollout (let's say the first six months of 2007) have not yet been signed by the Windows Hardware Quality Labs (WHQL), even though they are from popular manufacturers and work just fine.

And truth be told, there's really not *that* much to worry about. The worst that could happen is that your system crashes, in which case you should be able to reset things by booting into Safe Mode and then using a Restore Point. So, the advice, then, is to remember to make sure to set a Restore Point before installing an unsigned driver, right?

Not necessarily. Vista does this for you automatically anytime you install an unsigned driver.

I'll discuss recovering to a Restore Point in more detail in Chapter 14.

 In previous Windows iterations, you could set default options for handling unsigned device drivers with the System Properties dialog box. With Vista, you don't have this option; you get the "install or don't install" dialog box instead.

If you're an administrator who is concerned about unsigned device drivers and the system instability they are causing in your network, you can configure several options that govern an end user's options about using unsigned drivers. All it takes is a little knowledge of the Group Policy settings.

Here's what to do on a local machine:

1. Open the Group Policy Object Editor, and then open the Group Policy Object (GPO) that links to the local machine. There are a few ways to do this, the easiest of which is to type **gpedit.msc** at the Vista Start menu.

2. Now, navigate to the following node:

    User Configuration\Administrative Templates\System\Driver Installation

3. Here you will see three configuration settings. The relevant one for our purposes is the one labeled "Code signing for device drivers." Double-click it.

4. Now choose Enabled. As seen in Figure 7-17, you will then be able to configure one of three settings in a drop-down menu. These selections will govern behavior when Vista stumbles across a driver that is unsigned:

Ignore
> Vista will install all unsigned drivers without interruption.

Warn
> This is the default behavior; you are prompted with a dialog box asking you whether to install.

Block
> Vista will not install an unsigned driver.

You don't always have to tighten security. On a testing computer, for example, you probably *don't* want any notifications about unsigned drivers, and you can safely choose Ignore.

We'll explore GPOs in more detail in Chapter 13.

> There are some drivers, by the way, that Vista "black-flags." If Vista "knows" that drivers are prone to causing instability problems, it simply will block installation. You get a dialog box that allows only one option: to cancel the installation.

One more thing: the 64-bit version of Vista *requires* that all drivers be signed. If you don't have anything else to do, you can read more about it at:

http://www.microsoft.com/whdc/system/platform/64bit/kmsigning.mspx

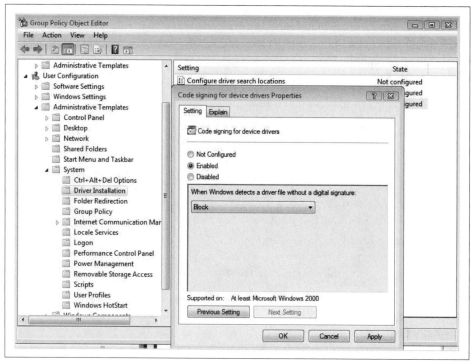

Figure 7-17. Configuring unsigned driver options

Installing a New Hard Drive

A very common computer device upgrade is to create additional storage by adding a hard drive. There are several ways to add this storage, and the specific installation instructions will vary depending on the choices.

One option is to add an external hard drive with a USB 2.0 connection. This probably involves the least amount of hassle, and the steps are exactly the same as adding any other USB device: just plug it in and it should work.

> Yes, you can attach FireWire drives as well, but they aren't nearly as common for several reasons that are really beyond the scope of this book. If you have a high-end Sony or Dell laptop, you probably have a built-in FireWire port, although Sony calls it i.Link. For maximum compatibility between computers, you're probably better off with a USB 2.0 external drive. Speed differences are comparable.

Unlike many other USB devices, however, there are still a few more configuration details to take care of before you're able to use the storage. You need to take the same steps with an external drive that you do with an internal drive. Namely, you will still have to make decisions about partitions and formatting. The next couple of sections examine each task.

 Adding a new hard drive in some ways resolves the whole HD-DVD versus Blu-Ray conundrum. Of those two technologies, which is better? It doesn't matter. They both were antiquated technologies the minute they came out, and they both are a complete waste of money. You'll be no more likely to carry around movies on plastic discs in the next five years than you have carried around music on plastic discs in the previous five years. All content, HD or otherwise, will be stored on hard drives.

Before getting into the specific details, though, we first need to discuss installation of an internal drive.

Adding an Internal Drive

I'll assume you're already familiar with the concept: the internal hard drive is your computer's filing cabinet. The bigger the cabinet is, the more stuff (music, pictures, movies, etc.) you can cram into it. And over the next few years, humans are going to be involved in a race to take as many items off physical media (film, tapes, paper, etc.) and cram them onto any hard drives they can find.

We're going to need bigger filing cabinets.

Fortunately, additional storage—especially internal storage—can be had for less than a dollar per gigabyte. Adding an internal hard drive is a very likely upgrade for you in the near term.

When upgrading, you essentially have two choices: you can either transfer the contents of your current system to a larger-capacity hard drive, or simply add more cabinet space. If you're doing the former, a few other considerations enter the picture, such as imaging what's already there and then deploying that image onto the larger-capacity drive. We won't discuss those options here. Lots of third-party software solutions can help with this task, and if you need additional help, feel free to drop me an email (*hmsbrian@brianculp.com*).

What we'll discuss instead is the second option: adding more "filing cabinet" space. To add another hard drive, you must crack open the computer case. You should bear in mind that most laptops have room for only a single hard drive, so adding a new internal drive isn't usually an option.

If you're installing an IDE device, you have to decide whether to designate the drive as a master or a slave, which you usually do with a jumper setting on the drive. Alternatively, most desktop motherboards have two IDE connectors for fixed storage devices, and you could install one drive on IDE channel 1 and the other on IDE channel 2. Again, it all depends on the particular hardware you have. Refer to your system and drive documentation for instructions.

If you're attaching a second Serial ATA (SATA) hard drive, you won't face any of these concerns. SATA is a newer hard drive technology that offers several advantages over IDE drives, including increased speed and reduced power consumption. With SATA, each drive is connected to a single destination on the motherboard. Because SATA devices do not share an interface, there's no need for master/slave jumper settings. Nonetheless, IDE drives are still in use on a great number of machines.

After you have added the drive to the motherboard, you can start using Vista's disk management tool, Disk Management. To access this utility, do the following:

1. Open the Computer Management MMC console. You can type **comp** at the Start menu, or look in the Administrative Tools grouping.

2. From the Computer Management MMC console, expand the Storage node, and then select Disk Management. You'll now see the interface shown in Figure 7-18.

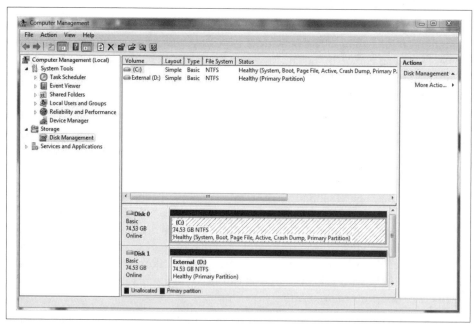

Figure 7-18. Most disk management tasks can be done from here

Assuming you've properly installed the new hard disk, you should now see it in the list of storage devices. Its capacity should be recognized, and the status should be set to Online. If you're attaching a blank hard drive for the first time, the available space will appear as Unformatted.

But simply recognizing the new drive is not enough. Before you can start using its space, you still have a few more steps to complete. But before discussing these steps, I'd like to explore a hard drive technology available in Windows Vista that can have a major impact on the drive's future capabilities.

Basic Versus Dynamic Storage

Windows Vista can use two *types* of storage on hard drives: basic and dynamic. Here's a brief summary of each storage type's capabilities:

Basic

This is the traditional method of storing data. Basic disks use *partition*-based logical storage, which carries with it several rules and regulations. In brief, a basic disk can contain up to three primary partitions and one extended partition. Each primary partition gets assigned a logical drive letter; extended partitions can be subdivided into multiple logical drives. (There are exceptions, which I'll discuss.) When dealing with partitions in Windows Vista, they are known as basic *volumes*. The main benefit of a basic disk is its flexibility, as a basic disk can be read by MS-DOS and all Windows operating systems.

Dynamic

This is not new to Windows Vista, but it is a more powerful and flexible (i.e., dynamic, get it?) storage choice. Dynamic disks use *volume*-based logical storage rather than partition-based storage, meaning that dynamic disks just take a chunk of space from the hard disk and treat it as a logical drive—leaving you with none of the rules or regulations to deal with when working with basic storage.

By default, Windows Vista installs using basic storage. You have to upgrade a basic disk to make it dynamic.

Just know as we start the discussion here that the terms *partition* and *volume* are used interchangeably throughout almost all technical documentation. And for practical purposes, they are interchangeable: a logical chunk of physical disk space that can be formatted with a filesystem and used to store information. The picture becomes clearer as we go along.

For the time being, I'll pretend I'm an economist and make assumptions that will serve our hard disk discussion. The first is that I'll assume you're setting up a basic disk, and therefore you will need to prepare that disk.

Partitioning the Drive

A physical hard drive cannot store data unless it is first partitioned and then formatted. Partitioning divides the real estate of the hard drive into discrete logical sections.

Formatting, then, takes those chunks of logical sections and divides them into storage containers, and then creates a tracking system so that the BIOS and operating system can keep track of what files are stored where. You can think of the tracking system as sort of like the table of contents of a book.

As mentioned previously, a hard disk won't store anything until a partition has been defined. And of course, there's no reason you can't create more than one partition if it better suits your needs.

One of the main reasons admins might consider multiple partitions is to use different filesystems on a single physical drive. One partition can use the FAT filesystem, for example, and the other can use NTFS. (I define these filesystems later in the chapter.) Another reason is performance. Generally speaking, smaller partitions make more efficient use of disk space.

To partition a newly added hard drive:

1. Right-click an area of unused hard drive space in the Disk Management utility and choose New Simple Volume.

2. In the New Simple Volume Wizard that launches, click Next from the welcome screen, then select the volume size, as shown in Figure 7-19.

3. The following dialog box lets you select the volume drive letter. Alternatively, you could mount the new volume in an empty NTFS folder or not assign a drive letter at all.

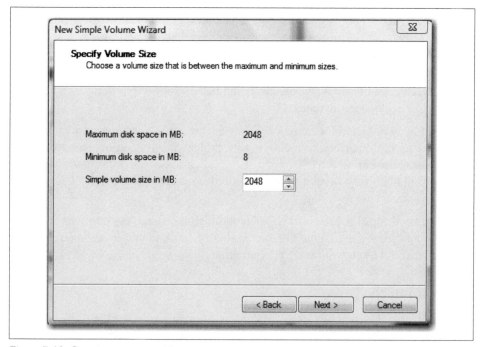

Figure 7-19. Creating a new partition

4. You can assign any drive letter other than B, which (believe it or not) is still reserved for a second floppy drive. (It dates back to the days when computers needed two 5.25-inch floppy disks—one for the operating system and one for whatever data you wanted to work with.)

5. After clicking Next once more, you will then see a dialog box that lets you immediately format the new simple volume using the filesystem of your choosing. Note, however, that you don't necessarily have to decide at this time. You can leave the new volume unformatted as well.

6. The last dialog box in the New Simple Volume Wizard confirms your choices. Click Back to return to the Wizard screens, or click Finish to complete the operations.

You should now have a chunk of disk space that is ready to store data.

If you choose not to format the volume at the time it's created, you will still see the new volume displayed in the Disk Management utility as a separate storage entity. The only difference is that this new space will still appear as "unformatted," with diagonal stripes across it.

 Vista Explorer shows you logical drives, not physical drives. The only way to verify that you're using a single physical drive or multiple ones is to use the Disk Management tool.

Furthermore, several rules govern partition behavior:

- A single disk can have either four primary partitions, or up to three primary partitions and one extended partition.

- A primary partition can be assigned only a single drive letter. Extended partitions can be subdivided into multiple logical drives.

- Once set, partitions cannot be resized with the built-in Vista tools.

I've discussed a lot of terms so far, especially if you don't have much experience administering a Windows environment. (Just wait until we get to the printing section.) Now let's talk about what happens after you create a partition.

Formatting the Volume

You need to complete one more step before you can actually use the new disk space. To keep track of files, you must format simple volumes with a filesystem. Filesystems essentially represent a set of rules that is followed by the operating system for the storage and retrieval of information on a logical drive.

Not available yet: the Windows File System (WinFS). In, oh, about 2003 or so, the operating system you're reading about right now was supposed to ship with something called WinFS. It promised (and still does) a quantum change in the way you manage and access files and folders.

The hope for WinFS is that you'll be able to aggregate information in multiple applications to make much more powerful use of that data. Wikipedia has a great article where you can read about it—hey, why don't you add Wikipedia as a search provider in Internet Explorer 7 and look it up? (Turn to Chapter 10 for instructions.) There's one hypothetical query in the article that pretty neatly summarizes the promise of WinFS, capturing the reason Mr. Gates himself has referred to it as the "Holy Grail." It reads like this:

"...it is nearly impossible to search for 'the phone numbers of all persons who live in Acapulco and each have more than 100 appearances in my photo collection and with whom I have had e-mail within [the] last month' ...WinFS solves this problem...."

Someday. At any rate, formatting a simple volume using the currently available filesystems takes only a couple of steps:

1. Right-click on a partition space in the Disk Management tool and choose Format from the context menu.

2. You'll see a dialog box asking you which filesystem to use, as shown in Figure 7-20. Note that you can also redefine the volume label and choose the allocation unit size. Further, you can enable file and folder compression with a single click.

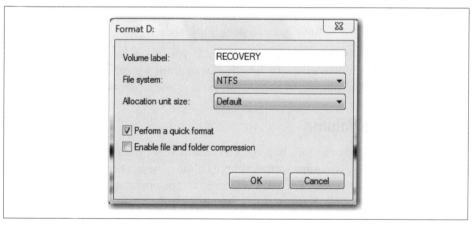

Figure 7-20. Filesystem selection

Now, try to perform the preceding steps with the C: drive. I'm betting that your C: drive is the one marked "(System, Boot, Page File, Active, Crash Dump, Primary Partition)." Yes, that one. Go ahead.

What happens? You can't, of course. The Disk Management tool includes a little safety mechanism that won't let you reformat these partitions. To do so would be disastrous for your computer (and by disastrous I mean really bad, which is the technical jargon for wiping out the entire contents of the volume, rendering your Vista computer unusable). Also, know that these System, Boot, and so on partitions don't always have to be located on the same logical drive. You can designate other logical drives with these roles, which I'll touch on in a bit.

So, which filesystem is best? Well, that depends on your storage goals, of course, as I'll detail more in the sections that follow.

FAT and FAT32 filesystems

The FAT filesystem divides space on a fixed disk into exactly 65,536 (16 bits' worth, or 216) storage locations, and each location is assigned a number. The storage locations are also known as clusters. A *cluster* is the smallest unit of storage space on a FAT partition.

File location in these storage spaces is tracked by the File Allocation Table, which, as mentioned earlier, works very much like the table of contents for this book—in cluster (page number) x lives file (topic) y.

FAT32 is an updated version of FAT that generally uses smaller cluster sizes, simply because it creates so many more of them (2^{32} of them, to be exact). Smaller cluster sizes generally result in more efficient use of a logical drive's disk space, and moreover support much larger drives.

But it is not the default filesystem for Windows Vista. NTFS is the default, and it makes even better use of larger drives, not to mention the host of improved security features in Vista.

So, why on Earth would you want to format a drive using the FAT32 filesystem? In a word: *compatibility*. The FAT32 filesystem was first introduced with the release of Windows 95 OEM Service Release 2 (OSR2), and it has been supported on all Windows versions since then. If your goal is to store data on a drive that will be used on earlier Windows versions, FAT32 might be your best choice.

However, it is not compatible with Windows NT versions 4.0 and earlier.

NTFS filesystem

NTFS (NT File System, depending on whom you ask) was first used with the Windows NT operating system many years ago and has been steadily improved ever since. It provides the highest level of performance and features for Windows Vista computers, and thus is the default filesystem used at installation.

Many of the enhancements to Windows operating systems over the years are technically enhancements to the filesystem, which continues to evolve much like any other software component. At the time of this writing, Vista uses NTFS version 3.1. The filesystem technologies included with NTFS 3.1 include compression, quotas, and encryption, technologies that haven't always been a part of the Windows NTFS environment. All of these technologies are covered within this book.

NTFS supports volumes of up to 2 terabytes, and as with FAT32, cluster size is relatively small. This means NTFS makes efficient use of disk space and is well suited for larger drives.

One other significant advantage of NTFS is that it allows for *local* security of files and folders, which is especially important when two or more users are accessing the same computer. With NTFS, different users can be assigned different levels of access to a resource. For example, one user may have access permission to change a particular file, whereas another user only has permission to read that file. This kind of local security is not possible with a FAT partition.

The biggest drawback when using an NTFS volume is in terms of compatibility, although this is becoming less of an issue as time goes on. Windows 9.*x* computers don't have the necessary filesystem drivers to read data from NTFS partitions. Windows 2000, XP, and Server 2003 operating systems do. About the only instance in which you would need to format your Vista system drive with the FAT filesystem is if you plan to dual-boot with Windows 98.

 Sometimes confusing is the fact that a Windows 9.*x* computer can still access data housed on an NTFS partition as long as that access occurs over the network. In that case, the Vista computer fields the request from the Windows 9.*x* system and then retrieves the appropriate filesystem drivers needed to access the data. In practice, that means you can have a workgroup set up with some computers running Windows 9.*x* and some running Vista without having to worry about formatting all your Vista drives with FAT.

Although we'll perform most disk administration tasks with the graphical utilities, we need to take a brief detour here to mention the command-line utilities that achieve the same objectives.

Partitioning and Formatting Utilities

Besides the graphical disk management utilities just discussed, Vista includes a couple of command-line utilities you might find useful.

The first is DiskPart, the command-line utility that lets you view and manage volumes. To launch DiskPart, open a Command window and simply type **diskpart** from the command line. You'll be asked for administrative confirmation if User Account Control is turned on.

A second command window then opens at a DISKPART prompt. From here, you can mark a partition as active; create, delete, shrink, and extend partitions; and even perform repairs on advanced volume configurations such as RAID 5. For a full listing of the possible commands as well as syntax on usage, type **help** from the DISKPART command prompt.

One of the advantages of DiskPart is that it can be used in scripted operations.

The other utility worth mentioning here is FSUtil, which allows administrators to configure disk quotas, view filesystem information, and manage volume size and number.

To launch FSUtil from the command line, you need to first open the Command Prompt in administrative mode (an elevated command prompt). One way to do this is to right-click the Command Prompt Start menu shortcut and choose Run as Administrator from the context menu. You'll then be prompted for administrative confirmation if User Account Control is turned on (see Figure 7-21).

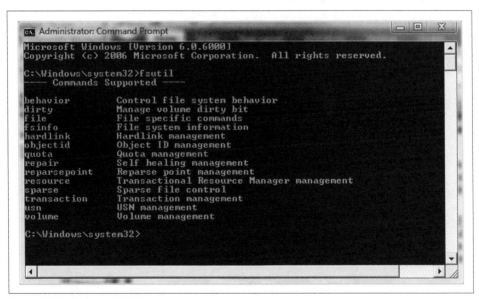

Figure 7-21. Running FSUtil

For full details about the possible commands and their syntax, type **fsutil help** at the elevated Command Prompt.

Changing Volume Properties

New to Windows Vista is the ability to change the size of a basic volume. This is a major, major departure from basic disk behavior of the past, where partition size was locked.

Using the old rules, anytime an admin wanted to change a partition's size, she had to delete and resize from scratch. This was not a huge deal from a button-clicking standpoint, but it was a huge headache when the actual data was factored in. That's because deleting a partition wipes out all data on that partition, and admins had to be careful about backing up before changing partition size—restoring from backup was the only way to get that data back.

The only other option prior to Windows Vista was to deploy a third-party utility such as Partition Magic.

But thankfully, that's no longer the case. At least sort of. It depends.

The click-steps to extend a basic volume are very straightforward:

1. Open the Disk Management console and right-click the volume you'd like to extend.

2. From the context menu, choose Extend Volume, and then follow the instructions in the wizard, as seen in Figure 7-22.

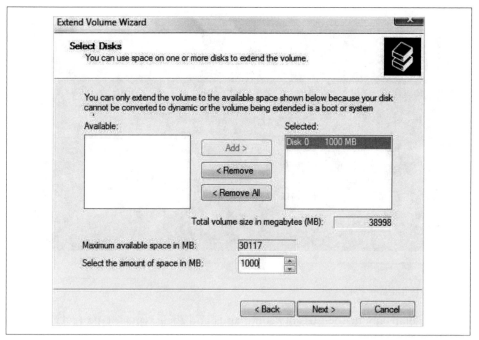

Figure 7-22. Extending a basic volume

You can also accomplish the same goal with the DiskPart command-line utility, as mentioned earlier.

But you might not even have the option of extending a basic volume. Here are the caveats:

- The volume you want to extend must be either raw (no filesystem yet) or format-ted with the NTFS filesystem.
- You can't extend volumes formatted with FAT or FAT32.
- You can extend only simple volumes. You can't extend a striped volume.
- You can't extend a system or boot volume, no matter the filesystem, unless you upgrade to a dynamic disk.
- You can extend a spanned volume only after you upgrade to a dynamic disk.
- You can extend a drive within contiguous free space in the extended partition that contains it. If you extend a basic volume beyond the available free space in the extended partition, the extended partition grows by the same amount.

Shrinkage

I'm not referring to theft in the retail business, but rather another administrative function available on Windows Vista basic volumes. You can reduce volume size as well.

As with expansion, you can shrink a simple or spanned volume. Again, the tool is either Disk Management or DiskPart. After right-clicking the volume you'd like to take down a notch, choose Shrink Volume from the context menu.

The Shrink dialog box appears, shown in Figure 7-23. Choose the amount of space to remove from the volume and click the Shrink button.

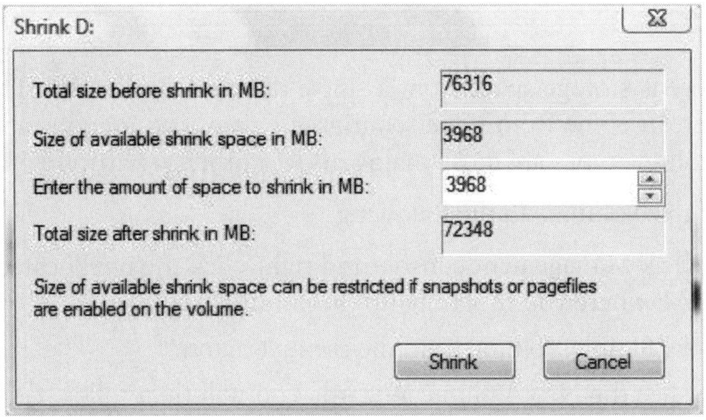

Figure 7-23. Reducing volume size

Granted, it may have a funny name, but believe me, this is a great feature, allowing administrators to reclaim lost space due to partitions being created with too much disk space. For example, let's say that at setup time, you divide your 300 GB hard disk into two partitions: a 200 GB C: drive and an E: "data" drive where you're going to store music and movies.

Now you realize you should have configured it the other way around: your "data" drive is stuffed to the gills, but the C: drive shows that you've got well over 100 GB of free space. What to do? Use these two techniques to complement each other and reclaim the wasted space. In the example given, you could shrink the C: drive by 100 GB and then expand the E: drive by 100 GB.

Problem solved.

Using Dynamic Storage

So far, we've looked at the process of formatting a basic volume. As introduced earlier, though, we have a lot more control over our hard disk storage when we opt for dynamic disk technology. It removes many of the constraints encountered in the basic storage world.

For example, dynamic storage gives admins the ability to set up some fault-tolerant volume configurations on Windows Server 2003 systems, also known as RAID arrays (not every RAID array is fault-tolerant, though). On Vista machines, dynamic disks let you combine storage from multiple disks onto a single logical unit with the use of a spanned drive. For internal storage on a Windows Vista machine, it's hard to beat dynamic storage.

Dynamic storage first appeared with Windows 2000. As mentioned, it divides the usable space on a hard disk not into partitions, but rather into volumes. On a Vista machine, a volume can be one of three varieties: simple, striped, or spanned.

Simple

A *simple volume* is storage space from a single dynamic hard drive. The cool part is that the space can come from either contiguous or noncontiguous space from that drive. These volume types are most analogous to a primary partition on a basic disk.

To set up a simple volume, do the following:

1. Open the Disk Management console and right-click the unallocated space on the dynamic disk where you're setting up the volume.

2. Choose New Simple Volume from the context menu.

3. You'll now see the New Volume Wizard. You will then follow the same volume creation steps as previously outlined in the discussion of basic storage.

4. As shown in Figure 7-24, the Completing the New Simple Volume Wizard dialog box lets you confirm your choices before clicking Finish to begin the operation.

You can also use the DiskPart utility for this very task, which is handy if you need to automate this for multiple machines.

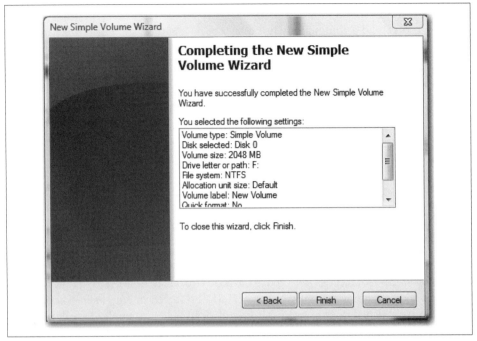

Figure 7-24. Setting up a simple volume

Spanned

A *spanned volume* contains slices of disk space located across multiple *dynamic* hard drives. Spanned volumes help you take advantage of unused space across multiple drives, or let you combine two or more drives into a single, monster partition. Data is still written sequentially, accessing only one physical disk per I/O request; spanned volumes will not enhance performance.

For example, a spanned drive lets you take 250 GB from one drive, and another 200 GB from another, for a total volume size of 450 GB. All the space would be addressed by a single name, usually a drive letter such as Z.

 You can't upgrade a removable disk—a floppy, ZIP, and so on—to a dynamic disk.

The ability to create a spanned drive can make a huge difference if you start to run out of space on the Z: drive, or any other drive, for that matter. If you're leveraging Vista's capability to record TV and you're working with a dynamic disk, for example, you can add another drive and extend the volume using Vista's built-in tools instead of having to delete saved shows.

A few caveats about this:

- You can extend a volume only if it does not have a filesystem or if it is formatted with NTFS. You cannot extend a volume formatted with FAT or FAT32.
- To perform this procedure, you must be a member of the Backup Operators or Administrators group on the local computer.
- You cannot extend a system volume or boot volume.
- You cannot extend a simple volume *if* that volume was originally created as a basic volume and was converted to a dynamic volume on Windows 2000. If you've upgraded a basic disk to dynamic on Vista, you should be just fine.

 You can upgrade external drives to dynamic storage, but it's best practice to leave external disks as basic disks. You can upgrade, but that disk should be used on only a single machine.

Striped

Striped volumes—sometimes referred to as RAID 0 arrays—are a dynamic volume type that allows administrators to set up data to be stored in equal slices across two or more physical disks. The entire set is still denoted by a single drive letter, and Vista handles read/write requests alternately and evenly across all disks in the set.

Why create a striped volume? Performance. Striped volumes can take advantage of I/O operations across two separate drive controllers simultaneously. As a result, hard drive read/write operations are handled more efficiently than using a single drive. A striped volume is not fault-tolerant, however, and is in fact a bit less so than its simple volume counterparts. If a single disk in a striped volume fails, the entire volume is lost.

Now that you understand the purpose, here are the click-steps:

1. From the Disk Management console, right-click the unallocated space on one of the dynamic disks where you'll set up the striped volume and choose New Striped Volume.
2. The Select Disks dialog box appears, as shown in Figure 7-25. Use this dialog box to choose which disks will be part of the striped set, and to configure the size of the stripe on each.

    Now the steps are the same as creating any other volume. All that's left is to assign a drive letter and format.

As before, you can also use the DiskPart utility to set up a striped volume.

And now, the striped volume stipulation section:

- Unlike simple volumes, a striped set cannot be extended once it's been created. Plan accordingly.
- Disk striping requires dynamic disks.
- You can create a striped volume onto a maximum of 32 disks.

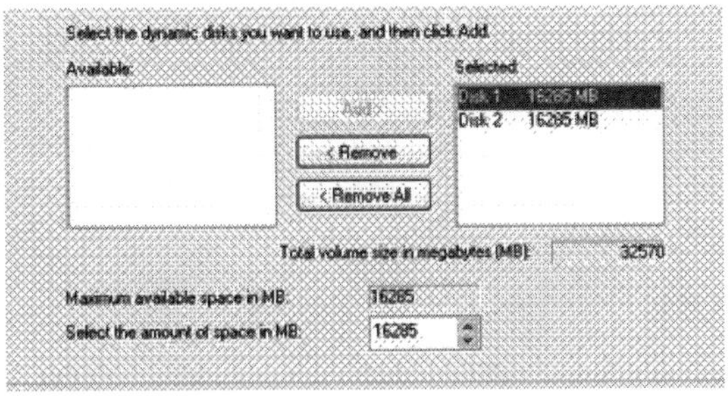

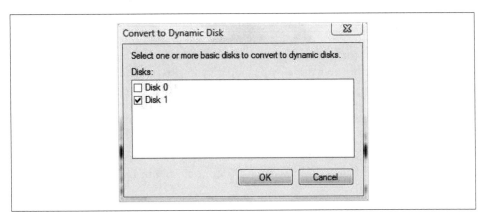

Figure 7-25. Setting up a striped volume

As mentioned, Windows Vista uses basic storage as the default. So before we can take advantage of this new storage technology, we must first upgrade our basic disks into dynamic disks.

Upgrading to a Dynamic Disk

No matter how excited you get about using dynamic storage, you're going to be stuck with basic storage out of the box. The only exception here is if you are upgrading from Windows XP and are already using dynamic disks. If not, you're going to have to perform an upgrade to benefit from dynamic storage.

It's awfully easy, though, and the process is not even worthy of a numbered list.

To perform the disk upgrade, open the Disk Management utility and then right-click the *drive* you want to convert. Choose Convert to Dynamic Disk from the context menu. And make sure you right-click the disk itself, not space on the disk.

As seen in Figure 7-26, you'll then get a dialog box asking you which disk you want to convert, followed by a Summary dialog box.

Figure 7-26. Upgrading a basic disk to dynamic

Yes, the confirmation dialog box is a tad redundant, but this is a significant change, so Vista steps you through this process slowly, giving you ample opportunity to change your mind.

Yet another dialog box warns you that any filesystems mounted on the disk will be dismounted, and then you at last see a final warning that informs you that a reboot will take place to complete the operation.

A few words of warning about the upgrade procedure:

- There is no equivalent downgrade procedure. If you change a dynamic disk back to a basic disk, all volumes are lost, and you have to start from scratch by creating brand-new basic volumes. That means, of course, that all data is lost, and you have to restore from backup.

- To upgrade a disk from basic to dynamic storage, the target disk needs at least 1 MB of free, nonpartitioned space for the operation to complete. Fortunately, Vista setup reserves 8 MB for this very purpose, even if you think you're partitioning the entire hard drive at setup time.

- Once converted, a dynamic disk will not contain basic volumes. Any existing partitions or logical drives on the basic disk become simple volumes on the dynamic disk.

Finally, notice that a single hard disk can be either basic or dynamic, but not both. The process of upgrading a disk is done at the disk level, not at the partition or volume level.

 You can use both basic and dynamic disks on the same Vista machine, but in order to use a spanned volume, both disks must be of the same type.

Changing a dynamic disk into a basic disk

Most of the time, changing a basic disk into a dynamic disk is a one-way operation. Occasionally, you'll want to redeploy a dynamic disk, but you will do so to a system that uses only basic storage. Another prime example is when you want to redeploy a dynamic disk as a removable drive by placing it in an external enclosure.

Here's what to do:

1. Back up everything on the dynamic disk that you will be converting back to a basic disk.

2. Using the Disk Management console, right-click each volume on the dynamic disk and choose Delete Volume from the context menu. Do this for all volumes on the disk.

3. Once you've cleared all volumes from the dynamic disk, right-click the disk (not the unallocated space), and choose Convert to Basic Disk. You'll see a warning dialog box to confirm your last step.

The DiskPart utility is up to the job as well.

Notes about this kind of conversion:

- As seen in the click-steps, the dynamic disk must be free of any data or volumes before the down-conversion.

- Once you change a dynamic disk back to a basic disk, you can create only partitions and logical drives on that disk.

- Be careful if you have valuable data on that dynamic disk. Make sure to back up and *verify* a successful backup before proceeding.

Using the Computer Console

There's one last disk management utility we haven't yet discussed: the Computer console. Among other ways, you can access this by opening a Vista Explorer window and choosing the computer item in the tree to the left.

It's easy to overlook this routine Vista window as a management utility, but we absolutely *can* perform disk management tasks with it.

As seen in Figure 7-27, the Computer console divides storage into these categories:

Hard disk drives
> This section lists all the logical drives available on the computer, including external hard drives. You can perform routine management tasks on these drives by right-clicking and choosing Properties, which will retrieve the System Control Panel application. Visual cues will also draw attention to conditions such as a drive running out of space.

Disks with removable storage
> This grouping displays removable storage drives such as optical disks and floppies. Routine management here includes accessing a Properties dialog box and ejecting, both done by right-clicking and making selections from the context menu.

Network location(s)
> Shows any available network drives hosted on other machines. This listing should include all drives for which you have mapped a logical drive letter. For example, if you've set up a fileserver location and mapped all users' H: drives to this location, it should appear here.

Other Hard Disk Considerations

There is one more topic left to explore before we leave the section on storage, and that's the five types of special designations given to drives, listed in order of how they appear in Disk Management.

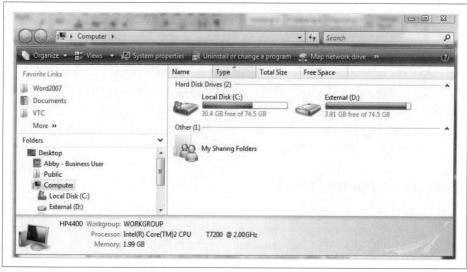

Figure 7-27. Using the Computer console to view and manage storage

Included are any noteworthy items about the behavior of, or restrictions placed on, a volume with such a designation:

System

> This is a little counterintuitive, but the System volume contains the files needed to *boot up* the computer. It cannot be part of a striped or a spanned volume.

Boot

> Again counterintuitive, the boot partition contains the Vista operating *system* files, and does not have to be the same drive as the system volume. As discussed in Chapter 6, one of the main functions of the Vista boot configuration data (BCD) is to help locate the boot volume.

Page File

> This contains the page file used by Vista. It can take advantage of volume configurations such as striping.

Active

> This designates the volume from which an x86 computer starts. If you're wondering what the difference is between an Active volume and a System volume, the answer is not much, functionally. The System volume and the Active volume should be one and the same. In most cases, it's the first volume or partition on Disk 0.

Crash Dump

> Here's where Vista attempts to write dump files in the event of a crash. By default, the Crash Dump volume is the same as where the Vista operating system files are stored (*%systemroot%*), but it can be located on any volume.

Each computer has only one Active, System, and Crash Dump volume. Some dual-boot machines may have two boot volumes, although you wouldn't see this from within the native disk management utilities. The only designation that is sometimes used across multiple volumes is the Page File. As you've already seen when looking at the Disk Management console, sometimes a single drive can be tagged with all of the roles just discussed.

And finally, don't confuse an Active volume with the Healthy designation.

Printing in Windows Vista

We begin this section with a quick discussion of printing terminology. I know, I know. But before you flip immediately to the next section, know that in order to truly understand printing, we have to be very precise with our vocabulary. Just as the entertainment attorney focused on negotiating contracts between actors and movie studios had to take constitutional law, for example, so, too, does a Windows expert have to understand basic printing vocabulary to proceed to more advanced printing tasks. (By the way, if you do flip to the next section, make sure you read about the new print management stuff; pretty cool.)

We have to be clear, for example, whether we're talking about a piece of software (the printer) that prepares electronic words and images before they're translated into ink dots, or the piece of hardware that applies ink to the page (the print device). It's a necessary distinction because we perform different administrative tasks on each.

What follows, then, is a quick overview of the terms used in a Windows Vista print environment.

Printer
> A piece of software that provides the necessary translation so that Windows can send information to a print device. The printer is there to provide access to the print device on your desk.

Print device
> What is normally referred to (before this section, anyway) as the printer. This is the piece of equipment that turns your electronic files into readable output on a sheet of paper.

Print driver
> A part of the printer installation that translates document formats into a language that the printer can understand. In other words, because of the work that printer drivers do, all documents look the same to the printer, no matter what application they are sent from. Each different print device usually ships with its own unique print driver, although many print devices can at least function with drivers that have not been specifically designed for them.

Print server

> A computer that has made the printer software resource available on the network by sharing it. Print clients and print servers use the same common language to speak to one another, the same one that they use to share and request file resources. Therefore, the client and server components between computers must be compatible in order for print clients to submit jobs to a print server. All Windows 9.*x* and later computers can be print servers.

Port

> A printer needs a way to send its translated information to the print device. It accomplishes this through a specifically defined pathway, known as a *port*. These information pathways can be of several varieties, as you'll soon learn.

Print spooler

> An area of buffer storage (usually an area on a disk) where documents wait to be serviced. The printer pulls the waiting jobs off the buffer at its own rate. This lineup of print jobs is also known as the *print queue*, and the two terms are often used interchangeably. Because the documents are in a buffer where the printer can access them, you can perform other operations on the computer while the printing takes place in the background. Spooling also lets you place a number of print jobs in a queue instead of waiting for each one to finish before specifying the next one.

And now that we have a little vocabulary to serve as a foundation, we also need to briefly identify the different types of printers you'll be administering in a Windows environment.

Printer Types

So, we've established that a printer is a piece of software and not a piece of hardware. It really shouldn't be too much of a leap, then, to imagine that this piece of software—the printer—is just another disk resource that can be made available to other computers on a network. How this is actually implemented is the focus of the rest of this printing section.

We should also be aware that printer devices can be further subdivided into one of three categories, depending on how they handle print jobs: local, network, and virtual. Each classification looks at which computer is managing the print job.

Local

Local printers are local because the software managing the devices is physically installed at your computer. Traditionally, local printers submit their jobs through a USB or parallel port to a device that is sitting right next to your desk, although that isn't always the case (covered in the discussion of "Installing a Network Printer," later in this chapter.

Network

These print devices are managed by printers that aren't directly installed on your system. They are accessible over the network, however, as their name implies, and they may or may not be located in the same room.

Virtual

These printer types show up as printing options in the Print dialog box of software applications, and they are represented as icons in the Printers Control Panel application. These printers don't send jobs to a device that puts ink on paper; instead, they convert a document to a widely readable format.

As we saw in Chapter 1's coverage of the new printing specification, one of the big improvements in Windows Vista is its capability to print to the XML Paper Specification (XPS). Yet another example of printing to a virtual printer is to use Office 2007's capability to print a document to a PDF Writer, which produces output in the form of an Adobe Acrobat *.pdf* file rather than a piece of paper.

Installing a Local Printer

OK, I'll grant you that setting up a printer won't present the greatest of administrative challenges, but it's still a task worth covering. Mundane as it may be, it remains one of the most mission-critical computer uses in many computer networks.

If, as an administrator, you stumble with this, it can really shake users' confidence in you to accomplish much else.

Nonetheless, the steps should ring fairly familiar to those who have set up Windows printers before. Here's how to attach a computer to a local machine:

1. Open the Printers Control Panel application. Type **print** in the Start menu, or look under the Hardware and Sound grouping if you're using the Classic View.

2. From the Printers console, click the "Add a printer" button in the toolbar located just under the address bar.

3. The Add Printer Wizard starts, giving you two options. Choose "Add a local printer."

4. Now select the port the printer will use to send its print jobs. By default, the computer's first parallel port (LPT1) will be selected. Change this if necessary.

5. You'll then see the "Install the printer driver" page, shown in Figure 7-28. This shows a list of drivers already included in the operating system, and you won't have to locate a driver disk or download anything to use any of the drivers you see here. Select the printer manufacturer and the printer name, and then click Next. If you have a disk with print drivers, you can use them at this time.

6. At this point, you'll be asked to give the computer a name. Click Finish on the final confirmation dialog box.

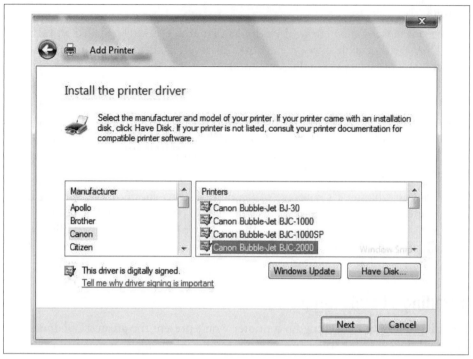

Figure 7-28. Setting up a local printer; note that the drivers are digitally signed

As you're told when stepping through the Add Printer Wizard, you should never have to do this when adding a USB printer. The steps for adding a USB printer are really no different from adding any other USB device, as mentioned earlier in this chapter. Essentially, you just plug the thing into an open port and Vista takes care of the rest. It will detect the device and install the appropriate drivers.

Installing a Network Printer

Setting up a *network* print environment can be even more critical. Laser printers are cheaper than they were 10 years ago, no doubt, but there still aren't many companies that can afford—or need—a printer on every desktop.

There are lots of variations on how administrators can set up a network print environment. What follows are the instructions that will help you connect to a printer that is not physically attached to the Vista machine. These instructions apply whether you use a standard network printer, a wireless (802.11) printer, or a Bluetooth-enabled printer:

1. Open the Printers Control Panel application. It's a standalone icon when using the Classic View, or again, type **print** in the Start menu.

2. From the Printers console, click the "Add a printer" button in the toolbar located just under the Address bar.

3. From the Add Printer Wizard, select the "Add a network, wireless or Bluetooth printer" selection, shown in Figure 7-29, and click Next.

4. Vista then searches for available printers on the network. Included in the list are printers that are reachable, and that have been shared on the network. From the list of available printers, choose the one you want to connect to and click Next.

5. After making the selection, you may be prompted to install the printer driver on your computer. You may then be prompted for administrative confirmation if User Account Control is turned on.

6. A few more tidying-up steps will complete the process. Click Finish from the last confirmation page.

Figure 7-29. Adding a network printer

Installing a network printer, Part 2

Now that you've learned how to use the Add Printer Wizard, it's time to learn about an even quicker way to install a network printer: to avoid all that clicking, just enter the printer's Universal Naming Convention (UNC) path (if you know it) using the Run dialog box. (Click Start and then type **run** for quick access; create a Start menu shortcut for even faster access.)

And…that's it. In a Windows-only environment, everything happens automatically: the print server makes the appropriate print drivers available, and the client downloads and installs the drivers automatically.

 If you're using a print server located on a non-Windows machine, you might have to install drivers locally in a separate installation routine.

The printer will now be set up and will appear the next time you navigate to the Printers Control Panel application. Upon successful connection to this shared printer for the first time, the contents of the print queue are displayed, as shown in Figure 7-30.

Figure 7-30. Use the UNC path to quickly connect to a network printer

There's yet a third way to connect: you can install a network printer simply by browsing for it in Windows Explorer. You can navigate Explorer in lots of ways; I recommend clicking the Network button from the Start menu. You can then browse to the desired (or suspected) print server and double-click the printer you want to set up. After a connection is established, you see the icon shown in Figure 7-31.

Figure 7-31. The "pipe" on a network printer indicates that it's not local

When you confirm your choice, the appropriate print drivers for the network printer will need to be installed on your local machine.

Removing a Printer

You won't need every printer installed on your machine forever, and it certainly won't hurt to delete those that you don't need. Although it won't really affect performance to have an additional printer or two installed (you can install all the printers you want without connecting an actual print device), it can prevent confusion when sending out print jobs.

The click-steps are easy: just open the Printers Control Panel application, right-click the desired printer, and then choose Delete from the context menu.

If you can't delete the printer, make sure you're using administrative credentials. You don't even need to be logged on as an administrator to do so. Use the Run As capability instead. To do so, right-click, select "Run as administrator" from the context menu, and *then* click Delete.

As always, you will be prompted for administrative confirmation if User Account Control is enabled.

 If a printer is currently servicing print jobs, you won't be able to delete it. Instead, Vista will wait until printing is complete, and then remove the printer. If you really, really can't wait to delete the printer, you can open the print queue and cancel all print jobs. You should now be able to remove the printer. (This might be necessary if the printer has stalled and you're deleting it as part of your troubleshooting actions.)

Changing the Default Printer

As you've seen, it's very possible to set up more than one printer on your Vista computer. In fact, it's very *likely* that you have more than one. To confirm, just open the Printers Control Panel application. If you see more than one icon, you have more than one printer installed.

But only one will be the default printer. This default printer is the one that applications use when no printer is specified in a Print dialog box. This is usually done when clicking the Print button on a given application's toolbar.

And of course, you can easily change the default printer used by Vista applications. All you have to do is right-click the desired printer in the Printers console and then choose "Set as default printer" in the context menu. A green checkmark appears next to the default printer (see Figure 7-32).

No matter what your default printer is, you still have the ability to select a specific printer with each print job.

Figure 7-32. It is easy to spot the default printer

Sharing a Vista Printer

Once you've gotten a local printer up and running, you now have the ability to make that printer available on the network by sharing it. How much additional software is needed to do this? None. Everything you need to get started is built-in. The only thing you have to decide is how and when other computers will connect.

Once an administrator is familiar with the concept of sharing folders over a network, the fundamentals are in place for network printing. Just as file sharing is the act of making a file resource available on the network, print sharing makes a print resource available to users who have connectivity.

And even if you're *not* familiar with this concept, it's still very easy to set up. All you really need to get started is a printer and a Vista computer. And beware: the steps aren't very much like those used to enable this same function on Windows XP.

Here's what to do:

1. Open the Network and Sharing Center Control Panel application.
2. Look in the section called Sharing and Discovery. Click the arrow button next to the "Printer sharing" option, and then choose the "Turn on printer sharing" radio button, as shown in Figure 7-33.
3. Click Apply, and network print sharing will be enabled (you may be prompted for administrative confirmation).

It's important to note that this procedure will share all printers attached to the Vista machine. To verify, just open a Run prompt and type this UNC syntax:

    \\computername

You'll see a Vista Explorer window showing all available network resources. You can even use this syntax to connect to the computer you're currently using from "over the network."

The printer sharing feature just demonstrated is quick and easy, but if you're setting up Vista as a print server, you may want a little more control. To share just a single printer, follow these steps:

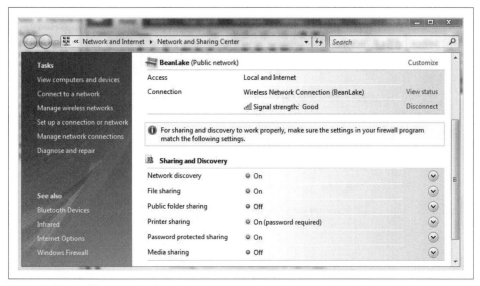

Figure 7-33. Enabling printer sharing

1. Open the Printers Control Panel application. It's in the Hardware and Sound grouping if you're using the Standard View.

2. Right-click on the printer you'd like to share, and then choose Sharing from the context menu.

3. In the *printername* properties dialog box that follows, you should now be on the Sharing tab. (If it's grayed out, see the following section.)

4. Click the "Share this printer" checkbox and give the shared printer a name, as shown in Figure 7-34. Click OK to complete the operation.

Once you've shared the printer, a little "people" icon appears under the printer icon (in previous Windows versions, this was a hand). If you see a printer with this people icon, congrats—you've just turned an ordinary Vista machine into a print server.

This will work on all Vista versions, by the way.

Print sharing considerations

You might also have stumbled across this: the printer sharing options are unavailable. This is because Vista's new security settings don't open ports—in this case, printer ports—to the outside world.

The share name you assign does not have to match the printer name. Users will use the share name to make a network connection to the printer, and you can use more intuitive names than are sometimes given to printers at setup time. Furthermore, you should bear in mind that any MS-DOS clients of your shared printer will not be able to see names longer than eight characters.

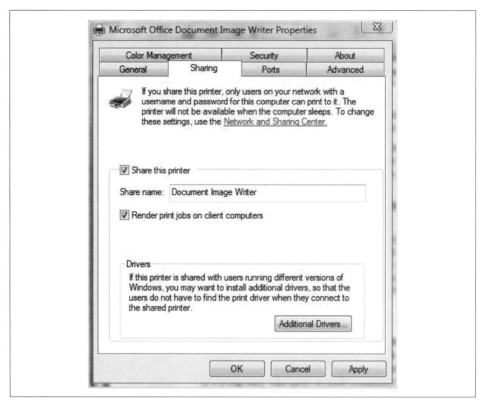

Figure 7-34. Sharing a Vista printer

Also, as you'll note in the dialog box when sharing the printer manually, users can connect to the network printer even if they're running different versions of Windows. In that case, you can follow the advice in the dialog box:

> …you may want to install additional drivers, so that the users do not have to find the print driver when they connect to the shared printer.

You can do so by clicking the Additional Drivers button and directing Vista to the location of the additional driver files, as seen in Figure 7-35.

As you'll notice, you won't be able to share every printer, notably the XPS Writer virtual printer. You should be able to share any printer that produces paper output, though.

And now that we've gotten some of the print basics out of the way, let's roll up our sleeves and look at some of the ways in which Vista has changed the network printing game. Actually, it's really only one way, but it's a big one. The next section examines this new feature.

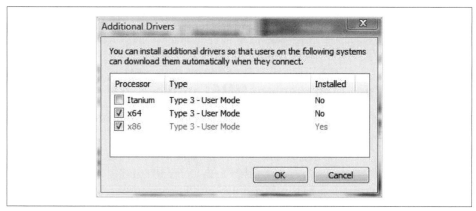

Figure 7-35. Installing 64-bit printing drivers

Managing Printing with Print Management

Yes, the printing environment can be administered in a variety of ways, some of which we've just seen. You want to make the printer available during only certain hours; fine. Just open the printer's Properties dialog box and configure away.

But Windows Vista network printing can be enhanced and managed like never before with a new MMC snap-in called Print Management.

The Print Management console allows Vista admins to set up, view the status of, and just generally manage all of the enterprise's printers from *any* computer running Windows Vista. Cool, huh? You can even use Print Management to set up printer connections for an entire group of computers simultaneously.

With its status reporting function, for example, Print Management helps you quickly track down printers that have an error condition. It can send email notifications that a certain printer is low on toner, or otherwise perform some action whenever a printer needs attention.

If the printer comes with an HTML interface, admins can even access information about that printer remotely—through a web page or over an Internet connection.

But merely explaining what Print Management does is of little use. To get a full appreciation of the new Print Management functionality, it's important to see the console in action. Setup and use is a multistep process. I'll tackle each step with individual instructions in the subsections that follow.

One thing to note before we begin is that there won't be any Print Management console installation instructions. The new snap-in comes as part of the normal Vista installation, so its availability should never be a problem.

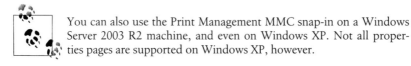

You can also use the Print Management MMC snap-in on a Windows Server 2003 R2 machine, and even on Windows XP. Not all properties pages are supported on Windows XP, however.

Opening the Print Management MMC Console

The first step in using Print Management, naturally, is to open the utility. This one is easy.

From the Start menu, type **print**. The Print Management console should appear at the top of your Programs list. As with other management utilities, you are asked for administrative confirmation if User Account Control is turned on. You'll now see the Print Management tool as shown in Figure 7-36.

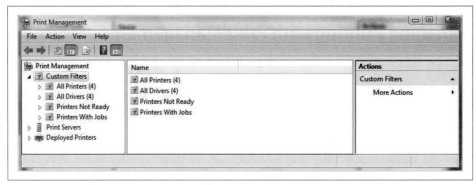

Figure 7-36. Ready to start administering the Vista print environment

Alternatively, you can open a blank MMC console and then choose File → Add/Remove Snap-in. From the Add or Remove Snap-ins dialog box, you can then select the Print Management console. You need to complete a few subsequent steps before you can actually manage a printer, and I cover them in the following sections.

The possible advantage to using the second method is that you can also add administrative snap-ins to this "blank" console, and then save the customized console. This lets admins create a custom MMC environment best suited to their common administrative tasks.

Adding Print Servers

One of the subsequent steps I just mentioned concerns adding the print server that the console is to manage. This applies when you're either using the preconfigured Print Management console or building your own from scratch.

Here are the specific steps for adding the local machine as a print server to manage:

1. In the Print Management tree, right-click the Print Servers item and choose Add/Remove Servers.

2. From the Add/Remove Servers dialog box, shown in Figure 7-37, click the Add the Local Server button.

3. Click OK once you've confirmed the local machine in the list of print servers.

Figure 7-37. Adding a local server

 By default, the preconfigured Print Management console adds the local machine as a print server automatically. The custom console will not.

You unlock the real utility of this tool when you add servers to manage from across the network. Here's how:

1. As before, navigate to the Print Servers item, right-click, and then choose Add/Remove Servers.

2. In the Add/Remove Servers dialog box, you'll be able to do one of the following:

   • Type the name of the managed print server using the *servername* UNC syntax.

   • Browse for the print server.

3. Click Add to List once you've specified the desired server. You can repeat this process to add as many print servers as you want.

4. Click OK to complete the operation.

 Recall that a print server describes what the computer is doing, not what the name of the operating system is. You can add plenty of print servers that are running Windows Vista, Server 2003, 2000 Server, XP, and whatever Microsoft ends up calling the next server operating system (Longhorn, as of this writing).

Managing the Printers

As you will now see in the Print Management console, there are three groupings of information about the print environment:

Custom Filters
Contains four separate subheadings: All Printers, All Drivers, Printers Not Ready, and Printers With Jobs. Depending on your circumstances, each can be expanded to reveal additional information and perform management tasks.

Print Servers
Contains information about each print server in the environment (more technically, each server managed by the Print Management console). There are four subheadings here, shown in Figure 7-38: Drivers, Forms, Ports, and Printers. To access the properties of the print server, just right-click the Print server item and choose Properties from the context menu.

Deployed Printers
Contains a list of printers that are managed by GPO. We will discuss print management with a GPO later in this chapter.

You can then manage any of the print server's subheading groupings by right-clicking and choosing Manage *item*.

The best way to illustrate this is with an example. If you want to delete one of the forms available on a particular print server's printer, for instance, expand the print server's name and then expand the selected printer to reveal the four subheadings. Now right-click the Forms item and choose Manage Forms.

You'll now see a dialog box similar to what is shown in Figure 7-39. From here, make sure the Forms tab is active, and then just select the targeted form from the list and click the Delete button.

Custom views

The Print Management console also provides a filtering feature that lets admins view only the printers or printer details of their choosing. You can use a filter to quickly track down a specific printer or set of printers that are reporting error conditions, for

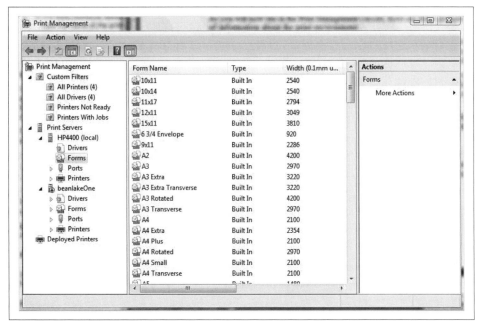

Figure 7-38. The Print Servers grouping has four items you can manage

example. You could similarly narrow down huge printer populations into more manageable groupings, such as printers in the sales department or printers in a specific office.

Four filtered views are built-in: All Printers, All Drivers, Printers Not Ready, and Printers With Jobs. You can get started with your own Custom Views by following these steps:

1. In the Print Management console tree, right-click the Custom Filters item and choose Add New Printer Filter from the Properties dialog box.

2. The New Printer Filter Wizard launches. From here, give the Custom View a name and a description if desired. You can also specify that the number of printers found by the filter be displayed as well. Click Next.

3. Now for the meat and potatoes: in the dialog box shown in Figure 7-40, you'll specify the criteria the filter uses. For example, if I want a view that shows all the HP printers in the network, I can choose the Printer Name field in the drop-down menu, set Contains as the condition, and then type **HP** as the value.

4. You can populate as many criteria as you like. In this example, I also want the Print Management console to send an email if any of these printers is reporting an error condition.

5. Click Next again and then specify what, if any, actions to take if the filter conditions are met. Choose Finish to complete the setup of the Custom View.

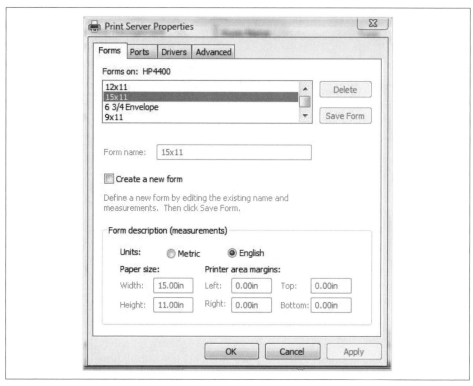

Figure 7-39. Managing a particular form for a particular printer on a particular print server

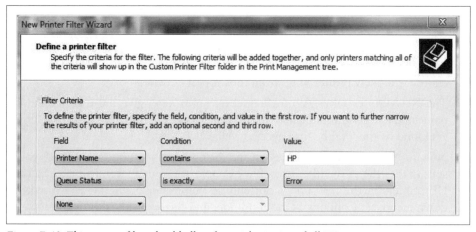

Figure 7-40. This custom filter should allow for quick viewing of all HP printers

The new view, along with any other changes made to the Print Management console, should now show up every time you open the console.

Stopping trustworthy site pop ups

One pesky little annoyance that can crop up when using Print Management is a stream of pop-up messages. This is because some printer software is written such that it provides extra functionality and status reporting through HTML pages. As a result, you may see intermittent warning messages from Internet Explorer as it communicates with these pages.

You can address this situation using two techniques:

- Add each printer's web site to the list of trusted web sites in Internet Explorer.
- Turn off the Enhanced Security Configuration option in Internet Explorer by using the Add or Remove Windows Components application in the Control Panel.

For additional information about how this will affect overall Internet Explorer security, refer to Chapter 10.

Deploying Printers with a Group Policy Object (GPO)

Another hands-off method for deploying printers is to use GPOs. With a GPO, an admin can "prestage" a computer for printer deployment, and automatically add printer connections to newly added systems.

Note before you begin, however, that this requires an Active Directory domain. Deploying on a Local Computer Policy object wouldn't serve any purpose; the idea is to automate deployment to many users and/or computers all at once.

The tool you'll use to facilitate this is our friend, Print Management, and the specific option is called Deploy with Group Policy. The details are spelled out in just a bit.

First, though, understand that Group Policy settings—at least those that have to do with printing—are applied at either computer startup/shutdown or user logon/logoff. The printer connections are deployed to those users or computers that are associated with the GPO.

This is a great weapon in the administrator's arsenal for deploying printers to large groups of users or company departments with a minimum of overhead, thus freeing the admin for less mundane tasks than deploying printers over and over again.

Depending on the options selected, this method can be used so that an entire company floor will always have the same printer available, or so that everyone in the marketing department has access to the color laser printer, no matter if they change desks, move to another floor, or undergo other company reorgs.

Here's how to leverage a GPO for easy printer deployment:

1. Open the Print Management console. Again, typing **print** from the Start menu spots it pretty quickly.

2. Navigate to the desired print server from the Print Management tree. Expand and choose Printers.

3. Look to the Details pane on the right. Now, right-click the printer you want to deploy to users and select the Deploy with Group Policy context menu option.

4. In the Deploy with Group Policy dialog box, shown in Figure 7-41, click Browse, and then choose the GPO where you want the printer deployed.

   As discussed in further detail in Chapter 12, GPOs can contain users and computers (as well as lots of other objects). You can then tailor most GPO settings to apply to only the computer or only the user.

5. Once you've selected the GPO, you deploy a specific printer connection setting by performing one or both of the following:

   - For a per-user setting, choose "The users that this GPO applies to (per user)" checkbox.

   - For a per-machine setting, choose "The computers that this GPO applies to (per machine)" checkbox.

   For example, a per-user setting will ensure that a given user always has the GPO-deployed printer available to her, no matter what computer she uses in the domain. If the GPO setting specifies a computer, anyone who uses the computer has a connection to the deployed printer.

6. Finally, click Add. You'll see the selected printer listed in the Deploy with Group Policy dialog box. You can repeat the process before closing and add the same printer connection setting to another GPO. Click OK to complete the procedure.

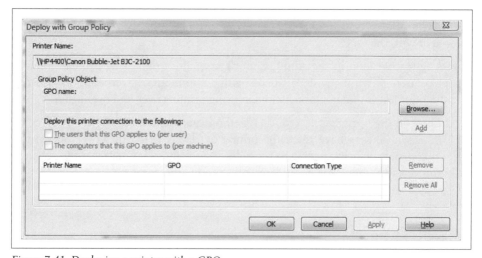

Figure 7-41. Deploying a printer with a GPO

When you deploy a printer using this method, the printer should show up in the Deployed Printers object of the Print Management console. If you're not on a domain, deployment with GPOs will not be available, and nothing will display here.

Adding Printers Automatically with Print Management

A great feature of Vista's Print Management that will save you much time in setting up a print server is the ability to detect and install printers automatically. With it, you can detect all printers that are on the same subnet as the print server.

Once it detects printers, Print Management carries out the following tasks:

- Installs print drivers for detected printers
- Sets up the print queues
- Shares the printers

The only time you need to step in is if the proper drivers cannot be located. Other than that, few administrative tasks could be more hands-off. Here's all you have to do:

1. Open the Print Management MMC console. If you have the Administrative Tools folder displayed in your Start menu, you could look there.

2. Expand the Printer Management tree until you see the computer you want to function as the subnet's printer server.

3. Right-click and choose Add Printers.

4. In the Add Network Printers dialog box, shown in Figure 7-42, choose the "Search the network for printers" option, and then click Next.

5. Follow the instructions to complete the wizard, choosing as many printers as you wish from the local subnet.

Figure 7-42. Adding printers automatically

If that didn't blow your mind sufficiently, there's this: you can even extend this capability beyond the local subnet. Let's say, for example, that you get a call in your Kansas City company headquarters to set up printers in a remote office in Omaha. You could take your private jet, of course, and manually set up the printers, but you could also accomplish the same goal using a combination of Print Management and Remote Desktop.

To do so, just log on to the remote print server from the Kansas City headquarters, and then start the Print Management automatic printer detection process from the remote computer. Alternatively, you could run a utility called fnprinters.exe from the remote computer's command line. Of course, this requires that the remote user has administrator privileges on the computer where the printers will be added.

Securing Vista Network Printing

Once a printer is made available from a print server, Vista assigns a default set of permissions. These default permissions allow the Everyone group (that is, all users) to print. Other select groups have the ability to manage the printer, manage documents sent to it, or both. But you might not want just any user to print to the shared printer. Instead, you might want to limit access for some users by assigning specific printer permissions.

For example, you might give all standard users in a department the Print permission, and then give all managers the Print and Manage Documents permissions. In this way, all users and managers can print documents, but managers can also change the print status of any document sent to the printer.

If you investigate the permissions for the CREATOR OWNER special group, you'll see that this special group has the Manage Documents permission. What's the significance? It simply means that an individual user can manage all documents he sends to the printer. For example, an ordinary user can send a job to the print queue and then cancel printing if he changes his mind. He will not be able to manage other users' documents in the queue, however.

Because ordinary users won't have the ability to do anything other than send jobs to the printer and then cancel their own jobs, admins won't typically have to do much security configuration when it comes to printers.

If you need to change printer permissions, you can do so using the Security tab on the printer's properties dialog box, as seen in Figure 7-43. To change permissions for an existing user or group, you can either check or uncheck the Permissions buttons, or click the Advanced button to open the full security settings dialog box.

Access the printer's properties dialog box by right-clicking the printer and choosing Properties.

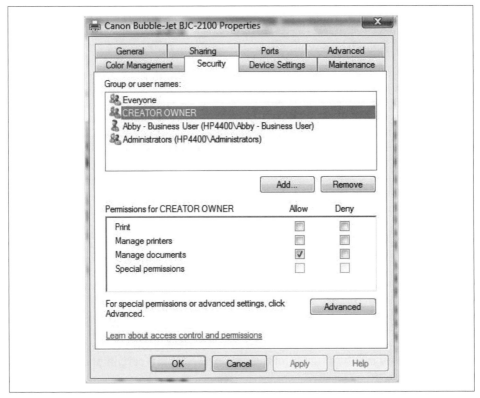

Figure 7-43. Setting printer permissions

Printer availability

Administrators have the added management ability of restricting the hours when people can print to a given network printer. You do this by setting the printer's hours of availability.

Let's say, for example, that you're worried about the printer's use for personal purposes. You're going through reams of paper and cartridge after cartridge of ink, and yet a monitoring of the print queue reveals nothing out of the ordinary during the workday.

If that's the case, you can place restrictions on when a printer can be used:

1. Access the printer's Properties dialog box by right-clicking and choosing Properties from the context menu. Now click the Advanced tab.

2. The default option for the printer is "Always available," but we're about to change this. To do so, select the "Available from" radio button, as seen in Figure 7-44, and then set the time when the printer will be available to service jobs.

3. Click OK to commit the change.

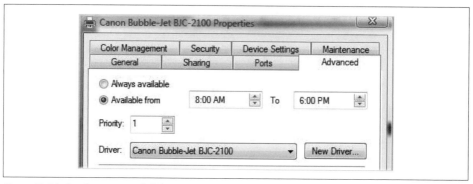

Figure 7-44. Configuring availability

It sounds nonsensical, I'll grant you, but the printer is technically able to receive jobs even when the schedule dictates that the printer isn't available. The received print jobs just don't print right away. They simply wait in the print queue until the schedule says the printer is available.

Assigning priority

Another way administrators can take control of a network print environment is by assigning priority to jobs in the print queue. This will allow certain print jobs to "cut the line" in order to be serviced next by the print device.

To change a print job priority, all you have to do is this:

1. Access the printer's print queue by opening the Printers Control Panel console and then double-clicking the printer you want to manage.

2. You will see multiple print jobs listed (if you don't, there's really no need to manage priority). From here, right-click the specific document you want to configure priority for and choose Properties.

3. In the Properties dialog box, make sure the General tab is selected, as seen in Figure 7-45.

4. Use the slider to set the document priority. You can rank a document anywhere between 1 and 99, but the default is 1; just about any higher number will do for 99 percent of instances where this is needed.

Why would this even be necessary?

Let's say, for instance, that you have only a single laser printer deployed for an entire subnet. Now the boss or legal team or marketing department has sent over a print job that is time-sensitive. The problem: 12 other print jobs have been sent in the past five minutes as well, one a 50-page draft of a book chapter that is currently tying up the print device.

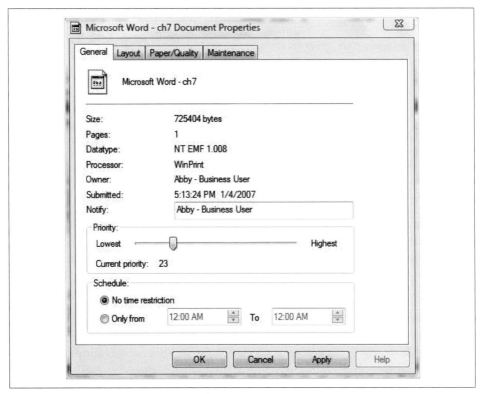

Figure 7-45. Configuring a higher print job priority

To get the last marketing department's print job serviced before the others once the printer frees up, an admin can open the print queue and change priority. (If you're really in a hurry, you could pause printing, cancel the print job, set priority, and then resume printing. A printer won't interrupt a job that is currently printing.)

Redirecting a Print Job

Another way to leverage your newly gained understanding of Vista print terminology and technology is to apply it to troubleshooting a faulty print device. How? By redirecting a print job. If it sounds a little like a cop rerouting traffic after a car accident, that's because it is.

Sometimes your local printer will not work for various reasons, including:

- It's out of ink.
- There's a nasty paper jam.
- It's just printing poorly, which in turn could have many causes.

But you still need to get the document printed. This is where the ability to redirect the printer can really help. It can keep work flowing while you troubleshoot the faulty print device.

Here's how it works: the administrator will instruct the printer to send print *jobs* to alternate printer *ports* that will then send the jobs to alternate print *devices*.

Let's say, for example, that a coworker has just "accidentally" kicked the print device connected to your computer. Now the device is malfunctioning, and you have a big report that's due. You're in luck, though, because it just so happens that the coworker has also configured his Vista machine to allow for network printing, and has the very same kind of printer attached.

Here's what you can do to get that report to the coworker's printer:

1. Open the Printers Control Panel console and access the Properties dialog box for the printer.

2. Choose the Ports tab, and then click the Add Port button to open the Printer Ports dialog box (see Figure 7-46).

3. With the Local Port option selected, click the New Port button to open the Port Name dialog box.

4. In the "Enter a port name" box, use the UNC syntax of *computername*\ *printername*, just as though you were setting up any old network printer.

5. Now click OK to close the Port Name dialog box. *Make sure the new port is selected* in the Printer Ports dialog box, and that the old port is deselected. Click OK to close.

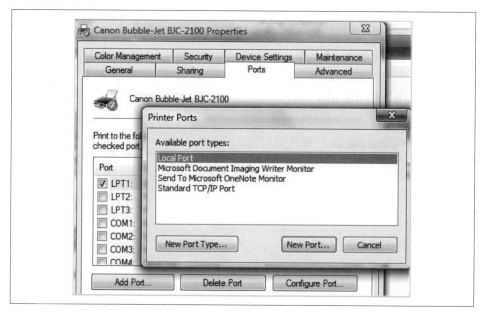

Figure 7-46. Redirecting a print job

You have now set up a new local port. Obviously, you can use this technique for multiple troubleshooting scenarios in addition to the one just described. (If you were thinking "he could just as quickly install a new network printer rather than redirect," you'd be right; there are many different ways to address most problems.)

And remember, even though print jobs will now be sent over the network, the port is considered local because the printer software installed locally at your machine manages these print jobs.

I have a few more printing tips and techniques for you to put into your back pocket, but I decided they were a better fit in Chapter 14's iteration of tips and tricks. Stay tuned.

Summary

We've certainly covered a lot of ground in our discussion of Vista hardware management. We've focused on getting things to work, and getting them to work quickly.

Along the way, you've seen how to install a hardware device for the first time, how to update the driver for that device, and what to do should you ever need to roll back that recently updated driver.

More important, you've seen how to manage and configure those hardware devices, whether it be partitioning disk space on that new 500 GB hard drive, or setting up a print environment that will automate network printer distribution for the entire company with the Print Management MMC console.

And speaking of hardware and software installation, the next chapter takes this discussion one step further. In it, we'll look at how to perform a Vista installation that will go smoothly, what to do with data from an older system, and when it's best to roll out multiple Vista installations using the unattended deployment technologies.

CHAPTER 8

Working with Software

After Vista has recognized all available hardware, you'll want to leverage that hardware to run applications at maximum efficiency. This chapter looks at that very objective, and will help administrators make sure software will run as well as it can.

In this chapter, we'll look at a few of the recommendations for best use of Vista as an application platform. After all, this is what has helped propel Microsoft to the top of the operating system heap—other vendors can make the hardware, and other creative minds can develop software to solve the world's problems. Microsoft makes the stuff that ties these two components together.

Although this chapter deals with *application* software, we haven't forgotten about the many productivity features that are built into the Windows Vista software itself. You'll learn about many more of these features that haven't already been covered, and how to make the operating system behave just as you want.

We'll start with a task that can be as simple as you think it can be, yet it's something over which we can have complete administrative control: installing a new program for use with Windows Vista.

Installing and Removing Software

Before working with an application, we of course have to install it. Under previous versions of Windows, this sometimes took a bit of work. Today, it's a fairly automated process that usually involves just inserting the installation media and clicking a button or two.

Nevertheless, we have to start a chapter on applications somewhere, and it might as well be here. If nothing else, this rather elementary task will provide a good foundation for the more complicated application tweaks that are to come.

You'll usually get a new piece of application software in one of two ways:

- From a CD or DVD
- From a network location, including over the Internet

What installation steps you follow will then depend on where the installation files reside.

Installing from CD

Here's what you'll do if you're holding an installation CD or DVD:

1. Insert the disc into your computer. AutoPlay should launch the disc's installation program automatically, from which you'll follow the instructions on the screen. I'll discuss how to manage this AutoPlay behavior in more detail later in this chapter.
2. If User Account Control is enabled, you will be prompted for an administrator password or confirmation.

If a program doesn't launch the install routine automatically, check the program's documentation. Application developers have distributed their software on discs to be installed, not because they feel there's a shortage of drink coasters; I assure you that you'll find instructions.

If you can't locate this product documentation, the next suggestion is to browse through the disc using a Vista Explorer window and double-click the program's setup file, usually called *setup.exe* or *install.exe*.

Installing from the Network

Here's what to do for programs downloaded from the Internet or another network location:

1. From an Internet Explorer 7 window (other browsers are up to the task as well, although installation steps may vary somewhat), follow the hyperlink to the program.
2. You'll see the dialog box shown in Figure 8-1. You have a couple of choices from here:
   - Choose Run and the program will install. Follow the instructions on your screen to complete the setup. Again, if you're using User Account Control, you will be prompted for an administrator password or confirmation.
   - Choose Save to download the installation file to your computer and install it at a later time. When you're ready to install it, just double-click the saved file and follow the on-screen instructions.

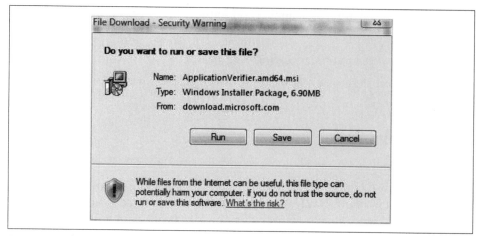

Figure 8-1. Choices when downloading a program over the Internet

 Of the two options, Microsoft recommends the second one because you get a chance to scan the file for viruses before performing the installation. Most virus-scanning programs today should catch an infected file during install, however, so in practice it really doesn't make much difference.

In any event, you should download and install programs only from a publisher you trust. As we've seen, Vista and Internet Explorer 7 combine new security features that help prevent program installation without the knowledge (and permission) of the system administrator.

Also, realize that in some implementations, performing a network install will more closely resemble the CD install. In this case, users typically browse for a network share and launch the setup routine by double-clicking the *setup.exe* or *setup.msi* file. Vista then proceeds with the installation, using the network location as the directory for the installation files rather than the optical drive.

Uninstalling or Changing a Program

Although a program that isn't being used anymore probably isn't causing any harm, administrators can certainly free up disk space by uninstalling it. (The unused application can cause system performance to drag, however, if it's being loaded at startup time and uses a chunk of memory that could be better put to use by one of your applications.)

For this reason alone, program uninstallation becomes a valuable skill.

Furthermore, some programs require that you uninstall the old version before you can install the newest version.

In addition, applications often have setup routines that provide a default installation. Often these default installations don't install some feature you might desperately need later on. Fortunately, you can use this uninstall routine to change some of the features or install additional ones.

Here's how to use the Programs and Features application to uninstall or change programs:

1. Open the Control Panel's Programs and Features application by typing **prog** at the Start menu. It should appear at the top of this list.

2. You'll see the dialog box shown in Figure 8-2. To remove the app, select the program from the list and then click Uninstall from the toolbar. Some programs provide an option to change or repair (see the next paragraph) in addition, but all should offer an option to uninstall.

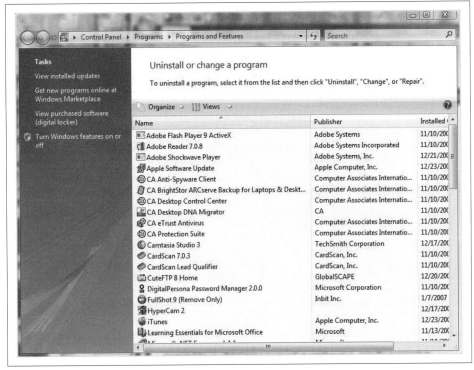

Figure 8-2. The Programs and Features application

To change a program, choose either the Change or the Repair button, shown in Figure 8-3. The options you see afterward will vary depending on the particular application. Note that you may be prompted for administrative confirmation if User Account Control is turned on.

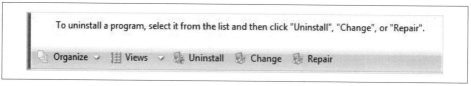

Figure 8-3. Change or repair an application

Removing a Program That Has Been Uninstalled

Huh? How do you *remove* a program once it's already been uninstalled? Or am I confused about the meaning of the word *uninstall*?

Maybe I should have been more specific. Sometimes you will still see a program listed here, even though it's been uninstalled using the Programs and Features Control Panel application. A registry entry determines all the programs you see in this list. It's located here, as shown in Figure 8-4:

HKLM\SOFTWARE\Microsoft\Windows\CurrentVersion\Uninstall

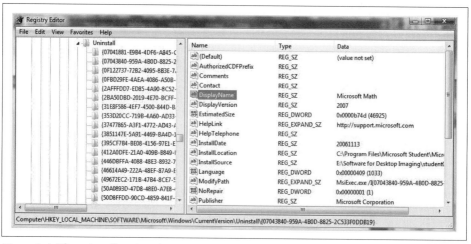

Figure 8-4. The uninstall registry key

As you can see in the figure, there are several keys here, and all of them are assigned numbers that don't hold much meaning for humans. Further investigation of specific keys reveals what programs they represent. The one I've selected is for Microsoft Math.

When uninstalling Microsoft Math with the Programs and Features Control Panel application, this registry key should be removed. Of course, that's not always the case. If you uninstall something but still see it listed, just open the Registry Editor and delete the entire program subkey. It will no longer be listed in Programs and Features.

Installing Vista Components

You don't always need an installation disc or connection to the Internet to use a new piece of software. Lots of Windows Vista components are residual from the Vista setup, ready at a moment's notice.

For example, Windows Vista includes a perfectly capable web server component called Internet Information Services (IIS). But before you can use this Vista application, you have to turn it on. Alternatively, administrators can turn off components they don't use or don't want other users to use.

The enable/disable behavior of Vista components represents a departure from earlier versions of Windows, where many times admins had to manually locate installation files to add a Windows component. In Vista, the optional components are stored on your hard disk, making it easy to toggle the particular feature on and off at will.

This also gives admins the flexibility to turn off a feature without uninstalling the bits, which in turn allows them to turn back on a feature without hunting down Vista source installation files.

The only possible drawback to this behavior is that the Vista components take up hard disk space regardless of whether they are actually turned on.

To get started with a change to one of the Windows components, follow these steps:

1. Open the Control Panel and choose the Programs grouping if you're using the Standard View. Follow the "Turn Windows features on or off" link, displaying the Windows Features dialog box shown in Figure 8-5.

2. From here, it's just a simple matter of selecting the checkbox next to the feature you want to enable. To turn off a Vista feature, clear the checkbox. Notice that Vista does not ask for files; once you check or uncheck a checkbox and click OK, Vista proceeds with installation.

Also, note from the preceding dialog box that some of the features are grouped together in folders. If a checkbox appears "colored in," some additional features are available—some are turned on and some are turned off. To view the contents of a folder, expand the plus sign or double-click it.

Disabling User Account Control

You saw this in Chapter 1 where we looked at some of the new Vista features. I'm including a précis of it here just to save you from flipping back and forth. For a full discussion, however, refer to Chapter 1.

As noted in Chapter 1, Vista introduces User Account Control, making it easier for companies to limit the rights of the average user while still protecting the computer from accidental installations of malware (read: mission-critical ActiveX controls).

Figure 8-5. Enable and disable additional Vista features

In Vista, there are now two basic kinds of user accounts:

Administrator accounts

These accounts can perform any and all administrative tasks on the machine, including device driver installation and system settings changes—changes that affect *all* user accounts on the machine.

Standard user accounts

These are the equivalent of the standard user accounts in previous versions of Windows. Standard accounts can install applications, but not those that install into the *%systemroot%* folder. Also, they cannot change system settings or perform other administrative tasks.

Now here's where Vista has made a big improvement over the past: a standard user can still perform administrative tasks if she provides proper account credentials. Figure 8-6 shows an example of a standard user being prompted for such administrative credentials.

When User Account Control is enabled, even a member of the local Administrators group will be prompted to approve a process in which a standard user would be asked for administrative credentials. In other words, even the admin behaves as a standard user until she's trying to perform an administrative task, at which time Windows Vista asks permission, as shown in Figure 8-7.

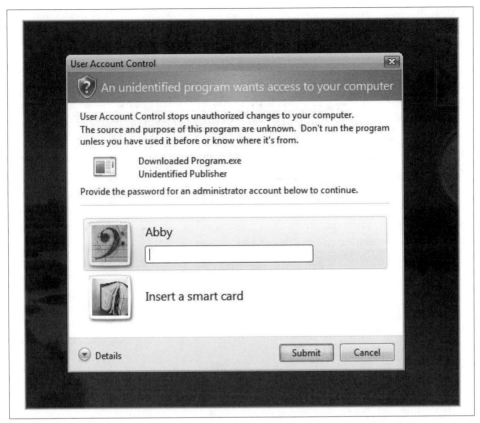

Figure 8-6. User Account Control asks a standard user for administrative credentials

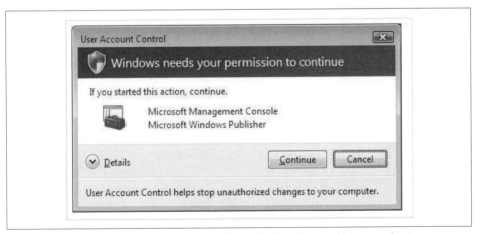

Figure 8-7. With User Account Control, even the local admin is treated like a regular Joe

(If you investigate further by clicking the Details button, you'll even notice the reason why: you're trying to launch an executable living in that darn *%systemroot%* folder.)

So even when the administrator is trying to install that "mission-critical" ActiveX control, User Account Control ensures that, at the very least, said administrator is aware that she's installing a piece of software. Vista allows no access to the *%systemroot%* folder, for example, without permission to proceed.

Turning it off

With that said, this great new security feature can really be intrusive. In fact, I'm guessing that it will become a big complaint for average users as they quickly tire of having to provide confirmation every time they do something like open Parental Controls. (It's already made more than a few top five-ish lists of the "Worst features of Vista"; see my comments in Chapter 15 for more.)

 Throughout Vista's interface, User Account Control provides a visual aid that identifies when administrative privileges are needed to perform a certain task. If you see a link or an icon with the little security shield icon next to it, you will be asked for administrative confirmation if User Account Control is enabled.

There are actually several options for turning off User Account Control. Here's one:

1. From the Control Panel, open the User Accounts console. It's under the User Accounts and Safety grouping if you're using the Standard View.

2. Follow the "Turn User Account on or off" link. Because you're turning User Account Control off, you are asked for administrator confirmation.

3. Uncheck the "Use User Account Control (UAC) to help protect your computer" checkbox (shown in Figure 8-8). Click OK and then restart your computer.

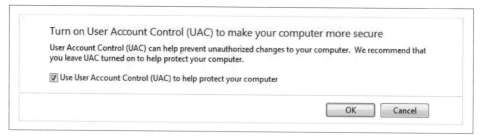

Figure 8-8. Uncheck this box to disable User Account Control

You can also disable User Account Control using the System Configuration utility. Follow these steps:

1. Launch *msconfig.exe* by typing **msconfig** at the either the Start menu or the Run dialog box. (Note that you have to type the entire thing.)

2. Because you haven't turned off User Account Control yet, you're asked for administrative confirmation.

3. From the Msconfig utility, select the Tools tab and scroll until you see the Disable UAC option, as shown in Figure 8-9.

4. Select that option and click the Launch button. A Command Prompt window briefly opens. When the command finishes, close the window.

5. Lastly, close the System Configuration utility and reboot the computer for changes to apply. You can then turn User Account Control back on by performing the same procedure and selecting Enable UAC instead.

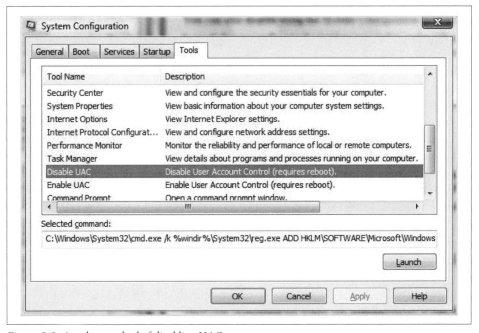

Figure 8-9. Another method of disabling UAC

If you noticed the syntax of the System Configuration command in the preceding example, you probably noticed that the underlying command edited the registry. You can do the same thing yourself to turn off User Account Control:

1. Open the Registry Editor by typing **regedit** at the Start menu. You're asked for Administrative confirmation.

2. Navigate to this key:

   HKEY_LOCAL_MACHINE\Software\Microsoft\Windows\CurrentVersion\ Policies\System

3. Locate the EnableLUA DWORD value. Double-click and give EnableLUA a value of 0, as seen in Figure 8-10.

4. Close the Registry Editor and reboot. You can then turn on User Account Control once again by changing the EnableLUA value to 1.

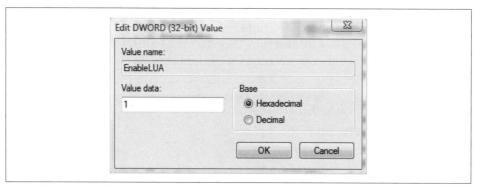

Figure 8-10. Editing the registry directly to disable User Account Control

Finally, and most powerfully, you can let Group Policy do the work for you. Here's how:

1. Open a blank MMC console and add the Group Policy Object Editor. For full instructions, turn to Chapter 12's discussion of Group Policy. You can also type **gpedit.msc** from the Start menu.

2. From the Group Policy Object Editor, shown in Figure 8-11, navigate to Computer Configuration → Windows Settings → Security Settings → Local Policies → Security Options.

3. Locate the set of User Account Control policies. There are nine at the bottom of the window. You now need to configure these User Account Control policies:

   User Account Control
   Behavior of the elevation prompt for standard users; *No Prompt*

   User Account Control
   Detect application installations and prompt for elevation; *Disabled*

   User Account Control
   Run all Administrators in Admin Approval mode; *Disabled*

4. Once configured, exit the Group Policy Object Editor and reboot computers where the policy settings apply.

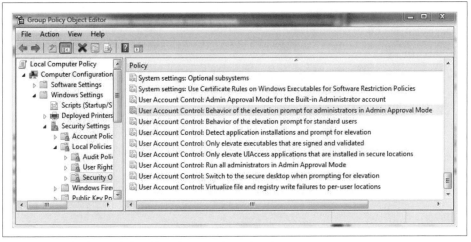

Figure 8-11. The Group Policy User Account Control options

As you can see, administrators have much more flexibility when using a Group Policy over simply toggling User Account Control on and off. One great option that you have is to turn off the User Account Control prompt for administrators only by using the "UAC: Behavior" of the elevation prompt for administrators in Admin Approval mode and configuring the setting to Disabled, as seen in Figure 8-12.

As a last thought on this topic, note that administrators have the option to configure on a single machine using the Local Group Policy Object (GPO), or to configure many groups of computers with an Active Directory-based GPO. For more about Active Directory and GPO deployments on Windows server domains, see Chapter 12.

If you're deploying to multiple computers in an Active Directory environment, the steps are roughly the same. Just browse to the Active Directory object to which you want to link the GPO, and configure away.

 Because User Account Control applies only to Windows Vista computers, it has no effect on a Windows XP or 2000 machine.

As you've seen, the Group Policy options take a little more work, but that work is paid off in terms of flexibility and administrative control.

And there's always third-party software that lets you disable User Account Control. At the time of this writing, you can get a tool called TweakVista at *http://www.tweakvista.com*. TweakVista, among its other capabilities, includes what's essentially a script that disables User Account Control without going through any of the steps mentioned earlier.

Once you've disabled the ability of administrators to run in Admin Approval mode, you have effectively turned off User Account Control; you've made your brand-new

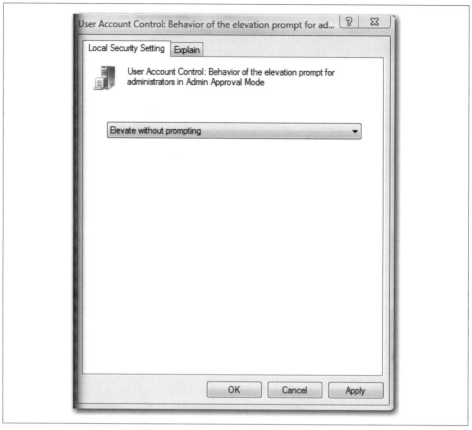

Figure 8-12. Turning off the User Account Control prompt for administrators only; an excellent option made possible via Group Policy

operating system behave more like the old one, where users logged in as local administrators carry the full access token with them at all times.

Starting a Program Automatically

Previously in this book, we looked at how to start programs automatically. Essentially, there are two quick and easy ways to get an app to launch as Vista starts up:

- Use the Start menu's Startup folder, at Start → All Programs → Startup. Just drag and drop a program shortcut here and the program launches automatically.

- Use Vista Explorer. Navigate to this folder:

    %username%\AppData\Roaming\Microsoft\Windows\Start Menu\Programs\ Startup

  where *%username%* is the directory for a user of the machine. Then, just create program shortcuts in this folder.

These two methods give most average users easy control over which programs should start automatically.

A third method is within reach of the average user, but is a little more convoluted. Nonetheless, it's worth identifying here. You can use the Task Scheduler and configure a startup or logon task. That task, in turn, can launch a program of your choosing.

Here's what to do:

1. Open the new Task Scheduler by typing either **task** or **sched** at the Start menu. (It's located under the Administrative Tools Control Panel grouping as well.)

2. In the Actions pane, choose the Create Basic Task item.

3. Give the task a name and general description, and click Next.

4. Now you'll set the task's triggers, two of which will occur when the computer starts and when a user logs on. Select the desired startup trigger, as shown in Figure 8-13.

5. The next dialog box has you specify the task. In this case, you want to select "Start a program." Click Next.

6. Now, you have the ability to specify the program executable or startup script from the next dialog box.

7. The Summary dialog box lets you review your selection and go back to make changes if needed. Click Finish to complete configuration of a startup program.

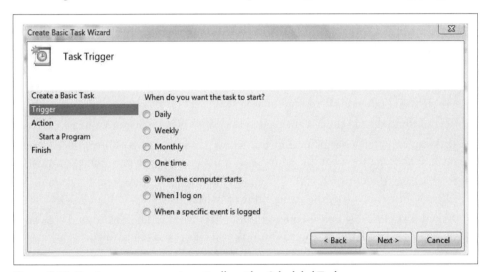

Figure 8-13. Starting a program automatically with a Scheduled Task

Again, this is not as easy as simply dragging and dropping a program shortcut into the Start menu's Startup folder, but it might be more permanent if others use the computer and tend to reconfigure the Start menu.

If you want to bypass the startup programs for a given Vista startup, just hold down the Shift key right after logging on and just as Vista generates the desktop.

There's a more powerful way to control startup behavior, however, which should be more appealing to administrators. As you've seen, users still have a fairly large amount of control over startup behavior using the methods previously described.

Startup and the Registry

For more authoritative command of startup, use the registry. Two keys here will dictate that a certain program runs no matter who logs on to the machine:

HKLM\Software\Microsoft\Windows\CurrentVersion\Run
> The values in this key tell Vista to run a program automatically at startup time for any user of the system.

HKLM\Microsoft\Windows\CurrentVersion\RunOnce
> As this key name suggests, these values will prompt a program to run only the next time a user logs on. Vista then deletes the entry.

Administrators can now add string values to these keys by setting the value to the full pathname of the program executable. For example, if I want Outlook to run at startup time no matter what items are added or deleted from the Start menu's Startup items, here's what I do:

1. Open the Registry Editor by typing **regedit** from the Start menu or the Run dialog box.

2. Navigate to the following key:

    HKLM\Software\Microsoft\Windows\CurrentVersion\Run

    Then I right-click in the Details pane and choose New → String Value.

3. It doesn't matter what name I give the new string value, so I'll call it Mr. Outlook. It *does* matter what the value is—it must point to the program executable.

4. In this case, the Outlook 2007 executable file lives in *C:\Program Files\Microsoft Office\Office12*. So I set the string value to match, as shown in Figure 8-14.

5. Now I just click OK and then exit the Registry Editor. The next time I—or anyone else—reboots the machine, Outlook will be up and ready to go.

What's more, you can specify that a program loads in the background by appending the registry's pathname value with */background*. (No period at the end.)

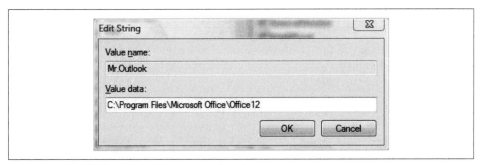

Figure 8-14. Configuring a startup program for all users

 You can do this for individual users as well. For example, maybe you're using Vista in a home environment and you want certain programs to launch automatically for just you and not the kids. Yet sometimes the kids use the computer under your user account and stuff has been known to go missing—such as a Start menu shortcut.

Instead of editing the *HKEY_LOCAL_MACHINE* top-level registry key, you'll edit the same entries in the *HKEY_CURRENT_USER* key. The rest of the procedure is exactly the same.

Naturally, you will open the Registry Editor once more and remove the registry value to undo your changes.

Startup and Group Policy

Administrators can also manipulate the startup environment using GPOs. In fact, there are actually two different methods for managing startup with a GPO. One is to specify either a Startup or Logon script (or both), and the other is to edit one of Group Policy's Administrative Templates.

What's more, all changes to the Administrative Templates write their changes to the registry. Therefore, much like using the Control Panel, you're using a graphical interface to make changes.

For more background information about Windows Vista's GPOs, please see Chapter 13.

Here are the specific steps:

1. From the Start menu, open a blank Microsoft Management Console by typing **mmc**. You'll be asked for administrative confirmation if User Account Control is turned on.

2. Now, use File → Add/Remove Snap-in to add the Group Policy Object Editor and select the Local Computer as the object. (As a shortcut, you can also type **gpedit.msc** at the Start menu, but you have to type the entire string.)

3. In the Group Policy Object Editor, navigate to Computer Configuration → Administrative Templates → System → Logon.

4. From here, look for the "Run these items at logon" setting. Double-click and then choose Enabled.

5. Now, in the Items to Run entry, click Show to open the dialog box shown in Figure 8-15.

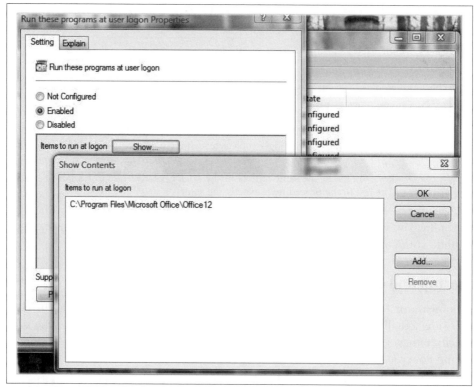

Figure 8-15. Adding startup items

In this dialog box is another button called Add from which you'll specify the full directory path to the application executable you want to start automatically.

To undo changes, edit the setting properties once again. You can either configure the "Run these programs" setting to Not Configured, or open the same dialog box and choose Remove.

The changes made here will make corresponding edits to a different registry key than was discussed in the preceding section. The Group Policies edit a key located here:

HKLM\Software\Microsoft\Windows\CurrentVersion\Policies\Explorer\Run

The result will be the same, however. Programs listed in either of the registry's startup locations will launch as Vista loads. Note, however, that the new keys won't appear in the registry until you use a Group Policy to specify a startup program. The keys outlined in the preceding section are called *legacy keys*.

Other keys in the *Computer Configuration\System\Startup* node that will affect computer startup activity include the following:

Do not process the RunOnce list
 This setting will determine whether Vista will process the RunOnce registry key. Because the items in RunOnce are deleted after processing, it's very rare that you will have to enable this setting.

Do not process the Legacy Run list
 This setting determines whether Vista will process the legacy Run keys as discussed in this section. Administrators could use this setting to override direct registry edits to the legacy keys, although if you need to enable this policy, you should probably rethink your user rights privileges as well.

You can also edit the settings in the same node found under User Settings; the complete path is:

User Configuration\Administrative Templates\System\Logon

The only difference here is that configured startup applications would then apply to just the user, and not the entire computer. It would make corresponding registry changes to this key:

HKEY_CURRENT_USER\Software\Microsoft\Windows\CurrentVersion\Policies\ Explorer\Run

Most of the time, administrators will want to use a Group Policy to change startup behavior for the computer, not the user.

Logon and startup scripts

The Group Policy Object Editor can also make changes to the startup environment by specifying that a script be run at either startup or logon time.

Admins will use Computer Configuration to specify a *startup* script, because that's what computers do: they start up. Admins will use User Configuration to specify logon scripts, because that's what users do: they *log on*.

No matter what type of script you specify, the click-steps will look almost exactly the same. For example, if you want to associate a startup script with computer startup, just do this:

1. Open the Group Policy Object Editor using the instructions previously detailed.

2. Now, navigate to Computer Configuration → Windows Settings → Scripts (Startup/Shutdown). From there, you will see two possible settings: Startup and Shutdown. Configuration is very straightforward.

3. For a Startup script, double-click the setting to see the dialog box shown in Figure 8-16. Now click the Add button to point to the appropriate script.

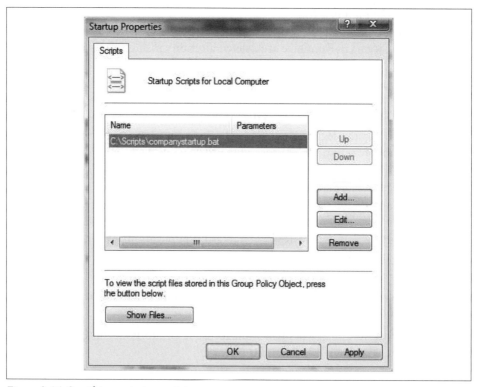

Figure 8-16. Specifying a startup script

Note that you can add multiple scripts for any given action (start up, shut down, log on, log off). Scripts will be processed in the order listed in the dialog box here. To change order, use the Up and Down buttons.

 You will rarely process a startup or logon script on a standalone Vista computer, or even one in a workgroup environment. Most of the time, scripts are deployed in a Windows server domain Active Directory enterprise.

For even more administrative command, there's a Group Policy setting or two that can control how the scripts are processed. To govern script processing, look in this Group Policy node:

Computer Configuration → Administrative Templates → System → Scripts

From here, you will see six Group Policy settings, three of which govern startup script behavior. They are:

Allow logon scripts when NetBIOS or WINS is disabled
This allows user logon scripts to run if NetBIOS or WINS is disabled during cross-forest logons without the DNS suffixes being configured. Without this setting enabled, logon scripts in a cross-forest logon will not run when DNS suffixes are not configured.

Maximum wait time for Group Policy scripts
This setting places a time limit for all logon, logoff, startup, and shutdown scripts applied by Group Policy to finish running. If the scripts have not finished running when the specified time expires, the system stops script processing and records an error event. The default time allowed for the combined set of logon scripts is 600 seconds (10 minutes), but the setting here will override this default interval.

Run logon scripts synchronously
This setting prevents the user from using the computer until scripts have finished. It directs the system to wait for the logon scripts to finish running before Vista creates the desktop.

Run shutdown scripts visible
This script setting displays the contents of shutdown scripts as they run. When enabled, the shutdown script instructions appear in a command window.

Run startup scripts asynchronously
This setting does not coordinate the running of startup scripts, overriding the default behavior of running startup scripts one at a time. As a result, all startup scripts run simultaneously.

Run startup scripts visible
This setting causes Vista to display a command prompt as each script runs. Instructions in the startup script display in this command window. This setting is designed for advanced users.

And not only can we control what software runs when Windows Vista starts up, we can also control what programs handle a particular file format. The next section looks at Vista's default actions and programs, which govern this very behavior.

Setting Default Actions and Programs

You click on a *.docx* file, and Microsoft Word 2007 opens to deal with the contents of the file. You double-click an *.mp3* file, and Media Player 11 opens. Or maybe it's iTunes. Or maybe the Media Center. What's defining all this behavior, anyway?

The answer is Vista's *default programs*. The default programs determine which programs open when you're using a particular type of file. Naturally, there are options that allow administrators to take charge of which programs Vista uses to open a web page, for example, or a *.jpg* graphics file, or a video.

Here's what to do.

Open the Default Programs Control Panel application by typing **default** at the Start menu. If you're browsing through the Control Panel, look in the Programs grouping when using the Standard View.

You have four options from the Default Programs application. You can:

Set your default programs
> Computer admins will use this selection to configure which programs Vista will use by default for a particular type of action, such as playing a movie. Note, however, that the settings here apply only to that specific user and not to all users of the computer. There is a separate option in the Default Programs application for managing computerwide settings.

Associate a file type or protocol with a program
> This lets admins pair a particular file extension with a particular program. You can specify that one music-playing program opens an *.mp3* file, for example, and another program opens a *.wma* file.

Change AutoPlay settings
> This lets you manage which programs start automatically when Vista recognizes a certain type of media, such as a DVD. We will deal with AutoPlay settings separately in a later section.

Set Program Access and Computer Defaults
> This lets computer admins configure the default programs for activities such as web surfing and email. Setting Program Access and Defaults is discussed more in the following section.

To get started with setting Default Programs for the currently logged-on user, just follow the "Set your default programs" link. You'll now see the dialog box shown in Figure 8-17.

From here, you select an application from the left pane and then decide how that program will behave with the choices on the right. You will see information about how the program is already configured.

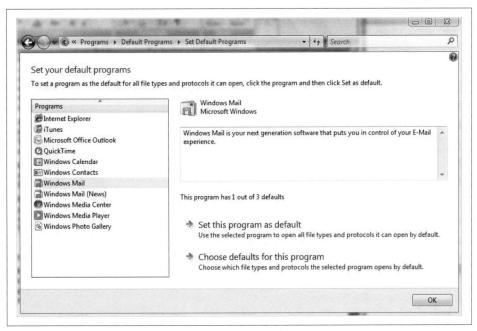

Figure 8-17. Setting default programs for a specific activity, such as dealing with email

In the figure, you see that Windows Mail is currently the default application for one of its possible three types of default activity. There are two selections below the informational message. You can:

Set this program as default
> In this example, clicking this would configure Windows Mail as the default program for handling all possible file extensions and protocols.

Choose defaults for this program
> Clicking here opens the dialog box seen in Figure 8-18. From here, you place checks in the boxes for the file extension or type of activity.

 You are not given any kind of confirmation once you click the "Set this program as default" selection.

In the figure, you see that my Vista machine is set up so that clicking the E-mail link on the Start menu launches Microsoft Outlook, not Windows Mail. I can change this with the checkbox in the "Set associations for a program" dialog box.

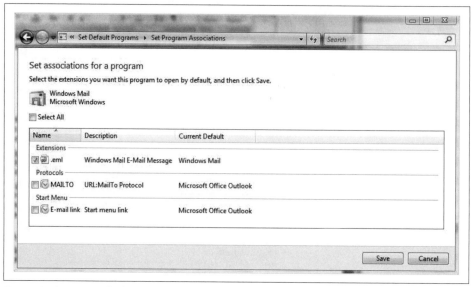

Figure 8-18. Setting which programs do what

Using Set Program Access and Computer Defaults

As you saw in the preceding section, another choice in the Default Programs Control Panel application lets administrators configure default programs for all Vista users. Set Program Access and Computer Defaults lets you specify which programs can be launched with the Start menu, desktop, and other common locations.

It's best to see it in action:

1. Open the Default Programs Control Panel application using the instructions in the preceding section and choose the Set Program Access and Computer Defaults link. You will be prompted for administrator confirmation if User Account Control is enabled.

2. You'll see the dialog box shown in Figure 8-19. From here, you will see three main categories, and possibly a fourth, depending on the computer manufacturer. To set a default action, expand the program grouping and choose an option from the drop-down menu. If you're not able to change the action, you won't see the drop-down menu.

In the figure, notice that I have the ability to change the default email programs for all Vista users from my currently configured program (Microsoft Outlook) to Windows Mail. I don't have the option here to change the computer's default media player. If I want to change the default media player, I do so on a per-user basis using the Default Programs steps outlined previously.

Here is a summary of the options you can expect from each of the four (or three) Program Access and Computer Defaults category groupings:

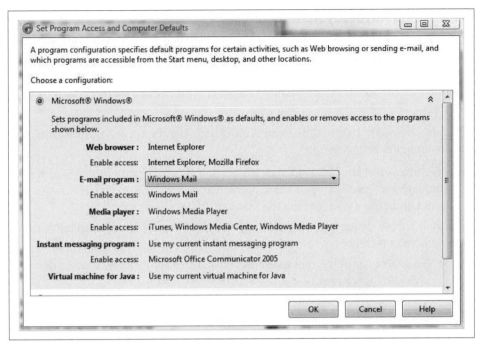

Figure 8-19. Setting Program Access and Computer Defaults

Microsoft Windows

Sets defaults for programs that are included with Vista. Even though Microsoft programs will be used by default, you can still access other programs installed on your computer. For example, if you install Firefox, it should appear here as a program with "enable(d) access." An individual user could then use Firefox as the default browser.

Non-Microsoft

Allows use of non-Microsoft programs that are installed on your computer as the defaults. If you choose this option, access to the specified Microsoft Windows programs will be removed. You should have the option to restore access to a Microsoft program at any time by changing the setting to Custom.

Custom

Allows configuration of a combination of Microsoft and non-Microsoft programs as the defaults. A custom configuration allows you to specify default programs for each activity. If you do not want a program to appear on the Start menu, the desktop, or other locations where programs typically appear, clear the "Enable access" checkbox next to the program name.

Computer Manufacturer

Restores settings to the defaults as selected by the manufacturer of your computer. You will see this option only if the computer OEM installed this version of Windows on your computer and established settings for this feature.

Configuring AutoPlay Actions

When you turn AutoPlay on, you can choose what should happen when you insert different types of digital media into your computer. For example, you can choose which digital media player is used to play CDs. When AutoPlay is turned off, you are prompted to choose what you want to do when you insert digital media into your computer.

Generally, there are two options with AutoPlay. It can be turned on or off. Here's how to configure behavior:

1. Open the AutoPlay Control Panel application by typing **auto** at the Start menu. Alternatively, you can open the Control Panel and look to the Hardware and Sound grouping if you're using the Standard View.

2. You'll see the dialog box shown in Figure 8-20. For the global AutoPlay options, you have two choices:

   • To enable AutoPlay, make sure the "Use AutoPlay for all media and devices" checkbox is selected.

   • To disable AutoPlay, uncheck this box.

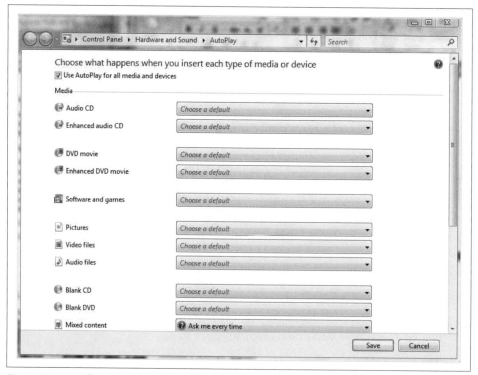

Figure 8-20. Configuring AutoPlay options

The rest of the AutoPlay application then provides a lot of specific choices that let administrators tweak behavior. Without going over each and every option, I'll point out a few of the more significant choices.

Changing the default action for a CD or DVD

To change the default action for a CD or DVD, open the AutoPlay Control Panel application. Use the drop-down menus next to the particular media type and choose the new action you want to use (see Figure 8-21).

Figure 8-21. Select the default action for a given media type

Stopping the AutoPlay dialog box from launching

There are actually two ways to stop the AutoPlay dialog from launching:

- Turn off AutoPlay completely using the instructions previously detailed.
- Turn off AutoPlay for only a particular type of media by opening the AutoPlay Control Panel application and using the "Take no action" drop-down option (see Figure 8-22). Then click Save.

Figure 8-22. Disable AutoPlay for a game or an application

Making sure you get the AutoPlay dialog box

To make sure you get the AutoPlay dialog box, open the AutoPlay Control Panel application and then use the drop-down menu to select the "Ask me every time" option (see Figure 8-23). Then click Save.

Finally, note that there's a quick way to reset all AutoPlay actions to the default. Just click the Reset All Defaults button at the bottom. You may have to scroll down to see it. There's no confirmation dialog box; just click Save to reset your choices.

Figure 8-23. Configuring AutoPlay for a prompt

Using an Application Path

Try this: open a Run dialog box and enter **snippingtool**, then press Enter. What happens? The Vista Snipping Tool application opens, that's what.

But why is this? You didn't necessarily specify an executable file (*.exe*). How does Vista know that you want to open the application, and moreover, how does it know where to look without you specifying the exact location?

What you just experienced is the result of what Vista calls an application-specific *path*, which is simply the set of folders and subfolders in which the application's executable file lives.

In the case of the Snipping Tool, Vista is able to locate the program because it has a list of paths where program executables are likely to be found. If Vista looks in one of these locations and finds a file called *snippingtool.exe*, it knows to open the program. (Vista also assumes that anything you enter into the Run dialog box is an executable file, by the way, and will append the *.exe* part automatically.)

All of this is governed by a specific registry key, located here:

HKLM\Software\Microsoft\Windows\CurrentVersion\App Paths

Under the App Paths key, you should find a lengthy list of applications in separate subkeys. The Snipping Tool, for example, has a string value of *C:\Windows\System32\SnippingTool.exe* stored in its subkey. This tells Vista to "remember" that *snippingtool.exe* is located in the *C:\Windows\System32* directory. If you type **snippingtool** at the Run dialog box, then, Vista looks here to find and run the executable.

Note that many application installs create a path subkey automatically to facilitate their launch from the Run dialog box.

So the big question now is this: can you create your own application-specific path? Absolutely.

To do so, follow these steps:

1. Open the Registry Editor by typing **regedit** at the Start menu.
2. Navigate to the key just introduced:

    HKLM\Software\Microsoft\Windows\CurrentVersion\App Paths

3. Again, each 32-bit application *should* have its own App Path subkey already set up. Each subkey will have one or both of these string variables defined:

Default

This details the full directory path to the application executable.

Path

This will point out the location of any other files needed to run the application. By default, Vista will look in the Default folder location for any other files that are necessary. Otherwise, it uses the Path locations. Most Office programs, for example, use a Path setting.

4. To set up a manual application-specific path, just create a new subkey under the App Path key, giving it the name of the application's executable file. If you're feeling froggy, you can even use this to create a sort of alias to an existing executable.

For example, I can create a new App Path subkey and call it something really clever, like *brianrocks.exe*. For the Default string value, then, I can point it to the snipping tool's executable: *C:\Windows\System32\SnippingTool.exe*, as shown in Figure 8-24.

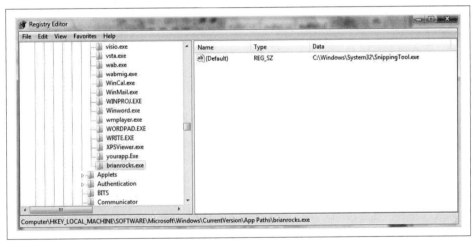

Figure 8-24. Creating your own application path

Now, I open the Run dialog box once again and type **brianrocks**. What happens? The Snipping Tool opens, which I use to take the screenshot shown previously in Figure 8-24.

And yes, as you have just borne witness to, I do indeed rock.

 You don't necessarily have to use the exact name of the program executable itself when naming your manually created subkey. If something else would better help you identify what the program is used for, go for it. The only constraints are that the subkey must end in *.exe* and must not already be in use.

What's the big, fat point of all this if you use the Start menu to launch applications, and never the Run dialog box, especially given that a 32-bit application writes an App Path subkey automatically?

There are three possible real-world application scenarios for the tweaks just discussed:

32-bit applications that don't create the subkey
This should be rare, but not unheard of. It depends on the setup routine, and whether common setup behavior has been followed.

16-bit applications
Older programs don't store paths to their executables in the Vista registry.

Documents
If you want to open a document using the Run dialog box, you have to type the entire pathname—unless, that is, you've created an App Path entry for the document. (The only other exception is if you're at the Command Prompt and are opening the document while currently in the folder where the doc is stored.)

Oh, and there's one more scenario. In a word, it's scripting. If scripting is used to automate certain actions such as running a program, it's better if Vista knows where to locate the executable.

Using Speech Recognition

Vista also includes a very powerful productivity tool: the ability to use your voice to interact with Windows and most installed applications. That's right; you talk to Vista, and it listens. Better, it obeys your commands.

When working with applications such as Microsoft Word or Notepad, you can also dictate text. Not only can this dramatically increase "typing" speed among those of us who were not exactly Mavis Beacon pupils, but it can also be a huge productivity boost for those with limited use of their hands.

We already touched on speech recognition fairly extensively in Chapter 5, however. For instructions on how to set up the microphone, please refer to that chapter.

Even if you don't flip back to Chapter 5 this second, you should be able to find your way easily enough by typing **speech** at the Start menu and launching Speech Recognition. Just follow the on-screen instructions, and you're on your way.

For reference, then, I'm including a table of Speech Recognition commands (Table 8-1) for working with windows and programs. Most of it is directly from Microsoft; I'm augmenting a few items that I thought were unclear.

If something appears in replaceable font, it means several variables would work to produce a desired result.

Table 8-1. Commands for working with folders, files, and Speech Recognition itself

To do this...	Say this...
Select a file or folder	Select *Pictures*; Click *Chapter 8*
Open a selected file or folder	Open; Open that; Launch that; Open *Pictures*; Open *Chapter 8*
Click any item by saying its name	File, Start, View, Tools, and so on
Double-click an item	Double-click *Recycle Bin*; Double-click *Computer*; Double-click *Chapter 8*
Minimize all windows to show the desktop	Show Desktop
Switch to an open program	Switch to *Word*; Switch to *Outlook*; Switch to *program name*
Scroll in a specified direction	Scroll up; Scroll down; Scroll left; Scroll right
Insert a new paragraph or new line in a document	New paragraph; New line
Select a word in a document	Select *word*
Select and delete specific words	Delete *word*
Show a list of possible voice commands	What can I say?
Update the list of currently available speech commands	Refresh speech commands
Turn on speech recognition	Start listening
Turn off speech recognition	Stop listening
Minimize the microphone bar	Minimize Speech Recognition
Move the Speech Recognition microphone out of the way	Move Speech Recognition

To unlock the dictation capabilities of Speech Recognition, it helps to have several of the most common dictation commands at your disposal. After all, dictation will be severely hampered if you have to spend a lot of time at the keyboard doing things like repositioning the mouse and pressing the Enter key to make new paragraphs. Once again, Table 8-2 is from Microsoft, with a few of my editorial changes.

As in the preceding table, replaceable font denotes that there are several possibilities for the particular command.

Table 8-2. A few of the more commonly used dictation commands

To do this...	Say this...
Insert a new line in the document	New line
Insert a new paragraph in the document	New paragraph
Insert a tab	Tab
Insert the literal word for the next command. If you say "question mark," for example, Vista inserts a ?. If you want the words *question mark* instead of the ?, use the word *literal* first.	Literal *word*
Insert the numeral form of a number	Numeral number
Set the insertion point before a specific word	Go to *word*

Table 8-2. A few of the more commonly used dictation commands (continued)

To do this...	Say this...
Set the insertion point after a specific word	Go after *word*
Go to the start of the sentence that the cursor is in	Go to start of sentence
Go to the start of the paragraph that the cursor is in	Go to start of paragraph
Go to the start of the document	Go to start of document
Go to the end of the sentence, paragraph, or document	Go to end of sentence/paragraph/document
Select a word range	Select *word* through *word*
Select all text	Select all
Select the last text you dictated (useful for training Speech Recognition)	Select that
Clear the selection	Clear selection
Delete the previous sentence or paragraph	Delete previous sentence/paragraph
Delete the next sentence or paragraph	Delete the next sentence/paragraph
Delete the selected or last dictated text	Delete that

Remember, you can open the Control Panel's Speech Recognition Options application and print pretty much this entire table plus a whole lot more (there are well over 100 speech commands in the entire set of tables).

To print this table, simply follow the Open the Speech Reference Card link at the bottom of the window. The Help and Support Center then opens to the Common Commands section. Use the Options in the upper-righthand corner to access the Print command, and then select the appropriate Print options.

Administrators can take advantage of this ability to distribute reference material to those in the organization who frequently use Vista's Speech Recognition features.

Or you can just bookmark these couple of pages; whatever's easier.

Configuring Application Compatibility

Most 32-bit applications, especially those that were developed for use on Windows 2000 or XP, will run on the Windows Vista platform without issue. Sometimes, however, that's not the case, and an administrator needs to step in and prod the application just a bit.

The prodding technology built into Vista is called *application compatibility*, and it allows Vista to run programs written for earlier versions of Windows. If you find yourself in a situation where your company is using a mission-critical application that won't run correctly on Vista (if at all), you need to know about the Program Compatibility Wizard.

Essentially, the Program Compatibility Wizard makes the application think it's running on an earlier version of Windows. Here's how to get started:

1. Open the Programs Control Panel application by typing **prog** from the Start menu. Choose the Programs grouping if you're using the Standard View.

2. Launch the Program Compatibility Wizard by clicking the "Use an older program with this version of Windows" link.

3. From there, just follow the instructions in the wizard. The first dialog box, for example, provides three options. You can:

   • Choose from a list of programs.

   • Use the program in the optical drive.

   • Locate the program manually.

4. The specific steps will then vary depending on the option chosen. Choosing from a list, for example, will produce the dialog box seen in Figure 8-25.

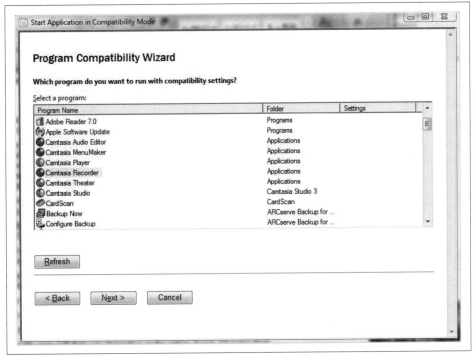

Figure 8-25. Choosing the program to run in compatibility mode

You can then choose the operating system for the particular application, and other settings such as screen resolution, visual theme options, and whether to run the program as an administrator (many older programs require either full administrative access to the machine, or membership in the Power Users group).

Microsoft recommends that you not use the Program Compatibility Wizard on older antivirus programs, disk utilities, or other system programs, as this might lead to data loss and a reduced level of security for the application and, thus, for Vista.

If you cannot install a program at all, use the Program Compatibility Wizard and browse to the program's setup file. It should be called either *setup.exe* or *install.exe*, which is an older installation utility. The Program Compatibility Wizard is not designed to work on programs that utilize the newer Microsoft Installer (*.msi*) file extension.

Using the Compatibility Tab

You can achieve this same objective by accessing the application's Compatibility tab and then specifying which Windows version Vista should emulate in order to make the program function.

And the good news is that you don't even have to know where the application's executable file is. All an administrator needs is the ability to find it in the Start menu.

To access the Compatibility tab, locate the program's shortcut. You can do this from anywhere; it doesn't matter where the shortcut is located, but the Start menu is generally the best place to look.

Right-click the shortcut and choose Properties. From the Properties dialog box, choose the Compatibility tab, shown in Figure 8-26. Now, choose the compatibility options—they will be similar to what you can set using the Program Compatibility Wizard.

By default, these compatibility settings become part of the user profile. If you want to configure these settings for all users, click the button at the bottom of this tab; you'll see a dialog box similar to the one in the figure. Also, note that the little security shield icon on the "Show settings for all users" button lets you know that you'll be prompted for administrative confirmation if User Account Control is turned on.

Table 8-3 details Microsoft's suggestions about when it might be best to try a given compatibility option on the Compatibility tab.

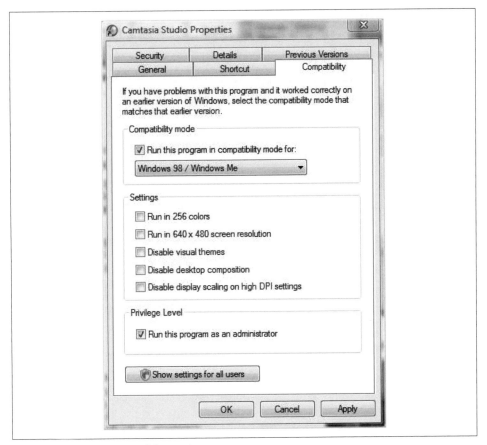

Figure 8-26. Setting compatibility options

Table 8-3. Compatibility options

Setting	Description
Compatibility mode	Runs the program using settings from a previous version of Windows. Try this setting if you know the program is designed for a specific previous version of Windows.
Run in 256 colors	Uses a limited set of colors in the program. Some older programs are designed to use fewer colors.
Run in 640 x 480 screen resolution	Runs the program in a smaller-size window. Try this setting if the graphical user interface appears jagged or is rendered improperly.
Disable visual themes	Disables themes on the program. Try this setting if you notice problems with the menus or buttons on the title bar of the program.

Table 8-3. Compatibility options (continued)

Setting	Description
Disable desktop composition	Turns off transparency and other advanced display features. Choose this setting if window movement appears erratic or you notice other display problems.
Disable display scaling on high DPI settings	Turns off automatic resizing of programs if a large-scale font size is in use. Try this setting if large-scale fonts are interfering with the appearance of the program.
Privilege level	Runs the program as an administrator. Some programs require administrator privileges to run properly. If you are not currently logged on as an administrator, this option is not available.

Note that although you can configure a program to always run in the context of an administrative account, this will not bypass the User Account Control confirmation message as long as User Account Control is enabled.

Running an application as an administrator once

Administrators have another compatibility option that allows for less dramatic changes to the program's overall behavior. You can run an application just once in the context of an administrator account. This can be useful when diagnosing a problem.

Here's what to do:

1. Find the program's shortcut icon in either the Start menu or Windows Explorer.

2. Right-click the shortcut, and then choose "Run as administrator" from the context menu.

3. You'll now see a User Account Control dialog box that's a little different from what you've seen many times before. It's titled "An unidentified program wants access to your computer," and it's shown in Figure 8-27. This dialog box gives you two options:

   • Allow access by clicking on Continue.

   • Prevent access by clicking Cancel. The program will not launch.

Also, the preceding assumes you're already logged on as an administrator in Administrator Approval mode. If you are logged on as a standard user, you'll need to enter the appropriate credentials and then click Submit.

 For some applications, the "Run this program as an administrator" context menu selection is unavailable. This means that either the application does not require administrative credentials to run, or it is blocked from always running with administrator credentials.

Figure 8-27. Running a program as an administrator

The Application Compatibility Toolkit

Microsoft's Application Compatibility Toolkit (ACT) is a set of tools that helps administrators better manage a company's overall application portfolio. Among its many capabilities, it helps to:

- Analyze applications, web sites, and computers
- Evaluate existing operating system deployments
- Evaluate the impact of operating system updates before deployment
- Report information about application compatibility
- Deploy automated solutions for compatibility issues, usually through the Windows Update mechanism

In its role as application analyzer, for example, the ACT includes a User Account Control agent, whose main job is to identify applications that require administrator privileges in order to run properly.

These ACT features help to lower the total cost of ownership (TCO) for an enterprise's applications, reducing the effort and resources spent resolving application compatibility issues.

The ACT works with the Standard User Analyzer (SUA) tool (which I cover in the next section) in that you can export SUA information into an ACT database. This will help administrators track application compatibility issues, not just on a single machine, but across the entire enterprise.

 Version 5.0 of the ACT for Windows Vista will not exactly be the least complex application you'll ever run, as it performs a wide variety of tests and collects a vast amount of information about application behavior. You can find complete ACT setup and use instructions at the Windows Vista Tech Center: *http://technet.microsoft.com/windowsvista*.

Using the Standard User Analyzer

If one tool in the ACT proves its value above all others to administrators considering migrating to Windows Vista, it's the SUA, which can help determine how a company's vital programs will behave when running under Vista's new security enhancements.

The SUA tool is included in the ACT, and its function is exactly as the name implies: it tests an application in the context of a standard user account in order to ensure that the prospective application does not depend on full administrator access to run properly. To use it, you'll first need to find and install the ACT, currently in version 5.0. You can get it at *http://www.microsoft.com/downloads*.

From there, just search for "Application Compatibility Toolkit," and you're on your way.

The SUA performs a series of tests that require no direct administrative intervention, and then returns the results of these tests in a graphical interface that's fairly easy to decipher. It includes results for:

- File access
- Registry access
- INI files
- Token issues
- Security privileges
- Namespace issues
- Other issues

Here's how to test an application you're thinking of deploying using the SUA:

1. From the Start menu, type either **standard** or **user**. The Standard User Analyzer should appear in your list of programs. Alternatively, the path is Start → All Programs → Standard User Analyzer → Standard User Analyzer.

2. As seen in Figure 8-28, the App Info tab is where it all starts. Click Browse to locate the desired Target Application. You can also just type the full path to the executable if you know it.

3. In the Parameters field, enter any launch parameters, if applicable.

4. To launch the application in the context of an administrator account, select the Launch Elevated checkbox. Most of the time, you *should* leave this checked. The tool will still test the application for issues when run in the context of a standard user.

5. Click Launch. You may see a dialog box asking you to download an Application Verifier. Click Yes. You may also be prompted for administrative credentials if User Account Control is enabled.

Figure 8-28. Use the App Info tab to begin analysis

During the test, the SUA launches the application. You can then use the application as you normally would. In the example here, I used an application called Camtasia Studio—which at the time of this writing does *not* work with Windows Vista—and recorded a screen capture movie.

Meanwhile, the SUA monitors Camtasia's actions until the application is closed. It then generates a log for the application, which, depending on how large the file is, might take some time.

Now that the SUA has completed the analysis process, it's able to generate a report that is doled out among the SUA's various tabs. As you can see in Figure 8-29, Camtasia Studio has spawned several processes that have made Vista unhappy.

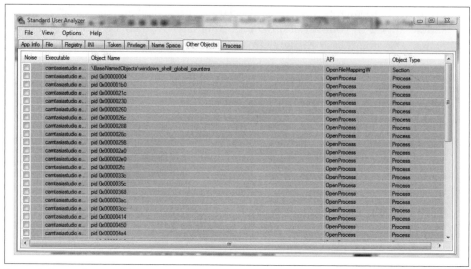

Figure 8-29. Gathering information from the Standard User Analyzer

If you don't see any logfile information right away, it may be because a child process might still be running even after the main application has exited. Click the Refresh Log button on the App Info tab to remedy the situation.

As you can see, now eight tabs provide feedback about the tested application. Microsoft has provided Table 8-4 to help explain what to look for on each tab.

Table 8-4. Examining the information generated by the Standard User Analyzer

Tab	Details
File	Lists filesystem access issues; for example, an application attempting to write to a file that normally only administrators can access.
Registry	Lists system registry access issues; for example, an application attempting to write to a registry key under HKLM, a location that normally only administrators can access.
INI	Lists WriteProfile APIs issues. WriteProfile APIs were originally used for 16-bit Windows but are still popular in some modern applications.
Token	Lists access token checking issues. If an application explicitly checks for the Built-in\Administrators security identifier (SID) in a user's access token, the application most likely will not work for a standard user.
Privilege	Lists privilege issues. For example, if an application explicitly enables SetDebugPrivilege, it will not work for a standard user.
Name Space	Lists issues that are caused when an application creates system objects (e.g., events, memory mappings) in restricted namespace. Applications that have this error will not work for a standard user.
Other Objects	Lists issues related to accessing objects other than files and registry keys.
Process	Lists issues related to process elevation. On Vista, if an application uses CreateProcess APIs to launch executables that require elevation, the application will not work for a standard user.

If you can believe it, the SUA crashed while I was trying to diagnose the problem with Camtasia Studio. I should note that the SUA was still in beta at the time of the test, however. ACT 5.0 should be "live" (and able to diagnose my issue with Camtasia) by the time you read this.

Further, the SUA is built such that is can easily be used in conjunction with the ACT 5.0.

Using the Application Verifier

Although more commonly used by Windows developers, administrators can also deploy a tool called the Application Verifier *before* a program is released to help ensure compatibility.

The Application Verifier is a runtime verification tool that helps track down programming errors that can be very difficult to identify with normal application testing. It was created specifically for detecting memory corruptions and critical security vulnerabilities. Once it finds these programming errors, the tool can then suggest corrections.

In terms of how this is especially useful to developers writing for Windows Vista, it includes several probes to determine how well the application will perform under least-privileged User Account operation—in other words, how Vista runs programs when using User Account Control.

Using the Application Verifier is very similar to using the SUA—a developer will install the Verifier and then run the program. The Verifier conducts its tests in the background. Once it's finished with the program test, it logs any errors it detected so that developers can make necessary corrections.

Again, this is not normally the purview of a system admin. Developers mostly use this tool as they're in the process of writing the app. Usually, the best thing an administrator can do is to make the developer aware of the Application Verifier's existence.

You can get the Application Verifier at the Microsoft Download Center, at *http://www.microsoft.com/downloads*.

Summary

As we've seen, using applications on Windows Vista is a *tad* more complicated than just inserting a CD and letting it install using the AutoPlay behavior. Or at least it can be, which is great news for Vista administrators.

For instance, we looked at how ordinary users and Vista administrators can govern AutoPlay behavior. You now know where to go to specify what AutoPlay will do automatically when you're inserting a DVD movie, for example, and what it will do when you're inserting a blank DVD-R.

We've also seen how to manipulate the many Windows components by using the designated Control Panel application. We've seen that, at last, you won't have to search for the installation media every time you want to add another component that is "built into" the OS. With Windows Vista, the built-in components really are built-in.

Part of this chapter served as a companion piece to Chapter 5, where we examined the many accessibility options, including Speech Recognition. You now have a handy reference for using many of the most useful commands, and you know how to quickly retrieve even more.

Finally, we looked at the many options administrators have to tackle the challenges of Vista startup programs and application compatibility. Along the way, you saw how easy—and how enforceable—startup program configuration can be, and you were introduced to the technologies that will get older programs working with this latest version of Windows.

In the next chapter, we look at Windows Vista deployment. Many new features have been developed to smooth the deployment of customized Vista images to multiple computers; Chapter 9 examines these technologies and will get you headed in the right direction.

CHAPTER 9

Deploying Windows Vista

Installing a single instance of the Windows Vista operating system on either a new or an existing machine is a fairly straightforward operation. Usually, it involves little more than inserting the installation DVD into the drive and answering a series of questions. Although I will briefly discuss single, unattended installation, this book won't spend that much time on the topic. That's because the *Vista Admin Definitive Guide* assumes that its audience already has a fairly high level of computer expertise when it comes to the single deployment; you've been there, done that.

Deploying enterprise-wide—multiple, simultaneous installations across an entire company—is another matter entirely. This chapter focuses on the administrative task of performing mass Windows Vista installations, and addresses the various challenges that go along with it. In this chapter, we'll look at several deployment scenarios, always with an eye toward what to do with user data during installation.

This chapter also touches on what to do *after* the Vista installation. Protecting and preserving users' data is usually one of the most central concerns at installation time, and this chapter provides a full discussion about what options administrators have at their disposal to achieve this objective. Specifically, we'll cover the User State Migration Tool (USMT) and Windows Easy Transfer.

Vista Deployment Overview

So, you've already seen some of the changes that ship with Windows Vista. In other words, you've seen some of the *whats*. Now we'll focus on some of the *hows*, as in how you will roll out the new OS under a variety of deployment scenarios.

Of course, the rest of the chapter explores the multifaceted answer to this very question. But before we venture too far in answering, let's take stock of some of the tools Vista places at an administrator's disposal.

To aid in your deployment tasks, Vista introduces several new utilities and offers improvements on existing technologies. Following is a list of some of the new and/or improved deployment technologies:

USMT 3.0
> An upgrade from USMT version 2.6, it captures user settings and data for transfer from one computer to another; discussed in this chapter.

Windows System Image Manager (SIM)
> Use this to create and modify *unattend.xml* files, which in turn facilitate unattended installations; discussed in this chapter.

Windows Deployment Services
> In a parallel world, this might be called Remote Installation Services 2.0 (RIS 2.0), as it functions as an upgrade of said utility. The difference is that it can deploy both Windows Vista and Windows XP images in large rollouts. It can also deploy Windows Preinstallation Environment (PE) images; discussed in this chapter.

Application Compatibility Toolkit 5.0
> This upgrade toolkit allows you to determine whether applications will work with Windows Vista; discussed in Chapter 8.

Sysprep
> This is new and improved for Windows Vista.

Setup
> This is the new executable that starts Windows Vista installation.

ImageX
> This is a new command-line tool for creating Windows Image Manager images.

PnPUtil
> This is used to add and remove drivers from the Windows Vista driver store, and it's especially useful when you're deploying machines with specialized hardware requiring drivers not included in the Windows Vista installation files.

OCSetup
> This utility replaces Sysocmgr. Both are used for installing Windows components.

PkgMgr
> Similar to the OCSetup tool, this tool services the Windows Vista operating system.

When new technologies are introduced, it usually means that some old technologies have been cleared out to make room. Here's what *not* to look for when performing mass installs:

Remote Installation Services (RIS)
> In the Vista environment, RIS is now RIP (it was right there, I couldn't help myself). It's been replaced by Windows Deployment Services, although you can still use it in Windows XP deployments if necessary. RIPREP and RISETUP, utilities that helped prepare RIS images, are not available with Windows Vista.

MS-DOS boot disks
> You won't need these anymore with the advent of Windows PE.

Setup Manager
> Functions once carried out by the Setup Manager are now being handled by the Windows System Image Manager.

Winnt.exe and win32.exe
> These Windows setup executables are now the stuff of folklore. Use Setup to start a Vista installation.

Sysocmgr
> As mentioned, this has been supplanted by OCSetup and PkgMgr.

Not only are there new tools to help you with your chores, but there is also a host of deployment considerations that good admins will contemplate prior to widespread Vista rollouts. A few of the more significant ones are handled in the next section.

Deployment Considerations

When deploying Vista, you must consider several factors that will come into play. A quick scan of these factors prior to installation will save you lots of time and headache, and will go a long way toward ensuring a successful operation. Here's what you need to know.

Vista images are bigger

The fact that Vista images are bigger affects options such as distribution media, and it can bring network bandwidth into play. A Windows Vista image size starts at 2 GB, and that's for a compressed image. Once the image is uncompressed, you're looking at a 5 GB installation at the very least. When you throw in the line-of-business applications such as Microsoft Office, you're talking about deployment image sizes that can stretch the capabilities of many forms of media that administrators have relied on in the past.

So then, how will you choose to deploy? You could distribute on CDs, but you'll need three or four to handle all of the necessary files. A DVD is probably a much better choice, but then again, not every computer that can run Windows Vista will have a DVD drive. Consider this when making a purchase decision.

Alternatively, you could install over the network, but a 10 Mbps network—still the norm in many an office park—will not sufficiently handle the workload. The same goes for a nonswitched network.

You could deploy from a bootable USB drive. This is becoming increasingly viable as prices for such drives continue to drop. If this sounds like a good plan, make sure you have computers that support booting to a USB drive. You may have to tweak Basic Input/Output System (BIOS) settings.

Vista has been broken into components

From an architecture standpoint, one of the most significant changes is that Vista is now broken into several distinct components. Deployment is affected because administrators now have an easier time specifying which technologies get to the desktop. Tools such as the Windows SIM, shown in Figure 9-1, assist in rolling out specific options.

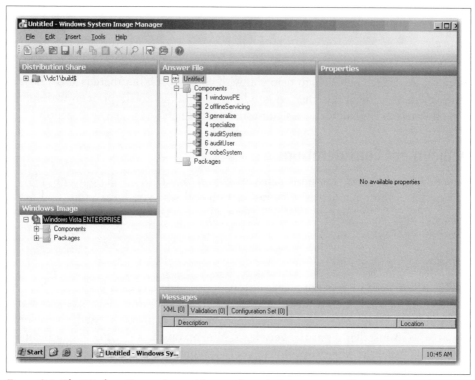

Figure 9-1. The Windows System Image Manager lets administrators enable certain Vista features for deployment

The Windows SIM allows administrators to configure "no-touch" Vista setup, language selection, product keys, and license agreement information, just to name a few (more on the Windows SIM later in this chapter).

Hardware drivers, language packs, and even service packs are now treated simply as components, and are deployed with a tool called Package Manager, which behaves very much like the System Manager utility. This lets admins deploy new drivers even while in the middle of the deployment process: a new driver can easily be applied to an existing deployment image.

No more text installation

You know the drill: you start a Windows installation and then stare at the computer for several minutes, looking at text during an initial text-only installation step. During this time, Windows was decompressing and installing system files, creating registry entries, and setting security. Now, at long last, the text-mode phase of Windows installation has been removed. A new setup program handles the chore of applying the Vista image to the computer.

Further, Vista changes, or can indeed eliminate, the image creation process. Although you can still "sysprep" (discussed shortly) a Vista machine to prepare it for disk imaging, you should be aware that the Vista DVD ships with an image that has already been "sysprepped" and is ready to deploy. Many an admin will be able to deploy this image with only minor additions of drivers or fixes, if any changes are needed at all.

Deployment settings are stored in XML

Same name, same general purpose; different file extension; better deployment options—what am I talking about?

Prior to Windows Vista, administrators were able to automate installations by storing configuration information in a text file called *unattend.txt*. Its job was simply to answer questions asked of users during installation, such as computer name and domain information.

Now, the *unattend.txt* file has been replaced by a file called *unattend.xml*. It also negates the need for several other installation configuration files:

Sysprep.inf
>   Used for configuring how a Windows XP machine was customized when using a mini setup wizard

Wimbom.ini
>   Used to configure Windows PE

Cmdlines.txt
>   Used to execute a list of text commands during mini setup

Note that you can still use these files with Vista deployments if you're comfortable with the function of each. Just use the Notepad application to make the appropriate edits. With the Windows SIM, however, you can inspect the Vista image, determine what modifications can be made, and then configure each one using a graphical interface.

Security has been improved

Security is still not perfect, but it definitely steps in the right direction. (No one operating system can lay claim to perfect security.) Some of these security developments may have an impact on rollout.

One big change to Windows Vista, as you've seen, is the ability for nonadministrators to load device drivers. An even bigger change, though, is in application compatibility. Apps that failed to work on Windows XP because they required the user to have full access to the system drive and registry can now work just fine on a Vista machine.

Because of this, Vista removes the Power Users local group. If your situation requires the Power Users group, you can apply it through a security template that is applied to the Vista installation.

Highly secure computing environments may opt to deploy the new BitLocker technology, available in the Vista Enterprise and Ultimate editions. However, admins must be aware of the requirements and implications before doing so. BitLocker encrypts an entire Vista volume, operating system files included. It then stores the encryption keys in a Trusted Platform Module (TPM) chip, but only chips version 1.2 or later are supported. Alternatively, the encryption keys may be stored on a USB flash drive, but accessing the computer in the event of a lost or stolen USB drive would be impossible without an administrator's help.

Also, the Windows Firewall has been updated and improved, and can now monitor both incoming and outgoing traffic. However, administrators still retain their ability to govern Windows Firewall behavior with new Group Policy settings.

Vista Deployment Scenarios

So, the decision's been made and the CIO has allocated the funds. It's time to begin Windows Vista deployment. But how? What options are available? And what are you going to do with the old machines? Will they be used for the Vista rollout, or is the company getting a hardware upgrade as well?

Prior to installation, the network administrator has many questions to ponder, many factors to consider. Let's start with a look at available deployment scenarios. When installing the Windows Vista operating system, admins perform one of the following installations:

- New computer
- Upgrade
- Computer to computer

That's really all the choices you have. Of course, the techniques you'll choose for deployment of 1 system will likely be different than if you're deploying for 100. The concepts will not change, however. This section looks at each deployment scenario separately. As the chapter progresses, we'll explore how mass Vista deployment might affect each of these.

New Computer

In the context of Windows Vista deployment, a new computer means a system with a clean install of the operating system. It doesn't necessarily mean a brand-new machine. OEMs, for example, use new-computer deployment methods when crafting new systems or even refurbishing existing systems.

Installing a new computer involves these steps:

1. With the desktop engineering tools, deployment professionals can modify the Vista image so that the necessary hardware drivers are included with the operating system installation. If you receive a *restore disk* from a manufacturer such as Dell, HP, or any other OEM, you're getting the (eventual) work product of an installation modified by the desktop engineering tools. Of course, companies can create their own deployment disks using the same tools.

2. Install this image on a test computer.

3. Install additional line-of-business applications such as Outlook or Excel.

4. Save the image, usually to DVD. Sometimes this image is saved to a network share.

5. The user installs the image using the desired media. If this is a DVD, you make the disk available and boot from disk (the restore disk, as mentioned in step 1). In many company-wide deployment scenarios, this installation image is then available for a client's access during a network boot.

6. Once the installation starts, the user is presented with a series of questions that help personalize deployment. An administrator can also create an answer file to provide these answers for the highest degree of "hands-free" deployment.

 In many deployment scenarios, the USB flash drive is the preferred device, as it is more portable and administrators can update the Windows PE environment without burning another DVD.

Upgrade

If preserving the existing desktop environment—including the user's data—is a main concern, you'll probably want to perform an upgrade of an existing system. A system upgrade is usually the least disruptive to the end user, but can also preserve a lot of settings admins may want to see changed.

Here's what's involved in an upgrade. Note that for the most part, the steps look fairly similar to those for installing to a new computer:

1. As in a clean install, admins can use the desktop engineering tools to modify the Windows Vista image so that necessary hardware drivers and components are included.

2. Install to a test system and then add the line-of-business applications.

3. The newly created image can then be saved to the medium of choice.

4. With the installation medium available, the end user performs an install of Windows Vista. (Again, if deploying from DVD, the user simply plops the disk in the coffee holder and clicks the upgrade button.)

During an upgrade, Vista's Setup program does not ask any questions of the end user. Instead, it uses all of the user's old settings and data, making them immediately a part of the user's new desktop environment. If the user has placed a bunch of desktop shortcuts on his desktop because that's how he likes to launch apps, for example, the shortcuts remain in the Vista desktop. (Conversely, Vista likes to keep the desktop as clean as possible during a new computer installation.)

Another important administrative consideration is what kind of Windows operating system can be upgraded in the first place. Table 9-1 looks at what can and cannot be upgraded to Windows Vista.

Table 9-1. What can and cannot be upgraded to Windows Vista

Can be upgraded	Cannot be upgraded
XP Professional	Windows 98
XP Home	Windows 95
Windows 2000 Professional	Windows 3.x
Windows Vista	Windows Me

 You may have noticed that Windows Vista was listed as an upgrade candidate. If you recall from Chapter 2, the Vista operating systems represent a departure from previous Windows operating systems in that you can more easily migrate from one version to another. For more information, please refer to the discussion in Chapter 2.

If your computer is one of those listed on the right side of the table, you'll be performing either a new computer installation or a side-by side migration. (Although, really now, I don't see how any system running Windows 3.x is going to have the horsepower for Vista anyway.)

The Windows Vista Upgrade Advisor

In Chapter 2, we discussed the requirements needed to run Windows Vista. But what if you haven't committed them to memory? Is there a tool available that can just tell you whether your computer can handle Vista, and if not, can it make recommendations about what needs improvement before performing the upgrade?

There is. It's called the Windows Vista Upgrade Advisor, and Microsoft has made it available for download from the Vista web site at:

http://www.microsoft.com/windows/products/windowsvista/buyorupgrade/ upgradeadvisor.mspx

Once there, you can grab the Upgrade Advisor (at the time of this writing, you could find it by following a link called, appropriately, Download Windows Vista Upgrade Advisor).

Now that you've downloaded this tool, using the new Vista Upgrade Advisor is fairly straightforward. Just double-click the *.msi* file you've downloaded, and the Advisor does most of the rest. Here's a brief iteration of the tasks carried out by the Upgrade Advisor:

1. The Vista Upgrade Advisor first asks your permission and then performs a system scan of your computer's hardware and software.

2. The results are then displayed in a dialog box, as seen in Figure 9-2.

As you can see, the Upgrade Advisor identifies the hardware and/or software components that, if upgraded, would enhance the Vista user experience.

Computer to Computer

Sometimes a user wants to prepare a new computer with Windows Vista while keeping her old system exactly as is. This is known as a computer-to-computer installation, in which user settings and data are migrated to the new system running Windows Vista, but the old computer is left essentially as is.

Here's what happens during a computer-to-computer installation:

1. Admins use a utility such as the USMT to save the settings and data from the existing machine to some storage location. Again, it doesn't really matter whether the storage location is on removable media or on a network share.

2. A new computer deployment image is created and deployed to the new machine.

3. This new computer image then utilizes the settings and data gathered in step 1 to deploy Vista on the new machine. These installations are unattended, and data/settings are then immediately available on the new machine.

Figure 9-2. The Windows Vista Upgrade Advisor helps assess your system's capabilities

 It's usually good practice to load necessary applications on the target machine before transferring the user state. Many applications require installation and registration before data is moved.

The USMT does not support every migration scenario, however. It supports movement of settings and data only from Windows 2000 (with Service Pack 4) or newer machines, and the target computers must be running either Windows Vista or XP.

For migration of settings/data from an older machine—such as one running Windows 98—to Windows Vista, third-party tools must be utilized.

In the following subsections, we'll examine the use of each migration and deployment tool.

Upgrade utilities

Whether we're simply upgrading to Vista on a home computer or rolling out a company-wide upgrade, it's usually vital that we keep existing settings. By keeping our existing favorites, shortcuts, program settings, and the like, we can smooth the transition process and quickly become comfortable with Vista's new features. For companies, this can save hours of potentially lost worker productivity as users re-create their desktop environments.

Vista places two tools at your disposal for the job of migrating settings. They are:

The USMT
> Now at version 3.0, the USMT is a command-line tool built with larger-scale, corporate migrations in mind. This newest release of the USMT contains several enhancements that are detailed later on. The main advantage of USMT from an administrator's point of view is that it can use scripting. This, in turn, allows for batching of several migrations at once.

Windows Easy Transfer
> Unlike USMT, this is a graphical, wizard-based interface that helps individual users port information from an old computer to a new one running Windows Vista. Such information can include email accounts and messages, application settings, Windows preferences such as the desktop and Internet Explorer favorites, photos, and music.

So, although both utilities perform essentially the same tasks at the end of the day, they do so utilizing different means. The PC Migration Assistant requires user interaction; someone has to be sitting at the migrated computer answering prompts and instructing the utility about which profiles are to be moved. If a system has more than one profile, the process must be repeated for each one being migrated. And while there's no law against using it in a company environment, it's built more for individuals moving from older OSs to Vista on a "onesey-twosey" basis.

A USMT migration, on the other hand, requires no user interaction. The utility can capture and migrate every profile on a system.

Here are a few important factors to keep in mind when using Vista-supplied migration utilities:

- The Windows Vista migration tools support only Vista, XP, and Windows 2000 SP4 as sources of migration data.
- The PC Migration Assistant only allows Vista as a migration target.
- The USMT allows both Vista and XP as migration targets.

Before we discuss the utilities themselves, we should segue for just a bit to understand better what these utilities transfer in the first place. For the most part, they're responsible for collecting *profile* information and shepherding it from computer A to computer B. But just what exactly is a profile?

A word about profiles

In Windows XP and 2000 systems, application settings and other personal data—such as the Outlook mailbox data (*.pst*) file—are stored in a *profile*. If it sounds mysterious (or looks so because I italicized the word), it's really not. The profile is actually just a folder hierarchy where applications and tools (such as Outlook) store the data that makes them behave the way they do. On Windows XP and 2000 machines, the profile folders are stored in the *\Documents and Settings\%username%* folder, where *%username%* is the name of the user in question. Figure 9-3 shows you one such profile.

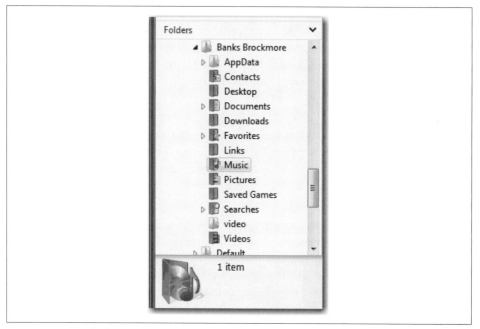

Figure 9-3. A profile folder hierarchy for Banks Brockmore

So, when you add a certain web site to your list of Favorites, for example, Internet Explorer places that URL in the Favorites folder. Other applications and tools, such as the Start menu, also reference this location. That's why you see the same list of Favorites when clicking Start → Favorites on an XP machine.

Of course, applications have to be written such that they place their settings in the profile folders, but that's the subject of much finger pointing, which I won't go into here.

Roaming profiles. Another way to mitigate the transfer of profiles is to use roaming profiles, a strategy that centrally stores a user's profile folders. With a roaming profile, a user logs on to any computer in the domain and then retrieves his settings from this central location, usually one of the Active Directory domain controllers.

A few roaming profile caveats, however, make this relatively uncommon in most companies:

- Roaming profiles consume resources, namely disc space on the server and network bandwidth as settings, files, and so on are sent to whatever machine the roaming user is currently using.
- Not many users really have any *need* to use several computers. Think about it: when you go into the office each day, do you normally sit at the same desk and log on to the same machine, or do you float around from computer to computer throughout the day, logging on to multiple machines? That's what I thought.

Running an Attended Installation

On the one hand, running an attended installation is a fairly simple operation, beyond the purview of most system admins. On the other, it is a crucial administrative task, one that still consumes many hours, especially for administrators of either home networks or small businesses.

Because this is a reference guide, it's important to include the attended installation steps. It might provide you with a few helpful pointers if you're relatively new to Vista administration. For those who have installed Windows hundreds of times before, feel free to skip ahead to the following section.

An attended installation means simply that you will be prompted for information during the setup process (also referred to as the mini setup or out-of-box-experience [OOBE]); hence the need, naturally, to attend the Vista installation. But even if you're new at this, it shouldn't prove too daunting a task.

Here's what you'll need handy during an attended installation:

- The installation media.
- The Windows Vista product key.
- Your computer name if you plan to connect to a network. Computer networks don't operate like the George Foreman family. In a network, no two computers can use the same name.
- If you're joining a domain, you'll also be prompted for user account credentials with the right to add a computer to the network. Which accounts have this right is up to the domain administrator.

You will then choose from one of three attended installation scenarios: the *clean* install, the *upgrade*, or the *reinstall*. We'll look at the steps for each individually.

Clean Install

The clean install involves either preparing a blank hard drive for Windows installation, or wiping out all existing data before proceeding with the install. Either way, the result is a computer with Windows Vista installed and nothing else. It bears repeating: nothing else. Make sure before you perform a clean install that either there's nothing on the existing hard drive that you want to keep, or that what you do want to keep has been copied somewhere else. Once you complete the steps listed here, all data is gone.

More advanced installations involve installing both Vista *and* the line-of-business applications, but we'll get to that in later sections.

1. The clean install begins when you insert the Windows installation DVD into your system. Two considerations come into play immediately:

    • If you're dealing with a computer with no operating system, you will probably have to reboot. Note also that you may have to edit your system's BIOS settings to boot to the DVD drive first before looking to the hard drive.

    • If your system does have an existing Windows OS, the AutoRun feature should present you with the dialog box shown in Figure 9-4. If not, look for the *setup.exe* file on the root directory of the optical drive.

2. If you choose Clean Install from this dialog box, you'll be prompted to restart your computer, getting you to the next step in the process.

3. The computer goes through its Power On Self Test (POST), and then detects bootable media in the optical drive and loads Windows PE. The next screen you'll see is the Install Windows page, where you'll click on "Install now."

4. You should now see the "Get important updates for installation" page, shown in Figure 9-5. Thanks to Windows PE, you might be able to get these updates even if you're setting up Vista on a blank disk. Getting the updates is recommended, because they can help facilitate less configuration work once setup is complete.

5. In the next dialog box, shown in Figure 9-6, you're prompted for the 25-character product key. Using the product key now can help avoid problems during activation.

6. You handle the next dialog box by clicking the box to "Accept the license terms."

7. And now we arrive at the crucial part of the Vista attended installation. After accepting the license agreement, you're asked which type of installation you want, as shown in Figure 9-7. To perform a clean install, choose the Custom option.

 You don't necessarily have to enter a product key at this point; you can do that later on. This will allow you to test different versions of Vista, using the 30 days to activate as an evaluation period. This note will also come in handy when used in conjunction with a valuable tip in Chapter 15.

8. The next dialog box asks where you want to install Windows. Here's your chance to either configure or reconfigure the hard drive to best suit your needs using the "Drive options (advanced)" selection.

9. If Vista will be the only OS—as is the case on most computers—you might just create a single partition out of the entire drive. (You can change your mind later. See Chapter 7 for details.)

10. If you plan to install another operating system—as is the case with many administrator or lab machines—you have the option of partitioning off your disk as seen in the dialog box shown in Figure 9-8. Note that installing Vista into a partition that already holds an operating system is not recommended by Microsoft and is not supported by any of its technical support staff.

11. If the hard drive already has a defined partition you're happy with—as is the case when performing a clean install on a system with an existing OS—you can just click Next, and installation will start automatically.

Figure 9-4. Options if you have an existing Windows OS such as Windows XP

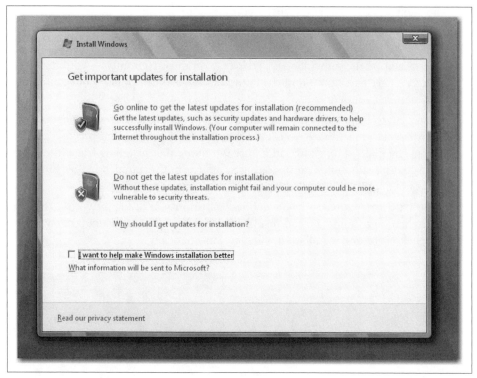

Figure 9-5. If possible, let Vista try to find updates, such as your computer's latest Vista drivers, before installing

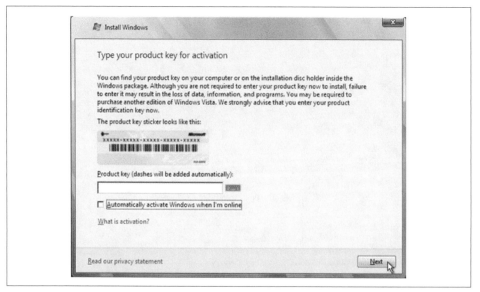

Figure 9-6. Entering the Vista product key

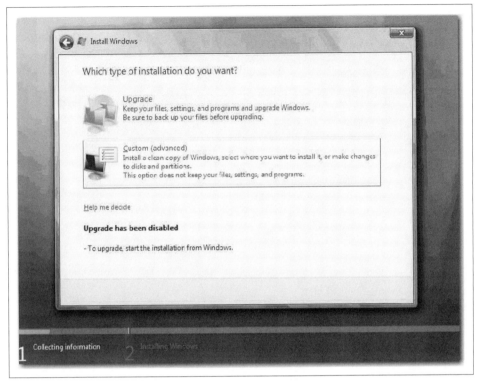

Figure 9-7. Choose Custom for the most control over a clean install

Performing a clean install of Windows Vista is really the easy part. The other part of the clean install is making sure all drivers are present and that all devices have been detected and are working properly. You will also likely have to install a series of applications before your system is ready to go from a productivity standpoint. An upgrade, on the other hand, typically reduces the amount of postinstall work.

 If you do a Vista install on a partition that already contains an OS, it will likely cause that OS to no longer be bootable.

Other notes regarding the clean install process:

- Vista is distributed only on DVD. If your system doesn't have a DVD drive, or is without an optical drive altogether, you must boot using an alternative device. Speaking of which…

- …if you're downloading Vista from the Internet, it is possible to create a bootable USB hard drive with the install bits on it, so it may not only be from DVD.

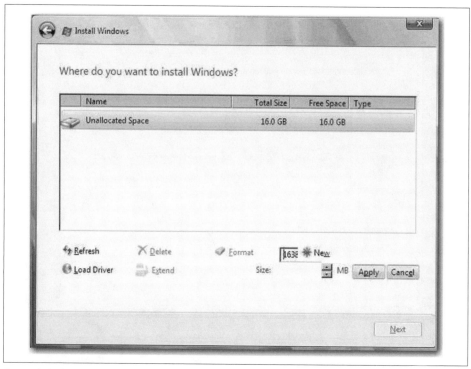

Figure 9-8. Creating a partition for Vista installation

Upgrading from Windows XP

A Vista upgrade is a less drastic operation than a clean install, because all files, settings, and programs are retained from the previous operating system. The only thing that's touched is the existing operating system files, which are replaced with the ones for Windows Vista.

Also, it's always a good idea before upgrading to run the Windows Vista Upgrade Advisor, available for download from the Microsoft web site. I presented specific instructions on the Upgrade Advisor earlier in this chapter. The Advisor can help you identify any potential issues and can offer resolution suggestions prior to installation. A simple video card drive upgrade flagged by the Advisor, for example, can go a long way toward maximizing the Windows Vista experience. And you certainly don't want to discover that you can't run your favorite application *after* the upgrade is complete.

 You might also see a compatibility report just after your install selection that lists which programs and software drivers won't work after the installation. This is for information only; you'll have to wait until installation is complete to troubleshoot.

At any rate, the process starts by inserting the Vista installation disc into your computer's optical drive. AutoRun should present you with the Install Windows dialog box. Click "Install now" and then follow these steps:

1. You should first see the "Get important updates for installation" dialog box. Once again, it's good practice to grab these updates. Because you're installing over the existing OS, you shouldn't have any difficulty connecting to the Internet to retrieve these updates.

2. You're now prompted for your 25-character product key in the activation page. As before, using the product key now generally ensures a problem-free activation. If, on the other hand, you're just setting up a test system, you can skip this step until you purchase (or use) an activation key later on.

3. The licensing terms come next. Click "I accept the license terms" to proceed.

4. Now we arrive at the attended upgrade's most critical step. In the "Which type of installation do you want?" dialog box, shown in Figure 9-9, choose Upgrade. Vista's setup may then present you with a compatibility report.

5. Now, just follow the instructions to complete the setup procedure. Your computer will restart automatically when done.

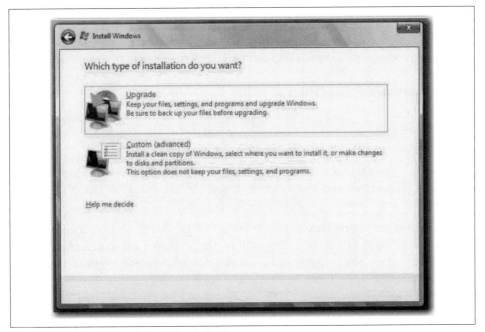

Figure 9-9. Choose Upgrade from this dialog box

Once the restart completes, inspect your desktop for changes. Other than the background, the environment should contain everything you had before.

Upgrading a Vista Installation

As first introduced in Chapter 2, you can also upgrade an existing Vista computer to a different version of Vista. For example, you might want to upgrade a Home Basic installation to Home Premium in order to take advantage of the Media Center, or you might upgrade Home Premium to Ultimate to use the Media Center and be able to join a domain.

This involves a few different steps, as described shortly. As you will see, upgrading a Vista machine with another version of Vista is a breeze, thanks to the new "nesting toy" approach Microsoft has taken with the operating system features.

To get started with the Vista-to-Vista upgrade, launch Internet Explorer 7 and navigate to the Windows Vista Anytime Upgrade web site, located here:

> *http://www.microsoft.com/windows/products/windowsvista/buyorupgrade/*
> *windowsanytimeupgrade/overview.mspx*

From there, you'll initiate a procedure that starts with ordering a disc of your new Vista version. But you won't have to wait for the disc to arrive in order to perform the upgrade. At the end of the procedure, there's an Upgrade Now link to follow that will lead you the rest of the way.

During the actual upgrade, your system will reboot and complete the upgrade. Note also that you may be instructed to insert a Windows Anytime Upgrade disc created during this process. This Upgrade disc contains the version to which you are upgrading.

Vista upgrades and the digital locker

Another interesting thing happens during the Vista-to-Vista upgrade process: Microsoft creates a personal digital locker for you during the upgrade process.

Just what is a digital locker, and what's stored within it? Simply put, the digital locker stores your original product keys and purchase information. If you ever need to reinstall the upgrade you just purchased, you can use this information. A copy of your upgrade key is also stored in your digital locker.

When creating the digital locker, you're prompted for Windows Live account information, as shown in Figure 9-10. This will be the account used to access the digital locker in the future, should you need to. If you don't have a Windows Live account, you can create one at this time.

This is a great feature that gives you peace of mind when 1) you're purchasing a new computer with Windows Home Basic, say, and then later 2) you're performing an upgrade to Home Premium or Ultimate. You'll never have to prove that you made the purchase or hunt for product keys should you ever decide to either reinstall or just get a new computer.

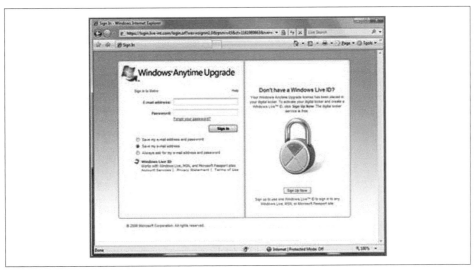

Figure 9-10. Use Windows Live account credentials to access your digital locker

Reinstall

A third installation option is the reinstall. A reinstall is a kind of hybrid between the clean install and the upgrade, where the Vista operating system files will be installed anew, but the existing data will be left alone.

This is usually performed as a troubleshooting step, when you're having a problem with Vista that isn't being resolved through other troubleshooting means. (In the past, this has been the troubleshooting option of choice when Windows will not start, although with Vista, you have additional options that don't require a complete reinstallation. For additional information, please refer to Chapter 11.)

Additionally, it's always a good idea to back up personal data before performing the reinstall. For example, if you choose to format your partition during a reinstall (technically making it a clean install), you'll erase everything.

As with the first two attended installation options discussed in this chapter, whether to reinstall will mostly be based on how you answer this question during the Setup Wizard: "Which type of installation do you want?" Follow the steps presented in the previous two sections for complete instructions. Then do this:

1. Once at the aforementioned dialog box, choose Custom to begin the reinstall process.

2. Now, as shown in Figure 9-11, choose "Drive options (advanced)." Select the partition where Vista already exists and then click Next to begin the installation. Once again, you may be presented with a compatibility report.

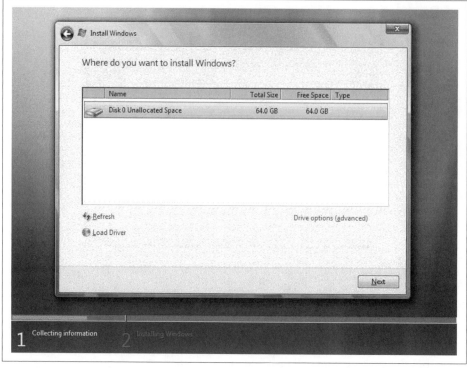

Figure 9-11. You can also install over the existing instance of Vista

Now you've seen how to deploy Windows Vista on a single computer. This is the only rollout strategy many organizations need. Workers are added only one at a time, and configuring a more exhaustive deployment strategy would be a waste of time and effort.

For larger organizations, the opposite is true. Trying to install Vista using one of the attended installation methods described earlier would have workers waiting days, if not weeks, for their new Vista computers. A method for deploying multiple installations at once is needed, and there must also be a way to automate deployment.

This can be handled by imaging software, which in turn facilitates unattended installations.

Deploying with Imaging Software

In addition to its improved migration tools, Windows Vista includes new capabilities for system imaging, remote system installation, and enhanced software deployment. In particular, the Windows Imaging (WIM) format provides enhanced deployment capabilities because it uses file-based disk-imaging technology.

Once captured, imaging files can be mounted as system volumes. The big advantage here is that they can then be edited more easily. As a result, administrators spend less time performing reimaging tasks—mounting image files as system volumes gives admins the option of making incremental adjustments to images that have already been created. In other words, WIM goes a long way toward simplifying disk-imaging maintenance.

Here's why this is significant: in the past, a single operating system image has been created for each kind of computer in the network. This is because Windows XP was hardware abstraction layer (HAL)-*dependent*.

What does that mean? In practical application, it means that if two users had laptops from different manufacturers, often each user had to get a different image for successful installation (a successful installation here refers to one in which all devices are set up properly). And even if deploying with a single image, for example, Windows XP administrators often had to be creative with scripting in order to deploy to both single- and multiple-CPU machines.

Now, however, Windows Vista is *independent* of the HAL. WIM enables a *single* image to be deployed to *different types of computer hardware*. And thanks to the componentized nature of Vista, it can even be used to deploy with different language requirements.

Before we discuss imaging further, though, it's important to take a moment and examine one of the technologies that make deploying WIM images a breeze. It's the Windows Preinstallation Environment, or Windows PE.

Windows Preinstallation Environment (Windows PE)

Windows PE is actually an operating system, albeit a very, very scaled-down version of Windows meant only to let a computer operate just enough to install one of the full-blown Windows OSs. It's used to detect and enable hardware such as keyboards, mice, displays, and optical drives (so that you can insert a CD or DVD and perform an installation), and it can usually load the network card drivers and TCP/IP stack.

It can even launch some Windows Vista applications.

But it's built with very specific objectives in mind. It won't *look* much like the Windows Vista you'd expect, and it won't do much other than get your system up and in some sort of operational state. In other words, while you may be able to move and copy files using Windows PE, don't try to play *Halo 3*. Windows PE is used mostly to facilitate deployment of multiple operating systems.

 Windows PE is available only to volume licensing agreement customers. It is also now available for license to Certified Partners. If this doesn't describe you, there's really no point in reading much further in this section.

Originally intended solely for the purpose just described—operating system rollout (for Windows XP)—Windows PE now has evolved to a version that's included with Windows Vista. You can use version 2 in the following instances:

- Large-scale Vista deployments.
- OS preinstallation on computers sold to end users by system builders.
- As a recovery platform for use in Windows recovery.
- As a substitute for MS-DOS. Because it's an operating system, system technicians can use Windows PE for diagnostics or repair.
- Third-party utilities, such as the latest release of Symantec Ghost, can also use Windows PE to facilitate image deployment.

With its power to replace what used to be handled by a DOS boot-up disk, Windows PE can take on the following tasks:

Create and format disk partitions
>One huge advantage of Windows PE is its capability to format disks with NTFS. Prior to Windows PE, the only way to format using NTFS in an MS-DOS environment was to use third-party utilities. Further, all filesystem utilities provided by Windows PE are fully scriptable, enabling administrators to automate disk preparation.

Access network shares
>With the capability to boot and access the network, Windows PE opens up a world of preinstallation possibilities. Again, this used to be done by customizing an MS-DOS boot disk with the appropriate networking drivers. Windows PE uses the same network drivers used by XP and Vista. Administrators now have a quick and easy way to reach troubleshooting tools when necessary, and can initiate image deployment over the network.

Load and access 32-bit and 64-bit device drivers
>This means a more fully functioning computer, even when in a command environment such as Windows PE. This also reduces the need to customize a DOS boot disk, freeing up the administrator for other tasks. With Windows PE, administrators can install drivers for a host of devices that use Vista, Windows 2000, XP Professional, or Server 2003 drivers.

Customize Windows PE
>Windows PE can be easily customized to suit a variety of deployment and troubleshooting scenarios. It is based on the XP Professional and Windows Server 2003 operating systems, so most administrators should already be familiar with the techniques and tools used to customize Windows PE.

In short, Windows PE's capability to replace DOS boot disks will help speed deployment and troubleshooting tasks because administrators will be using an environment (i.e., Windows) with which they are already comfortable, rather than one (MS-DOS) with which they are not.

What's more, most of the MS-DOS scripts that are currently being used to deploy images to recover from failed installations can be used in Windows PE.

Don't look for this on the shelves of your local computer retailer, however. You cannot purchase Windows PE. As you've just seen, it can be used for purposes other than deploying disk images, purposes that are of special note for administrators. But you'll need to create a Windows PE bootable device first. With that device in hand, you can then perform a variety of troubleshooting tasks.

Troubleshooting with Windows PE

You don't have to use Windows PE solely for deployment scenarios. Because of its capability to load and run applications such as file and disk utilities, it can also be very useful in a variety of troubleshooting scenarios. Examples include:

Replacing system files
> You use Windows PE to grab a file from installation media and replace a corrupted file. For example, if a corrupted system file is preventing a computer from starting, use Windows PE to start the computer. Then, use Windows PE's file utilities to replace the corrupted file.

Recovering data
> Pinpointing the exact file that's causing a system not to start can be a chore. Sometimes the most expedient troubleshooting for a cranky system is a hard drive wipe and reinstall. But what about all your data? Windows PE can be the perfect solution.
>
> Windows PE provides full access to both FAT and NTFS filesystems and can usually load the network stack. As such, you can boot the computer to Windows PE prior to the hard drive reformat and copy user data to either another disk or another network location.

Running diagnostic tools
> If disk management or network access is part of the troubleshooting approach, Windows PE is up to the task. It includes common command-line diagnostic tools such as these:

DiskPart
> DiskPart is a text-mode command interpreter that allows you to manage disks, partitions, or volumes from a command prompt or script.

Drvload
> You use the Drvload command to add device drivers, such as audio, video, and motherboard chip sets, to a Windows PE image. You can also use Drvload to dynamically load a driver after Windows PE has started.

Net

> The Net command-line tool allows you to manage the local user database, start and stop services, and connect to shared folders.

Netcfg

> This network configuration tool configures network access. When using Windows PE as a custom deployment tool, you might use Netcfg to manually configure network settings as part of a startup script.

Use of these utilities, of course, assumes that you can first successfully boot your system to the preinstallation environment. To do so, administrators might first need to create a bootable Windows PE disk. Here's what you'll do.

 The following example assumes use of two computers, one I'll call *source* and one I'll call *target*. You will use the CD created here to capture an image of your source computer and later deploy that image onto your target computer.

From the source computer. First, using your source computer, run the *copype.cmd* script to create a local Windows PE build directory. The most likely choice is from a Command Prompt window. You can use the following syntax:

```
cd Program Files\Windows AIK\Tools\PETools\
copype.cmd <arch> <destination>
```

where *<arch>* can be x86, amd64, or ia64, and *<destination>* is a path to a local directory. For example,

```
copype.cmd x86 c:\winpe_x86
```

You can now copy additional tools such as ImageX (discussed in the following section) into your Windows PE build directory. For example:

```
copy "c:\program files\Windows AIK\Tools\x86\imagex.exe"
c:\winpe_x86\iso\
```

You also have the option of creating a configuration file called *wimscript.ini* using any text editor you choose, such as Notepad, for instance. The configuration file will instruct ImageX to exclude certain files during the capture operation. You might use the following syntax, for instance:

```
[ExclusionList]
ntfs.log
hiberfil.sys
pagefile.sys
"System Volume Information"
RECYCLER
Windows\CSC
[CompressionExclusionList]
*.mp3
*.zip
*.cab
\WINDOWS\inf\*.pnf
```

Now, save the configuration file to the location you just specified in the preceding step as the storage location for the ImageX files:

```
c:\winpe_x86\iso\
```

ImageX will automatically detect the *wimscript.ini* file if it's located in the same spot.

Now you're ready to create the image (*.iso*) file. You can do so using the Oscdimg tool. For example, open a command prompt and type:

```
cd program files\Windows AIK\Tools\PETools\
oscdimg -n -bc:\winpe_x86\etfsboot.com c:\winpe_x86\ISO c:\winpe_x86\winpe_x86.iso
```

That's it. What did you just create? A brand-new, bootable Windows PE CD is what.

You can create a wide variety of bootable devices using Windows PE, including USB flash drives.

You now have the ability to burn the *.iso* image file to a CD using any disc-burning utility of your choice. Note that the Windows Automated Installation Kit does not include disc-burning software.

Recall that all this has happened on the source computer, and you've now taken the first step toward duplicating that computer across the network. Once again, Windows PE is a big help with the deployment chore as well.

Using Windows PE to capture and deploy images

Now that you've prepared the *.iso* image and burned it to CD, you can use it to quickly deploy multiple Windows Vista images throughout a corporate network. For the most part, this deployment is independent of the hardware platform used.

You can then store an installation image onto a network share for future deployments.

Here's how to proceed:

1. From your source computer, insert the newly created Windows PE media and restart the computer, booting to the optical drive. Windows PE then displays a Command Prompt window.

You may need to change your computer's boot order to perform the preceding step by editing the BIOS settings. Usually this is done by pressing either one of the Function keys or the Delete key as the system performs its Power On Self Test (POST), and then changing default values. Refer to your computer's documentation for specific steps.

2. Now, capture an image of the master installation by using ImageX, which is located on your Windows PE media. You could use the following syntax:

```
d:\tools\imagex.exe /compress fast /capture c: c:\myimage.wim "my Vista Install"
/verify
```

3. Next, copy the image to a network location. Because you've booted into Windows PE, you should also have the ability to access the network using the net-utilities. For example, you could type:

```
net use y: \\network_share\images
```

and then:

```
copy c:\myimage.wim y:
```

4. If necessary, provide network credentials for appropriate network access.

Now you're ready to deploy an image across the network. For example, if your company hires a new employee, he can have his new laptop set up for him in just a few easy steps.

Imaging the new system

In this step, you will use DiskPart to prepare the hard drive, and then copy an image down from the network share. For this example, use your master computer as your destination computer.

From the target computer. Here's the procedure:

1. On the target computer, use the Windows PE media and restart the computer. As before, Windows PE presents the user with a Command Prompt window.

 As before, you may need to change the computer's boot order using the system BIOS program. If the computer has a brand-new hard disk, however, it should be unformatted and this step could be skipped.

2. Use the DiskPart tool to create a hard drive partition that will serve as the destination for the image according to configuration requirements. You might use the following command-prompt syntax:

```
diskpart
select disk 0
clean
create partition primary size=20000
select partition 1
active
format
exit
```

To save time with multiple deployments on unformatted disks, the preceding commands can also be scripted. Just save the commands to a text file and store it in the same location as your image. Then, to run the script from a Windows PE command prompt, you type **diskpart /s *scriptname*.txt**.

3. You'll now pull the disk image from the network location to the local hard drive, using a command similar to the following:

```
net use y: \\network_share\images
copy y:\myimage.wim c:
```

4. If needed, supply administrative credentials.

5. The heavy lifting is almost done. All that's left is to apply the image using ImageX. Again, it should be located on the Windows PE media. Once located, here's how you could apply the newly copied image from the Windows PE command prompt:

```
d:\tools\imagex.exe /apply c:\myimage.wim 1 c:
```

That's it! Your custom image is now installed, and the system is ready for deployment. Users can now sit down and log on.

Windows PE and the WIM format

One of the most exciting developments surrounding Windows PE is the ability for it to be distributed within a WIM file.

There are two big advantages to structuring a Windows PE deployment around the WIM format. One is that WIM can deploy both Windows Vista and Windows PE images. This means that the procedure for creating and storing Windows PE files will look very similar to the procedure for creating Vista images.

The other big advantage is that through WIM, images (again, both Vista and PE) can be updated with drivers, upgrades, and Windows components. These changes can even be made offline without ever starting the operating system.

There is one important difference between the Vista WIM image and the Windows PE image, however. When storing a Vista image in a WIM file, the only way to start Windows Vista is to copy the image to the computer's hard disk.

Windows PE works differently. It can start directly from a WIM file without being copied to a hard disk. With this feature, you can create a WIM file, store it on bootable media such as a CD or USB flash drive, and start Windows PE directly from that medium. In fact, Windows relies on just this mechanism to deploy Vista: Windows PE loads and launches without having to be copied to disk. The Windows PE operating environment then facilitates Vista image installation.

Now let's look at how to set up and alter a Windows Vista image using this tool, the Windows SIM.

Using the Windows System Image Manager

One great tool that administrators have in their deployment toolkit is the Windows SIM. This graphical utility speeds the creation and management of Windows Setup answer files using an interface such as the one shown in Figure 9-12.

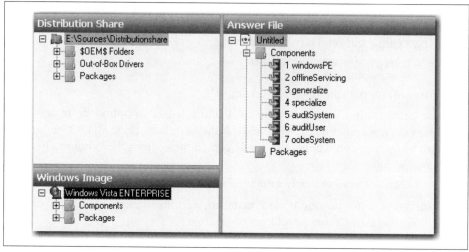

Figure 9-12. The Windows SIM interface

The answer files generated with the Windows SIM tool are XML files. They're used during Vista setup to customize an image-based deployment. The answer file will specify such installation parameters as the destination partition, changes to the Internet Explorer 7 home page, and the computer name, just to name a few.

What's more, administrators can alter the answer file to automate the installation of device drivers, language packs, and third-party applications. In other words, the computer can be completely set and ready for use with proper deployment of a Windows SIM answer file.

To get started with the answer file creation process, use the buttons in the Windows SIM toolbar. Each button's function is listed in Table 9-2.

Table 9-2. Getting started with the Windows SIM

Button name	Button function
New Answer File	Creates a new answer file.
Open Answer File	Opens an existing answer file.
Close Answer File	Closes the currently selected answer file.
Save Answer File	Saves the currently open answer file.

Table 9-2. Getting started with the Windows SIM (continued)

Button name	Button function
Cut, Copy, Paste, Delete	Manipulates data.
Find	Enables you to search a Windows image and answer file, a distribution share, or within the Messages pane.
Validate Answer File	Validates the answer file against the settings in the opened catalog file.
Create Configuration Set	Creates a configuration set.

You can use the answer file for several Windows Vista installation purposes. Instead of editing the XML file with a text editor, the administrator can find herself using the SIM for these tasks:

Create a new Windows image answer file
> The Windows SIM enables admins to create an answer file to be used during Windows setup. The graphical tool lets administrators easily view all of the components available in a Windows image, add component settings to the answer file, and choose when to apply a component setting. And once component settings have been added, the Windows SIM lets administrators customize the available answer file settings for each component.

Edit an existing answer file
> Just as when creating the *unattended.xml* file, the Windows SIM lets administrators easily add updates to an existing answer file. Further, you have the ability to validate an answer file against a Windows image. This gives administrators the power to troubleshoot a particular image file proactively. The Windows SIM lets you open a Windows image, test an existing answer file, and then make changes to the answer file if necessary.

Add drivers to an existing answer file
> Administrators can use the Windows SIM to add the device drivers needed to make sure the Vista system's devices are working properly. Microsoft refers to three types of device drivers that can be applied with the Windows SIM. They are:

In-box drivers
> These are handled the same as packages.

Out-of-box drivers
> These are *.iof*-based device drivers that must be stored in a distribution share subfolder called Out-of-Box Drivers.

In-box drivers installed with an .msi file
> Drivers that install using an *.msi* file are treated the same as applications.

Add applications to an answer file

Administrators can further customize Vista deployment by installing additional applications using a set of folders called a *distribution share*. A distribution share stores any and all applications, device drivers, scripts, or other resources that are available during a custom Windows setup.

Add updates to a Windows image

The Windows SIM allows addition of Vista updates to an existing Windows image. For example, if a network administrator wanted to deploy a language pack as part of image deployment, he could do so by adding these files using the Package Tool.

Using a Windows SIM answer file

What's more, the Windows SIM answer files are used in conjunction with these technologies, which help prepare and capture disk images for deployment:

Sysprep

Sysprep removes all information specific to a particular computer, which in turn makes it ready for disk image capturing. With the unique information about the computer removed, administrators can use a copy of that computer to deploy on multiple systems.

ImageX

As mentioned, ImageX enables corporations and OEMs to capture, modify, and apply file-based disk images for deployment. ImageX creates Windows image (*.wim*) files for copying to a network. It can also work with other technologies that use Windows images, such as Windows Setup.

In other words, the unattended answer files will be used to supply information needed when applying a Vista deployment image. The Sysprep and ImageX tools help create these deployment images.

You can obtain the Windows SIM as part of the Windows Automated Installation Kit, which you can download from *http://www.Microsoft.com/downloads*. Once here, search for "Automated Installation Kit." (You can also just search for "AIK.")

Migrating User Information

In this chapter's introduction, I specifically mentioned two migration utilities by name: the USMT and Windows Easy Transfer. After reading this section, you'll have a better understanding of the best uses of each. Better yet, you should be able to perform a migration with confidence (or at least refer back to this section should confidence be found wanting).

Of these two, we'll first talk about the one with the most administrative horsepower, so to speak: the USMT.

The User State Migration Tool

As mentioned previously, the USMT has been available to Windows administrators for some time now. Its previous release, version 2.6, allowed for migrations between Windows XP or Windows 2000 machines to either the 64-bit or the 32-bit version of Windows XP and Server 2003.

Now some of the rules have changed for USMT's version 3.0. Here are a couple of changes worthy of note:

- It supports migrations in which the destination operating systems must be either Windows Vista or Windows XP. No other destination OS is supported.
- If the destination system is Windows XP, the cookies, network drives, and printer settings will not be migrated.
- Source operating systems must be only Windows Vista, Windows XP, and Windows 2000. Migrating from previous Windows versions is not supported.
- USMT now allows admins to move profiles that contain files encrypted with the Encrypting File System (EFS).
- If the target machine is running Windows XP, only the mail files from Outlook Express and the phonebook files from Remote Access Settings are migrated. If the target machine is Windows Vista, all Outlook Express and Remote Access settings are migrated.
- The ScanState and LoadState commands can be driven by key scripts that are in XML format.

The mention of XML, of course, merits another brief subsection covering the different kinds of files you may use for scripting.

XML and the USMT

The USMT now includes several XML files to help you handle migration work, all of which you can customize to meet specific migration objectives. Here are the XML files included with USMT, along with an explanation of each one's function:

MigApp.xml
This file controls which application settings are migrated. There are sections in the file to specify which applications are included and which are excluded from the migration.

MigUser.xml
This identifies which user folders, files, file types, and desktop settings are migrated. Although the name might suggest otherwise, it does not specify which *users* are migrated.

MigSys.xml

This is used only when the target machine is running Windows XP. It stores information that governs migration of operating system and browser settings. Windows Vista migrations do not require this file; they rely on a different mechanism.

Config.xml

This is a custom file that can capture a list of user, application, and operating system settings used for a specific organizational migration. The *config.xml* file is created with a special ScanState switch, /genconfig, and can be used only if the target system is running Windows Vista. Typical use of the *config.xml* file includes loading a single target system with migrated applications, and then running ScanState /genconfig on this system to capture the list of user, operating system, and application settings to migrate. If *config.xml* is not included, USMT migrates all default components in Windows Vista.

A few additional notes on the XML files:

- You can edit XML files in any plain-text application, such as Notepad.
- If the target computer is Windows Vista, use the *MigApp.xml* and *MigUser.xml* files.
- If the target computer is Windows XP, one additional file is required. It's called *MigSys.xml*.

Regardless of the enhancements in this latest version of the USMT, using it will still include three basic steps to transfer information. While using the USMT, you will:

1. Scan the source machine for files and settings, and then copy these files and settings in a compressed format to some storage location.
2. Deploy the operating system to the new computer. If you've stored settings on a removable drive or network location, this can even mean a clean wipe of the source's hard drive and installing a fresh copy of the OS and line-of-business applications.
3. On the target machine, the files and settings are then restored.

Configuring the USMT

Now that you have a better understanding of what the Windows PC migration utilities do, let's get into some specifics about behavior and configuration. First up, a look at a few of the items migrated by the USMT:

- Internet Explorer settings
- Outlook Express settings (migrated to Windows Mail)
- Desktop
- Accessibility options
- Favorites

- Folder options
- Fonts
- Quick Launch toolbar shortcuts
- Sound settings
- Regional options
- My Documents
- Mouse and keyboard settings

This, of course, merits a list of items that won't be moved:

- Hardware settings
- Drivers
- Passwords
- Applications
- Synchronization files

Now that we've seen what the USMT does, it's time to look at how it does it. Here are the specific steps for migrating all user accounts from one system to another with the USMT:

1. Log on to the source computer as an administrator and open a Command Prompt session (Start → All Programs → Accessories → Command Prompt). From the command prompt, type the following:

   ```
   scanstate \\fileserver\migration\mystore /i:miguser.xml /i:migapp.xml /o
   ```

2. Now, log on to the destination computer as an administrator, and perform one of the following tasks:

   If you are migrating domain accounts, specify:

   ```
   loadstate \\fileserver\migration\mystore /i:miguser.xml /i:migapp.xml
   ```

   If you are migrating local accounts along with domain accounts, specify:

   ```
   loadstate \\fileserver\migration\mystore /i:miguser.xml /i:migapp.xml /lac /lae
   ```

By default, all users are migrated. You can only specify which users to include using the command line. You will not be able to specify users in the *.xml* files. You can use the following procedures to migrate user accounts.

Migrating a domain account

In the preceding example, we looked at how to move user environments from one computer to another when each machine is a standalone system—that is, the computer does not have an account in a domain.

In most companies, however, administrators *will* be moving users who exist within a domain environment. Fortunately, the USMT can handle domain migrations just as easily. In this example, we'll look at how to migrate two domain accounts to the new Vista machine. Here's what to do:

1. Log on to the source computer as an administrator. Open a command prompt and type this command:

   ```
   scanstate \\fileserver\migration\mystore /ue:*\* /ui:Domain\user1 /ui:Domain\
   user2 /i:miguser.xml /i:migapp.xml /o
   ```

2. Now that the USMT has gathered the necessary files and settings, it's time to log on to the destination computer. As before, open a command prompt and specify the following:

   ```
   loadstate \\fileserver\migration\mystore /i:miguser.xml /i:migapp.xml
   ```

That should be all you have to do. As long as you've stored the settings to a network location and the network is still available, the USMT should automate things from here, which is the whole idea.

Migrating settings while changing domain membership

Sometimes a new physical configuration will prompt a new logical configuration as well. If a user moves from a branch office in Los Angeles to one in Dallas, for example, it's a fairly good bet that the domain membership will change as well.

It's also possible to move an account from one domain to another while performing the migration operation. Here's the syntax:

1. As we saw in the previous examples, it starts by logging in at the source computer as an administrator. Then type the following into the command prompt:

   ```
   scanstate \\fileserver\migration\mystore /ue:*\* /ui:fareast\user1 /ui:fareast\
   user2 /i:miguser.xml /i:migapp.xml /o
   ```

2. Next, use administrative credentials at the destination computer and use this syntax:

   ```
   loadstate \\fileserver\migration\mystore /mu:fareast\user1:farwest\user2 /i:
   miguser.xml /i:migapp.xml
   ```

Using these two commands, administrators have just ensured a seamless transition from one location to another. And assuming that the USMT commands have been executed while the worker is in transit, the user will now see the same desktop he left behind when reporting to the new office for the first time.

For migrations that involve fewer computers, or for those of us who simply don't like to type, another tool is available in Windows Vista for quick and painless migration of the user environment. We'll discuss it in the following section.

Migrating with Windows Easy Transfer

Besides the USMT, Vista includes another tool for easy migration of files from an old system to a new one. It's Windows Easy Transfer, and the migration process it uses can be generally described as consisting of two distinct parts. What follows, then, is a breakdown of each part of Windows Easy Transfer.

Part one: Preparing the target (Vista) machine

The migration begins at the destination machine. For our purposes, I'll assume the target is a Vista machine. Here's how to transfer user data and settings with Windows Easy Transfer:

1. From the Vista machine, close any open programs. (Although you don't necessarily *have* to, it's a good idea to do so. Vista won't let you use either of the computers during the Windows Easy Transfer process—this is why it's a good idea to save and close work first.) Now, launch Windows Easy Transfer by clicking Start → All Programs → Accessories → System Tools → Windows Easy Transfer. Windows Easy Transfer takes over your desktop with a Welcome screen. Click Next to proceed.

2. If you had any open applications, you'll be prompted to close them now. Fortunately, Windows Easy Transfer allows you the option of saving your work. You also have the ability to just close all open programs at once. (See why it's easier to just close applications before running Windows Easy Transfer?) Click Next.

3. Click Start, and Windows Easy Transfer begins gathering information from the computers involved in the migration operation.

4. Because you're on the Vista machine, choose the "This is my new computer" option.

5. Now, select the destination for Windows Easy Transfer files. You have the following options, shown in Figure 9-13:

   - CD or DVD
   - Removable media
   - Network drive

 Both computers must support the selected transfer method. You can't choose the CD or DVD transfer method, for example, if the destination computer lacks an optical drive. Choosing the network drive option requires that the computers be connected on the same network.

6. Choose the location for the Windows Easy Transfer files. The default directory is *C:\migwiz*. Note the location because you'll need this to complete the process. Click Next.

Figure 9-13. Three ways to use Windows Easy Transfer

Now you're ready for part two of the process, in which you will gather your existing settings as files from your existing computer.

Part two: Gathering settings from the existing machine

Here are the steps for transferring across a network:

1. Again, it's a good idea to first close any open applications. Now, launch Windows Easy Transfer on the existing machine. Here's where you'll need to locate the Windows Easy Transfer directory created in part one. In this instance, you'll browse to the network location containing the *migwiz* directory and then double-click migwiz.exe.

2. If you ignored my advice in part one, you'll now be prompted to close open apps. Once more, you will have the ability to save work in each program before closing it. Click Next.

3. Select the "Through a network" option for the transfer method.

4. Now choose "Connect directly via network," and the transfer begins. Note that you could also save your migration files to a network location and complete the transfer at a later time if you prefer. If you choose to store the data in a network location, you will be prompted to provide the path.

5. Now you're given the option about what gets sent to the new Vista installation. Windows Easy Transfer recommends that all user accounts, files, and program settings be transferred, although in my experience this is hardly ever what you want. I prefer to choose exactly which files should be migrated by clicking "Only my user account, files, and program settings," or by clicking Custom.

 If you click Custom, you'll see another dialog box where you select exactly what gets transferred from the old machine to the new machine.

6. In the final dialog box, you can review the list of files and settings to be transferred. Choose Customize to add and remove certain files or settings. Click Start to begin the transfer.

The steps for each of the other two Windows Easy Transfer options will vary slightly, of course, but the basic principles will remain the same: you'll launch the utility by double-clicking migwiz.exe, and then specify what files and settings to gather, choose where they'll be stored, and be prompted to complete the operation.

If you're saving migration files to a CD, for example, you'll have to move the media to the new Vista computer, launch Windows Easy Transfer again, and then select an option called Continue a Transfer in Progress.

This requires a few more steps, to be sure, but you should be able to take it from there. The network option will be the most commonly used, in my estimation.

Summary

We've spent several chapters so far examining the various technologies built into Windows Vista. But you won't be able to use those technologies without first installing the operating system. Fortunately, Vista's innovations and improvements include many that make deployment easier than ever before.

As we've seen, the installation of a single Vista machine is quite an easy task, not much different from installing just about any application. And if your computing environment calls for more massive rollouts of Windows Vista, there are lots of new features, technologies, and utilities that make this administrative task easier and more flexible than ever before.

This chapter looked at the tasks and tools involved in Windows deployment, and most specifically at the challenge of deployments across the enterprise. In it, we touched on some considerations that will affect deployment, such as the image size of the operating system, and then we discussed the tools that will make rapid deployment possible.

In the next chapter, we'll look specifically at a single application—Internet Explorer 7—and how it has changed the game for surfing the Internet. Although you can use it on Windows XP machines as well, you'll see that not every new feature is enabled on the older OS. As you'll learn, this new application includes many new features that are congruent with Vista's overall engineering mantra—more secure, clearer, and better connected.

CHAPTER 10

Internet Explorer 7

Although not unique to Windows Vista, Internet Explorer gets a major facelift in conjunction with the new OS release. And because it will be the application used as much as or more often than almost any other, it merits a separate discussion here.

Relying heavily on input from customers, developers, IT professionals, and even other browser providers, Microsoft has created what can be described as its most progressive browser release to date. With its final release, Microsoft has addressed some major security concerns, which should serve to counteract the lip sweat of IT admins worried about the next Internet-borne attack.

The new features of Internet Explorer 7 (IE7) are designed to enhance two main areas of browser use:

For the audience
> Users can find comfort in the addition of features such as tabbed browsing, Tab Groups, a simplified user interface, the Instant Search box, the Favorites Center, advanced printing capabilities, and in-browser Really Simple Syndication (RSS) support.

Behind the curtain
> Administrators can breathe a sigh of relief with massive security improvements, beginning with a new architecture, ActiveX Opt-in, a Security Status bar, cross-domain access barriers, redesigned URL parsing, a Protected Mode option in Vista, new Address bar protections, and a native phishing filter.

What's more, IE7 includes additional elements that are exclusive to Windows Vista. These elements are functionally significant and beyond mere bells and whistles, meriting their own little niche in this chapter.

I should also add that part of this chapter serves as a sort of ersatz history lesson about IE version 6. Why? To understand many of the IE7 improvements, we must also know that features are being improved. Further, nothing is more frustrating than going to use one of your tried-and-true actions within a program, only to discover that it's no longer there.

A similar foil has been deployed throughout much of this book's discussion of Vista features, but in a less overt way. It's Windows XP, if course, which is our departure point for so much of the discussion of Vista. In this chapter, however, the compare/contrast nature of the conversation has been compressed, that's all.

And along the way, I've sprinkled in a few tables that might help you navigate the program more quickly than ever before. Their placement is pretty much random; just thought you'd want to know.

So, let's begin.

For the Audience

We begin with a look at enhancements that will be most apparent to the casual end user. These improvements should save the user time when surfing the Internet, which also makes the experience safer than ever before.

What's the Big Deal?

Your first indicator of the marked changes in IE7 will be immediately evident. Upon the application's initial launch, you'll be struck by the new user interface—simpler, less cluttered, and streamlined for productivity and efficiency. How so? Simply put, more of your screen is now dedicated to viewing the web page, not viewing the browser that's framing the web page.

While not exactly coded with a stone tablet and chisel, IE6 was also by no means a breakthrough in functional design...big buttons, lots of buttons, and isolated action panes (i.e., Search, History). Figure 10-1 should jog your memory.

Adhering to the "more is more" school of design, IE6's aesthetics were, at times, matched by erratic performance. With enough security concerns to warrant the nickname *Internet Exploder* (coined by crafty Linux folks, no doubt, who, as evidenced by their creative twist on language, are clearly way, *way*, smarter than any of us simple Windows saps), IE6 is not likely to be missed by many.

It's worth noting, in fact, that if you're still using Windows XP, Internet Explorer 7 is a recommended *security* update.

To be fair, IE6 did have an initial release date of August 2001. Yep, you read that right...with Internet Explorer 6's Service Pack 1 released in September 2002, and SP2 in August 2004. A lot of browsing has happened since then.

So, when you consider that an average PC's life span is three years, IE6 has more than held up its end of the bargain. It's also worth noting that it's much better still than any Internet browser that either I or any Linux wonk has ever written. (Don't worry, no Linux people will be offended; they're too busy conversing in Latin on their blogs.)

At any rate, now that we've briefly laid out what *was*, let's now touch on what *is* with the new browser.

Figure 10-1. IE6 having a bad day

Browser Viewing Improvements

Beyond the overall more polished appearance—one that incorporates much of the Aero glass styling of Vista no matter what OS it's used on—the redesigned user interface of IE7 provides navigation that is cleaner and more streamlined than ever before. Figure 10-2 shows this new look and feel when IE7 is used on a Windows XP machine, and Figure 10-3 shows IE7 running in Windows Vista.

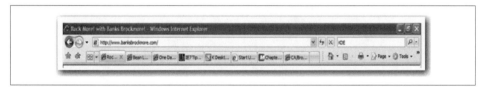

Figure 10-2. The IE7 interface in Windows XP

Figure 10-3. The IE7 interface in Windows Vista

As you can see in both the XP and Vista versions, IE7 has significant navigational enhancements:

- The browser frame has been reorganized with the Address bar appearing at the top of the window, replacing the drop-down menu list in IE6.
- The Back and Forward buttons are smaller and moved to the left of the Address bar.
- Flanking the Address bar on the right are the smaller Refresh and Stop buttons.
- The new Instant Search box lives in the upper-righthand side of the Refresh and Stop buttons. We'll discuss the new Instant Search in more detail later in this chapter.

The changes in the navigational design of IE7 continue onto the next row of buttons, beginning below the Back/Forward buttons with a new star icon.

Favorites Center enhancements

In exploring the second row of navigational buttons, IE7 users will also find significant usability enhancements. These usability enhancements are immediately evident within the new Favorites Center:

Adding to favorites

    The Favorites menu is now positioned to the *left* of the tabs and is represented by a star icon. It is paired with an icon comprising a star and a plus sign, indicating quick access to the Add Favorites/Feeds options. You can see these menu options in Figure 10-4.

Favorites/Feeds and options

    As seen in Figure 10-5, clicking on the star icon provides the user with access to her Favorites, RSS feed subscriptions, and browser history. This is done without interfering with browser window viewing.

Figure 10-4. Adding an item to the Favorites

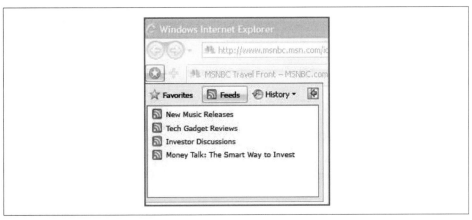

Figure 10-5. Accessing Favorites/Feeds/History

Microsoft has also provided the option of docking the Favorites/Feeds/History panel, similar to Microsoft browser behavior of the past. You can do this with the Docking button to the right of the History button.

For those who want a little more browsing real estate, the menu interface allows us to take care of business and then get back to our full-screen browser window.

The Add Favorites/Feeds menu operates in the same manner as the Favorites/Feeds/ History menu, but without the option of docking the menu. However, if you choose to organize your Favorites from within this menu, you will get one of the few pop-up menus in IE7. For those who may be pop-up-window phobic, rest assured that basic organizing can be performed in the Favorites menu using drag-and-drop.

In Table 10-1, submitted for your enjoyment, are a few more keyboard shortcuts that will help you navigate the IE7 Favorites with a little more ease.

Table 10-1. Favorites Center keyboard shortcuts

IE7 action	Keyboard shortcut
Open Favorites	Ctrl-I
Open Favorites in pinned mode	Ctrl-Shift-I
Organize Favorites	Ctrl-B
Add current page to Favorites	Ctrl-D
Open feeds	Ctrl-J
Open feeds in pinned mode	Ctrl-Shift-J
Open History	Ctrl-H
Open History in pinned mode	Ctrl-Shift-H

Using tabs

Continuing to the right are some of the best new features of IE7:

Quick Tabs button
   The tab with four rectangles arranged on it is the Quick Tabs button.

Tabs List
   A mini tab with a downward-pointing arrow indicates access to the Tabs List.

I will cover both tabs in more depth shortly.

Following the Quick Tabs and Tabs List buttons are open tabs and a blank, smaller tab (roughly the same size as the Quick Tabs tab) for adding new tabs to the browser window.

Then, as I'm sure most people could guess, is the house icon, which grants quick access to the browser's home page. This is followed by the RSS Feeds icon and the print menu icon, as shown in Figure 10-6.

Figure 10-6. Close-up of icons

Finally, the Master Control Program (*Tron* fans everywhere are geeking out) of sorts for the IE7 browser resides in the Page Actions menu and the Tools menu.

From the Tools menu, you can find controls for the Pop-up Blocker, Phishing Filter, and add-ons, all of which we'll discuss later in the chapter. Users will also find the Internet Options menu here, which launches a dialog box that should look fairly familiar to IE6 users, as seen in Figure 10-7.

 How do you see the Tools menu in the first place? Part of the stream-lined interface is that the menus are hidden. To show the Tools menu—or any other menu, for that matter—just press the Alt key. Press it again to toggle the traditional menus off.

How can these seemingly cosmetic changes lead to increased job security? Improved access means increased functionality, which means increased efficiency, which means increased productivity, which, as we all know, means more money to spend on IT department salaries.

Precisely because the changes go beyond the surface, they represent (at times) vast improvements over anything Microsoft has ever done with Internet Explorer.

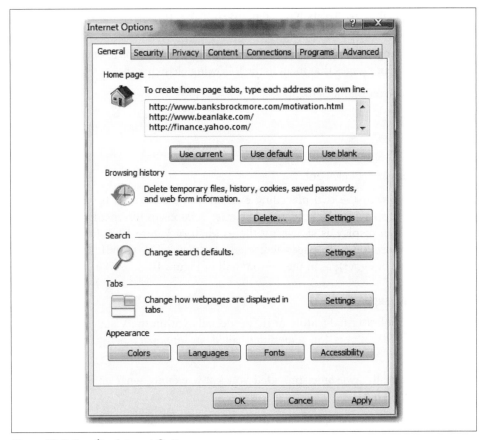

Figure 10-7. Familiar Internet Options menu

Content Viewing Improvements

With IE7, the browser architecture has been re-engineered for greater compatibility and quality page viewing for a variety of users. In early betas of IE7, it was clear that improved support for Cascading Style Sheets (CSS), as well as transparent Portable Graphics Network (PNG) support, were priorities for Microsoft. The IE7 final release confirms this intent, providing users with a view of web sites like never before experienced in Internet Explorer.

At the core of this change is IE7's capability to support CSS. CSS has become one of the most widely used standards for creating web pages. It allows designers to create complex designs without losing their minds having to apply/reapply style settings manually to each element of the site.

With IE7, Microsoft intelligently decided to begin shoring up its CSS support by first enabling the features most sought after by developers. As a result, IE7 has resolved many of the major inconsistencies that previously would devastate a developer's beautiful, interactive web page.

With these changes in how IE7 exhibits CSS elements, web-page-deprived viewers can now experience pages that include the following elements:

- Ability to hover on all elements
- Fixed positioning
- CSS 2 selectors
- HTML 4.01 improvements
- Windowless Select element

As you can see with the two preceding examples, the difference between CSS and non-CSS page display can be immense. In earlier versions of Internet Explorer, a CSS page would often display as shown on the top half of Figure 10-8. In IE7, with the increased support for CSS, pages will likely be viewed in their full splendor (as intended by the designer), as in the bottom half of Figure 10-8.

Transparent PNG support

Probably the coolest visual feature of IE7, especially within the Vista environment, is the newly added support for something called an *alpha-channel-transparent* PNG file.

This is really, really awesome, provided you know exactly what an alpha-channel-transparent PNG file is.

PNG is a graphics format specifically designed for use on the World Wide Web that enables compression without any loss of quality. With an alpha channel, designers can use special effects that were not previously supported—such as transparency. As shown in Figure 10-9, they can create web page images that can layer, yet still not obscure the background image.

This PNG transparency support enables web site developers to create more visually appealing sites.

Improved Ajax support

Microsoft is also happy to repost that IE7 provides improved functionality for viewing web sites that are designed with Ajax. In case you're not familiar with Ajax, it's a web development technique that incorporates JavaScript with XML and is extremely useful for making interactive web applications.

The most practical application of Ajax is its capability to allow data manipulation without rerendering the entire page in the browser. A popular example of an Ajax-enabled site is Google Maps, shown in Figure 10-10.

Figure 10-8. A web site as it displayed in earlier IE versions (top), and how it is supposed to look (bottom)

But there's a catch: according to the Ajax and web design community at large, the improvements here amount to little more than a polite mentioning. The Web Standards Project (*http://www.webstandards.org*) has provided a program called the Acid2 Browser Test, a test page for evaluating browser performance and support of current web technology, such as Ajax.

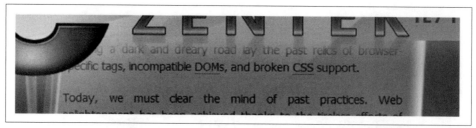

Figure 10-9. Close-up of PNG transparency

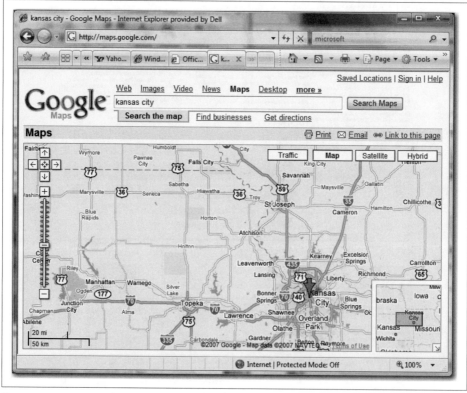

Figure 10-10. Ajax application shown in Google Maps

When subjecting IE7 to evaluation via Acid2, the results were not very positive, as demonstrated in Figure 10-11.

Microsoft has even admitted that Ajax support was not at the top of its priority list with IE7, so the improvements in this arena should be considered with this information in mind.

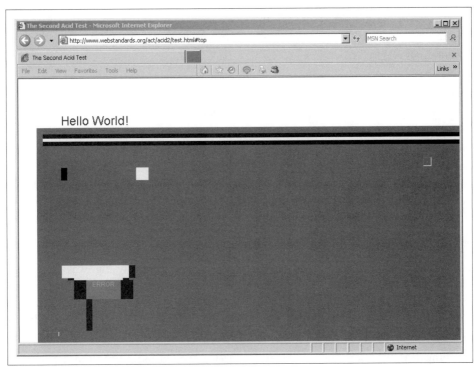

Figure 10-11. Acid2 test result for Ajax support in IE7

JavaScript compatibility

It's also important to mention that, especially when discussing how IE7 displays Ajax objects, little more has been done to support viewing JavaScript-driven sites. There are still enough JavaScript bugs in IE7 to keep the bloggers at *Quirksmode.org* frothing at the mouth indefinitely. Quite frankly, based on the lack of changes evident in IE7, it appears that smooth JavaScript functionality was also not a priority with Microsoft.

Keyboard shortcuts: general usability

Along with general usability information, I'll throw in a few handy keyboard shortcuts that should enhance IE7 productivity (see Table 10-2).

Table 10-2. IE7's general keyboard shortcuts

IE7 action	Keyboard command
Turn Full Screen Mode on or off	F11
Cycle through the Address bar, Refresh button, Search box, and items on a web page	Tab
Find a word or phrase on a page	Ctrl-F

Table 10-2. IE7's general keyboard shortcuts (continued)

IE7 action	Keyboard command
Open the current web page in a new window	Ctrl-N
Print the page	Ctrl-P
Select all items on the page	Ctrl-A
Go to the home page	Alt-Home
Go backward	Alt-Left Arrow
Go forward	Alt-RightArrow
Refresh page view	F5
Refresh page view and the cache	Ctrl-F5
Stop page download	Esc

A Closer Look at IE7's New Features

During the early days of Internet Explorer 6, tabbed browsing was the most requested browser upgrade. And it's easy to see why: users typically want more than one web site open simultaneously. With browser tabs, users can manage multiple web sites within one browsing window instead of having to open 2, 4, even 10 Internet Explorer windows at once.

As competing browsers such as Mozilla's Firefox wooed users onto the dance floor with their tabbed-browsing capabilities, Microsoft seemed content to play wallflower. Content, that is, until users began to actively seek and install these competing browsers as substitutes for Internet Explorer.

 Firefox is essentially Netscape reborn…with a cooler logo.

With integrated browser tabs, users can access multiple sites within a single browsing window instead of being forced to open multiple Internet Explorer windows at once.

While Windows XP somewhat addressed this issue by adding the option of grouping taskbar buttons for each program that was running, this still did not alleviate the total number of windows open at any given time. So, while the taskbar in Windows XP may have looked tidier, users still had to deal with multiple open windows, as evident in Figure 10-12.

Microsoft did finally add a non-native tabbed-browsing capability to Internet Explorer 6, a feature that was added with the installation of the MSN Desktop Search toolbar. This is no longer the case with IE7, even in the Windows XP environment. Tabs are no longer an add-on feature, but rather are now a vital part of the

Figure 10-12. Taskbar buttons in Windows XP

Internet Explorer experience. Moreover, the additional tab options that Microsoft has included makes IE7 one of the most flexible and robust Internet browsers available, whether you're using Vista right now or not.

Are you ready for tabs?

First and foremost, to use the new tab toys in IE7, you must verify your tabbed-browsing capabilities. You access the tab settings by first pressing the Alt key and then choosing Tools → Internet Options → Tab Settings.

Then look at the General tab, as shown in Figure 10-13.

Configuring which tabbed settings are the best is another matter entirely, of course, and will be the subject of much debate among users. It's therefore up to you, the administrator, to determine the optimum settings that will balance your users' browsing needs, the network's security, and your sanity.

Based on your determined tabbed-browsing settings, you may then use some or all of the following tools.

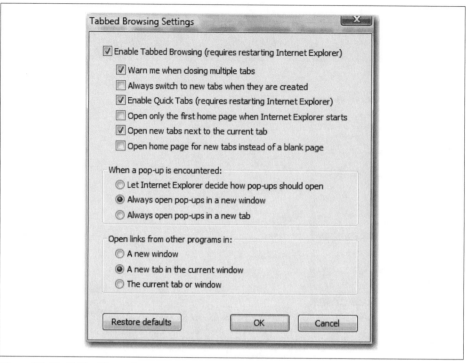

Figure 10-13. Tabbed browsing menu

Configuring tab options. Getting started is simple: to create or open tabs in IE7, users can simply click on the empty tab to the right of the open tabs, or use the shortcut keystroke combination of Ctrl-T (see Figure 10-14).

Figure 10-14. Open multiple sites with tabs

That was easy enough, and even the most novice user can quickly figure this one out. But if you thought those crazy Microsoft developers were going to stop there, you've got another thing coming. If there are other options for opening new tabs that require a little more digging, consider this book your shovel.

If you right-click on any hyperlink in a web page and choose Open in New Tab from the context menu, for example, the new site magically opens in a new tab. This can be a great way to avoid unnecessary typing in the Address bar or, even more useful, as a way to view linked web pages without navigating away from your current page.

It's particularly useful when you're viewing a site, for instance, that has multiple articles referenced on a page. You can maintain your linking page for reference while opening and viewing each linked article in a separate tab.

Here are two other handy ways to expediently open a new tab:

- Hold down the Ctrl key while clicking on a hyperlink.
- Hold down the Alt when pressing Enter in either the Address bar or the Search bar.

In each case, your results will automatically open in a new tab. Nifty, eh?

But wait—the fun doesn't stop with mere tab creation.

Users have the ability to right-click on a tab and perform one of several other browser actions, including:

- Refreshing each page as an individual tab
- Refreshing *all* tabs as a group
- Closing individual tabs or the entire group

And what if you want to group two tabs side by side? Do you have to close any intervening tabs? Absolutely not. Users can reorder tabs by simply clicking on the tab and then dragging and dropping. It's an extremely useful feature that, amazingly, doesn't appear in some of the other tabbed browsers. Along with the tabbing functionality are some awesome tools that help manage and maximize the usefulness of those tabs. First among our discussion of the various tab tools is Quick Tabs.

The Quick Tabs feature

Exhibit A in our discussion of all that is new and rocking in IE7 is the Quick Tabs feature. By using this feature, users can easily manage multiple tabs by viewing thumbnail images of all open tabs in a single window, as seen in Figure 10-15.

To begin your first experience with the Quick Tabs feature, click the leftmost tab with the square of rectangles. This will present you with a new window showing a single-page thumbnail representation for each open tab within this particular browser window.

At the risk of stating the obvious, do note that the thumbnails shown are *only* for the tabs associated with the browser window within which you clicked the Quick Tabs icon. If you have any additional browser windows open, those browser tabs will not appear in this particular Quick Tabs window.

However, a thumbnail quick tab will appear for each tab, regardless of how many tabs you have open in this particular browser. The thumbnail images will merely scale as necessary to show all open tabs in a single window.

Now, here's where it gets really cool. Each quick tab shows not only the thumbnail image of the page open in the tab, but also the associated page's title above the thumbnail. To the right of the title for each quick tab is an X icon.

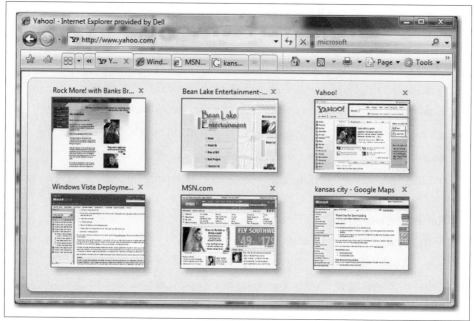

Figure 10-15. Quick Tabs in the house

So, what do you do with all of this once you've got it?

To navigate to one of the displayed quick tabs, simply click on the thumbnail image. You may also click on the X icon above the thumbnail image to close the associated tab, which is extremely useful when trying to scale down the number of open tabs so as to increase the size of the Quick Tabs thumbnail images.

I've found this most useful when I have multiple tabs open from the same site, and that particular site shows incredibly long page titles, such as "WebSiteName.com—This is your open page." With multiple tabs open, it is impossible to know which tab is which, a problem that is easily alleviated using the quick tab image.

The Tabs List feature

Just in case the Quick Tabs viewing option is a little too extreme for some users, Microsoft threw in the option of viewing a comfortable, familiar drop-down list of all open tabs.

To the right of the Tab Groups viewing tab is a tab with a down arrow. Clicking on this tab will provide users with a drop-down listing of all open tabs, as seen in Figure 10-16. Users can then click on whichever tab they wish to view, and IE7 will make it so.

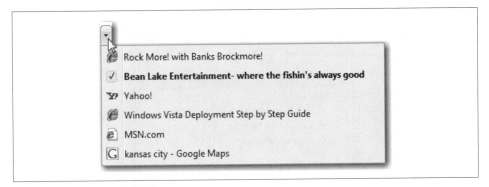

Figure 10-16. View of Tabs List

The Tab Groups feature

Another tab-management utensil built into Internet Explorer 7 is Tab Groups, which allows users to group different URLs together in a single location.

Instead of opening a tab for this site, a tab for that site, and so on—making multiple trips to the Favorites Center along the way—users can launch all associated tabs at once with a single click. IE7 pulls off this impressive feat of efficiency by allowing tab groups to be saved as a single Favorites entry.

To create a tab group, open all sites as tabs within a browser window. Once open, click the Add Favorite button, and then click the Add Tab Group to Favorites option from the menu, as shown in Figure 10-17.

Figure 10-17. Creating Tab Groups

Once created, the tab group will appear as a seemingly regular old folder in the Favorites menu, as shown in Figure 10-18. Clicking on the folder makes the tab group expand to show all of the unique sites organized within the folder.

Better still is the fact that the user can open all the sites within the tab group with a single click of the arrow shown to the right of the folder in the Favorites list (see Figure 10-19).

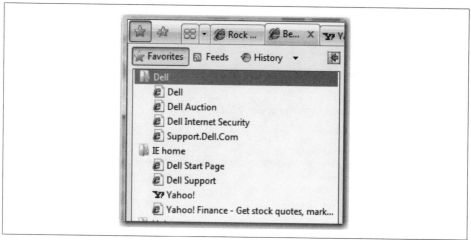

Figure 10-18. View of tab group within Favorites

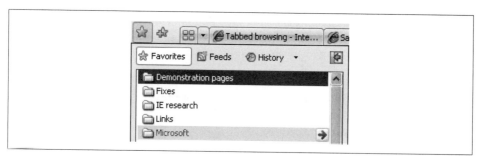

Figure 10-19. Clicking the tab group arrow to open the entire group

Setting a tab group as your home page. The preceding words pretty much say it all. That's right: you don't have to set just a single URL as your IE7 home page. In fact, setting just one home page will seem downright homespun once you learn about setting up an entire tab group as your home page.

Why? Let's say that each time you hop onto the Internet, you check your email via the web mail login, check the daily movement in your current stock holdings, watch the Star Wars kid for the 135th time on YouTube, and then see whether Dane Cook has responded to your MySpace friend request (he probably has; he's just cool like that).

As we discussed earlier, you can open each of these web sites as a separate tab and then save all open tabs as a tab group, as shown in Figure 10-20.

And now that you have a saved tab group, you can set this group as your home page. To set the tab group as IE7's home page, use the Home button drop-down menu and choose Add or Change Home Page.

From there, you receive a dialog box asking you what to set as the default location. You have three choices here, seen in Figure 10-21.

Figure 10-20. Adding a tab group

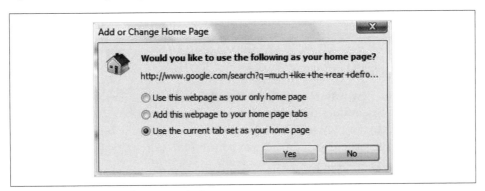

Figure 10-21. Setting a tab group as the home page

Obviously, you'll use the third selection, "Use the current tab set as your home page."

If you want to set a specific site or tab group as your home page without opening the page(s), you may also use the Internet Options menu that is accessible through Tools → Internet Options → General Tab. Enter the desired home page address, or if you want to use multiple sites, enter each site address on a separate line, as shown in Figure 10-22.

Figure 10-22. Setting the home page manually

A tab group can contain an unlimited number of tabs or sites, and users can create an unlimited number of tab groups within Favorites.

Keyboard shortcuts: Tabbed browsing

Table 10-3 lists some additional keyboard shortcuts.

Table 10-3. Tabbed-browsing keyboard shortcuts

Tabbed-browsing action	Keyboard command
Open link in new background tab	Ctrl-left or middle mouse button
Open link in new foreground tab	Ctrl-Shift-left or middle mouse button
Close tab (closes window if only one tab is open)	Ctrl-W or Ctrl-F4
Open Quick Tabs view	Ctrl-Q
Open new tab	Ctrl-T
View list of open tabs	Ctrl-Shift-Q
Switch to next tab	Ctrl-Tab
Switch to previous tab	Ctrl-Shift-Tab

The Instant Search feature

Another powerful new feature is the way that IE7 makes it easier to locate information on the Internet. It does this with the new Instant Search box. The search interface allows users to not only search the Internet directly from the browser frame, but also deploy their favorite search provider to perform the search.

Users can choose a search provider from the drop-down list, as shown in Figure 10-23, and easily add more providers to the list.

Figure 10-23. Pick your search provider

When you're upgrading to IE7, the Instant Search box will inherit the default search setting from IE6.

To offer users a greater degree of choice, however, Internet Explorer has expanded the definition of a "search provider" to include both broad- and vertical-search providers as potential candidates for inclusion in the Instant Search drop-down list.

From the Instant Search drop-down menu, users can click on Find More Providers to view the linked Windows Search Guide, shown in Figure 10-24.

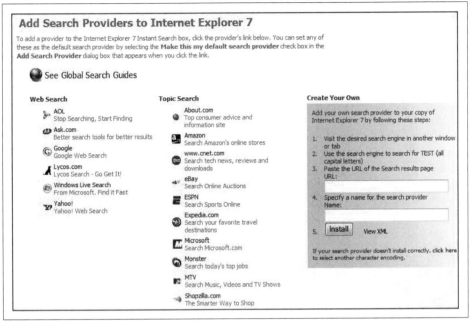

Figure 10-24. Add more search bar options

Once a search provider has been added, users can toggle between providers with the drop-down arrow on the right. Doing a research paper on Kansas City barbecue? Maybe Expedia is a better starting point than Goog—excuse me—Windows Live Search.* Trying to find a great price on Zune? Maybe Shopzilla can point you in the right direction.

That last one was funny, huh? *No one's* looking for good prices on Zune.

Keyboard shortcuts: Instant Search

Some search shortcuts heighten the levity even further (see Table 10-4).

Table 10-4. IE7 Search keyboard shortcuts

Search action	Keyboard command
Select the Search bar	Ctrl-E
View search providers list	Ctrl-down arrow
Open search results in new tab	Alt-Enter

---

* You'll quickly find Arthur Bryant's and Fiorella's Jacks Stack if Googling. Should you be in the Kansas City area, you can't go wrong with either one, although I'd like to add Hayward's Pit BBQ to the list as well.

The page zoom feature

For myriad reasons, IE7 has added a page zoom feature. By choosing the Page Zoom option, users are able to increase or decrease the page size to meet their viewing needs.

Not only does the zoom feature change the appearance of the text size, but any graphics or text embedded in graphics will also be visually modified. This can be especially helpful when dealing with spreadsheets and other lists of data that have been saved as web pages.

Looking at a web page at normal view, as shown in Figure 10-25, it is easy to see why a user might want to use the zoom feature. While the site's designer might not have had any difficulty reading the site within the design application, live text on the Web can often be difficult to read due to size, color, or even the page design itself.

Figure 10-25. A web page at normal size

As Figure 10-26 shows, a zoom to 150 percent makes all the difference in the world.

The easiest, most obvious way to accomplish the zoom view is to use the Zoom menu on the status bar, located in the lower right of the browser window, as shown in Figure 10-27.

Figure 10-26. Zoom in to a particular area

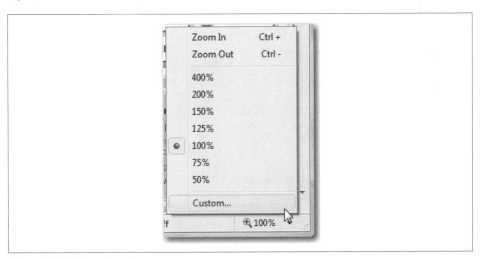

Figure 10-27. Zoom interface

Instead of using the actual Zoom menu, and if you happen to have a wheel mouse at your disposal, you can also hold down the Ctrl key while spinning the wheel. Spin up to zoom in and spin down to zoom out.

As I just implied, zooming in on a page is not your only option. Should you find yourself wanting to view the entire page at once, maybe to evaluate a web site layout or something of the sort, you can do so in IE7. As shown in Figure 10-28, a zoom out to 50 percent is available.

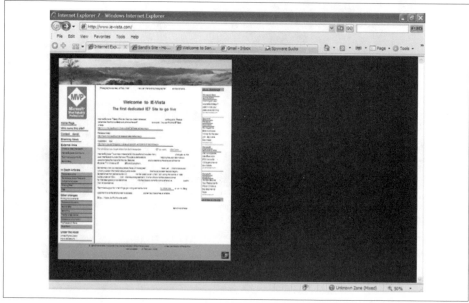

Figure 10-28. Zoom out to view the entire web page

In other words, IE7 offers a cornucopia of options to meet your every viewing whim.

Keyboard shortcuts: Page zoom

Table 10-5 provides some zoom commands that will make life easier for the two of you who do not own a wheel mouse.

Table 10-5. Page zoom shortcuts

Zoom action	Keyboard command
Zoom in	Ctrl-plus sign (+) key
Zoom out	Ctrl-minus sign (−) key
Zoom to 100 percent	Ctrl-0

Advanced printing capabilities

Amid the oft-trumpeted additions of tabbed browsing and RSS feeds, one of the most useful and dynamic new features of IE7 is often left by the wayside. Not so in these pages.

With IE7, Microsoft has helped users win those annoying and time-consuming print battles waged against the printer.

For instance, how many times have you printed a web page, only to find that the righthand side has been cut off? What about that mysterious, unexplained blank page that prints at the end (or sometimes the beginning, depending on how the printer's configured) of a print job? Or what about the page that prints with one line of text?

IE7 makes all of these issues a thing of the past. In IE7, web pages are automatically scaled for viewing within the browser window by using Shrink to Fit (see Figure 10-29) and Orphan Control (for unnecessary whitespace). With these two options, pages should always fit the paper when printed.

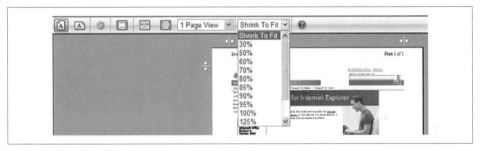

Figure 10-29. Using Shrink to Fit

Printing of useless blank pages can be easily avoided as well. Follow these steps:

1. Click the Print drop-down arrow in the IE7 toolbar.
2. In the Print menu, select Print Preview.

From here, you have several options. You can choose from multiple view options, ranging from a single page all the way up to a 12-page view. You can also view each page at full width or at full page, and switch between landscape and portrait view modes.

What's more, you can choose to print headers and footers or leave them out entirely while in the preview window. To do so, click the little "gear" button on the Print Preview toolbar, opening the Page Setup dialog box. To remove the header and/or footer, select and remove the field entries in the Header and Footer sections, respectively.

This ease of use means no more looking at the preview, canceling the print, and then having to adjust the document properties in another dialog box prior to resuming your print operation.

Add to this the new Live Margin sliders in the preview, as shown in Figure 10-30, and you feel a much greater sense of control over what is sent to the printer.

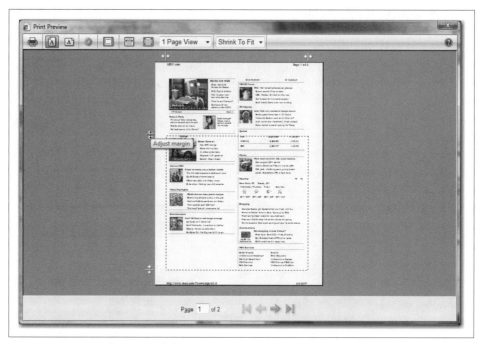

Figure 10-30. Using the margin sliders

RSS Feed Support

Another significant enhancement in IE7 is integrated support for Really Simple Syndication (RSS) feeds. Using this feature, users can easily discover, subscribe to, and read RSS feeds directly in the browser, allowing them to receive a variety of different subscriptions delivered directly to them. The RSS reader capabilities mean that users can subscribe to multiple feeds and read new entries without visiting individual web sites, and without having to open a separate feed reader.

In previous versions of Internet Explorer, RSS feeds were rendered in the browser in raw Extensible Markup Language (XML), which was virtually useless.

In IE7, however, users can find feeds, subscribe to them, read them directly in the browser, scan them for important stories, and view a synopsis of the story's content.

Users can also subscribe to a feed with a single click within IE7, a process that is virtually identical to the process of adding a new Favorite.

Here's what to look for when using IE7 as the RSS reader application:

Feed Discovery button
> The Feed Discovery button tells users whether a feed is detected on the web page being viewed (see Figure 10-31). It lives on the Command bar and lights up when a feed is found. Clicking on it navigates the browser to the Feed Reading page.

Figure 10-31. RSS button options in the toolbar

Feed Reading page
> This is the view of the feed for reading. When you subscribe to a feed, you can determine the new content versus the content that you've seen before. To assist users in accessing the content that is of interest, IE7 makes controls for inline search, sorting, and filtering available *within* the reading page.

Feeds List
> By clicking the Favorites/Feeds List star icon, as shown in Figure 10-32, users can access their list of subscribed feeds. A feed is bold if there is new content available for users to access.

Figure 10-32. Feeds List

IE7 incorporates an RSS platform that any application can use. This cross-platform availability provides different applications the capability to share access to the same set of RSS subscriptions, enabling the possibility of a whole new range of options for RSS feed use.

Getting started with RSS

So, just how do you set all this up so that information is delivered without additional searching? Glad you asked.

Generally speaking, there are four parts to the feed reading experience: discovering, subscribing to, reading, and managing the content.

Discovering the content. To get started with RSS using IE7, users must find a feed and then subscribe to it.

Most users will encounter a feed through the Feed Discovery button located on the Command bar.

A web site may advertise that it has one or more feeds available. How will you know? If available, the RSS button is active and appears orange. If unavailable, the RSS button remains grayed out or inactive.

The default action of the browser button accesses the first discovered feed. If multiple feeds are associated with the page, click the drop-down arrow to see the menu of all discovered feeds.

Subscribing to the content. There are two modes to the IE7 Feed Reading page: preview and subscribed mode. In preview mode, users see the web site's live RSS feed. By subscribing to the feed, IE7 automatically checks the web site (even if IE7 isn't running) to see whether there are new updates as designated in the feed's settings (see Figure 10-33).

Figure 10-33. Subscribing to an RSS feed

Users can set these subscription settings in the Feed Settings menu. Users can reach this menu by right-clicking on any feed entry and selecting Properties.

From this menu, users can rename the feed entry, change how often Internet Explorer checks for new content, automatically download enclosures (eek…every admin's nightmare), and control the archiving of old items.

Once the user has subscribed to the feed, the feed will be listed in the Feeds List within the Favorites Center. If a feed appears in boldface in the Feeds List, new content is associated with that feed that the subscriber has not yet viewed. Any downloaded content generated via the user's designated subscriptions is available for reading in the Feed Reading page.

For many, RSS feeds are nothing new. In fact, some readers may have current RSS feed subscriptions at a place such as Bloglines. Instead of having to abandon your feeds, though, you can just import them into IE7, as shown in Figure 10-34.

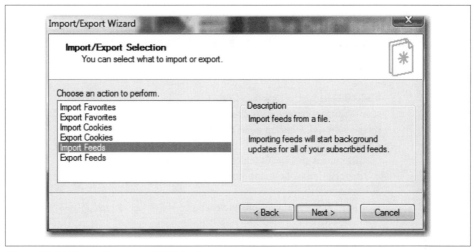

Figure 10-34. Importing a set of RSS feeds

Merely click on the + button next to the Favorites Center icon and select Import and Export. This takes you through a wizard to import your feeds into IE7.

Once users successfully discover and subscribe to a feed, they can begin to read the feed immediately.

Reading and managing feeds. The feed reading experience in IE7 is, in my opinion, amazing—superior to other RSS offerings, especially those enmeshed in other browsers.

When you view the feed, accumulated feed content is displayed in one simple, scrollable view, much like a web page. This is great for news feeds and blogs where you want to scan the feed content to catch an interesting post.

Again, it's important to contrast this with Internet Explorer experiences of the past, or even with some current browsers, whose RSS feeds display as shown in Figure 10-35.

This stands in stark contrast with what IE7 does with the same content, shown in Figure 10-36. IE7 makes managing and reading RSS feeds a much more human experience.

In some feeds, it may be important for users to see every new item on which to take action. For instance, such item-level management is suited for an email application that provides an integrated feed reading experience (which is exactly what occurs with Outlook 2007, another RSS feed reader option).

This is possible because the IE7 reading experience is built on a shared RSS platform. An email application such as Outlook 2007 can then build on this very platform without the user having to go through the same discover-and-subscribe experience in a different application.

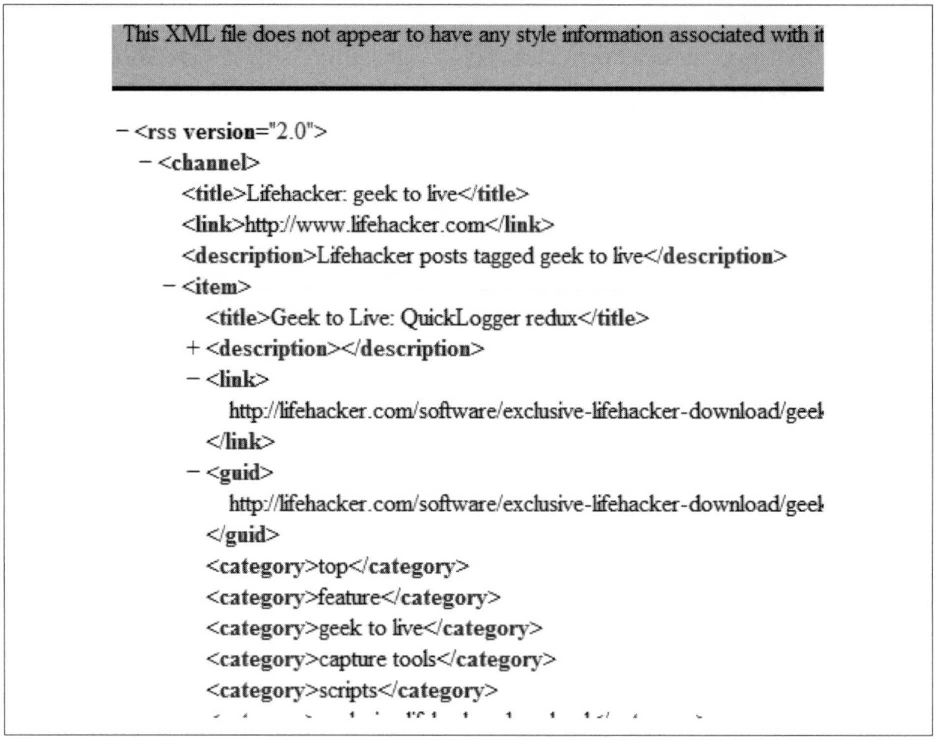

```
This XML file does not appear to have any style information associated with it

- <rss version="2.0">
  - <channel>
      <title>Lifehacker: geek to live</title>
      <link>http://www.lifehacker.com</link>
      <description>Lifehacker posts tagged geek to live</description>
    - <item>
        <title>Geek to Live: QuickLogger redux</title>
      + <description></description>
      - <link>
          http://lifehacker.com/software/exclusive-lifehacker-download/geek
        </link>
      - <guid>
          http://lifehacker.com/software/exclusive-lifehacker-download/geek
        </guid>
        <category>top</category>
        <category>feature</category>
        <category>geek to live</category>
        <category>capture tools</category>
        <category>scripts</category>
```

Figure 10-35. An RSS feed display with IE6's reader capability

In the subscribed mode of the Feed Reading page, users can quickly identify new content (listings appear in blue) making the IE7 RSS model for identifying and then determining whether a feed is new truly ideal for the RSS newbie.

Once the article has been viewed and the user has navigated away, the article is marked as viewed. The next time the user visits, the previously viewed content is gray, providing visual cues that separate new content from old.

Users can also deploy filters to quickly locate a specific category if categories are included in the feed. In Figure 10-36, note how I'm able to jump to the 26 feeds that are marked as having "Downloads." Just like sorting, a web site publisher can include different filtering fields such as region and color.

To reset your control settings, press the Show All link within the controls box.

As discussed earlier in this chapter, users can individually manage their feeds. All that's needed is to select the feed in the Feeds List, and then right-click to view the Properties dialog box for the feed, as seen in Figure 10-37.

However, users can also manage the general feed discovery/download activity within IE7. You can access these controls via Tools → Internet Options → Content tab.

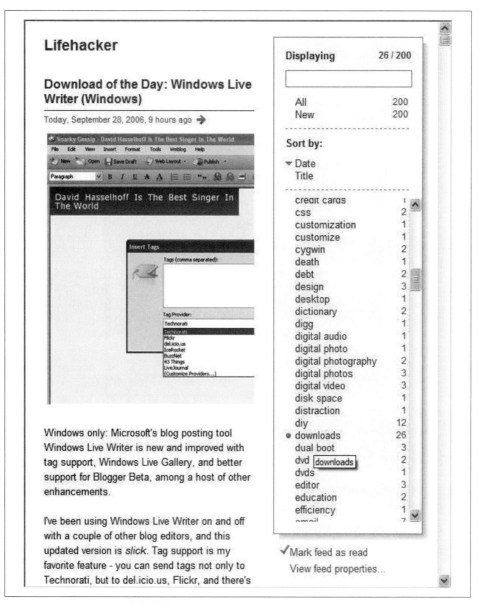

Figure 10-36. Using an RSS feed filter

Now, click on the Settings button to access the Feed Settings menu.

Also note that IE7 restricts downloads in RSS feeds by default. Attached files can be downloaded only upon determination that they are safe (no executables, for example). IE7 then stores the files separately from any personal files, much like a virtual quarantine.

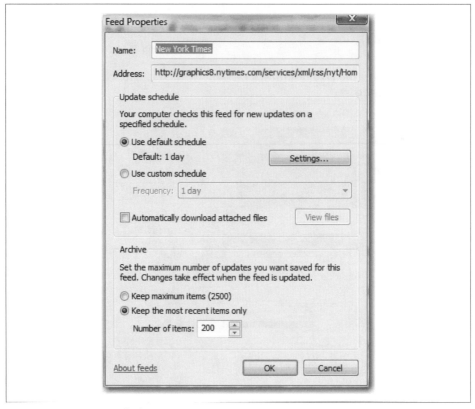

Figure 10-37. Managing feed properties

Behind the Curtain

Besides the improvements to overall look, feel, and functionality, Internet Explorer 7 also includes many exciting features that aren't as apparent to the naked eye.

This doesn't make them any less significant, however, and can mean a much more pleasant Internet browsing experience for users and admins alike.

Administrative Improvements

By integrating additional controls within Group Policy, setting security standards for Internet Explorer has never been easier.

In addition, Microsoft has continued to pour on the love to network admins by providing an enhanced Internet Explorer Administration Kit (IEAK). Add the new User Account Control in Microsoft Vista, and you have the makings of a beautiful friendship.

CSS fixes

With IE7, Microsoft does its best to offer a much-improved rendering engine with fixes made for several major CSS issues that developers have been cursing for years. These previous issues made workarounds a necessity for displaying CSS pages in Internet Explorer. IE7 eliminates the need for many of those workarounds. The fallout to this is that any site that employs a workaround might experience some rendering or layout issues in IE7.

In its desire to assist developers in discovering these issues in their sites (and associated workarounds) as quickly as possible, Microsoft has designed IE7 to create a log whenever it discovers a workaround that has been rendered unnecessary by the improvements in IE7.

Microsoft has provided the following list showing some of the CSS filters associated with the CSS fixes in IE7. However, it's important to note that CSS style rules that rely on nonparser bug filters are considered CSS filters only when used to detect specific browsers or versions.

* HTML filter
> This CSS filter is based on a parser bug. It was used to show rules exclusive to Internet Explorer. These constructs will now be ignored by IE7 and later.

_ Underscore filter
> This CSS filter is based on a parser bug. It was used to show properties exclusive to Internet Explorer. These constructs will now be treated as a "custom property" by IE7 and later. *Custom property* means that it is still in the Operations Manager and can be queried through script, but does not natively apply its value.

/**/ Comment filter
> This CSS filter is based on a parser bug. It was used to hide properties exclusive to Internet Explorer under the strict doctype (this filter did not work under quirks mode). In IE7, the property will now be parsed and applied.

"html > body" Child Selector filter
> This CSS filter is based on a previously unimplemented feature in Internet Explorer. It hid declarations exclusive to Internet Explorer. Starting with version 7, Internet Explorer will apply the properties within the declaration.

"head + body" Adjacent Selector filter
> This CSS filter is based on a previously nonimplemented feature in Internet Explorer. It hid declarations exclusive to Internet Explorer. Now Internet Explorer will apply the properties within the declaration.

"head:first-child + body" First Child and Adjacent Selector filter
> This CSS filter is based on two previous nonimplemented features in Internet Explorer (the `:first-child` pseudoclass and the adjacent selector). It hid declarations exclusive to Internet Explorer. Now Internet Explorer will apply the properties within the declaration.

If you find your web page design is less than desirable when displayed in IE7 strict mode, you'll find yourself with basically three options:

- Try to create standards-based, cross-browser designs. By simplifying your page, you might remove the problem. While this probably sounds labor-intensive at the outset, this change should minimize any future compatibility issues.

- Use conditional comments to work around issues that exclusively affect Internet Explorer.

- If you need to use CSS filters, try to limit yourself to filters that exclusively target older browser versions. This will minimize your risk of problems with IE7 and subsequent versions.

Fix My Settings

From a network administration perspective, the addition of Fix My Settings to IE7 should never be available to users, as User Account Controls should restrict users to safe settings.

Nonetheless, should you have the misfortune to administrate a low-security network, this may be a feature that you should highlight with your users.

Protection against spyware with Windows Defender

Initially released in January 2005 as Microsoft AntiSpyware, Microsoft Windows Defender is designed to prevent, remove, and quarantine spyware. This final release is designed specifically to enhance security and privacy protections when used with IE7.

In the Windows Defender Options, you can configure the following Real-Time Protection options:

Auto Start
Monitors lists of programs that are allowed to automatically run when Windows is started

System Configurations
Monitors security-related settings in Windows

Internet Explorer Add-ons
Monitors programs that automatically run when you start Internet Explorer

Internet Explorer Configurations
Monitors browser security settings

Internet Explorer Downloads
Monitors files and programs that are designed to work with Internet Explorer

Services and Drivers
Monitors services and drivers as they interact with Windows and other programs

Application Execution
Monitors when programs start, and any operations performed by the programs while running

Application Registration

Monitors tools and files in the operating system where programs can register to run at any time

Windows Add-ons

Monitors add-on programs for Windows

Although Windows Defender cannot prevent non-browser-based spyware from infecting the machine, using it with IE7 will provide a solid defense on the browser front. Windows Defender is available for Windows XP and is included in Windows Vista. You can obtain additional product information, including product downloads, from:

http://www.microsoft.com/athome/security/spyware/software/default.mspx

Microsoft Phishing Filter

One technique used by many malicious web site operators to gather personal information is known as *phishing*—presenting information online (or via email) as a legitimate person or business for the purpose of acquiring a user's sensitive information. Such fake sites are often referred to as *spoofed sites*.

Over the past year, phishing attacks have been reported in record numbers, and identity theft is a very real threat to financial security, as indicated in the "Phishing Trends" report shown in Figure 10-38.

In the past two years, the number of confirmed phishing sites, as reported by the Anti-Phishing Working Group in April 2006, has grown from 580 to more than 11,000.

Internet scam artists attempt to capitalize on limited sharing of information, and subsequent public ignorance. By updating its reference definitions several times per hour, the Phishing Filter in IE7 consolidates the latest industry knowledge with updated statistics to best assist customers. The filter is designed on the belief that early warning systems must derive information dynamically and update it frequently to be effective.

After opting in, users running the Phishing Filter will be assisting in client-side scans for suspicious sites. According to Microsoft, performing such a function helps protect users from phishing scams in three ways:

- It compares the addresses of web sites a user attempts to visit with a list of reported legitimate sites stored on the user's computer.
- It analyzes sites that users want to visit by checking those sites for characteristics common to phishing sites.
- It sends the web site address that a user attempts to visit to an online service run by Microsoft to be checked immediately against a frequently updated list of reported phishing sites.

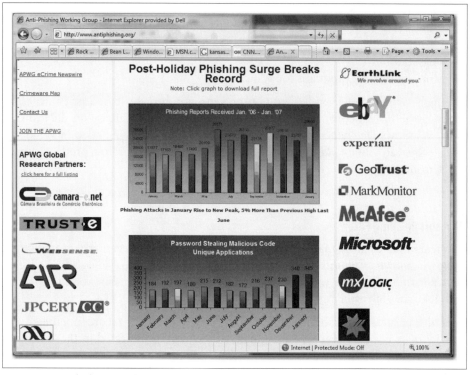

Figure 10-38. Phishing trends

If IE7 is unsure about the security of a site, it uses the Security Status bar to notify users (in yellow). As shown in Figure 10-39, this site is attempting to spoof a legitimate site.

If the requested site is a confirmed phishing site, IE7 notifies the user of the threat level in red, and then automatically escorts the user safely away from that site.

Security Status bar

IE7 also offers better protection against unscrupulous site operators with the Security Status bar, located next to the Address bar. The Security Status bar also assists administrators in enhancing awareness of web site security for their users, providing color-coded Address bar notifications (see Figure 10-40).

These colors coordinate logically with the various levels of web site certificate security (including the new High Assurance SSL, or EV-SSL, certification), Phishing Filter notifications, and other various site security notifications. (See Figure 10-41.)

E-commerce web sites need certificates as much as consumers. While certificates help consumers by preventing phishing scams, the very same certificates assist businesses by assuring a new Internet shopper that his transaction is safe.

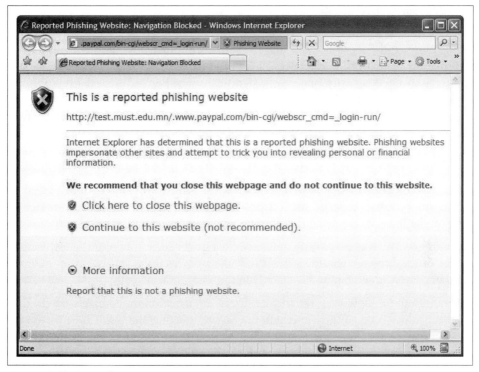

Figure 10-39. A spoof attempt

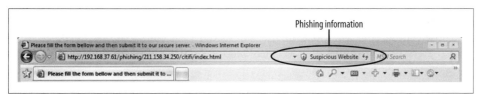

Figure 10-40. A suspected phishing web site

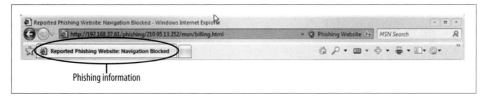

Figure 10-41. A known phishing web site

The Security Status bar in IE7 allows users immediate access to security certificate information, placing it more noticeably in front of users at the same time single-click access to the certificate is provided.

Extended validation certificates

Over the past few years, web browser users have been exposed to encrypted communications and Secure Sockets Layer (SSL) technologies to better protect their information from third-party access. Although most users are familiar with SSL and its associated security benefits, a significant number of Internet users remain unacquainted with the dangers of providing personal information to any web site requesting it. With the explosion of web sites selling goods that span the pricing spectrum, as well as web sites selling other sites' goods by proxy, users are even more likely to encounter unknown entities asking for their financial information. The combination of these factors creates a situation ripe for abuse.

A site's security can now be easily verified in IE7 with color-coded cues to assist in confirmation. Using the information provided by IE7, users can more confidently shop on the Internet, knowing that they are buying from a legitimate business.

Web site security was previously indicated by a gold padlock icon in the lower-right corner of the browser window. With IE7, the new Security Status bar is incorporated into the Address bar and is directly in the users' line of sight.

Further, users can now view security certificate information immediately by clicking on the padlock icon. When encountering a site meeting the guidelines for better entity identity validation, the Security Status bar can provide users with the associated Extended Validation certificates information. The included support in IE7 for Extended Validation certificates benefits users immensely, providing instant visual access to the increased security authenticity for a given web site.

On the opposite end of the spectrum, the padlock now appears on a red background if IE7 detects any irregularities in the site's certificate information. This contrasts with the gold background of a verified secure web site, indicating that users can safely provide confidential data.

High Assurance SSL certificates work with high-security web browsers to clearly identify a web site's organizational identity. For example, if you use IE7 to access a web site secured with an SSL certificate that meets the High Assurance standard, the URL window will turn green. A display next to the green bar will toggle between the organization name listed in the certificate and the Certification Authority that issued the certificate (VeriSign, for example, as seen in Figure 10-42). Older versions of browsers will display High Assurance SSL certificates with the same security symbols as existing SSL certificates (see Figure 10-43).

To purchase a High Assurance SSL certificate, an organization has to go through a validation process that meets the High Assurance Standard established by the Certificate Authority/Browser Forum (*http://www.cabforum.org*). The CA/Browser Forum is a group of leading Certification Authorities (e.g., Entrust, VeriSign, DigiCert, etc.), Internet browser providers (Opera, Microsoft, Mozilla, and KDE), members of the Information Security Committee of the American Bar Association, and the Canadian

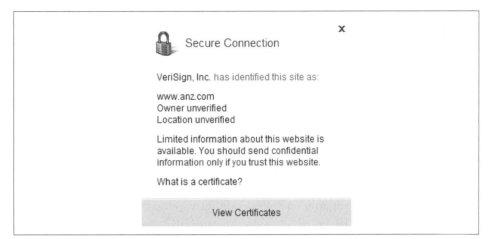

Figure 10-42. IE7 reports on site certificates

Figure 10-43. IE7 has established a secure connection

Institute of Chartered Accountants, who have come together to develop these new standards and guidelines for the enhanced type of digital certificates.

Beyond confirming domain name ownership, the process includes entity identity verification, a valid incorporation registration number, a valid registered agent, verification of domain name ownership, and verification of the business with government or third-party business registries. In addition, the Forum may incorporate other verification methods deemed necessary.

So, at least at the outset, this appears to be a rather laborious and intensive review and authorization process that administrators can rely upon. Not to constantly play the role of Chicken Little, but a "wait-and-see" approach for inclusion into User Account Controls would probably be a wise administrative decision nonetheless.

URL Display Protections

Hackers commonly attempt a sort of technological sleight of hand, fooling users into believing that what they are viewing is a known, trusted source of information. One of the most common techniques hackers use to accomplish this goal is presenting unsuspecting users with faulty URLs through various methods.

To try to help users and administrators deal with the browser aspect of the equation, Microsoft has implemented two major security enhancements within IE7:

- Requiring that the Address bar be displayed in every browser window
- Internationalized Domain Name (IDN) support

An Address bar in every window

Hackers have a history of utilizing pop-up windows to achieve their objectives, executing scripts to display windows with spoofed information.

Because Microsoft can't very well combat each individual attacker, it has chosen to try to take away one of the tools of such an attack. To do this, IE7 now requires that any generated browser window, including pop-up windows, must have an Address bar, as shown in Figure 10-44.

Figure 10-44. Requiring an Address bar

Further, with the security status display integrated with the Address bar, users should be able to more readily determine whether the site is legitimate.

Now, recently there have been some grumblings, most notably from the security company Secunia, that this Address bar requirement may be exploited by a malicious script that displays a spoofed Address bar. However, only time and real-world use can confirm the extent of this vulnerability.

IDN display protections

IE7 supports Internationalized Domain Names (IDNs). While this might not mean much in its mere mentioning, it's important to understand that an IDN is an Internet domain name that contains non-ASCII characters, as seen in Figure 10-45.

Figure 10-45. An IDN

With an ever-increasing global economy, the prospects of encountering such a web site are growing as well. Previously, without installation of a plug-in (which was available only for IE6), the browser could not resolve the domain name and would have no way to access the web site.

In IE7, IDN support and conversion is a native process. This is accomplished by using the API provided by the new Microsoft IDN Mitigation APIs 1.0, which ships with Windows Vista and IE7.

Previously, IDN support was achieved using the Internationalizing Domain Names in Applications (IDNA) conversion standard, which allows the browser to actually convert the non-ASCII characters to ASCII characters that are acceptable to the program. Algorithms called ToASCII and ToUnicode accomplish this domain name conversion. These algorithms are not applied to the domain name as a whole, but rather to individual labels within the address. For example, if the domain name is *www.banksbr⌷ckmore.com*, IDNA would assess and deal with the labels as *www*, *banksbr⌷ckmore*, and *com*, with ToASCII and/or ToUnicode being applied to each of these three separately.

The ToASCII algorithm takes the non-ASCII characters in a label, runs a Nameprep algorithm, and then translates the result to an ASCII-compatible label using Punycode. Oftentimes, this Punycode conversion results in address strings that can exceed the 63-character limit for Domain Name System (DNS), which is why the ToUnicode algorithm is necessary.

ToUnicode cleans up the Punycode conversion to ensure that the address meets DNS standards. It was this Unicode that left users open to homographic spoofing attacks, wherein different characters in a certain language look the same.

IE7 applies its IDN support with the understanding that the IDNA conversion process can provide a tempting homographic spoofing opportunity. Thus, in creating its conversion standard, Microsoft decided to restrict the Unicode conversion. IE7 restricts the scripts allowed to be displayed inside the Address bar.

These restrictions are based on the user's configured browser language settings. Using the new IDN APIs, IE7 detects what character set is used by the sought-after domain name. If the domain name contains characters outside of the user's designated languages, the address is displayed in Punycode form to help prevent spoofing.

According to Microsoft, IE7 will display a domain name in Punycode if any of the following is true:

- The domain name contains characters that are not a part of any language (e.g., *www.banksbr☐ckmore.com*).

- A label within the address contains a mix of scripts that do not appear together within a single language.

- A label within the address contains characters that appear only in languages other than the user's list of chosen languages.

It is this Punycode conversion that IE7 focuses on. IE7 will create a log each time a domain name is changed to a Punycode hostname and will log the hostname.

Barring application of any of the aforementioned conditions, the domain name will be displayed in Unicode. IE7 will allow different languages to appear in different labels if the user has designated the languages as approved languages. This is so that domain names such as *http://www.bobo.fait.com*, where *bobo* and *fait* are composed of characters from different languages, can still display as intended in the Address Bar.

As is the continuing theme, IE7 will notify the user via the Information bar whenever an IDN domain name has been prevented from displaying in Unicode. Users do have the option, however, to add languages to the Allow List using the IDN Information bar.

By default, the user's list of approved languages will contain only the language designated during Windows installation.

Parental Controls

This is the first of several features in Internet Explorer 7 that are available only in Windows Vista.

Parental Controls use a network layer filter component to provide added security and privacy. The Parental Control functionality extends to all Windows Vista applications that use IE7, providing a network layer service to allow parents to control accessible content or restrict browser navigation to specific web sites, no matter what application originates the request.

Logging information and settings are managed via a single interface for managing Parental Controls settings of IE7 in Windows Vista, as seen in Figure 10-46.

The first of the available restrictions is blocking file downloads. If set to block downloads, IE7 in Vista will block all downloads that do not present an administrative

Figure 10-46. Using Parental Controls with IE7

password. If Parental Controls are set to permit file downloads, all downloads will be logged for review at a later time.

Additional controls, as shown in Figure 10-47, include the following:

Activity reporting

When enabled, this feature collects enough information about the restricted account's activities to make the CIA jealous. Reports are generated for viewing at any time, with a fairly impressive amount of information collected: list of sites visited, list of sites to which access was attempted yet blocked, files downloaded, attempted file downloads that were blocked, the dates and times of activity (or attempted activity) on the system, any applications run, review of any and all email and instant messages sent and received, and any media files that were accessed.

Web filtering

Using the IE7 for Vista web filter allows for specific web sites, or types of web sites, to be restricted. Ways to configure this feature range from allowing certain sites or domains that are actively approved, to use of the automated content blocking feature. Specific sites may also be listed for blocking.

Time limits

You can use the Time Restrictions dialog box to block out the periods during which logon and use are restricted. By using a simple hourly grid interface, access may be restricted by both time of day and day of the week.

Games

Microsoft has surely made Tipper Gore's day with the games restriction option that integrates with the Entertainment Software Rating Board (ESRB) game ratings to allow and block games based on their respective ratings. In addition, as with web sites, specific games may be whitelisted or blacklisted.

Application restrictions

Keep the kiddies out of specific applications.

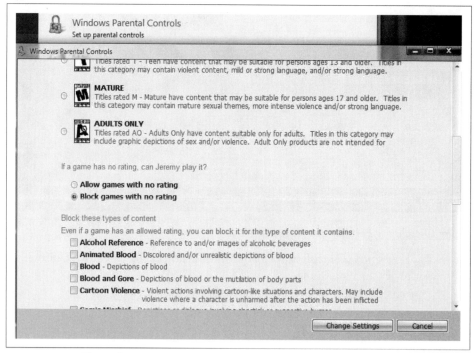

Figure 10-47. Additional IE7 Parental Controls

While some of this may seem a little (or a lot) overboard, the reality is that this is a major selling point for a number of people.

 Parental Controls are available only in the Home Basic, Home Premium, and Ultimate editions. Other technologies such as Group Policy Objects (GPOs) and System Management Server (SMS), as well as System Center Configuration Manager 2007, can be used to govern Internet Explorer behavior with the Business and Enterprise editions.

Protected Mode

Also available only in Vista, Internet Explorer Protected Mode provides a new level of security by preventing unauthorized users from obtaining administrative privileges. In doing so, it protects against hackers attempting to assume control of the browser.

In Protected Mode, IE7 runs completely secluded from all other processes. All communications with the operating system must occur via a mediation process. The mediation process is initiated only when the user interacts with the browser. Microsoft claims that all workarounds of this mediation process are prohibited in Protected Mode. Any scripted actions or automatic processes are unable to download data or directly affect the system. Specifically, Component Object Model (COM) objects are standalone, having no reference information that may be mined for attack of other applications or the operating system.

Protected Mode is, in essence, a way to protect users from themselves. Writing to the Windows registry or other locations outside of Internet Explorer requires elevated permissions that can be verified only by a direct browser interface. While Protected Mode is not a panacea against all forms of attack, it significantly reduces a hacker's options for modes of attack.

Configuring Protected Mode

You can configure Protected Mode in Internet Explorer's Internet Options dialog box. To do so, click the Security tab, select a web content zone, and then check the Enable Protected Mode checkbox. By default, Protected Mode is enabled for the Internet, Intranet, and Restricted Sites zones. To verify that Internet Explorer is running in Protected Mode, look for the words "Protected Mode: On" next to the web content zone displayed in Internet Explorer's status bar.

You can also just double-click the words "Protected Mode: On" to display the same dialog box and make changes.

 Protected Mode is also configurable through a GPO.

Extensions can perform common tasks while in Protected Mode, explaining how to find low-integrity object locations, save files outside low-integrity file locations, elevate processes out of Protected Mode, and debug Protected Mode access failures.

Resetting Internet Explorer Settings

For years, Microsoft has been fielding complaints that users need a way to recover Internet Explorer to a workable state if it becomes unusable due to spurious add-ons, incompatible browser extensions, spyware, or malware. With the release of Internet Explorer 7, users finally have a way to accomplish this feat without a lot of laborious changes to individual settings. Now, when IE7 problems arise, the Reset Internet Explorer Settings (RIES) feature is here to save your day.

RIES provides a one-button solution to get Internet Explorer settings to a workable state. It's a welcome addition, as spyware, malware, or other such malicious code are not the only sources of browser instability. Normal Internet browsing and configuration changes occasionally lead to a browser that does not quite work as well as it once did.

Now that IE7 allows users more options regarding incorporating third-party add-ons, Internet Explorer functionality can be brought to a screeching halt by badly written add-ons. RIES allows Internet Explorer 7, and thus users, to recover from such situations.

After RIES is run, the user will notice default settings of Home Pages, Search Scopes, Browsing History, Form Data, Passwords, Appearance Settings, Toolbars, and ActiveX controls. However, it's important to note that the following settings are *not* reset:

- Enable FTP folder view (outside of Internet Explorer)
- Use passive FTP (for firewall and DSL modem compatibility)
- Always use ClearType for HTML
- Check for publisher's certificate revocation

We'll discuss what to do about this later in this section, but first let's discuss how to use the RIES feature.

Using RIES

Just follow these steps:

1. With the Internet Explorer window active, press the Alt key.
2. Now select the Tools menu (you can shortcut this a bit by clicking the "gear" icon on the IE7 toolbar), and then choose Internet Options.
3. Choose the Advanced tab. Then, simply click the Reset button, as shown in Figure 10-48.

 If Internet Explorer is in a state in which it cannot be started at all, users can access RIES from the Internet Options application located in the Control Panel.

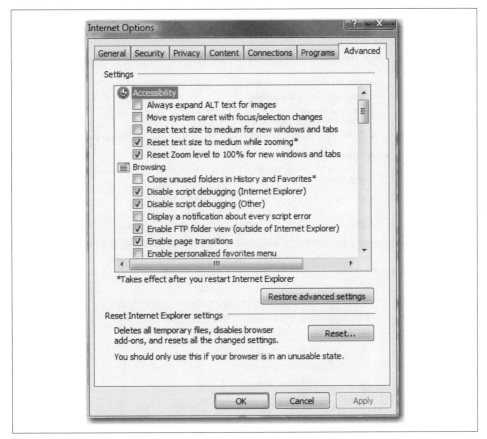

Figure 10-48. Resetting Internet Explorer options

After choosing Reset from Internet Options, a confirmation dialog is displayed, warning users about the settings categories that will be reset during the RIES operation. This dialog box is shown in Figure 10-49.

As usual, Microsoft provides extremely helpful information for the novice computer user in the form of a link in the dialog, which takes the user to a Help pane explaining all settings that will be reset. When continued, a dialog provides feedback of progress on these categories and finally asks the user to restart her Internet Explorer, as seen in Figure 10-50.

Internet Explorer settings for all users will be reset if an administrator runs RIES with admin privileges.

 This immediately affects users who begin a new browser session and users currently running a browser session. Because of this, Microsoft suggests RIES use by administrators be a scheduled action communicated to all affected users.

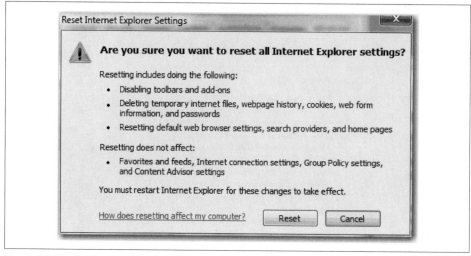

Figure 10-49. Confirming the selection

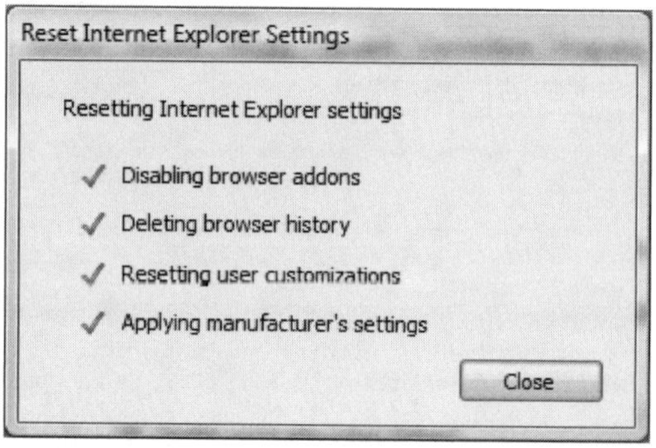

Reset Internet Explorer Settings

Resetting Internet Explorer settings

✓ Disabling browser addons

✓ Deleting browser history

✓ Resetting user customizations

✓ Applying manufacturer's settings

Close

Figure 10-50. Restarting IE7 after resetting

As previously mentioned, RIES does not affect Group Policy. However, RIES will affect any branding settings applied using the Internet Explorer Maintenance Extension in the Group Policy Object Editor.

Because most of these branding settings are preferences and not policies, however, the settings will be lost after running RIES.

Practical advice for running RIES

As you are no doubt aware, many applications interact with Internet Explorer launching or embedding as needed. For example, many applications now include hyperlinks to a help menu or program tutorial that will launch an instance of Internet Explorer when clicked. Any such interactions with IE while you're running RIES can lead to very nasty results, though, so make sure that any and all such applications are closed prior to running RIES.

If one or more of the RIES tasks fail (as indicated by that big ol' X against the task in the Progress dialog), the logfiles (*ried.log* and *brndlog.txt*) detailing the failed actions can be found in *%userprofile%\Local Settings\Application Data\Microsoft\Internet Explorer\.*

To reset these settings on Windows XP or Microsoft Windows Server 2003, perform the following actions:

1. Click Start → Run. Type `inetcpl.cpl` in the Run dialog box, and then click OK.

2. In the Internet Options dialog box, select the Advanced tab and click "Restore advanced settings," or manually check or clear the boxes for the settings that you want to change.

To reset these settings on Windows Vista, perform the following actions:

1. Click Start, then type `inetcpl.cpl` in the Search bar. Choose inetcpl.cpl in the Programs list.

2. In the Internet Properties dialog, select the Advanced tab and click "Restore advanced settings," or manually check or clear the boxes for the settings that you want to change.

RIES does *not* affect the following four settings:

"Automatically detect intranet network" setting
It's enabled by default.

"Require server verification (https:) for all sites in this zone" checkbox
It is not selected for the local intranet.

"Require server verification (https:) for all sites in this zone" checkbox
It is selected for trusted sites.

Lock the Toolbars setting
It's enabled by default.

To change the "Automatically detect intranet network" setting, follow these steps:

1. Select the Security tab on the Internet Properties dialog box. Select the "Local intranet" zone icon and then click Sites.

2. In the "Local intranet" dialog box, toggle the checkbox next to "Automatically detect intranet network."

To restore the "Require server verification for the local intranet zone" setting, follow these steps:

1. Select the Security tab in the Internet Properties dialog box. Select the "Local intranet" zone icon and then click Sites.

2. In the "Local intranet" dialog box, click Advanced.

3. Toggle the "Require server verification (https:) for all sites in this zone" checkbox.

To restore the "Require server verification (https:) for all trusted sites" setting, follow these steps:

1. Select the Security tab in the Internet Properties dialog box. Select the "Trusted sites" zone icon and click Sites.

2. In the "Trusted sites" dialog box, select the "Require server verification (https:) for all sites in this zone" checkbox if it is not already checked.

To configure toolbar locking behavior, use the View menu and choose Toolbars. Then toggle Lock the Toolbars on or off with a click.

With the safety net provided by RIES, and armed with additional knowledge about how to use and further specify RIES behavior, administrators should take comfort in the fact that there's a relatively easy way to reverse any damage to IE7 that a user is able to dish out. Heck, maybe that user is you.

Administrative improvements

Vista also includes several new Internet Explorer administrative settings that can be configured with a GPO. To get started, use the Local Group Policy Object shown in Figure 10-51.

From the Start menu, simply type `gpedit.msc` and then launch the Microsoft Management Console that appears. You'll be asked for administrative confirmation if User Account Control is enabled.

From there, you can locate the IE7 settings by expanding User Configuration, then Administrative Templates, then Windows Components. The Internet Explorer settings are about halfway down the list, and in turn they contain several subfolders' worth of settings.

A similar node is located under Computer Configuration.

We will discuss GPOs in further detail in Chapter 13.

Compatibility in Internet Explorer 7

The introduction of IE7 may pose, according to Microsoft, "compatibility challenges." This is Microsoft's polite way of saying, "Dude, sorry about your web site." However, the company has been nice enough to provide resources to help developers deal with incompatibilities. The following are a few of these resources:

Application Compatibility logging
Application Compatibility logging allows IT professionals and developers to discover incompatibilities that Internet Explorer 7 has with older versions of Internet Explorer running on Microsoft Windows XP Service Pack 2 (SP2). It works with Windows Application Compatibility, implemented in Internet Explorer 6.

Figure 10-51. Managing IE7 behavior with Group Policy

User Agent String

Web developers should verify that their web sites can access IE7's new User Agent String value of MSIE 7. If problems are encountered when attempting to access a site after Internet Explorer 7 installation, check the site's use of User Agent strings for some early troubleshooting.

Notification of Clipboard access from scripts

IE7 notifies users, by default, when any scripts from the Internet, regardless of zone security designation, attempt to read or write to the Clipboard.

Scriptlets

IE7 disables Dynamic HTML (DHTML) scriptlets by default. You can re-enable scriptlets by changing URLActions with the Internet Control Panel (INetCPL) The INetCPL text should read "Allow Scriptlets." It is recommended that any programs relying on scriptlets use DHTML behaviors, which are more efficient.

Status bar update

IE7 limits the capability of web pages to write information in the Status bar. This capability is restricted by default in the Internet zone and is subject to user-configurable settings in security zones. Any calls to the browser's Status bar will silently fail unless the feature has been "enabled" by the user.

Search bar update

IE7 now disables "_search" by default. All searches should now use the Search box, located in the top-right corner of the browser. "_search" may be re-enabled by system administrators or by changing URLActions with the INetCPL. The INetCPL text should read "Enable Search Pane." A restart of IE7 is needed for the setting to take effect.

No more phishing

To cope with the escalating problem of phishing, IE7 has added the Microsoft Phishing Filter. The Phishing Filter automatically checks the web sites visited against a list of known phishing sites, warning users if the site has been identified as a phishing site.

If you prefer not to have sites checked automatically, you can check specific sites when you suspect they might be phishing sites. Here's what to do.

From the Internet Explorer window, click Tools → Phishing Filter → Check This Web Site.

If the site is indeed a known phisher, it should immediately be identified as such. Figure 10-52 shows you what to expect.

Figure 10-52. IE7's phishing filter in action

However, any site that is believed to be a phishing site and is not identified by the Phishing Filter may be reported to Microsoft for investigation. If the site is deemed to be a phishing site, it will be added to the database of identified phishing sites. However, if the suspected phishing site submitted is on a list of known good sites, Microsoft will not waste time and resources to investigate it.

Microsoft likes to proclaim that the Phishing Filter uses "heuristics" to determine whether a site displays common characteristics of phishing sites before flagging it as suspicious. It is important to note that heuristics is a problem-solving method that is little more than trial and error, so don't expect perfection immediately.

The Phishing Filter may be disabled, or automatic checking may be turned off/on through the Advanced Settings tab in Internet Options.

Summary

I don't have to reiterate the subject of this chapter: it's all been about Internet Explorer 7. This new web browser is the default browser available with Windows Vista. Even if you don't yet have Vista, chances are that this will be the one browser with which you'll be spending the most time flexing your administrative muscles.

In this chapter, we covered all that was new and improved in IE7, often using IE version 6 as the benchmark.

Some of the comparison included a discussion of tabbed-browsing features and handling RSS feeds. We identified the significant security enhancements, including Protected Mode, something available only in Windows Vista's version of IE7. We also covered, as we do in all chapters, how admins can manage and manipulate these new enhancements.

In the next chapter, our focus turns to another vital administrative task: optimizing and troubleshooting the Windows Vista environment. We'll look at some of the new ways to tune Vista settings so that Internet Explorer and all your other software and hardware are running at optimal levels.

CHAPTER 11
Optimize Performance

So now your Vista system is up and running. It's hosting your company's mission-critical applications, and you've subscribed to a few RSS feeds to keep you current with the latest industry information, configured a few programs to launch automatically at startup, attached to all necessary networks, and joined the appropriate logical groupings. You've even installed a game or two, and, well, those monsters shooting at you have never looked so scary.

In short, the computer is humming along just like you want it to. For now.

But what about later? You've been down this road before, after all. Right after getting everything set up initially, Windows performance is snappy; apps open within seconds, and multitasking is a breeze.

But what about six months from now? What about when it's been used every day to perform your daily work, when the antivirus software has run a hundred complete system scans, when a dozen or more software updates and driver updates and new pieces of hardware have been added?

How can you make sure the computer is humming along then as well?

This, of course, presents a bigger challenge to Vista users and admins alike: how should we configure our systems so that they're running at optimal efficiency? We will want the same performance later that we have now, right after installation.

This chapter looks at some of the new Vista technologies that will give you the best chance possible of getting the most out of your systems today, and more important, keeping things that way in the days and months to come.

In it, we'll examine each main component of system performance—memory, processor, network, and disk—and the techniques and technologies that will let us maximize performance.

Gathering System Performance Information

It begins with information.

Before optimizing performance on a Windows Vista machine, administrators generally need some way to measure current conditions. You should be able to measure and quantify your performance observations, if not for your administrative benefit, then at least for the people who are responsible for releasing the funds so that your system can be upgraded.

This is commonly referred to as either benchmarking a system, or establishing a baseline. But as with Shakespeare and his roses, its purpose is the same no matter what name you choose: it helps to quantify what is *normal* use on a system so that we can later measure improvements.

In real-world use, there is probably no great need to establish baselines for each and every one of your enterprise's computers. Administrators can instead take snapshots of just one or two of the machines that are used for similar purposes. *When* is actually a more important consideration when setting baselines than *how many*. In fact, Microsoft recommends as good practice that you measure baselines at the following times:

- When the computer is first brought online and begins operation. This lets you accurately state what users should expect from a system.
- When any changes are made to the hardware or software configuration. This lets you measure the effect made by any upgrades.

The reason baselines are useful for these situations is evident: when any changes are made to the system, you will have something to which you can compare the changes.

In this section, we'll examine some of the Vista tools that can help administrators gather this vital performance information, helping us take the "before" and "after" snapshots.

The System Console

We can view performance parameters and, more important, manage those parameters by using the System console. You can open it in a number of ways:

From the Start menu, right-click the Computer button and choose Properties.

The System console provides quick access to several performance tools in the Tasks pane on the lefthand side. They are:

- Device Manager
- Remote Settings
- System Protection
- Advanced System Settings

We'll look at each tool in this chapter.

The System console also has four basic areas that provide links for performing common tasks, and a system overview. As shown in Figure 11-1, these four areas are:

Windows edition
> The operating system edition and version

System
> The processor, memory, performance rating, and type of operating system installed (32-bit or 64-bit)

Computer name, domain and workgroup settings
> The computer name, description, domain, and workgroup details

Windows activation
> Whether the operating system and the product key are activated

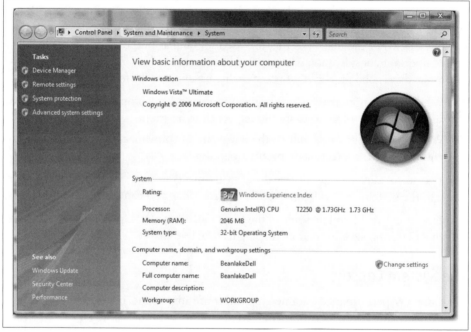

Figure 11-1. An overview of Vista performance with the System console

The Windows Task Manager

Press Ctrl-Shift-Esc. A window opens and presents you with six tabs. As most Windows administrators already know, you've just opened the Windows Task Manager, which presents a graphical display of open programs, processes, and services that are currently running on your computer. It's been available for many years on various Windows operating systems, and has now been updated with a few new features for the release of Vista.

In short, it can do everything the Windows XP Task Manager could do, and it includes additional functionality that makes it more powerful.

In the following few sections, we'll examine many of the troubleshooting tasks that you can handle with Vista's Task Manager. We will examine one tab at a time, and we'll look at a specific instance or two of a troubleshooting task that you can perform on each.

The Applications tab

The Applications tab is one of the simpler tabs visually; it displays a list of any open applications in alphabetical order, and it includes a Status column to indicate whether the application is running or, worse, not responding.

The following three buttons appear at the bottom of the Applications tab:

End Task
> This is the most commonly used command on the Applications tab, and it's used for just what the button name suggests. I'll discuss how to end a task later in the chapter.

Switch To
> This button can act as the equivalent of Windows Flip or Windows Flip 3D. Simply select the application in the program list and click the Switch To button. The selected app becomes active.

New Task
> This lets you launch a new application using a dialog box called, appropriately, Create New Task, which looks and behaves exactly like the Run dialog box.

Recovering a frozen application. One of the main reasons you'd visit the Applications tab during the course of troubleshooting is to close an application that has stopped responding. The click-steps are minimal, and they have not really changed in this iteration of the Task Manager.

Here's what to do:

1. Open the Task Manager. Either use the keyboard shortcut introduced previously (Ctrl-Shift-Esc), or right-click the taskbar and choose Task Manager from the context menu.

2. Choose the Applications tab. The Applications tab is the default, but note that the Task Manager always opens with the previously selected tab.

3. Select the program with a Status of Not Responding, and then click the End Task button.

Note that you usually will not get any kind of confirmation before the application closes when you're using this technique. Also, it's usually a good idea to give the frozen application a minute or two to try to resolve the issue on its own, because closing a program in this way will cause any unsaved changes to be lost.

Troubleshooting a frozen application. OK, you know how to close an application that's frozen, but wouldn't it be even better if the Task Manager could help you figure out why the application froze in the first place?

Guess what: it's time to point out one of the new features of Vista's Task Manager. You now have the ability to create a dump file for a specific application that's frozen. You can then use this dump information in a debugging application to determine the root cause of the problem.

To create a dump file for a frozen app, just right-click it from the Applications tab and select Create Dump File from the context menu. When the procedure completes, you'll see a dialog box like the one shown in Figure 11-2.

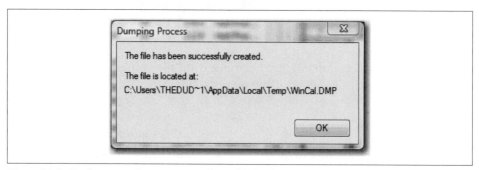

Figure 11-2. Confirmation that a memory dump file has been created

This will help you retrieve the dump file for later parsing in the debugging app of your choosing. Naturally, interpreting debugging files is something of an art unto itself, and it requires a good understanding of the various operating system mechanisms that govern how data is used and executed. You can find more information on how to use Windows debugging tools at:

http://www.microsoft.com/whdc/devtools/debugging/debugstart.mspx

The Processes tab

One of the improvements on the Processes tab is the ability to access the properties of a particular process. To do so, just right-click the process and choose Properties from the context menu. The nice thing about accessing properties for a process is that you can set specific compatibility options for an application's process. Try this if you can't get a program to run as well as you'd like.

 You can combine this technique, of course, with the ability to select an application on the Applications tab. To do so, select the running application, right-click, and then choose Go To Process from the context menu.

Setting processor affinity. Another helpful task that you can perform from the Processes tab is setting processor affinity for a particular process. Setting processor affinity should not be a task you perform regularly, but it can be especially helpful in optimizing performance in Vista systems that are running either two processors or single processors with a dual core (Intel's Core 2 Duo, for instance).

What's processor affinity? Essentially, it's instructions that specify that either one processor or another will be used to handle instructions in a multiprocessor system. It is used to avoid performance problems that may occur when moving an application's instructions between two (or more) processor caches.

To set processor affinity, right-click the process on the Processes tab and choose Set Processor Affinity from the context menu. You'll see a dialog box like the one shown in Figure 11-3.

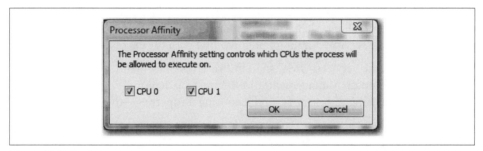

Figure 11-3. Setting processor affinity

Troubleshooting excessive CPU usage. One of the biggest benefits of the Processes tab is the ability to see how much processing horsepower a particular process is using. Obviously, a process that is taking between 50 and 100 percent of the processing cycles is most likely going to cause problems for anything else running on the system.

Vista tries its best to manage processing time so that all apps and background processes get their instructions processed, but often you'll notice an app hogging more than its share.

Sometimes it's easy to tell where the problem lies—the application's process is taking up a lot of time; killing the process fixes the problem. But at other times, the problem is with related processes such as svchost.exe. Services such as these can sometimes be responsible for hosting multiple child processes, and killing the svchost.exe process can cause a lot of cascading problems.

In this case, two different tools can help. One, of course, is the Task Manager. The other is the Tasklist command, which you can run from the Command Prompt. With these two tools in hand, Vista administrators can quickly pinpoint the problem and correct it.

Here's an example of how to use the two applications to fix an excessive CPU usage issue.

First, launch the Task Manager and choose the Processes tab. Now, add the Process Identifier column—you'll need this later on. To do so, choose View → Select Columns, and then check the PID (process identifier) item.

Sort the list of processes by CPU time by clicking the CPU column heading. Obviously, you're looking for the highest number. Also, make sure you're seeing processes from all users by using the button at the bottom of the Processes tab.

Now you have two items that will help your troubleshooting efforts: you've identified the process that's taxing system performance, and you have the Process ID (PID) in hand. It's time to open a Command Prompt.

From the command line, type in the following:

```
Tasklisk /svc /fo list
```

You should see a rather extensive list of all processes, their PIDs, and the services that each one is controlling. Using the information gathered from the previous steps, make note of all the services running under the PID with the excessive CPU usage.

Now you can use the Services MMC snap-in (from the Start menu, type **services.msc** or open the Computer Management tool). You can determine the actual service name by right-clicking the service and choosing Properties—the service name is listed at the top.

Alternatively, you can use the Services tab on the Task Manager. Again, you can sort the services using the PID column heading. You can even right-click the process on the Processes tab and choose Go to Process from the context menu.

Now, simply stop the services listed under your PID in the task list one at a time, using either the Services MMC snap-in or the Services tab on the Task Manager (instructions to follow), checking each time with the Task Manager to see the results. If the processor usage remains high, restart the service and try another. If the CPU usage drops dramatically, you've just discovered the source of the problem.

The Services tab

Similar to the Processes tab, the Services tab lists all services currently running on the computer and lets you sort them according to column headings. You can use the Status column to quickly locate a service that is not running.

The Services button on the bottom launches the Services MMC console, which is the same as launching *services.msc* from the Start menu.

The Performance tab

The Performance tab provides a quick peek into Vista system performance, listing several critical performance parameters and a graph of CPU and processor usage. As seen in Figure 11-4, the graphs here display the current value on the left and a history chart on the right.

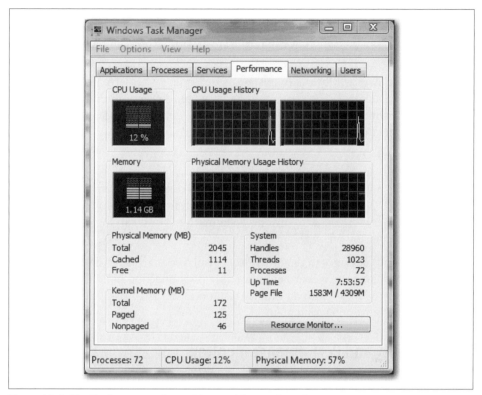

Figure 11-4. The Performance tab provides a quick snapshot of system usage

Here are a few things to look for:

A flat memory graph

A flat Physical Memory Usage History graph means that open applications aren't continuously asking for more system memory, also known as a *memory leak*. A graph that looks like a ramp will lead to poor performance as other applications fight for remaining memory.

The amount of free physical memory

As the value approaches zero, memory is running low. You might want to close an application or two, especially one that's using large amounts of memory.

The physical memory cached

If the value is less than half of the total available memory, Vista is having trouble storing recently used information in memory. Again, the solution here is to close applications you aren't actively using. Vista gives up some of the system cache when it needs RAM, so closing the programs should alleviate this problem by reducing the demand for RAM.

The Networking tab

The Networking tab provides another graphical representation of performance, this time on the network adapters on your system. On a desktop computer, you might see only one adapter. On a laptop, three (or more) network connections may be displayed: a local area connection, a wireless network connection, and a Bluetooth network connection.

The information here will help administrators determine whether a networking connection is being stressed. Such a circumstance would be very rare, and you could address it by disabling the network connection before determining the root cause (i.e., what's sending all that traffic).

The Users tab

The Users tab is not new to Windows Vista, and it's used for the same purposes as it was in Windows XP. With the Users tab, administrators can see who is currently logged on or otherwise connected to the Vista machine, and can force such users to either disconnect or log off.

You can also send messages to the other users displayed on this tab. It's often a good idea to send a message to a user before forcibly disconnecting him. This allows the user to close any open work in an orderly fashion rather than risk losing data when the connection is abruptly terminated.

The Reliability and Performance Monitor

The most comprehensive way you can gather information about the performance of your Windows Vista machine is with the Reliability and Performance Monitor. While Windows has offered the Performance Monitor in the past (it was called the System Monitor), this Vista update includes many new enhancements that make it better than ever.

For example, let's examine the "Reliability" part of the utility's name. In the past, it was very difficult for administrators to determine how often programs were crashing and a system required a reboot. Now, Vista's Reliability and Performance Monitor tracks that information. As seen in Figure 11-5, the tool even gives your system's reliability a grade.

And besides the new Reliability portion of the Reliability and Performance Monitor, this utility includes several other advances, discussed in the following sections, that will help administrators optimize performance.

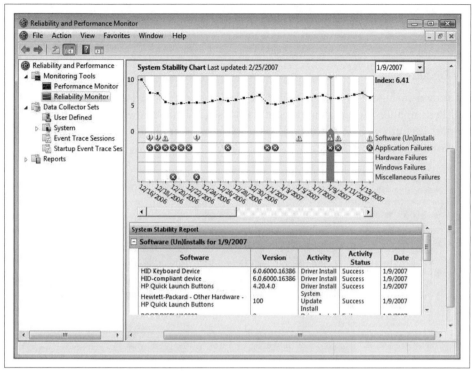

Figure 11-5. Just how reliable is my system? It's a 6.4, if you must know

Data Collector Sets

Notice in the preceding figure the expanded Data Collector Sets node. This node groups data *collectors* into elements that administrators can reuse in a number of different circumstances. The grouping of data collectors works much like the grouping of user accounts: a single change to the collector set, such as scheduling, will apply to the entire set.

Also, the Data Collector Sets work as templates, helping administrators to collect performance data immediately instead of having to manually configure a number of performance counters for a specific monitoring scenario.

Wizards and templates for creating logs

In Vista, gathering performance information is more intuitive than in previous iterations of the Performance Monitor. Instead of having to learn and understand the data collected by each performance counter, administrators can add counters or data collector sets by answering questions about their monitoring goals.

What's more, administrators can save time by saving a manually created data set as a template that they can use on other systems without having to regenerate the data collection set.

The Resource view

As shown in Figure 11-6, this might be the most often-used part of the Reliability and Performance Monitor in terms of daily usage. This "home page" of the Reliability and Performance Monitor displays a real-time graphical overview of CPU, disk, network, and memory usage.

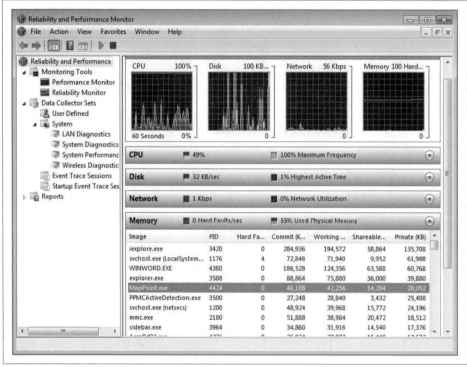

Figure 11-6. Real-time performance information with the Reliability and Performance Monitor home page

Administrators can then obtain further information about each monitored subsystem. For example, I can easily obtain information about which programs are using the most system memory by expanding the Memory heading. Again, refer to the figure. Under previous versions of Windows, a real-time view at performance data was available only in the Task Manager, and even then it was in a very limited form.

The Reliability Monitor

The Reliability Monitor was previously introduced, but it merits further discussion here. The reliability score that this tool generates has a name: it's called the System Stability Index, and it reflects whether unexpected problems have compromised the system's reliability.

This graph is particularly helpful in answering the following question: when did the problems start? You can easily roll the graph back to a particular point in time using the drop-down calendar in the upper-righthand side.

Below the Reliability Graph is a System Stability Report, which provides additional troubleshooting details. As seen in Figure 11-7, you can see exactly what crashed and when, and you can compare this information to any other reported changes to the system. These changes can include:

- Installation or removal of applications
- Updates to the operating system
- The addition or modification of drivers

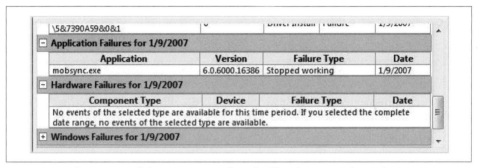

Figure 11-7. The System Stability Report provides valuable information about what went wrong and when

With this information in hand, administrators can often "connect the dots" to help them get to the root cause of the problem.

User-friendly diagnosis reports

Administrators can also use the same data collector set to generate a diagnosis report that they can then share with other system admins or archive for the purposes of establishing a baseline. The report also can help them determine how efforts to optimize Vista have actually impacted performance.

This reporting capability is the same as what you can deploy with the Server Performance Advisor under Windows Server 2003.

The Performance Monitor

As you just saw, the Reliability and Performance Monitor's home page does a pretty good job of providing basic information about the current performance of your Vista system.

But it is just basic information. The Performance Monitor part of the Reliability and Performance Monitor also lets you collect data about a huge range of computer behavior, both from the hardware and from the software.

In fact, the computer performance *counters* available in the Performance Monitor tool are too numerous to list by name here. For example, there are no fewer than 17 different performance measures you can gather that provide information about what data is being executed by a system's processor, and how fast.

So while the Reliability and Performance Monitor's home page will provide much of the day-to-day graphing of system performance, the Performance Monitor will allow administrators to gather more specific information when necessary. It also includes a few additional options that the Reliability and Performance Monitor home page does not.

Here's how to set up a real-time Performance Monitor graph:

1. From the Start menu, type **per**. The Reliability and Performance Monitor should appear in the list of programs (you can also find it in your Accessories program group, or by typing **perfmon.msc** in the Start menu's Instant Search box).

2. With the Reliability and Performance Monitor open, choose the Performance Monitor node.

3. You'll now see the Performance Monitor graph. By default, the %Processor Time counter is displayed.

4. Now, right-click anywhere in the graph and choose Add Counters from the context menu.

5. You'll now see the Add Counters dialog box, as shown in Figure 11-8. Click the down arrow to use the Available Counters selector. You can then pick from one of the counter categories.

6. Each category has multiple individual counters. Select the counter that will provide the information you're trying to gather. For example, a common counter of memory performance is "Page Faults/sec." This is generally a measurement of how often Vista is utilizing virtual memory, which is much slower than physical RAM.

7. Click Add. Repeat steps 4, 5, and 6 for each counter you want to add (you can click the + button in the Performance Monitor taskbar as well). Also note that you can add all counters for a particular category (subsystem) by selecting just the category heading and choosing Add.

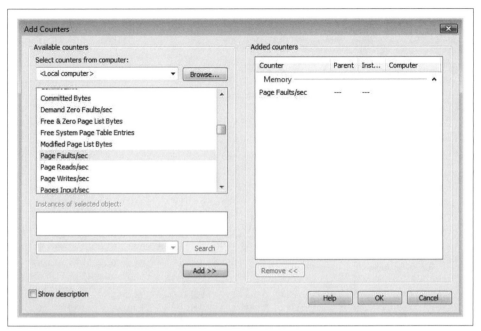

Figure 11-8. Adding a Performance Monitor counter

Some of the counters will have instances such as when dealing with multiple hard disks, network cards, or processors. This lets you gather performance information about processor 1 independently of processor 2, for example. (You'll actually see them as processor 0 and processor 1 in the Reliability and Performance Monitor tool.)

Now you should see why the data collector sets can be so valuable. Adding individual counters can be a painstaking process. But whether you're using a data collector set or manually tracking performance information, you'll end up with a graph of information similar to what you see in Figure 11-9.

One of the advantages of the Performance Monitor is that you can generate graphs of logged data rather than real-time information. To graph the same information about something that has occurred in the past, right-click the Performance Monitor graph and choose Properties. Then, from the Properties dialog box, use the Source tab, shown in Figure 11-10, to specify a logfile instead of current activity.

Sharing Performance Monitor information

Another handy feature of the Performance Monitor is the ability to save and share performance graphs. To do so, you first need to save the display in a format that is easily shared, i.e., a web page or a picture that you can email or paste into other documents.

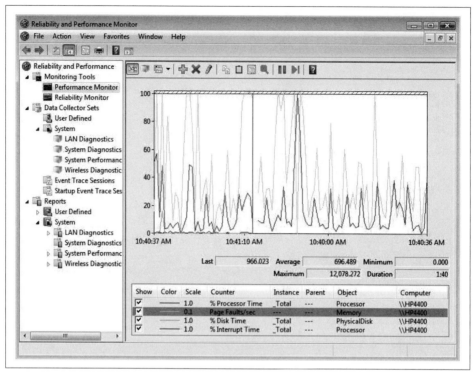

Figure 11-9. A Reliability and Performance Monitor graph

Here's how to save a Performance Monitor graph as a picture:

1. Right-click in the Performance Monitor graph and choose Save Image As from the context menu.

2. Now, just choose a directory and name for the saved image.

Sometimes the Performance Monitor graphs are hard to read. Maybe a bar graph (histogram) would better suit your purposes, or maybe the occasion calls for sheer numbers alone. Fortunately, this tool also allows you to change the appearance of the graphical elements.

Here's what to do.

1. Right-click the Performance Monitor graph and choose Properties from the context menu.

2. Choose the Graph and Appearance tabs to make any desired changes.

3. Click Apply to change the graph without closing the Properties dialog box. Click OK when you've made the changes to your satisfaction.

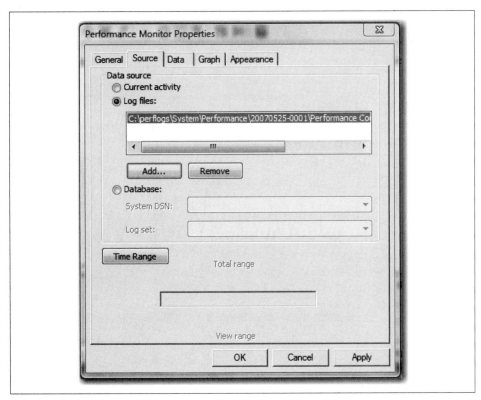

Figure 11-10. Using a logfile

You can even use a highlighting feature to call attention to a particular counter in the display. Select the counter, and then toggle on the highlight of that counter with the Highlight taskbar button (see Figure 11-11).

So, how to we put all of this information to use? By identifying a subsystem bottleneck, and then optimizing the performance of that subsystem.

When we looked at how to gather information about performance, you probably noticed that much of the information gathering kept coming back to the same core components: memory, processor, disk, and network. Indeed, these are the computer subsystems that have the most influence on Vista performance, and we'll spend the next section discussing how to get the most out of them.

For each, we'll point out a few of the yardsticks that you can gather using the preceding tools which, in turn, will help you learn the most about the particular subsystem.

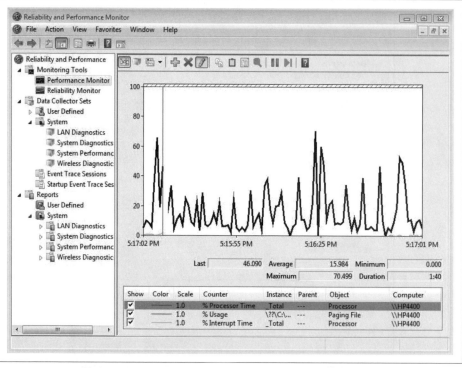

Figure 11-11. Highlighting a particular counter

Performance Subsystems

We all want Vista to run as fast as possible (more specifically, we all want our Vista *applications* to run as fast as possible). But what factors influence that performance?

As we've seen already in Chapter 6, Vista introduces a new measurement benchmark that gives your computer a score: the Windows Experience Index (WEI), which examines five computer subsystems. As you noticed, the WEI rates both the graphics and the gaming graphics subsystems separately, and each does indeed have an impact on overall Vista performance.

But graphics card benchmarking and recommendations are not the focus of this section. Instead, the first part starts with a look at four major computer subsystems that will play an important part in Vista performance, and what we can do to measure and maximize that performance. The four subsystems are:

- Memory
- Processor
- Disk
- Network

Memory Performance

Consider the long-standing metaphor: the desktop of your computer is like the top of a real desk onto which you might set that computer.

Microsoft and other operating system manufacturers have been using this metaphor for decades now because it is an *anchor*—it provides a link to something that we already understand. So whether the desktop we're talking about comprises particleboard, stainless steel, rich mahogany, or an LCD display, we also understand that we can be more productive if we have a bigger desktop.

The larger the desktop area, the more things we can have right at our fingertips to be "processed" by our brains, and the less time we have to spend retrieving stuff from places such as filing cabinets, storage boxes, and so on. In computing terms, the more memory we have, the more data that can be accessed—and thus, acted upon—quickly by the computer's brain, the CPU.

In other words, the more memory, the better our computers will behave. In fact, memory is the most common cause of system bottlenecks. There is almost no way for a system to have too much memory, and it is a great starting point as you begin to look for bottlenecks.

As you examine memory performance on a Windows Vista machine, keep in mind that memory performance is a byproduct of two factors:

- Physical memory
- Virtual memory, also known as the pagefile (aka the swap file)

Physical memory is the physical sticks of RAM that hold all of the instructions for an application, an operating system, or a hardware device. Each location in memory is given a *memory address*, which is how the CPU keeps track of what application is placing instructions where. In other words, RAM is simply a long list of numbers that represent storage locations for either a 1 or a 0. When optimizing physical memory, administrators focus mostly on one simple task: adding more of it. Yes, there are some considerations about the type and speed of that memory, but as long as you know how to refer to the computer (or motherboard) documentation, you should be in good shape.

Not all memory addresses exist on the chips of physical RAM, however. As a rule, Windows Vista machines run out of physical memory addresses at some point no matter how much physical memory is installed, and thus they have to store some working data in *virtual memory*. This virtual memory is simply additional memory addresses stored on hard disk space.

The bad news is that virtual memory, as unavoidable as it is on occasion, is much, much slower than physical RAM. The good news is that administrators have the most control over *optimizing* virtual memory, and they can use the following techniques, among others, to improve virtual memory performance. They can ensure that:

- The virtual memory file is stored on the fastest disk possible.
- The virtual memory file is not fragmented.
- They use virtual memory as infrequently as possible by adding more physical memory.

To implement virtual memory, Windows uses a *pagefile*. As with prior versions of Windows, Vista creates this file to increase the efficiency of available RAM on a system.

The pagefile is logical memory that exists in a file called *pagefile.sys* and is located on the root of the Windows installation drive. To the applications running under Vista, this is just another file. Vista, however, treats the file as just another list of addressable locations meant for storing data as it waits to be processed.

In fact, applications have no idea whether the instructions they are sending to memory are kept on the pagefile or in physical RAM. The one who can tell the difference is the end user, who notices a considerable slowdown in performance when the pagefile is accessed frequently.

This is a great time to dispel any myths about what the *pagefile.sys* file (the swap file) is, and more important, how the operating system uses it. The discussion is necessary because of the speed difference between data traveling into and out of RAM and data traveling into and out of the hard disk.

Namely, it's this: RAM speed is calculated in millionths of a second (nanoseconds), and hard disk speed is calculated in thousandths of a second (milliseconds). To save you a trip to the calculator, a nanosecond is roughly 1 million times faster than a millisecond.

So what? So the operating system can send and receive data into and out of RAM a million times faster than it can with the hard disk, is what. For that reason, the operating system moves data from RAM into the pagefile only as a last resort.

For example, I have five programs running on my laptop as I type this: Outlook 2007, Internet Explorer 7, Microsoft Excel 2007, Vista Explorer, and of course, Microsoft Word 2007. As I type in Word, the application caches my keyboard input into a temporary copy of the file. And until I save the file or close Word and discard the typing, the operating system is tracking the memory requirements that Word needs in relation to the memory needs of the other four programs.

Complicating the RAM picture is the Excel spreadsheet. Because the spreadsheet has several sheets of data, it requires more memory than an empty spreadsheet. But as long as I continue typing in Word, the spreadsheet will eventually need to be moved out of RAM and placed temporarily into the pagefile. Items are usually placed into the pagefile only if the program that is hosting the data is not needed or accessed frequently.

Now, if the computer does not have enough RAM, data is continually being moved into and out of the pagefile. If this goes on too often, it can lead to a condition known as *disk thrashing*.

Yet, when I save my Word file and make Excel the foreground application, the operating system will remove Word from RAM and then, as quickly as possible, will move the spreadsheet from the pagefile back into RAM. This process makes the operating system more efficient in its use of the hardware (RAM) and, thus, more responsive to the user. After all, that's what it's all about.

In the next few sections, we'll examine how administrators can configure the pagefile for optimum performance.

Configuring Virtual Memory

While virtual memory and pagefiles have been implemented in prior Windows incarnations, Vista does a much better job of automatically managing the paging file.

Under previous iterations, many admins found themselves manually managing virtual memory to prevent the paging file from becoming fragmented and acting like a boat anchor on the system performance. Vista seeks to avoid this problem by allocating a *dedicated* virtual memory space equal to 150 percent of the system's installed physical RAM. So once again, Vista helps to shoulder some of the admin load.

Vista will automatically create a paging file on the drive containing the operating system, but all other drives will not, by default, contain paging files. You can remedy this easily, however, by manually creating a paging file with the appropriate settings.

Under normal use, you should not need to do this. This is usually necessary only if the (Windows server) system is performing in dedicated roles such as a SQL server or an Exchange server, both of which require unique memory configurations depending on their workloads and other system hardware parameters (CPU, HD-subsystems, NICs, etc.).

To do this, complete the following steps:

1. Open the Control Panel and then the System console (look under the System and Maintenance grouping).

2. In the System console, choose *one* of the following two options (because you're opening a tool that can make a change that can/will affect all users, you will be prompted for administrative confirmation if User Account Control is turned on):

   • Click the Change Settings link
   • Click Advanced System Settings in the Tasks pane

3. From the System Properties dialog box, choose the Advanced tab, and then choose the Settings button under Performance.

4. You'll now see the Performance Options dialog box. Click the Advanced tab, and then the Change button.

5. You now have the ability to make paging file adjustments using the Virtual Memory dialog box shown in Figure 11-12.

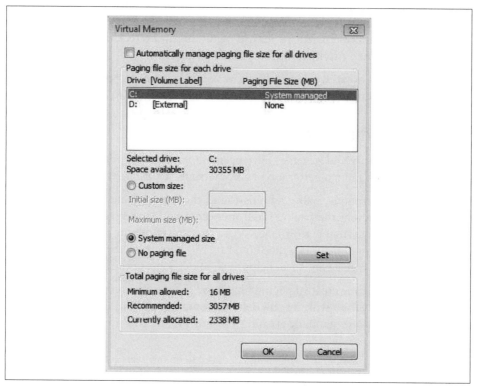

Figure 11-12. Configuring paging file settings

By default, Vista manually manages the paging file. To manually configure paging file settings, clear the "Automatically manage paging file size for all drives" check-box. You will now be able to review information about two settings:

Paging file size for each drive
   This shows the current configuration, with each volume listed with its associated paging file (if any). The paging file range shows the initial and maximum size values.

Total paging file size for all drives
   This provides a recommended size for virtual RAM on the system and displays the amount currently allocated.

To make changes to the paging file parameters, first select a volume label, and then choose from one of the following three radio buttons:

Custom size
> To create a custom size paging file, you must configure an initial and a maximum size.

System managed size
> Select this radio button if you want Vista to manage the paging file.

No paging file
> You can specify no paging file for certain drives.

Click Set to save configuration information, and then click OK. You may be prompted to overwrite an existing *pagefile.sys* file.

 An external hard drive will not have a paging file by default.

Note that if you've changed settings for a current paging file, you'll need to restart the system for the changes to take effect.

Windows Memory Diagnostics

If you have questions concerning the stability of your physical memory, Vista provides built-in diagnostics to test for both memory leaks and failing memory. These tools automatically work in concert with the new Microsoft Online Crash Analysis tool. Together, this dynamic duo prompts the user to schedule a memory test when it detects that a system crash has occurred, possibly due to failing memory.

If you believe that a system may have a memory problem, regardless of notification from the system, it is possible to run memory diagnostics manually via the Command Prompt. Merely type **mdsched.exe** from a Command Prompt window, and then choose to immediately restart the computer, running the Memory Diagnostics utility immediately upon system restart.

Also note that you need to have launched the Command Prompt in Administrator mode in order to be able to launch the utility. To do so:

1. Type **Command Prompt** at the Start menu. The Command Prompt should appear.
2. Right-click and select "Run as administrator" from the shortcut menu.
3. When the User Account Control dialog box appears, click on the Continue button, or provide administrative credentials if you're logged on as a standard user.

For instructions on how to make this the default action, turn to Chapter 15.

Assuming that the request is made appropriately, Windows will restart and provide the option to choose the memory testing type.

We'll discuss other ways to measure memory performance later in the chapter.

Processor Performance

If the computer's CPU is the brains of the machine, logic dictates that it could really help boost performance to get a faster processor. In reality, however, it's rare that a processor is the source of a true performance bottleneck on a Vista machine.

A quick review of the hardware requirements bears this out: Vista requires only an 800 MHz processor to run, and a 1 GHz proc is all that's needed for the Windows Vista Premium experience. Compare that to the 1 GB of memory and 128 MB of dedicated video RAM needed for the Vista Premium minimums, and then ask yourself: "Which of my one-year-old computers' subsystems is most likely to require a facelift in order to run Windows Vista?" The fact is that most people buy much more processor than they really need. After all, how fast do you need that email to open anyway? I've got a three-year-old desktop that's awaiting a hardware upgrade before switching over to Vista as I write, in fact. Its processor? A 2.4 GHz Pentium 4. It doesn't need a processor upgrade.

With that being said, applications can sometimes perform some processor-intensive tasks, and having a fast processor can certainly save time if that's the case. I'm primarily thinking of tasks that require a lot of rendering time, such as video-editing or animation tools.

We'll look, then, at how to gather information about processor performance, and at ways in which performance can be optimized.

Disk Performance

If a hard drive is a filing cabinet for all the information we want to work with, it stands to reason that the cabinet's performance can suffer when we cram too much stuff into it.

This is especially true of the system volume, which, as was briefly mentioned earlier in Chapter 7, typically holds the pagefile. Furthermore, adding more disk space just because we've filled up what's there is sometimes just not an option. In particular, this affects laptop computers, which rarely have space to add more fixed storage.

And besides, we generally end up with much more "stuff" than we need. We can safely remove hundreds, if not thousands, of files without altering computer performance in the least (indeed, deleting unused files usually *improves* performance).

The Disk Cleanup utility

For these and other reasons, it's important that admins know how to use the Disk Cleanup utility. It presents an easy graphical interface to help you get rid of unused files, including these:

- Temporary files that have not been removed
- Downloaded program files
- Offline files (you get the offline files back by reconnecting to the server where the offline files reside)

By default, the Disk Cleanup utility also empties the Recycle Bin and compresses files that haven't been opened recently.

Here's the procedure:

From the Start menu, type **clean**. The Disk Cleanup utility appears in the list of available programs. You'll see a Disk Cleanup Options dialog box, shown in Figure 11-13, asking you which files to clean up. You have two choices: your files or files for all users.

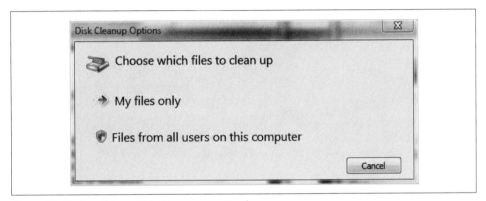

Figure 11-13. Specifying which files you want to clean

If you select All Users, the Security shield icon hints at the next action: you'll be asked for administrative confirmation if User Account Control is enabled.

Note that the utility may take a while to launch; it's checking just how much space can be freed up if you allow it to do its magic. After it calculates, the Disk Cleanup dialog box appears, as shown in Figure 11-14.

From here, it's just a matter of using the checkboxes to control exactly what gets deleted. The interface also lets you see how much disk space will be freed by each chore.

Note also that the More Options tab lets you delete more than just mere files; you can use the Programs and Features section or the System Restore section to free up even more disk space. Clicking the Clean Up button in the Programs and Features section, for example, opens the Programs and Features Control Panel application, letting you remove a program that's stayed a little past its welcome.

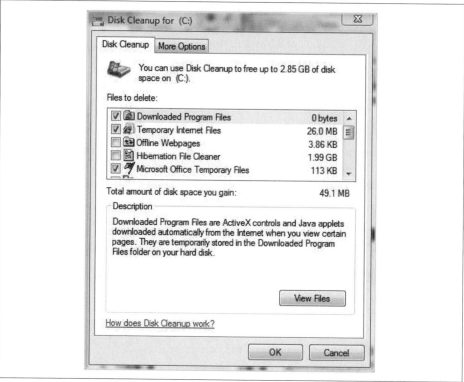

Figure 11-14. The Disk Cleanup dialog box

To keep your hard disk free of too many unnecessary files, it's recommended that you run the Disk Cleanup utility at least once a year. Make it a part of your spring cleaning program.

> You need to run Disk Cleanup for each logical drive on your computer. The utility examines only the logical space, not the physical drive.

The Disk Defragmenter utility

You can find another friendly face in the Disk Defragmenter utility. As we all know by now, the Disk Defragmenter utility is used to reorganize files on a disk drive. When files are initially stored on a drive, or over the course of time, data from the files can become fragmented, with parts of a single file stored in different locations on a drive. This leads to sluggish performance and instability of both the file and the drive.

The Disk Defragmenter corrects this problem by reuniting all data from files, in addition to combining most free space on the drive. When choosing to run the Defrag utility in previous versions of Windows, users could actually watch as colored sections of the files were realigned in a contiguous manner, as shown in Figure 11-15.

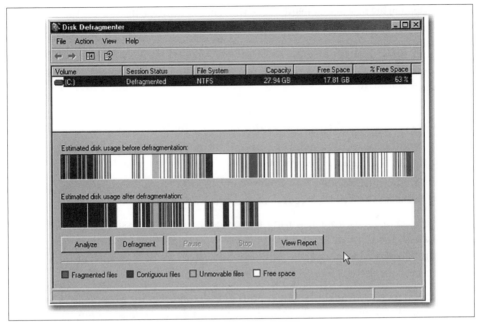

Figure 11-15. Files realigned in a contiguous manner

However, as the preceding statement implies, defragmenting the drive was an action that the user had to initiate. Microsoft has since altered its course on that requirement.

Within Vista, the Disk Defragmenter is now automatically scheduled to run once a week, with the default time being 4:00 a.m. on Sunday. Users can adjust this schedule or elect to run the utility at any time manually (I discuss both options in the following sections).

The Vista Disk Defragmenter interface is different from that in previous Windows versions, where users were supplied with a visual representation of the fragmented nature of their drive. Users merely elect to run the Disk Defragmenter utility, and then wait for confirmation from the system that the process is a) done, and b) successful. This may be a little disconcerting, but seriously, who really sat and watched the little colored blocks move and believed that to be a realistic portrayal of the defrag status?

A slightly annoying feature of the new interface is that, well, there really isn't one. No "current status" or "estimated time remaining" is provided while the defragmenting process takes place. This can cause a real problem for some users, because as you know and as the Vista interface reminds you while defragmenting, the process can take "between a few minutes and a few hours."

Although Windows reminds users that they can continue to use their computer while defragmenting, this is often a risky proposition. Allowing the defragmenting process to finish without any interruptions is always a good idea.

Manually running the Disk Defragmenter. As with most utilities in Windows, users can opt to run the Disk Defragmenter utility in many different ways:

- Choose Start → All Programs → Accessories → System Tools → Disk Defragmenter.
- Choose Start → Computer, right-click a disk, and choose Properties → Tools tab → Defragment Now.
- Choose Start → Search box, type **command**, and press Enter to access the Command Prompt, and then type **dfrgui** and press Enter.

  You can also open the same version of the Command Prompt by typing **cmd** and pressing Enter from the Search box.

- Press the Windows logo key-R key combination to open the Run dialog box; type **\windows\system32\dfrgui.exe** and press Enter.

A security prompt may appear during the process, which necessitates an administrator password to confirm the requested action. If defragmenting is unnecessary, Windows will display the message "You do not need to defragment at this time." Translation: your drive is less than 3 percent fragmented.

If you don't receive this kind notice, start the defragmenting process and go get a latte. While Windows claims that the process can take as little as "a few minutes," I have yet to experience a defrag that takes less than 15 to 20 minutes.

Should you start a defragment and find that it's taking too long, or some other action needs to be performed immediately, all is not lost. The Cancel Defragmentation option is available throughout the process.

Modifying/canceling scheduled defragmentation. As mentioned earlier, it is possible to modify or cancel either the default defragmentation schedule or any other scheduled defragmentation. Assuming the user has administrative privileges, modification/cancellation can be achieved by the following steps:

1. Choose Start → Computer, right-click a disk, and choose Properties → Tools tab → Defragment Now. This displays the Disk Defragmenter dialog box, shown in Figure 11-16.
2. To *cancel* the automated defragmentation, clear the "Run on a schedule" box and then click OK twice to save changes.
3. To *modify* the defragmentation schedule, click the "Modify schedule" button, located to the right of the "Run on a schedule" box. Use the Modify Schedule dialog box to set the new run schedule. Within the schedule options, users can enter the How Often, What Day, and What Time dialogs to specify the appropriate run schedule options. When done, click OK twice to save changes.

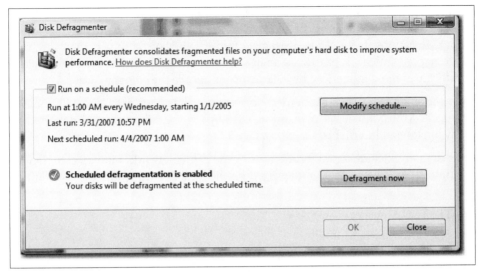

Figure 11-16. Running a scheduled defragmentation

Network Performance

For most administrators, network performance is the most difficult computing performance to govern, yet it is often the one factor that has the most impact on the user's experience.

First, know that many, many variables can influence network performance, such as:

- Physical components such as network cards, cables, switches, and routers
- Logical components such as protocols, authentication, and encryption
- Complimentary services such as Domain Name System (DNS), Dynamic Host Configuration Protocol (DHCP), WINS, and the Address Resolution Protocol (ARP)
- Applications that use the network, such as browsers and email programs

That's why entire books are devoted to network technologies; that's why entire certification tracks concern themselves with nothing other than getting data from point A to point B.

What's more, network performance is usually measured by looking at the network as a whole, and not at the performance of any one particular computer. In fact, one computer's *good* performance can sometimes means *bad* performance for the rest of the network.

If we limit our discussion to just the Vista machine, administrators will have the most direct influence over the network cards used and the security deployed for network connections. It would be extremely rare if either of these was the cause of a performance bottleneck on the company network. Overall network performance is usually much more influenced by what happens *outside* the company walls.

Even the slowest network cards used on Vista machines, for example, will transmit data at 11 Mbps, much faster than the 512 Kbps or 1.2 Mbps that are delivered by many broadband Internet connections.

Vista does not include a tool for monitoring the *entire* network, but you can monitor the traffic that is being sent and received on the local network card with one of two utilities:

- The Task Manager
- The Performance Monitor

These two tools serve as your primary means for gathering information about system performance. And once you know what's going on, of course, you can then take steps to improve performance.

Other Optimization Techniques

One of the nicest aspects of Vista is the number of "tweaks" users can make. Depending on the needs of both the user and system, users can optimize Vista to run for maximum performance.

Optimizing for application performance

While the more common applications do not have excessive requirements for performance, the higher-end, advanced applications are rather needy. The Aero application is at the front of the pack. With these high-demand applications, it is paramount that your entire system be designed with that goal in mind.

Adding more memory. Memory…if you've got it to spare, you never think about it. If you don't have enough, your system *constantly* reminds you of that fact.

Vista, in and of itself, weighs fairly heavily on your RAM. Add to the equation the weight of all running applications and the storage of excess program data in the pagefile on the hard drive, and you have a massive performance hindrance.

While in the midst of your normal activities, take a peek into the Available Memory display located in either the Task Manager or the System Monitor. If this number is getting low, a RAM upgrade might be just what the doctor ordered. ReadyBoost might help alleviate some of the processing strain, but this will need to be evaluated on a case-by-case basis.

Installing to the fastest hard drive. Failing to install to the fastest drive is, frankly, more common than you'd think. Now, we'll argue that it's only common among the average Joe user, not among admins, but it's easy to do.

Many systems have multiple hard drives installed. Those hard drives may have not only different storage sizes, but also different performance ratings. Vista will install to the default drive (usually C:) unless directed otherwise. So, ensure that your Vista install goes to the fastest drive by understanding the different specs of your drive array and then choosing the fastest as the install destination.

Several parameters govern hard drive performance, and different combinations of these will produce a hard drive of varying speeds. They are:

Bus
> Either Parallel or Serial ATA. You get a little more storage for your dollar from a Parallel ATA drive, but Serial ATA drives are a newer technology and generally perform a little better; they draw less power, are less susceptible to electromagnetic interference, and are faster.

Cache
> The amount of data held in the RAM of the drive. The more cache, the better; a Parallel ATA drive with 16 MB of cache is going to perform better than a Serial ATA drive with 2 MB.

Transfer rate
> The sheer amount of data the device is able to send out to the motherboard. The higher the transfer rate, the better. Drives today are capable of transferring 3 GB of data per second.

Access time
> How long it takes for the drive's read/write heads to locate, or access, a piece of data on the disk platters. The lower this is, the better.

Disk Revolutions Per Minute (RPM)
> The higher this number is, the better. A 7,200 RPM disk will perform faster than a 5,400 RPM disk, for example (and is usually more expensive). This measure usually influences the disk's transfer rate and access times.

Optimizing for program performance

It is also possible to optimize Windows Vista to run programs. This involves adjusting processor scheduling. When you adjust processor scheduling, your adjustments dictate how the computer will allocate processor priority between foreground and background tasks.

When optimizing for programs, this establishes priority with foreground tasks. While optimal program functioning is the goal of Vista (and the default for processor scheduling), the setting may have been changed in a number of different ways.

To ensure that your system is still set to prioritize for foreground programs:

1. Click Start, right-click Computer, and then select Properties → System window.

2. Click the Advanced System Settings link, enter your User Account Control credentials. In the System Properties dialog box, click the Advanced tab.

3. In the Performance group, click Settings to open the Performance Options dialog box.

4. Select the Advanced tab, as shown in Figure 11-17.

5. In the "Processor scheduling" group, activate the Programs option and click OK.

6. If you're told that the changes require a restart, click OK to open the System Properties dialog box. Then click OK again.

7. When prompted to restart, click Yes.

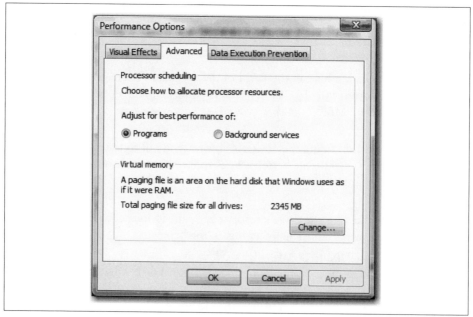

Figure 11-17. Optimizing Vista performance for applications

Setting the program priority in the Task Manager

While the overall performance of Vista is designed for program priority, there is a way to establish a higher priority for specific programs.

Vista, by default, not only assigns program priority, but also evaluates the frequency at which each program is used. Vista then assigns a base priority ranking to each program. Using this base priority ranking, Vista distributes processing power. If a program is used more frequently, that program is provided a higher base priority ranking and, consequently, will receive more turns with the processor (in a sort of "one for you, two for me" way).

Although Vista sets this base priority, it is possible to manually change that ranking. To do this, follow these steps:

1. Launch the program whose priority ranking you would like to alter.
2. Open the Task Manager and click the Processes tab.
3. Right-click the program to display its shortcut menu.
4. Click Set Priority, and then click either Realtime, which is the highest priority, High, or Above Normal, which is the lowest priority above the Normal setting.
5. Click OK.

You should be very judicious when setting a process to the Realtime priority setting. This can draw all processing attention to the Realtime process, and away from other important tasks such as writing a file to disk. Using Realtime on the wrong process can effectively crash your system.

Optimizing the hard disk

Vista calls upon your hard drive like no previous version of Windows. With Super-Fetch, increased use of pagefiles, and other such applications, optimizing the hard disk can result in drastic performance improvements.

New Vista Performance Tools

Within Vista, Microsoft has incorporated three new tools for improving disk drive performance. These tools are unlike anything ever incorporated in an operating system by Microsoft or, for that matter, by any other company.

Of course, new technology is usually associated with unforeseen complications. These new tools are no exception. Some members of the IT community have come out in strong opposition to Vista's incorporation of these tools. At the time of this writing, these issues are merely intellectual conjecture (and may amount to little more than the "Chicken Little Syndrome"), but I would be remiss in failing to discuss these new tools.

Thus, in this section we'll discuss:

Windows ReadyBoost
A performance-boosting tool that makes it possible for Windows to use external solid-state media including, but not limited to, USB flash drives as an additional source of system cache.

Windows ReadyDrive
Specific to mobile computers, a new hybrid disk drive that boosts performance by incorporating flash memory into normal drive function.

Windows SuperFetch
An updated version of XP's Prefetching that tracks program and data usage by user. It boosts performance by anticipating the data that might next be used and preloading it into the designated flash memory for immediate access.

Flash memory and performance

Traditional operating systems have always relied upon a computer's disk drives for storage/use of system cache and paging files. All of this changes with Vista.

Microsoft developers recognized that flash memory could be accessed much faster than normal disk drive data. The developers also understood the limitations of flash memory when it came to large, sequential input/output (I/O) data streams, as standard disk drives are superior for handling this type of data. However, the random I/O data handling is where flash memory makes its money.

Associating these attributes prompted Microsoft to incorporate flash memory for Vista in a number of unconventional ways. We discussed most of these new tools already, so here we're going to talk about how to tweak these tools to best meet your needs.

Windows ReadyBoost

As we already discussed, ReadyBoost in Vista uses a solid-state memory device as an additional source of system cache. Before enabling ReadyBoost on your system or network, there are a number of caveats to consider.

Before even getting to the Vista compatibility requirements for using a USB device for ReadyBoost, you should verify that the USB port is at least USB 2.0. Once you've ensured that the USB flash device is designated as Vista-compliant (Vista can't use just *any* device), you must ensure that the USB device has at least 512 MB of free space. The device can be no larger than 4 GB.

It's also important to note that if a USB device uses both fast and slow flash memory, Vista will utilize only the fast portion.

Should you or your client decide that ReadyBoost is a Vista feature you'd like to take advantage of, what next? I'm glad you asked!

Enabling ReadyBoost. Windows ReadyBoost is not enabled by default. If you want to incorporate ReadyBoost into your Vista environment, you must enable it by following these steps:

1. When you first insert your USB flash device, Vista will analyze the device for compliance and speed. If the device meets the ReadyBoost requirements, a dialog box will ask you how to handle it (see Figure 11-18). The AutoPlay prompt will also offer the option to "Speed up my System." If you want this device associated with this computer for ReadyBoost, select this option.

2. The Properties dialog box for the device will be displayed. After designating the amount of space you want Vista to use for ReadyBoost, click OK.

3. If you decide that you want to use the device in a different computer, all you need to do is right-click the drive icon for the device in Windows Explorer and select Properties. Then select the ReadyBoost tab. Now you will need to click on the option button labeled "Do not use this device," and then click OK. Remove the device and be prepared to start the process all over again the next time you plug the device into a Vista computer and want to use ReadyBoost. You can even plug the device into a computer with a legacy operating system and it will work just fine without any formatting of any kind.

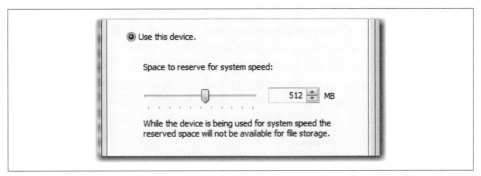

Figure 11-18. ReadyBoost technology

If your USB device is not ReadyBoost-compliant, there is no way to force the system to form that association. You either is or you ain't—there's no in-between.

Configuring ReadyBoost. So, let's assume that you and your USB device are members of the ReadyBoost club. Your next step is to establish a ReadyBoost setting for that device that best meets your needs. You can set the device configuration by following these steps:

1. Click Start → Computer.
2. Right-click the USB device and then select Properties.
3. Select the ReadyBoost tab and adjust the "Space to reserve for system speed" slider as desired; see Figure 11-19. (Any space not used for ReadyBoost can be used for other data.) Notice that toward the bottom of the dialog box in Figure 11-19 is a statement that reads "Windows recommends reserving 350 MB for optimal performance." The recommendation is based on what Vista can safely utilize without actually generating any extra system overhead. That would defeat the purpose of adding memory if it took more work to manage the memory than the system received from the memory.
4. Click OK to apply settings.

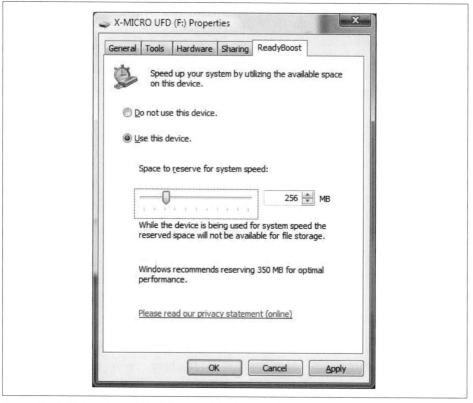

Figure 11-19. Using a removable drive to speed system performance

Ejecting a flash device that ReadyBoost is using. Now, according to Microsoft, you can safely remove a USB ReadyBoost device at any time. Even if you remove it accidentally, you should suffer no data loss because ReadyBoost merely serves as a faster cache of data that is also written to the hard disk. The data will remain intact, the system will remain functional, and the only effect will be a return to the performance level experienced prior to the device's removal.

This is the claim about which I am probably the most skeptical. I think everybody has seen an XP system freak out when a peripheral has changed. And this is just a peripheral, not a system-enhancing device.

So, choosing not to tempt Murphy's Law, I suggest these steps to remove the device:

1. Select a system viewer, such as Computer or Windows Explorer, that will show the device.

2. Right-click the device and then select Safely Remove.

3. Hold your breath, cross your fingers, close your eyes, pray to Hephaestus (the Greek God of technology)...OK, this last one is optional, but I know I'll be doing it.

Windows ReadyDrive

As we already discussed, Windows ReadyDrive is a new form of hybrid hard drive that has large amounts of Non-Volatile RAM (NVRAM) flash memory built into the drive itself. This memory acts as a cache of sorts, providing accelerated performance. This can speed up everything from boot-up and resume from various sleep states to better overall battery life (which is especially nice for laptop users). Hybrid hard drives should also be more reliable than their standard drive cousins, again because the moving parts won't need to spin so often.

You can implement this technology through what was almost a dead technology: the PCMCIA slots. The Personal Computer Memory Card Industry Association slots that were found on many legacy desktop systems nearly became extinct. Were it not for the digital camera craze of the early 1990s, the PCMCIA slots that are now on nearly every laptop computer might be the location of a sleek "coffee cup" holder. The PCMCIA slots, specifically the type III slots, are the target home for the new ReadyDrive technology.

While these drives will be backward-compatible with any other operating system (barring a change of heart by the drive manufacturers), Vista supports this technology by default with nothing to enable, add, or configure.

 Both the Basic Input/Output System (BIOS) and socket services of the mobile computer will need to support ReadyDrive technology. Look for such systems to hit the shelves sometime in the middle of 2007.

Windows SuperFetch

As we already discussed, Vista improves system performance by changing the I/O priority of main processes and background processes. In XP, all processes were assigned equal prioritization, oftentimes leading to a bottleneck for memory access requests and subsequent performance lags. Vista solves this internal battle by implementing priority assignments for memory access requests: high-priority I/O (user process and application read/write to physical drives) and low-priority I/O queues (background read/write to physical drives). Vista implements this I/O prioritization via a new data management algorithm called SuperFetch.

Previous versions of Windows have used data management algorithms. Prefetching, introduced in XP, was a data management algorithm that monitored and anticipated future data use, loading the anticipated data into memory before the actual request was made. While it was a wonderful technology at the time, SuperFetch leaves it in its wake.

Unlike prior memory management algorithms, SuperFetch optimizes memory usage based on user-specific activity. Cool... that's about all I can say.

Performance optimization considerations

Perhaps the most innovative technology introduced with Windows Vista is the integration of flash memory into the core activities of the operating system for the purpose of enhanced performance. These enhancements take form in a new data-access system within the operating system itself, as well as new data storage hardware that may be employed within the operating system.

According to Microsoft, these enhancements—Windows ReadyBoost and hybrid hard disk drives with Windows ReadyDrive technology—produce drastic improvements in Vista's global performance. A viral video is on the Web that shows a Windows Vista machine during startup. According to the creator of this video, and as shown in the video, the normal startup duration for his Vista system is 43 seconds, whereas the startup time with ReadyBoost is a mere 14 seconds. While we all know that video can easily be manipulated, this differential is reflective of Microsoft's claims.

The big question, however, is whether this technology is a good thing. Sure, everybody wants increased quality of performance, but what is the cost of reliance upon flash technology to achieve this goal? A significant number of folks in the tech industry believe that the risk is too high. While a number of arguments have been made (and there will undoubtedly be more), the crux of most antiflash claims is the following: flash memory, even NVRAM flash memory, just doesn't have the durability or reliability for incorporation into the operating system or hard drive environments, and to do so is inviting disaster.

I have yet to decide how I feel about this, but it is important for you as an administrator to consider this argument before deploying, or advising clients to deploy, any of these Vista features. Data stability is at the core of all computing activity—nobody wants to work in an environment where work is likely to be lost at any time. However, as we all know, balancing data stability with user satisfaction is half the battle. Whether the leap is justified should be evaluated on a case-by-case basis.

The Windows Experience Index

We saw this before in Chapter 6. I'll provide a brief review here.

During Vista's initial setup time, your computer is being subjected to a sort of technology performance boot camp. It is being prodded with a number of processing hurdles, and if it can complete all of the tasks presented, Vista will then assign separate scores for each of five component areas to your system in addition to the overall PC score.

 This isn't terribly important unless you're building Vista systems for a living, but the performance hurdles have a name: the Windows System Assessment Tool, or WinSAT, which is what determines your WEI system score. It runs in the background when you click the Refresh Now button in the Performance Information and Tools Control Panel application.

This overall score will be equal to the lowest component score…we're only as strong as our weakest link and such. The five component areas are as follows: Processor (CPU), System RAM, Hard Drive subsystem, Video Card Processor & Drivers, and Dedicated Video RAM.

As of now, the highest possible score is 5.9, with a range between 1 and 5.9.

Sleep

Also discussed in detail in Chapter 6, this is a whole new Sleep. Again, a brief recap is in order.

With Vista, Standby and Hibernate as we know them are primarily replaced with a new power management mode called Sleep. While it is still possible to enable Hibernate, the new Sleep combines the best features of Standby and Hibernate and, according to Microsoft, is more reliable than Standby ever was.

The new Sleep state is the default power management mode on Vista notebooks. After "shutting down" into the Sleep state, the system resumes normal function in a mere two to three seconds—that's right, two to three seconds. If the system sits in Sleep long enough, it will enter the old-fashioned Hibernate automatically before the battery dies.

So, Vista is more efficient in its energy usage, quicker in resuming functionality from Sleep, and more reliable in its function.

Command-Line Administration

For some, typing commands into a computer conjures up images of 1980s-era computing and the movie *WarGames*, in which people had to set a phone earpiece on a cradle in order to communicate on the Net.

And although typing at a Command Prompt is certainly done less today than it was years ago, there are still some legitimate reasons why an administrator would want to use typed commands to get a computer to do what he wants it to do. Already in this book, you've seen many examples of how tasks carried out through the GUI can also be performed using the Command Prompt. And one of the reasons some administrators prefer the Command Prompt, believe it or not, is speed.

Not so much the speed at which you can type commands, mind you, but rather the speed at which the commands are carried out. It takes far less to process a string of text than to paint a picture on a screen and present a GUI.

Another reason for the Command Prompt is because sometimes certain tasks performed at the command line just can't be done any other way.

Also, some legacy programs require a Command Prompt. If this is the case for you, the pointers in this section will be a big help.

Using the Command Prompt

You can't take advantage of the command environment, though, unless you first know how to open it. We've seen instructions throughout this title when detailing specific tasks, but just to review, you can use any of these methods to begin a command session:

- Type **comm** at the Start menu. The Command Prompt should appear at the top of your programs list.
- Choose Start → All Programs → Accessories → Command Prompt.
- Choose Start → Run to open the Run dialog box, type **cmd** in the Open box, and then press Enter.
- Double-click the CMD icon in your *\System32* folder.
- Double-click any shortcut you create for the *cmd.exe* utility.

 There are actually two command environments. If you type **command** at the Run menu, you open a command window, but it won't be the Vista Command Prompt. More on this later.

No matter what method you choose, you'll see a Command Prompt window like the one in Figure 11-20.

```
C:\Windows\system32\cmd.exe                                    _ □ ×
Microsoft Windows [Version 6.0.6000]
Copyright (c) 2006 Microsoft Corporation.  All rights reserved.

C:\Users\Abby - Business User>
```

Figure 11-20. The Command Prompt awaits

What's more, administrators can open an unlimited number of Command Prompt sessions simultaneously. Vista opens each one in its own memory space. This gives the administrator the ability to perform multiple concurrent tasks without the fear of one task crashing and subsequently interrupting all other tasks.

Contrast this behavior with the behavior of programs such as Microsoft Word, or utilities such as Parental Controls. You can have several documents open in Word, for example, but if one encounters a problem and needs to close, it takes the others down with it. The entire app shuts down. And with Parental Controls, you can have only one instance open at a time. It's impossible to conduct reporting on two accounts at once, for instance.

To open additional Command Prompt windows:

1. From the Command Prompt, type **start** and press Enter.

That's it. There is no second step. (Additionally, any of the methods listed earlier work just as well.)

Closing the Command Prompt

There are three ways to close the Command Prompt:

- Type **exit** and then press Enter.
- Click the Close button (the X).
- Use the Control menu in the Command Prompt window's upper-left corner. It's the little icon that looks like the Start menu Command Prompt icon.

Note that the steps just listed merely close the command session. Usually, whatever is running within has had time to execute the command and commit any changes, but some legacy applications running in a Command Prompt window require that you quit the *program* before quitting the Command Prompt *window*. If you don't take this step, you might lose unsaved data in the DOS program.

Vista does include behavior to combat this occurrence, however. If you try to close the Command Prompt window without first closing the DOS program, a dialog box should appear asking if you really want to end the program.

The executables: cmd.exe and command.com

As you saw earlier, two command environments are included with Windows Vista. I'll list them here using their executable filenames: *cmd.exe* and *command.com*.

So what's the big, fat difference? In a word, it's Windows NT. Here's the quick rundown.

Windows NT was developed to exist entirely separately from the Disk Operating System (DOS), Microsoft's first operating system. Meanwhile, the operating systems that Microsoft is most famous for—Windows 3.*x*, 95, 98, and Me—were essentially graphical shells that executed DOS commands behind the scenes.

And while both utilities—Command.com and Cmd.exe—are command environments (they process text instructions), Cmd.exe is the Windows NT tool, the one that launches when you open the Command Prompt from the Start menu, and is thus the one we focus on here.

Command.com, on the other hand, is the 16-bit version of DOS that is launched in a virtual machine. It's included for backward compatibility with older MS-DOS text-interface programs running in compatibility mode. You cannot run a 32-bit program in a Command.com window.

In fact, when using Command.com, the program that actually runs is NTVDM.exe, the NT Virtual DOS Machine. Unlike Cmd.exe, a failure in one NTVDM program *will* affect all other programs running in the Virtual Machine.

So how will you know the difference? Again, Cmd.exe is the default method for passing text instructions to the Windows Vista kernel, and will be launched using almost any method of browsing around the computer, including the Start menu. Command.com is not listed there. You sort of have to *look* for Command.com.

Another difference between the two command processors, this one easily recognizable, is that only Cmd.exe understands long filenames. Notice in Figure 11-21 that the 16-bit Command.com can deal with only DOS 8.3 naming conventions. Directory names such as "Users\Abby – Business User" are therefore truncated into DOS-digestible "B~1."

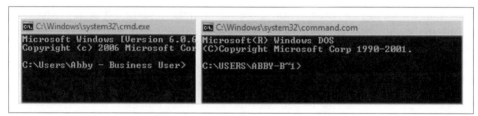

Figure 11-21. Note how Command.com handles long directory or filenames

So, because Cmd.exe is the default and is the 32-bit version of Vista's command environment, the rest of this section deals with Cmd.exe. In fact, not everything detailed here even works with the older Command.com.

Command Prompt Usage

With very little additional know-how, your Command Prompt can prove to be a valuable time-saving utility.

Before we get started with examples, one feature alone can make the Command Prompt less intimidating because it reduces the amount of typing you'll do: it's called AutoComplete. Many users have experience with this feature in other programs such as Excel and Word. At the Command Prompt, AutoComplete has the same purpose.

Using AutoComplete

Know before reading another word that the feature just introduced isn't really called AutoComplete. AutoComplete is just what the feature *does*. In Command Prompt terminology, this feature is called File and Directory Name Completion (FDNC). See why I used AutoComplete instead?

At any rate, you don't have to worry about enabling this feature; FDNC is turned on by default. This allows you to start typing the start of your text string, and then use the Tab key to scroll through an AutoComplete list. It will then offer to complete your typing based on the text you've started to type.

For example, a user launching the Vista Command Prompt will open to her own user directory location by default (*C:Users\username*). This directory contains several sub-folders, some of which start with the letter *d*:

- Desktop
- Documents
- Downloads

To see FDNC behavior in action, type the **cd** command (for Change Directory) and then press the Tab key.

You should see the Desktop, Documents, and Downloads folders, in that order, completed for you. Now press Enter, and you have just changed the working directory to *C:\Downloads* with a minimum amount of typing.

Note, however, that AutoComplete makes suggestions based on the contents of the current directory. If you were in the *C:* root directory trying to do the same thing, the preceding steps wouldn't work (unless you did have folders under the *C:* drive called Desktop, Documents, and Downloads, that is).

The Command Prompt buffer

Another huge timesaver when it comes to typing at the Command Prompt is something known as the Command Prompt buffer, which stores a list of recently typed commands, keeping even the ones you've mistyped.

Using the buffer is easy: you just use the up and down arrow keys. When you reach the desired command, press Enter to execute it again. Needless to say, this can be a huge timesaver when repeating a command such as the following:

```
net use z: \\beanlakeone\writing_projects /u:brianculp.beanlake.com password
```

The preceding command maps a drive to a share called *writing_projects* on a server called *beanlakeone*. If you need to reconnect, just press the up arrow key and then Enter.

What's more, you can change the behavior of the Command Prompt buffer by clicking the Control Menu icon and choosing Properties from the menu. The Command Prompt buffer is governed by three selections from the Options screen:

Buffer Size
Click the spin box to specify the number of commands you can access again with the up and down arrow keys.

Number of Buffers
Specify the number of command history buffers to use.

Discard Old Duplicates
With this enabled, the history buffers work more efficiently by not saving duplicate commands. This setting is disabled by default, however.

To commit changes, click OK in the Properties dialog box. The Cmd.exe utility remembers the setting changes the next time you launch.

 There are many other Command Prompt options, of course, and most are accessible from the same Properties dialog box as the one you've just seen. Much is self-explanatory, and none is terribly functional. If you want to increase the font size used, for example, use the options on the Font tab. It won't change how the commands are processed.

Using the Clipboard

Because it's a Vista application, the Command Prompt can also take full advantage of the Windows Clipboard. You can use this to import a command that has been emailed, for example, or it can help generate output to be manipulated further in another program.

Either way, just follow these steps:

1. Choose the Control menu, point to Edit, and then click Mark. (Alternatively, you can right-click the title bar of the Command Prompt window to access the same menu.)

2. The cursor changes from a blinking underscore to a blinking box. Click the beginning of the text you want to copy. You can also navigate using the arrow keys.

3. Now, just click and drag to select the text you want to work with. You can also hold down the Shift key, and then click the end of the text, or use the arrow keys.

4. Right-click the title bar, and either point to Edit and then Copy, or just press Enter.

The text is now on the Clipboard. To use it, just employ the target application's Paste command. In most Windows apps, this means the Ctrl-V keyboard combination.

The reverse of this is even easier. To paste Clipboard text from another application into the Command Prompt:

1. Position the mouse somewhere in the active Command Prompt window and right-click.

2. Choose Paste from the shortcut menu. You can also just use the Control menu.

That's it! The text is now inserted at the Command Prompt's insertion point.

Quick Edit Mode

And there's an even easier way to copy and paste text. It's called Quick Edit Mode. When enabled, you can select text by simply clicking and dragging over a line instead of using the Mark command first.

Quick Edit Mode is not enabled by default, however. To turn it on, open the Command Prompt's Properties dialog box using one of the methods described earlier, and then turn on Quick Edit Mode with a single click.

 You can have both the Insert Mode and the Quick Edit Mode enabled at the same time.

Once you're familiar with a few Command Prompt basics, getting started with administrative tasks is just a few keystrokes away. To give you a feel for how Command Prompt administration is done, I'll introduce two common utilities, providing correct syntax and usage for each.

Command Prompt Administration

Administrators do things such as add users, change accounts, set passwords, create groups, and so on. We've seen already in this book how to perform tasks such as these using the graphical tools.

But the Command Prompt is available as well. Two commands in particular are handy when the job calls for scripting user and group chores. They are:

- NET USER
- NET LOCALGROUP

As long as you are able to run the Command Prompt in Administrative mode, you can unlock a number of administrative possibilities, performing almost any necessary account task. In addition to those mentioned earlier, you can also add and remove users from groups.

The NET USER command

First we'll look at NET USER, which is probably one of the most often-used administrator Command Prompt utilities.

You use the NET USER command to add users, set account passwords, disable/remove accounts, and set miscellaneous account options such as network availability.

It uses the following syntax:

```
NET USER [username [password | * | /RANDOM] [/ADD] [/DELETE] [options]]
```

Table 11-1 explains each part of this general usage syntax.

Table 11-1. NET USER switches

Switch	Description
Username	The account name you want to add or work with. If you run NET USER with only the name of an existing user, the command displays the user's account data.
Password	The password assigned to the user. You can use the asterisk (*) to have Vista prompt you for the password. You can also use the /RANDOM switch when setting up an account; Vista then assigns a random strong password of eight characters containing letters, numbers, and symbols. This random password is then displayed on the console.
/ADD	Creates a new user account.
/DELETE	Deletes the specified user account.
Options	Lets the administrator specify additional account options.

Options that you can further specify with the NET USER command include the following:

/ACTIVE:{YES | NO}
: Specifies whether the newly created account is active or disabled.

/EXPIRES:{*date* | NEVER}
: Sets the date (expressed in the system's Short Date format) at which the account expires.

/HOMEDIR:*path*
: Lets you specify a home directory folder for the user. It should be a subfolder within *%SystemDrive%\Users*.

/PASSWORDCHG:{YES | NO}
: Specifies whether the user is allowed to change his password.

/PASSWORDREQ:{YES | NO}
: Configures whether the user is required to have a password.

/PROFILEPATH:*path*
: Sets the user's profile directory.

/SCRIPTPATH:*path*
: Sets the user's logon script directory.

/TIMES:{*times* | ALL}
: Sets the times of day when the user is allowed to log on. Some examples follow:

- M-F,3am-1pm
- M,W,F,07:00-15:00
- Sa,4pm-6pm;Su,2pm-7pm

But wait. That's all well and good if I want to use the NET USER command, but what if I want to use a different Command Prompt utility such as NET USE instead of NET USER? Where's the reference section for that?

Good news; it's already in the Command Prompt, waiting to provide guidance. If you know what to do, you can pull up a list of commands such as the one I just showed you without having to remember where they're located in some book.

The most valuable lesson you can take from any discussion of the Command Prompt, then, is how to get help. There are just too many commands, and switches, and arguments that can be combined in countless ways for this or any other book to detail them all.

Fortunately, it's not that hard to access the built-in help. Just type the following at the end of any command:

```
/?
```

So, let's say you want to use NET USE in order to script a connection to a network share at logon time. To get the exact syntax, just enter this:

```
Net use /?
```

An online help tutorial then displays, looking much like the example I just gave regarding NET USE. This is known as the utility's online help, and this help should include all of the switches that are available, along with examples of proper syntax for each.

Furthermore, you can even type **help** at the Command Prompt all by itself. Why do this? Maybe you've forgotten a command, or you are simply wondering whether a command-line utility is available for the job. Typing **help** with no arguments displays a list of all the internal commands and utilities provided with Vista, as shown in Figure 11-22.

And with that knowledge in hand, you could then figure out the purpose and syntax of the NET LOCALGROUP command on your own. You can probably guess its job: it creates and manages groups on the local Vista computer. As you'll learn in more detail in Chapter 12, these groups are used to control access to resources.

The NET LOCALGROUP command

But just to save you a trip to the Command Prompt, here's what you would see if you're running the NET LOCALGROUP /? command. Its correct syntax reads like this:

```
NET LOCALGROUP [group name1 [name2 ...] {/ADD | /DELETE}
```

Table 11-2 lists the switches and their descriptions.

Figure 11-22. A list of all of Vista's internal help utilities

Table 11-2. Syntax of the NET LOCALGROUP utility

Switch	Description
group	The name of the security group with which you want to work
name1 [name2 ...]	The username(s) to add or delete, separated by spaces
/ADD	Adds the user or users to the group
/DELETE	Removes the user or users from the group

So why use NET LOCALGROUP instead of the Computer Management console for your group management tasks?

Again, scripting comes to mind, but there's another case in which the Command Prompt trumps its graphical equivalent: speed over the network. If you're connecting remotely to a system, conducting command-line administration is often much faster than doing the same with the graphical equivalents.

But no matter where or how you use the Command Prompt, remember: help on using the utility is just a question mark (?) away.

Summary

In this chapter, we covered ways to keep that "new computer feeling" going strong throughout your system's life span. To that end, we noted many new Vista technologies that help us get the best performance possible.

We touched on ways to measure performance with tools such as the Task Manager and the Reliability and Performance Monitor, talked about how to make sure the disk drive is defragmented automatically, and covered how to keep the hard disk free of unwanted files.

Along the way, we saw many new performance-enhancing technologies, such as hybrid drives and ReadyBoost, which should make computing on a Vista machine a speedier experience than ever. Also, we covered one potential performance booster that is often overlooked: the Command Prompt.

In the next chapter, we move into another key area of Vista administration: securing the computer. That chapter will help make sure that you're actually able to take advantage of the performance boosts presented in this chapter. In other words, it will help ensure that you don't have a hard disk that is really, really fast, but is currently being hacked by a data thief.

CHAPTER 12

Securing the Vista Environment

In this chapter, we will look at security in Microsoft Vista.

Rather than just jump in and describe everything you need to do to secure your Vista system, I first explain the security "big picture." This includes a discussion of the kinds of threats that exist "out there" that could impact your system. It doesn't happen just to other people; it could happen to you, too.

Security isn't just about configuration—passwords, antivirus, and such. It's also about your behavior—how you use your computer and the risks you bring upon yourself as you use it. A momentary lapse in good judgment can result in catastrophic damage that no technology on your computer can prevent.

Security doesn't only mean protection from bad people. Sometimes bad things just happen. A software or hardware malfunction (whether as a result of a bug or of unintended or unanticipated interaction) can cause events that lead to the disclosure of—or damage to—your information. Also, a user malfunction, what is sometimes known as a PEBCAC (Problem Exists Between Computer And Chair) error, can produce the same results. (Try dropping the word *PEBCAC* during a dinner conversation; it's a *great* way to cut short a bad date.)

Why You Need Security

You need security because your data is important; because it represents hours upon hours of hard work; because it represents your livelihood, or, in the case of a corporate network, the livelihood of many others.

You need security because bad things can and will happen to your information, and to your computer, unless you make a concerted effort to protect them. And ultimately, this is *your* responsibility. No one else is going to do it for you.

And even though Vista proves to be a powerful ally in keeping information safe, it still cannot do *everything* to protect your information. This is not because of any specific design flaw or bug in Vista, but because of the nature of computers and information. In other words, it's not *possible* for an operating system such as Vista—or for any other operating system, for that matter—to do a perfect job of safeguarding your information.

We'll start by examining a few important data security concepts.

CIA: Confidentiality, Integrity, and Availability

At the conceptual level, security is concerned with three things in relation to an information system (in this case, your Vista machine): confidentiality, integrity, and availability. In the security profession, this is known as CIA. Let's look at these concepts in more detail:

Confidentiality
> This involves the protection of information and services so that only authorized and intended persons may view or access it.

Integrity
> This concerns the protection of information and services from unauthorized and improper modification.

Availability
> Information and services need to be available, or there when they are wanted.

Everything in information security leads back to these three principles. Frequently in this chapter I will reference these concepts in discussions of specific configurations, measures, and behaviors that are needed to ensure that your information and your system are safe.

Threats

Merriam Webster's Online Dictionary defines *threat* as "an expression of intention to inflict evil, injury, or damage" and "an indication of something impending." In the context of computers (including those running Vista), this translates to a number of real-life scenarios that you need to be aware of.

Malware

Malware is the collective term that means viruses, Trojan horses, worms, spyware, key loggers, and rootkits. The following list describes these in more detail:

Viruses

These are computer code fragments that attach themselves to working programs in your computer. Viruses contain instructions that activate when you start the program to which a virus is attached. The program may or may not perform its expected function, but meanwhile, the virus code *will* perform its intended function—which may be destroying information, harvesting information, altering settings on your computer, emailing copies of itself to everyone on your address book, and (of course) propagating to other files on your computer and other computers. Viruses are among the oldest types of malware in existence.

Trojan horses

Like the old Greek legend, a Trojan horse is a way of describing a program that is purported to perform one function, but that actually does something else. An example of a Trojan horse is an attractive screensaver that instead steals information from your hard drive and sends it to the Trojan's owner without your knowledge. Trojan horses require human intervention to activate and spread.

Worms

This type of malware attempts to copy itself to other computers on a network. Requiring no human intervention, a worm can rapidly spread and cause widespread disruption, partly because of its effect on infected computers, and because of the potential flood of network traffic it produces as it tries to spread. The Slammer worm of 2003, for example, doubled in size every 8.5 seconds and infected 75,000 systems less than 10 minutes after the start of the attack.

Spyware

This is an entire class of malware, all designed to collect personal information without consent. Spyware often does not itself have the necessary instructions to further its own spread; instead, spyware is implanted on computers one at a time, (usually) through email and web sites.

Key loggers

These take two forms, hardware and software. Hardware versions are small devices that usually plug inline with a computer's keyboard. It's difficult to get these through email or a web site (unless you agree to purchase one by those means). Most key loggers are of the software variety. Either way, a key logger records your keystrokes (some also record mouse movements and clicks) and sends them back to its owner (not you, but the malicious person who is operating it). Key loggers are used to capture login information for high-value web sites and applications such as online banking and other financial transaction sites.

Rootkits

These newer and nastier forms of malware are designed to hide themselves and be nearly (if not completely) impossible to detect. Rootkits are often propagated the same way as other forms of malware, but they implant themselves in ways that help them avoid detection.

Today there are well over 100,000 variants of viruses, not counting Trojan horses and the rest. Viruses got their start in PCs in the early 1980s, and every year since then the rate of production has increased dramatically. Today thousands of new virus variants are released every month. It's no wonder that most antivirus programs configure themselves to update at least once per day!

How malware spreads

The broad category of malware signifies the computer code that can get into your computer by various means and cause damage in a number of ways, including:

File sharing
> This includes the use of formal file-sharing programs such as Kazaa, BitTorrent, and LimeWire, as well as ad hoc file sharing such as when people download files from web sites or FTP servers, and even when one person gives files to another.

Email
> Unquestionably the most popular means for transporting data, email has become a common way to exchange information among people and organizations. Malware can propagate through email between persons who unknowingly send files that are infected with it.

Spam
> It doesn't matter anymore how spam got its name. Everyone knows that spam is the horde of unwanted and unsolicited email that now accounts for more than 90 percent of all email messages on the Internet.*

Instant messaging
> Popular IM programs such as MSN Messenger, Yahoo! IM, AOL Instant Messenger, and Google Talk have file transfer capabilities that can be used to propagate malware. There have also been some IM "worms" that self-propagate through users' IM programs, jumping from computer to computer.

Visiting web sites
> Embedding malware right on web pages or web sites is a very popular means of spreading it. A web site contains some scripting code that will attempt to perform some unauthorized (and usually hidden) action on your computer. There are two ways in which this malware will get into the web site: first, the web site operator may have set up the web site with the purpose of spreading malware; second, an honest web site operator may have had a vulnerability in his web site that permitted a hacker to break in and implant malware on it without his knowledge or permission.

---

* An article in the IT security web site Dark Reading on January 10, 2007, claims that spam accounted for more than 94 percent of all email, according to a spokesperson from Postini, a well-known spam-blocking service provider.

Installing software

Sometimes a new software program that you would install on your computer will have, in addition to the program that you intended to install, one or more pieces of malware. Like web sites, sometimes this is deliberate, and sometimes a hacker is able to get his malware into a commercial company's software distribution, resulting in malware being distributed in that company's CDs and downloads. This is rare, but it does happen.

I discuss the detection and elimination of malware later in this chapter.

Theft of information

Sometimes (but not always) the result of malware, information theft is one of the most serious threats today. Persons with ill intent may target you personally, or you as a worker in a specific organization, and use any of several means available to steal information from your computer. These include:

Malware

See the earlier discussion.

Breaking into your computer through a wireless connection

An intruder might try to break into your computer through an unsecured wireless network.

Stealing your desktop or laptop computer

This is pretty easy to do; more than 100,000 laptops are stolen in the United States every year.

Breaking into your high-value accounts

Intruders often try to break into online user accounts in order to steal information or money.

Stealing paper documents

Sufficiently motivated, your would-be thief might consider going through your trash or breaking into your place of work or residence. This is a good reason to get a shredder, eh?

Some of this goes way beyond the scope of Vista, and even computing in general. But I'm a big-picture thinker and I think you ought to be as well, even if just once in a while.

Sabotage

Individuals may be intent on damaging your information. As we discussed in the preceding section on theft, many of the same means can be used for sabotage. Be on your guard.

Accidental events

Things can and do go wrong. But in case you think we're getting off-track, remember that I'm talking about CIA—confidentiality, integrity, and availability. Security is designed to ensure these goals and protect your system from whatever threat. Accidents are part and parcel to the story.

Here are just a few of the calamities that can threaten the CIA of your information:

Hardware failure
Hard drives can and do fail.

Software malfunction
Whether it's with the OS or an application program, sometimes unexpected things happen and your data is destroyed. This can be the result of a software bug, or an unexpected interaction between two or more programs, or an untested configuration.

User error
You might accidentally damage or erase important data, or forget an encryption password, rendering your information safe—even from you.

Physical damage
You could drop your computer, spill a drink or other liquid on it, or even leave it on the roof of your car. It could be knocked over or fall from a height. There are floods, tornadoes, hurricanes…you get the idea here.

Accidental loss
You left your computer somewhere, but where?

You can probably think of many more. I discuss several strategies for protecting your information against these events later in the chapter.

Vulnerabilities

If you are reading this chapter in linear order and your head is spinning from all of the preceding talk of threats, hang on for a bit longer as I complete the picture by discussing common data vulnerabilities.

Software vulnerabilities

The primary set of vulnerabilities that we need to worry about is software vulnerabilities. I'm not just talking bugs here; there's more to it than that. Software vulnerabilities include:

Unsecured configuration
> Vista ships with most software configurations set for more-secure operation, but partly this depends on what you do on your computer or in your company. Microsoft can't please everyone or magically autoconfigure your computer to be "most secure" for your individual or company needs. To its credit, Microsoft is getting better about disabling less-safe features, but we live in an imperfect world. Administrators should be aware at least of what the most secure configurations are.

Software design vulnerability
> While less common than in earlier years, a flaw in the design of software may be discovered that could lead to a serious weakness. An example of this is the original Telnet and FTP protocols, which transmitted unencrypted usernames and passwords. Another example of this is something known as a *SQL injection attack*. Programmers did not anticipate such an attack, although they are commonplace today.

Software bug
> Even well-designed software programs may have flaws in their source code that permit unsafe actions given the right conditions or inputs. An example of a software bug is a program that does not properly filter out SQL injection attacks (to continue the example from the preceding point).

Hardware vulnerabilities

Akin to software vulnerabilities, flaws in design or manufacturing processes can result in hardware that is prone to problems. A few examples are:

Electrical problems
> This includes things such as defective or downright unsafe batteries, wiring defects, and bad power supplies. You get the idea.

Faulty components
> From motherboards that crack to keys that stop working, many things can and do go wrong here.

I won't belabor the point of hardware defects here, but again, cautious admins should keep their ears to the ground. Why can hardware vulnerabilities place data at risk? Let's just say that a laptop whose battery is on fire is not exactly a safe haven for your novel.

User issues

You know, the person attached to the keyboard. Us. Briefly, we are capable of making mistakes (please send me an email if you know anyone who hasn't), either because we don't understand how a particular piece of hardware or software is supposed to be used, or because we type something in like FORMAT C: or DEL /S /Q /F C:*.* without thinking about what we're doing.

Now that I've mapped out threats and vulnerabilities, let's get started with the real focus of the chapter: how to configure Vista to ensure the most secure environment possible.

Security Features in Vista

Security has progressively improved with each version of Windows. Vista has a number of welcome changes that I describe here. We'll start with a mention of one of the most significant security changes, the User Account Control feature. Its full discussion occurs in other chapters.

User Account Control

Something you probably noticed within the first five minutes of using Vista is User Account Control. Generally speaking, this new mechanism prompts you to approve every operation that makes a change that will affect all users of the machine.

If you have permission to perform the task, Vista will still stop and ask whether you want to do this. You'll see a pop-up window such as the one in Figure 12-1.

Figure 12-1. With User Account Control, even the local admin must confirm privileged operations

If you don't have the necessary privileges to perform the operation, Vista demands more credentials, as shown in Figure 12-2.

Figure 12-2. User Account Control requires regular users to provide credentials if they want to perform privileged functions

There are several good reasons for this, including:

Making sure you're sure
> This prevents accidental changes by making you think twice about what you intend to do (provided you do think about it and you don't just blindly click OK).

Making sure it's you
> If some piece of malware is trying to perform a privileged operation, it's gonna generate one of these pop ups. If it's not you, you'll want to click Cancel and figure out what's going on (did you just download and launch a freeware program that was only supposed to tell you your horoscope?).

Like seatbelts, User Account Control will slow you down a little bit, but someday it's going to save your life. Well, maybe just your data.

Disabling User Account Control

If you want to live on the wild side and do away with those User Account Control pop ups, you can disable them. Here's how to do it:

1. Open the Control Panel. There are lots of ways to do that. Pick your favorite.

2. Select User Accounts.

3. Select "Turn User Account Control on or off" (if it's on, you'll have to give yourself permission one last time).

4. Uncheck "Use User Account Control (UAC) to help protect your computer."

5. Click OK.

There, you're now climbing without a safety rope.

User and Group Accounts

The single most important aspect of information security is controlling and knowing who has access to a system. Often, the only things between an unauthorized person and desired information are a user ID and password—two simple strings of characters. It makes sense to get a little creative about the composition of the user ID and password to ensure that an outsider cannot reach the information you need to protect.

First, a few principles; if you learn *nothing else* in this book, learn these principles. They are vital, and they apply universally to information systems, not just your new Vista system.

Use strong passwords
> Don't use easily guessed passwords that others might know.

Do not share your user account with others
> User accounts are secure only if one person is able to use the account.

Do not write down your passwords
> Well, OK, maybe you do need to write them down so that you do not forget them. If you do, keep those passwords locked away.

Use separate accounts for each user
> If you are in a work or home setting where several people use a single computer, create a separate user account for each user, and make sure every user account has a password. There are some good reasons why users should have their own accounts:
>
> - Each user will have her own session and user cookies. This will prevent users from seeing each other's email and other sensitive information.
> - Each user will have her own preferences that she can set without adversely affecting other users.
> - Each user's Documents folder is kept separate from others, enabling the privacy that each may expect.

Later in the chapter, I discuss good ways to keep your passwords reliably locked away but readily available when needed.

Standard Versus Administrator Users

Windows Vista still distinguishes between standard users and administrators. Let's dig in a little more and see what this means.

Standard users

Standard users are able to perform everyday functions on the computer, including (but not necessarily limited to):

- Starting programs
- Connecting to the Internet
- Sending and receiving email
- Using a web browser and surfing the Net
- Opening and closing gadgets
- Creating, working with, moving, and removing documents and files
- Changing wallpaper and many other appearance settings
- Playing and burning CDs and DVDs
- Connecting a Bluetooth device
- Printing
- Shutting down and restarting the computer

Even if you are a power user, this probably meets your needs most of the time. More important, on a shared computer, most users will be fine with the *Standard User* role.

Administrator users

Administrators can perform all of the *Standard User* functions, as well as the following:

- Changing security settings
- Installing patches
- Running Windows Update and Microsoft Update
- Installing software and hardware
- Accessing all of the files on the computer
- Adding, changing, and removing user accounts

When you first set up Vista, the first user account that you set up is an Administrator account. However, Microsoft rightly recommends that you use a *Standard user* account for your everyday computer use.

Some power users frequently change computer settings and perform other activities that require Administrator user privileges. Prior to Vista, power users really had to stay logged into their Administrator accounts all day long. But with Vista, even power users can run as Standard users and provide the necessary password when installing software or performing other privileged actions.

Creating an Account

Microsoft strongly recommends that every person who uses your computer needs her own user account. Follow this procedure to set up a user account.

1. Open the Control Panel. Click on "Add or remove user accounts." The Manage Accounts window will appear, showing you the user accounts that already exist on your computer. See Figure 12-3.

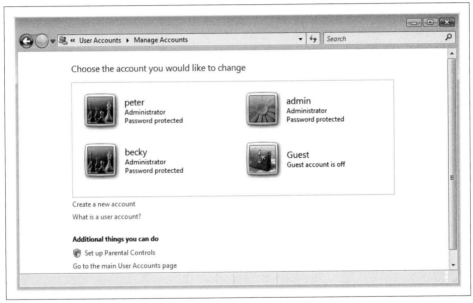

Figure 12-3. These are the users on your Vista system

2. Click "Create a new account." A new window will appear, as in Figure 12-4.

3. Type in the user ID in the field provided. Windows presumes the new account should be a standard user versus an administrator. Select Administrator only if the user will be managing hardware and security settings. Click the Create Account button. You will be returned to the Manage Accounts window, and you'll see the new user among those listed.

4. Next, you need to set a password for the user account. Click the new account; the Change an Account window will appear.

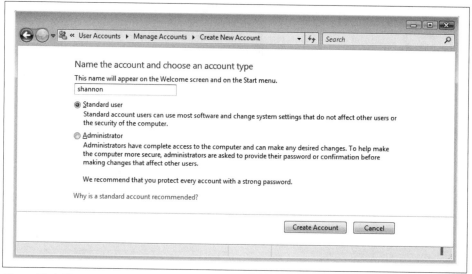

Figure 12-4. You are creating a new user account

5. Click "Create a password." The Create Password window will appear.

6. Type in the new password in the password fields. Also, you can type in a password hint, or something that will remind the user of the password. Remember, though, that all users on the computer can see the password hint, so you've got to think carefully about what you put here.

7. After you input the password, click "Change the password." You'll be returned to the Change an Account window. (See Figure 12-5.) Below the username you'll see that it now says "Password protected."

Figure 12-5. This user account is now protected by a password

Creating a Local Group

Groups are sets of one or more users on a system. Groups facilitate administration of user permissions. Assigning permissions to a group effectively assigns permissions to each member of that group.

By default, two groups are set up on a Windows system: Administrators and Standard users. Sometimes other groups are needed—for instance, when setting file access permissions for several users at a time, it's easier to assign permissions to a group than to several individual users.

> Groups can be administered only on Business, Enterprise, and Ultimate editions of Windows Vista.

Follow this procedure to manage groups:

1. Open the Microsoft Management Console by going to Control Panel → System and Maintenance → Administrative Tools → Computer Management.

2. Click Local Users and Groups in the left panel. In the center panel, click Groups. Your window should look like Figure 12-6.

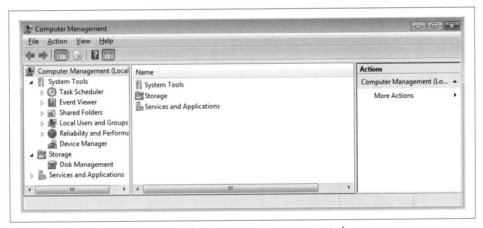

Figure 12-6. Creating a new group in the Computer Management window

3. In the right panel of the same window, click More Actions → New Group. The New Group window appears.

4. In the New Group window, type in the name of the group in the "Group name" field and a verbal description in the Description field. To select members of the group, click the Add button. The Select Users window appears.

5. Type in usernames, separated by semicolons (;). Click the Check Names button. If you typed in the names correctly, they will appear in the same field where you typed them in. See Figure 12-7.

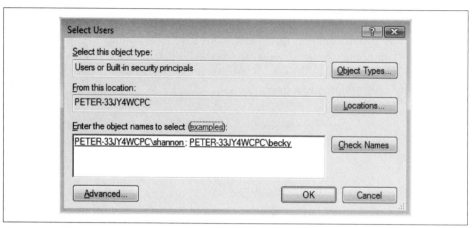

Figure 12-7. Selecting the group's users

6. Click OK. The New Group window will now list the users you added. See Figure 12-8.

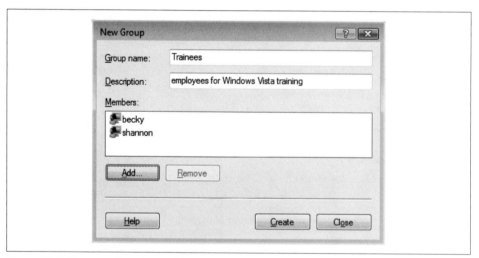

Figure 12-8. Two users have been added

7. Click the Create button. The group will be created. Click the Close button.

8. The group you created will appear in the middle panel of the Computer Management window. When you are finished, close the window.

You can add users to groups, and add groups to groups.

This may sound like a lot of work, but creating a group is actually pretty easy, and it is definitely the way to go if you anticipate the need to set permissions for users on your system. If more users need to have the same permissions as others in the group, you just add them to the group and *voilà*; they will instantly have the same permissions as the other users.

Account Policies

You can easily configure additional user account security settings on your system. These settings may enhance the security of your system, depending on your specific needs. The settings are described in the following subsections.

Password policy

Here you can change several settings that have to do with user account passwords. These settings are:

Password history
The system will "remember" previous passwords and prohibit the user from recycling passwords.

Maximum age
This is the maximum number of days after which a user will be required to change his password.

Minimum age
This is the minimum number of days before a user is permitted to change his password again (this can help to prevent a user from immediately going back to his old, familiar password).

Minimum length
This is the minimum number of characters required in the password.

Complexity
This states whether passwords must meet complexity rules—for example, at least six characters long; must contain characters from at least three of the following categories: 1) English uppercase characters, 2) English lowercase characters, 3) Digits (0–9), 4) Nonalphanumeric (!, $, #, %, etc.) characters, 5) Unicode characters; or cannot contain three or more characters from the user account name.

Store passwords using reversible encryption
It's recommended that you not use this setting, as it would permit an intruder to determine your accounts' passwords.

Account lockout policy

You can change system characteristics related to account lockouts—what happens when someone tries to log in unsuccessfully. The available settings are:

Account lockout threshold
>This is the number of unsuccessful login attempts that triggers an account lockout condition. If set to zero, an account will never lock out, despite the number of unsuccessful login attempts.

Account lockout counter reset
>This is the period of time (in minutes) before the lockout counter will be reset to zero.

Account lockout duration
>This is the period of time (in minutes) in which an account remains locked before it unlocks. Then the user would be permitted to try to log in again.

Setting account security policies

Follow this procedure to view or change account security policies:

1. Go to Control Panel → System and Maintenance → Administrative Tools → Local Security Policy. The Local Security Policy window appears.

2. Click on Account Policies, then Password Policy or Account Lockout Policy. Figure 12-9 shows the Password Policy selection.

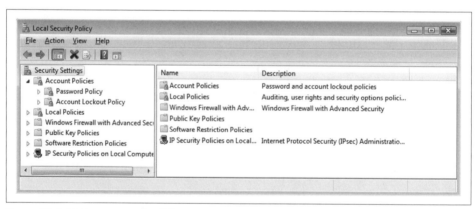

Figure 12-9. Setting password policies

3. Double-click the policy you wish to change. A new window will open, showing you the possible choices. The window has an Explain tab that describes the setting in detail. Select your setting and click OK.

4. Windows may automatically make other policy changes; if so, it will tell you so, such as in Figure 12-10.

5. You can edit those other policies if you need to. When you are finished, close the Local Security Policy window.

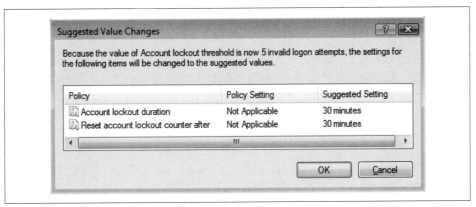

Figure 12-10. Windows may make other policy changes for you

Most policies are not effective for users until after they log out and log back in again.

Managing Auditing

Windows keeps a system log that is a record of events that take place on the computer. Examples of such events include:

- Device driver problems
- Hardware errors
- Logon and logoff
- Reboots
- Service startups and shutdowns
- Creation of, and changes to, user accounts
- Program errors

These events and more are kept in the event log and are viewable with the Event Viewer. But before we talk about that, let's go into more detail on auditing, which also results in event log entries.

Auditing gives you the ability to watch certain types of events even more closely.

 Microsoft uses the terms *events* and *audit* in the same context. Audit log entries and event log entries are the same thing.

Enabling Auditing

Follow these steps to enable auditing:

1. Go to Control Panel → System and Maintenance → Administrative Tools.

2. Double-click Local Security Policy. The Local Security Policy window appears.

3. Open Local Policies → Audit Policies. Click Audit Policies. The window should now appear as in Figure 12-11.

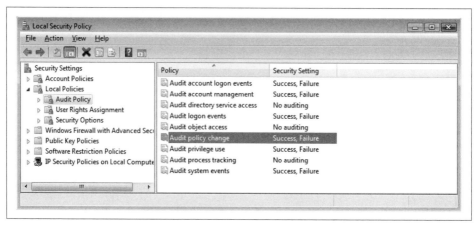

Figure 12-11. Viewing and setting audit policies

4. Double-click the audit policy you wish to change. For instance, you may wish to turn on auditing for privilege use. See Figure 12-12.

5. Select the events you wish to audit (or uncheck those you do not wish to audit). Click Apply and then OK.

6. The Local Security Policy window will be updated to reflect any changes you make for individual audit policies. Close the Local Security Policy and Administrative Tools windows when you are done with them.

Thereafter, any changes you make to audit policies will be reflected on the system, and any audited events that occur can be viewed.

Changing Audit Settings on Files

You can turn on auditing for individual files on the system if you want Windows to track who is opening the file. Follow this procedure to turn on file auditing:

1. Using Windows Explorer, navigate to the file you wish to audit. Right-click the file and click Properties.

2. Click the Security tab, then Advanced, and then Auditing. See Figure 12-13.

3. Click the Edit button. Another window will open. Click Add.

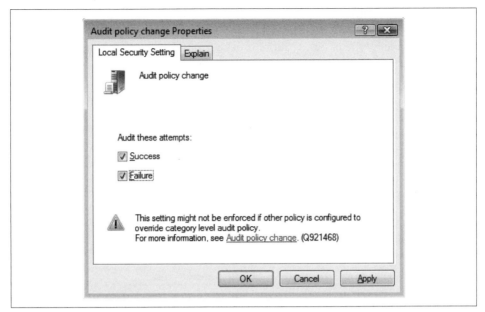

Figure 12-12. Changing audit privilege use properties

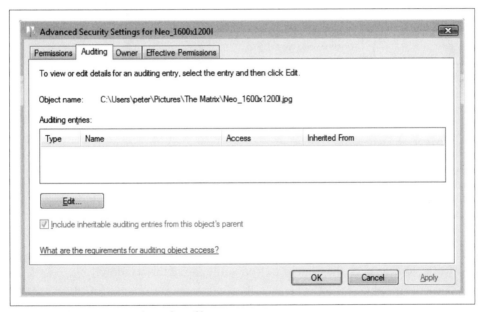

Figure 12-13. Setting up auditing for a file

4. You can add which individual users or groups you wish to monitor. However, if you want to see everyone who opens a file, you can easily do that, too. In the field provided, type in one or more user or group IDs, separated by semicolons. Type **everyone**, for example, if you want to audit any user's access to the file. Now click Check Names.

5. Click OK. You are not done yet. Now the "Auditing Entry for *filename*" window opens. Here you specify which specific actions you wish to have audited. Talk about detailed! See Figure 12-14.

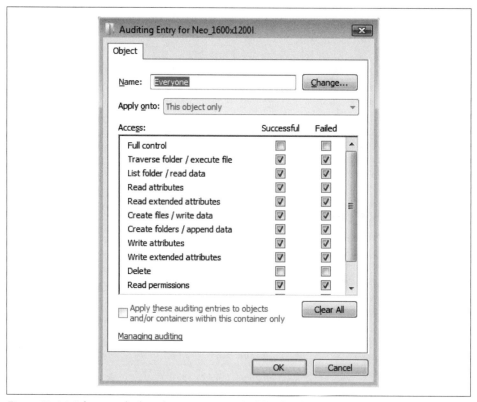

Figure 12-14. Selecting which audit events are tracked for this file

6. Click OK. Note that you can change your mind about which users you want to track; you can click the Change button at the top of this window.

7. The Advanced Security Settings window will show what actions will be audited for which users. See Figure 12-15.

8. Click Apply, and then click OK and then OK again. Now you should be back to the file's Properties window. Are you tired yet?

The next section describes how to read audit logs, which are just another type of event in Windows.

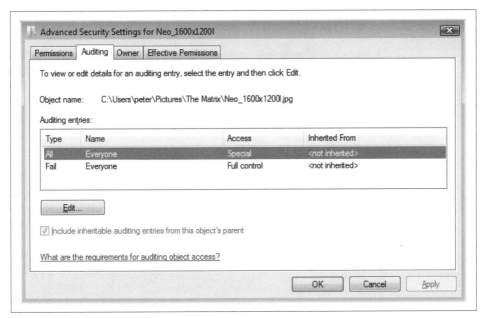

Figure 12-15. Results of the audit selections

Viewing Audit Logs and Events

To view audit logs and system events, open the Event Viewer. Click Control Panel → System and Maintenance → Administrative Tools → View Event Logs. The Event Viewer appears, as seen in Figure 12-16.

Select the types of logs on the panel on the left. The middle panel will show the events; the names will be listed on the top half of the panel and details of the events will be listed on the bottom half. Actions such as Filtering, Properties, and Save Events As are on the right panel.

 Your system can really consume a lot of disk space if you turn on auditing. If you are serious about auditing, you'll need to read more about it and be prepared to make some major system changes to accommodate the disk space required by audit logging.

Protecting Against Malware

As mentioned earlier in the chapter, *malware* is the inclusive term meaning viruses, Trojan horses, worms, and similar malicious software (for more on this, see the section "Why You Need Security," earlier in this chapter). While Windows security has incrementally improved with Vista, you must still have antivirus software, and you should also have a firewall. We'll go into lots more detail in this section on protecting yourself against the plague of malware that is constantly trying to worm its way into your computer (pun intended).

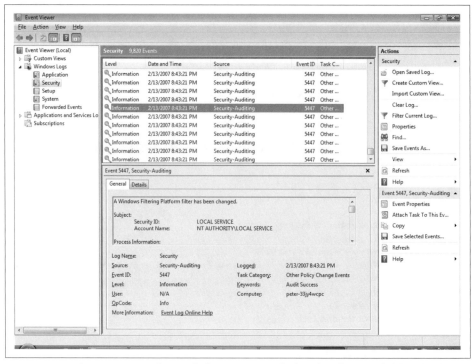

Figure 12-16. The Event Viewer lists audit logs, events, and a lot of stuff you probably didn't know Windows kept track of

The Windows Security Center

The Windows Security Center is the nerve center for security on your Vista system. It is basically a "dashboard" that shows you the status of many security systems on your computer, including:

- Firewall
- Automatic updates
- Malware protection
- Internet security settings
- User Account Control

Figure 12-17 shows the Windows Security Center.

In this example, "Automatic updating" is set as "Not automatic." It is yellow, not red, because Automatic Updates are configured to automatically download but not install security patches and other updates. "Other security settings" is red because we turned off User Account Control earlier in this chapter when discussing that feature.

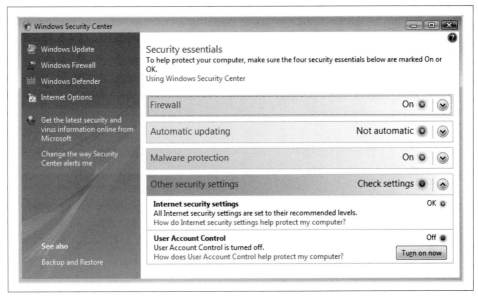

Figure 12-17. The Windows Security Center shows us the status of security in Vista

The Windows Security Center provides a convenient means for viewing and managing security. You can see your security status, quickly drill down and see even more detail, and be just a click away from changing security configurations.

Antivirus and Antispyware

Unless you are never going to connect your computer to a network and never receive files or programs from any other person or entity, you need to have antivirus software. This is so very important that Microsoft strongly recommends that you obtain and install antivirus software before you *ever* connect your new Vista system to any network. Without antivirus software, your computer can become infected with a virus within *minutes* of connecting to the Internet, often without your even having to visit web sites or read email.

Many brands of antivirus software are available today, and for the purposes of virus protection, they are all more or less the same. Some may argue the point, but any of the following (listed in alphabetical order) should be sufficient for the average user's needs:

- AVG, *http://www.grisoft.com*
- BitDefender, *http://www.bitdefender.com*
- eTrust EZ Antivirus, *http://www.ca.com*
- Kaspersky AntiVirus, *http://www.kaspersky.com*
- McAfee VirusScan, *http://www.mcafee.com*

- NOD32, *http://www.eset.com*
- Norton AntiVirus, *http://www.symantec.com*
- Panda, *http://www.pandasoftware.com*
- PC-cillin, *http://www.trendmicro.com*

Several others are available. A handy place to check is Microsoft's Antivirus Partner site, *http://www.microsoft.com/security/partners/antivirus.asp*.

 If you have upgraded your system from an earlier version of Windows, you need to make sure your antivirus software is supported on Vista. Visit your antivirus program's web site for more information.

Recommended settings

After you buy or upgrade your antivirus software (or even if the antivirus software you already have is sufficient for Vista), you need to examine the configuration for your antivirus program to confirm *all* of the following:

Real-time protection is turned on
> The default for most (if not all) antivirus programs, you need to make sure that your antivirus program is configured to detect a virus the instant it tries to get into your system.

Checking for virus updates at least once per day
> Viruses are coming out at such a high rate that it is vital that your antivirus program check for updates at least once per day.

Scanning the entire computer at least once per week
> It's possible for viruses to sneak through your outer defenses. The best way to detect viruses that sneak around is to scan your hard drive weekly. This can be pretty resource-intensive and make your computer act like it's got a flat tire, so you might want to schedule this for the middle of the night (or whenever you aren't using your computer).

The System Tray status icon is always on
> The System Tray icon helps identify times when settings are not as safe as they should be, and can help warn when a virus programs is using outdated pattern information.

The heuristics setting is turned on
> Antivirus programs are signature-based, which means they are looking for viruses based upon the patterns in them. But many antivirus programs can also do what's called heuristics-based virus detection, which means they watch certain system activities and can detect a virus by its activity alone.

In addition to these settings, Microsoft also recommends that you view the console of your antivirus program at least once per week to make sure everything looks healthy.

Get second opinions often

Even with a good antivirus program, the antivirus companies occasionally miss a virus that is released into the world. For this reason, we strongly recommend you get a second opinion by using another antivirus program to scan your system.

Wait! It is a very bad idea to try to install two antivirus programs on your system. They'll definitely get into arguments over who's really supposed to watch for viruses. Fortunately, there's an easy way to do this: online virus scans. Many of the reputable antivirus software companies have online virus scanners that scan your entire system looking for viruses and other malware. Good computing habits dictate that you use one or more of these online services to scan your system for viruses at least once each month.

Some of the vendors that have good online virus scanners are:

- Panda, *http://www.pandasoftware.com*
- Trend Micro, *http://www.trendmicro.com*
- Symantec, *http://www.symantec.com*

There are probably other good virus scanners, but you can start with these.

 Some web site pop ups claim to be security scanners for your computer. These are not the same as the reputable online virus scanners mentioned in the preceding list. Avoid the pop-up security scams at all costs!

Oh, and I should mention another nice online tool: Secunia's Software Inspector. This tool examines the software on your system and lists any unsecure versions. Software Inspector also detects which Microsoft patches you may need to install. The tool provides detailed explanations on any actions you need to take, including URLs to software updates and patch downloads.

And don't forget Microsoft Update, the online tool from Microsoft that examines your system and identifies all missing patches and updates. We discuss this later in this chapter, in the section "Staying Current on Security Issues."

Antispyware programs

Spyware became an issue in the late 1990s, and several good antispyware programs became available. Most were free, and the better ones had fee-based versions.

Antispyware programs work pretty much the same as antivirus programs: they have real-time filesystem sensors that watch for spyware trying to get in; they are signature-based; they require downloaded signature updates; and you can use them to scan your entire hard drive for spyware.

The antivirus companies have seen this, and they are slowly coming around and are including antispyware capabilities right alongside their antivirus capabilities. Why not use the same tried-and-true mechanism to detect both viruses *and* spyware? Great idea!

Some of the good antispyware programs are listed here. As with the antivirus programs, this is an incomplete list. Other good ones are also available.

- Ad-Aware, *http://www.lavasoftusa.com*
- Pest Patrol, *http://www.pestpatrol.com*
- Spy Sweeper, *http://www.webroot.com*
- Trend Micro Anti-Spyware, *http://www.trendmicro.com*
- Windows Defender, *http://www.microsoft.com*

As with antivirus programs, you should configure your antispyware software to update its signatures daily and scan your computer weekly (or more frequently for high-risk users, or those who click before they think).

Windows Defender

Windows Defender is Microsoft's antispyware program that is bundled with Vista. Defender works like most antivirus and antispyware software, given its basic functions:

Signature-based
> Defender works by recognizing the signatures of known spyware programs.

Real-time protection
> Watching all disk activity, Defender can block spyware from getting installed on your system.

Hard drive scan
> Defender can scan your hard drive to look for and remove spyware. You can perform these scans on demand or configure Defender to perform them on a schedule.

To run Defender, just click on Windows Defender on the left side of the Windows Security Center.

Defender's control panel is straightforward, as shown in Figure 12-18.

A complete breakdown and tutorial on Windows Defender is beyond the scope of this book, but I'll describe its basic functions here.

Scan

If you click on Scan from the Defender window, it will immediately start to scan your computer for spyware. If you click the down arrow next to Scan, you'll have some more choices for scanning.

You can stop the scan at any time after you start it.

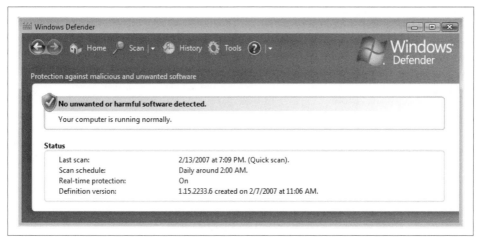

Figure 12-18. Windows Defender's main screen provides access to all of its functions

Tools

Windows Defender options and other functions are found under Tools. When you click on Tools, Defender shows another window with six more things you can do:

Options

Here you can set the scanning schedule, and tell Defender how to alert you if it finds spyware. There are also a lot of other options here; Microsoft provided plenty of buttons and knobs for controlling Defender's behavior.

Microsoft SpyNet

This is the part of Defender where you can report suspected spyware to Microsoft. This helps Defender do a better job of blocking new pieces of spyware. You can choose basic or advanced membership, or opt out altogether.

Quarantined Items

Here you can examine pieces of spyware like insects in a jar. This is interesting if you want to look at recent specimens.

Software Explorer

This is a pretty cool feature that lets you look at all of the software that's running on your computer, right now. I've included a screenshot of this in Figure 12-19.

Allowed Items

This lets you look at software programs that you've told Defender to ignore.

Windows Defender website

This is just a link to…you know.

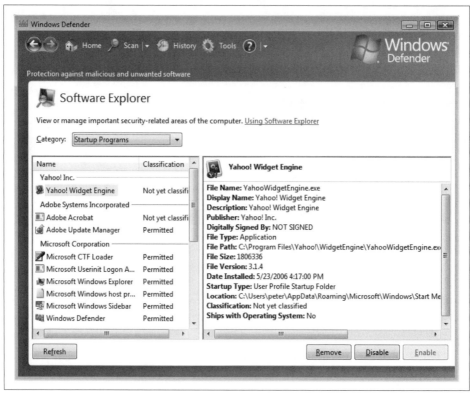

Figure 12-19. See what programs are running on your computer with Software Explorer

Windows Firewall

Windows operating systems have included a firewall for some time now. One of the big advances with Windows XP's Service Pack 2, however, was that the firewall was enabled by default. Vista carries forward this behavior.

 Windows Firewall is a "personal firewall," a software program that controls what traffic is permitted to enter and leave the computer. It uses rules to decide whether individual network packets should be permitted to enter and leave.

Like Defender, you can access Windows Firewall from the Windows Security Center. Just click on the Windows Firewall link on the left side. Figure 12-20 shows what Windows Firewall's main window looks like.

There aren't many settings with Windows Firewall, not that there need to be a lot of buttons and knobs here. Most settings are available from the "Change settings" link.

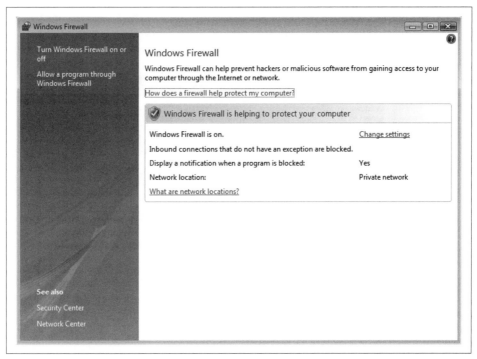

Figure 12-20. Windows Firewall control panel

When you click the link, you'll see the Windows Firewall Settings window, as shown in Figure 12-21.

In the main window, you can turn Windows Firewall on or off. You can also block all incoming connections if you're on a public access point or other unsecure network.

The Exceptions tab lists the programs that are permitted to communicate through the firewall. You can also access this window by clicking "Allow a program through Windows Firewall" from the main Windows Firewall window.

The Advanced tab lets you specify whether Windows Firewall will be active on each of your network connections. For instance, you might always want the firewall on for wireless network connections, if you connect to the Internet via unsecure wireless access points, but you might want the firewall off for local area connections that could be protected by network firewalls.

The firewall in action

Windows Firewall watches all network traffic closely. If you are running a new program that Windows Firewall doesn't know about, and that program wants to communicate on the network, Windows Firewall will ask you whether it's OK for that program to communicate. See Figure 12-22.

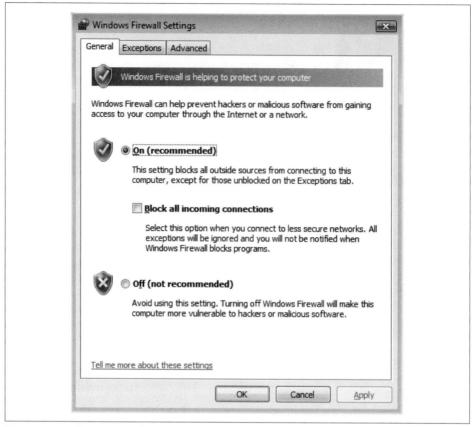

Figure 12-21. The main Windows Firewall Settings window

Automatic Updates

You can access Windows Automatic Updates through the Windows Security Center, although Microsoft doesn't place a link for Automatic Updates on the left side of the window. Instead, you need to open Automatic Updates by clicking on the little down arrow, and then clicking the "Change settings" button. You'll see the Automatic Updates window, as shown in Figure 12-23.

Microsoft's default here is for updates to be installed automatically. If you don't want to bother with the details of updates, this option is fine.

I prefer "Let me choose," however. In other words, I want more control over when and how patches are installed. If you click on "Let me choose," you'll see another window, as in Figure 12-24.

My choice is to have updates downloaded to my computer, but then installed when *I* want them installed.

Figure 12-22. Windows Firewall asks whether each new program is permitted to communicate over the network

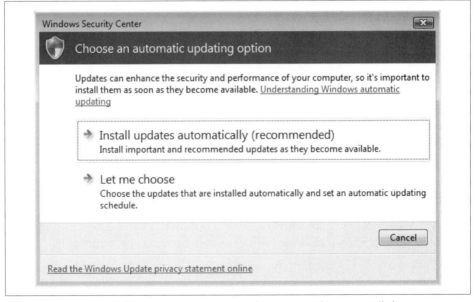

Figure 12-23. Automatic Updates lets you determine how new patches are installed on your Windows system

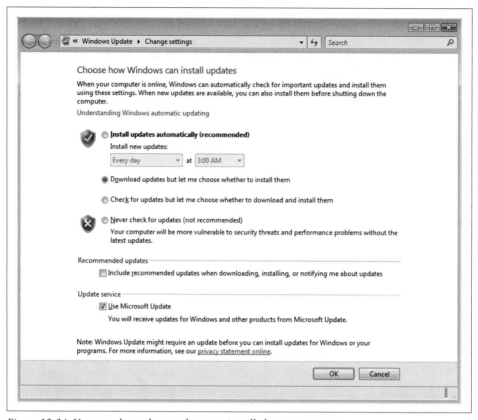

Figure 12-24. You can choose how updates are installed on your system

When updates are available for installation, a new System Tray icon appears; if you hover over the icon, you'll see the text "New updates are available." If you click on the icon, you'll see the Windows Updates window that shows updates that are available for installation.

Malicious Software Removal Tool

The Windows Malicious Software Removal Tool (MSRT) is a program that scans your computer for known malicious software and, if it finds any, removes it.

The MSRT is usually downloaded during Windows Update or Microsoft Update and is run automatically without any intervention required. Just to be sure, I used Microsoft Update to download the latest MSRT (Microsoft comes out with a new version every few weeks, it seems), and sure enough, it ran without even telling me. The tool runs one time only and then uninstalls itself. You'll find more on the MSRT in Chapter 14.

Internet Explorer Security

Another vital area of network security is to make sure your Internet browser is configured with the most secure settings for your purposes. After all, most of the security measures we've dealt with so far in this chapter have to do with threats from the Internet, and most of your interaction with the Internet will be done through a web browser.

This section, then, reinforces the discussion of the many new security features in Internet Explorer 7. For more information on Vista's new browser features, refer to Chapter 10.

Internet Explorer includes some security settings and indicators on the status bar at the bottom of the Internet Explorer window, as in Figure 12-25. These indicators are:

Privacy Report
> This is the little eyeball that indicates whether any cookies have been blocked.

Zone
> This indicates whether the page you are viewing is in the Local Zone, Trusted Zone, or Internet Zone. I explain these in detail later in this section.

Protected Mode
> This is a setting that makes it more difficult for web sites to plant malicious code in your computer.

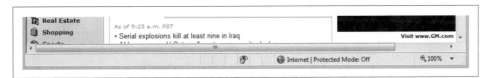

Figure 12-25. Internet Explorer 7 status bar showing security settings

You can double-click any of these to view settings or status. For instance, if you double-click the Privacy Report (the little eyeball), you'll see the Privacy Report window, as shown in Figure 12-26.

You can find Internet Explorer security settings in two sections: Privacy Settings and Security Settings. I describe both in detail in the next few subsections.

Internet Explorer privacy settings

You can find Internet Explorer's privacy settings in Tools → Internet Options → Privacy. You'll see the Privacy window, as shown in Figure 12-27.

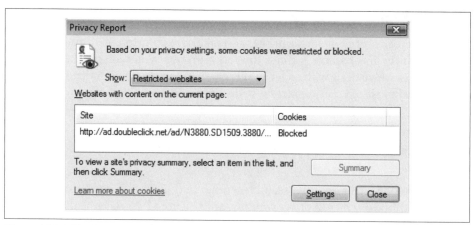

Figure 12-26. The Internet Explorer Privacy Report shows blocked cookies for the web page you're viewing

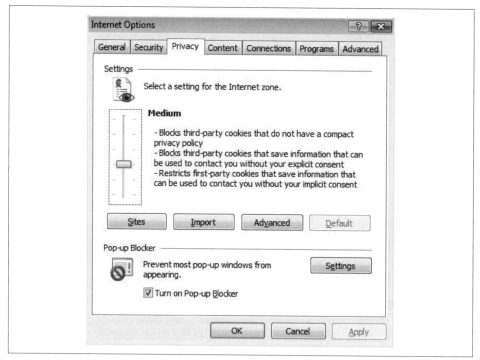

Figure 12-27. Internet Explorer's Privacy window

Here you can select your security settings for the Internet Zone. In other words, you tell Internet Explorer what sorts of cookies you will accept when you are visiting untrusted web sites on the Internet. Six settings are available when you move the slider up and down. These settings are:

Block All Cookies

> You block all cookies from all web sites. Cookies that you have already stored on your computer are not accessible by web sites. Effectively, this means you have no cookies and accept no cookies. This is the most secure setting, but it will also prevent any convenience features that cookies make possible, such as a web site displaying weather or news specific to your locale.

High

> You block all cookies from web sites that do not have a "compact privacy policy" (that are not P3P-compliant). You also block all cookies that save contact information for you.

Medium High

> You block all third-party cookies that lack a compact privacy policy, as well as cookies that contain contact information for you.

Medium

> You block all third-party cookies that lack a compact privacy policy, and all third-party cookies that can be used to contact you without your explicit consent. Cookies that can be used to contact you without your implicit consent are restricted (this means Internet Explorer will ask you whether to accept specific cookies of this type). This is the setting that I use.

Low

> You block all third-party cookies that lack a compact privacy policy, and you restrict cookies that can be used to contact you without your implicit consent.

Accept All Cookies

> You accept all cookies; cookies that are already on your computer are accessible by web sites you visit. I strongly recommend you not use this setting.

 You can configure which sites are in the Internet Zone, as discussed in the next subsection.

On the Internet Options Privacy tab, you can also specify the sites that should never send you cookies. Internet Explorer comes preloaded with a long list of such sites, and you can edit this list if you wish. Click the Sites button to view or change the list. The Per Site Privacy Actions window will appear, shown in Figure 12-28.

If you saved privacy settings on another computer, you can import those settings; click the Import button to pull in those settings that you saved on another computer.

You can override cookie handling using the Advanced button; see Figure 12-29. Here you can Accept, Block, or Prompt cookies from first parties and third parties, and you can always allow session cookies if you want to.

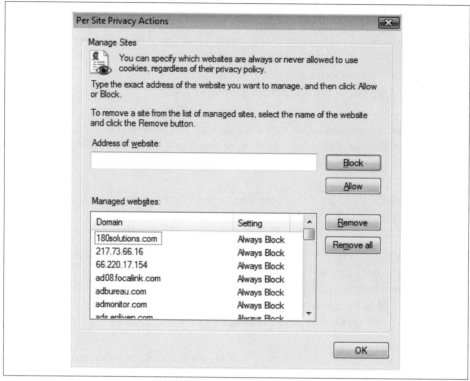

Figure 12-28. The Per Site Privacy Actions window permits you to manage restricted sites

Figure 12-29. Advanced settings permit you to enact your cookie policies

Finally, you can also configure the Internet Explorer Pop-up Blocker on the Privacy tab. From here, you can enable or disable the Pop-up blocker, and click the Settings button to manage additional settings. There you can manage the list of sites whose pop-up windows you will always accept, as well as set a filter policy.

When Internet Explorer blocks a pop-up window, a message bar appears at the top of the viewing screen. You can then unblock pop ups for that site if you wish, or ignore the message if you wanted the pop up blocked.

Internet Explorer security settings

Many security settings are available in Internet Explorer. To access them, go to the Security tab in the Internet Options window. See Figure 12-30.

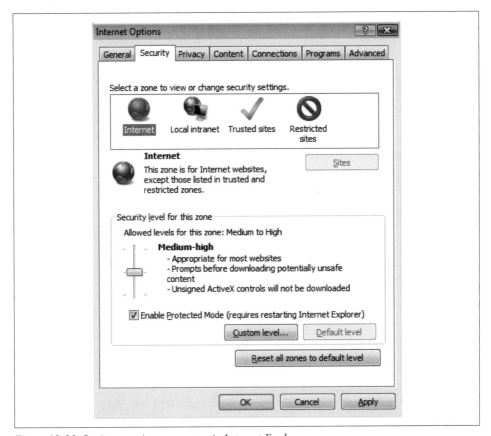

Figure 12-30. Setting security parameters in Internet Explorer

The principal feature in Internet Explorer's security settings is the management of sites that belong in one of the four available zones, which are:

Internet
> This is the big zone of all sites on the Internet.

Local intranet
> These are sites that are inside your organization's network. This really applies only to computers in organizations that have web sites that are physically within the premises.

Trusted sites
> These are Internet sites that you explicitly trust.

Restricted sites
> These are Internet sites that you do not trust. More than that, these are sites that you wish to avoid.

Internet Explorer lets you change its security behavior for each zone in two ways. First, you can use the slider on the window to move your security levels up and down. Text to the right of the slider describes settings for that level.

The second way to change security settings for each zone is through the custom settings; to access this, click the "Custom level" button. Here, you'll be able to change dozens of fine-grained settings. We recommend this only for experts who understand the technologies involved. Have a look at this in Figure 12-31.

If you start making changes and then decide that you're in over your head (and this should not make you feel bad), you can just click the "Reset custom settings" button to easily go back to square one.

 If the slider is grayed out for any of the four security zones, this means custom settings have been set for that zone, in which case you must go back into Custom Settings to make more changes.

To manage the list of intranet, trusted, and restricted sites, click on one of those zones, and then click the Sites button. You'll get the Sites window, where you can see what sites are in the list, and you can add more if you like. Figure 12-32 shows the list of restricted sites.

 For the Intranet Zone, Internet Explorer can use additional settings to automatically detect sites in this zone. You can also edit the sites in the Intranet Zone manually, like you can for trusted and restricted sites.

Finally, you can turn Protected Mode off and on in the Security tab. Protected Mode is a setting that makes it more difficult for web sites to install malicious software onto your computer. Microsoft recommends you turn Protected Mode *on*.

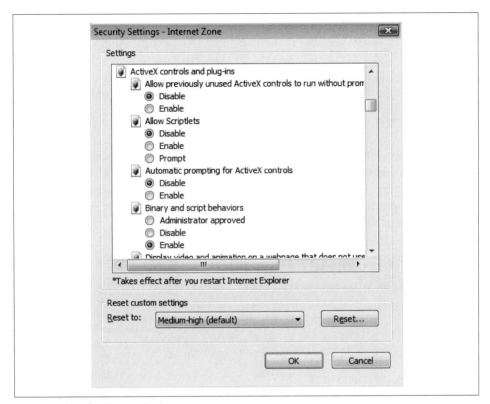

Figure 12-31. The Custom Settings screen

Figure 12-32. Sites you trust the least are in the Restricted Sites list

Phishing Filter

Internet Explorer now has a filter that it uses to try to detect phishing sites.

 A phishing site is a fraudulent web site that masquerades as a high-value site such as banking or financial services. Viewers are enticed to visit phishing sites via spam email messages that originate from the owner of the fake site.

To view Phishing Filter settings, click Tools → Phishing Filter → Phishing Filter Settings. Clicking that takes you to Internet Explorer's Internet Options Advanced tab, as shown in Figure 12-33. You'll need to scroll down to the bottom, where you'll find the only setting where you can disable the Phishing Filter, or turn automatic web site checking off or on.

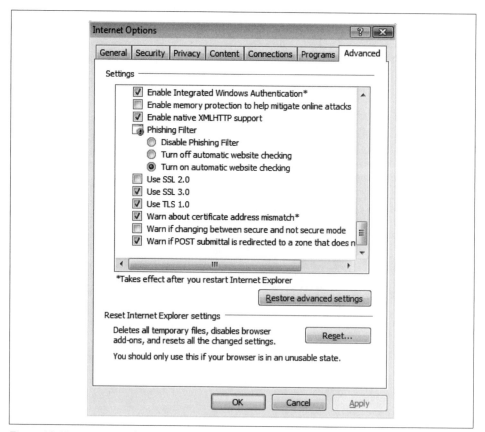

Figure 12-33. Internet Explorer's Phishing Filter settings in the Advanced Internet Options tab

If you aren't sure whether you are on a phishing web site (a site that exists in order to defraud you in some way), you can check it by clicking on Tools → Phishing Filter → Check This Website. Internet Explorer will then check with Microsoft's central phishing site database and tell you whether the site is a reported phishing site, as seen in Figure 12-34.

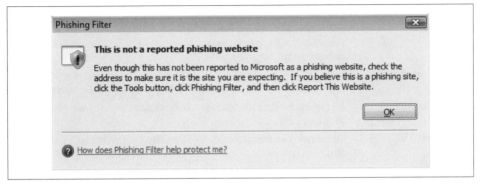

Figure 12-34. The page viewed is not a reported phishing site

If you suspect that you are on a phishing site, you can report the site by clicking Tools → Phishing Filter → Report This Website.

If you do visit a reported phishing site, Internet Explorer will display a message that warns you that the site is suspected to be a fake.

File Encryption

Encryption is a means of scrambling information to prevent unwanted persons from being able to read it. It's been used to transmit information for, oh, thousands of years or so, but as it applies to computers, it describes a mathematical process of transforming blocks of data using an *encryption algorithm*. Examples of well-known encryption algorithms in use today are DES, AES, CAST, and Blowfish.

So, why encrypt? It's especially valuable if your computer is ever lost or stolen—unless the thief knows your username and password, files that are encrypted will not be readable. As introduced in Chapters 1 and 2, Windows Vista provides two methods for encrypting files: the Encrypting File System (EFS) and BitLocker Drive Encryption.

EFS has been around since Windows 2000, whereas BitLocker is brand-new. Table 12-1 lists the differences between EFS and BitLocker.

Table 12-1. EFS and BitLocker comparison

	EFS	BitLocker
What is encrypted	Individual files and folders.	All personal and system files on the hard drive.
Encryption's association with user accounts	Encryption is associated with the user who encrypts files or directories. When one user encrypts a file, no other user will be able to read it. This can be a problem when a user wants to share files with another user, but still provide the protection that encryption provides.	Encryption is performed at the system level and is not associated with any user accounts.
Hardware support required	None.	BitLocker uses the Trusted Platform Module (TPM), a special chip found in newer computers.
Administrator status	Any user, whether standard or administrator, can use EFS.	Only administrators can manage BitLocker.
User control	Users can selectively encrypt and decrypt files as they wish.	Users cannot turn off BitLocker, unless they are an Administrator user.

In everyday use, EFS is "visible" to computer users (I'll explain how in a minute), whereas BitLocker is largely invisible and automatic.

File Encryption with EFS

EFS permits users to encrypt and decrypt any files or directories, as desired, at any time. Standard and Administrator users may encrypt any files and directories that they own.

To encrypt files or directories, follow this procedure:

1. Open Windows Explorer and navigate to the directory that contains the directories or files that you wish to encrypt.
2. Right-click the file(s) or directory(ies) you wish to encrypt. Click Properties → Advanced. The Advanced Attributes window appears.
3. Check "Encrypt contents to secure data." Click OK.
4. In the Security Properties window, click Apply.
5. The Confirm Attribute Changes window appears, and asks whether only the current folder should be encrypted, or whether all files and subfolders should also be encrypted. The default, "Apply changes to this folder, subfolders and files," is usually what you will choose. Click OK. (See Figure 12-35.)
6. Windows will encrypt the file(s) and directory(ies) you selected. This can take quite a while if you have selected a large amount of data to encrypt. You'll see a window that shows the progress of the encryption, as in Figure 12-36.
7. If you are using EFS for the first time, a System Tray balloon will appear that reminds you to back up your encryption key. After the balloon disappears, the System Tray icon will remain.

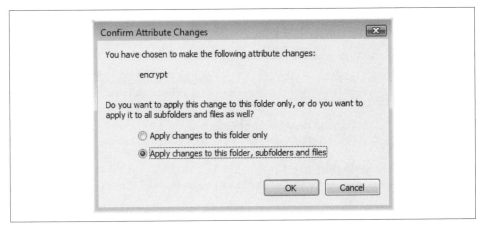

Figure 12-35. The Confirm Attribute Changes window lets you select or deselect encryption

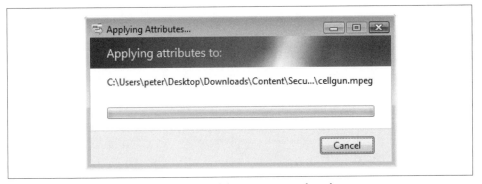

Figure 12-36. Windows encrypts the files and directories you selected

8. Click the EFS System Tray icon. The EFS key backup window appears, as in Figure 12-37.

9. Click "Back up now (recommended)." The Certificate Export Wizard appears and will guide you through the steps to export your EFS encryption key, which is really a digital certificate. Click Next.

10. The next window asks which format you want to use. The only available format is "Personal Information Exchange—PKCS #12 (.PFX)." The other options are grayed out. You may check "Include all certifications" and "Export all extended properties" if you wish; it's not required that you do so. Click Next.

11. You must type in a password to protect your exported certificate. You should use a good, strong password that others cannot guess. You should write down the password and keep it in a safe place.

12. Next, you must choose the name and location of the file where you want your certificate written. This must be a new file. If you choose an existing file, it will be overwritten. Navigate to the directory where you want your certificate saved. Click Next, and then click Finish.

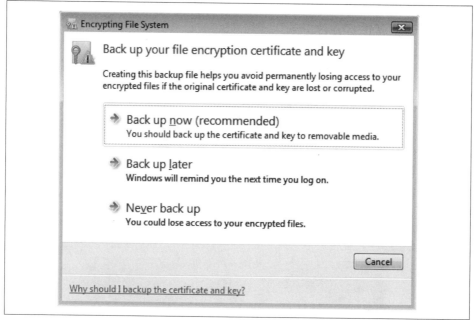

Figure 12-37. You need to back up your EFS file encryption key

 You should copy your exported certificate to a CD-ROM or other file that is stored on a different computer, in case you ever need to recover your certificate.

You can easily tell whether a file or directory has been encrypted. Windows Explorer will show the name of the file or directory in green text or black text.

 Windows permits you to either compress your data *or* encrypt it, but not both.

EFS permits you to encrypt files or entire directories. If you need to encrypt your entire hard drive, you should consider using BitLocker.

File Encryption with BitLocker Drive Encryption

Vista is the first Windows OS to offer *drive* encryption, in which all files on the drive are encrypted, instead of just selected files and directories. BitLocker even encrypts all of the Windows operating system, including logon information, installed programs, and all other files on your computer. Once set up, BitLocker is fully automatic.

BitLocker requires a small (about 1 GB) partition on your computer. If you have upgraded from an earlier version of Windows, you probably do not have this extra partition. But do not fear: BitLocker will create it for you.

Before BitLocker encrypts your hard drive, you will be prompted to set up a Startup Key and a Recovery Key. When you start your computer, you will be prompted for the Startup Key before your computer will start. If you lose your Startup Key, you must provide the Recovery Key to recover your data. If you lose both the Startup Key and the Recovery Key, your data will be irretrievably lost.

Setting up BitLocker (no TPM)

To set up BitLocker, go to Control Panel → Security → BitLocker Drive Encryption.

On many systems, especially those upgraded from a previous version of Windows, you'll see a warning message that says your drive configuration is unsuitable for Bit-Locker. To continue, click "Set up your hard disk for BitLocker Drive Encryption." See Figure 12-38.

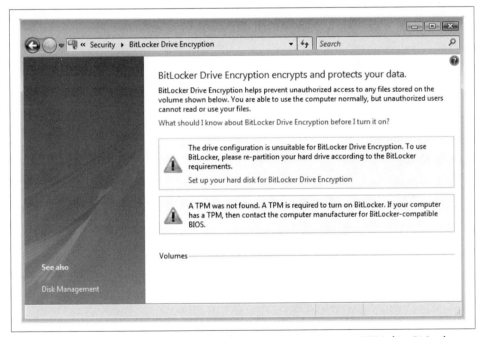

Figure 12-38. If your disk doesn't have either the necessary partitions or a TPM chip, BitLocker will tell you so

If your disk doesn't have the necessary second partition, you will have to create one. Click on the "Set up your hard disk for BitLocker Drive Encryption" link. This will display a help page that contains instructions on how to shrink your main volume and create a new 1.5 GB volume for BitLocker. See Chapter 7 for full instructions on how to shrink a drive.

When you have completed that task, continue here:

1. When you click on Control Panel → Security → BitLocker Drive Encryption, you will see the window shown in Figure 12-39.

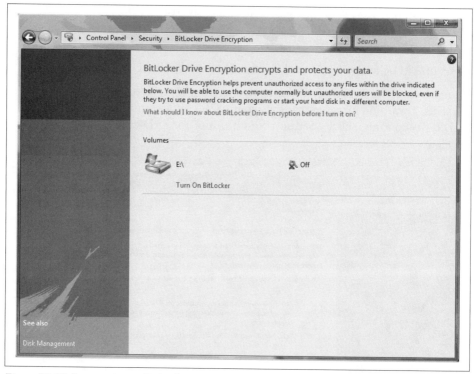

Figure 12-39. Start setting up BitLocker

2. Click on Turn On BitLocker. BitLocker will prompt you for a Startup Key or PIN, as shown in Figure 12-40. If your system does not have a TPM chip, you will have to create a Startup Key on a USB drive.

3. You are required to insert a USB key. Select it from the list and click Save.

4. Next, you will be asked to type in a 4- to 20-digit PIN. Note that in a domain environment, administrators may disable PIN creation.

   Most systems don't have a TPM chip unless you've just recently bought a system.

5. Now you will be required to create a recovery password. When you create the password, you have four options. You must save it to a USB drive, a network folder (it makes no sense to save it on *this* computer!), print it, or display it on the screen. See Figure 12-41. Select one of the options and continue.

Figure 12-40. Choosing your USB drive from the list

Figure 12-41. You have four options when saving your BitLocker recovery password

6. The recovery password is set for you; you don't have the option of typing it in. It's a long string that you are not likely to remember. If you choose the Show option, you'll see the window shown in Figure 12-42.

After creating the PIN on a USB key and creating the recovery password, BitLocker is ready to encrypt your drive. How long this takes depends on your hard drive size and your computer's performance. Encryption takes place in the background.

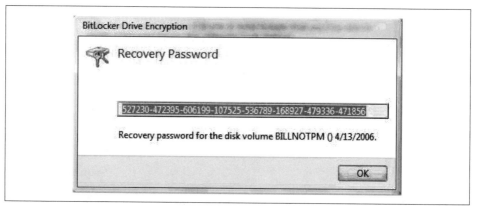

Figure 12-42. The recovery password is not for the faint of heart

Booting with BitLocker (no TPM)

Once BitLocker is set up on your system, your boot-up sequence will look a little different. You will be required to have that USB key, and you'll have to remember your PIN. If you have neither, your only option will be to type in the recovery password.

When your system boots, you'll see the following message:

```
If the Startup Key is not present (screen 1):
The key required to unlock this volume was not found.
Please insert removable storage media containing the Startup Key or the Recovery Key.
Then press ENTER to reboot.
```

Insert your USB key; then you'll see:

```
You may now remove the media.
```

If you are required to type in your PIN, you'll see the following message instead:

```
To start this computer, type its BitLocker Drive Encryption startup PIN and then
press Enter.

Use function keys F1 through F9 for 1 through 9, and F10 for 0. Use the Tab, Home,
End, and Arrow keys to move the cursor.

If you do not have the correct startup PIN, press Escape.
```

If you have neither the USB key nor the PIN, you'll have to reboot and try again.

Recovering data encrypted with BitLocker. If you do not have the USB key or the PIN, the only option available to you is to recover your data using your recovery password.

When the system boots, you can type in the recovery password at the initial prompt, or insert a USB key that contains the recovery password:

```
If the Startup Key is not present (screen 1):
The key required to unlock this volume was not found.
Please insert removable storage media containing the Startup Key or the Recovery Key.
Then press ENTER to reboot.
```

Then you will want to create a new PIN and Startup Key using BitLocker's key management program in the Control Panel.

Managing a TPM environment. If your system has the new TPM hardware, you can opt to utilize the TPM when setting up BitLocker. With TPM present, you have three implementation options:

TPM-only encryption
The user does not need to provide a USB key or PIN on startup. The end user will not be required to enter a password on startup.

Two-factor protection: PIN and TPM
The user will be required to type in a PIN each time he starts. A recovery password is still created when BitLocker is set up, and is required if the user cannot remember his PIN.

Two-factor protection: USB and TPM
The user will be required to insert the USB key containing the Startup Key at system boot time. The recovery password can be used to recover the volume if the USB key is lost.

 At first glance, TPM-only encryption might seem a moot point. After all, if a user is not required to enter a PIN or a key to boot the system, can't any intruder also boot the system?

This is true, but the intruder will *not* be able to put the computer's hard drive into another computer in order to extract files from the user's hard drive, because they're all encrypted.

One potential vulnerability is a weak password. If the user used a weak password on the computer, and if an intruder was able to guess the password, the intruder would have full access to all of the user's information (and everything else on the computer, if the user account is Administrator level).

Managing Disk Quotas

If you are sharing your computer with other people and you've ever been in a situation in which one of those people filled the hard drive with pictures or MP3 files, you will want to consider turning on Disk Quotas.

Disk Quotas controls how much space each user is allowed to consume on a computer. This can prevent any one user from consuming all the free space on the hard drive, which would prevent other users from being able to open files or create new files.

Disk Quotas allows you to specify whether you will have users *warned* if they are exceeding their quota, or whether you will actually *block* users from exceeding their quota. Blocking further disk use is a lot better than repeated "This is the last time!" warnings that may just irritate computer users without actually changing their behavior.

You can set two thresholds in Disk Quotas: one level where users will receive a warning that they are consuming excess disk space, and another level where Windows will actually block users from using anymore space.

You can also set up logging, where Windows will track every instance in which users exceed their warning levels, their quota limits, or both. Then, even if they aren't paying attention (or are trying to tell you that they never received a warning), you have logging to prove it.

 Disk Quotas is an administrative control that is configured on a per-user basis. You cannot set it up on a per-group basis.

Setting Up Disk Quotas

To manage quotas, follow this procedure:

1. Using Windows Explorer, navigate to your Computer where you can see the hard drive(s) your computer uses.

2. Right-click Local Disk and then click Properties. Find and click the Quota tab, and then click the Show Quota Settings button.

3. Unless you or someone else turned on Disk Quotas, it's probably disabled. To enable Disk Quotas, check the "Enable quota management" checkbox. The remaining options will now activate. See Figure 12-43.

4. Now that Disk Quotas is enabled, you can choose how Disk Quotas should work on your system. You can specify whether Windows will actually block users from using additional space, by checking "Deny disk space to users exceeding quota limit." You can set the disk space and warning levels, and you can specify whether warnings or quota limit events should be recorded. Warnings are logged. But notice that in this example, I don't actually block users from exceeding their quotas (the "Deny disk space to users exceeding quota limit" box is not checked).

5. Click Apply. If you haven't used Disk Quotas before, Windows will warn you that it will scan the entire hard drive to calculate how much space each user is consuming. Click OK if you want to continue.

Figure 12-43. Once you activate Disk Quotas, you can select options

Running a Disk Quotas Report

Once you're using Disk Quotas, you can run a report to see how much space users are using. Follow this procedure, referring to figures earlier in this section:

1. Using Windows Explorer, navigate to your Computer where you can see the hard drive(s) your computer uses.

2. Right-click Local Disk and then click Properties. Find and click the Quota tab, and then click the Show Quota Settings button.

3. Click the Quota Entries button. Windows will create the Quota Entries report in a new window, as shown in Figure 12-44.

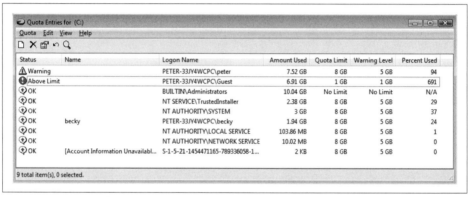

Figure 12-44. A typical Quota Entries report

 The report shows the quota limit and warning level for each user. Also note in this example the last entry, where the username reads [Account Information Unavailable]. This is for a user that has been deleted from the system. For this reason, it is usually good administrative practice to never *remove* user accounts from a system, but instead to disable them.

Setting Individual Quotas

In the preceding section, you may have noticed that there is no apparent ability to set quotas for individual users. The main Disk Quotas user interface doesn't provide a way to do it.

Yet, there is a way, through the Quota Entries *Report* user interface. Yeah, this is a bit odd: aren't reports supposed to just *show* us things? Well, this one also has the means for changing disk quotas for individual users. It makes sense as long as you don't think about it.

Anyway, here's how you set quotas for individual users:

1. Run the Quota Entries report per the preceding instructions.

2. Right-click a user whose quota you want to change. Click Properties. The "Quota Settings for *user*" window appears. See Figure 12-45.

Figure 12-45. Setting disk quotas for individual users through the Quota Entries report

3. Select the desired settings, depending upon whether you want disk quotas imposed upon the user, or nondefault settings instead. When you're done, click Apply and then OK.

4. Your settings will be immediately reflected on the Quota Entries window. The screenshot I took for the Quota Entries report was actually after I changed the settings for user Guest. Did you notice that earlier?

5. When you're done with your settings, quit the Quota Entries window by selecting Quota → Close, or by clicking the Close Window control.

> You can also create new quota entries from the Quota Entries window. Click Quota → New Quota Entry, which will then display a Select Users window that is similar to what you'd find in other procedures where you're selecting users or resources on a system.

Network Security

In this section, I'll discuss security as it relates to networks. When you connect to a corporate network or to the Internet, your system needs to be protected from the threats that are present in those settings.

The network security features in Vista that are discussed here (or elsewhere in this chapter) include:

Firewall

Whenever you take your computer outside of the protection of a network that includes a firewall, you must use Windows Firewall. In Vista, Windows Firewall is turned on by default. Specific firewall settings are discussed in the section "Windows Firewall," earlier in this chapter.

File sharing

You can control which files and directories are shared with other computers over the network.

Network Access Protection

This is a network security policy enforcement feature set up and controlled by network administrators.

Wireless network configuration

If your computer has a built-in or plugged-in Wi-Fi adapter, it can connect to a Wi-Fi network if one is nearby.

Network Access Protection

Network Access Protection (NAP) is a tool that network administrators use to help protect the security of an organization's network. When you connect your computer to a NAP-enabled network, the network checks your computer's security settings and environment before permitting connection to the network. If anything is missing or outdated, the network will automatically make the necessary changes, and then connect your computer to the network. Some of the things that can be checked include:

Antivirus capabilities

NAP can check your computer to make sure your antivirus software is installed, running, and using up-to-date signature files.

Firewall

NAP can verify that your firewall is enabled and properly configured.

Defender

NAP can also verify that Windows Defender is running properly and is up-to-date.

Patches

NAP can examine the Windows patches, as well as patches for other programs.

Installed programs

NAP can check whether your computer has programs that are required in your organization's environment. Examples include system management agents and business tools.

NAP is entirely set up on the corporate network; you do not need to do anything on your Windows Vista computer to enable it.

Wireless Network Access

Several configurations are related to wireless networks, and some are security-related. Because not all wireless networks are friendly, there are some settings you need to confirm and perhaps change on your computer.

To manage wireless network settings, go to Control Panel → Network and Internet → Network and Sharing Center → Manage Wireless Networks. The first window you'll see is a list of the wireless networks already configured in your computer. If you've been getting around like I have, you may have many wireless networks already in the list. See Figure 12-46.

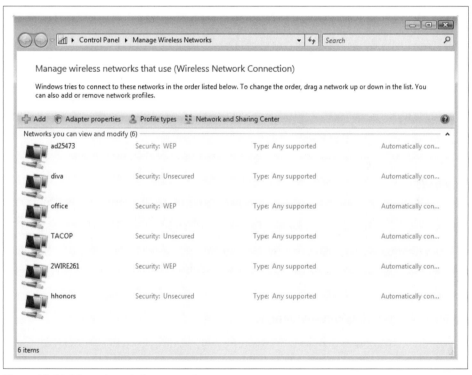

Figure 12-46. Managing wireless networks

Each item on this list is called a *profile*. Profiles store settings that are specific to each wireless network, such as SSID (network identifier) and encryption keys. There are two ways to create a new profile entry:

Automatically

If a network that you wish to connect to is in range of your computer, Windows will automatically sense it and ask whether you wish to connect to the network. An example appears in Figure 12-47.

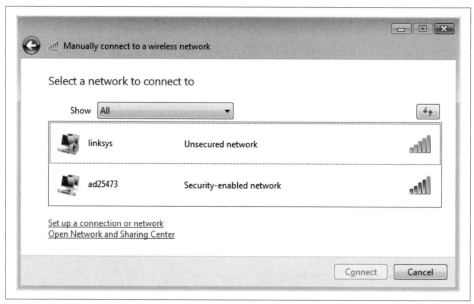

Figure 12-47. Windows asks whether you wish to connect to a new in-range network

Manually

If you wish to connect to a wireless network but are not presently within range of the network, you can set it up in advance. You will need to know the network's SSID and encryption key (if it uses one). To set up a new wireless connection manually, click Add on the Manage Wireless Networks window, then click Manually on the next window. You'll see a third window where you type in specific network configuration information, as shown in Figure 12-48.

Recommended wireless network settings

If you are setting up a wireless network at your home or small business, I recommend you set up the network access point with the following settings:

Use a nonstandard SSID (access point name)

A standard access point name such as "Linksys" or "mshome" will invite strangers and other unsavory folks to try to connect to your network.

Turn off SSID broadcasting

Most access points "broadcast" (make public) the SSID by default. You're better off not broadcasting your wireless network to the world (or at least to the neighborhood).

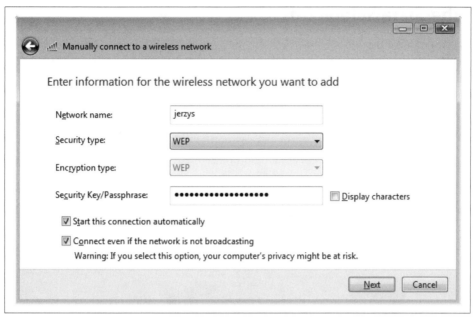

Figure 12-48. Entering wireless network information manually

Change the administrative password
  If you don't change the administrative password, anyone who knows the default password can potentially break into your home or office network.

Use the strongest possible encryption
  If your access point supports 128-bit or 256-bit Wired Equivalent Privacy (WEP) encryption, use the strongest encryption that your access point and your computer support. If they support WPA encryption, that's even better.

Turn down the transmit strength
  Many access points are set up with their transmit power turned to maximum, which may push your signal far past the range you need. Turn back your transmit power a little at a time until you have trouble receiving a signal, and then bump it back up a notch.

Don't share with your neighbors
  While sharing is neighborly, sharing your Internet access point with neighbors is not only risky, but probably also violates your terms of use with your Internet service provider.

You should not indiscriminately connect to unknown wireless networks. Many "rogue access points" are really traps that are set up to intercept your private information, such as logon passwords.

Other Data Safeguards

Network-based threats are not the only ones you need to worry about. Because this chapter deals with all manner of protecting your information, such a discussion should include protecting the computer *itself*, yes? That was a rhetorical question, one that I answer fully in the sections that follow.

Physical Protection

More than 100,000 computers are stolen every year in the United States alone. You probably know someone whose laptop was stolen. Notebook computers today come with a little slot designed for use with a cable lock that you use to secure the computer to a piece of heavy furniture. Most newer desktop computers have the same kind of locking slot, or some other means for attaching a cable. Figure 12-49 shows what these look like.

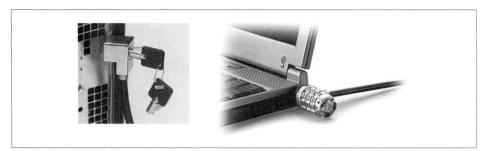

Figure 12-49. Lock up your computer to prevent it from being stolen

Here are other guidelines for laptop theft prevention:

- If you must leave your laptop computer in your vehicle, lock it in the trunk. Do not let others see you put your laptop in your trunk, or else a mischievous onlooker might just steal it.
- When traveling, always keep your laptop with you and bring it in your carry-on luggage. Never include a laptop with checked baggage.
- Avoid checking your laptop in with a hotel's bell desk, but instead keep it with you.
- Affix your business card to the top or bottom of your laptop computer; this can avoid mix-ups, confusion, and an attempted theft.

Preventing Others from Shoulder Surfing

If you use your laptop computer in public places (such as airports) where there are lots of people, some will be watching what's on your screen, if only out of curiosity. If you are working on sensitive information, you should consider purchasing a privacy filter, a film that goes over your screen to prevent onlookers from being able to see what's on your screen. See Figure 12-50 for an example of what these look like.

Figure 12-50. Privacy filters make it more difficult for others to see what's on your screen, yet they are easily removed

You should also make sure that people aren't gawking when you are typing in a password. The last thing you want is for an onlooker to write down the password that you just keyed in.

Strategies for Protecting Information

There are plenty of other things you need to do in order to protect your information from loss. This section describes a few strategies that you should consider.

Backups

Unless you've been living under a rock for the past several years—or are just getting started with computers—you are probably aware that bad things happen that can (and eventually will) destroy or remove your data. Here is a *short* list of the things that can happen to your data:

Hardware failures
> Disk crashes and malfunctions, power-supply glitches, and other events can result in your data being wrecked or inaccessible.

Software failures
> Bugs in operating systems (yes, even Vista) and application software can cause your data to be messed up.

Errors
> This includes removing and overwriting data that you later realize was a mistake.

You get the idea.

Backups are essential, unless you flat-out don't care about your data. (What, then, are you using your computer for? Surfing the Net and nothing else? Well, maybe you really don't!) For the rest of us, backups are a necessary part of computing.

I cover backups fully in Chapter 14.

Defense in depth

The concept of *defense in depth* is about not relying upon a single mechanism to protect you. Here are some examples of defense-in-depth strategies:

Malware defense
> Antivirus software on the firewall, email server, fileservers, and user workstations: viruses will usually have to pass one or more outer defenses before reaching users' computers, increasing the likelihood that viruses will be caught.

Firewalls
> Home broadband firewalls and firewalls on PCs increase the chances that network-based threats will be stopped by one of the two firewalls, because ordinarily a network-based attack would have to penetrate both.

Backups
> Keeping a copy of backed-up data where you work/live, and copies in another location, better ensures that you will be able to recover data in almost any situation (even if your home or place of business burns down).

Medieval castles also have an excellent defense in depth. Moats, drawbridges, high ramparts, and inner walls makes it difficult for attackers to reach the innermost parts of the castle.

Sometimes it is difficult to avoid having only a single layer of defense. When you have your laptop out in public and connect to the Internet using a public access facility, often the only antivirus software, the only antispam software, and the only firewall will be what you bring with you. Laptops are in their most vulnerable state when they're in public, connected to unprotected networks. Not only are such laptops more easily attacked and compromised, but they're also more likely to be stolen from a public place.

Password Storage

You might remember from the section "User and Group Accounts," earlier in this chapter, that passwords are often the only things separating your data from any possible intruder. How many user accounts in all of the online systems and applications you use do you have today? I have well over 100 user IDs and passwords. Do you think there is any chance in the world that I can keep these user IDs and passwords in sync with one another? No way, not when different web sites and applications have different formats for user IDs, and different complexity rules and expiration schedules for passwords. And besides, it's a bad idea to use the same password in too many different environments; otherwise, if someone guesses a password, she could have access to many of the web sites or applications that you want all to yourself.

I strongly discourage you from storing your passwords in a Word or Excel document, even one that is password-protected, because the password protection provided by Word and Excel is weak. And realize that EFS and BitLocker are no help if someone steals your system while it is turned on and you are logged in. Here are some recommended ways to store your passwords that provide a reasonable safeguard against third-party access:

Electronic password vault
> A specially encrypted repository just for passwords, a password vault offers strong security against intruders. Good examples are Password Safe and KeePass.

Write them down
> And keep the list well protected!

Encrypted text file
> You may keep your passwords in a *.txt* file if you encrypt it with PGP or WinZip version 9 or newer. I want to discourage you from encrypting Word and Excel documents, even with PGP or WinZip, because Word and Excel often leave temp and backup copies of your files lying around. Encrypting *.txt* files is safer, as long as you use Notepad to manage them.

Do not rely upon the password protection in Word or Excel. It is easily defeated with free and low-cost tools that can recover passwords in seconds.

Staying Current on Security Issues

Unless your Vista system is managed by a well-run IT shop that does a good job of staying on top of security issues, you will need to stay in the know yourself. Fortunately, you can do this in a plethora of ways. So, how do you choose?

Before we dive in, let's talk about just what you need to be aware of, in general:

Microsoft Vista patches
> Yes, even Vista will have security patches.

Other Microsoft patches
> If you have Office and other Microsoft software, you'll need to be aware of these patches, too.

Patches for other software tools
> Whatever you run on your Windows system, I'm sure that patches or updates of some sort will be released now and then. You want to use current versions of important software; older versions go off of support and no longer get patches issued for them.

Security threats
> It helps to be aware of new techniques that the black hats are using to try to steal your identity and your money.

Security trends and events
> It helps to know what's going on in the world.

It definitely pays to stay current on issues. The data you save could be your own!

Obtaining Patches

There's really only one good place for patches for Microsoft software: Microsoft. Once in a great while, a third party will develop patches for Microsoft software, but in most situations you are better off just waiting for Microsoft to release a patch.

There are several ways to get Microsoft patches installed on your system, including:

Microsoft Update
> Point your browser to *http://update.microsoft.com*.

Windows Update
> Almost the same as Microsoft Update. Go to *http://windowsupdate.microsoft.com*.

Automatic Updates
> This is the easy and automatic way to get patches into your system.

Microsoft Download Center
> If you want to sift through all of the things that users download, go to *http://www.microsoft.com/downloads*.

TechNet
> Go to *http://technet.microsoft.com*. You'll have to download and install them yourself.

Are all patches really needed? Well, for the most part, yes. If you are willing to take the time to do a risk analysis on every single patch, maybe you can avoid putting a few patches on your system. But if you don't have the time or the expertise to understand each patch and whether it's truly needed, you are better off just installing every applicable patch.

Sources for Security Advisories

Security advisories are notices that inform you about security issues that you may need to know about. Unless you have enough free time and a good task management system, it's probably best to have security advisories emailed to you so that you can find out about an important issue as soon as it is released.

There are more good sources for security advisories than you can shake a memory stick at; here are my favorites:

Microsoft
> You'll find everything on Microsoft's security page, at *http://www.microsoft.com/security*. Look around; Microsoft rearranges this page and I'm hesitant to tell you exactly where to look. It has a couple of different security newsletters and advisory services available.

US-CERT
> This is one of the premier sites on security. US-CERT has a free security-alert mailing list that will inform you of any new security risks and what you need to

do about them. Sign up for their alerts at *http://www.us-cert.gov*. The precursor to US-CERT is the older and highly respected CERT, which you can find at *http:// www.cert.org*. CERT also has an email security-alert service. Both are very good.

Secunia

Secunia is a highly respected security research organization that has a free alerts service. I warn you, however, that if you sign up with Secunia, you will truly be gulping from the fire hose. Sign up and brace yourself for alerts on Microsoft and other popular software, as well as software you may have never even heard of, at *http://www.secunia.com*.

Summary

In this chapter, you learned about some of Vista's most prominent security features, including these:

- The facets of data security are confidentiality, integrity, and availability (CIA).
- Vista doesn't do all of the security automatically for you.
- It is up to you to know what security measures you need to take, given your unique computing and business requirements.
- You are primarily responsible for the CIA of your data.
- Security is a moving target. Data thieves and other threats are constantly changing their tactics, which requires us to continually change ours.
- Ignorance is not bliss. Often, it leads to a compromise of your data.

Along the way, users and administrators with previous experience with other Windows operating systems may have noticed that much of Vista's redesign concerns areas of security. And while computer security under Vista can still be a complex subject, it is a little easier than in earlier versions of Windows.

Essentially, using Windows Vista means that you have a few more weapons at your disposal—User Account Control and BitLocker come immediately to mind—and that many of the default settings will help the average user navigate the often dangerous waters of safe Internet usage without much background computer know-how.

In the next chapter, we'll go beyond security to examine the most powerful tool administrators have to govern a Vista network: the Group Policy Object (GPO). As you'll soon see, these GPOs can give administrators authority over a vast range of Vista behavior. Enforcing secure computing is but one area that might be preconfigured by the settings of a GPO.

CHAPTER 13

Vista and Group Policy

In this chapter, we will look at one of the most powerful tools in the administrator's arsenal: Group Policies. A Group Policy lets an admin control almost every single aspect of the user environment, whether it be what appears on the desktop, what programs are available and when, what software is available, what group membership is in a domain, whether computer activity is audited, and what security and audit settings are in effect.

Just to name a few.

And even though we have the option of deploying them to manage a single Vista machine, it's much more likely that you'll deploy a Group Policy while participating in a Windows domain. Further, in the Windows world, domains are implemented via a technology called Active Directory. Essentially, an Active Directory database stores all information about the domain.

But I won't dare to explain it all in the introduction. It's a topic that simply takes a little time to flesh out, so we'll start this chapter with a general overview of the Windows Server Active Directory domain environment.

After you have a good understanding of what you're working with, we'll then move into some specific implementation examples, and then concentrate on some of the Group Policy changes that have been made with the release of Vista.

Whether you're a new Vista user or an experienced admin, you'll come away from this chapter with an enhanced appreciation of the power of Group Policies and a better understanding of how the new Vista settings can help you better manage your network.

Windows Group Policies

After a dozen chapters of Vista configuration joy, we now get to the *really* fun stuff; at last, we get to roll up our administrative sleeves and do some heavy-duty Vista administratin'.

We'll do that with Group Policy. Group Policies offer an administrative lever—a lever that will help admins implement a written administrative policy. Your company doesn't want ordinary users to access the Control Panel? Fine, you enforce the wish with a Group Policy.

Like folders and files, like users and groups, a Group Policy Object (GPO) is just another software object, typically stored in the Windows Server Active Directory database. (I say *typically* because one is stored in Vista's local directory database as well, but mostly Group Policies are used to manage Active Directory-based computing environments.)

This software object contains a collection of settings that can potentially affect almost any aspect of user and computer configuration. They're independent pieces of software, stored somewhere on the hard drive, just like everything else. (And like files and folders, the Group Policies are sometimes stored on network locations.)

We'll start this chapter with a look at Group Policies in the most general terms, discussing how Group Policies are created, managed, and processed when a user logs on. We'll then look at some specific implementations later in the chapter, focusing most specifically on deployment on a Windows Vista machine. Bear in mind, though, that these are just some examples of how Group Policies can be used. It would be impossible to examine every Group Policy scenario no matter how many pages were in the book.

But if we're going to discuss application of Group Policies to Active Directory objects, it helps to have the proper foundation: we need to better understand what those objects are. For seasoned Windows network administrators, this should be old hat. But not everyone is a seasoned Windows network administrator.

The next section is a necessary, if lengthy, segue to help those who might be new to Windows server enterprise computing concepts. We pick up with the discussion of how to apply Group Policy once the segue is done.

Understanding the Components of Active Directory

As we start the discussion of Group Policies deployment to Active Directory objects, we can't help avoiding a particular question: what, exactly, is an Active Directory?

That's an excellent question. In the simplest of terms, Active Directory is just another piece of Microsoft software, built upon the networking technologies that preceded it.

There's certainly nothing unique in that regard. Microsoft, along with software companies everywhere big and small, has taken existing technologies and/or the ideas from existing software and made it theirs by taking what, in its view, is the next evolutionary step.

In the case of Active Directory, Microsoft already had a working (if somewhat grumbled about) domain model built into its server products. When Microsoft moved to the NT operating system, it added the capability to link domains together with trust relationships. When this capability was carefully implemented, the enterprise could still be managed centrally or, conversely, could be distributed among multiple administrative groups. This linking also provided for easy access to resources, and it accommodated business mergers and subsidies as organizations redefined themselves.

The problem with NT 4's domain model was one of scalability. To wit: NT 4's domain model was flat, affording no levels of hierarchy. As you started to add multiple domains to the NT mix, several problems occurred, and these problems usually compounded themselves as the organization began to grow.

In its next iteration of its server family, Windows 2000, Microsoft set out to address this scalability problem by seeking an enterprise model that could meet two primary design objectives. The Windows 2000 domain model would need:

- A global list of each domain's directory available at every domain
- A system to automatically manage trust relationships, lessening the administrative overhead when deploying multiple domains

The result was Active Directory, which made its debut in Windows 2000, and it came with a handy little side benefit. By storing all Windows domain information in a centralized database, users and admins could then perform queries such as "Which one of the printers on the fourth floor of building 22 prints in color?" or "Is that computer located in the North building or the South building?"

Windows Server 2003 includes many improvements to Windows 2000's version of Active Directory, making it even more versatile, dependable, and economical to use. Windows Server 2003 provides the following benefits:

Easier deployment and management
> This includes improved migration and management tools, better tools with drag-and-drop capabilities, multiobject selection, and the ability to save and reuse queries; in essence, improvements in Group Policy that make it easier to manage groups of users and computers in an Active Directory environment.

Greater security
> Cross-forest trusts provided a new type of Windows trust for managing the security relationship between two forests. (I'll define forests in a bit.) Users can securely access resources in other domains without sacrificing administrative benefits of having only one user ID and password maintained in the user's home domain.

Improved performance and dependability
> Windows Server 2003 more efficiently manages replication and synchronization of Active Directory information. In addition, Active Directory provides more features to intelligently select only changed information for replication; it no longer requires updating of entire portions of the directory.

All of these improvements have been made in one area: the Windows directory database. But just what is stored in an Active Directory database? GPOs, for one. I discuss the other things in the section that follows.

Objects Managed by Active Directory

At its core, the Active Directory database is simply a collection of things in a Windows computing enterprise. The list of exactly which things are stored in an Active Directory database is exhaustive, and certainly most of these things are of little to no import, at least to a human being.

Of most concern to the administrator, of course, is a listing of what things can be managed.

Computers

A computer object is a software representation of a physical entity, namely, the computer.

It represents an important level of participation in the Active Directory domain. This level of participation usually has to do with security. When thinking of computer accounts, you should also understand that only certain operating systems have this capability to create a computer account in the domain:

- Windows Vista (Business, Enterprise, and Ultimate editions)
- Windows XP Professional
- Windows 2000 Professional
- Windows Server 2003
- Windows 2000 Server

The Vista Home Basic and Home Premium editions cannot participate in a Windows domain.

This can be terribly significant, of course, if your aim is to administer security options or the desktop via a GPO.

Users

All computing activities, whether it be access to a resource or backing up a file, occur in the context of a user account. An account is needed to interact with the local computer and the network, and is issued an access token at logon time. This access token is presented against a resource's access control list (ACL) to determine what level of access a user has.

Most often associated with domains, user accounts are also essential for standalone Vista computers.

Groups

A group object is just another type of account, much like a user account. However, this account's purpose is to contain a list. In this list is an inventory of all the user accounts that belong to the container account (i.e., the group). It is also used at logon time, in conjunction with the user account, to help generate an access token.

The advantage of a group is straightforward: it simplifies administration of permissions and rights. When you grant a level of access permission to a group, the permission applies to all members of that group. This is especially significant as domain accounts grow into the hundreds and even thousands of accounts, but can be deployed locally on a standalone Vista machine as well.

Printers

In a Windows domain environment, you have the option of creating a software object in Active Directory for each shared printer in your enterprise. The advantage is that it enables users to find an enterprise's printers more easily by conducting a search through Active Directory.

Additionally, printers deployed with Active Directory can be managed with some of the new Group Policy settings released with Windows Vista.

Shared folders

Much like printers, these resources are shared out from file servers in your enterprise. But also like printers, information about the shares can be published in Active Directory, facilitating easier searches when users are looking for resources. The computer hosting the share will still be responsible for managing the security permissions on that shared folder when it is accessed from the network.

Also keep in mind that these are just a few of the more common objects you create in an Active Directory database. You can also create Contact, InetorgPerson, and MSMQ Queue Alias objects, along with many others, as your needs require.

So now that we understand some of the things we can store in an Active Directory database, we turn our attention to some of the containers we can store them in.

And what's the significance of these containers? We can manage the objects in the Active Directory containers with a GPO.

Logical Active Directory Components

When we examine the Active Directory container objects into which we can place other objects (such as users, computers, printers, etc.), we're looking at the logical structure of a Windows server enterprise environment. The logical structure consists of several components, as discussed in the following subsections.

Domains

If the logical structure of a Windows server environment describes container objects, a domain is the main container. Simply defined, it's a logical collection of users and computers.

This is where all other Active Directory objects, such as user accounts, are stored. In other words, while there may be multiple domains in your enterprise, all objects will be stored in one of these domains.

More significantly, a domain represents a unit of administration. The objects in one domain are—or can be—administered very differently than the objects in other domains.

With a server domain in place, your computing enterprise gains several benefits over Windows Vista workgroups, including the following:

- They enable you to organize objects within a single department or single location. Further, all information about the object is available throughout the domain.
- They act as security boundaries. Domain administrators exercise complete control over all domain objects. Additionally, Group Policies, which are just another type of domain object, can be applied to manage domain resources.
- Domain objects can be made available to other domains.
- Domain names follow established Domain Name System (DNS) naming conventions, permitting the easy creation of child domains to best suit your administrative needs.

Not only does Active Directory store the list of objects in your domain, but it also provides a set of services that make those objects available and searchable by clients of the domain.

What kinds of services? Active Directory provides services to facilitate:

- User logons
- Directory replication
- Domain security
- Resource publication
- Application of Group Policies

And just where is this Active Directory database stored? On any Windows server that is designated as a domain controller. How is this accomplished? By running the Active Directory setup application. (Specific instructions are beyond the scope of this book; any Windows Server 2003 or Longhorn tome will provide detailed instructions, and you can find them easily enough online at sites such as Microsoft's TechNet.)

As mentioned, a domain is created using a single DNS namespace. But isn't it possible for some enterprises to have more than one namespace? Of course it is; Microsoft is a perfect example.

Larger enterprises such as this end up needing Active Directory trees.

Trees

The hallmark of an Active Directory tree is a contiguous linking of one or more Active Directory domains that share a common namespace. In other words, the domains are linked together in parent/child relationships

Think of the multiple Microsoft domains and you have the idea, demonstrated in Figure 13-1.

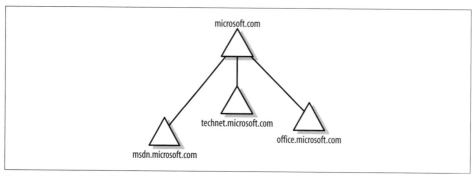

Figure 13-1. Multiple domains can be linked in a tree

 I'm not sure why, but the geometric shape given to a domain in every Windows book you'll ever see is a triangle.

In some cases, however, a single tree full of domains will not work for your enterprise. Say, for example, you run a company such as Microsoft, and you decide to purchase another company. Let's *pretend* that said company is Hotmail.com. The computing resources—users, computers, and so on—of one enterprise need to be merged with another so that they can be managed in a single administrative structure.

In this case, you'll create another logical entity, an Active Directory forest.

Forests

A forest lets administrators link together multiple domain trees in a hierarchical arrangement. The goal is to create an administrative relationship between several Windows server domains that do *not* share a common namespace.

By creating a forest, administrators have the computing to reflect the real-world business flexibility of acquisitions, mergers, and spinoffs, as represented by the illustration in Figure 13-2.

Organizational units

One of the most significant logical components of an Active Directory environment is the organizational unit (OU). OUs are container objects within a domain used to

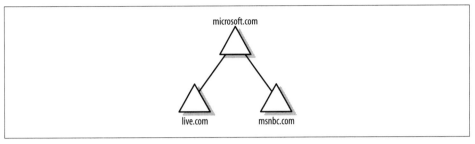

Figure 13-2. An Active Directory forest

group domain computers, users, and other domain objects into separate logical units. These separate units are also administrative entities.

Don't confuse an OU with a standard group. The only things groups can contain are users or other groups. OUs, on the other hand, can contain computers, shared resources, printers, as well as groups and users.

More significantly, you can manage the objects in an OU with a GPO. Although it looks strange in a sentence, you don't apply Group Policies to groups.

This also gives administrators almost unlimited control over how the domain objects are administered. A Group Policy security setting could dictate encrypted network traffic on one OU's set of computers—say, in a research department, for example—but not on another.

And it's entirely possible—likely, in fact—that more than one GPO is applied to the computer/user session. For this reason, it's important that administrators understand how GPOs are processed.

Group Policy processing

Many Group Policies can play a hand in determining the end-user environment. It is therefore important for administrators to understand the default Group Policy processing order.

Here's how the computer configuration and user configuration settings are applied at (computer) startup and (user) logon time:

1. At computer startup time, a computer obtains a list of GPOs that will be applied to the computer. This list depends on the following:
   - Whether the computer is a member of a Windows Active Directory domain
   - In what site the computer resides in Active Directory
   - Whether the list of GPOs has changed
2. After the list has been obtained, the computer configuration settings are processed synchronously in the order dictated by the processing hierarchy, which I discuss later in the chapter.

3. Any startup scripts assigned to the computer are run synchronously: each script must complete before the next one is run. All this occurs before the user gets any user interface, including the Windows logon dialog box.

4. The user presses Ctrl-Alt-Delete and submits user credentials.

5. After the user is authenticated, a list of GPOs for the user is obtained. This list is also dependant on several factors, including:

   • Whether loopback is enabled, as discussed later

   • Where the user account resides in the Active Directory tree structure (assuming a domain account is used; a logon using a local account to a local machine would not have any domain-based policies take effect)

   • Whether the list of GPOs has changed

6. The user settings are then processed using the processing hierarchy.

7. Any logon scripts assigned run asynchronously—all scripts are run at the same time by default.

Now that you have a better feel for the broad range of Group Policy options and how they can be leveraged in a larger Windows enterprise, let's turn our attention more specifically to Group Policies on Windows Vista computers.

Group Policy and Vista Administration

In very broad terms, here is what an administrator can accomplish with Group Policies:

• Provide a desktop environment that enables users to accomplish job functions while also ensuring that applications cannot be changed or removed

• Control the user experience by managing the appearance of the desktop, including what software is or can be installed

• Ensure that company-written policies regarding computer use and security settings have a computing mechanism for application

• Enforce centralized control of user and computer settings at the site, domain, or OU level

As mentioned, this can and usually does apply to Windows server sites, domains, and OUs.

But again, our focus is on what's new. For now, let's concentrate on the one GPO that is available on every Vista computer, no matter where that computer is deployed (i.e., domain or workgroup): the local GPO.

The Local Group Policy Object

Group Policies were first introduced with the Active Directory domain model with the release of Windows 2000. Since that time, every computer running Windows 2000, XP Professional, Server 2003, and now, Vista, has a local GPO linked to it.

This doesn't necessarily mean the local GPO has *any* effect on the user environment, however. By default, none of the GPO settings is configured.

For network admins, the advantage of a local GPO is the possibility of configuring just a single computer without affecting any others. In an Active Directory environment, these local settings can be overwritten by settings configured at the site, domain, or OU level. When Vista is operating in a workgroup, the local GPO is the only way to apply a Group Policy setting.

Opening the Group Policy Object Editor

A good way to get a feel for all the Group Policy capabilities is just to configure one. To do this, we'll start with an unconfigured GPO. Here's what to do to open the Group Policy Object Editor and get started with a local policy:

1. From the Start menu, open an empty MMC console by typing **mmc**. It should appear at the top of the program list. You'll be asked for administrative confirmation if User Account Control is turned on.

2. An empty MMC opens. From the File menu, choose Add/Remove Snap-in.

3. In the Add or Remove Snap-ins dialog box, shown in Figure 13-3, choose the Group Policy Object Editor and then click Add.

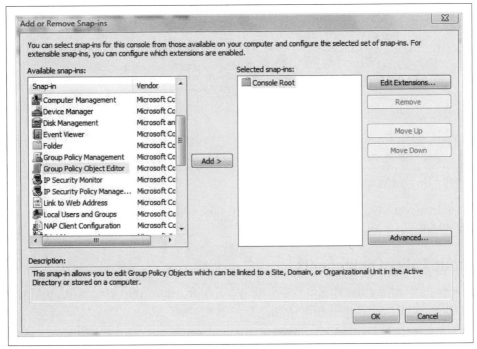

Figure 13-3. Adding the Group Policy Object Editor snap-in to the MMC console

4. You'll now see the Select Group Policy Object dialog box, seen in Figure 13-4. The default object here is the Local Computer object, which is what we want. If you're in an Active Directory environment, you can browse to edit Group Policies that would apply to other domain objects.

5. You're taken back to the Add or Remove Snap-ins dialog box. You can continue to add more management snap-ins to create an MMC console that best suits your needs. Click OK to finish.

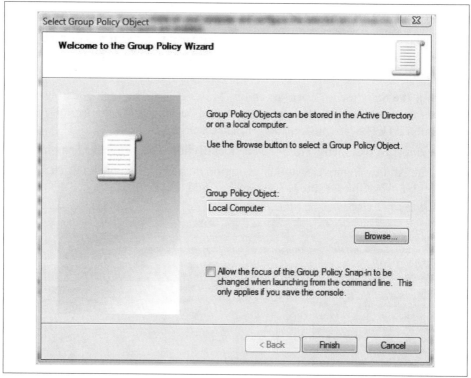

Figure 13-4. Linking to an object

Now that you have a point of reference, I'll take some time to explain what you're looking at.

Group Policy Components

You will now have the Group Policy Object Editor loaded into your custom MMC console. Now you can edit your computer's local policy.

As you can see in Figure 13-5, there are two main categories of Group Policy settings:

Computer Configuration settings

These are used to set policies that affect the computer regardless of who logs on. They are applied as the operating system initializes, before the user is presented with the logon screen.

User Configuration settings

These are used to set policies that apply to users regardless of the computer they are using. User settings are applied after a user identifies himself, usually through a username and password, and before the desktop is presented.

Figure 13-5. Settings in a GPO

If you expand each main grouping, you will see several subheadings of policy settings. Each grouping then includes a collection of software settings, Windows settings, and administrative templates. This does not mean that individual settings for users and computers are the same.

Generally speaking, you can expect three types of settings in each category heading, as discussed in the following subsections.

The Software Settings section

Found in both user and computer configurations, the software settings specify software installation options. These settings help you deploy and maintain installed software for the computers and/or users in your organization.

For example, you could use the software settings to ensure that all computers in a site get a service pack update to an application, or to ensure that a particular user has an accounting program available to her regardless of the computer from which she logs on.

The Windows Settings section

Found in both user and computer configurations, the Windows settings contain subgroups of scripts and security settings. The Scripts node is where we can most clearly see the difference between what settings affect the user and what settings affect the computer.

Notice that the scripts assigned to computers are startup/shutdown scripts, as computers engage in starting up and shutting down. Users, though, are assigned logon and logoff scripts, because that's what they do: log on and log off.

In the Scripts node, administrators can attach a script to a group using Group Policy. There aren't any limitations on the scripting languages used, ActiveX, VBScript, JScript, Perl, and DOS-based scripts such as *.bat* and *.cmd* are all acceptable.

The Deployed Printers node allows for management of printers deployed through Active Directory policy. I discussed these in more detail in Chapter 7.

The Security settings node allows for manual security configuration. These settings include Audit Policies, Password Polices, and User Rights Assignments, to name a few. Hundreds of security settings are available.

The Policy-based QoS settings node allows administrators to configure policies that will affect application traffic depending on network performance and availability. Quality of Service (QoS) describes an industry-wide set of mechanisms for ensuring that applications receive the required amount of network performance to ensure high quality.

In the User Configuration group of the Windows settings, you'll also find policies used for Internet Explorer maintenance and Remote Installation Services (RIS). If you're creating a GPO that will apply to an Active Directory container, you'll see a Folder Redirection node. You won't see one when working with a Vista local GPO.

The Administrative Templates section

Many policy settings are configurable in the Administrative Templates section, and they will have the most visible impact on the end user environment.

Further, these settings are all registry-based, meaning that they all write changes to the registry when they are processed. For computer settings, these settings are processed at startup time. For users, they are processed at login time.

The Administrative Templates section includes settings for Windows Components, System, Desktop, Control Panel, and Network. You configure the System node to control Group Policy itself, and we will examine it later when we discuss processing exceptions.

When you make changes to the status of an Administrative Template setting, you will simply double-click the setting (or right-click and choose Properties) to open the dialog box shown in Figure 13-6. In it, you will notice three options regarding configuration. A setting can either be:

Enabled

This setting will enforce the selected GPO setting. A setting that's enabled will edit the registry of the computer where the GPO is applied. These settings are usually the equivalent of editing a registry setting with a value of true (1).

Disabled

This setting will not enforce the GPO setting. Admins use the Disabled setting to specifically configure something they don't want to happen. These settings are usually the equivalent of editing a registry setting with a value of false (0).

Not Configured

This is the default for all local policy settings. It simply means the setting will not be configured one way or another, and that the setting (display of the Control Panel, for example) will be controlled somewhere else.

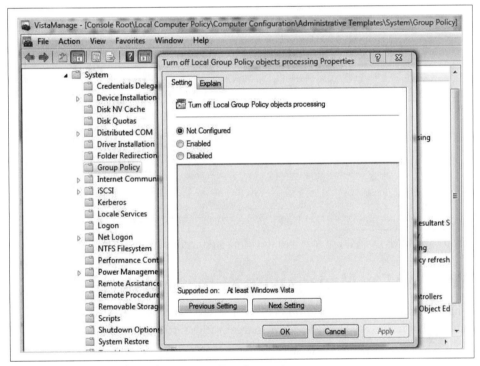

Figure 13-6. Configuring an Administrative Template setting

When you configure an Administrative Template setting, the change will be written to the registry, thus increasing processing time for the GPO. Note that this includes configuring the policy setting in the negative. Therefore, you want to configure as few of these settings as possible while still meeting your administrative objectives.

If you don't want to scroll through all of the many hundreds of Administrative Template settings, you can display only those settings that have been configured. To do so, choose the Administrative Templates node, and then from the View menu, choose Filtering. You will see the dialog box shown in Figure 13-7, where you can check the option to "Only show configured policy settings." Of course, this won't be effective when you are configuring the settings in the first place.

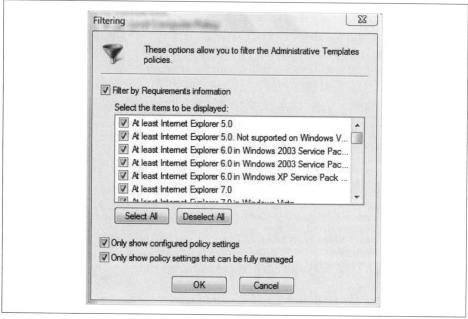

Figure 13-7. Filtering display of Administrative Templates settings

What You Can Manage with a Group Policy

What can you manage with a Group Policy? The short answer: almost anything you can think of. If it relates to Vista, you can manage it with a Group Policy.

If you need to impress friends and coworkers, know that with Windows Vista you can manage 2,400 settings, give or take a few. You read that right: two *thousand* four *hundred* settings.*

---

* That reminds me: I could probably pose this question at the end of Chapter 15, but why isn't there a way to search the Group Policy Object Editor? Vista lets us index the contents of an entire hard drive so that we can do things quickly like locate a single phrase in an email sent over a year ago, but it won't let us type what setting we're looking for in the Group Policy Object Editor. I don't get it. The best Microsoft has been able to come up with is a spreadsheet of all possible settings, which you can then open in Excel and search.

But don't worry, in this chapter we'll concentrate only on the settings that have been added to Vista. That'll narrow down our discussion to a scant *eight hundred* or so. Better settle in with a glass of merlot or something; we're gonna be here a while.

OK, not really. Instead of a data dump of all 800 new settings (never mind the 2,400 available settings), I'll include only a summary of the changed categories in the sub-sections that follow. Following that will be a table highlighting some of the most significant changes to help you get your bearings.

Painting with the broadest brush for now, here are the Group Policy categories where settings have been *enhanced*:

- Wired and wireless networking policy
- Windows Firewall and IPSec
- Print management
- Desktop shell
- Remote Assistance
- Tablet PC

And note that the new wired and wireless networking policies may require a forest-wide schema update, a discussion of which is beyond the scope of this book. For more information, go to *http://www.microsoft.com/technet* and search for "Vista Active Directory extensions."

Not only have there been enhancements to what was already there, but some new groupings have also been added. Here are the *brand-new* GPO groupings in Windows Vista:

- Removable storage device management
- Power management
- User Account Control
- Windows error reporting
- Network Access Protection
- Windows Defender

And bear in mind that in order to edit a GPO setting that will specifically affect Vista machines, you must launch the Group Policy Object Editor from either a Vista or a Windows Server Longhorn system. The new settings won't appear when you're using previous versions of Windows.

Changes to Group Policy Settings

A few of these new changes require more explanation. The next subsections provide that explanation.

Removable storage device management

Device installation presents a considerable challenge to network admins. Your network firewall can be a paragon of secure computing, for example, but do nothing to combat the user with a USB drive on his keychain. The new Vista GPO settings offer control over the installation and use of these devices so that there is a reduced threat of viruses, worms, and other malicious applications using removable media as a conduit.

You can disable removable device installation altogether using the setting shown in Figure 13-8.

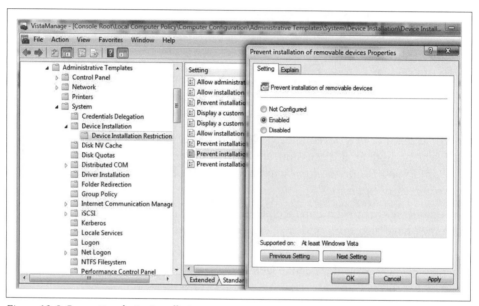

Figure 13-8. Preventing device installation

You can even configure removable storage installation policies so that only approved devices can be attached.

Power management

As discussed earlier in the book, the new Vista Power Options such as Sleep can save a considerable chunk of money per year on a single machine. Implemented across an enterprise, this can have a substantial impact on the bottom line. Prior to Windows Vista, companies had to enforce Hibernate and other power management edits with third-party tools such as Desktop Standard and Full Armor. Now you can control them with the Power Management options, an example of which appears in Figure 13-9.

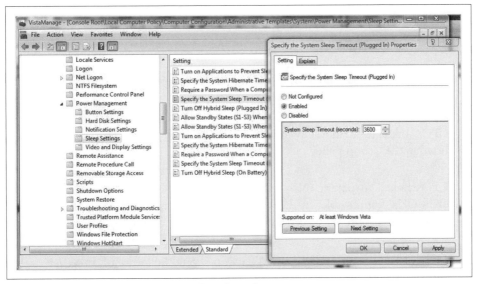

Figure 13-9. Managing a sleep timeout when plugged in

Security settings

With Vista, both the Windows Firewall and IPSec have been combined, allowing network admins to have greater control over client-to-server and server-to-server communications, both inside and outside the firewall. These are crucial security settings; GPOs enable them to be better managed centrally.

Printer assignment

Employees are on the move more than ever. They want simply to boot up their computers and be able to print. Vista addresses this by allowing printers to be configured based on Active Directory membership, letting computers move from site to site and automatically install the right printer for the site.

Group Policy Processing

Even though we deal with just the local computer policy object in a book on Windows Vista administration, several Group Policies might ultimately affect the user experience. As mentioned, GPOs can be linked to domains, sites, and OUs, and your user or computer may exist in one or more of these logical containers.

It's important, then, to understand GPO processing order so that administrators know where the local GPO fits into the picture. Here's the order in which GPOs are processed by default:

Local

Each Windows Vista computer will have at least a single local GPO, which will get processed first.

Site

Any GPOs associated with a site to which the computer belongs, or from which a user is logging in, will be processed next.

Domain

GPOs linked to the domain container are processed next, according to the order listed in the Group Policy tab.

OU

GPOs linked to parent OUs are processed next, followed by GPOs linked to child OUs if applicable. In this way, the immediate parent object of the user or computer account will be processed last, which has a significant impact on effective settings.

So, the local GPO is processed first. What you should be aware of, however, is that this actually makes local settings lowest in the GPO pecking order, for lack of a better term. This means that a setting applied by a local GPO can be overwritten by any setting applied at the site, domain, or OU level.

This doesn't mean the setting *will* be overwritten, just that it *can* if there's a setting conflict. For example, if you've configured a local GPO so that the Control Panel is not available to the computer, but a domain setting specifies that the Control Panel *is* available, the Control Panel will be available at logon time. Why? Because the domain setting is processed after the local setting, and will therefore override the local one.

However, if no Control Panel settings are configured for any other GPO that would apply to the session, the Control Panel will be disabled as dictated by the local GPO.

In other words, the last setting processed becomes the effective setting, but only when there is a conflict between settings.

See? It's simple.

Group Policy processing considerations

OK, it's not really that simple, especially when we throw in a few of the many Group Policy exceptions to default GPO processing order. Keep in mind, however, that all of these characteristics are meant to provide administrators with more flexible control over their desktops.

Here are some of the exceptions:

Workgroup computers process only the local GPO

Because all of the other containers you can link a GPO to—sites, domains, and OUs—reside in Active Directory, workgroup computers can process only the local GPO. This is especially significant in our discussion of Vista.

Admins can block policy inheritance

Inheritance behavior of some GPOs can be blocked. This applies only to GPOs that are linked to domains and OUs, however. It will not affect Vista machines in a workgroup.

There is a no override feature

This is the antidote for the Block Policy Inheritance option, but once again it does not affect the local GPO. Any GPO linked to the site, the domain, or the OU can be configured so that its settings cannot be overridden by other GPOs lower in the processing chain.

You can set a loopback setting

This one is probably the most confusing, and it is definitely the method used least often to configure an exception. A much better way is with the multiple local GPO, as discussed later on. It is designed for computers that are part of a closely controlled environment, such as laboratories or kiosks. In essence, the loopback setting makes the Computer Configuration settings the effective settings, no matter what other GPOs might apply to the user account at logon time. It's actually a setting of the Group Policy itself.

Configuring GPO loopback. To configure the loopback setting, you must edit the local GPO and then edit one of the Computer Configuration settings. The full path to the loopback setting is Computer Configuration → Administrative Templates → System → Group Policy → User Group Policy loopback processing mode (see Figure 13-10).

Figure 13-10. Configuring the loopback setting

Double-click this setting to enable loopback. Once in the Enabled state, the loop-back behavior will operate in one of two modes:

Replace

>This replaces the GPO list obtained for the user with the GPO list obtained for the computer at startup time. It effectively overrides any user-specific settings the user might have.

Merge

>This appends the computer GPO list with the user GPO list. Because the GPO list for the computer is applied after the user's normal GPO list is received from Active Directory, any settings configured with the local GPO settings override the user's normal settings where there are conflicts.

An example might help you make better sense of all of this. Let's say you have a computer in an office reception area. But now, rather than walk back to her desk, a user who is part of a Marketing OU logs on to check email before lunch using that very computer.

Here's the complication: you've set a GPO on the Marketing OU such that a large software package is distributed to all users of that OU. Without loopback, the user would have to wait until the software package deploys, and the reception computer would have an unnecessary application loaded. With the loopback setting, however, the user would not have the application sent and installed on the reception computer.

For more information on the loopback setting, choose either the Explain function or the Extended View in the Details pane of the Group Policy Object Editor.

In a Windows Vista workgroup environment, there's an even better option for tweaking Group Policy processing.

Multiple Local Group Policy Objects

Vista adds a new wrinkle to the local computer policy mix with the ability to apply multiple local GPOs, or as some people describe it, MLGPOs (pronounced *milg-pos*). Come to think of it, I may be the only one who describes it like this until now.

At any rate, it works very much like filtering the scope of a GPO with the ACL, but generally with much less confusion and configuration headache than before.

Here's why: prior to Windows Vista, admins working with a computer that wasn't joined to a domain had but one local GPO they could apply—by default, settings applied to admins and everyday users alike. This could present quite a challenge to administrators who wanted to change a setting or two—a local policy not really meant for an admin locked the computer from changes, and working around this could require a lot of effort.

But now, with a MLGPO, administrators can apply two different local GPOs to the local machine: one for admins, for example, and one for users. In fact, they can configure one for a particular user, as we'll see. This might come in especially handy where you're deploying a standalone Vista computer in a kiosk setting or other public locale.

Here's how it all works:

- When a user logs on to a local machine, Vista checks whether that user is a member of the local Administrators group. If so, a special "Administrator LGPO" is processed for the session.
- If the user is not an administrator, the "Non-Administrators LGPO" is processed instead.

 Applying these two local GPOs is an *either/or* proposition, not an *and* proposition.

So, let's set one up.

Creating a multiple local GPO

Here's how to create and apply a multiple local GPO:

1. Open the Microsoft Management Console and add the Group Policy Object Editor snap-in.
2. From the Select Group Policy Object dialog box, click Browse.
3. As seen in Figure 13-11, select the Users tab and click the user or group for which you want to create or edit Local Group Policy.
4. Click OK, click Finish, and then click OK.

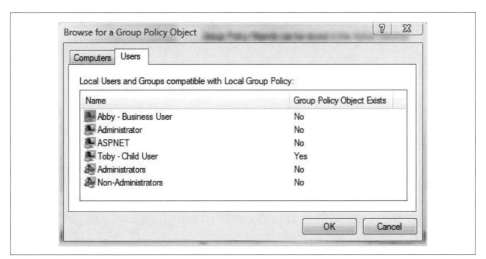

Figure 13-11. Configuring a multiple local GPO

You now see an item in the MMC that allows editing of policy settings that will apply only to selected users. For example, if you choose the Non-Administrators item, the settings will look like Figure 13-12.

Figure 13-12. Edit the policy settings for Non-Administrators

Note the absence of computer configuration settings as you edit the GPO. Only the user settings are present.

Once you've set it up, it's also important to understand the order of processing for multiple local GPOs. Here's that order:

1. Local Group Policy

2. Administrators or Non-Administrators Local Policy

3. User-specific Local Group Policy

As we discussed previously in this chapter, the last setting processed is the effective setting. For instance, any local GPOs that would lock down the computer can be overridden by more relaxed settings in an Administrators Local Policy. This lets admins log on to a kiosk type of Vista computer and make quick changes without facing a lot of Group Policy obstacles.

Further, a new computer policy is released with Vista called "Turn off Local Group Policy objects processing," shown in Figure 13-13. If you enable this setting, the system will not process any local GPOs. It is meant for use in domain environments to ensure that no other policies are applied at startup/logon time. This setting will be ignored on standalone systems.

MLGPO practical use

Now, you can use a combination of several local GPOs to tailor the user environment in almost any conceivable way. Let's say you have a child user on your home network. You can configure a rather lax set of Group Policy settings—except for the child account.

To lock down the desktop, create a MLGPO for just the child user and then configure setting restrictions as you please. If you want to take Internet Explorer off the desktop completely, for example, navigate to User Configuration → Administrative Templates → Desktop and then configure the "Hide Internet Explorer icon on desktop" setting, shown in Figure 13-14.

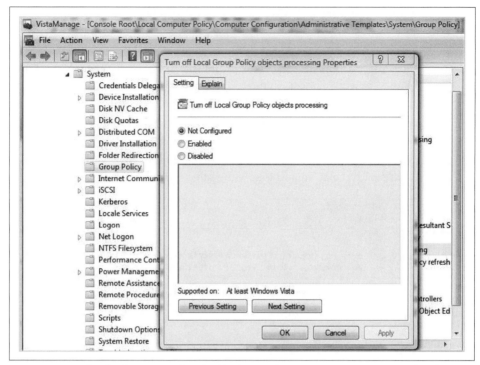

Figure 13-13. A local policy setting that disables local policy settings; very Ouroboros-like, huh?

Remember to save as a custom MMC on exiting. That can save a lot of clicking around when you need to edit these same settings later on.

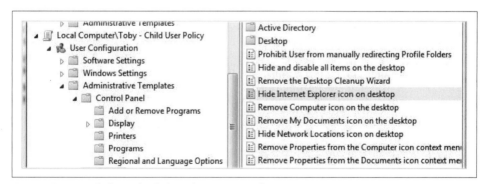

Figure 13-14. Lock down the desktop for just a specific user

Deleting a multiple local GPO

Removing the MLGPOs is a breeze. You don't have to fish around to undo all the setting changes; just delete the particular MLGPO instead. Here are the specific steps:

1. Open a Microsoft Management Console instance and add the Group Policy Object Editor snap-in.

2. Chose Browse, and select the Users tab.

3. Right-click the Administrators, Non-Administrators, or User-Specific Local Group Policy object. Choose Remove Group Policy Object from the context menu.

4. Click Yes to confirm, as shown in Figure 13-15, and close the Microsoft Management Console.

5. If you've saved a previous custom MMC, you can open that as well. Then, click File → Add/Remove snap-in and follow the same procedure as just described.

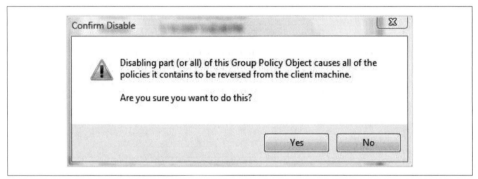

Figure 13-15. Deleting a local GPO for a specific user

 You can delete a user-specific GPO or the Administrative/Non-Administrative one. You cannot delete the built-in local GPO, however. To disable the configured settings of a local GPO, my suggestion is to reset all settings to the default of Not Configured.

Disabling User Configuration and Computer Configuration settings

As you have already seen, not all of your settings in a particular GPO need to be configured. In fact, it's a safe bet to say that the vast majority of settings *won't* be configured.

For example, if you configure a GPO whose only function is to configure a sleep timeout, the User Configuration settings will remain untouched. However, these unconfigured settings still have to be processed at logon time.

You can boost performance just a bit by disabling one of the two setting headings (User or Computer) if the only configured settings are in the other heading.

In fact, Microsoft recommends this practice; disabling a part of a GPO can speed up its processing. Generally speaking, however, you'll notice the biggest performance increase when several GPOs apply to a user logon. Disabling the user or computer setting won't have much of an impact if you're applying just the local GPO.

Nonetheless, it's a tweak all admins should have in their back pockets just in case. Here's how to disable the user or computer setting for a given GPO:

1. Open the GPO that you want to edit. On a Vista workgroup system, this means opening the custom MMC where you built the GPO or adding the Group Policy Object Editor.

2. Right-click the policy name and choose Properties. In the case of a standalone Vista deployment, you right-click the Local Computer Policy item.

3. From the GPO's General tab, select either the Disable User Configuration Settings or the Computer Configuration Settings checkbox as shown in Figure 13-16. You'll then see a warning as shown previously in Figure 13-15.

4. Click OK to accept the changes, and then click OK again.

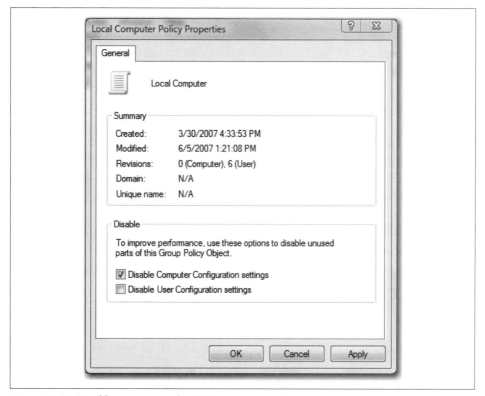

Figure 13-16. Disabling a section of a GPO

Configuring the User Environment with Administrative Templates

Once you learn the fundamentals of GPOs, the rest of the discussion just looks at specific examples of what GPOs can manage. And as you've already seen, they can manage quite a bit. What follows, then, are a few sections that examine just a couple of ways to effectively manage this Vista environment.

To briefly review, there are generally two ways you'll manipulate the Vista desktop environment for your users:

- You can change settings with the various applets in the Control Panel, as discussed numerous times throughout the book.
- You can use the administrative templates in the Group Policy Object Editor.

Obviously, this section focuses on the latter option.

When you edit the Control Panel, essentially you edit registry settings for a single system. Depending on what changes are made, they will apply either to all users of the machine or to just a single user.

What's more, the changes made with the Control Panel can be overwritten by a user with sufficient privileges, and remember that there are multiple pathways to access the Control Panel. Just because you remove the Start Menu option doesn't prevent a curious user from discovering another way.

The advantage of a GPO, on the other hand, is that the changes become a permanent part of the user's desktop, and these changes can then be easily ported to multiple computers. If you take away access to the Control Panel with a GPO, for example, it's gone; there is no pathway to open it.

Keeping this in mind, let's say that I want to make sure users—all users—have to enter a password when the computer resumes from either Hibernate or Sleep. I have two options: one is to open the Power Management Control Panel application. The other, longer-term solution is to do as follows:

1. Open a Microsoft Management Console instance and add the Group Policy Object Editor for the Local Computer Policy.
2. Navigate to User Configuration → Administrative Templates → System → Power Management.
3. In the User settings, there is but one power management option: the requirement of a password on resume.
4. Double-click the setting and then choose Enable, as seen in Figure 13-17.

Of course, as an administrator, you're worried about security settings that have a more substantial impact. You can also configure a host of security settings with a local GPO.

Configuring Security Settings with Group Policy

Another major subheading of Group Policy settings includes security settings. As with the end user environment, admins can exert control over wide swaths of computer security with GPOs. The challenge is to understand how each setting meets a particular challenge.

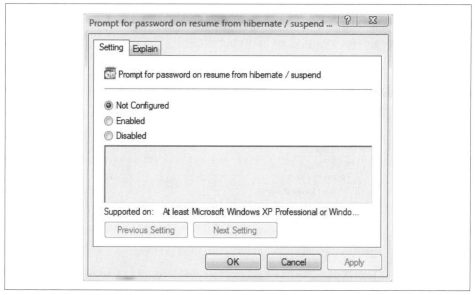

Figure 13-17. Enforcing a password policy upon resume

You can access all security areas from under the Windows settings in each of the User and Computer Configuration nodes, as shown in Figure 13-18. They include:

Account Policies
> These settings apply to user accounts, including password and account lockout policies.

Local Policies
> These settings are based on the computer you are logged on to, and they affect the abilities a user has over that system. The Local Policies settings include audit policies, user rights assignments, and security options.

Windows Firewall with Advanced Security
> This node lets you specify rules for Windows Firewall behavior. You can configure sets of rules to specify how the firewall responds to incoming and outgoing traffic.

Public Key Policies
> This setting allows admins to enforce data encryption on NTFS volumes and to define encrypted data recovery agents.

Software Restriction Policies
> These policies let you manage what software can run on a particular machine. This can be an important security level if you are worried about users downloading and running untrusted software in your network. For example, you can use these policies to block certain file type attachments from running in your email program. Other rules include path rules, which have the potential to restrict users from running software unless it resides in a specific directory or registry path.

IP Security Policies on Local Computer

The settings here are for configuring secure IP traffic. You can use this area to set encryption rules for inbound and outbound traffic, and to specify particular networks or individual computers your system can communicate with. Much like the software restriction policies, IP security policies are exception-based, configured by either accepting or rejecting traffic based on a set of conditions. The different permutations of IP security polices are virtually infinite.

Figure 13-18. Lots of security-related settings

Configuring a firewall setting

Once again, we could look at almost any of the security settings in more detail to give you a better feel for the configuration steps/possibilities; I lean toward the Firewall settings because these are new in Vista.

With a Windows Firewall GPO setting in place, admins can dictate several aspects of firewall behavior. For example, Windows Firewall can inspect incoming packets to determine whether they meet specific criteria in a firewall rule. If there's a match, Windows Firewall security carries out the specified action. If Windows Firewall cannot find a match, it discards the packet and writes an entry in the firewall log if logging is enabled.

To start creating a Windows Firewall with Advanced Security rule, follow these steps:

1. Open a Microsoft Management Console instance and add the Group Policy Object Editor for the Local Computer Policy.

2. Navigate to Computer Configuration → Security Settings → Windows Firewall with Advanced Security.

3. Right-click the Windows Firewall with Advanced Security item and choose Properties.

4. As seen in Figure 13-19, you now have a dialog box with four tabs: Domain Profile, Private Profile, Public Profile, and IPsec Settings. In this example, we'll configure a setting that ensures that the Windows Firewall is on.

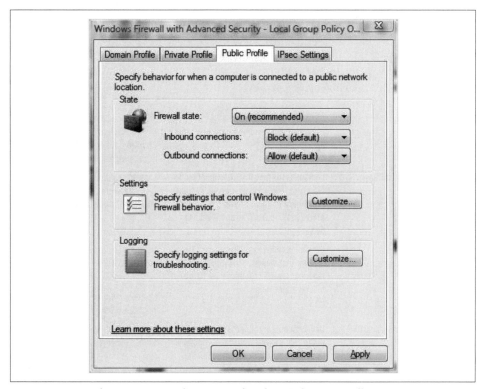

Figure 13-19. Configuring a setting that ensures that the Windows Firewall is on

Additionally, we'll configure a rule so that the Windows Firewall blocks all inbound connections and allows all outbound connections (the firewall will still allow responses initiated from the local system, such as routine web surfing).

Other New Group Policy Settings

This is just the overview. Table 13-1, provided by Microsoft, summarizes several of the new or expanded Group Policy settings. I include it here not because I expect anyone to actually read the whole thing, but instead to provide a quick point of reference in case you're wondering whether there's a Group Policy setting that will address a particular challenge.

For example, if you're wondering whether you can manage DVD burning on a Vista machine with a Group Policy setting, this table might be a good place to look. If you'd like to know whether there's a way to have applications install with an elevated account automatically so that you don't have to disable User Account Control completely, you can find out here. I generally hate printed tables, but this one can save you a lot of fishing around with the Group Policy Object Editor.

The table specifies the setting category, followed by a brief description of what it does, and then its location. You can review Table 13-1 now, or just skip ahead and use it when you need it.

Table 13-1. The new Vista Group Policy settings

Setting category	Description	Location
Antivirus	Manages behavior for evaluating high-risk attachments.	*User Configuration\Administrative Templates\Windows Components\Attachment Manager*
Background Intelligent Transfer Service (BITS)	Configures the new BITS Neighbor Casting feature to facilitate peer-to-peer file transfer within a domain. This feature is supported in Windows Vista and Windows Server Longhorn.	*Computer Configuration\Administrative Templates\Network\Background Intelligent Transfer Service*
Client Help	Determines where your users access Help systems that may include untrusted content. You can direct your users to Help or to local offline Help.	*Computer Configuration\Administrative Templates\Online Assistance*
		User Configuration\Administrative Templates\Online Assistance
Deployed Printer Connections	Deploys a printer connection to a computer. This is useful when the computer is shared in a locked-down environment, such as a school, or when a user roams to a different location and needs to have a printer connected automatically.	*Computer Configuration\Windows Settings\Deployed Printers*
		User Configuration\Windows Settings\Deployed Printers
Device Installation	Allows or denies a device installation, based upon the device class or ID.	*Computer Configuration\Administrative Templates\System\Device Installation*
Disk Failure Diagnostic	Controls the level of information displayed by the disk failure diagnostics.	*Computer Configuration\Administrative Templates\System\Troubleshooting and Diagnostics\Disk Diagnostic*
DVD Video Burning	Customizes the video disc authoring experience.	*Computer Configuration\Administrative Templates\Windows Components\Import Video*
		User Configuration\Administrative Templates\Windows Components\Import Video

Table 13-1. The new Vista Group Policy settings (continued)

Setting category	Description	Location
Enterprise Quality of Service (QoS)	Alleviates network congestion issues by enabling central management of Windows Vista network traffic. Without requiring changes to applications, you can define flexible policies to prioritize the Differentiated Services Code Point (DSCP) marking and throttle rate.	*Computer Configuration\Windows Settings\Policy-based QoS*
Hybrid Hard Disk	Configures the hybrid hard disk to allow management of nonvolatile cache, startup and resume options, solid state mode, and power savings mode.	*Computer Configuration\Administrative Templates\System\Disk NV Cache*
Internet Explorer 7	Replaces and expands the current settings in the Internet Explorer Maintenance extension to allow administrators the ability to read the current settings without affecting values.	*Computer Configuration\Administrative Templates\Windows Components\ Internet Explorer* *User Configuration\Administrative Templates\Windows Components\ Internet Explorer*
Networking: Quarantine	Manages three components: the Health Registration Authority, Internet Authentication Service, and Network Access Protection protocol.	*Computer Configuration\Windows Settings\Security Settings\Network Access Protection*
Networking: Wired Wireless	Applies a generic architecture for centrally managing existing and future media types.	*Computer Configuration\Windows Settings\Security Settings\Wired Network (IEEE 802.11) Policies* *Computer Configuration\Windows Settings\Security Settings\Wireless Network (IEEE 802.11) Policies*
Power Management	Configures any current power management options in the Control Panel.	*Computer Configuration\Administrative Templates\System\Power Management*
Removable Storage	Allows administrators to protect corporate data by limiting the data that can be read from and written to removable storage devices. Administrators can enforce restrictions on specific computers or users without relying on third-party products or disabling the buses.	*Computer Configuration\Software\ Policies\Microsoft\Windows\ RemovableStorageDevices* *User Configuration\Software\Policies\ Microsoft\Windows\ RemovableStorageDevices*
Security Protection	Combines the management of both the Windows Firewall and IPSec technologies to reduce the possibility of creating conflicting rules. Administrators can specify which applications or ports to open and whether connections to those resources must be secure.	*Computer Configuration\Windows Settings\Security Settings\Windows Firewall with Advance Security*
Shell Application Management	Manages access to the toolbar, taskbar, Start menu, and icon displays.	*User Configuration\Administrative Templates\Start Menu and Taskbar*

Table 13-1. The new Vista Group Policy settings (continued)

Setting category	Description	Location
Shell First Experience, Logon, and Privileges	Configures the logon experience to include expanded Group Policy settings in roaming profiles, redirected folders, and logon screens.	*User Configuration\Administrative Templates\Windows Components*
Shell Sharing, Sync, and Roaming	Customizes AutoRun behavior, creation and removal of sync partnerships, sync schedule, and creation of and access to workspaces.	*User Configuration\Administrative Templates\Windows Components*
Shell Visuals	Configures the desktop display to include the Aero glass display, new screensaver behavior, and new search and views.	*User Configuration\Administrative Templates\Windows Components*
Tablet PC	Configures Tablet PCs to include tablet Ink Watson and personalization features, Tablet PC touch input, input personalization, and pen training.	*Computer Configuration\Administrative Templates\Windows Components* *User Configuration\Administrative Templates\Windows Components*
Terminal Services	Configures Terminal Services remote connection properties to enhance security, ease of use, and manageability. You can prevent redirection of devices, require use of the TLS or RDP encryption, and require additional encryption settings.	*Computer Configuration\Administrative Templates\Windows Components\ Terminal Services* *User Configuration\Administrative Templates\Windows Components\ Terminal Services*
Troubleshooting and Diagnostics	Controls the diagnostic level from automatically detecting and fixing problems to indicating to the user that assisted resolution is available for application issues, leak detection, and resource allocation.	*Computer Configuration\Administrative Templates\System\Troubleshooting and Diagnostics*
User Account Protection	Configures the properties of user accounts to determine behavior of the elevated command prompt, and elevate the user account during application installs.	*Computer Configuration\Windows Settings\Security Settings\Local Policies\Security Options*
Windows Error Reporting	Disables Windows Feedback only for Windows or for all components. By default, Windows Feedback is turned on for all Windows components.	*Computer Configuration\Administrative Templates\Windows Components\ Windows Error Reporting* *User Configuration\Windows Components\Administrative Templates\ Windows Error Reporting*

Which of these new settings you might need to configure for your environment will be a matter of exploration, trial, and error.

You can configure the new Group Policy settings in a mixed Windows Vista and Windows XP environment, but they will be effective only on Vista machines. A Hybrid Hard Disk setting, for example, won't have any influence on a Windows XP system even if that computer is using a hybrid disk.

Background information: .adm and .admx files

Under previous versions of Windows, administrative templates were stored using a file with an *.adm* extension. These files represented the central nervous system of the administrative templates, providing the underlying definition of what is possible with Group Policy. They defined everything that was stored in User Configuration → Administrative Templates and Computer Configuration → Administrative Templates.

When an administrative template is changed or created, a *registry.pol* file is created. The *.pol* file simply points to the corresponding *.adm* or *.admx* files where the actual settings are defined in the templates. The machine or user receiving the policy doesn't need the *.adm* files at all; he just needs to be aware of a *.pol* file at logon time. In Windows domain environments, these files are stored in the SYSVOL folders on domain controllers.

But two of the big problems with *.adm* files in Windows domain environments were the *.adm* file size and replication. In previous Windows versions, several *.adm* files were copied to the SYSVOL folder every time an administrator created a new GPO. With several of these *.adm* files being placed in the domain controller's SYSVOL folder, and each file running about 5 MB, well, you see the problem.

Now, Vista and Windows Server Longhorn utilize the XML file format, and store settings using the new *.admx* file extension. The *.admx* format supports a central store that eliminates replication of duplicate information and makes it easier to update the file.

If a future service pack updates one of the *.admx* files, for example, all you need to do is drop the updated file in the central store and you're done. (This central store needs to be created manually on a domain controller, however.)

Vista comes with roughly 130 *.admx* files preinstalled. As shown in Figure 13-20, you can find them in the *Windows\PolicyDefinitions* directory.

But again, this is largely background information, and it will escape the notice of most Windows administrators unless they stumble across book sections such as these. As we've already seen, the tools used to edit these files—namely, the Group Policy Object Editor and Group Policy Management Console—are not significantly changed. You can edit the *.admx* files directly if you're so inclined.

There is also no *.adm* to *.admx* conversion tool to convert custom *.adm* files that your network may already be using.

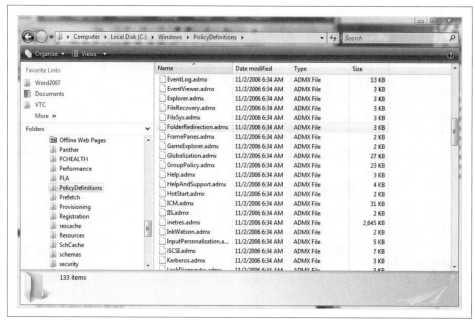

Figure 13-20. The administrative templates

Group Policy storage location

As I mentioned previously in this chapter, every system running Windows Vista will have a single local GPO stored in the following location:

%systemroot%\System32\GroupPolicy

Domain-based GPOs, on the other hand, are stored in two locations. The Group Policy container is a directory service object, and it stores all properties for the GPO including the latest version of the object, as well as the list of all settings that have been configured.

The other storage location is the Group Policy template, a folder structure located under the SYSVOL directory, which is a folder location stored on Windows server domain controllers that clients connect to when logging on to the domain.

Settings that have been configured with Administrative Template settings are stored here, along with security settings, script files, and any information about applications that will be deployed or managed via software installation settings. The Group Policy template is located in the *\Policies* subfolder for its domain.

Group Policy Behavior

To best administer Group Policy, it's vital that you understand how these policies behave. This will help you avoid confusion when troubleshooting settings, and also help you avoid unnecessary configuration. I mentioned some of these rules in other parts of the chapter; others introduce new concepts. I've gathered them all in one place for easy reference:

- All GPO settings apply, including those on the local machine and those from an Active Directory domain—unless a conflict is detected. The effective settings are then a combination of all settings of all site, domain, and OU Group Policies that might apply to a user login.

- If there is a conflict, the rules of policy inheritance are followed: local, site, domain, OU. The last setting applied where there is a conflict becomes the effective setting.

- If more than one GPO is linked to an Active Directory container object, GPOs are processed from the bottom to the top as they are listed in the Group Policy tab in the Properties dialog box. Again, where there is a conflict in settings, the last setting applied becomes the effective setting.

- Computer settings take precedence over user settings. If a setting is specified from a user and a computer at the same level of GPO processing, the computer settings override the user settings where there is a conflict in settings.

Remember these four items, and you will be well on your way to leveraging the full management capabilities of GPOs.

Summary

This chapter introduced you to one of the most powerful and flexible tools in the administrative tool chest. With proper implementation of Group Policies, you can enforce exactly the user and computer behavior you want.

We started with a general look at what Windows Group Policies are, and how they fit into the overall Windows enterprise. The simple fact is that you most likely won't be implementing many Group Policies unless you're in a Windows server domain. We touched on the role of Group Policies in these domains, and we touched on the interplay between local Group Policies and those implemented on domain objects.

We also stressed the changes to Group Policies introduced with Windows Vista. There have been many, as we have seen, and they provide new ways to make the network more productive and more secure.

In the next chapter, we'll take all that we've discussed in this book and examine what to do when the features and technologies don't behave exactly as I've described.

CHAPTER 14

Troubleshooting Essentials

In the previous 13 chapters, we established a good foundation. You now have a better understanding of how Windows Vista works, what technologies it is built upon, and how it represents a departure from previous versions of Microsoft's operating systems. Now we'll get to put some of that knowledge to use in solving some of the everyday problems that can arise.

Computer troubleshooting is in many ways more art than science; it's more of a marriage between your basic computer understanding and all the peculiarities of your specific environment. Truth be told, this chapter actually possesses very little capability in terms of helping you troubleshoot your network. What it can do, however, is get you pointed in the right direction so that you have a better idea of the troubleshooting resources that are at your fingertips.

Of course, there's no way any computer book can possibly foresee every possible computer troubleshooting scenario. If you want to really know whether a particular troubleshooting approach will work, my best advice is to give it a try. It's just a machine, after all, and you aren't going to break it with a few clicks of the mouse.

OK, you might break it, but if you follow some of the advice laid out in this chapter, you shouldn't be able to do anything that you can't undo. Here, we focus mainly on some of the troubleshooting tools that Windows Vista places in the hands of the administrator. As always, the focus is mainly on what's new: we will examine a new utility called Problem Reports and Solutions, and I'll bet you don't need to read much further to guess what the nature of that one is. Also, we'll explore some tools that an administrator might already know from previous operating systems like the System Restore utility, and we'll look at situations in which System Restore just might save the day.

We start this chapter with a look at a troubleshooting task that is meant to prevent many problems from happening in the first place. It's the Vista Automatic Updates, which Vista admins should absolutely use to enforce good preventive health.

Automatically Updating Vista

You should probably view Vista's Automatic Updates the same way you view a yearly physical checkup. It's just something that you should do to prevent as many issues as possible *before* they become issues in the first place.

The Windows Update engine handles two kinds of updates:

Critical updates
> Can help speed up your system, secure it, and keep it from crashing

Recommended updates
> Will address noncritical problems and help enhance your computing experience

A third kind of update, the optional update, is not downloaded automatically. You must get these updates manually by running the "Check for updates" task in the Windows Update Control Panel application.

By default, Windows Updates turns on the Automatic Updates feature, so it's very likely that this is something you'll never have to do in your administrative career. It's still a good idea to know where to look, though.

Here's what to do:

1. Open the Windows Update Control Panel application by typing **update** at the Start menu. It's under the System and Maintenance grouping if you're going through the Control Panel.
2. In the list of tasks on the left, click "Change settings."
3. From the dialog box shown in Figure 14-1, choose the desired update options.
4. Click OK to commit your changes. You may be asked for administrative confirmation by User Account Control.

Additionally, if the Automatic Updates feature is ever turned off, the Vista Security Center will yell at you (assuming that the Security Center notifications about Automatic Updates defaults haven't been changed). Once you're in the Security Center, you'll see a "Change settings" button, shown in Figure 14-2, that will take you right back to the Automatic Updates settings dialog box.

 The Windows Updates are applied to the computer, and therefore affect all users of a particular system.

Sometimes during troubleshooting, you will want to double-check to confirm that a particular update has been installed. If this is the case, you can choose the "View update history" link on the right side of the Windows Updates dialog box.

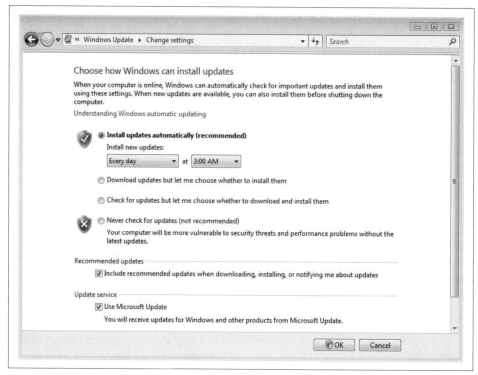

Figure 14-1. Configuring Automatic Updates

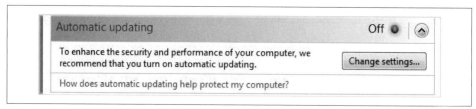

Figure 14-2. The Security Center when detecting that Automatic Updates are off

Automatically Checking for Solutions to Problems

Each time you encounter a significant error using Windows Vista, you'll be asked whether you want to send the information to Microsoft. You might think this is just a one-way street, where you're providing information that will help Microsoft write software in the future that will prevent whatever problem you're having.

If you think about it for a moment, that must be one huge store of information being generated by the planet's users of Windows computers.

So, why should one entity be the only beneficiary? Surely there must be a way for ordinary users to leverage this information as well, right? Surely some other user in another corner of the computing globe is—or has had—the same difficulty as you. Right?

The answer is yes, and yes. Users can use the information gathered from other users to try to troubleshoot issues, using a utility called Problem Reports and Solutions. If there's a known solution to a known problem, you can use Problem Reports and Solutions to easily retrieve the fix.

Here's how to put it all to work:

1. Open the Control Panel, and then open Problem Reports and Solutions. As always, you can type **problem** from the Start menu.

2. You'll see the Problem Reports and Solutions window. In this window are several tasks on the left pane and a status area on the right.

3. To see a list of problems that Vista has detected, click the View Problem History link. You'll see a dialog box such as the one shown in Figure 14-3. You can view further details about each problem using the links herein.

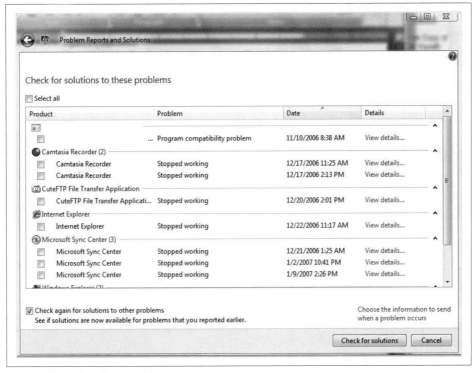

Figure 14-3. A list of Vista problems

4. After visiting the Problem History page, you can run a check for solutions by navigating back to the Problem Reports and Solutions home page and clicking the Check Now button.

   Vista then checks online for any available solutions. If it finds one, you'll see a dialog box similar to what you see in Figure 14-4.

5. From there, simply follow the "Solution found" link for instructions on how to resolve the detected issue. Most times, it will involve a software download and install.

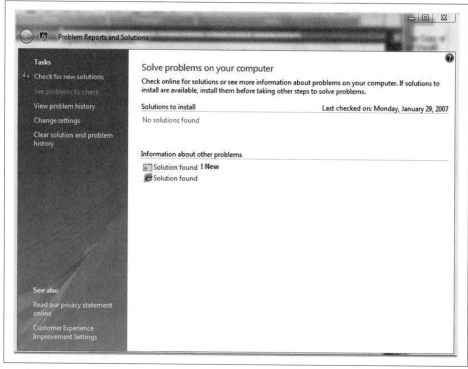

Figure 14-4. A fix is discovered

Note that much of this problem-checking behavior is completely automated by default. Administrators can govern this, however, by following the "Change settings" link on the left.

After clicking this link, you will be able to toggle automatic reporting either on or off, and you will be able to configure a few other options. As seen in Figure 14-5, administrators can set exceptions if they have a program that they want Vista to ignore when it reports a problem.

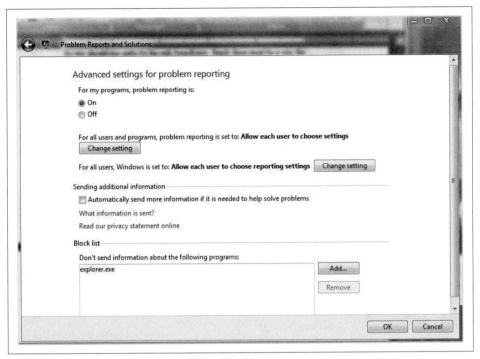

Figure 14-5. Configuring Problem Reports and Solutions options

In Figure 14-5, I added Vista Explorer as an exception. No information about it will be sent if and when it crashes.

Note here that one user's setting doesn't necessarily have to be the setting for other users. If you're changing the reporting settings for all users, you will be asked for administrative confirmation if User Account Control is turned on.

Checking Security Using the Microsoft Baseline Security Analyzer

Another excellent tool that's freely available to Windows Vista administrators (or anyone else, for that matter) is the Microsoft Baseline Security Analyzer (MBSA). This tool scans a system and quickly identifies security holes such as missing software patches or accounts with a blank or weak password.

Better yet, it recommends corrective action. The only bad news of sorts is that it's not built into Windows Vista. You have to download this one from the Microsoft web site:

http://www.microsoft.com/technet/security/tools/mbsahome.mspx

At the time of this writing, the tool was in version 2.0.1, the version whose click-steps I describe here. The install steps are straightforward; just follow the steps in the wizard.

During installation, the MBSA places a shortcut on the desktop by default. To launch the tool and perform a scan, follow these steps:

1. Double-click the desktop icon, and then, from the MBSA home page, choose Scan a Computer. Note here that admins can also use the MBSA to scan multiple computers in a network from a central location.

2. In the Computer to Scan page, you should see the local machine listed if you've chosen the "Scan a computer" option. (The other selection produces a page from which you can select a range of machines.) Furthermore, the options in this screen let you specify exactly what components get checked during the scan.

3. Once you verify the machine to scan, click the "Start scan" link. You'll now see a Scanning page with a progress bar that can take several minutes to complete.

4. When the scan finishes, you'll see a report screen similar to what appears in Figure 14-6.

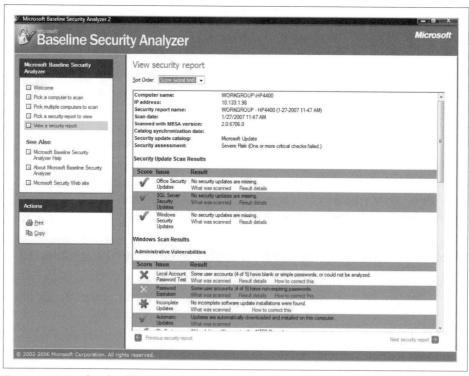

Figure 14-6. Results of an MBSA scan

As you can see, this provides extremely valuable information to administrators who are interested in doing everything they can to stop problems before they start. For example, the administrator of this machine (me) has been very diligent about installing necessary software updates, it seems, and has gotten passing grades in most areas of computer security.

But the MBSA scan also revealed a very significant threat: local user account passwords are weak, and have received a failing grade. However, the MBSA makes it easy to investigate the exact nature of the failing grade by clicking the "Result details" link, revealing the dialog box shown in Figure 14-7.

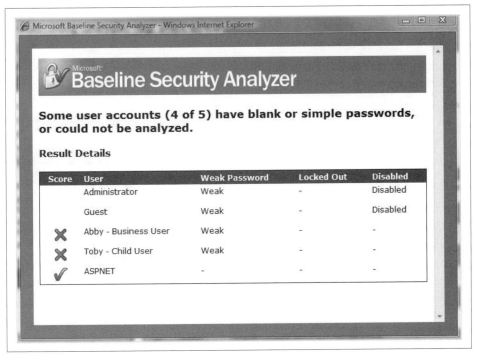

Figure 14-7. Investigating the nature of a failing grade

The passwords for both the Business User and the Child User are weak (in fact, they are both blank). The passwords for the Guest and Administrator accounts are weak as well, but they don't receive a formal score because both accounts are disabled.

Removing Software Using the Malicious Software Removal Tool

While we're on the subject of freely available software, a mention of the Malicious Software Removal Tool (MSRT) is in order. Like Automatic Updates and the MBSA, you should view the MSRT as an essential tool in your toolkit.

Unlike Automatic Updates and the MBSA, though, this is a utility that you will call in *after* the problem has occurred. As the name implies, it is meant for both detection and removal of software that has already infected a system.

Also like the MBSA, it is not included as a Windows Vista built-in component. You can download it from this web resource:

http://www.microsoft.com/security/malwareremove/default.mspx

Once you locate the MSRT, running it is a fairy automated process. Note that it will *not* install software locally on the Vista computer by default, although the Microsoft Download Center offers a version that you can install locally. From the aforementioned web site, it is instead an entirely web-based application.

To run it, follow these steps:

1. From the MSRT web site, follow the download links. When you're prompted by the download, click Run.

2. You'll now see a dialog box like the one in Figure 14-8. You have three MSRT scanning options here:

   Quick scan
   This scans the areas that are most likely to contain malicious software.

   Full scan
   This scans the entire machine. It's more exhaustive in its check, and it can take several hours. Usually, you'll be prompted to run a full scan when a quick scan reveals malicious software.

   Customized scan
   This option provides administrators with the most flexibility. To scan specific folders, click the Choose Folder button.

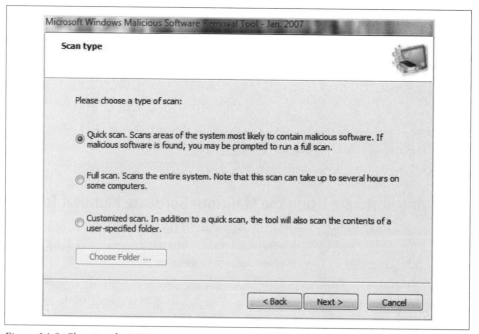

Figure 14-8. Choosing the MSRT scan options

The MSRT then performs a scan and finishes with a report. You'll want to see a report that looks like the one in Figure 14-9.

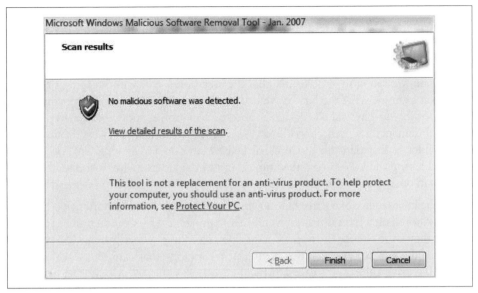

Figure 14-9. Results of a clean MSRT scan

You can follow the "View detailed results of the scan" link to find out more about the scan. You'll see a list of what the scan checks for, as well as whether any malware was detected. The MSRT checks for common viruses such as bugbear, mydoom, mywife, blaster, and netsky.

 It's worth reiterating that the MSRT is not a replacement for antivirus software. Antivirus software protects the machine before the infection occurs. The MSRT is meant for post-infection cleansing, and it scans for a larger scope of programs that are classified as malicious without necessarily being considered computer viruses.

The MSRT is also available for Windows XP machines. It's a good practice to run an MSRT scan before performing an upgrade from XP to Vista.

Troubleshooting the Hard Disk

Obviously, the hard disk is a critical component to the overall Windows Vista experience. After all, Vista won't load in the first place without a working hard drive.

Throughout this book, we examined many hard drive administration considerations. Now let's try to focus on a few of the things we can do when things start to go wrong.

Disk Diagnostics

If you'll allow a little journalistic license here, I will cite from memory with 99 percent certainty that the hard drive is the one computing component that fails more often than any other—more than processors, monitors, memory, video cards, and so on. (I'm excluding peripherals such as printers and scanners from the equation.) I read this somewhere before; if someone has evidence to refute it, I'm open to correction.

At any rate, we can fairly well *assume* that the assertion is true without further research when you examine what the hard drive has going against it: it has lots of moving parts, it's susceptible to physical shock, it's connected to a power supply, it's susceptible to electrical damage, it's used almost every day, and it's susceptible to overheating. The real wonder is that data on modern hard disks survives for as long as it does. (I've dropped laptops and iPods countless times, and to date I have never lost data this way. Knock.) In other words, drive failure is not a question of *if*, but rather of *when*.

Given the inevitability of a drive failure, combined with the vital importance of what is typically stored on a hard drive (I haven't met many folks who wouldn't go nearly catatonic if they were to lose their entire hard drive like, now, yours truly included), hard drive manufacturers have included a built-in technology that can help warn users of impending drive failures. It's called SMART technology (for Self Monitoring, Analysis, and Reporting Technology), and it's been around for more than 10 years, no less.

The problem, at least until now, has been that Windows operating systems had no way to access this information without a third-party utility. Windows Vista, however, comes with a feature called Diagnostic Policy Service (DPS) that includes the capability to monitor SMART. If SMART detects a hard drive problem, Vista shows a message that the hard disk is at risk.

There's nothing to configure, really; it's just an informational message. The idea is that SMART gives you enough time to perform backups before it's too late—the SMART error messages will even nudge you to start a backup session. You should replace the disk as soon as possible, however.

And if you're wondering about the chances that Vista and SMART will be able to save your hard drive bacon, know that it is estimated that SMART technology can predict about one out of every three disk failures. Don't for a moment think that this is a good replacement for a regular backup.

Checking for Disk Errors

You can also manually check for disk errors at any time by following these steps:

1. Open Vista Explorer and select the Computer object. Right-click the hard disk you want to check for errors and choose Properties from the context menu.

2. As seen in Figure 14-10, select the Tools tab and then click Check Now in the Error Checking section. You will be prompted for administrative confirmation if User Account Control is turned on.

Figure 14-10. Click Check Now

3. You'll now see a little dialog box with two options:

- To automatically repair problems, select the "Automatically fix file system errors" checkbox. Otherwise, the scan will simply report problems rather than fix them.

- To perform a thorough disk check, choose the "Scan for and attempt recovery of bad sectors" option. This will try to repair physical errors on the hard disk itself. The drawback is that this option will take much longer to complete.

4. Click Start to begin the scan. You can continue working while it is conducted.

This scan will help solve problems caused by corrupted files and folders, and it is part of a good preventive maintenance routine: it helps improve overall performance by making sure that the hard disk is error-free.

Memory Diagnostics

If you've ever troubleshot a problem that was traced back to bad physical memory, you understand just how frustrating this diagnosis can be. Often the problem cannot be reproduced, and the seeming randomness makes problem isolation next to impossible.

Again, Vista now includes a tool to help administrators test physical memory in order to either pinpoint or eliminate physical RAM as the source of the trouble.

It's called the Windows Memory Diagnostics tool. What's more, Vista will automatically monitor memory during system use. If a possible memory problem is detected, you'll see a notification that asks whether you want to run the Memory Diagnostics Tool. You can select from two options here: either run it now, or run it the next time the computer is restarted. Note that in either case, however, the tool requires a system reboot.

If you want to run it without prompting, you can do so at any time. Here's how to run a memory scan:

1. From the Start menu, type **memory**. The Windows Memory Diagnostics Tool should appear at the top of your programs list.

2. You'll now see the dialog box shown in Figure 14-11. As mentioned, you can either run the tool immediately or run it the next time your computer restarts (essentially creating a scheduled task).

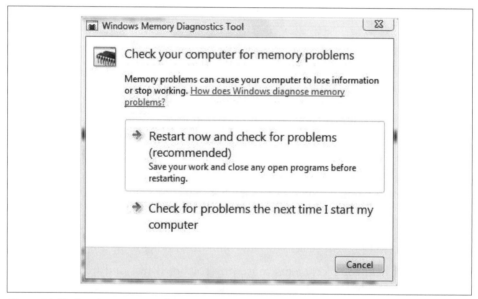

Figure 14-11. Starting a memory diagnostic test

Once the computer reboots, you'll be presented with a results report. If the Memory Diagnostics Tool has not detected any errors, you'll get a message that no errors were found. If it has, you should be prompted to contact your computer or memory manufacturer for additional troubleshooting steps and/or replacement of the memory modules.

Administrators can also configure a few advanced options in the Memory Diagnostics Tool. You can set three additional options:

Test mix
Select which type of test you want to run. These options are listed when you run the Memory Diagnostics Tool.

Cache
Select the cache setting you want for each test.

Pass count
Choose the number of times you want to repeat the test.

To configure these advanced settings, press F1 as the Memory Diagnostics Tool starts.

Resource Exhaustion Detection

Another common cause of general computer flakiness is when resources are taxed to their limit. If it's making extensive use of virtual memory, for example, the computer will often become unstable. If it's out of virtual memory altogether, it can simply hang.

But Vista has provided an early warning mechanism for this very condition, with the Windows Resource Exhaustion Detection and Resolution tool, which gets the oh-so-kitschy acronym of RADAR (it has all the earmarks of a backronym, though, doesn't it?).

Windows Resource Exhaustion Detection and Resolution works its magic by tracking the commit limit used by virtual memory, which is essentially the total amount of virtual memory that Windows Vista can use. If the commit limit reaches a value of 100 percent of the available paging file size, the RADAR tool notifies the user.

What's more, the warning includes a list of applications that are using the greatest amount of virtual memory resources. Administrators can then shut down the offending applications rather than take a scattershot approach of closing apps in an attempt to free system resources.

You can keep track of the commit limit manually by launching the Reliability and Performance Monitor and then using the Performance Monitor to track the "% Committed Bytes in Use" counter under the Memory object. As the commit percentage approaches 100, you can expect to receive the RADAR warning.

If you're administering Vista and can't stand the thought of the RADAR tool running on a particular machine, you can prevent it from running by killing the service on which it depends. The RADAR tool relies on the Diagnostic Policy Service.

Using Remote Assistance

Another valuable troubleshooting resource available for Vista computers is Remote Assistance. This feature has been available on previous version of Windows, and its purpose is the same here: it lets other people you trust—family members, friends, support personnel, and so on—connect to your computer and either demonstrate how to perform a certain (troubleshooting) task or just perform the task themselves.

And as the name suggests, the person helping you troubleshoot doesn't have to be in the next room. He can connect from anywhere in the world provided that there's an Internet connection between the two computers and the firewalls in between allow the traffic (discussed shortly).

After the Remote Assistance Connection has been established, the support person can view your computer screen, exchange instant messages, and even take control of your computer, but only if you grant him permission to do so.

Before you begin, understand that although Remote Assistance has been around for a while, it is not available on every version of Windows. You can use it on these operating systems:

- Windows Vista (all versions)
- Windows XP
- Windows Server 2003
- Any later versions of Windows

In other words, you won't be able to use Remote Assistance from your Windows Vista machine to help out a friend using Windows 2000, but you will be able to help someone using Windows XP.

Once the prerequisite operating systems are in place, the next part is actually setting up a Remote Assistance session. The next section looks at some of the considerations involved.

Setting Up a Remote Assistance Connection

The Remote Assistance Process starts in one of two ways:

- The person in need of help (the user) can initiate a Remote Assistance session by requesting help from a support person.
- A support person can initiate the session by offering help.

What's more, there are two methods whereby the Remote Assistance request—either *for* help or *offering* help—can be generated. The two methods are:

Email invitation

The Remote Assistance invitation in an email is sent as an attachment to a standard email message. The session is initiated when the attachment is opened. In an enterprise environment, it might be good practice to create a dedicated support email so that support personnel can more efficiently respond to Remote Assistance requests.

File invitation

A file invitation is saved as a Microsoft Remote Control incident file, and it's given the file extension *.MsRcIncident*. Now it can be treated as just about any other file on your computer, such as a Word document or Excel spreadsheet. Like the email invitation, the file has to be received and opened by the recipient for it to be useful. It can be attached to an email, yes, but in that case, why not use the email invitation? More practically, in an enterprise where file invitations are used rather than email requests, administrators might consider setting up a share where all Remote Assistance file invitations can be saved. Support personnel can then connect to the share and open the invite.

From there, the click-steps are little more than a matter of stepping through a wizard that does a pretty good job of laying out the necessary steps. If you're requesting help from a support person, for example, do this:

1. Open the Remote Assistance tool by typing **remote** at the Start menu. Windows Remote Assistance should appear at the top of the screen.

2. The first Windows Remote Assistance dialog box you'll see has two paths. To request help, choose the "Invite someone" option.

3. You'll now see a dialog box, shown in Figure 14-12, where you will either send the invite as an email or save the invite as a file. What's more, you will be able to reuse an existing invitation if you're sending to the same support person. Let's say, for instance, that you invited someone to help, but she got tied up before she was able to respond. If she's now available, you don't have to generate a new invitation again. Just use the old one instead.

The instructions from there will depend on what you're doing with the invite. Under either option, you'll be creating a password for the Remote Assistance session.

Click Finish to complete the Remote Assistance request. You'll then see a narrow dialog box like the one shown in Figure 14-13 until the Remote Assistance request is received and acted upon.

By default, the Remote Assistance invitation will be valid for six hours, but you can change this using the System Properties dialog box. Use the Remote Settings task to configure these defaults.

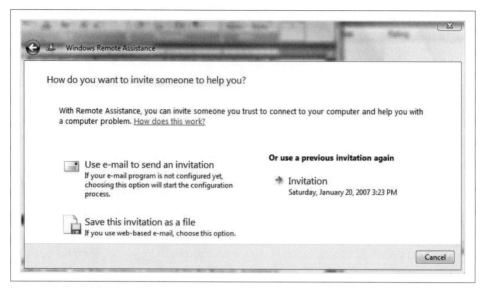

Figure 14-12. Sending a Remote Assistance invitation

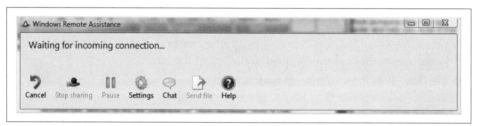

Figure 14-13. Waiting for a connection

The other Remote Assistance option is to offer help. You might want to use this option on the heels of a phone call in which the other person is confused by your instructions, or when it will just save time, effort, and a car ride to perform a quick fix.

Here's how to offer help:

1. Once again, open the Remote Assistance tool as shown previously, and choose the second option, "Offer to help someone."

2. You are now given a dialog box where you can choose how to connect, as shown in Figure 14-14. If the user has sent out a request, you can use this dialog box to locate that invitation (you don't have to, however; just opening the invitation file is enough). If you're making an "unsolicited" offer, you have to type the IP address or computer name in the second entry box.

3. Choose Finish.

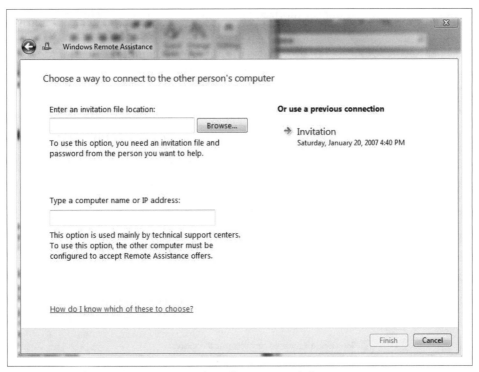

Figure 14-14. Choosing how to connect when offering remote help

Assuming someone's on the other end waiting to accept the offer, the remote session should now commence. If you don't get a response, it could be because the user you're offering assistance to is not using a compatible operating system. I will discuss these considerations in more detail shortly.

No matter how the Remote Assistance session is established, its use should be fairly intuitive, even for the user who has sent out the Remote Assistance request. If she can figure out how to send the Remote Assistance invitation, she will probably have little trouble with its actual use.

And even if the user can't figure it out, she can always be walked through the process over the phone. She can then be walked through the process of allowing remote control, and she won't have to do a thing. I've just made an excellent business case for upgrading the sullen 19-year-old computer whiz to Windows Vista—he can help the rest of the family for the price of the new OS and, possibly, a copy of *Halo 3*.

Remote Assistance and security

As mentioned in the click-steps, you have to create a password that will be used to control the Remote Assistance session. This is a feature new to the Windows Vista version of Remote Assistance, and it provides an additional layer of security to the session. It ensures that only authorized people are able to open a Remote Assistance invitation—they have to know the Remote Assistance session password to do so.

Another security consideration is whether the target computer is configured to accept incoming Remote Assistance offers. To ensure that your Vista computer is even capable of hosting a Remote Assistance connection, make sure you do this:

1. Open the System Control Panel application by typing **system** at the Start menu or by right-clicking the Computer desktop icon (if applicable) and choosing Properties.

2. Follow the Remote Settings task link on the dialog box's left side. You will be asked to provide administrative confirmation if User Account Control is turned on.

3. You'll see the System Properties dialog box. The Remote tab should be selected, and you'll want to confirm that the "Allow Remote Assistance connections to this computer" checkbox is selected, as shown in Figure 14-15.

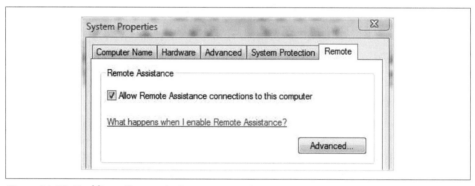

Figure 14-15. Enabling a Remote Assistance connection

More configuration settings are available by clicking the Advanced button. This will conjure the dialog box shown in Figure 14-16. This is where you can adjust the six-hour default expiration of the Remote Assistance request, or specify that the invites be used only from Windows Vista or later systems.

More interesting, though, is the first checkbox, which can toggle the Remote Control feature. If you'd like to have your system seen remotely but not controlled remotely by support technicians, you can always uncheck the option here. Remember, though, that Remote Assistance's security allows the user ultimate control; you can always decline an offer to take over remotely.

Remote Assistance and Group Policy

As you learned a chapter ago, Windows Vista offers a host of Group Policy settings that control a vast range of computer behavior. As you might expect, you can also manage Remote Assistance behavior with a Group Policy Object (GPO) linked to the local machine.

Figure 14-16. You can disallow remote control out of hand

Here's how to configure a Group Policy to set more universal and flexible Remote Assistance options:

1. Open the Group Policy Object Editor and add the Local policy object. Refer to Chapter 13 for full instructions. Alternatively, you can type **gpedit.msc** from the Start menu.

2. Navigate to this folder of settings:

   Computer Configuration\Administrative Templates\System\Remote Assistance

3. As seen in Figure 14-17, you will now be able to work with six settings that can further control the use and behavior of Remote Assistance. If an administrator wants to configure the system so that it can never accept a "solicited" offer (i.e., one that is not in response to a request for assistance), use the fifth setting in the list, Solicited Remote Assistance. By default, none of the Remote Assistance settings is configured.

Remote Assistance and User Account Control

It's very likely that the support person will perform an administrative task while remotely controlling your computer, which then leaves us with a quandary: how do we handle the User Account Control behavior?

One method, of course, is to disable User Account Control before initiating the remote session. But there's another way that's built into Remote Assistance and doesn't require such drastic steps.

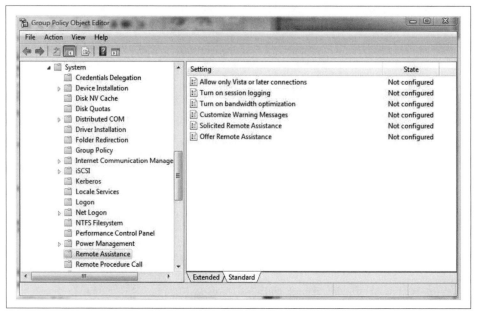

Figure 14-17. Configuring a Remote Assistance policy

When the support person asks to take control of the desktop, the user sees a message asking whether the helper can "respond to User Account Control prompts." Selecting this checkbox permits the support person to respond to requests from User Account Control for administrator consent or administrator credentials.

 Two other characteristics concerning granting User Account Control permission to the support person are worthy of mention: one, the user is asked for consent before handing over such control, and two, the user can grant this permission only if she has rights to run administrative-level programs.

Remote Assistance and the Windows Firewall

With Remote Assistance, you're allowing traffic into your computer—just the opposite of what the Windows Firewall is configured to do. Its job, for the most part, is to keep traffic out.

For these two features to work in harmony, then, it's necessary to make sure the proper exceptions are configured on the Windows Firewall.

Because the Windows Firewall restricts communication between your computer and the Internet, you might need to change settings for the Remote Desktop Connection so that it can work properly.

Here's how to do it:

1. Open the Windows Firewall. To do this, you could open the Control Panel's Security Center first, but I prefer typing **fire** at the Start menu. It will appear in the program list.

2. In the firewall console's left pane, follow the "Allow a program through Windows Firewall" link. You will be prompted for administrative confirmation if User Account Control is turned on.

3. You should be taken directly to the Firewall Settings dialog box with the Exceptions tab selected. In the list, select the checkbox next to Remote Assistance and then click OK (Figure 14-18).

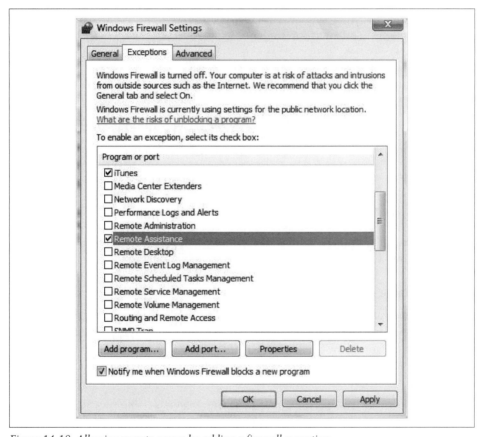

Figure 14-18. Allowing remote access by adding a firewall exception

Now, a look behind the scenes: for the Windows Firewall to work its magic and allow Remote Assistance traffic, it will open TCP port 3389. On two computers directly connected to the Internet, the Windows Firewall will handle this just fine. By setting up with a single click as just described, or by "Allow"-ing Remote Assistance when asked, Vista will manage the connection just fine.

But when other firewalls sit between the two computers, they may prevent the Remote Access traffic. This is not only a consideration for businesses that might have users in one office building and support personnel in another, but it also must be on the mind of the home user who is sharing out a broadband Internet connection to his house's three computers with a wireless router. Oftentimes, port 3389 will *not* be open by default.

I can offer few pointers here other than to read the documentation that came with your router regarding how to open certain ports. Fortunately, most SOHO wireless routers today come with an HTML-based configuration utility that allows router changes via a web page. In most cases, you just open a web browser and enter the router's IP address in the address bar, as in *http://192.168.1.1.*

You should then be prompted for a username and password. Now, you'll configure firewall exceptions in an interface similar to what you see in Figure 14-19.

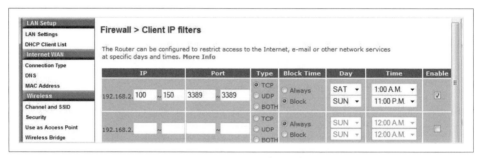

Figure 14-19. Opening port 3389 on a common router/firewall

You could also just disable the firewall capability for the duration of the session and let the Windows Firewall monitor all incoming and outgoing traffic.

Remote Assistance and compatibility

As I mentioned earlier, this isn't the first rodeo for Windows Remote Assistance, and you can happily use the Vista version in combination with other operating systems that support Remote Assistance. You can use Remote Assistance from your Vista machine, for example, to provide help to users still running Windows XP. There are a few considerations, however:

- In Windows XP and Server 2003, you can't pause a Windows Remote Assistance session. If you are using Vista to help an XP user and you pause the session, the person running XP won't be notified. There's no stopping you from using the chat function to say "I've got to step away for a bit," however.

- There is no voice support in this version of Remote Assistance. Under Windows XP and Windows Server 2003, you could transmit voice over the Remote Assistance session. If you're using Windows XP to help someone with running Windows Vista and you click the Start Talk button, nothing will happen.

- You cannot *offer* Remote Assistance help from your Vista computer to users running either XP or Server 2003. You can, however, respond to Remote Assistance requests.

Remote Desktop

Another troubleshooting tool is built into Windows Vista and is a very close cousin of Remote Assistance: the Remote Desktop. You can think of it as Remote Assistance, except that no one has to be at the other end of the connection requesting that a remote session be established.

The Remote Desktop can be a huge benefit for network administrators or for any other professional who needs to access his office (or home) computer from a remote location. Think hotel; think coffee shop; think about remotely administering a Vista machine in your boxer shorts. Think convenience.

Of course, there are a few setup considerations before implementing a Remote Desktop session, but hey, that's what I'm here for. O'Reilly doesn't hand out these book contracts lightly. I'll walk you through everything you need to get started.

Also, like Remote Assistance, this is not an entirely new feature in the Vista operating system, although also like Remote Assistance, there have been some feature improvements. Essentially, this means that you will be able to mix and match Remote Desktop in an XP/Vista environment. And before you begin, know that Remote Desktop is not available on every version of Windows Vista. Because it's mostly meant for companies in which remote access to office computers is a must, you can host a Remote Desktop connection only on these versions:

- Business
- Enterprise
- Ultimate

The Windows Vista Home Basic and Home Premium versions will only allow for the creation of outgoing connections. In other words, you can use a Vista Home Premium machine to connect to your Enterprise computer back in the office, but not the other way around.

And although this is available on XP computers as well, you can't connect to computers running Windows XP Home Edition.

Deploying Remote Desktop

At any rate, how that we've seen what Remote Desktop is used for and some of its usage constraints, let's get into a few of the implementation steps.

First, let's discuss the computer that will be connected *to*. In Remote Desktop nomenclature, this is known as the *host* machine. In most cases, this will be your office system. To establish a Remote Desktop connection, the host must first be configured to allow such connections. We'll deal with the other end of the equation, the *client* machine, in just a bit.

Here's how to prepare the host machine for a Remote Desktop session:

1. Open the System Control Panel application by typing **system** at the Start menu or by looking to the System and Maintenance Control Panel grouping.

2. Follow the Remote Settings link on the left side. You will be prompted for administrative credentials if User Account Control is turned on.

   We saw this dialog box previously in the Remote Assistance discussion. This time, the focus is on the bottom half.

3. There are three choices here, as seen in Figure 14-20.

   Don't allow connections to this computer
   > This is self-explanatory.

   Allow connections from computers running any version of Remote Desktop (less secure)
   > This is the best choice in a mixed XP/Vista environment, as it allows connections from previous versions of Remote Desktop.

   Allow connections only from computers running Remote Desktop with Network Level Authentication (more secure)
   > This is more secure (the parenthetical phrase will tell you this as well),* and will check to see whether the connecting computer supports Network Level Authentication, which is simply a protocol that identifies the user before the remote session is established.

 Only a user with a password-protected account can establish a Remote Desktop connection.

And notice that by default, Vista will not allow any Remote Desktop connections (I had just changed this before taking the screenshot).

Establishing the Remote Desktop connection

Now we turn our attention to the remote computer that is making the connection—in this context, the *client* computer. Good news: all the necessary software needed to establish this client connection is built into Windows Vista. This was not the case

---

* If you have ever wondered what the definition of *meta* is, you need look no further.

Figure 14-20. Setting up the host computer to allow a Remote Desktop session

under Windows XP, as I will detail in just a bit. For now, we'll assume a Vista-to-Vista connection.

So, then: if you're at home on a Sunday night and desperately need to update a file that's sitting on your work machine, just follow these steps to establish a remote session:

1. Open the Remote Desktop Connection dialog box by typing **remote** at the Start menu. It's also under All Programs → Accessories if you're not into the whole brevity thing.

2. You'll see the Remote Desktop Connection dialog box shown in Figure 14-21. From here, type either the name (usually the Fully Qualified Domain Name [FQDN]) of the remote computer, or the IP address.

3. Click the Connect button and Vista will then ask you for your security credentials. The next screen you should see, assuming the credentials are valid, is the desktop of the remote machine.

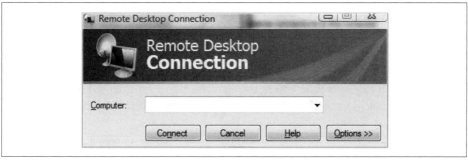

Figure 14-21. Establishing contact

This can be a *lot* more complicated if you'd like it to be, by the way. Click on the Options button to see what I mean. You'll get a new Remote Desktop Connection dialog box that looks like Figure 14-22.

Figure 14-22. The Remote Desktop Connection with additional options

As you can see, there are six tabs here that you can use to further govern the behavior of the Remote Desktop session.

The General tab. Here you will see four additional options:

Computer

OK, this isn't really an additional option, but it's still necessary.

Save

This tells Vista to remember your connection settings so that you won't have to retype them the next time you make a connection to the same host. If you find yourself using Remote Desktop to connect to the same computer (your office machine, for example), this can be useful.

Save As

> This saves your connection settings to an *.rdp* file that can be used later on. It's better put to use to save typing when connecting to multiple computers, such as when an administrator uses Remote Desktop to administer multiple machines.

Open

> This opens a saved *.rdp* file.

The Display tab. The three options here control the Remote Desktop window's look and feel:

Remote Desktop size

> Use the slider here to set the Remote Desktop screen resolution. Dragging all the way to the right will configure Remote Desktop to use the entire client screen.

Colors

> This sets the number of colors. Vista uses the least number of colors available at either the host or the client, so there are times when the color setting has no effect.

Display the Connection Bar when in Full Screen mode

> This is a default setting that, when active, displays a Remote Desktop bar that lets you minimize, restore, and close the session. I recommend you leave this option enabled.

The Local Resources tab. There are three options on the Local Resources tab that control specific interaction between client and host:

Remote Computer Sound

> The drop-down box here determines how Vista handles sound on the host computer. By default, the client hears sounds from the host, such as a chime when an error message is displayed.

Keyboard

> This determines which computer receives special keyboard commands. When you press Ctrl-Shift-Esc to bring up the Task Manager, for example, it shows activity on the host or the client machine. By default, keyboard combinations such as Ctrl-Shift-Esc will apply only to the host when in full-screen mode.

Local Devices and Resources

> Options here determine whether the client's printers are displayed in the host's list of printers, and whether to use the client's Clipboard during the session to cut and paste data from client to host.

The More button lets you specify even more options, as shown in Figure 14-23.

Figure 14-23. Additional remote resource options

As you can see, the options here will determine the level of interaction of other client devices and peripherals such as smart cards, serial ports, and drives. For example, if you choose the Drives checkbox, any drives you select here will also be available in the host's Remote Desktop window. This can be very useful if the purpose of the connection is to transfer files from client computer to host, or vice versa.

Supported Plug and Play devices would make items such as digital cameras, printers, and media players available as well.

The Programs tab. With the Programs tab, administrators can specify a particular program to be run on connection. The caveat here is that selecting a program to run in this dialog box pretty much sets the parameters for the entire Remote Desktop session. Once connected, the remote administrator can work only with the program here, and when the program ends, so does the Remote Desktop session.

The Experience tab. Several options on the Experience tab govern the Remote Desktop session itself. Some or all might be selected by default, depending on the choice of connection speed. Here's what they do:

Desktop background
Turns the host background on when enabled.

Font smoothing
Smoothes the fonts of the host machine.

Desktop composition
>Turns the desktop composition engine on.

Show contents of window while dragging
>Enables content in a window that's being moved.

Menu and Windows animation
>Enables the menu animations.

Themes
>Turns the host desktop theme on or off.

Bitmap caching
>Improves performance by storing host images on the client computer. Note that this is the only experience feature that is enabled in all speed configurations.

For example, the desktop background and font smoothing are both turned off if you're connecting over modem connection speeds (56 kbps or lower). If the remote connection is over a 10 mbps LAN, on the other hand, all experience options are on.

The Advanced tab. The Advanced tab allows you to specify warning options if authentication fails, and lets you configure a connection to a Terminal Services Gateway (TS Gateway) server.

A TS Gateway server (Figure 14-24) can make it easier to allow Remote Desktop connections to a corporate network using an Internet connection. TS Gateway servers use the Remote Desktop Protocol (RDP) along with the HTTPS protocol to help create a more secure, encrypted connection.

A TS Gateway server provides these benefits:

- It enables Remote Desktop connections over the Internet without setting up a virtual private network (VPN) connection.
- It better enables connections across firewalls.

Remote Desktop and Windows XP

It's very possible that network administrators will use Vista's Remote Desktop to remotely connect to computers running Windows XP. In other words, the XP machine will be the host machine. In that case, the setup instructions will differ somewhat. It's probably best to have them handy:

1. Insert the Windows XP installation disc and wait for AutoRun to present you with the Welcome to Microsoft Windows XP screen.
2. Follow the "Perform additional tasks" link.
3. Choose the Set Up Remote Desktop Connection option.

If you don't have the Windows XP installation disc handy, you can also visit the Microsoft download center and search for "Remote Desktop Connection." It should appear at the top of your search results.

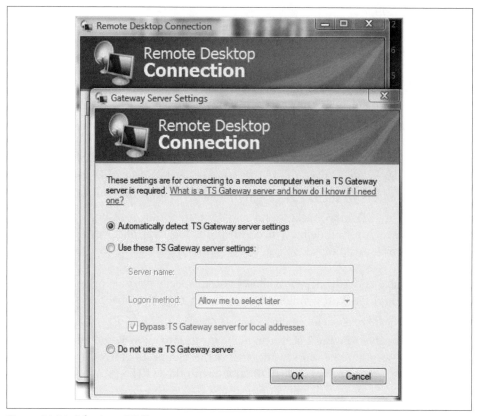

Figure 14-24. Selecting a TS Gateway server connection

For your "believe it or not" file: you can even connect to a Vista computer hosting a Remote Desktop session from a Mac. And no, I'm not talking about a Mac running Parallels or Boot Camp with Vista as the operating system. I mean a Mac running OS X. For more information, visit *http://microsoft.com/downloads*.

Making the Remote Desktop connection

Actual use of the Remote Desktop connection is very straightforward, because you're really just using the computer on the other end of the connection. All you're really doing is substituting one keyboard, mouse, and monitor that's a long way away for another set a little closer at hand.

The Remote Desktop session looks like just another application, albeit one that looks like a Windows Vista desktop. The only thing to focus on here is the connection bar at the top. This lets you perform tasks such as minimizing the Remote Desktop window, restoring it, and closing the session.

In fact, there are two ways to end a session: by clicking the Close button on the connection bar, and by using the host's Start menu. Choose Start → Disconnect to end the remote session, and the window closes.

Remote Desktop and the Windows Firewall

Like its cousin, Remote Assistance, the Remote Desktop will not be able to pass data back and forth across the Windows Firewall until it's allowed to do so. If you remember the steps from earlier, you're in good shape. If not, you'll need to tweak settings using these steps:

1. Open the Windows Firewall and choose the "Allow a program through Windows Firewall" task. (If you open the Control Panel, there's a link under the Security grouping as well.)

2. After supplying administrative confirmation, you'll see the Exceptions tab of the Windows Firewall Settings dialog box.

3. In the list of programs, place a checkmark next to the Remote Desktop box, as seen in Figure 14-25.

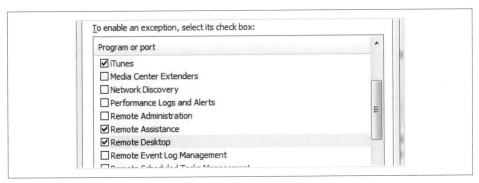

Figure 14-25. Allowing the host to use Remote Desktop

And of course, it's worth stating that you need to make sure you take these steps on the remote host *before* attempting the connection. You can't remote in and then try to set things up.

Remote Desktop and NAT

Often, the system you want to "Remote Desktop" into is living behind a router. This router is usually configured with what's known as Network Address Translation, or NAT. This is especially true on most SOHO networks where 3, 4, maybe 10 computers are all sharing a single broadband Internet connection.

If you're curious, you can type **ipconfig** from a Command Prompt window right now. If you see an address that starts with 192.168, you're using NAT. NAT *translates* a public IP address such as 64.151.*x.y* into a private IP address such as 192.168.2.1 during both outgoing and incoming communications.

Can Remote Desktop work when NAT is in place? Absolutely. We do have to know the *public* IP address of the router that's between the client computer and the host computer, however—thousands, if not millions, of computers have Internet access with a private IP address of 192.168.2.1, but only one device is connected to the Internet with a public address of 64.151.x.y. We can't remote into 192.168.2.1; we need to send the Remote Desktop request to the public location.

And just how do we figure out what the public address is? There are several ways, actually. We could use the router utility as discussed earlier. Oftentimes, the utility will display the router's public address.

We can also use free web site services such as these:

- *http://whatismyip.com*
- *http://broadbandreports.com*
- *http://checkip.dyndns.org*
- *http://whatismyipaddress.com*

There are many others.

Once you know the public IP address of the router connected to the Remote Desktop *host*, use that address to connect.

There's one more thing to remember: just because you've configured the Windows Firewall correctly doesn't mean the router will let the Remote Desktop traffic pass. You still need to configure either:

- An *exception* on your router, as discussed previously
- *Port forwarding*, where you configure the router to forward specific port requests to a specific private IP address such as 192.168.2.1

Again, you'll have to refer to the router's documentation for full instructions, because they vary from device to device. Because of its reliance on Terminal Services as its underlying connection technology, Remote Desktop exchanges information on TCP port 3389 by default.

Securing the Remote Desktop connection with a different port

The problem with the preceding advice and instructions is that just when you feel comfortable with your understanding of how Remote Desktop works and all the configuration details needed to get it up and running, you realize that every hacker in the world is well aware of the same information already, and those who don't can pick up a book as easily as you can.

Using freely available software, they can sit at their computers (in their parents' basements, no doubt) and scan the Internet for open 3389 ports. With an open port in hand, they have just found a doorway into your computer.

So what's the answer? Well, first, you should take comfort in the fact that just because someone finds a door doesn't mean that he has a key. The best way to "lock your doors," as it were, is to use a sound password strategy. If you're doing this, chances are that most hackers will look for easier prey. If, on the other hand, you've allowed a Remote Desktop connection to a user called Admin with a password of *password*, you may have what I call "issues."

For an even more secure Remote Desktop strategy, you can change the port used by Remote Desktop from the default of 3389. It's just a number, after all, and Remote Desktop doesn't care which one you use.

Follow these steps to change the Remote Desktop listening port:

1. Open the Registry Editor by typing **regedit** at the Start menu, and navigate to this key:

    HLM\System\CurrentControlSet\Control\TerminalServer\WinStations\RDP-Tcp

2. From there, you'll see a PortNumber setting. Open this setting and replace the 3389 value with any number between 1024 and 65536, as shown in Figure 14-26.

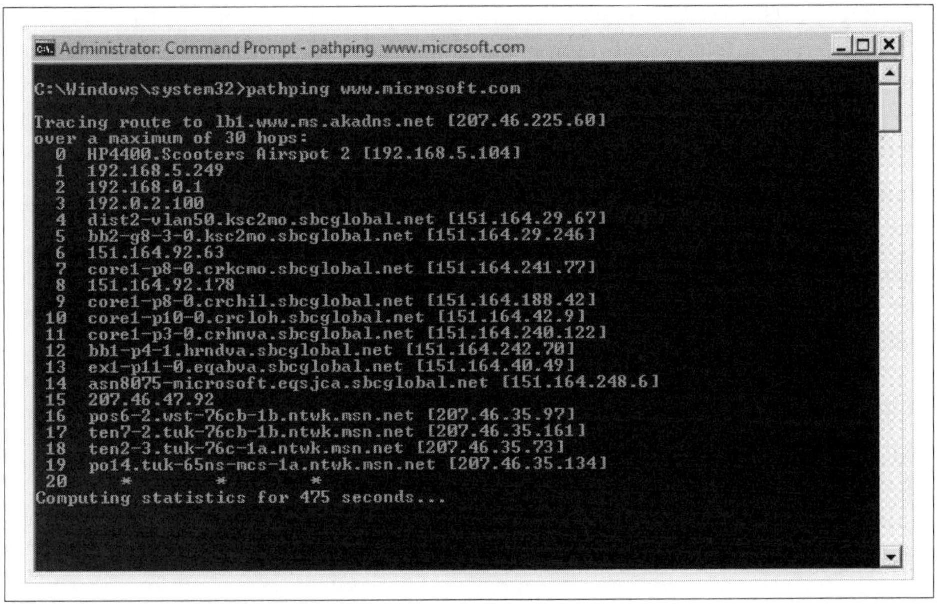

Figure 14-26. Configuring an alternative Remote Desktop port

Now, to make the connection, you just specify the public IP address (discovered using one of the techniques described earlier) and the port number. Using the earlier value, I would type the following into the Remote Desktop connection's Computer entry box:

```
65.43.123.98:10012
```

Remote Desktop. What could be simpler?

Troubleshooting Network Connectivity

You've probably already noticed that many of the troubleshooting steps presented in this chapter—shoot, many of the features in the entire book—require a connection to the network. Troubleshooting that connection becomes a very important tool for the Vista administrator.

As with so many other troubleshooting procedures, network connectivity troubleshooting usually begins with the physical: is it plugged in? Is it attached properly? Usually, the answer is yes, but it doesn't hurt to double-check. I've seen several occasions where a laptop "just stopped being able to get on the Internet." The problem? The user had inadvertently pressed or clicked a button that disabled the network card.

On one of my laptops, for example, is a little button flanked by the power switch and a USB port. This button toggles on or off the wireless networking card, and it's dreadfully easy to accidentally press this thing when either resuming from a Sleep session or plugging in a USB device. The only indicator I have (besides loss of connectivity) is a little blue light on the front of the laptop housing, which is easy to overlook.

At any rate, once you determine that everything is *physically* attached properly, it's time to start your *logical* networking investigation.

There's no right or wrong in how to go about this investigation, but a good place to start is with a check of the Device Manager. I recommend visiting this first to make sure the device driver is still installed and operational. If everything checks out, you can then start the process of checking Vista's network protocols, namely the Transmission Control Protocol/Internet Protocol (TCP/IP).

TCP/IP includes several complementary troubleshooting utilities, such as IPCONFIG.EXE, PING.EXE, PATHPING.EXE, and TRACERT.EXE. Each one is run from the Command Prompt, each has its place in the troubleshooting process, and each is discussed briefly in the sections that follow.

IPCONFIG

TCP/IP troubleshooting usually begins here, with answers to questions such as these:

- What's my IP address?
- Do I have a static or a dynamic IP address?
- What is my assigned Domain Name System (DNS) server?
- How many network cards are configured with an IP address?

The answers to these questions and more can be provided by IPCONFIG. Its job is straightforward: it displays IP configuration information. When it is run without any switches (just **ipconfig** at the Command Prompt), it will provide four pieces of basic information:

- The IP address
- The subnet mask
- The default gateway
- The connection-specific DNS suffix

This is sometimes all you need. If you see an IP address of 169.254.x.y, for example, you know that the Dynamic Host Configuration Protocol (DHCP) component in the network is down, and you've been assigned an address from the APIPA space. Your troubleshooting can then focus on the DCHP server (the wireless access point in many cases), rather than on the Vista machine.

You can also use IPCONFIG with one of several switches that you can list by running the /? (help) switch, as in ipconfig /?. Table 14-1 shows a few of the more common switches.

Table 14-1. Common IPCONFIG switches

Switch	What it does
/all	Shows information about your IP connection, including any DNS and WINS servers used and whether the address is dynamic or static. It also shows the hostname.
/release	Releases the IP address that has been assigned through DHCP. You cannot release a leased IP address through the TCP/IP Properties dialog box.
/renew	Renews a DHCP address. This is not possible through the TCP/IP Properties dialog box.
/registerdns	Reregisters the DNS name with the configured DNS server. This can be useful for troubleshooting name resolution problems.
/flushdns	Clears the contents of the DNS resolver cache located on the workstation. A client will check its DNS resolver cache before checking a DNS server. This will clear out an incorrect entry made by an improperly configured DNS server.

As mentioned, you need to run all of these utilities from a Command Prompt. What's more, you need to run them from a Command Prompt with administrative privileges. To do so, make sure to right-click the Start menu Command Prompt icon and choose Run As Administrator in the Context menu. (I provide a shortcut so that this is the default action; see Chapter 15.)

PING

Now that you have a valid IP address, the next step is usually to test connectivity to another computer. The Packet Internet Groper (PING, although it's really a backronym) utility is used to do just that.

It works by sending a packet of information that behaves much like sonar does for submarines. If a PING is successful, the receiving computer responds, and you've just confirmed that both systems can send and receive TCP/IP packets. Thus, other communication *should* work as well.

Typical PING syntax goes like this:

    ping IP Address

or:

    ping computername

If you're not able to PING using the IP address, for example, something's amiss in the network in between the source and destination (assuming the target computer is on). If you can't PING using the computer name, the problem lies with name resolution.

Further, you can use PING with a series of modifiers that change the default behavior of sending four 32-byte packets out to the designated host for response. Some can change the size of the PING packet, others can modify the duration of the ping test. Again, use the /? (help) switch to see a list of these modifiers.

Firewalls can (and often are) also set to block PING traffic, as PING attacks are an unsophisticated way to tamper with a server—you just tie up its resources responding to PING requests. In other words, you won't be able to ping *www.microsoft.com* even though it can be reached. PING is best used to troubleshoot in a private, corporate environment.

When communication is failing, the general flow of PINGing to verify TCP/IP connectivity from a computer is as follows:

- PING the loopback address of 127.0.0.1.
- PING the local computer's IP address.
- PING the default gateway.
- PING the remote computer you are trying to reach using first the IP address (if known) and then the computer name.

You can also do this in reverse order to try to isolate the cause of broken network communication.

TRACERT.EXE

How does a packet of information get from point A to point B? The TRACERT utility addresses this very question.

It works by employing PING packets, albeit ones with slight modifications. If you test a connection using a normal PING packet, you'll note that each packet has a time-to-live (TTL) value of 128, meaning that it can stop at up to 127 different routing points along its way. (When the TTL value reaches 0, the packet is dropped. Without this characteristic, *all* undelivered traffic on the Internet would still be out there, passing from one router to the Net in a neverending attempt to find a destination.)

The TRACERT utility uses this same PING packet, but one with an initial TTL value of 1, meaning that the packet will die at its first stop. When it dies, TRACERT notes the IP address of the device that dropped the packet.

The next PING packet sent to the destination has a TTL value of 2. This packet dies two hops away from its source, and TRACERT logs where it dies; and so on and so on until the PING reaches its destination, at which time the route from sender to receiver has been reconstructed.

Because it steps through the complete path taken by information, it can be very helpful in identifying slow or broken links in the information chain.

The syntax is very similar to that for PING, and it looks like this:

```
tracert IP Address or computername
```

PATHPING

The title of this one *sounds* like what TRACERT actually *does*, but PATHPING actually *combines* features of TRACERT and PING to provide information about problems at a router or a network link.

It does so by providing information about network latency (slowness) and network loss (dropped packets) at all points between a source computer and a destination computer.

PATHPING has no functionality without parameters, which are essentially used to specify the network path you are trying to diagnose. Again, `pathping /?` can help get you started with these parameters.

Also, note that PATHPING generates a report that will take some time to create. The first results you see list the route taken from source to destination, which is the same information you could generate with TRACERT.

You will then see a busy message displayed for approximately 90 seconds, although as seen in Figure 14-27, it can be even longer on larger networks. During this time,

PATHPING gathers information from all routers between source and destination. At the end of this "busy" period, PATHPING displays test results. You can now use this information to determine where problems lie in the network infrastructure.

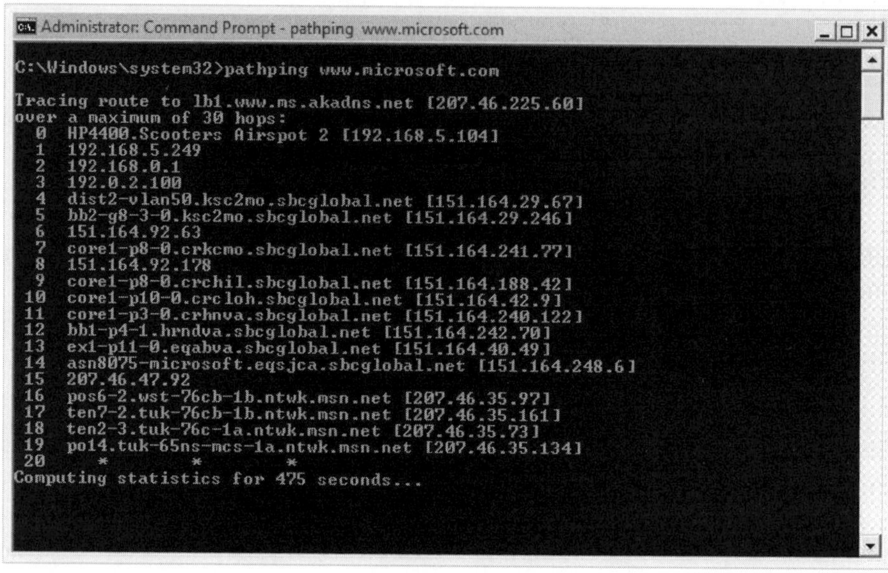

Figure 14-27. Using PATHPING

NSLOOKUP

NSLOOKUP is a handy utility that you can use to troubleshoot DNS infrastructure problems. There are two modes of NSLOOKUP:

Interactive
    Where you are at an `nslookup` command and can enter a series of commands

Noninteractive
    Where you enter a single command and then are returned to the Command Prompt

Which one is appropriate? It depends on the kind of information you're trying to gather. As always, use the /? command switch to retrieve exact syntax.

If you need to look up only a single piece of data, for example, use the noninteractive mode. For the first parameter, type the name or IP address of the computer that you want to look up. For the second parameter, type the name or IP address of a DNS name server.

If you omit the second argument, NSLOOKUP uses the default DNS name server. Here's what it will look like in practice. To find out what IP address a DNS server called SERVER1 has for a computer called GROY, use this syntax:

```
Nslookup groy -server1
```

If you need to look up more than one piece of data, you should use interactive mode. To enter interactive mode, type **nslookup** at the Command Prompt. You will then see a prompt without the directory pathname, as is the default. Now you can just enter the nslookup commands without specifying the -nslookup part first.

 The preceding examples assume that a Reverse Lookup zone has been properly configured at the DNS server. This is needed because you're looking up the name of the DNS server based on the IP address gathered from your client's TCP/IP properties information.

Status and repair

Vista also includes a simplified graphical interface for viewing the status of a network connection. You can use this interface to automatically run many of the network troubleshooting steps that I introduced in the previous sections.

It's called the Connection Status dialog box. In it, there's a button called Diagnose that runs through the troubleshooting steps. To view, follow these steps:

1. Open the Network and Sharing Center.

2. Under the network name section, click the View Status link. You'll then see the dialog box shown in Figure 14-28.

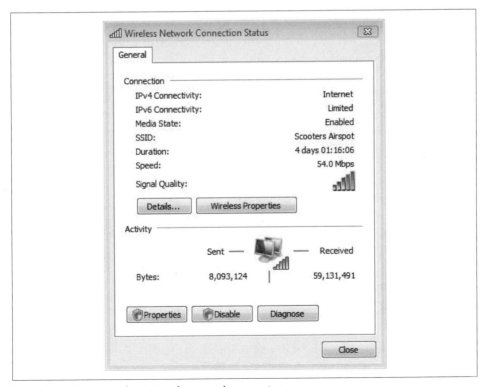

Figure 14-28. Viewing the status of a network connection

From here, you have several options. You can click the Details button, for example, to call up a dialog box that displays much of the information shown using the IPCONFIG utility.

And if you're having problems with network connectivity, you can use the Diagnose button. This carries out each of the following tasks and commands while a status window is shown. Note also that these are a part of normal troubleshooting resolution. In order, the Diagnose feature:

- Disables and enables the network card.
- Runs `ipconfig /renew`, which automatically renews the IP address from a DHCP server or service.
- Runs `arp -d`, which flushes the Address Resolution Protocol (ARP) cache, which resolves IP addresses to physical network card addresses (aka MAC addresses). Any incorrect entries in the ARP cache can cause information to be sent to the wrong destination, even if other name resolution services in the network are working properly.
- Runs `Nbtstat -r`, which reloads the NetBIOS name cache.
- Runs `ipconfig /flushdns`, which reloads the DNS cache.
- Runs `ipconfig /registerdns`, which registers the computer name at the configured DNS server.

This essentially describes startup behavior, by the way. It's the equivalent of what used to be accomplished by rebooting the system, although with the Diagnose utility, you're just rebooting the network card instead.

Backup and Restore

Yes, you should back up all the time, and no, you do not back up as often as you should unless you are the exception to the rule, and blah blah blah, and so forth and so on.

I won't waste either your time or this book's (rather impressive) page count extolling the virtues of a good data backup strategy. We all know that it's a good idea to back up critical files. And for reasons that will become clear in just a moment, I won't waste a lot of time discussing the Vista Backup utility, either. After you see what it can—or more specifically *can't*—do, I think this is one new Vista feature you'll avoid.

Microsoft has never seemed to get its poor Backup utility just right, it seems, and Vista's Backup and Restore Center is no exception. It does a few things very well, but it does others either really badly or not at all. See Chapter 15 for a full explanation.

But since I'm (briefly) including it in this chapter on troubleshooting, I might as well touch on some of Vista's backup capabilities. They are:

- The capability to back up to multiple drive types, such as USB drives, external hard drives, and optical drives such as DVD-R and CD-R
- The capability to back up to a network share
- The capability to automate backup

So, then, to back up files using Vista's backup program:

1. Open the Backup and Restore Center by typing **backup** at the Start menu.
2. You'll see the Backup and Restore Center, as shown in Figure 14-29. Don't confuse the Backup and Restore Center with the Backup Status and Configuration console. I'll discuss this in a bit.
3. You're prompted for administrative confirmation if User Account Control is turned on. From here, just click the "Back up files" button and then follow the instructions.

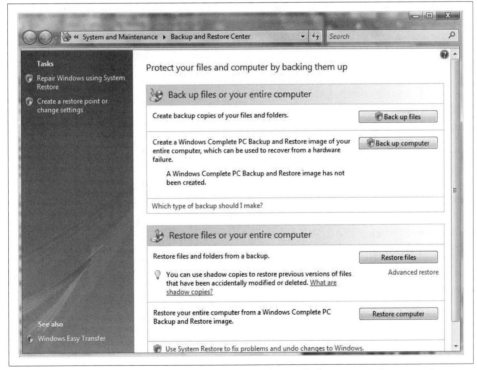

Figure 14-29. Vista's "improved" backup utility (reminds me of when Coca-Cola improved its signature beverage)

Oh, and note that Vista Backup won't back up anything that's either encrypted with the Encrypting File System (EFS) or stored on a FAT disk.

So, then, if you've lost a bet or are otherwise forced to use Vista Backup, I suppose you'd better know how to restore a backup as well:

1. Open the Backup and Restore Center. Choose the "Restore files" button.
2. Follow the instructions in the Restore Wizard.

Alright, I've taken my shots; it's time to pay Vista's backup a compliment. It does have one significant capability that previous Windows Backup utilities did not: the capability to create a backup image.

Vista Backup and the Complete PC Image

Probably the best administrative use for Vista Backup that I can think of is the ability to create a complete disk image. A Complete PC Backup creates a copy of all programs, all system settings, and all files. As the saying goes, it's the whole enchilada.

But before you begin, know that the Complete PC Backup is available only on these Vista versions:

- Business
- Enterprise
- Ultimate

Home Premium owners, I know what you're thinking: I told you you wouldn't like Vista Backup.

With the complete backup in hand, you can quickly restore the entire computer to the exact state it was in at the time the backup was made. Note also that, like most disk imaging programs, the Complete PC Backup capability built into Windows Vista is all-or-nothing: you can't select individual files, programs, or components to restore. When you restore the image file, it replaces anything else that's on the hard drive where it's being copied.

Further, the Complete PC Backup will save your drive configuration as well. In other words, it will save *all* files on *all* volumes on your computer. Well, it might, as I will explain later.

At any rate, to get started with a Complete PC Backup, follow these steps:

1. Open the Backup and Restore Center.
2. Choose the "Back up computer" button. You'll be asked for administrative confirmation if User Account Control is turned on.
3. Now, follow the steps in the wizard.

Microsoft recommends that you create a Complete PC Backup image at the moment you have your computer entirely set up—all programs installed, all drivers present and accounted for, everything working just as you'd like. You can think of it as a quick little reset switch for your computer should anything go terribly wrong, and it can be a whole lot faster than trying to troubleshoot. Keep in mind, however, that this "original" PC backup won't contain any of your data since then. You'll want to restore that data with a separate backup routine.

Also, there are some caveats that will probably have you looking elsewhere for an imaging utility. Among them:

- You can do a Complete PC Backup only if all volumes are formatted with NTFS.
- The drive where you store the image must also be formatted with NTFS.
- You can't *save* the image on a dynamic disk.
- And speaking of dynamic disks, if you have a computer with multiple drive types (basic and dynamic), forget about the Complete PC Backup.

Did I pay this utility a compliment earlier? I may have to take that one back.

And there's another way to create this Compete PC Backup besides using the Backup and Restore Center. Use the Backup Status and Configuration dialog box instead and choose the "Create Backup now" button to start the same procedure. We'll discuss this dialog box in a bit more detail in the next section.

Restoring a Complete PC Backup

The other side of the coin, of course, is to perform a Complete PC Backup Restore operation. If you have a Windows installation disc, follow this procedure:

1. Insert the installation disc and restart your computer. Make sure the system is configured to boot from an optical drive.
2. Choose your language settings, click Next, and then choose "Repair your computer."
3. Select the operating system you want to repair, and then click Next.
4. On the System Recovery Options menu, click Windows Complete PC Restore, and then follow the instructions.
5. Naturally, you should make sure your Complete PC Backup image is handy on the external media before beginning the operation.

Backup status and configuration

Adding a layer of confusion is the fact that the Backup Status and Configuration is a separate tool, yet contains only three buttons; I'm not sure why this wasn't incorporated into the Backup and Restore Center. You will have seen this—what, utility? dialog box? I'm not sure what to call it—when launching (see Figure 14-30).

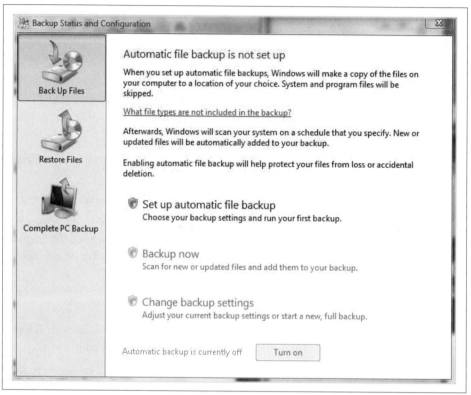

Figure 14-30. The Backup Status and Configuration dialog box

Its job, ostensibly, is to help you configure automatic file backups and perform Complete PC Backups, but its buttons don't really do much besides launch you into procedures you can get to through the Backup and Restore Center.

And although the word *status* appears in its name, the only backup status it provides is the date of your last Complete PC Backup. I suppose it will step you through an automated backup easily enough, but you won't use this clunker of a backup program anyway, so why bother?

I might as well just continue to pile it on here: you can't just simply create a scheduled backup when creating a scheduled backup. "Huh?" you say. Yes, Vista's Backup utility makes you actually perform the backup at the time you set the schedule, which pretty much defeats the purpose of a schedule in the first place. What if the backup is going to take an hour or two, and you don't want the computer tied up with extra overhead while doing an unscheduled scheduled backup? Am I really supposed to wait until 5:00 p.m. Friday to configure my scheduled backup and then wait at the office for another two hours so that the job I just scheduled for 11:00 p.m. that night will run now?

OK, I think I've made my point.

Using System Restore

Somewhat related to the Complete PC Backup is the System Restore feature, which is a lot more pleasant to use, not to mention write about. System Restore is a Vista service that runs in the background, continually monitoring changes to essential system files and the registry, and it's used to roll back the operating system without affecting any of your data.

The System Restore is especially effective in the following situations:

- You install an application that causes a conflict with other software on your system. If uninstalling the program doesn't fix the situation, you can restore to a point before the program was installed.

- You install one or more updated drivers, creating subsequent instability. System Restore can restore *all* previously installed drivers instead in a single procedure. (You can use the Driver Rollback feature of the Device Manager to restore a previous driver, but this is a one-at-a-time operation.)

- The Vista machine develops performance or stability problems for no apparent reason. Consider a situation in which a computer is shared by many people. Any time a computer is shared, those users usually do not document changes they make. They can also install untested or unsupported devices without compatible drivers. If this is the case, a computer administrator can restore to a point where she is reasonably sure the system was functioning properly.

In other words, System Restore acts as a sort of time machine, transporting your Vista installation to a point where it was working properly. And as I mentioned, the really cool part is that rolling back the Vista operating system will not affect personal data such as Word documents or email files. It allows a user to make Vista behave the way it did three months ago, yet still have all the changes you made to your latest novel.

You should not view System Restore as a substitute for a good antivirus program or a regular backup. A system can become infected and not exhibit any symptoms for a while, and files identified in restore points can be infected without your knowledge. Most times, the virus is treated as another piece of data anyway, and data is not rolled back. Additionally, a system can become infected and then spread the virus to other computers. Rolling back one system, even if that cures the problem, will not help the other infected machines in the network.

So what do you need to do to configure System Restore? In most cases, not much. Windows Vista turns on System Restore by default, and creates restore points every day without user intervention (assuming you leave your computer on).

If you'd like to override the default behavior, or turn System Restore on or off for a particular disk, follow these steps:

1. Open the System Control Panel application and then click the System Protection link.

2. Clear one of the checkboxes next to the system drives, as shown in Figure 14-31. Unchecking all drives here effectively disables System Restore.

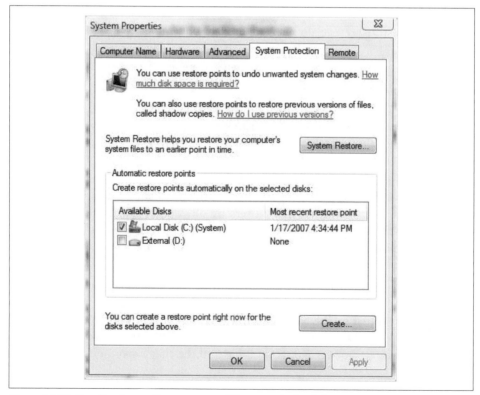

Figure 14-31. Toggling System Restore on or off for a particular disk

There's more. At regular intervals, System Restore takes snapshots of the Vista system files and settings. If it detects a major change, it creates a restore point. For example, if you install a program such as Microsoft Office, chances are that a restore point will be generated.

The restore points are stored on the same disk as the operating system, so in this way they are not like a backup that is stored on separate media. And note that you shouldn't be too concerned about the amount of disk space; restore points will use up to 15 percent of a volume's free disk space, but will automatically delete older restore points to make room for new ones.

 You can run Disk Cleanup to claim additional space taken up by System Restore.

Creating a manual restore point

Additionally, you can create a System Restore point manually any time you feel one is merited. It is good administrative practice, for example, to double-check System Restore points after a major change or upgrade. If you don't see one there, go ahead and create it.

Here's how to create a manual restore point:

1. Open the System Control Panel application by typing **sys** in the Start menu.

2. In the left pane, follow the System Protection link. You will be prompted for administrative confirmation if User Account Control is turned on.

3. The System Protection tab should already be selected, as shown previously in Figure 14-31. Click Create.

4. You now see the System Protection dialog box shown in Figure 14-32. From here, give the manual restore point a description, and then click Create.

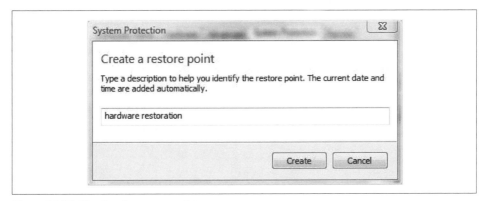

Figure 14-32. Naming the restore point

Using a restore point

No matter how a restore point was created, using one is very straightforward. All you have to do is open the System Protection tab using the method described previously, and then click the System Restore button.

You'll then see a "Restore System files and settings" dialog box, which kicks off the restore procedure. From there, click Next and choose the restore point in the dialog box shown in Figure 14-33.

You'll be warned about the computer having to reboot as the restore process commences.

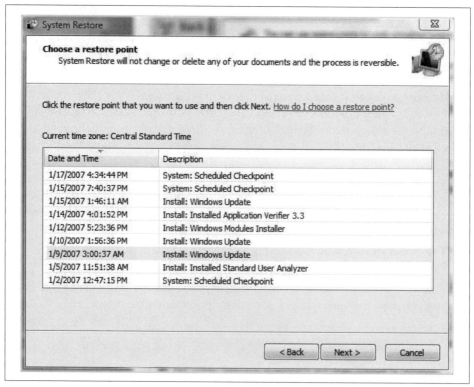

Figure 14-33. Performing the restore

Note that in the System Restore window, daily restore points are identified with the label "System: Scheduled Checkpoint."

Using the Vista Logs

Windows Vista makes vital information about itself available in a series of logfiles, which you can review using an old standby of an application, the Event Viewer.

Administrators have been poring over the Windows Event Viewer logs for years, and they still perform essentially the same troubleshooting task. If you have previous experience with the Event Viewer, you won't find the new Vista Event Viewer to be substantially different.

Here's what to do.

Open the Event Viewer by typing **event** at the Start menu. It should appear at the top of the list of programs. Alternatively, you can open the Computer Management MMC snap-in and choose the Event Viewer node.

However you open it, you will now see four main Event Viewer categories, as seen in Figure 14-34:

- Custom Views
- Windows Logs
- Applications and Services Logs
- Subscriptions

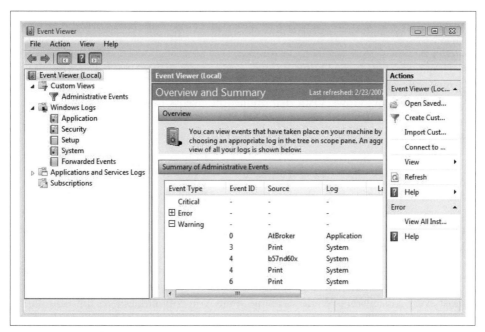

Figure 14-34. The four main Event Viewer categories

The Subscriptions node, new to Windows Vista, will let administrators collect Event Log information from other computers in the network. It's also related to one of the new Windows Logs nodes. I'll deal with Event Viewer subscriptions separately in just a bit.

The Windows Logs node has several subnodes where the event logs themselves are stored. These logs contain information that applies to the Vista system as a whole. They include three logs that were available on previous versions of Windows: Application, Security, and System logs. There are also two new logs: Setup and Forwarded Events.

Application
> Contains events logged by applications or programs. Just about any application running on your computer has the potential to write an event to the Application log. What events are logged is determined by application developers.

Security
> Contains events relevant to the security of the machine, such as valid and invalid logon attempts. Unlike Application logs, administrators have the most say as to what gets written to the Security log, as the results of auditing policies are posted here. If an administrator is auditing resource usage, for example, events related to opening, deleting, or creating files in that resource are noted here.

Setup
> New to Vista, it is used mostly to troubleshoot Vista application installation issues. It contains events related to application setup.

System
> Contains events logged by Windows system components. If a driver or other system component fails to load during startup, an event is typically recorded in the System log. Windows Vista determines the events logged here; administrators have no say.

Forwarded Events
> This logfile is used to store events collected from remote computers, but only if you have first created an event subscription. More on subscriptions later.

Under the Windows Logs node is a category of Event Logs new to Windows Vista: Applications and Services Logs. Unlike the Windows logs that capture events that affect the entire computer, the Applications and Services logs collect information about just a single application or component.

Expand Applications and Services Logs, and you'll see individual logfiles that are too numerous to list. There's also a Windows category that collects information about almost every conceivable Windows component. You could look here, for example, to find out more information about a printer that is not working properly, or about the wired network connection.

Within each logfile, you may come across four categories of individual log events:

Admin

Of particular interest to administrators (and help staff) will be the Admin logs. Not only do the events collected here identify a particular problem, but they also *suggest a solution that an administrator can act on.* An example of an admin event is an event that occurs when an application fails to connect to a printer. These events either are well documented or have a message associated with them that gives the reader direct instructions for what to do to rectify the problem.

Operational

These can also be helpful to administrators or other help staff, but they require a bit more interpretation in order to help determine a course of action. What's more, they can be configured to tasks based on the problem or occurrence.

Analytic

These events describe program operation. They are used to identify problems that cannot be handled by user intervention.

Debug logs

These events are not used by administrators, but rather by developers trouble-shooting issues with their programs.

 You won't see any of the Analytic or Debug log events by default, as they typically require further parsing by additional applications or specialized support professionals. To view the Analytic and Debug logs, go to the View options on the right pane and choose "Show Analytic and Debug logs."

Getting Help from a Newsgroup

Of course, you know how to use the Windows Help and Support feature. There it is, right there on the Start menu, ready for you to ask a question at any time, and the kinds of users who need directions using the Help and Support Center probably aren't the ones who have made it to the end of Chapter 14 of this book.

If you're looking for immediate help using the Windows Firewall, for example, you can open Help and Support and either navigate through the Table of Contents or type `Firewall` in the search bar. You'll receive a list of topics that provide instruction and background on the Windows Firewall.

And while Help and Support has gotten a facelift, and much of the help content has been rewritten to be more direct and useful, trying to get a computer to help you is one task that really highlights the limitations of a machine. No matter what's done to help files, they will never be as good as asking a human being a question.

Ah, but Help and Support facilitates this as never before. To see what I mean, open Help and Support and then click in the Troubleshooting item on the home page.

From the ensuing help page, look toward the bottom and expand the Get Help From Other People topic. You'll see this sentence:

> Newsgroups are a great place to start. Post a question or search for an answer in Windows communities.

Windows Communities is a hyperlink that will take you to the Windows Vista Community. From there, you can browse through the many Vista newsgroups to try to find answers to your questions. It's very possible that someone has encountered the same problem, and you just may be able to benefit from his previous posting.

If you don't see the discussion thread that will help you resolve your issue, you can always post a new question. There's not much in the way of step-by-step help I can offer here; it pretty much falls under the category of surfing the Internet. I just want to make sure you know that you have this troubleshooting resource available as well.

Summary

In this chapter, you got a solid foothold on troubleshooting concepts, and you saw some of the tools Vista provides to make troubleshooting easier. It will never be easy or completely automated; the best troubleshooting tool is, and will remain, experience.

This chapter is also one that will likely benefit most from the augmented material that will be available on *http://www.brianculp.com*.

The next chapter wraps up this book's several-hundred-pages-long discussion of Windows Vista. It's a big operating system, so a book covering it should merit a page or two as well, I suppose. In the closing chapter you'll find some fun stuff, however, gathered together with an eye toward making you—whether you are an administrator, an ordinary user, or some combination thereof—more productive while at the computer.

CHAPTER 15

Vista Tips and Tricks

If O'Reilly books had chapter subtitles, this one would read "Several Really Cool Things You Can Do with Windows Vista, and Six Things That Wouldn't Be There If They Had Asked Me First."

Alas, they don't have subtitles; the preceding paragraph will have to do.

At any rate, the idea of this chapter is that it provides a nice little catchall for the things I wanted to put into other chapters of this book, but couldn't for some reason. Sometimes the tips or pieces of information just didn't fit the surrounding material in those chapters. Other times, what you see here doesn't require much in the way of preamble or setup; it's just my way of saying "By the way, did you know that Windows Vista can do *this* as well?"

And yet other times, leaving it out of other chapters was just a matter of editorial license. Despite the length of this book, I can't write about *everything* in Windows Vista. I don't know who keeps count of these things, but apparently there are 2,750 new features in Microsoft's latest operating system.

What follows in this chapter is a loosely organized listing of some tips and tricks that can help you get the most out of the Vista operating system. Of course, not everyone will find every tip useful, but for those of you looking for instructions on how to perform that *one* little change, this chapter will prove invaluable.

And yes, it's possible that I've mentioned some of these quick little tips and tricks in one form or another elsewhere in this book. This will be the exception, though, not the rule. I wrote the other chapters so that you would come away with a fairly thorough understanding of the underlying material; I'm not fool enough to think that many readers are actually seeking this understanding. I write this chapter fully aware that many people flip directly to the back of the book to pick up a few cool new tricks that will impress friends and coworkers.

It should be fun. If nothing else, you'll come away from this chapter saying to yourself "Hey, I didn't realize Vista could do that" at least a couple of times.

Warm up your keyboard; let's get started.

Several Really Cool Things, in No Particular Order

We'll start this chapter with a look at what's new and cool—ways you can tweak Vista performance and/or appearance and/or function to get the most out of your computing experience.

And as the section heading suggests, there's really no overarching organizational MO at work here; these are just some tips that have worked for me, and now I'm passing them along.

We begin with one I've deployed on my desktop computer. Since it's not going anywhere and I've got backups of critical data, I'm not too worried about the security provided by the logon process, and have configured a feature that speeds up Vista logon.

Enabling Auto-Logon in Windows Vista

There's an easy way to configure a specific user account to always log on when starting Vista. If you're not concerned about anyone else using your computer, or what he might see or access if you got up for a latte after booting your machine, this can help smooth the startup process.

1. From the Start menu, type **netplwiz** and then launch the application of the same name. The User Accounts dialog box appears, shown in Figure 15-1.

2. Uncheck the "Users must enter a user name and password to use this computer" checkbox, and click Apply.

3. You'll now see the "Automatically log on" dialog box. From here, type the name of the account and the password for the account for which you want to enable auto-logon.

4. Click OK and then OK again to commit the changes.

To reverse course, just open the same *netplwiz* application once again and recheck the checkbox.

Removing Tool Tips

You know what a tool tip is, right? You hover your mouse pointer over something such as a button on the taskbar and text materializes, often explaining what you're about to click. But is there a way to turn that off?

Turns out that there is. It's a registry edit, but as long as you follow these instructions carefully, you should be OK. We've edited the registry plenty of times together with no ill effects, right?

Figure 15-1. You can enable auto-logon from here

Follow these instructions to remove Vista's tool tips:

1. From the Start menu, type **regedit** and then launch the corresponding application from the Program list.

2. From the Registry Editor, navigate to the following key, shown in Figure 15-2:

    *HKEY_CURRENT_USER\Software\Microsoft\Windows\CurrentVersion\
    Explorer\Advanced*

3. Now, set the DWORD value called ShowInfoTip to 0 (i.e., off).

Exit the Registry Editor. You must now reboot Vista for the changes to take effect. To reenable the tool tips, set the ShowInfoTip DWORD value back to 1.

Removing the Splash Screen in Windows Mail

A nuisance for some users is the splash screen in Windows Mail, which can interfere if you're trying to work on something while launching Windows Mail in the background.

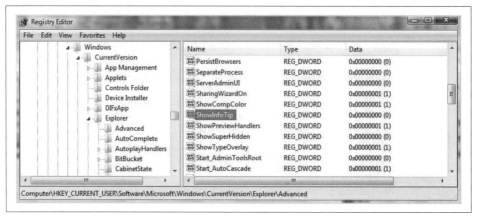

Figure 15-2. Remove Vista's tool tips with this registry hack

Here's how to get rid of it:

1. Open the Registry Editor; you can do this by typing **regedit** from the Start menu.

2. Navigate to this key:

   HKEY_CURRENT_USER\Software\Microsoft\Windows Mail

3. Look for the NoSplash DWORD value and set it to 1.

4. Exit the Registry Editor and reboot Vista.

Deleting the Hibernate File

Upon hibernation, Vista creates a hibernate file called *hiberfil.sys* in which all contents of the current session are stored.

If you don't emerge from hibernation properly, that *hiberfil.sys* file can stick around, and because this file is as large as the system RAM, getting rid of it can free up a considerable amount of disk space.

A simple way to delete it is to type **powercfg -h off** from an elevated Command Prompt, and then to press Enter. That's it. You've just freed up at least 1 GB of storage on most Vista machines.

To verify your handiwork, you can open Vista Explorer and look for the *hiberfil.sys* file. It's a hidden system file, so you'll have to make sure you can see it by using the Folder and Search Options dialog box:

1. Click the Organize button, and then choose Folder and Search Options.

2. On the View tab, choose the "Show hidden files" option and uncheck the "Hide protected operating system files (recommended)" checkbox.

Starting Vista Explorer at the C: Drive

It's a small annoyance of mine, but an annoyance nonetheless: when I open Vista Explorer, it automatically takes me to the user's Documents folder.

But I usually open Vista Explorer to browse through the contents of my entire hard drive(s), not just the contents of the Documents folder.

What to do? Try the following options.

Option 1:

1. Create a shortcut to *Explorer.exe* on the desktop.
2. Right-click the shortcut and choose Properties from the context menu.
3. Choose the Shortcut tab and note the Target field.
4. Change the Target value to `C:\Windows\explorer.exe /n, /e, c:\`.
5. Click OK and exit.

Now, you can double-click the desktop shortcut and Vista Explorer launches with the focus on the C: drive (you can choose another drive besides the C: drive, of course).

Option 2:

1. Add the Computer icon to the desktop by opening the Personalization Control Panel application (right-click the desktop and choose Properties).
2. Choose the "Change desktop icons" link on the left, opening the dialog box shown in Figure 15-3. Place a check in the Computer checkbox.
3. Now, right-click the Computer desktop icon and choose Explorer. You're not opening exactly to the C: drive, but you're close; you're a lot higher in the folder hierarchy than when using the Windows key-E key combination.

 You can also use the Computer desktop icon to launch the Computer Management console by right-clicking and choosing Manage.

Option 3:

1. Open a Vista Explorer window.
2. Expand the Computer item to expose the logical drives.
3. Drag-and-drop the Local Disk (C:) drive icon to the desktop. You can do this for any logical drive on your system.

Figure 15-3. Adding the Computer desktop icon

Getting Rid of Arrows on Shortcuts

If the little arrows on the program shortcuts are simply more than you can bear, you can get rid of them with a registry edit.

Here's what to do:

1. From the Start menu, type **regedit** and open the corresponding application. You will need to provide administrative confirmation if User Account Control is turned on.

2. Now, navigate to this registry key:

    HKEY_CLASSES_ROOT\lnkfile

3. Rename the `IsShortcut` string to `AriochIsShortcut`.

4. Close the Registry Editor and reboot.

This is an old trick, but it should still work on Windows Vista machines as well.

Always Running the Command Prompt in Admin Mode

Althogh administrators can do more with the graphical interface than ever before, the Command Prompt has yet to go away completely. It still remains the best way to accomplish more than a few administrative tasks.

There's one problem, though. Even though the Command Prompt is used mostly by system administrators, it doesn't run in the context of an administrator account by default. You can fix this easily enough by right-clicking the Command Prompt Start Menu shortcut and choosing "Run as administrator."

But there's another way to make this even more permanent. You can set the properties of the Command Prompt shortcut so that it always runs in the context of an administrator account.

Here's the procedure:

1. Pin a Command Prompt shortcut to the Start menu. You should know how to do this, especially after reading Chapter 4, but just in case, here's one way:

    a. Navigate to Start → All Programs → Accessories → Command Prompt. Now, right-click the Command Prompt shortcut you just created and choose Properties.

    b. Choose the Shortcut tab on the Command Prompt shortcut and click the Advanced button.

    c. As seen in Figure 15-4, check the "Run as administrator" checkbox in the ensuing dialog box.

2. Click OK to save your changes and then exit the Command Prompt's shortcut properties dialog box.

Figure 15-4. Always run an elevated Command Prompt

Enabling Aero Glass Without a Supported Graphics Card

Believe it or not, there's a way to cheat Vista into using many of the Aero glass effects even if you don't have a graphics card that supports the full Vista Aero theme.

Try out this registry edit instead:

1. From the Start menu, type **regedit** and open the corresponding application. You'll need to provide administrative confirmation if User Account Control is turned on.

2. Now, navigate to this Registry key:

   HKEY_LOCAL_MACHINE\Software\Microsoft

3. From there, you need to create a new key and name it DWM.

4. In the DWM key, create a new DWORD value called `EnableMachineCheck`.

5. Set the `EnableMachineCheck` value to 0 (false).

6. Create another DWORD value, name it `Blur`, and set that value to 0 as well.

7. One more to go. Again in the DWM key you just made, create a DWORD value called `Animations` and set that value to 0 as well.

All that's left now is to exit and reboot. The result is an Aero interface, but without the "blurring" effect that occurs when you're able to see "through" one window to whatever is behind it. Also, to lighten the load on your graphics card, the window animations such as the Mac-like (I went the whole book without using the adjective; sorry, it's Mac-like) "whooshing" of a window back down to the taskbar.

Try this on a graphics card with 64 MB of RAM. I think you'll be pleasantly surprised.

Fixing Red Eye with Windows Photo Gallery

I've found the Windows Photo Gallery to be quite a nice little application. It presents a reasonably intuitive interface for storing and managing your digital pictures.

It also includes a few little photo-editing capabilities that most people will find very useful. No, it's not a fully equipped photo editor, nor was it designed to be. It's good at what it does, which is more than you can say for some other Vista-bundled apps (discussed shortly). The Photo Gallery makes it easy to tag and rate pictures, quickly scroll through thumbnails, and even play a slide show of selected items (great for use when a Vista system is connected to a large external display).

One of my favorites is the Photo Editor's capability to quickly fix red eye. Here's how to use it to do that:

1. From the Photo Gallery, select the picture with the red-eye trouble.

2. In the toolbar, click Fix.

3. You're then given a window dealing with just that picture. In the right pane are several correcting options, including the red-eye fixer at the bottom, as shown in Figure 15-5.

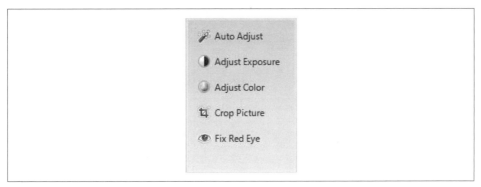

Figure 15-5. Quickly cleaning up a picture

Showing the Built-in Administrator Account on the Welcome Screen

If you open the Computer Management console to investigate/manage user accounts, you may notice that there's a built-in local Administrator account. Yet it doesn't show up in the Welcome screen. Is there a way to make sure it does?

Yes. Here's what to do:

1. From a Run dialog box (Windows key-R), type `netplwiz`. You'll be asked for administrative confirmation if User Account Control is turned on.
2. Choose the built-in Administrator account, and then reset the password using the Reset Password button.
3. Now, open the Registry Editor and navigate to this key:

    HKEY_LOCAL_MACHINE\SOFTWARE\Microsoft\Windows NT\ CurrentVersion\Winlogon

4. In that key, create two new subkeys: the first will be called *SpecialAccounts*. Create a subkey of that one called *UserList*.
5. Now, add a new DWORD value and name it `Administrator`. Give the DWORD a value of 1 (true), as shown in Figure 15-6.

You should now be able to click on the built-in Administrator account just like you can any other.

Getting Access to More Options from the Right-Click Menus

The tip couldn't be easier: just hold down the Shift key when performing a right-click.

To demonstrate the difference between a regular right-click menu and one that is generated using the Shift key, I'll show you two context menus side by side in Figure 15-7. To the left is the normal right-click context menu for a file; the Shift-enabled context menus are to the right.

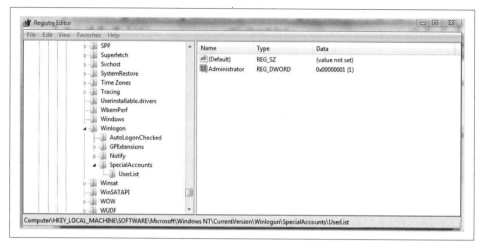

Figure 15-6. Adding the Administrator account to the Welcome screen

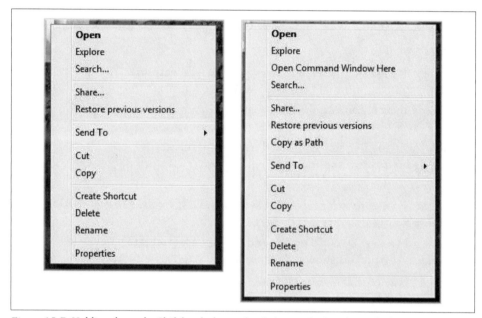

Figure 15-7. Holding down the Shift key before right-clicking unlocks a host of other options

For power users, one of the most significant differences is the ability to "open a Command Prompt here" to open a command window with the current directory already listed. Also, you can add any file to the Quick Launch toolbar, or copy the full path for a file or folder to the Clipboard.

One of the third-party tools mentioned a couple of times in this book, TweakVista, includes a little routine that in effect makes the Shift-right-click functionality the default right-click action.

Finding Something on a Web Page

Not all web sites present an interface as uncluttered as Google's home page. Some web sites are, shall we say, just a tad more "scholarly."

But let's say I'm looking for an article on Thomas Jefferson's Monticello home. I do a search, and I see several sites that might be relevant. The first one I land on, however, is as long as one of the chapters of this book, and I want to skip right to the part that deals with Monticello.

In Internet Explorer 6 (IE6), this was easy. I could just select Edit → Find on page to take advantage of this essential feature.

But there is no Edit menu in Internet Explorer 7!! Or at least it's not visible unless you remember to hold down the Alt key!! Does that mean that now I'll have to read the entire page!? (Note here the exclamation point and question mark to convey both worry and bewilderment *at the same time*. The things I can do at a keyboard.)

Fortunately, Microsoft hasn't taken away that functionality. To locate a specific item on a web page, use the Ctrl-F key combination to bring up Figure 15-8.

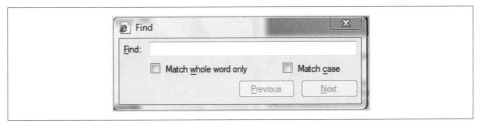

Figure 15-8. This can save a lot of time when looking for information

(A minor IE7 annoyance, while on the subject of what's been removed from IE6: you can't relocate the Home toolbar icon very easily, although you can change its order in the toolbar. Right-click, choose Customize the Command Bar, then use the Add or Remove Commands dialog box—not worth expanding into a full-fledged gripe as I do with a few features later in the chapter.)

Removing the IE7 Search Toolbar

While we're on the subject of IE7, I suppose I should tell you how to remove the Search bar. Personally, I *really* like the Search bar, especially its capability to utilize several search providers.

But plenty of folks out there use a third-party toolbar, and most of these already have a Search box built in (some even have the same IE7-like capability to change search providers).

If this describes you and you find the IE7 Search box redundant, follow these steps to remove the Search box from Internet Explorer:

1. Open the Registry Editor and navigate to this key:

   HKEY_LOCAL_MACHINE\Software\Policies\Microsoft\Internet Explorer\ Infodelivery\Restrictions

2. Create a DWORD value named NoSearchBox.

3. Set the NoSearchBox value to 1 (true).

The Search box disappears from IE7. To undo your changes, set the value back to 0 or delete the DWORD entry.

Blasting the Security Center Icon

Many Windows users didn't like the Security Center icon when it was introduced in Windows XP Service Pack 2, and many don't like it now in Windows Vista, either.

There is a way to get rid of the icon and its many associated reminders that pop up from the Notification Area from time to time:

1. Open the Security Center by typing **security** at the Start menu.

2. In the lefthand pane of the Security Center, choose "Change the way the Security Center alerts me."

3. You'll now see the dialog box shown in Figure 15-9. You can select the third option here to rid the System Tray of the icon and rid yourself of all Security Center reminders.

To undo your changes, just follow the same procedure again and choose the "Yes, notify me and display the icon (recommended)" option.

You could also go to the Computer Management console and look for the Security Center Service. Prevent the service from running automatically and it should accomplish the same goal. The first technique is a little more straightforward and a bit less risky, however.

Making Text Easier to Read

I mentioned this in Chapter 4, but it's worth another mention, if for no other reason than the fact that I've really included two tips here.

At higher display resolutions, text gets smaller, leading to potentially increased eyestrain. You can have your cake and eat it, too, by using the higher resolution yet increasing the font size used by Vista.

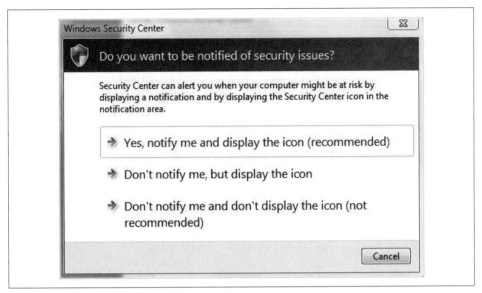

Figure 15-9. Changing the Security Center behavior

Here's what to do:

1. Open the Control Panel.

2. Recall that the Control Panel is essentially an Explorer window, and can therefore be searched just as easily as any other Explorer window (this is the other tip, in case you're wondering). Type **Adjust** in the Search box.

3. You will see a listing of all adjustments that you can make via the Control Panel interface. The first one listed should be to "Adjust the font size (DPI)." Click this link to continue.

4. You'll now see the DPI scaling dialog box shown in Figure 15-10, where you can select the preset value of 120 DPI or click Custom DPI. The slider will let you resize to whatever your eyesight can handle.

Purchasing Windows Vista Online and Downloading It for Installation

Microsoft has not only released many new features in Windows Vista, as you've seen, but the company also has updated the way in which Vista is *distributed*.

For the first time, Microsoft is making an operating system available for purchase and download online. The download is targeted for current users of Windows XP who want to upgrade. Just like upgrading almost any other application, you'll be able to complete the upgrade to a new OS online, too. This will be available for upgrades to Office 2007 as well.

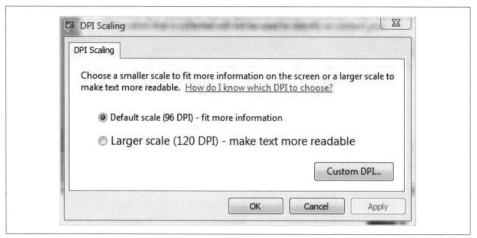

Figure 15-10. Adjusting font size with the DPI utility

This might be a good option for small/home businesses, because apparently a promotion is planned that allows for the purchase of two copies of Home Premium for $50 with the purchase of one copy of Vista Ultimate.

For more information, visit one of these web sites: *http://www.Microsoft.com/downloads* or *http://www.Microsoft.com/windowsvista*.

Optimizing the Sound

This is a tip that will be available if you have a PC with an Intel motherboard with High Definition Audio support. If this describes your system, read on to find out how to take advantage of this hardware package.

1. Open the Control Panel and then the Sound options from the Hardware and Sound grouping. For a short cut, type **sound** at the Start menu.

2. Choose the Playback tab, and then select the Speakers icon. Now click the Properties button.

3. You should now see an Enhancements tab, as shown in Figure 15-11. This tab will include a set of options that will control bass levels, use virtual surround sound on a two-speaker system, correct for room acoustics, and enhance loudness settings.

Very cool. Obviously, this is best utilized on desktops and/or Vista machines that function primarily as a media center.

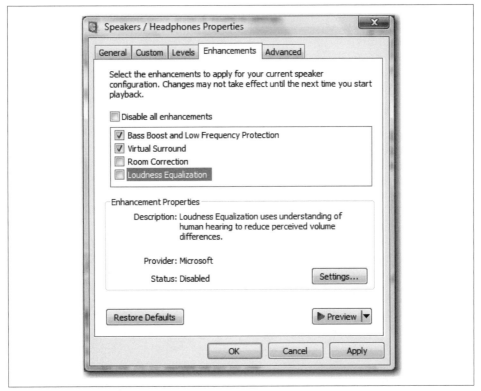

Figure 15-11. Using optimized sound settings

Restoring Run on the Start Menu

For current users of Windows XP (and 2000, for that matter), it's hard not to notice that one important feature is missing from the Start menu: the Run option. On Windows Vista's simple Start menu, it's no longer there.

How to access? Well, there are several ways; some I discussed previously, such as locating it under the Accessories submenu, or by using the quick Windows key-R keyboard shortcut.

But as you've explored the taskbar and Start menu customization options, you might discover that you can add Run to the Vista Start menu with just a few clicks:

1. Right-click the Vista Start button and choose Properties from the context menu.
2. Select the Start Menu tab of the Taskbar and Start Menu Properties, and then click the Customize button.
3. As seen in Figure 15-12, scroll down the list until you see the "Run command" checkbox.
4. Place a check here and click OK twice to commit the changes.

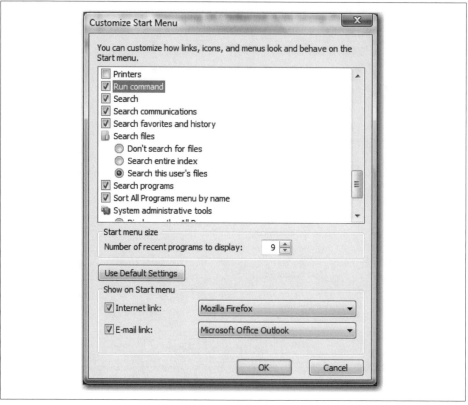

Figure 15-12. Adding the Run command to Vista's Start menu

You should now see this comforting little command on the bottom of the righthand side of Vista's Start menu.

Adjusting the Default Height of a Window

This is probably intuitive, but it's also worth pointing out: you can change the default height of an application window simply by resizing it and closing. Here are the specific click-steps:

1. To change window height, hover your mouse at either the top or the bottom of the window. It will change to a double-headed arrow, with which you can click and drag to resize the window.

2. To change window width, use the same procedure at either the left or right window border. The mouse pointer changes into a horizontal double-headed arrow.

3. To change both height and width simultaneously, hover over any window corner and click and drag. Here, the mouse pointer changes into a diagonal double-headed arrow.

Once you've got the window resized to your liking, close the application. Now, any subsequent windows of the same application should launch at the same size as what was just set.

This works with maximized windows as well. If you want Microsoft Outlook to be maximized each time it opens (I set it to launch at startup and then maximize, for example), just maximize it and then close from the maximized state.

Porting Video Output to an External Monitor

This tip applies especially to laptop computers that are connected to external displays used for presentations. If that pretty much describes why you were issued a laptop, you certainly need to know how to duplicate the laptop display to a second screen.

Fortunately, it's usually just a matter of using the correct keyboard shortcut. On most laptops, it's the Function key (Fn)-F4, or Fn-F5, but you have to check with your hardware manufacturer to determine for sure.

Another thing to check on laptops is that Vista is detecting the external display properly. The new Vista Mobility Center works wonders for performing this task. With the Windows Mobility Center open, look to the lower-lefthand corner for the External Display button, as seen in Figure 15-13.

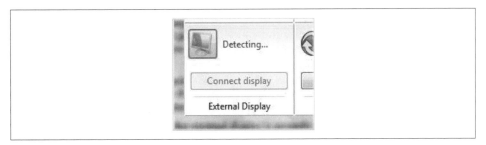

Figure 15-13. Make sure Vista detects the external display

If you've attached the external monitor and you don't see the Mobility Center report that an external display has been detected, try clicking this button first before using the keyboard commands mentioned here.

Leveraging the Quick Launch Toolbar with Shortcut Keys

I'm not sure this will speed up the function of the Quick Launch toolbar significantly—after all, the whole idea is to launch a program with a single click—but it can certainly be a handy tip when you want to keep your hands at the keyboard.

The tip is simple: use the Windows key-*number* combination to launch the Quick Launch application.

For example, look at my Quick Launch toolbar (see Figure 15-14).

Figure 15-14. My Quick Launch toolbar

To launch Microsoft Outlook, I would use the Windows key-4 combination. For iTunes, it's Windows key-5, and so on. Like I said, easy.

Checking Whether Your Device Is Compatible with Vista

As I have pointed out numerous times throughout this book, and as has been pointed out in countless other places such as web sites and even advertisements for iMac computers (the Mac versus PC commercials, like Donald Trump, can seem endearing in small doses, but they are *this* close to wearing out their welcome; I'm starting to root for PC to just turn and punch Mac—who's sounding more and more like a snobbish bully with every ad—right in the nose), not every hardware device will work with Windows Vista.

But lots of resources are at your disposal. For the most part, you can determine whether a product you plan to purchase is compatible with Vista by visiting the manufacturer's web sites, for example, and can always look at the side of the box. Then again, boxes are designed and printed and sit on store shelves for months, sometimes years, before you grab and read them.

With that in mind, here's a quick little tip that can save you time and trouble before installing that next upgrade: try the Vista Hardware Compatibility List (HCL) at the Microsoft web site, which is really more tool than list, per se. You can find it at *http://winqual.microsoft.com/hcl*.

The web site includes full instructions on how to use the HCL to find a specific device that has passed muster at the Windows Hardware Qualifying Lab. For example, if you're considering purchasing an ATI All-In-Wonder 9600 XT graphics card, and you want to know whether it's compatible with the 64-bit version of Vista (it is), you can select Components → Graphics Cards from the web site's lefthand panel.

You can also search for a specific string, such as "9600 XT," using the options at the bottom of the left pane.

It's one of those "stitch in time saves nine" kinds of tips.

Using Two Printers for One Print Device

Using two printers for one device can be a great advantage when you want to quickly make several changes to the way a job is printed.

This is a great way to take advantage of a modern printer's multiple options—paper tray, page size, page orientation, half-toning, print optimization, and so on—without having to access the printer's Properties dialog box with each and every option change.

For example, let's say that one of your common printing chores includes the use of your inkjet's photo-quality output, and on 3×5 photo-quality paper rather than 8.5×11 office paper.

Yes, you could make the necessary changes before printing using the Properties dialog box interface. However, you'd have to remember to switch back before printing that letter you have to get out the door, and you'd have to remember once again the next time you printed snapshots.

Here's a solution: instead of having to keep track of the print settings each time you send something to the printer, you can set up two different *printers*, each one printing to the same *print device*.

Using the example just cited, you could call one of these printers Photo Printer and the other one Text Printer. (You could take this one step further and configure specific applications to use different default printers—the Text Printer when using Microsoft Word, the Photo Printer when using the Vista Photo Gallery.) The magic, once properly configured, is this: you press the Print button in your applications and retrieve finished output from the same device, and each set of output uses the settings appropriate for the file. Cool.

What's more, this two printers/one device configuration gives you lots of flexibility. You can always switch an application's printer (and thus, the output settings) for any particular job by simply selecting the alternative printer in the Print dialog box. This way, all you'll have to think about when printing is loading the right paper.

At any rate, here's what to do in order to add a second printer instance:

1. Open the Control Panel's Printers console using the method of your choosing. Yes, you'll see that a printer is already set up there. We're going to add that same printer a second time. Click the Add a Printer toolbar button to get started.

2. The Add Printer Wizard launches. Use the steps in the wizard to add the same printer (usually it will be a local printer). You'll be asked whether you want to keep the existing driver files or install new ones, as shown in Figure 15-15. Keep the existing files.

3. Now that you've got the second printer instance set up, right-click and access its Properties dialog box.

4. Configure the printer's settings as desired. A suggestion: include a descriptive name so that you and possibly other users have a clue about the printer's settings and purpose. In the example in Figure 15-15, I used (Photos) and configured printer settings that include optimization for glossy photo paper.

5. Close the Properties dialog box.

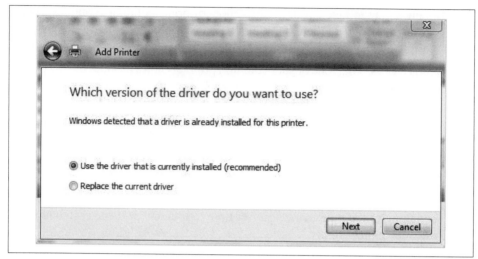

Figure 15-15. Adding a second printer instance

Follow these steps again to add other instances as needed, configuring their print properties as required. Before long, you'll end up with this: a Properties dialog box that lists multiple printers for a single port, as shown in Figure 15-16.

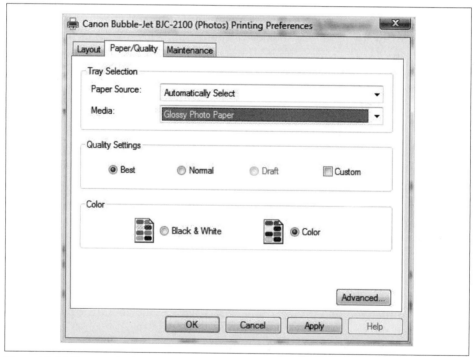

Figure 15-16. Using multiple printers for a single print device

Configuring a Printer Pool

Printer pools are typically used in high-volume printing environments, where many print devices serve the needs of network users. In the preceding Vista tip, we looked at how to manage the print environment using multiple printers to print to a single device.

Creating a printer pool sets up the exact opposite: it associates a single printer with multiple print devices.

Typically, printer pools are configured when many print devices of the same type are located on the network. This is to ensure that all devices understand the instructions sent by the single type of print driver.

When you're submitting jobs to a print pool, the first available print device services the job. But what if one of the print devices has just run out of ink? Can administrators specify that a job gets sent to a particular print device?

In a word, no. In this instance, your only solution is to take the inkless printer offline; in a print pool, you don't have any control over which print device will eventually service the job.

Here's how to quickly set up a printer pool, assuming you have several of the same print device:

1. Open the Printer Control Panel console, and then access the printer's Properties dialog box.
2. Choose the Ports tab. At the bottom, click the "Enable printer pooling" checkbox, and then select the checkboxes for all the ports to which you want the printer to send the job, as shown in Figure 15-17.
3. Click Apply or OK to commit the changes.

In the end, this looks very similar to redirecting a print job, a task discussed in Chapter 7. The biggest difference is the use of multiple ports simultaneously rather than one at a time, which is made possible with the "Enable printer pooling" checkbox. If you don't check this, you can configure only one port per printer.

Also, it's wise to locate your pooled print devices close together. Because there's no way to predict which device prints the job, you don't want to have these devices in separate rooms, never mind on separate floors.

Converting a Volume to NTFS

This isn't necessarily new to Windows Vista, but it's nice to know you can still take a volume that has been formatted as a FAT filesystem and convert it to NTFS.

Like its predecessors, Vista provides a utility that allows for conversion of both FAT and FAT32 volumes to NTFS without causing any adverse effect on the data. It's called Convert.exe. You launch it from the Command Prompt. Here's the correct syntax:

```
convert volume /fs:ntfs
```

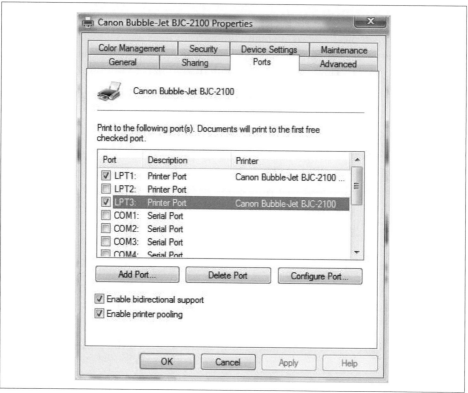

Figure 15-17. Setting up a print pool

where *volume* is the target FAT volume you're converting. If you convert the System partition, the conversion will be completed at the next operating system restart.

> Unfortunately, you can't convert a volume from NTFS to FAT. Well, I take that back—you can, but it's a bit of a hassle. It either involves third-party utilities or using the Vista tools, but you end up reformatting the entire volume. Of course, reformatting wipes out all data on the volume, so if you convert from NTFS to FAT and you want to keep the data, you must restore that data from a backup.

As is usually the case, a little planning can go a long way.

Mounting a Volume into an NTFS Folder

In Chapter 7, we looked at many of the management options you have when dealing with hard disk space, including creating volumes on basic and dynamic disks. Most of the time, you assign a volume a drive letter.

But there's another option: you can also *mount* a new volume into an existing folder. This creates more room on an existing volume without actually resizing it. It also allows you to store all information, no matter where it's stored, in a single directory hierarchy.

For example, if you have a C: drive that you want to store music in, but you can't expand the C: drive's capacity to do so (it's the System volume, for example), you could create a new volume of 50 GB or so, and mount the new volume in an empty folder called Music.

In Vista's Explorer, the Music folder looks like a drive instead of a folder. Now, the C: drive's overall capacity appears as though it has been expanded by 50 GB. In reality, however, any files stored in the Music directory are placed on the new volume.

There are two requirements for mounting a drive. First, the mount point must be an empty folder. The second is that the volume hosting the mount-point folder must be formatted with the NTFS filesystem.

The click-steps are exactly the same as when creating a new volume. Using the disk management tool, you'll arrive at the screen where you normally assign a drive letter. Here's where you have the option of mounting the drive, as seen in Figure 15-18.

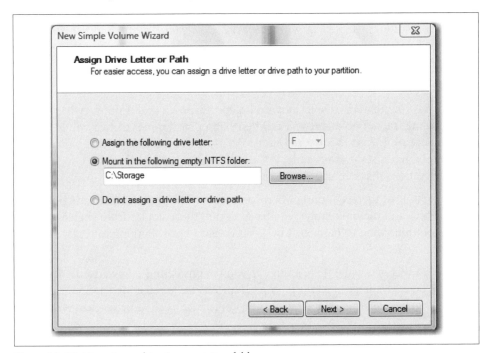

Figure 15-18. Mounting a drive in an existing folder

The "Ultimate" Vista Tip: Do a Clean Install of Vista Without Using the Full Version

The title of this tip is really the tip itself. Here's what I mean: as of this writing, you can purchase an Upgrade version of Windows Vista and perform a clean install.

How's that? Well, an Upgrade version of Windows looks for an existing installation of the operating system, and then upgrades it. But Windows Vista can upgrade *itself*, at least for now. Here's how it would work, if one were to do this:

1. Boot from the Vista Upgrade DVD. (I'm assuming you're doing the clean install on a blank disk.)

2. Choose the Install Now option, but *don't* enter the product key. Choose the Custom (Advanced) install.

3. After install, *don't* activate the copy of Windows. Instead, perform Vista installation again by doing the upgrade.

4. This time, select the Upgrade installation option. Vista will now upgrade itself, and you'll be able to activate just as though upgrading from Windows XP.

Awesome, huh? (Well, I guess it depends on whom you ask. I imagine that more than a few Microsoft stockholders flung this book across the room a sentence ago and are now uttering sentences with the words *liner*, *bird*, *wrap*, and *fish* sprinkled somewhere within.[*])

If you're considering the Ultimate edition, for example, this tip alone just saved you $140. Yes, this book just increased your net worth.

Now, be assured that Microsoft knows all about this trick and is not very happy that I'm including it in a book, and you can bet that a programmer or two will lose their jobs because of it. Also, be assured that Microsoft will figure out what went wrong and create a fix as soon as possible, but until that time, the shelves are chock-full of Upgrade editions that will upgrade over themselves.

But for right now, there's nothing Microsoft can do. The product is already boxed up and shipped, and the only immediate fix is to pull those copies from shelves. That's just flat-out not going to happen; Microsoft doesn't have anything to replace it with for now.

So jump on this one while there's time. If you're considering a move to the Ultimate edition to take advantage of all the laptop enhancements and the Media Center capabilities, this can be one instance in which acting immediately can be better than waiting.

---

[*] Or are they? They might be smiling about this one, knowing that this is going to cause many people to go out and pay for an Upgrade edition of Vista that they might not otherwise have purchased. After all, Microsoft did write the code to allow this to happen; it's possible that the developers did so on purpose.

And Now, What I Would Have Changed About Windows Vista If Only...

...Gates, Allchin, or heck, even J. Allard had bothered to ask (apparently, I'm not cool enough for someone who forgoes his first name, letting an initial act as a stand-in.)*

This book has been a chronicle of Vista's new features, and indeed, this last chapter has done nothing but sing its praises by pointing out a few cool little tips and tricks that will help you get the most out of Vista.

But it can't be all roses, can it? Surely there are a few dents in the armor, aren't there?

There are, and this section looks at six Vista features that would be different if Microsoft had bothered to ask me first.

User Account Control

Look, User Account Control's head is in the right place. According to Microsoft, software isn't the biggest threat to desktop security. Instead, poor decision-making causes the most problems. Users are fooled by phishing web sites; they install malware without realizing it; they open attachments they shouldn't; and so on. User Account Control is built to help—or at least force—the user or admin to make more informed decisions.

Unfortunately, the execution is just not there yet. If it was, it wouldn't have taken so many pages in Chapter 1 for me to explain it, nor would there be several more pages explaining how to disable the thing in Chapter 8.

But the big problem I see is one of security, not of hassle, although on the hassle side, I must admit that I've turned the thing off on my personal computer because it is just way, way too intrusive.

The security argument goes like this: because it's relatively easy to disable, why can't a malware program just include code for turning off User Account Control before installing? If an application such as TweakVista can do it with a click of a button, why not a program with a more pernicious intent?

And as the infomercial guy says, "But wait, there's more!" Apparently, there's a rather large flaw in the User Account Control architecture, which has been reported by WinAbility Software's Andrei Belogortseff.

His analysis from *http://www.tweak-uac.com* is as follows:

---

* As should be pathetically transparent, I would actually like to meet the guy and talk about the Xbox or Zune, or maybe just shoot the breeze about mountain biking.

I believe I've stumbled upon the first bug in Vista UAC (in the final release of Vista, not in a beta version).

It's very easy to see the bug in action:

Login to your computer with the Guest account. (You may need to enable the Guest account first, using the Control Panel).

Download any digitally signed program (such as TweakUAC), save it to the default download folder (*C:\Users\Guest\Downloads*).

Now run the file you've just downloaded, and take a look at the elevation prompt [displayed in Figure 15-19].

As you can see, UAC cannot recognize that the file contains a valid digital signature, and it warns you that the program is "unidentified." This is a bug, because you can check that the digital signature of the file is actually valid [see Figure 15-20].

This problem is not limited to the TweakUAC file, any other digitally signed executable (such as the installation utilities of most software packages) will produce the same effect. All you need to do to reproduce this bug is login to Vista with the Guest account and run a digitally signed file from the *Guest\Downloads* folder. Note that if you copy the executable into the *C:\Program Files* folder, and run the file from there, its digital signature would magically become recognizable by UAC! Move the file to the root folder C:\, and the file again becomes unidentified to UAC.

Is this bug dangerous? Yes, it is! The whole idea behind UAC is to shift the responsibility of distinguishing the bad programs from the good ones to the end user (you!). The only tool that UAC gives you in this regard is the digital signature information, and it turns out it's broken! How are you supposed to make the decision whether to trust a certain program or not if UAC does not provide you with the correct information?

Figure 15-19. The User Account Control warning

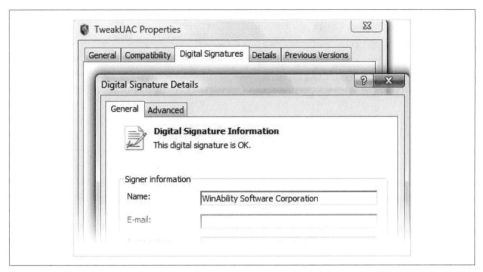

Figure 15-20. Checking to see whether the signature is actually valid

I will confess that I'm including the quote here mostly because of peer pressure, although I find it a bit over the top as well. There are blog entries and articles ad nauseam on the subject, but the most often-lodged complaint concerns User Account Control's incessant "chattiness." If you leave it on, you won't use a Vista computer for long before being reminded of its presence.

The New Logon Screen: A Step Backward

Vista machines will no doubt be installed in lots of domains the world over. Once that's done, users (and admins) will then be able to log on to either the domain or the local computer.

But it's now a lot more complex than it used to be. In previous versions of Windows, such as XP Professional, users could just select where they wanted to log on from a drop-down menu and then type a username and password.

Now, it "works" like this:

1. A default user appears at the Vista logon screen. Underneath, as shown in Figure 15-21, there's a button called Switch User. Click it, and you see a second screen where you have to click on "Other user."

2. Finally, you see an entry box where you can enter a new username. Notice, however, that you won't have the option of choosing the domain or local computer to log on to.

3. To log on locally, you must enter the computer name and then the username using the following syntax:

    Computername\username

Then enter the password in Figure 15-22.

Figure 15-21. Switching the user to log on locally

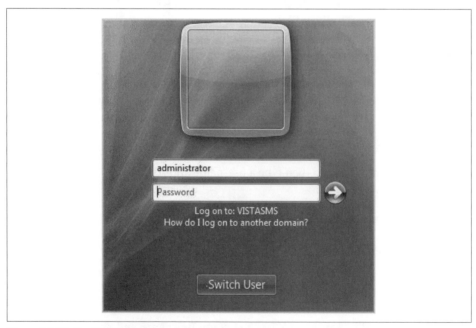

Figure 15-22. You'd better know the computer name

That leaves the following question, of course: what happens if you don't have the foggiest about the local computer name? You don't log on, that's what.

To further complicate things, if you log on locally, possibly to make a few administrative changes (I know, that's not how things are *supposed* to work), the next user has to follow the same procedure to then log on to the domain.

This time, however, the domain name appears below the logon fields. You see a "Logon to *domain*" entry box. But then after entering the logon name, the line changes again and displays the name of the local computer.

Huh? Users now have to enter the domain name to present logon credentials, like this:

    Domainname\username

I can't even dream up a more complicated logon scheme. What Microsoft is counting on here is that one person uses the same computer day in, day out, and further, that in a domain environment, that users always log on to the domain and never to their local machine. Unfortunately, real computer networks don't work that way, and this is a redesign I just don't get.

 There's a correlated tip with this, by the way. You can type `.\username` to log on to the local computer; easy enough, assuming you learned about this tip here. If you didn't, the new logon screen is anything but easy.

The Price

I don't quite know what to say about this, other than the following:

- I'm not suggesting that I know enough about the internal economics of Microsoft to suggest what its operating system should cost, nor am I suggesting that its bottom line would either be hurt or helped by lowering the cost.

- It's not as though other software vendors exactly give their software away. Case in point: Apple. For all its sneering, it hasn't released a major update in its operating system in five or six years, either. It just releases another version of the same operating system (OS X) every year and instead of calling it a service pack or hot fix or something like that, it calls it a new Earth-shattering breakthrough and gives it the name of an exotic cat. The real genius of Apple is that it charges $120 or more for the privilege of installing Widgets or Spotlight. As I write this, OS X 10.4 Leopard is promising computing sea changes such as the following, which appeared on Apple's web site:

  > "With Mac OS X Leopard, you get even more widgets," and "Mail transforms mere email into personalized stationery."

  So, there you have it. OS X 10.4: Widgets and stationery for email. Whoop-de-freaking-doo!! Where can I stand in line to pay for stuff I already have?

  The same behavior out of Microsoft would have Jobs *literally* thumbing his nose at Gates to wild applause during a MacWorld keynote. (What's more, Apple even gets people to *pay* for the chance to be a beta tester. Because features are constantly changing between beta and release, I was reluctant to install the beta version of Vista even for this book.)

The preceding disclaimers (and my own nose-thumbing) notwithstanding, Vista does seem a little on the pricey side. Here's how it breaks down for the full versions:

- Vista Ultimate: $399
- Vista Business: $299
- Vista Home Premium: $239
- Vista Home Basic: $199

So let me get this straight: I can get a brand-new computer to be the absolute center of my home entertainment universe for 400–500 bucks, and then have to pay another 400 bucks just to turn it on?* OK....

If anything seems overpriced in the era of the $300 laptop, it's the Vista Home Basic edition. For what you get for the extra 40 bucks (Aero, Media Center, etc.), Vista Home Premium is a far superior "value." Then again, you will be spending more than $300 to purchase a laptop that is Windows Vista Home Premium Ready. So just spend the extra $40.

I know the counterarguments: you won't *really* ever pay that much because you'll purchase Vista preloaded with your next computer, and so on. But I will want Windows Vista Ultimate on my next computer, won't I? I will want the Media Center, available in Windows Vista Home Premium, and I will also want the ability to join a domain and use Offline Files, which is *not* available with Premium. My only real option (if I purchase a Windows Vista computer) is to get Ultimate.

And I bet I'm hardly the only computer user who wants to use these three features on the same computer. By selectively turning off features in its code base (which is Ultimate), Microsoft has forced my hand—in terms of upgrading or buying new—into choosing the most expensive version of its operating system.†

---

* Or do I? Maybe the previous upgrade tip I mentioned right before this section is an entirely calculated move, and Microsoft is simply using the $400 price tag in the same way that clothing retailers use sale prices, as in: "This tie is normally $120, but it's on sale today for just $79. Great deal, huh?" So maybe, just maybe, Microsoft wants you to consider $260 to be a great bargain when compared to $400.

† Upgrading a laptop to Windows Vista Ultimate on Dell's Small Business web site will set you back an additional $200, for example. Plus, it's hardly hassle-free to get Ultimate. I tried to get Ultimate on HP's web site but couldn't—the Home notebooks only let you upgrade to Home Premium, and the Small Business notebooks force you to purchase Vista Business. I would have tried other manufacturers, but one only has so much time.

In Europe, the prices are even higher, thanks in part to the exchange rate of the U.S. dollar versus the euro. According to my research, Europeans are being asked to shell out more than $600 U.S. for a retail copy of Vista Ultimate. Sorry, but that's just a rip-off.

And at the risk of unleashing the Mac versus PC religious debate, let me close this rather overwrought price footnote with this comparison, which puts Apple Computers, Inc. in a much more favorable light than did my earlier broadside aimed at OS X 10.4: you can get five licenses of the compete OS X 10.4 operating system at retail for just $199 U.S. The same five retail licenses for the complete Vista operating system (Ultimate) would set you back—wait for it—nearly $2,000 U.S.

But then again, let me hedge my bet: there don't seem to be any compelling alternatives. Linux is still way too inaccessible and byzantine to the average user no matter the price tag, and you can get two or three really kickass laptops for what you pay for a similarly equipped MacBook Pro.

And let me further hedge by stating that I neither pay the salaries of, nor lease the office space to, the programmers who write Windows Vista code, so I'm only expressing the opinion of a software consumer.*

A final thought on price: when Apple makes its OS X software available for 120 bucks on the Intel/AMD platform, at last Microsoft will have met its match in the operating system world. Given that you can run Windows on a Mac today, I expect an announcement of the opposite will soon be in the offing.

Closely related to price: What else you'll have to upgrade when purchasing Windows Vista

This won't be factored into many Vista purchases, but I'm here to tell you that it should be: if you're upgrading a machine that you've had for a couple of years, you *will* be buying a new thing or two.

Here's why: despite assurances to the contrary from Microsoft, and despite how easy Vista makes it to find updated drivers/patches for existing hardware/software, something just isn't going to work. It will therefore be a lot cheaper in terms of headache and cash just to buy a new one than to try to get what you have to work with Vista.

And mind you, I'm not talking about the video card with 64 MB of RAM that seemed perfectly capable of running Windows XP, but that is no longer cut out for the Vista experience. Nor am I talking about the 512 MB of RAM on your XP laptop that was powering its way through spreadsheets and movies just fine while on the airplane. I'm not talking about stuff you'll have to replace because it's *inadequate* for Windows Vista; I'm talking about the stuff you'll have to replace because it *just won't work*.

The main culprits here will be security programs and peripherals such as printers and scanners. For example, I wrote the majority of this book using a brand-new laptop computer (purchased in December 2006; I won't embarrass the manufacturer), which has a built-in fingerprint reader. And while the laptop is fully capable of showcasing the Vista Aero interface—it's got the Windows Vista Capable sticker and all—it asks me to install the drivers for the fingerprint reader each and every time I reboot.

---

* I also think frequent flyer miles should be available whenever you want to redeem them, but airlines seem more willing to fly empty seats than let their best customers redeem gift certificates they've earned. It's also worth pointing out in this completely off-topic footnote that I do not purchase airplanes or hire pilots to fly them or sell tickets on said airplanes, so maybe they have their reasons as well. You get the point (and you should fly Southwest if you want to actually *use* your frequent flyer credits).

If the upgrade of hardware hasn't factored in to your Vista deliberations by now, I ask you again to review Vista's hardware requirements. If I recall correctly, the jump in minimum RAM from Windows Me to Windows XP Home was from 32 MB to 64 MB—a twofold increase. Compare that to the recommended minimum of Vista Home Premium: 1 GB of RAM. That's an increase not of twofold, but of 10- or 20-fold. Are we really getting a 10-fold increase in operating system capability in that tradeoff? My argument is no. I think that a laptop with 2 GB of RAM should run one *hell* of a lot faster than one with 256 MB of RAM, but I haven't found that to be the case. Code seems to be growing faster than the hardware can keep up. If my cell phone can handle email, music, and movies on a 200 mhz processor with 16 MB of RAM, then my laptop should be able to keep up with 20 times the horsepower.

Closely related to stuff that doesn't work with Vista: What's with Vista and communication with laptop batteries?

This will amaze you, but as I write this very sentence, I've been working on battery power using an extended-life battery on my laptop for about six hours. What's more, I have *29 hours* of remaining battery life.

I told you you'd be amazed. Here's the problem: about six hours ago, my battery indicated that I had 29 hours remaining. And in about another 30 minutes or so, if I'm still working, the system will abruptly shut off and I'll lose all work since my last save. Here's why this is worthy of mention:

This is the third laptop on which I've used Vista.

All are from major manufacturers.

They all do the same thing.

My batteries will *never* last for 29 hours, so I have no idea why Vista reports that they will. I also don't know why, after six hours of use, the battery meter doesn't display 23 hours or something like that, and still reports that 100 percent of battery life is remaining.

And when Vista isn't overreporting the amount of available battery time on one machine, it's positively *killing* the battery life on another. I've definitely experienced a decrease in battery life on computers that have been upgraded to Vista.

I'm finding other power "issues" as well as I go, such as Vista never going into Sleep mode when it's plugged in, even though I've clicked all the right things in the Power Management options.

And here's my biggest complaint: *Sleep doesn't work*. Not the way it's advertised, anyway. First off, it causes application crash after application crash. Resuming from Sleep is always a little bit of a roll of the dice. Obviously, this is a huge concern, but even little things like the Ultimate Extras DreamScene usually can't get going again when coming out of Sleep.

Furthermore, in my experience, Sleep is painfully, paaaaiiinfully slow. I thought the idea was to *quickly* resume from a low-power state and get back to work. But I've resumed from Sleep mode, gotten up, brewed a pot of coffee (not just hitting the Brew button, mind you; I'm talking the whole procedure: measuring the water, beans, etc., hitting the button, and then waiting for the coffee to brew), and returned to a computer that is *still* not responsive to clicks such as switching among tabs on IE7.

But this is highly anecdotal, and it could just be me and these three particular laptop/battery combinations. I'm interested to hear if it is. Drop me an email at *hmsbrian@brianculp.com*, and let's gather some anecdotal information.

Vista Backup

I know that lots of people groan about User Account Control. But just wait until you see the Vista Backup utility. This is not only the worst application built into Vista, it is quite possibly the worst backup application in the history of computing for its era.

I don't know how this one got past a whiteboard session, as you can go down to the local Microcenter and get a better backup for free with one of those Western Digital My Book or Maxtor One Touch external drives.

Here's why you should never use this, especially if you put the title "IT administrator" on your business card or résumé: you can back up only what Microsoft decides you should back up. Look at the interface in Figure 15-23.

OK, fine, you say. Just what a Home user needs—a simple way to back up all the stuff on her computer. There's probably a way to schedule this backup to run every Friday night or so.

No, there isn't. The ability to schedule a backup is not included with the Home Basic edition.

Got you covered, you say. You spent the extra money and have the Home Premium version. You therefore have a quick way to back up all your Word documents and pictures, and you're probably now wondering where the screen is that would let you alter these defaults—you know, just back up your latest book, as everything else you've worked on in the past year has already been tucked away.

THERE ISN'T ONE. (All caps: I'm shouting now.) That's right—there's isn't a way to back up just a few folders or files; instead of you telling Vista what to back up, Vista tells you. You just pick a category.

In other words, if you want to back up, say, 10 GB's worth of *.doc*, *.jpg*, and *.zip* files, from a possible 150 GB of such files, you can't. The Backup program instead forces you to back up every single Word document, every single graphics file saved in *.jpg* format, and every single *.zip* compressed file *on your entire hard disk—including the ones created by the operating system itself*. Yes. Depending on your selections here, you could be backing up all of your icons, wallpapers, Windows sounds, and so on.

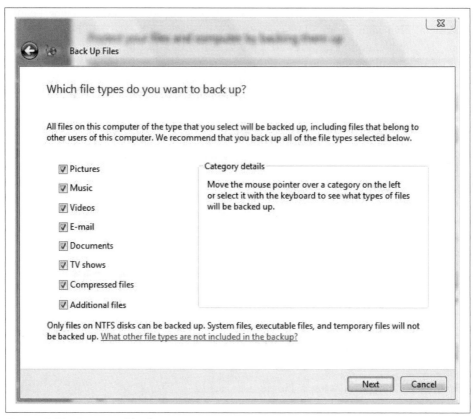

Figure 15-23. Nonsensical backup

And what if that handy little 2.5-inch 80 GB backup drive you tote around can't handle 150 GB's worth of stuff? Exactly. Don't waste your time with this one.

Oh, and just in case you like wasting time, try to run the Backup application while on battery power. Figure 15-24 shows what you'll see.

For an operating system that prides itself on being the ideal solution for laptop users, this one is absolutely inexcusable. What if I've got a 10-hour battery? Lots of laptops today come with extended battery options (such as the one I'm using right now). What if I'm flying from JFK to LAX and I want to back up my laptop to an external drive during the flight, while catching up on some reading?

Like I said, a complete head-scratcher.

Windows Mail

It's fine. Perfectly pleasant in most regards, it acts like Outlook Express and looks even better, making it easier to create, send, and reply to mail—an improvement, even, over Outlook Express.

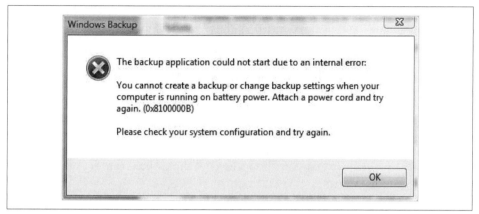

Figure 15-24. Don't do anything important while on battery power

Except for one glaring problem: *there's no integration with your Hotmail (Windows Live) account*. Or with any other Internet-based email accounts, such as Gmail and Yahoo! mail, for that matter. You could do this with Outlook Express; I'm not quite sure why this convenient feature was taken out.

If you want a Hotmail desktop client, you have to use Windows Live Mail Desktop instead, which as of this writing even Microsoft doesn't have a link to. No joke. I typed "Windows Live Mail Desktop" into a Windows Live search and was pointed to *http://ideas.live.com*. I clicked the Windows Live Mail Desktop link and was taken to…*http://ideas.live.com*.

Oh, and Windows Mail will let you try to set up your Hotmail account: there's a Hotmail option and everything on the Windows Mail "head fake" page where it looks like you can set up a Hotmail account, but you will then be taken to a page where you can sign up for a Hotmail account.

Wait. Huh? Isn't that what you were trying to do in the first place—set up a Hotmail account with Windows Mail? Why take you there? Even assuming you don't have one already, what good would signing up for one be? So you have something that doesn't work in Windows Mail?

It gets better. There's also a really helpful link called "here's why" on that page, as in, "Here's why Windows Mail doesn't support HTTP email." That link will take you to a support page that will tell you…that Windows Mail doesn't support HTTP email. (A page designed by the Microsoft redundancy division, no doubt, and there's nary a mention about why.) There's then a link on that page that will help you fix the issue—by linking to a page that will help you get started with a web-based email account from—are you sitting down, Steve Ballmer? Google.

To briefly recap…. The problem: Windows Mail cannot integrate with an HTTP email account. The solution as iterated by Microsoft: get a web-based email account like Gmail (which won't integrate with Windows Mail)* and a Windows Mobile device from your cell phone provider. Yeah, I don't follow the logic, either.

Makes you wonder whether the Windows Mail team wasn't infiltrated by someone trying to get people to use Mozilla Thunderbird instead. Thunderbird will happily handle all your Internet mail accounts. If you're curious, go to *http://www.mozilla.org*.

Gadgets

I know, they can be pretty useful, and they're a new feature and all, and yes, I spent a little time in Chapter 1 telling you about the cool things they can do, and they can indeed do a few cool things.

But there's just too much of a "me too" feel to the gadgets for me to get real excited about flogging them to the public; they don't do anything that Yahoo! Widgets (*http://widgets.yahoo.com*) or Konfabulator (*http://widgetgallery.com*) don't already do a whole lot better.

I find the widgets available at these two locations to be better in their visual polish, flexibility, and usability. Each complaint deserves a specific mention.

The visual polish is a fairly subjective topic, so you (or Microsoft) can dismiss my complaint out of hand. I can't really put my finger on it, except to say that the Yahoo! Widgets look more at home in the Aero interface than the Microsoft gadgets; Yahoo!'s widgets are glassier and more Aero-ey† than Vista's gadgets.

The flexibility complaint goes like this: try to resize a gadget. You can't. To your annoyance, you'll find the gadgets are either on the sidebar, where they are often too small to provide all the information you want to have handy, or on the desktop, where they can be large enough to be useful, but are often hidden behind other windows. I have used widgets on my XP machine for years, and I was excited when I heard Vista was including gadgets (maybe *excited* is a little strong), but I was then disheartened when I actually saw the gadgets in action.

I mean, really, do the Clock and Notes gadgets need to be the same size to provide the necessary information? Most Widgets on the other hand, generally resize beautifully, adapting themselves to whatever information they display.

On to my third and most important grievance about the gadgets: their usability. Yes, you can track your investment portfolio in real time (assuming you have an Internet connection) with the Stocks gadget. But spend a half hour setting up the list of your favorite 20 stocks. Now close the gadget. Poof! Your stock portfolio is gone, and you have to rebuild it all over. Other gadgets follow this very same aggravating pattern.

---

* Actually, Google can integrate with Windows Mail because Gmail accounts can be configured to support POP3 and SMTP email, so you can use Gmail in lots of email client applications.

† $10 to the first person who creates a Wikipedia entry for that word.

(I hope you want to know what the weather is like in Redmond, Washington—you'll be forced to check each time you open the gadget.)

Of course, Microsoft's counterpoint to this is that if you want to make the gadgets disappear, you should hide the sidebar instead of closing the gadget, but come on: it's 2007.

Also, don't try to get the three-day forecast with a quick glance at the sidebar, or see how five of your stocks are doing without scrolling back and forth. Even when you stop your work and drag a gadget onto the desktop to see it in a larger size (thus defeating its purpose), that usually isn't much of a help. Unfortunately, the inability to resize a gadget directly impacts its usability. If you want to see up-to-date information about, say, seven stocks at once, forget about it.

And also forget about gadgets being much of a help in staying more productive. Try a widget instead.

Summary

Especially on the heels of grievances I just listed in the latter portion of this chapter, I want to leave you on the following note.

After five years of development and a reported 50 million lines of code, Microsoft's Windows Vista is no small feat, and will beautifully address almost any given computing challenge. In other words, I wouldn't say that any of the listed gripes here is a deal-breaker. They are instead just what I called them in the section heading: a list of things that would have been done differently had Microsoft asked me first.

But Microsoft didn't ask me first (nor did it need to; it solicited advice from plenty of others), and I am fully aware that complaining about it has a bit of a "Monday morning quarterback" feel. I worked for Microsoft for two years; I suppose if I had really wanted to, I could have figured out a way to make my input heard.

And remember that most of this chapter was about either ways to make the OS *better*, or ways you can *better use* the OS. As you've seen, tons of features will enhance your productivity and enjoyment of this new operating system—tons that don't fit neatly into a book already jam-packed with 14 other chapters of tips and advice and pointers and explanation.

What I'm trying to say here, I guess, is that the pros outweigh the cons.

What's more, I could have easily expanded the size of this chapter threefold by continuing to name feature after tip after tweak. You'll discover many more by your own exploration, no doubt, and when you do, feel free to share them with me. I can then share them with the rest of the world.

I'll conclude, then, with this thought: Windows Vista sure is a lot better than any operating system I've developed, and the same is true for all but a handful of humans on this planet. So we'll deal with what we've got, recognize that because those 50 million lines of code were written by humans, they are prone to human error on occasion. And further recognize that there are some pretty smart people at Microsoft who are in charge of this sort of thing, people who pretty much skip to work because they love writing computer code and solving problems, and who will continue their work of making Windows Vista even better over the next few years just as they have done with the entire line of Microsoft operating systems.

After all, a perfect solution for *me* might be a huge pain in the keister for some other user. Not everyone wants to interact with Windows Vista in the way I do, nor in the way you do.

What we've got, then, is an operating system that does a whole lot of things under a whole lot of different operating conditions, and does them quite well. Armed with the knowledge and advice that this book provides, you'll be able to better use and deploy these amazing capabilities, putting them to use in a way that best suits *you*.

Happy computing.

—Brian
January 2007

Index

We'd like to hear your suggestions for improving our indexes. Send email to *index@oreilly.com*.

B

Back button, 6
Background Intelligent Transfer Service (BITS) setting (Group Policy), 658
backup and restore, 623, 704–712
  backup issues, 749–750
  Complete PC Backup, 706–709
    backup status and configuration, 708
    compatible OS versions, 706
    restoring, 707
  Encrypting File System (EFS), 705
  FAT disk, 705
  System Restore, 709–712
    effectiveness, 709
    restore point, manual, 711
    restore point, using, 712
Backup and Restore Center, 80, 704
Baseline Security Analyzer (MBSA), 669–671
baseline, establishing, 517
Basic Input/Output System (BIOS), 271
basic storage
  converting to dynamic storage, 354
  versus dynamic storage, 341
batteries
  laptop, 748
  status, 76
BCD (boot configuration data), 272
  editor
    BCDEdit utility, 275
    System applet in Control Panel, 274
    System Configuration utility (Msconfig), 274
  modifying, 274
  Startup, 273
BCD Windows Management Instrumentation (WMI) provider, 274
BCDEdit utility, 275
benchmarking, 517
binding IPv4 to network adapters, 109
BIOS (Basic Input/Output System), 271
BitLocker Drive Encryption, 15, 31–33, 83, 608–613
  operating system versions, 53
  versus Encrypting File System (EFS), 32
BITS (Background Intelligent Transfer Service) setting (Group Policy), 658
Block (or allow)
  games by name, 24
  games by rating, 24

Bluetooth devices, 257–262
  communication, 261
  passkey, 258
  proper location, 262
  removing and reinstalling, 260
  setting up connection, 257
  surfing with Bluetooth phone, 259
  troubleshooting connection, 259
Bluetooth personal area network (PAN), 130
boot applications, 272
boot configuration data (see BCD)
boot partition, 356
boot up (see power up performance)
boot.ini, 271
bootmgr, 272
bootstrap profile, 142
brightness settings, 76
Business edition, 80–82
  advanced backup and diagnostics, 80
  Backup and Restore Center, 80
  features, 80
  Remote Desktop Connection, 81

C

Calculator, 11
calendar-based task, 45
Certificate Authority/Browser Forum, 500
Change permission, 150
CIDR (Classless Inter-Domain Routing), 108–109
clean install, 436–439
ClearRecentItemsOnExit (DWORD value), 185
Click Computer (speech command), 243
Click File (speech command), 243
Click Recycle Bin (speech command), 243
Client Help setting (Group Policy), 658
Clock, 11
cmd.exe, 555
Cmdlines.txt, 427
Color and Appearance dialog box, 3
color scheme
  Aero (see Aero)
color schemes, 202
Command link, 6
Command Prompt, 554–563
  administration, 559
  always running in Admin mode, 723
  AutoComplete, 556

New line (speech command), 243
New paragraph, 243
New Simple Volume command, 342
news reader program, 61
newsgroups, 715
NoChangeStartMenu (DWORD value), 185
NoNetwork (DWORD value), 185
NoRecentItemsMenu (DWORD value), 185
NoSetTaskbar (DWORD value), 185
NoSimpleStartMenu (DWORD value), 185
NoSMHelp (DWORD value), 185
NoSMPictures (DWORD value), 185
NoStartMenuMFUprogramsList (DWORD
        value), 185
NoStartMenuMusic (DWORD value), 185
NoStartMenuPinnedList (DWORD
        value), 185
NOT (Boolean filter), 41
Notes, 11
notification of Clipboard access from
        scripts, 513
NoUserNameInStartMenu (DWORD
        value), 185
NoWindowsUpdate (DWORD value), 185
NSLOOKUP, 702–704
    interactive mode, 702
    noninteractive mode, 702
    status and repair, 703
NT Virtual DOS Machine (NTVDM), 556
NTFS
    converting volume to, 737
    filesystem, 345
    mounting volume into NTFS folder, 738
    permissions, 152–157
        behavior, 156
        best practices, 157
        file level, 155
        removing inherited permissions, 153
        standard folder, 153
        versus share permissions, 157
Ntldr program, 271
Number Puzzle, 11
NVRAM, 284

O

OCSetup, 424
offline files, 160–164, 255
    accessing files using network syntax, 162
    removing, 164
    status, 162
    Sync Center, 160, 162
    working with, 162

On-Screen Keyboard tool, 253
Operational log events, 715
optimizing
    hard disk, 547
    performance, 516, 544, 547, 563
    programs, 545
OR (Boolean filter), 41
Orphan Control, 487
Oscdimg tool, 449
Outlook 2003/2007, 44
Outlook Express, 751
Outlook Web Access (OWA), 132
out-of-box-experience (OOBE), 435

P

Package Manager, 426
padlock icon, 500
page zoom, 484
    keyboard shortcuts, 486
pagefile, 356, 534
    disk thrashing, 535
    pagefile.sys, 534
PANs (personal area networks), 130, 257
Parental Controls, 15, 21–27, 504–507
    activity reporting, 26, 505
    application restrictions, 506
    computer use, limiting, 21
    Entertainment Software Rating Board
        (ESRB) game ratings, 506
    games, preventing running, 24
    Internet use, limiting, 22
    programs, blocking, 23
    time limits, 506
    uses for, 21
    web filtering, 505
Partition Magic, 348
partitioning hard drives, 341–343
partitioning utilities, 346
partitions, 32
passwords
    policy, 579
    protected sharing, 145
    storing, 624
    strong, 573
patches
    Automatic Updates, 626
    Microsoft Download Center, 626
    Microsoft Update, 626
    TechNet, 626
    Windows Update, 626
PATHPING, 701
PC Migration Assistant, 433

S

T

Windows XP, upgrading from, 440–441
winload.exe, 272
winnt.exe, 425
winresume.exe, 272
Wired Equivalent Privacy (see WEP)
wireless networking, 115, 126–142
    access, 619
    ad hoc networks (see ad hoc networks)
    connecting, 126–130
        encryption, 129
        password, 129
        security protocol, 129
        SSID, 129
        VPN (see VPN)
        WAP, 128
    connection choices
        connecting to a Bluetooth personal
            area network (PAN), 130
        connecting to a workplace, 130
        connecting to the Internet, 130
        manually connecting to a wireless
            network, 130
        set up a wireless router or access
            point, 130
        setting up a dial-up connection, 130
        setting up a wireless ad hoc
            (computer-to-computer)
            network, 130
    connection status, 77
    disconnecting, 135
    managing, 136–137
    security, 137–142
        802.1x authentication, 137
        WAP (see WAP)
        WEP (see WEP)
    settings, 620
    single sign-on, 140–142
        bootstrap profile, 142
        network administrators preconfigure
            wireless computer to domain, 140
        user configures wireless computer with
            bootstrap wireless profile, 141
        user manually configures wireless
            computer with bootstrap
            profile, 141

System Tray, wireless network
    availability, 127
WAP, 130
WEP, 131
Wizard 97, 5
    Welcome and Completion pages, 5
Work network type, 119
workgroups
    changing affiliation, 100
    defined, 96–98
    joining, 100–102
        changing computer name, 101
    pros and cons, 97
worms, 566
WPA, 138–139
    AES (Advanced Encryption
        Standard), 139
    Protected EAP (PEAP), 139
    smart card, 139
    subcategories, 138
    TKIP (Temporal Key Integrity
        Protocol), 139
    types of connections, 138
    types of encryption, 139
WPA (Wi-Fi Protected Access), 137

X

Xbox 360 Media Center Extender, 78–79
XML
    USMT, and, 455
    Vista settings stored in, 427
XML Paper Specification (XPS), 49
XPS Document Writer, 49
XPS Viewer, 50

Y

Yahoo! mail, 751
Yahoo! Widgets, 752

About the Author

Brian Culp, MCSE, MCT, is a recognized Microsoft expert who has been teaching and writing about Windows for many years. He is author/coauthor of seven books including *Windows XP Power Tools* (Sybex) and *Outlook 2003 Bible* (Wiley); four MCSE study guides (McGraw-Hill); and several tutorials for the Virtual Training Company. Culp gives presentations for Microsoft on Windows XP, Vista, Small Business Server, and Office 2007.

Colophon

The animal on the cover of *Windows Vista Administration: The Definitive Guide* is a ruddy shelduck (*Tadorna ferruginea*). Native to Africa, Europe, and Asia, the ruddy shelduck can be found in freshwater, desert and semidesert, temperate grassland, and mountain habitats.

Members of the duck, goose, and swan family *Anatidae*, ruddy shelducks are large ducks, at 24–26 inches long and 2–3.5 pounds. They are characterized by ruddy orange–brown plumage and black tails. Adult males have cream-colored heads and a narrow black "collar" during breeding season. Females have a paler, whitish patch on the face. Ruddy shelducks are good swimmers and are also impressive in flight; in fact, they're often mistaken for geese due to their large size. Also similar to geese, the shelduck's call is a loud, coarse honking.

Ruddy shelducks spend more time away from water than most ducks. They pluck weeds, pick up insects from dry, grassy areas, and rummage around in the soil for insect larvae. Like other ducks, they search for tasty water weeds and insects by upending when they are feeding in shallow water. Ruddy shelducks are aggressively territorial around their nests, but are otherwise social, spending much of the year in the company of others, sometimes in flocks of several thousand. Family groups tend to stay together even after the chicks have left the nest.

In some Buddhist countries such as Tibet and Mongolia, the shelduck is highly revered, as its coloring resembles that of the robes the monks wear. It is also considered a sacred animal in Slavic mythology.

The cover image is from the Dover Pictorial Archive. The cover font is Adobe ITC Garamond. The text font is Linotype Birka; the heading font is Adobe Myriad Condensed; and the code font is LucasFont's TheSans Mono Condensed.

Better than e-books

Buy *Windows Vista Administration: The Definitive Guide* and access the digital edition FREE on Safari for 45 days.

Go to www.oreilly.com/go/safarienabled
and type in coupon code EQXOSBI

Search
thousands of
top tech books

Download
whole chapters

Cut and Paste
code examples

Find
answers fast

Search Safari! The premier electronic reference
library for programmers and IT professionals.